THE PLAID AVENGERS WORLD

#2 2008

$80.00/ US

KENDALL/HUNT PUBLISHING COMPANY
4050 Westmark Drive   Dubuque, Iowa 52002

Illustrations on the cover and cartoons throughout book created by Klaus Shmidheiser.

Copyright © 2008 by John Boyer
Copyright © 2006 by Kendall/Hunt Publishing Company
ISBN 978-0-7575-5881-8

Printed in the United States of America
10 9 8 7 6 5 4 3 2

Acknowledgments

Contributing Writers: Flash Clark, Cory Greenberg, Alexander Reniers, Nicholas Reinholtz, & Jason Hushour

Editors: Chris Drake, Stacy Boyer, Flash Clark, & Nick Reinholtz

Image Acquisitions: Katie Pritchard

Graphics Creation: Katie Pritchard

Plaid Avenger's Transcription Team: Renata L. Hafich & Steven Rich

Personal Assistant to the Plaid Avenger: Katie Pritchard

And a special thanks to the most awesome plaid artist on the planet:
 Cartoonist: Klaus Shmidheiser

PART ONE
UNDERSTANDING
THE PLAID PLANET

A Plaid World Intro

1

What is globalization?

How do the interconnections of the global economy and politics affect my life?

Why are some places rich while others are poor?

What does the future of the planet look like?

All great questions fellow world watchers—questions that deserve great answers. Thoughtful, intuitive and well-researched answers contained in a well-ordered and glibly constructed textbook.

This is not that book.

Welcome to my world. The world of the Plaid Avenger, where seeking knowledge of our planet is imperative, where blissful ignorance is not accepted, and where truth and justice can only be achieved by those willing to learn . . . willing to work . . . willing to fight. It is not a place most are ready to enter yet. But you are here. Good. Read on.

In the Plaid Avenger's world, we will strip off the shallow window dressing in which you have been trained to see the world donned, we will lay it bare to see what is really happening around the planet. We do this in order to gain enough insight about the current state of the world to truly understand the how and why and where things are happening right now. In this world, no single government or press dictates our views; no single political party shapes our opinion; no single religion or ethnicity tints our not-so-rose-colored glasses. We will see the world in plaid: a mystical weaving of facts, figures, cultures and viewpoints from every corner of the planet, culminating into the fabric that is today.

Many, if not most, in our society would say, "Why bother?" Here's why:

AGE OF GLOBALIZATION

Globalization: what is it and what does it mean to me? Economically? Technologically? Politically? Socially? Morally?

We constantly hear about how the world is getting smaller—is it? Hell, the world is the same damn size it has always been . . . *but* it is becoming more connected and more interdependent than ever before. More information flows faster from even the most remote parts of the planet. For the first time ever we can travel to any part of the world virtually overnight. Corporations move capital and jobs from one country to the next in a matter of days. News of international significance is reported seconds after it happens. We can communicate in real time with any part of the globe. The world is now one system . . . mostly.

We are the first generation of humans who enjoy foreign travel as a casual part of life, who communicate by direct-dialing to any country on all continents, who receive instant news of world happenings, who expect to work overseas or work for a company that deals overseas. Let me reiterate that—expect; it is not an exception. This is a really important concept, especially to you—the first generation that is living in the postindustrial, highly interconnected age.

Many if not all of you will work for multinational companies whose business is all over the world. Many if not all of you will work and live outside of the US at some point in your careers. Businesses and jobs are internationalizing as we speak—almost all jobs, not just the fancy ones. You guys are the people who are going to be running the world. You guys are the decision makers—when all is said and done, I'm just a single superhero out thwarting international intrigue. But *you* will be the ones building the bridges, and electing leaders, and stabilizing governments, controlling monetary exchange rates; you may even be setting up all sorts of private or national or even international businesses/programs/projects that will shape the world and its population.

Make no mistake about it, the AIDS rate in Africa *does* affect you, the increasing coal consumption in China *does* affect you, an earthquake in Japan, and the price of cocaine in Colombia *does* affect you. (allocation of your tax dollars, your jobs, the price you pay for goods, the amount of goods we sell, etc.) Globalization is pretty much a one-way street. We are not going back to medieval times, no matter what isolationist say, do, or think. Ignore the rest of the world at your own peril—you won't be hurting anyone but yourself.

Knowledge is power, or at least empowerment. The more you know about the world in which we live, the more power you have. So its good to have at least a minimal understanding of our planet. What's that? You don't know what geography is?

WHAT IS GEOGRAPHY?

Geography is one of those words, and subsequently one of those fields of study, which has become so generic that it seems to have lost its own definition in the modern world. The term is so truly holistic in meaning that many other social sciences, as well as a lot of the physical ones, are actually sub-branches of it, as opposed to geography's current designation as a sub-branch of one of them. What am I talking about? Consider for a moment the origin of the word and the discipline; *geography* has its roots in the ancient world, roughly translated as "describing the earth," and every culture and society with a written record has done just that—described both physically and culturally the environment around them as they understood it.

Be it Greek philosophers calculating the size of the known world in the 2nd century BCE, Chinese diplomats considering trade ties with Southeast Asia in the 11th century, military strategist planning the Boer War in Africa, or American scientist assessing the impact of the loss of Brazilian rainforest on world climate in the 21st century—all are geographers in

the sense that they are studying the physical and/or cultural components of their environments to gain understanding and make decisions. Just as all of us do every day in our own lives. How do I get from here to there? Should I buy an American car to support the American economy, even though their fuel efficiency is worse than imported cars? What is the foreign policy of the political party I support? Should I donate money to alleviate hunger in Ethiopia? Is this neighborhood I'm in a high-crime area? Paper or plastic? All questions require us to consider economic, social, political, and environmental knowledge and repercussions of that knowledge on the world around us.

I am intentionally pointing out here that the world around us, every place on the planet no matter where you are, has both physical traits and cultural traits that make it unique. Every place has a certain climate, particular landforms, and some kind

We are unique!

of soils, vegetation and animal life. These are its **physical** traits, much like every human has some natural hair color, skin color, a certain height and weight, and particular physical abilities—maybe to run fast or jump high. At the same time, every place has languages being spoken, religious practices, economic activities, political organizations, and human infrastructure like roads and buildings. These are the **cultural** traits of the place, just like a human has certain religious beliefs, spoken language, a job, a learned skill like archery, and/or a favorite alcoholic beverage. Defining any place in the world, or any region of the world, involves looking at both of these aspects, as well as their interaction with each other.

Every place on the planet is unique in that even when many of these factors are identical—say between two small towns in the Midwest located only 5 miles apart—there will still be tangible differences. Each town has a different history. The weather may be pretty much the same, but one will get more rainfall than the other. The people may all be of the same religion, but there will be different churches that do things just slightly different. The economies may both be based on corn, but there will be different business names, and different storefronts. There will be at least one Chinese restaurant in both towns, but they will definitely have different tasting General's Chicken. Like human identical twins, no matter how much is the same, there are always distinguishable differences upon closer examination. So to understand our world, we will look at the physical and cultural traits of regions of the planet, how these traits converge to form a distinct region, and perhaps more importantly for our assignment, how these regions interact with each other.

So what the hell is a region?

WHAT IS A REGION?

The world is just too damn big and filled with a hell of a lot of things going on and way too many facts and figures and images and names and places for us to know and comprehend everything all of the time. Hell, you can't possibly even know all the facts and histories and physical variables of your own home town, much less your county, your state, or your planet. There's just too much, and the story is added to daily. But don't give up hope! Don't become despondent! And for goodness sake, don't start drinking cheap Chardonnay. The human mind has a coping mechanism for this overflow of knowledge, which of course has gotten much worse with the advent of global communications and the 24-hour news cycle: We assess importance. We filter. We generalize. We are going to do the same geographically for the planet. By synthesizing and systematizing vast amounts of information from parts of the world and making pertinent generalizations, we create a unit of area called a *region.*

Regions are areas usually defined by one or more distinctive characteristics or features, which can be physical features or cultural features . . . or more often than not, a combination of both. We could identify a strictly physical region such as a pine forest, the Sahara Desert or the Mississippi drainage basin. Conversely, we could form up an area that we would identify culturally like the Bible Belt, a Wal-Mart store service area, or even Switzerland (defined by human-created political borders). However, since we have already pointed out that every part of the planet has both types of traits, most regions are identified as a combination of physical and cultural characteristics . . . such as the regions we refer to as the Midwestern US, tropical Africa, or Eastern Europe. These names typically make one think of both physical and cultural traits simultaneously, and may actually be meaningless in a context of just one or the other. This last type of world regional delineation is what we will mainly utilize in our journey.

That is a good jumping off point for what we will consider a region for our global guidebook. A region has three components:

1. Has to have some area.
2. Has to have some boundaries—although these boundaries are typically fuzzy, or imperfectly defined. Where does the Middle East stop and Africa start?
3. Has to have some homogeneous trait or traits which set it apart from surrounding areas. This is the most important thing to consider.

What trait is homogeneous is defined by the user. You can define any place on earth as being in an infinite number of regions, depending on what trait you pick. Your current exact position could be described as in a distinct political region like Charleston, California, or Canada. Or perhaps you're in a distinct physical region like the Everglades or the Appalachians or the Badlands. An simultaneously you may be in a distinct socially defined region like the Bible Belt, the Rust Belt, or the 'The Beltway'—what region do you think you are in right now? Play this exciting 'name your region' game with all your friends, and you will be the toast of the town. Or perhaps a big geek. But I digress.

Here is a quick breakdown of the world regions we will be examining:

Why these areas? Why these borders? Why these regions? Because they are defined by homogeneous traits as picked by me. These are the Plaid Avenger's world regions. The bulk of this book will be explaining these regions and their homogeneous traits. Your world regional map may be different than mine depending upon what traits you want to focus.

Don't like my regions? Then go write your own damn book.

A MATTER OF SCALE

When we are being geographers, or defining regions, or even just trying to get from point A to point B, we must always keep the *scale* of our endeavor in mind. How much area are we talking about? How far are point A and B from each other? Does this description of the environment in my hometown scale apply to a larger scaled area like my state or country? It rarely does. Thus we must always be wary about how far we can push our analysis. Changing scales typically calls for reassessment of the area being considered.

The other reason to pay attention to scale is because it plays an important component of our definition of regions. Since we have already expressed that regions have some sort of homogeneous factor which defines them, we must consider at what scale does this homogeneity apply—because it is defined by the scale itself. Let me give you an example.

Several presidential elections ago our country, by majority, elected Bill Clinton—a Democrat—to the presidency. Since more than half voted Democrat, we could say that the US, at the country scale, is a Democratic region, based on that singular homogeneous trait. However, if we looked at the state of Virginia, it voted predominately Republican—so at a smaller scale, we are in a Republican region. Fairfax County, a smaller region within Virginia, may have voted predominately Democrat . . . thus in that smaller region we are back to a Democrat-defined area. Maybe most of the people on a certain city block in Fairfax County, a smaller region still, voted Republican . . . so at the block scale you are in Republic territory again. Thus, defining regions based on voting preferences *demands* that you state the scale of focus. And most importantly, the larger the region you define, the more exceptions to your homogeneous trait you will find within your region.

FIGURE 1.1 WORLD REGIONS AS DEFINED BY THE PLAID AVENGER

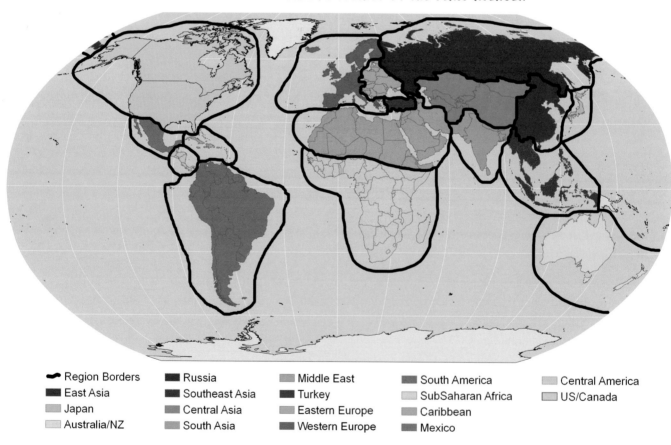

➤ Region Borders	■ Russia	▨ Middle East	▨ South America	▨ Central America
■ East Asia	■ Southeast Asia	■ Turkey	▨ SubSaharan Africa	▨ US/Canada
▨ Japan	▨ Central Asia	■ Eastern Europe	▨ Caribbean	
▨ Australia/NZ	▨ South Asia	■ Western Europe	■ Mexico	

This is what generalizations are all about—we are going to discuss and define our regions with *generally homogeneous* traits within the region, knowing full well our generalization won't apply to everyone and every place. For example: by any definition, the Middle East region would be identified as an area dominated by Islam. Oops, except for a radical and extremely important exception, that of the Jewish state of Israel. For our travels, we will be pointing out and elaborating mostly on those homogeneous traits which define our regions, but will also include those glaring exceptions to the rule when they are of particular significance to today's headlines. The other main goal of this guide is to describe each of the world regions' interactions with each other, and their role in the world at large. This is a tall order to be sure, but a goal worthy of pursuit by the mightiest of global superheroes . . . the Plaid Avenger.

SO WHO THE HELL IS THE PLAID AVENGER?

Yes, it seems that everything is growing into a singular world system. We speak of a world economy in which goods and services and businesses move all over the planet; they even have a club for everyone: the WTO. We have a great global transportation network which can transport us faster than ever to any point on the planet. We have the United Nations: a world legislative body that sets standards and rules for conduct on the planet (and I've heard rumors that they are also supposedly peace-keeping enforcers of these rules . . . although I won't swear to this). Thanks to mass media and global telecommunications, we can even speak of movement towards a more homogeneous world culture—where in the world can you *not* talk on your cell phone while you watch MTV and sip on a Guinness?

But wait, there seems to be something missing. Hmmm. . . . Global leadership . . . check. Global legislature . . . check. Global economy . . . check. Global judicial system . . . Global judicial system . . . Global justice??? Bueller . . . Bueller . . . Bueller? Where is it? I knew something was missing dammit.

Just as the world continues to become more interconnected, and every event across the globe becomes more pertinent to our daily lives, we gain more knowledge about inequalities and unfairness around the planet. This comes at a time here at the dawn of the 21st century when conflict proliferates around the globe; multinational corporations grow unchecked and unhindered by law; diseases have the capacity to truly create an unprecedented planetary epidemic; and trade in guns, drugs, and people continue unabated. Yes, even the trade in people . . . you know, slavery. Global inequality may be reaching a new zenith; that is, the gulf between the rich and the poor widens as every day passes. And those poor folks are growing in numbers. . . .

The Plaid Avenger is a product of this age. Somewhere at a major university on the eastern seaboard, a meek but smartly dressed college professor by day, he toils in an effort to educate the youth of America about the wider world, and their role in it. By night, he roams the planet fighting organized international crime, abusive multinational corporations, and corrupt governments, wherever they may be. He also has a penchant for fine wines and liquors from around the globe, but that is a different story. The Plaid Avenger: international equalizer and educator. A fighter for truth, global justice, and the international way, he also possesses an unstoppable urge to bring plaid back into fashion. And that brings us to your first assignment:

Your first mission to become globally literate . . . that is, smart . . . is to know the locations of the states of the world (in America, we call them "countries"; start calling them states now and just get over it.) Look back to Figure 1.1, and get to work. The reason? While I'm not an advocate of memorizing every damn town, district, and province on the map, we do need to have a working vocabulary to discuss things intelligently. Not that you need to be able to draw a map from memory, but you will be amazed how much more intelligent you appear when you are in a discussion about a news event and you know with authority that Senegal is in western Africa, not in Central Asia. Trust me, chicks dig it.

Got them all down? Then look at the following figures. A straight-up matching game with some style. As the Plaid Avenger must often work undercover around the planet, he has an endless array of outfits to help him blend into the environs he is investigating. He also enjoys the local beverages wherever he happens to be. Match the appropriate high-lighted country map to the outfit the Plaid Avenger would be wearing and the appropriate tipple he would be consuming. Good luck, and see you in Chapter 2.

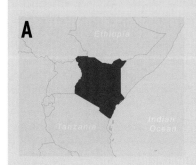

Vodka martini, stirred.

Fresh ginger beer

Vamanos dos tequilas!

Gandhi G's lager.

Sake to me, baby!

Das ist goot!

4

5

6

D

E

F

World Population Dynamics

BEFORE we get to the regions, we will focus on several topics that are better approached at the global scale; they involve traits that all regions possess equally (like people or religions) or that all regions participate in as a singular global unit (like the world economy or international organizations). Since people create, define, and operate all the cultural aspects of our planet, let's start with them.

INTRO TO PEOPLE AKA WORLD SEX ED 101

People, people, people, all over the world. Old ones, young ones, rich ones, poor ones, black ones, white ones, Asian ones, and even plaid ones. Some places got lots of people, some places got just a few. Are there too many people? Perhaps in some places not enough? Some states have growing populations while some states actually have shrinking populations. What's this all about? Although there are great differences in numbers of people around the world as well as differences in growth rates of populations around the world, it is best to approach this subject by looking at it systematically. That is, we can look at how human population dynamics operate as a whole, because the rules are essentially the same anywhere you go on the planet. Let's get to know how it works, and then you can apply your knowledge to understand what's happening in any state or region of interest. Game on.

For starters, you should know that we are currently closing in on 6.5 billion people alive across the world right now. This has not always been the case. In fact, numbers this huge for human population are actually quite recent. Consider Figure 2.1.

As you can see, for most of humankind's existence, population totals have been relatively small. It took approximately one million years, from the beginning of time until about the year 1800, for the first billion humans to appear on the earth at the same time. From then, it's roughly

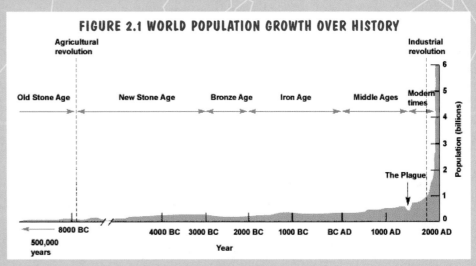

FIGURE 2.1 WORLD POPULATION GROWTH OVER HISTORY

→ 1927 that the second billion showed up

→ 1960 saw the crossing over to 3 billion

→ 1974 picked up number 4 billion

→ 1987 flipped the pop-odometer to 5 billion and

→ 1999 the predawn of the 21st century reached the 6 billion high-water mark. Or should I say the high-broken-water mark.

Point is that what you may be detecting here is a radically accelerated numbers increase in the last 40 years. The time it takes to add another billion people gets shorter and shorter every cycle, with the 7 billion humans mark showing up here very soon. This is because that population growth is exponential, not mathematical—meaning that adding 10 more fertile females to the pool doesn't equate to adding just ten more babies, but more like 100 babies, as each woman has the potential to spawn many more offspring, which in turn can produce many more offspring themselves down the road! Get it? And you can't blame it all on me either. I'm good, but not that damn good.

As a result of this exponential growth in the human population, many folks believe that the planet is already overpopulated. Is that true? I can't give you an answer for that, because it is a relative question. Where are we talking about? Siberia? It's certainly not overpopulated. Calcutta, India? Perhaps it certainly is overpopulated. Maybe. Many assume that Africa as a whole is overpopulated, but given the size of the place and its current population totals, it is actually quite sparsely populated per square mile, particularly if you compare it to a place like Western Europe. And if Western Europe is overpopulated, why do many of its governments encourage their citizens to have more babies? Hmmmm . . . things get complicated fast. Plaid Avenger rule of thumb: a place seems to be considered truly overpopulated only when there are not enough resources to supply the people who live there. Thus, the 70 million people in Ethiopia may all agree that their country is overpopulated, but the 80 million people in Germany would probably not consider themselves so, even given that Ethiopia is roughly three times the size of its schnitzel-eating friend. But enough for now on the theme of over- or underpopulation. Let's look at where people are in the first place.

CHART 1 TOP 20 POPULOUS STATES
COUNTRIES RANKED BY POPULATION: 2008

Rank	Country	Population
1	China	1,323,775,000
2	India	1,131,750,000
3	United States	305,000,000
4	Indonesia	240,000,000
5	Brazil	189,000,000
6	Pakistan	165,000,000
7	Bangladesh	158,000,000
8	Nigeria	150,000,000
9	Russia	142,000,000
10	Japan	128,000,000
11	Mexico	108,000,000
12	Philippines	90,000,000
13	Vietnam	87,000,000
14	Germany	82,000,000
15	Ethiopia	79,000,000
16	Egypt	75,000,000
17	Iran	72,000,000
18	Turkey	71,000,000
19	France	65,000,000
20	Thailand	63,000,000

REGIONAL DIFFERENCES IN POPULATION

Where are people, and where are they not? In some parts of the world, harsh climates and terrains are too formidable for large numbers of humans to hang out in. The cold Arctic areas in Canada and Russia, the great desert and steppe regions of the world in North Africa and Central Asia, and the high Andes and Himalayan ranges serve to keep population numbers low. Humans tend to proliferate in well-watered areas, along coastlines, and, generally speaking, favor the mid-latitudes (there are way more people in Eurasia and North America than in tropical areas). Draw on your own experiences to figure out why this is. Would you like to live in a tropical rainforest, a desert, or a mountain top? Why not?

FIGURE 2.2 HISTORICAL POPULATION DENSITY

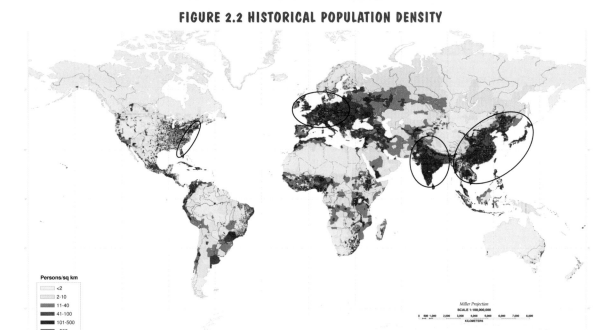

Persons/sq km
<2
2-10
11-40
41-100
101-500
>500

Miller Projection
SCALE 1:100,000,000

0 500 1,000   2,000   3,000   4,000   5,000   6,000   7,000   8,000
KILOMETERS

That's just the impact of the physical world, which by the way humans have a flair for overcoming if they really want to. People have adapted to living in just about every extreme environment our planet has—just not in great numbers. So what is the deal with the great numbers? It has a lot to do with history, culture and current population dynamics which we'll get to in just a second. First, a few points about the map in Figure 2.2, and as you can see I've circled the four biggest population clusters on the planet for our discussion.

Over half the world's people are found in Eurasia, particularly a people-packed arc from Japan to Eastern China, through Southeast Asia to South Asia. The common perception is that China is far and away the most populated place with over a billion people, but watch out! India, with about a billion people as of right now, will be taking the lead soon. And don't forget India's neighborhood—Pakistan and Bangladesh are both members of the top ten most populous states in the world as well.

The monster Asian population centers are in large part a product of history. People in these areas have been getting busy, in more ways than one, for thousands of years since the innovation of agriculture and the birth of civilization as we know it. They are stable civilizations for long periods of time, which also happen to be in physically conducive environments— you know, well-watered, mid-latitude lowlands; think India and China. This also helps explain why the cradle of Western Civilization—Mesopotamia, which is just as old—did not form huge populations over time. Its physical environment is arid, and cannot support large numbers of people.

However, due to great leaps in technology during the Industrial Revolution (including lots of technologies that helped keep more humans alive longer), Europe's population boomed in the last several hundred years, and so they are another significant center for people-packing on the planet. By contrast, not a lot of folks have been in the Western Hemisphere for very long, and when Europeans did arrive in the "New World," they brought diseases that wiped out significant numbers of people who were here. Thus, giving way to much lower numbers on our side of the planet. So history combined with the physical world has a lot to do with where most people are today.

Just two more global population points of interest: Africa, largely believed to be overpopulated, is a huge-ass place, but with half the people totals of South Asia or East Asia. And my favorite population fact deals with Russia and the US: the two Cold War adversaries. Look again at the map, and realize this: these two regions account for less than 10 percent of the world's population, but have effectively shaped the political and economic fate of the other 90 percent during the last 50 years. Interesting isn't it? Okay, maybe not, but it certainly was during the Cold War. Damn, those commies produced some fine vodkas, which apparently diminished their child-producing capabilities because Russia is a state currently in population decline. Which brings us to our next point: where are populations growing, where are they shrinking, and why?

HOW POPULATION IS CHANGING

To complicate matters further, not just total population but also **population growth rates,** are unevenly distributed around the world. Population growth rate refers to how fast or slow a group's population total is expanding . . . or shrinking, when referring to our Cossack friends. When you see a number like 3.5 for a population growth rate, that means that this time next year the population total for that country will be 3.5% bigger than it is right now. A negative number is the inverse: population growth of −0.5 means that population total for next year will be 0.5% smaller than now. See if you can detect any patterns in the map on page 23.

Saudi Arabia's population total is expanding very quickly which means a high growth rate. China's total population gets bigger every year, but not by much percentage-wise which is a moderate to slow growth rate. Belgium's population total remains the same every year—a stable or flat growth rate. Russia's population total is getting smaller every year—a negative growth rate. You may have also identified a major trend: the highest growth rates typically occur in states that we consider underdeveloped, a.k.a. the poor ones. Say again? You mean the poorest areas of the planet are where more people are being added faster than ever? That is correct. The developed, or richer, states all seem to have low growth rates. So the places that could afford to provide for more kids, have less kids? Yep, that's true as well. Why is this so? Good question. Answer: the Demographic Transition.

FIGURE 2.3 WORLD POPULATION GROWTH RATES

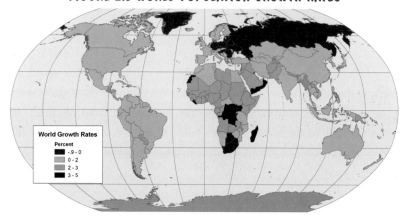

World Growth Rates
Percent
- −.9 - 0
- 0 - 2
- 2 - 3
- 3 - 5

Source: CIA World Factbook 2006

HOW/WHY/WHERE POPULATION IS CHANGING: THE DEMOGRAPHIC TRANSITION

The Demographic Transition is a lovely little model that goes a long way in explaining lots of things about human population change around the world today. Be forewarned: it is just a theory, but damned if it doesn't make a whole lot of sense when applied to just about anywhere, just about anytime. It helps us understand why population is booming in the poorer parts of the world, shrinking in richer parts, and even why women in Laos may have 10 kids, when women reading this book here in America may not want to have kids at all.

The model is based on the experience of the richer, fully developed states, which underwent a population surge on a smaller scale beginning about 1700 in Europe, and then later stabilized. Other states—typically ex-colonies of Western European powers (US, Australia) or states in close proximity to Western European powers (Russia, Eastern Europe)—followed suit in the last couple of hundred years. Every place else on the globe can be seen as somewhere in the transitional process that these states have gone through.

Generally speaking, this "transition cycle" begins with high birth rates and high death rates, passes into a high **birth**

FIGURE 2.4 BASE MAP, DEMOGRAPHIC TRANSITION

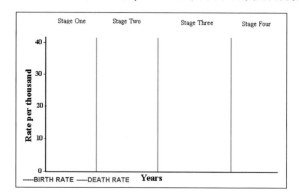

rate/lower **death rate** period for a variety of reasons, and ends with low birth rates and low death rates. The total population at the beginning and end of this cycle is stable or very low growth rate, perhaps even negative. However, it is the massive increases in population during the middle phases that makes the model so compelling, and explains so much about what is happening in today's world. But I'm getting ahead of the story. Let's take it one step at a time.

For the rest of this discussion, **birth rate** refers to how many children are born every year per 1000 people. To give you some context, the birth rate in the US right now is about 14/1000 every year. **Death rate** of course refers to how many people kicked the bucket that year per 1000 people. The US death rate is around 10/1000 right now. Now, on to the transition. . . .

DEMOGRAPHIC TRANSITION STAGE ONE

This whole concept hinges on the idea that all societies want to go *from* premodern, hunter-gatherer, stick-collecting goobers *to* postmodern, latte-sipping, Vespa-driving goobers. It does seem to make sense. Given the option anywhere in the world, I think most folks would choose the latte, that is, most societies are striving to become industrialized, richer, and all-around better off. You don't have to buy my theory, because quite frankly, I'm not selling it. There are those that argue that we would all be a lot better off living in grass huts somewhere weaving baskets from giraffe hair, because that would be true sustainable development in harmony with mother earth. Good luck with that one. Give anyone a chance not to live on a dirt floor, and I'll bet they pack their bags, set the giraffes free, and head out to a better life for themselves and their kids. But I digress . . . where were we . . . ah! Stage One . . .

STAGE ONE of societal development finds us making baskets from giraffe hair. We typically associate this stage with premodern times, wherein most folks are hunter-gatherers, living solely by collecting food naturally occurring out in, um . . . nature. This is pretty much the way things were for a great number of humans for a good long time in human history. Small groups of folks on the move, searching for food, waiting around for civilization to pop up. Of note for our model is that both the birth rates and the death rates are extremely high and erratic. Essentially you have a situation where lots of kids are born per 1000 people, and lots of people die per 1000 people, with some years being really good, and others being really bad. Why?

FIGURE 2.5 DEMOGRAPHIC TRANSITION STAGE ONE

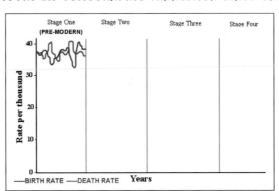

Why the high death rates? Because this lifestyle is hard, and it sucks, and it's easy to die from just about anything. Lack of health care, food shortages, poor food containment so things go bad fast, lack of regular clean water, lack of sewage disposal (worse yet, your sewage disposal plan involves your drinking water source), animals that want to eat you, animals that just want to kill you, animals just having fun with you, diseases of all sorts, simple infections you could contract from a hangnail . . . damn, this sounds like no fun at all. **Infant mortality,** the number of children that don't make it to their first birthday per 1000, is also high because of lack of immunizations and/or lack of adequate diet. **Life expectancy,** the average age the population lives to, is low because old people get sick easier, can't pull their own weight out picking berries and therefore don't eat as much, and in general, are slow enough to get caught by the animals that want to eat them. Poor Granny. I really liked her. Now she is cheetah food.

So why are the birth rates high? For the same reasons that they are high in some of today's underdeveloped world. For starters, it's a mindset; if you expect half your kids to die before they reach adulthood, then you should have twice as many. Makes sense. Also, children are often seen as a resource in these societies; maybe you have junior out picking berries at an early age to help out the fam. Plus, no health care = no health education = no sex education = no contraception use. Well, I guess people could always just abstain from having sex . . . yeah, right.

So why are the rates so erratic? For the simple fact that some years are good years, and some years are bad ones. A drought or a plague would cause births to drop and deaths to rise. A very good, wet season with lots of food around would cause the spikes in the opposite direction.

Because both birth and death rates are extremely high, they offset each other, equating to a total population that is low and a population growth rate that is slow or stable. Looking back at Figure 2.1, you can see that for most of human history, population growth rate has been very slow, or stable, right on up to the Industrial Revolution. Before we leave this rather boring phase, just a quick note: there really are no more societies like this left anywhere on the planet. You have to dig deep into the Amazon rainforest, the remote savannas of tropical Africa, or into the highlands of Papua New Guinea to find folks still living this lifestyle, and even then, they will be very small numbers of people in isolated pockets. No state on the planet today would be classified in Stage One.

STAGE TWO is the trickiest phase to consider, because we are going to pack a shitload of different human experiences under this single banner—which occur over long periods of time, but have this one big Stage Two result: the death rate will decline while the birth rate remains high and stabilizes. Less people die; same amount of people being born. What is going to happen to the total population numbers in such a situation?

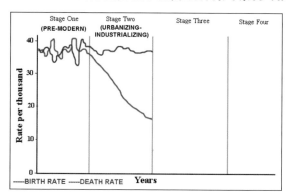

FIGURE 2.6 DEMOGRAPHIC TRANSITION STAGE TWO

Before we answer that, let's define the stage a little more. I said it is fairly all-inclusive of the human development spectrum, and I meant it. Stage Two includes the transition of humans from hunter-gatherer to agriculturalist to factory worker. Yes, this is a long stretch of time that also entails the formation of what we call technical innovation, civilization, and urbanization. Essentially, dudes figure out that staying put in a place and growing food is more productive than hunting all the time—an agricultural revolution. With increases in technology, there is so much extra food that not everybody has to be farmers; some become blacksmiths, butchers, priests, and rock stars—that's specialization. This leads to formation of villages, towns and eventually cities where larger and larger groups of dudes hang out—that's urbanization. Further increases in technology lead to creation of machines which do our work, which leads to the creation of machines making stuff, and even machines making machines—that's industrialization . . . kind of like The Terminator, but we'll call it the Industrial Revolution. So what's all this got to do with people having kids?

During this part of the societal transition, death rates just absolutely plummet. Why? In Stage One, I told you that everything sucked. In Stage Two, everything gets way better. Increases in food production and increases in food storage technology allow for a steady, stable food supply. There are no more "bad" food years (at least not as frequent).

Increased technologies in water resources, sewage treatment, and public health care, all based on growing scientific knowledge, serve to keep more people alive, for a longer period of time. Child mortality drops and life expectancy rises. We have developed the shotgun to ensure that Granny is not eaten by the cheetah. I missed you Granny, so glad you're back. More important though is the fact that more kids stay alive than ever before, and young kids become an increasingly bigger percentage of the total population than ever before. Education across the board, at all levels, also significantly increases quality of life and survivability.

During this vast sweep of progress, death rates drop and birth rates remain solidly high and even stabilize high. What is going on here? Basically, people are caught in a warp. Old habits die hard, and if mom had 10 kids and her mom had 10 kids and her mom had 10 kids, it is highly likely that you would be of the mindset to have 10 kids as well. It's just what people do. The society as a whole, and certainly not the individuals within it, does not understand that it is going through some transition. The mentality that large numbers of kids is good because half are going to die and the rest will work in the fields remains the same, even though conditions have changed—because half the kids are now not going to die. Maybe only one or two of them will die . . . maybe none at all. Granny had ten kids and only 5 survived. Mom had 10 kids and 7 survived. I had 10 kids and . . . dammit, all these little bastards are still here!

This mind warp is called *cultural lag.* Conditions have changed, but the culture is lagging behind. Folks with Stage One mentality are thinking "Hell, this is just a good year," without realizing that it is a good year after a good year after a good year, and they are still having kids like it's a boom-and-bust cycle. Result: *population explosion!* More kids beget more kids, and people just don't die like they used to.

FIGURE 2.7 CULTURAL LAG

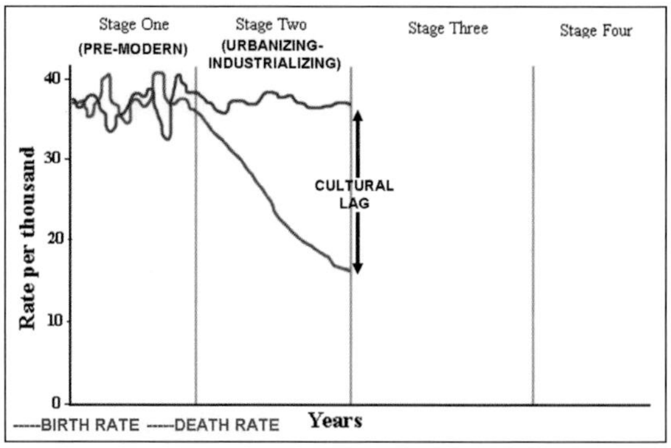

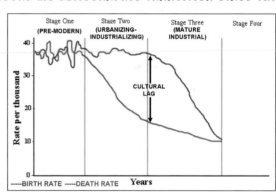

Stage Two main points: death rates decrease, birth rates remain the same, total population explodes, and the structure of the total population becomes more youthful. This last point is the most important for the rest of this story, as we have more potential baby-makers entering the scene. There are many states in the world that may fall into the later fringe of this Stage Two. Mostly in Africa, Central America, and dotted around Southeast Asia, many of these states are still heavily reliant on agricultural production as a main economic activity and also may have their death rates drop more from foreign external aid, importation of life-saving technologies, and humanitarian relief than from true evolution of the society upwards. This is important to note, since all of these things will help the death rate drop immediately, which means the period of cultural lag will likely be longer—significantly increasing total population overall. Examples of states in Stage Two would be Angola and Guatemala.

Now we can accelerate the telling of this story in **STAGE THREE** because we are getting onto ground of which we are more familiar. Stage Two ends with the beginning of the industrialization of the society, and Stage Three will take us the rest of the way through it, ending with what we refer to as the "mature industrial phase." Most states on the planet are currently located here, with varying degrees of development which can be quite radically different depending upon whether they are early Stage Three or late Stage Three.

FIGURE 2.8 DEMOGRAPHIC TRANSITION STAGE THREE

At this time, the society continues down the modern industrial path, and this is marked particularly by a shift in what the majority of folks do for a living. It is at this point that the scale gets tipped and more people are working in the processing/manufacturing and service sectors than are working as farmers. This is significant because this typically means that agricultural technology has superseded the need for vast amounts of human labor in the fields . . . and this equates to less farmers . . . which equates to more people leaving the countryside and heading to the big city to get a job: increasing urbanization.

Make no mistakes about it though; agriculture is still the number one job on the planet even today. But states within which agriculture is not the predominant occupation are further down the development road. That is, they are typically richer than states that still rely heavily on the agricultural sector to employ people. Food for thought—pun intended.

But we're just getting warmed up with the impacts of this age–to–industry and rural–to–urban shift. What happens to the ideas about having lots of kids when this shift occurs? Plenty! Life in the big city is more costly. Having more kids to feed costs more money. Plus, you've got to clothe them and house them and buy school books for them and throw birthday parties for them and eventually buy them cars. Wow! This is starting to suck as bad as Stage One. But it gets worse! Now the value of kids has changed too; junior used to be an asset picking berries and plowing the fields. Now junior is an added cost who only picks his nose and plows the family car into the side of the garage. Little bastard! The cultural lag is over thanks to you, junior! No more kids for us!

In addition to these changes, several other things of note are on the rise. Health care technology and accessibility continues to increase, and especially increasing knowledge about birth control and contraceptive use in general. Increasing education across the board helps more and more people, but I want you to think particularly of the education of women and how that effects the whole equation: more educated women = more women entering the workforce = more contraceptive use = more women delaying family formation = fewer kids.

Educating the women of any society decreases **fertility rate** instantaneously. Okay, maybe instantaneously is a bit strong, but it's a HUGE factor in affecting the fertility rate in today's world.

FIGURE 2.9 WORLD FERTILITY RATES

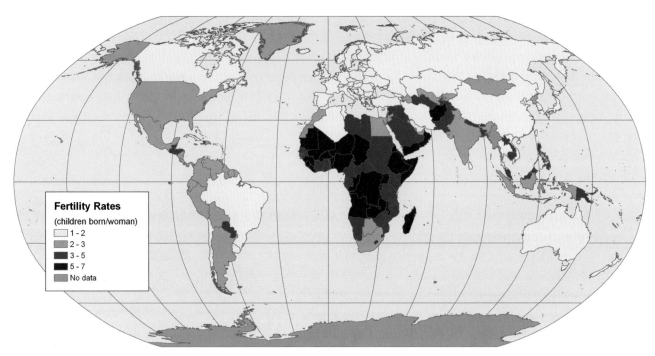

Fertility Rates
(children born/woman)
- 1 - 2
- 2 - 3
- 3 - 5
- 5 - 7
- No data

Source: CIA World Factbook 2006

Fertility rate is simply how many kids on average one woman will have in her lifetime in a particular state. Fertility rate of the US is about 2.1; of Italy about 1.3; of Mali about 7.5. So the average woman in Mali will have 7 kids and one half, say from the waist down. In the US, a woman will have 2 kids and a leg. For our international readers, that is what we call a joke. Actually, the US figure is a quite important fertility rate because it also happens to be something called the **replacement level.** A fertility rate of 2.1 is exactly what it takes to "replace" the current population. See, two people have to get together to create kids (at least still for now, thankfully) and if two people produce 2.1 kids, then when the parents die, there are still two humans they've created to take their place. Sweet! We'll return to this idea in a little bit.

Back to Stage Three. The result of increased health care, increased technology, increased childcare and increased education serve to knock the death rates down even further—but there is only so much that modern medicine can do, and eventually that line flattens out. Child mortality decreases and life expectancy increases a bit more, but we all got to die sooner or later, so we'll say goodbye to Granny once again.

Of a more radical impact, increasing urbanization due to the employment shift, revaluation of the cost and benefits of having children, increased education of women (and all that entails) combine to overcome cultural lag causing the birth rate to plummet and meet the death rate. People may still be getting busy like it's 1999, but they are not having the babies like they used to. After several generations, the fertility rates sink down closer to 2.1, the percentage of young people in the society about equals the middle aged cohort, and the older people as well. Good examples of early Stage Three states would be India and Brazil; late Stage Three, China and Chile.

And now we are through the transition, approaching life as we know it here in the fully developed, postindustrial, mostly western world. **STAGE FOUR** is characterized by population stability, where death rates and birth rates are both low and parallel each other nicely. The postindustrial world is one in which yet another economic shift has occurred; now most folks work in the service sector, and not quite as many in the manufacturing sectors, and virtually no one in agriculture. If these terms are confusing to you, just hang on; we will be delving into economics in the next chapter.

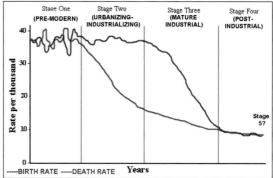

FIGURE 2.10 DEMOGRAPHIC TRANSITION STAGE FOUR

In this stage the population age structure has become older overall. Technology and education may still be increasing, but only in minute detail can they lower death rates anymore. The population of a Stage Four state is overwhelmingly urban, educated, uses some form of birth control, and spends way too much money on coffee. The US, France, and Japan are all great examples of Stage Four states. As a result of expected higher standard of living and higher costs of living, many people will plan to have one or two children at most, and some people will decide not to have any children at all.

This leads us to a possible expansion of the Demographic Transition to a Stage Five, in which birth rates actually dip below death rates. The effect? Net population loss—the state's population shrinks every year, and unless supplemented by immigration, the state would eventually disappear. *Immigration* is when people not born in the state move into it. *Emigration* is just the opposite perspective: when people leave your state, they are emigrating out of it. These concepts are increasingly critical in today's world, because many Stage 4 and 5 states rely on immigrants to fill jobs, pay taxes and boost slumping population growth rates. The US is a prime example whose population is only growing because of immigration; the locals like us aren't having lots of kids. This is actually much more pronounced in Europe where states may be fading away.

Of course the disappearing state thing has never happened before, but there are several states that are currently in this Stage 5 category. Russia, Sweden, Italy, and Japan are all losing people. Italy and Japan are both in dire straights, but for opposite reasons; both have declining fertility rates but people are emigrating out of Italy like never before, while Japan refuses to allow any immigration into its pristine palace. We shall see how that works out in the long run. Serves them right for creating Pokemon.

POPULATION PYRAMIDS

A final tool for our consideration of population dynamics on the planet is called a population pyramid. Population pyramids are constructed to show the breakdown of the population for gender and age groups. The x-axis across the bottom displays either a percentage of total population or actual population numbers, and the y-axis shows age cohorts, typically in 5-year increments. The two sides of the pyramid are divided up with

FIGURE 2.11 A POPULATION PYRAMID

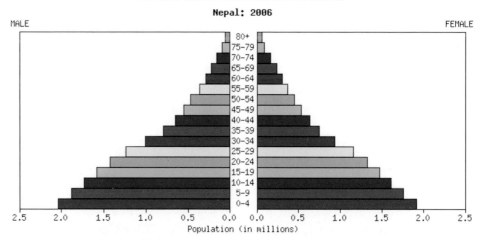

Source: U.S Census Bureau, International Data Base

males on one side, females on the other. Kind of like your junior high prom dance floor. In the figure below, you can see that in the rainbow of fruit flavors for Nepal in 2006, there are about 2 million males aged 0–4 years old, about 1.5 million females aged 10–14 years old, and about 0.5 million males aged 50–54.

Like I give a crap about how many Nepalese women are over 80 years old! What do these pyramids really tell us? They tell us all sorts of things about the current population of a state, the current economy of the state, and we can read lots into the standard of living in the state as well. But that's not all; these pyramids tell us a whole lot about what the future will hold too, and you don't even need a crystal ball. Consider the three basic shapes that these pyramids can take: *classic pyramid,* a *column* shape, or an *inverted pyramid.*

FIGURE 2.12 THREE TYPES OF PYRAMIDS: CLASSIC, COLUMN, AND INVERTED

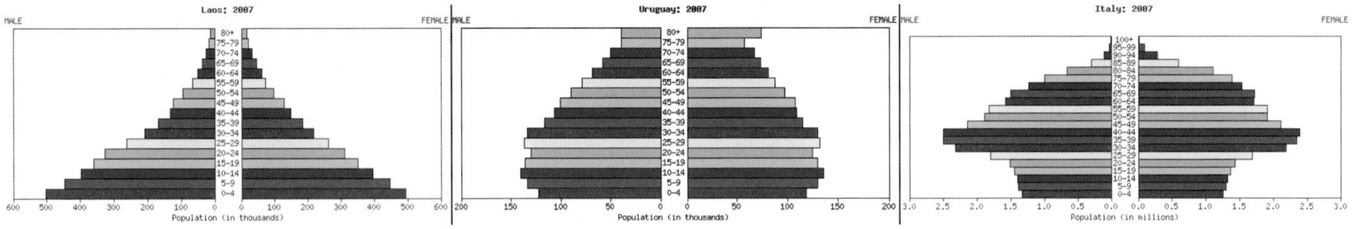

Source: U.S Census Bureau, International Data Base

THE CLASSIC PYRAMID

The classic pyramid shape is, um . . . shaped like a perfect pyramid. The wide bars at the bottom taper up gradually to smaller and smaller bars as age increases, displaying that there are more people in the younger brackets and the size of the group diminishes steadily with age. Broad-based pyramids, like this one, are characteristic of populations with high birth rates and low life expectancies. Why? You already know the answer! Look back at the Stage Two and Stage Three description of the Demographic Transition.

Industrialization and agricultural innovations, as well as increases in technologies across the board, result in advances in food supply and public health overall. This results in recently reduced infant and childhood mortality rates and slightly increased life expectancy. However, they are definitely in the cultural lag mode, as fertility rates continue to be high, resulting in high population growth rates and in many cases, outright population explosion. Each year the bottom bracket of 0–5 year olds gets wider than the previous year, and of particular significance is that the numbers of kids under the age of 15 is larger than the number of folks in the 15–35 brackets.

Why is this significant? Because the under 15s are dependents in the society. That is, they absorb resources. Typically the 15–35 year olds are the biggest providers in the society, both in economic means as money-makers for the state (GDP) and as family sustainers—of the young as well as the old members of the society. That is, they provide most of the resources. Perhaps now you are starting to see why countries with this type of pyramid are often poorer or less-developed; the dependents often vastly outnumber the providers. Stage Two and early Stage Three societies more often than not exhibit the pyramid shape demographic. The best examples of this type are any African country.

But there is ever so much more we can say about a society with this type of pyramid as well. It is probably heavily reliant on agriculture or other primary industries for much of its economic earnings. Most people definitely grow some food, either for sustenance, for an occupation, or both. It probably has lower literacy rates, has little or no social safety nets like welfare, and probably lacks adequate infrastructure like good roads, sewer systems, etc. Also, as pointed out earlier, many of the gains in health care, food availability, and life-sustaining technologies may be attributed to foreign aid and humanitarian aid programs. This is a distinctly 21st century dimension added to the transition model, and no one really knows what impacts this will have in the long run for less-developed countries.

THE COLUMN SHAPE

All columns are not created equal, and there can be radical variations on this shape, but the main thing to identify this type of population pyramid is the more overall fuller figure. No, I'm not talking about a full-figured gal, that's a different book altogether. The real distinguishing mark here is that the size of the 15–50 year cohorts are *roughly* the same size as the under-15 cohorts, giving the overall shape more of a cylindrical look. The older age brackets also grow slightly, and upwards, as more people stay alive longer, adding to the elongated shape.

When this is the case, we realize that the fertility rate must be much lower than in the true pyramid shape, usually hovering between 2.0–3.0. This of course means that those child-bearing folks (typically between 15–50 years old) are having just 2 or 3 kids each, roughly replacing themselves or even maybe just a bit more. Remember that term replacement level? Well, the closer a society gets to that 2.1 fertility rate, which constitutes the replacement level, the more perfect the column shape will become. Examples: The US, Lebanon, Norway.

Operative word in these states: stability. The population growth rate is low, or perhaps even zero, with the state adding just a few percentage points of population every year. What else can be said about these countries? They are fully developed industrialized or post-industrialized societies. The highs: GDP per capita, standards of living, health care quality and access, social programs available, life expectancy, education levels, technology levels, urbanization, use of birth control, service sector jobs, SUV ownership. The lows: fertility rate, infant mortality, illiteracy, farmers, miners, people who die from infectious disease.

INVERTED PYRAMID . . . YOU MEAN IT'S UPSIDE DOWN?

Indeed. This is an easy one to describe, because its essential ingredient is that the younger cohorts are smaller than the older ones—child-bearing peoples are creating less people than themselves, and total population is actually shrinking! Fertility rates are under 2.1 and thus the replacement level is not being reached, and ultimately, left unchecked, the population would shrink into nonexistence. This has never really happened before, and is not likely to ever come to its full conclusion either; to counter this effect, immigration is increased or some other government policy is put into place to encourage fertility rates to rise.

Why does this scenario happen? Perhaps a couple of different reasons. The first and foremost explanation is due to the same processes at work which serve to end cultural lag in developing societies; namely, the higher cost of living in highly urbanized areas coupled with the transition of children from asset to expenditure changes attitudes towards family size. Smaller is better in industrialized societies. They only have one or two kids, and invest heavily in them, as opposed to having lots of kids. In some places here in the 21st century, this has gone to an extreme; many people totally opt out of the family thing altogether, having no children, to maintain their own high standard of living. End result: fewer or no kids, replacement level for the state is not reached. The best examples of this today are Japan, Italy, and Sweden.

Another reason for declining populations in the world may be due to economic circumstances. Some countries, while considered part of the developed world, have gone through radical changes and economic collapse due to the end of the Soviet Empire. Russia, Belarus, and Ukraine are all in this inverted pyramid category due to lack of resources, jobs, health care, and many other services that the government used to supply. This is particularly evident in some of the measures of well-being for Russia, whose current life expectancy more approximates a poor, underdeveloped African country than a former world superpower. So hard times can also cause fertility rates, and a state's population, to decline as life becomes too hard and too expensive to maintain large families.

IT'S HARD TO STOP HAVING BABIES . . .

Many of you will look at these definitions and numbers and come up with some puzzling questions. You may wonder how China is the most populous state on the planet, with 1.5 billion people, but whose fertility rate is only 1.73. Or perhaps you may discover that projecting ahead in India, they will continue to grow their population rapidly for some time to come—and indeed will surpass China as the most populous state here very soon—but their fertility rate is only 2.73 . . . hey, that's not very much more than replacement level! How is this possible?

Simple. **Population Momentum** is the answer you seek. Consider India for the next 50 years:

FIGURE 2.13 INDIA: THE SNOWBALL GROWS

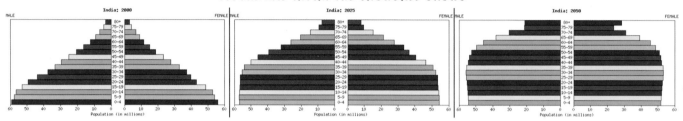

What these three images from 2000, 2025, and 2050 in India are showing you is the Demographic Transition model in action. In 2000, India was early- to mid-Stage Three, as you can just detect the perfect pyramid starting to round away the edges of the bottom age cohorts in an obvious sign that cultural lag is wearing off and fertility rates are starting to sink from what were highs of 4 to 6 kids average per fertile female. We see in 2025 that this has taken full effect, and India is certainly in the column shape as its late Stage 3 or early Stage 4 industrialization has knocked down fertility rates to a precise 2.1, the replacement level. It's a perfect column. So how can population totals continue to expand after this?

Population momentum is like a snowball rolling down a steep hill. Even after fertility rate stabilization, the population pyramid will have to "fill out its figure," as you can see by projecting further ahead to 2050. Everyone may be only having 2.1 kids, but a much bigger number of them are doing it, as represented by those bottom age cohorts back in 2000, where the stabilization actually starts. By the time the snowball reaches the bottom of the hill, it is massive—as will India be by the time its population total flatlines.

SOME FINAL THOUGHTS ON PEOPLE . . .

They disgust me! No, I'm joking. I love the peoples, especially the ladies. . . . What can we say about the future of population on our plaid planet? It shouldn't be too hard to figure out some general trends. Most countries will continue down the development path, and thus we should be able to track what's happening in societies and within population dynamics through the lens of our Demographic Transition model. Everybody in the world wants a good job, a good standard of living, access to health care, a better life for their kids. It's just the human way.

Having said that, there is nothing to lead me to believe that poorer states won't continue to try and modernize and industrialize like the rich ones have. Is this possible? That's a whole other ballgame we won't get into yet. But what will this mean for the peoples of the planet? The world population total will continue to go up for some time to come . . . but we can be more specific than that:

→ The least-developed countries are the places where population will truly grow the fastest, and the most. Regions like sub-Saharan Africa, the Middle East, Central America, and most of Asia will continue to pile on the humans, even though they are the regions perhaps most ill-equipped to handle more.

→ Regions further down the development path, like China, India, Mexico, and South America, will continue to grow too, albeit at a slower pace as fertility rates stabilize.

→ Fully developed regions, like Western Europe, US/Canada, and Australia are stabilized populations with no growth, but with the potential to grow bigger only through allowing immigration from other regions.

→ Regions that are currently shrinking in populations, like Russia, Eastern Europe, some parts of Western Europe, and Japan, will almost certainly not disappear—but most certainly will encourage folks to have more kids and allow more immigration as well.

This is the current state of the plaid world. This is the future state of the plaid world. How many kids do you want? How many can the plaid world support? All of the factors explained in this chapter combine to create the world population of today. Check out the regional totals in Figure 2.14 to see how these things are reflected in today's world. And know these figures well.

FIGURE 2.14 WORLD REGIONAL MAP WITH POPULATION TOTALS

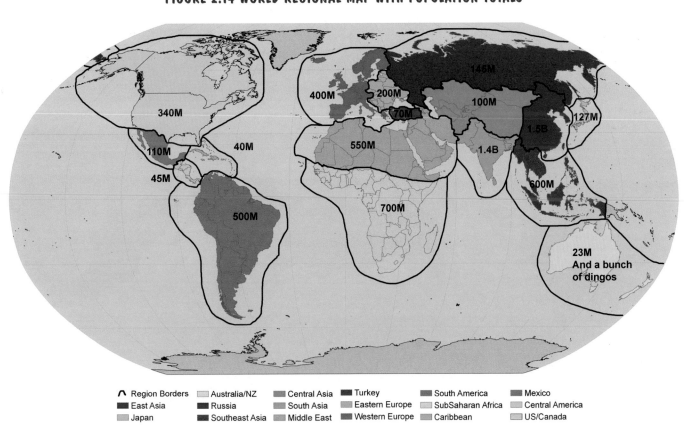

∧ Region Borders	Australia/NZ	Central Asia	■ Turkey	South America	Mexico
■ East Asia	■ Russia	South Asia	Eastern Europe	SubSaharan Africa	Central America
Japan	■ Southeast Asia	Middle East	■ Western Europe	Caribbean	US/Canada

Now let's see what you've learned about population dynamics, population pyramids, and fertility rates. Help the Plaid Avenger find his way home with his family. Match the Plaid Avenger fertility rate to the appropriate population pyramid and then to the country to which they belong. Be sure to notice the partial children! (ADD)

Fertility Rate

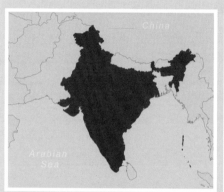

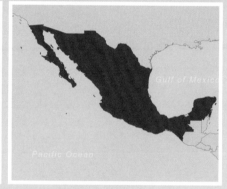

Country of Origin

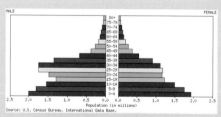
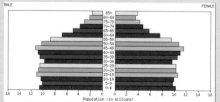
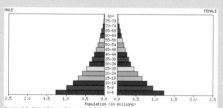

Population Pyramid

Source: U.S Census Bureau, International Data Base

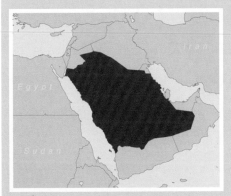

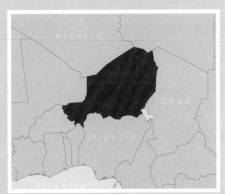

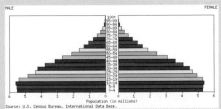

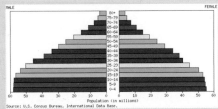

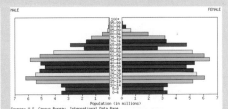

Source: U.S Census Bureau, International Data Base

Know Your Heads of State

3

WE'VE talked about peoples in the world, we've talked about what people do for a living, their economy, maybe we've even talked about people's religions, but where are they doing all this? Mostly they are doing it in some place we mostly call a "state." This textbook is all about the regions of the world, and indeed we're going to tackle 18 or 19 of those regions here in a little bit. That's first and foremost how the Plaid Avenger wants you to understand what's going on around the planet. But regions are user-defined, and even as good a user as I am, many edges around regions can be fuzzy. On the other hand, everybody is located in a legally and physically defined entity—a thing called a "state." And the borders of a state are not up for debate. What the hell's a state? What's that all about? Where did it come from? What's going on with it? And why is it important for understanding the world?

IDEA OF A STATE

The idea of a defined territory over which a political entity would rule is a fairly new concept. If you think back, for most of human history there have been kings, or rulers, or leaders of *peoples*, not of geographically defined political entities. Think back to, let's say, the French. I know most of us try not to think about the French, but bear with me for a moment. Throughout most of history, the king or leader has been referred to as the *King of the Francs*, not the *King of France*. It's only around the 16th and 17th century that this innovation of legally defining a space on the earth evolved—the idea that we're going to define a place on the planet in which those Francs cohabitate and call it France. In the 18th century the concept really spread to the European colonies and ex-colonies, and then on to the rest of the planet.

FIGURE 3.1 SOVEREIGN STATES BY AGE

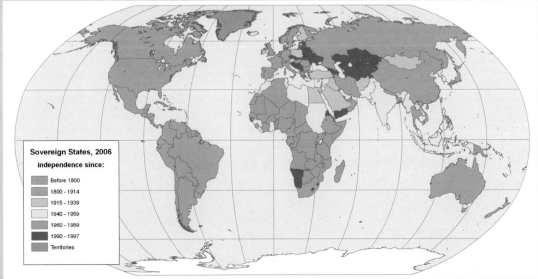

Sovereign States, 2006
independence since:

- Before 1800
- 1800 - 1914
- 1915 - 1939
- 1940 - 1959
- 1960 - 1989
- 1990 - 1997
- Territories

There are some truly old states in the world, China and Persia (Iran) in particular, where ethnically distinct nations of folks did mark off the borders of their empires for a good long time. While we can recognize this fact, the idea that these borders are recognized by all others is the truly European addition to the idea; it is also why most European states are counted among the world's oldest, even though they may be relatively new in the real scheme of things. One has to look no further than the United States to see how new this concept is; the US is in the "oldest" category of states despite the fact it is truly one of the youngest countries on the planet! We've only been around for 200 years total, but we are one of the oldest sovereign states!

A 19th century wave of new states cropped up as European colonies started declaring independence: the countries of Latin America, South Africa, and Australia. Some others popped up as a result of disintegrating empires in Europe: Germany, Italy, Bulgaria, and Romania. Another wave cropped up as the Ottoman Empire, which controlled a large chunk of the Middle East dissolved in the early 20th century. It didn't really get to places like Africa and India and Asia (large chunks of which were European colonial holdings) until they became independent countries (that is, states) in the second half of the 20th century. So if we looked around the planet, most states in the world are fairly new.

So a state, in its basic definition, is a politically defined area with people who are recognized across the planet. Most sovereign states on the planet are fairly new, having been reshaped or declared independent in the last fifty years or so. Maybe we should start defining these terms that the Plaid Avenger is throwing out here. What is a state? What is a nation? What is a nation-state? And before we even get to those, we have to tackle the critical issue of sovereignty, which is one of . . .

THE ESSENTIAL INGREDIENTS

What are we talking about? We hear these terms all the time, but what do they mean? Well, we kind of already hinted at it. A state has something to do with some defined boundaries. That's easy. A **state** is a legally defined and recognized political area on the planet. Lines are drawn like a deed, and all the neighbors agree to its parameters—at least mostly.

But it's not just about a legal description is it? When we think about the term **the state,** and if you ask people what was exactly needed to have a state, you would get a wide variety of answers. Many would say you need a government to head up the state, or a military to protect the state, or a fence around the state. Others would say you need an economy, or money, or official currency, or jobs to have a state. Some might point out that you obviously need some area and some people and some stuff to have a state. Maybe you need roads and buildings and sewer systems and hospitals and McDonalds to have a state. Perhaps you need a constitution, or laws, or courts to have a real state. What do you think a state needs?

I'll give you the brief answer: you really only need two things to have yourself a state. Number One is sovereignty. And the concept is so important, that the Number Two thing you need is also sovereignty. Yeah, I'm a goofball, but now you will always remember the two things you need to be a state. Sovereignty and sovereignty. If you've got it, you don't even need all that other stuff to be a state. So what is sovereignty, and why is it so darned important in today's world?

What state am I in, when I'm in the United States?

By the way, the term *state* is what we use synonymously with *country* here in the United States of America. It gets confusing. Here in the US we say we're in the state of Virginia, but we're not really. We're in the state of the USA. We just say *countries* because it makes it easier. Country equals state, state equals country; just use the term **state** when you're dealing with international politics. Everybody understands it better. What state of inebriation are you in right now as you are contemplating which state of the United States you are in, which of course is a state in its own right, right now. Right?

ALL YOU NEED IS LOVE . . . NO, I MEANT SOVEREIGNTY

What is sovereignty? Well, the concrete definition of sovereignty is really up for grabs nowadays. For the last couple hundred years, it has been a concept that everybody has agreed on and understood, but in the last couple of decades, there's been some serious debate about what it truly means now. Times have changed, and it appears the idea of sovereignty is changing too. And this redefinition is causing considerable consternation in the world, among big states, small states, and all states in-between. But I'm getting ahead of myself.

First we want to find out what it truly means for an entity to have sovereignty, and thus be called a state. The Plaid Avenger's simple interpretation is this: holding the ultimate power over the people in your territory constitutes true sovereignty. No other state can have power over your territory or the people in it. And how can you demonstrate that you hold ultimate power over your people? Kill them. Straight up. If you can legally get away with it, then you have sovereignty, and you are a sovereign state in the world.

What?

Let me say that again.

In the end game, does the political entity have the ultimate right to do the ultimate deed within its borders? And what is the ultimate deed? The ultimate, beat all, true test of power is the taking of life. When you think about it, everything else is quite trivial, isn't it? The right to tax, to boss around, to enact laws over, to make inferior products at crappy jobs, or sing crappy national anthems . . . that's all pretty tame stuff compared to death. If you can legally kill people within your state, that is, the leaders and government can kill their own citizens legally and nobody else in the world cares about it, or can do anything else about it, then you're in something we call a state.

Again, people want to say that sovereignty means a system, a government, some leadership, some people who vote, some walls . . . well you'll have all of that. But if you want the real test of "Is this place a state?" find out if they can kill their own citizens. Now that sounds extreme, and . . . it really is! Are we a sovereign state in the US? Can the US pass the ultimate sovereignty test? Absolutely. We kill people everyday; it's called capital punishment. The death sentence.

So the government kills people. They put criminals to death. But that's too easy. That's something we understand. That's just baby stuff to the real issue I'm talking about here. Let's take it a step further: How about innocent people? What would happen if the government of this country, or any country, just decided to kill 10,000 of its own citizens? Let's say the FBI or the CIA bungled some information (like that's never happened before?) and decided that the entire state of Delaware had to be eliminated by presidential directive, and then nuked it. Now, again, that's extreme. Nothing like that's going to happen . . . yet. But let's say it happened. What would France's response be? What would the UK do? What would China do? What would Angola do?

Save for giving the offender a great big collective hairy eyeball, the answer is . . . they would do nothing, *especially if it were France*. Even though it's an extreme event, and it may be of horrific consequences, the US is a sovereign state. We can legally kill our own citizens, as can all sovereign states. That is an agreed upon principle, and again, it's the extreme. If you can kill someone in your state, then you can pretty much do anything else. You can tax them, you can tell them what to do, make some laws, you can do all that stuff. If you can do the extreme, you can do all the lesser stuff, and that's the first big principle rule of sovereignty. So the *Number One Rule of Sovereignty* is: Does the state have the ultimate right to do the ultimate deed to its citizens, without the interference of other states? If the answer is "yes" then you're in a sovereign state.

Now, how do you get that status? What if I, The Plaid Avenger, created a Little Plaid World over here, and I said, "Well I'm giving myself the authority to kill all people who enter the royal domains of my backyard, which I have christened Plaidtopia." Obviously people would say no, you can't do that man, you are crazy. Because even if Plaidtopia had a constitution, some laws, an economy, some area, a fence, a military, a police force, and even a harem of women bodyguards who were trained to kill interlopers on my behalf, it still wouldn't be a sovereign state. The reason that I could not do it is because other political entities, namely states, wouldn't agree with it. That's the *Number Two Rule of Sovereignty*.

Number Two Rule of Sovereignty is that all the other states in the sovereign state club recognize your sovereignty. You are in the "country" club, so to speak. Indeed, the UN is kind of the country club, and if all the other sovereign states say, "Yes, not only can you kill your own citizens, we respect your right to kill your own citizens," then you indeed possess sovereignty. If you are in a legally defined political territory, recognized by other sovereign states, and no other state has power over your territory—as ultimately tested by killing your own citizens—you are a sovereign state. Everything else is inconsequential; it doesn't amount to a hill of beans.

BUT SOVEREIGNTY MAY BE REDEFINED

Why would I suggest that this concept is up for grabs? One of the reasons that today's world is so complicated is because the nature of the world has changed. It's one of the reasons the Plaid Avenger has gotten involved in international justice—the

I love cigars, and re-defining sovereignty.

concept has lost credibility in the 21st century. Everybody for centuries has said, "Yeah you can kill your own citizens, as long as you're not attacking another sovereign state; no one's got a problem with it." That's been the agreed upon, core, central component to sovereignty. Part of the base principle here is reciprocity: we will not intervene in your state affairs when you mess with your own citizens. In return, we expect you to respect our ability to mess with our citizens as well. That's the way it all goes. Even today we say, "Hey the US doesn't like what China's doing to its citizens; we think your human rights are atrocious." But we're not going to invade. No one's going to do anything about it, really. We might protest and say, "Hey! China you suck for the way you treat people but . . . here . . . be the host of the Olympics anyway." At most an official condemnation issued from a head of state or perhaps even a trade embargo would be the extent of any disapproval. But no active military intervention is going to happen, because that's what it is to be a sovereign state. We respect their sovereignty so that they will respect ours. Or at least that is the way it was . . .

Why is it changing? It's actually the United States' fault. Perhaps this is something that has been building up, and no, for those of you who are jumping the gun thinking I'm going to attack President Bush and the gang of hawks currently in the White House—I'm not. I'm actually referring to their predecessor, Billy Boy Clinton.

In March of 1999, during the Clinton administration, the United States led NATO on a bombing campaign of Yugoslavia. Why did the United States and NATO start bombing Yugoslavia, a sovereign state?

Because Yugoslavia invaded the US? No

Threatened US citizens? No

Because Yugoslavia invaded another fellow NATO country, which comes under article 5? No Threatened or invaded any other sovereign state? Ummm . . . No

Because Clinton wanted to re-enact the movie '*Wag the Dog*'? Mmmm . . . good one, but no.

Slobodan sez: "I can kill them if I want to . . ."

Does that attack seem important to you? Do you even remember hearing anything about it? I doubt it. But let me be the first to educate you on how big a deal it was to sovereign states. Here's an excerpt from the British *Financial Times:* "The enormity of NATO launching its first attack against a sovereign state is not to be underestimated. Unlike Iraq, Belgrade has not invaded another country. Nor is the situation akin to Bosnia, where the legitimate government invited outside intervention. Nor, finally, has the United Nations Security Council specifically authorized NATO to bomb."

The thing that happened was that this crazy guy, Slobodan Milosevic, started killing his own citizens. The who or why or how is not important right this second. What is important is that killing your own citizens was one of the baseline agreements of sovereignty. States respect the authority of every other sovereign state to kill its own citizens. Yes. You may remember that from seven paragraphs ago. It's the cornerstone. Well, in this circumstance it was an ethnic cleansing situation, perhaps where Slobodan—then the leader of Yugoslavia, currently worm food pushing up daisies, may have been persecuting and encouraging the national army to outright kill members of a specific ethnic group. And in hindsight, there is not much debate about it. Slobodan was actively pursuing genocide/ethnic cleansing . . . but only against his own citizens. And he is the leader of a sovereign state. Should be no problem, but . . .

Apparently it gets to be too much to bear. There's a large outcry about this in Europe and indeed in the United States. Perhaps it's the memory of the Jewish Holocaust that occurred in Europe, or perhaps the instability in this region that had previously launched World War II, or even as some have pointed out, it was simply because there were white people being slaughtered. For whatever reasons, President Bill Clinton decided to enact a bombing campaign, coordinated with NATO, to stop the genocide. Long story short, the United States bombed Yugoslavia into submission for what it was doing to its own citizens.

Why am I telling this long story that we really need to shorten up? Because this has changed the whole identification of a sovereign state. As we suggested, this whole "kill your citizens" thing used to be the standard. What a state did to its own people was not up for debate. But apparently this was the straw that broke the camel's back . . . and it's not an isolated incident. Since the 1999 bombing campaign on Serbia, the US and/or NATO have played an active role in Afghanistan, Bosnia, and Iraq under the umbrella of liberating the locals. Meanwhile, serious genocides have been occurring in Sudan and the Congo, for which many in the international community are calling for invasive action to remedy. Those are on the heels of the now famous Rwandan genocide of 1994, which no state, international organization, or otherwise, stepped in to stop.

All of the listed above are actions, or inactions, based upon unacceptable sovereign state behavior in dealing with their own citizens. Again, it used to be the hallmark of what a sovereign state was; now it's totally up for grabs and totally up for question. How much is the international community going to allow misbehavior, even when that misbehavior is confined inside of a single state?

This is causing a lot of consternation on the planet. Because if the golden rule for what defines a sovereign state is up for question, then what exactly is a sovereign state? Sorry, my friends, the Plaid Avenger doesn't have an answer for you right now, because nobody does.

With the current movement of UN troops around the planet, and unilateral actions by the United States in today's world, we don't really know. You can see this in today's news as a major point of contention particularly with the Chinese, and a lot of times with the Russians. Why those two? Just because they hate the United States? No, it's got nothing to do with that at all. These two countries, particularly the Chinese, are really big into the sovereignty thing because they want to cover their own asses. Remember, forever it's just been: don't invade other countries, respect everyone else's sovereignty, and you can get away with whatever you want in your own country. Well, that's up for grabs now. The Chinese and the Russians think, "We are not really keen with the US involvement in other countries because it is violating the sacred rights of sovereignty that we've all agreed to." Now we're rewriting the textbook and folks are a little troubled by it, particularly in countries where they might actively be doing stuff to their own citizens (e.g., see Russia, see China). So this is a conflicting issue, still up for grabs in the world. We're not really sure which way it's going to work out, as it's all being redefined right this second.

Sparked by the US bombing campaign in Yugoslavia, sovereignty has also been called into question by human rights groups and lots of folks around the planet who say, "Okay, you're right. We're in the 21st century, we cannot allow acts of genocide to occur, even if it is in a sovereign state." While Yugoslavia was the base-map for this, in terms of a trial flight on intervening into a sovereign state to protect its citizens, it will probably be used more. And indeed the Bush administration said, "One of the reasons we went to Iraq was to protect the Kurds and the Shi'ites there from what their own government was doing to them." There are folks around the world who are calling for more action from the UN and the world to stop genocide in other places. So right now people are saying, "Hey! What's the deal? You guys bomb Serbia to protect *those* guys, and you're currently in Iraq protecting *those* people from their government, so how come you didn't interject in Rwanda? Why aren't you in Sudan right now? Those are all acts of genocide too." This is really bugging people. This is a big debate on the world forum right now. And it's another reason why, you'll see, that people hesitate big time in the UN to use the word "genocide." Why is this?

What's the Deal with . . . Genocide?

The deal with genocide is that, well, we all recognize what it is. It's when a government, or a small group of people, kills or tries to completely exterminate another specific group of people, usually based on ethnicity or religion. The worst example of this in modern history occurred during World War II, when the Germans tried to exterminate all of the Jews out of German territory, actually out of all of Europe. This was such a horrific act that after World War II the world kind of agreed that we would never allow this to happen again. All the states in the world even passed a UN law making genocide an international crime. The ***Convention on the Prevention and Punishment of the Crime of Genocide*** says this: "any of the following acts committed with intent to destroy, in whole or in part, a national, ethnic, racial or religious group, as such: Killing members of the group; Causing serious bodily or mental harm to members of the group; Deliberately inflicting on the group conditions of life calculated to bring about its physical destruction in whole or in part; Imposing measures intended to prevent births within the group; and forcibly transferring children of the group to another group."

But the old rules of sovereignty were still in play. Things floated along pretty well, until the appearance of possible genocide in Serbia/Yugoslavia, in Rwanda, and in Sudan. Now wait a minute. Didn't we all agree we were not going to let this happen again? So shouldn't we do something?

That is one of the calls on the world stage right now. But the reason you did not hear about Rwandan genocide, or the situation in Sudan today, is because the use of that particular word demands a call for action. In other words, as long as everybody in the UN is just saying: "Yeah, well, they've got a civil war," or "They have some sort of internal conflict," or perhaps "They may have isolated acts of ethnic cleansing," (which was said about Rwanda) then there is no need to act. Sovereignty takes precedence. They say these things very intentionally because everyone is scared to whisper: "It's genocide." If everyone in the UN agrees that genocide is occurring, then they have to act. It's their law.

That's the deal with genocide and why people gingerly dance around the term, particularly the UN. And you also now know how genocide is calling into question the whole sovereignty theme. Plaid Avenger tip: Watch Sudan for the next big explosive test of sovereignty, and how far it can be pushed in relation to genocide.

NATION, STATE, OR NATION-STATE?

So now we've looked at what constitutes a state. Perhaps now you know more about what constitutes a state than you ever wanted to know. Yeah, me too. But it's my job. However, what about these other terms? What is a *nation?* Is it different from a *state?* And if so, then what in the living hell is a *nation-state?* It's easy. Let's break it down.

A ***state,*** you now know, is a legally defined political unit that possesses ***sovereignty.*** Fair enough. I've beaten you over the head with that for several pages now.

A ***nation,*** straight up, has really nothing to do with a state. You think it does, but it doesn't. A nation is about the people. Remember the intro paragraph of this chapter? This is what it *used* to mean in the world, a leader led a specific group of people. It's all about the peoples. A nation has much more to do with the people than any specific area. In fact, some peoples don't even have an area—but I get ahead of myself. A nation refers to a group of people who share a common culture, and who may even want to have their own government, and may want to rule themselves. Common culture could be just about anything, but often it is a combination of a lot of things: ethnicity, religion, historical background, diet, maybe they believe the same ideas about life and death, how to dress, how to dance, how to drink . . . whatever.

The number of nations is undefined. There could be thousands, hell, could be millions. It depends on what group of people and on what scale you're looking. Perhaps in every town there's a small nation of people who think that they're different; that they share a common culture, and perhaps would like to form their own country. Again, it's an undeterminable number, but it is all about the people. Let's think about some true examples on the planet that we can all agree are distinct groups of people who share a common culture. This is actually quite easy.

Distinct nations are all over the place . . . but are they in nation-states?

What common cultures are there around the world that are tied to people? How about the French? How about the Germans? Wow, this is getting easier; let's stay in Europe. How about the Italians? Think of all these guys. They all have distinct common cultures from each other; just think about cuisine if nothing else. Just think alcoholic beverages: Germans drink beer; the French drink wine. The Czechs, the Poles, the Russians. All distinct cultures and peoples. But it can get even more specific. We could look at the UK as a UK culture. Kind of, but there's definitely a Scottish culture within the UK, and an English culture, but we're stuck in the Old World. Is there a Saudi nation? Yes, I believe there probably is. Is there an Argentinean one? That one gets a little fuzzier, but it's possible. Japanese? Yes, definitely. Japanese is a nation, a distinct group of people, distinct common culture. The Chinese, yes, the Vietnamese, yes, Thai, Laotian, Indian, Kurds, the Turks, the Maasai tribesmen in Kenya? Sure. So we could go all over the planet and see this common culture, and an idea of a group of people who share something in common who, may or may not, want to rule themselves, under their own government. That's a nation.

Let's get to the final definition here: what is a **nation-state?** Simple. Let's just add a nation to a state, and presto, you got a nation-state. A **nation-state** is a group of people who share a common culture, who want to have their own government and

FIGURE 3.2 TYPICAL NATIONS WITH STATES

Turks in Turkey, Thais is Thailand. Yep, that's a nation-state!

FIGURE 3.3: SOME EXAMPLES OF NATIONS WITHOUT STATES

Nations sans statehood

want to rule themselves—a nation—and do so in a defined and recognized political area—a state—which has sovereignty to boot. That is a nation-state. Let's give an example of a nation-state. We look around the world, and see a lot of the ones we've already talked about. Germany: perfect nation-state. This group of people with a common culture in a distinct area that we call Germany. The French: same deal. The Japanese: even better. The Koreans: best example yet; a 100 percent ethnically homogeneous group of folks, with a distinct Korean culture, distinct cuisine. That's it; that's a nation-state.

But the list can go on and on, all over the world. Most of the places in the world are close to what we call a nation-state. Of greater significance than listing all that are nation-states would be to look at those places in the world that are not.

Which brings up the question: can we have a **nation without a state?** Indeed. We certainly can. And this is one of the causes for conflict on the planet today. There are lots of groups of people with a shared common culture, and a desire to rule themselves in a legally defined territory—but they don't have that sovereign state status. A prime example is the Palestinians in a place called Palestine, which is not yet a state (it might be soon) but who are still largely under the control of Israel. Both parties are working on making the Palestinians a nation-state.

Let's get more complicated. Places like Chechnya—yeah, good one! A very distinct culture in a place that's called Chechnya, but it's not sovereign. They'd like to be sovereign; they would love to not be part of Russia, because they are not Russian. But they are also not sovereign. Russia might yield someday to their nation-state aspirations.

Lama has no state.

And what about Tibet? You've heard of them. The leader of the Tibetans, the Dali Lama, is the spiritual leader of the Buddhist movement on the planet. Their spiritual and traditional homeland has been Tibet. Most of the people there share this Tibetan culture and Buddhist culture, but they are part of China. Thus, they are not a nation-state. It's one that's likely to *never* become a nation-state. That's a little Plaid insider tip for you. Sorry Lama. So, some very good examples of nations without states. Some of these are areas quite active in the world in the terms of conflict, with those people trying to become stand-alone nation-states, and full-fledged sovereign states at that.

HOW MANY STATES ARE THERE?

There are an unidentifiable number of nations. Groups of people that are self-defined, and at multiple scales, are all over the place. Every country will have small pockets or groups of folks that consider themselves culturally different. Like the Basque in Spain, the Scottish in the UK, or the French in Canada . . . maybe we should just say the French, everywhere. It's impossible to determine the number of nations. Now nation-states, that's a little bit easier. But even that definition gets a little muddled if you think about it too much. Is the US a nation-state? What's our common culture? Besides a shared hatred of Celene Dion, do we share any unequivocal commonality?

However, the number of states we can say with some confidence. Yes, we can look at some numbers. You'll hear this question a lot, and the number is growing so you have to keep up with world events to stay ahead of the curve. How many states are there? The magic number we're using right now is 192. Now if you look at the number of countries in the UN, that number will be 191. What are we talking about again? We're talking about sovereign states in the "country" club. They all recognize each other, and they recognize each other's sovereignty.

Pope sez: "Hell no" to UN.

Let's get back to the numbers. There are 191 members of the United Nations. Why 191? Because the Vatican City, which is a sovereign state (all the other 191 recognize it as a sovereign state), is not a member of the UN. That's why there's a little confusion here. The Pope and his buddies have said, "Nah, that's okay, the UN is cool, but we're kind of a religious people. We're going to keep to ourselves."

So 191 is the official ticker at the UN, and everybody recognizes the Vatican City, so that's 192 all together. Some folks would perhaps say there are 193 states. Now where is this confusion arising from? The confusion is Taiwan. It is somewhere in the middle, at least for a little while longer. Is it a nation? Yes, probably. Is it a state? No, probably not. Most other states recognize this fact. Others do not. There are about 23 sovereign states in the world that say, "Yes, we actually do recognize Taiwanese sovereignty. We think they should be in the country club." But the vast majority, the other 169, don't see it that way. There is no consensus, so Taiwan is not considered a fully sovereign state. Not at the UN, not in the US, and not in most of the world. In the future, you will see that group of 23 who do recognize Taiwan as a sovereign state shrink away to non-existence. Our boys over in China are working hard on those countries that do recognize Taiwanese sovereignty to make sure that they soon won't.

However, there will soon be a 193, and we might see 194 coming up in the next several years as well. The first tag-along is East Timor. It was formerly a colony of the Portuguese—a situation that made it distinct from the rest of the Indonesian territory that was controlled by the Dutch. In the last decade, they have had independence movements. When the Portuguese finally pulled out, they voted for sovereignty. Indonesia was not keen on that happening, so it turned into a bloody mess. We won't get into it here, but they are now on the path to becoming a sovereign state. They have a few more hoops to jump through, but people at the UN say, "Yes, when it comes up for a vote, we will vote to recognize East Timor as a sovereign state."

Number 194 will probably be Palestine. Now this is a big "IF," since it's the Middle East, and you can't predict its future from one second to the next, much less year to year. For the last decade, there has been a general movement toward Palestinian independence from the state of Israel. Indeed, given the track record of the last two years, it does seem, with a lot of trouble and turbulence, that they are heading toward that goal. So we might be looking at two years out, we might be looking at ten years out, but certainly at some point, there will probably be 194.

Speaking of Israel and Palestine, it is also important to note that the recognition of a state is not

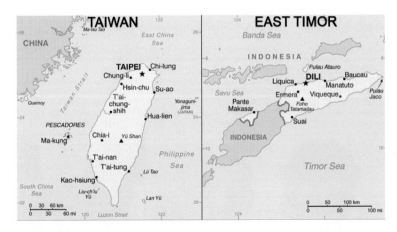

Future statehood? Taiwan out, Timor in!

always a given . . . depending upon who you are asking the question to. For instance, while Israel is certainly fully accepted as a state by most governments in the world and the UN, many Arab and Islamic countries continue to shun it; in particular,

Iran outright refuses to recognize it at all. North Korea refuses to recognize South Korea, and vice-versa. Turkey refuses to recognize Cyprus. And in what can only be called the most un-exciting recognition refusal of all time, Liechtenstein and the Czech Republic refute each other's existence because of some ancient WWII era decree. What a bunch of boneheads.

The most current, hottest sovereignty showdown has erupted in early 2008 when Kosovo declared independence from Serbia, and about 40 countries (the US and most EU states) immediately recognized it. This would perhaps be no big deal (like the Taiwan issue is not anymore) but for one small fact: this showdown is pitting major powers against each other. What do I mean? The US, UK, and France all recognize it, while China and Russia are firmly opposed. Hey, that's a major rift at the UN Permanent Security Council . . . a topic for later discussion.

Kosovo causing consternation.

And one more thing: let me point out a few places that are not states, that are often mistaken for states. Some of them are still colonies of other countries. For example, French Guiana, a fairly big place in South America, is a French colony; it's not a state. Places like Greenland, that's still a Danish colony. There are some extenuating circumstances too, some strange ones, like Western Sahara, which Morocco is claiming and is attempting to absorb legally and politically. It's in some "nowhere land status" in the middle. Bermuda is an overseas territory of the UK; not a sovereign state. And Puerto Rico! Not a state and not really an independent territory; it's not really a colonial holding either. It's just kind of associated with the United States. So that's a bit of a muddled situation there as well.

On top of that, you have a lot of nations around the world *without* a state, which are sometimes mistaken for states. Places like Tibet in China we have referenced already. Or like the Scottish, we think of Scotland—that is a political subdivision of the UK, not a state. It's a nation, a group of people who definitely think they're culturally distinct. You know, Scottish people, we'd all agree to that—they are the guys that wear kilts, play noisy instruments, and eat haggis. Damn, that is definitely a distinct culture—and let's make sure they stay that way. Keep that haggis shit distinct from my neighborhood. They are eating that stuff? The hell

Stateless hagis-eaters.

with them; give them the nation-state status! Of course they produce that lovely beverage, Scotch, which is distinct around the entire planet as well. But they are a sub-state, a province of the UK, for lack of a better word. They are not an independent state. There are 192 in the world right now that are true states; possibly 193 and 194 are coming up in the batter's circle.

Extreme Left
Anarchy . . .

Communism . . .

Direct Democracy . . .

Representative
Democracy . . .

One-Party State . . .

WHO CONTROLS THE STATE?

So we talked about what was a state, what is a state, who is not a state, it's all about the state . . . but who controls the state? That's what the rest of this chapter is all about: World governments and world political systems, the guys in charge of these sovereign entities. Before we get to that, we have to throw out a few terms that we hear all the time, and the Plaid Avenger is going to make sense of it for you, but boy, is it a mess. There are so many terms, they cross over, they refer to each other, and they refer not to just politics, but sometimes economics, and sometimes religions, and sometimes social issues. They are terms like the **Left** versus the **Right, Liberal** versus **Conservative, Communism** versus **Capitalism.** We'll get to some of these terms in later chapters, but let's start with the **Left** versus the **Right.** Throughout this book, we're going to talk about leftist governments and rightist movements and we're going to deal with them politically right this second.

So what does it mean to be the **Left** or the **Right** in the political spectrum? Often we've heard "lefty commies" and "extreme rightist" or "rightist fascist." What does this mean? Again, we're talking about the *world* political stage, not the politics within independent sovereign states. It's easy to get the terms mixed up; you might hear reference to "the liberal Left" or the "conservative Right" in America, but that stuff doesn't mean the same thing that we are talking about on the world stage.

So check out the world stage, the world political spectrum, from left to right as you can see across the bottom of these pages. Maybe you're starting to get a sense of what it means. Here's what I want you to know about it. On the extreme left would be government styles like communism or anarchy. These are ruling systems where there is little to no central government control. Another way to put it is as you head to the left, less government power, more power in the hands of the people. This is best displayed by anarchy, which we think of as a chaotic state, but indeed there are anarchists, political anarchists, and what they believe in is that there should be no government at all. Every single person within every single state in every single society should have the right to do anything they want. That's what anarchy really means. It's never existed anywhere, and probably never will, but the theory is that the people have *all* of the power. Never mind the bullocks, the government, or the rulers of the state, have no control over individual people. That's an extreme.

What's on the other side of the political spectrum, on the other extreme? That's on the total extreme right, which is just the reverse. All of the power is in the government hands. Control of the country is in the hands of the few, the people in charge. Most of the population has zero or limited political voice on the extreme right. To think of it in perspective—and extremes are always good to clarify the perspectives—is that the power pyramid is upside down in anarchy. The people are on the top; they get everything, and can do anything they want. On the extreme right are fascists like Hitler, who actually said something to the effect of "*I* am the state. An individual person. Me. I am the state. Everyone here in this state of Germany is here at my disposal at my will. *I am the state.* You work for *me.*" On the left, is just the reverse; the state works for *you.* The state as an apparatus that exists solely for the people. That's a huge difference to consider. That's what the real spectrum is all about. All of the political systems in the world fall somewhere between these two extremes, because (here's a little insider tip), these extremes don't exist anywhere. In fact, some of these systems hardly exist anywhere at all. So let's go through them really quickly.

Theocracy . . .   Monarchy . . .   Military Government . . .   Dictatorship . . .   . . . Extreme Right Fascism

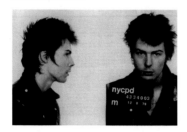
ANARCHY

We'll start on the left. Anarchy, as I already suggested, is essentially no government at all. Maybe the Libertarian party in the United States is close to ideological anarchy in that they don't want any interjection or interference by anybody overtop. Yeah, Ron Paul partying with Sid Vicious . . . now there's a good time! No superstructure, no hierarchy of folks that are in control of anything. In an anarchy state, there would be really no government to speak of, no national defense, no one taking care of roads, or any of that kind of stuff. So you're starting to get the flavor of this; high-schoolers with punk rock jackets may think that anarchy's really cool, but it doesn't sound too good when you really begin to define what's going on in this type of society. It's pretty much every man for himself. We already know in human society that this deteriorates fairly rapidly into people beating the living daylights out of each other for a cigarette. But in a political spectrum, when we're just thinking about this abstract idea politically, it's: "No, it's the individual right to do anything he/she wants." Long story short, ain't never happened anywhere, ain't gonna happen anywhere. Are there any anarchy states anywhere in the world today? There is perhaps one, but it's not intentional, and that would be Somalia. It is a state that has fallen into chaos—and we typically consider anarchy and chaos synonymous—and indeed, that is the case for Somalia. But they aren't really an anarchy; they didn't intentionally become anarchic; they've just deteriorated into chaos. In the sense of an intentionally instituted system of anarchy, the whole concept humorously contradicts itself. Much like Ron Paul running for president. So, really, there aren't any true anarchic states in the world.

COMMUNISM

Communism is another hilarious one because it doesn't exist anywhere either. What a barrel of laughs. The Plaid Avenger wonders if it actually ever did exist anywhere. So what are we talking about here then? Why are we talking about it at all if it doesn't exist? Because the ideology is powerful, and it has greatly shaped history, especially the last century. Communism as an idea is still a potent force that shapes judgments of decision makers around the planet. There are several confusing factors about Communism, and before I get to those confusing points, let's just say what it is.

Communism was a concept that had been around forever, but some folks in 19th century Europe (namely Marx and Engels) really put it into its modern interpretation. These guys were living in the environment of the Industrial Revolution. They were witnesses to flagrant excesses of capitalism, ruled by monarchs on the throne who controlled all political power, and rich factory owners who controlled the economy. Marx and his ilk looked around and said, "This really sucks. We have no power over our lives. We need more power to the people." So they wrote their manifestos and all that jazz, and long story short, came up with this: In a Communist political system there is a government, but the government is solely there (remember the inverted pyramid) to provide everything that the citizens need. To facilitate this provision of economic and political needs, the government would set up small *soviets*: that is, small groups of folks in cities of which every citizen is a member . . . everybody is attached to a specific soviet, kind of like voting districts here in the US, but much much smaller. These soviets would debate on every issue that affect the people. In this manner the government listens to the people directly and distributes resources or makes decisions based on the citizens' needs and requests.

How can a government afford to do that? In this society there is no private property, the state controls it all. In other words the government is kind of "by the people, for the people"—we think about that in democracy—but it's even beyond that. It exists solely to distribute everything as per the needs of the people in the society, and that means economic as well as political power. That's one of the reasons it's extremely confusing.

→ Confusing point #1: Communism is both a political and economic term, because it combines politics and economy into one system in which all ownership of property is communal, all resources are owned by the government; the entire economy and the political system is run by a singular government. It's the only kind of system that works that way. All of the other political systems we'll talk about are just politics, and the economy goes its own way and does its own thing. In true Communism, it's all one big happy family where the government, Big Brother, controls everything.

→ Confusing point #2: When we think about the manifestations of Communism in the world, we typically think of dictatorship. The big one, of course, is during the Soviet experience: the USSR under Stalin. Or even Chairman Mao. Communism in China turns into Maoist China, a singular leader that ends up being a dictator. Even when it's not a well-recognized singular leader, these systems tend to perpetuate a small group of people in charge of everything.

Indeed, that's exactly what has always happened. Politically, when Communism has tried to manifest itself, it never works because the whole thing is supposed to be a transition. What do I mean by that? During the Soviet experience, Lenin came to power in 1917 with his commie posse. They were attempting to implement a system that had never been tried before. To become politically Communist meant to be politically and economically Communist. So Lenin said, "Well, okay, this has never been done before. We want to get to this utopian society where everybody's equal, and all decisions are made communally, and all property is held communally, and all resources are distributed communally—that's what we're shooting for. But we're not there yet. In fact, we're very far from it. So we need to set up a small group of people in order to get from point A to point B. In other words, to get from where we are now to our perfect commie society, we basically have to become an oligarchy/dictatorship . . . just for a while." I'm paraphrasing here. That is not a quote from Lenin. He is not as good-looking as me, although the goatee is stylin' . . .

Main point: this is supposed to be a temporary thing, a transition, a transitory government. But here's the problem folks: Of all of the societies that have tried to go down the Communist path, not one single one has actually finished the transition. In other words, they start the transition, and they want to get to this pure utopian society, but it always ends up as a power grab by few people . . . or typically one person, who we then call a dictator. Good examples are in the Soviet system; Stalin becomes a singular dictator. In the Cuban system, Castro, who's still there, is a singular man in charge of everything. In China, Mao, and then his successors, are singular people. It never fully develops into equality for all. Plaid Avenger Tip: Communism will never, has never, and did I mention will never work the way it ideally should.

In fact, here's

→ Confusing point #3: There are no Communist countries on the planet right now. They don't exist. Even if we look at places like today's China, or even today's Cuba, these are something closer to what we would call one-party systems, because *purely* political Communist states can't exist—remember, the system is a political/economic combo. It's like peanut butter and jelly or 'Tango and Cash': they got to happen together. Today, everybody pretty much now has some form of capitalist economies. In other words, the economies of even the "Communist" countries are not communist. Everybody's given up on that. Since Communism in its pure form is both politics and economy, it does not exist. So we've got to re-classify everything that *was* categorized a commie in some other category.

Those are the three confusing points about Communism. Let's move onto something more sound, and that is . . . direct democracy.

DEMOCRACY

Now we're getting into familiar territory; this is the stuff that we all get and understand, 'cause we live in it. Democracy: *ocracy* = "ruled by" and *demo* = "the people." We are still in this inverted pyramid in which the government is here mostly for the people, as a service for the people. Not the other way around. We are not here to serve the US government, it is

here to serve us. It protects us; it does things that are in our interest, not its own interest. That may be up for debate on some issues, but that is the system as it is in the abstract form. Direct democracy, doesn't really exist anywhere; we don't even have it in the US. Direct democracy says, "We think everybody's so equal that every single issue and every single person we vote for and every law we enact must be voted upon by every single person involved in democracy, that is, everyone in the state." You can probably figure out why there's not too many of these in the world—because it's impossible. In countries that have millions of people you can't have millions of people trying to come to a common consensus on what's going on—even if it were something as simple as a dog-leash law. Direct democracy, that is, democracy that involves every single person, really only exists in one place that I know of, and these guys are screwed up on several fronts, and that is the Swiss. I mean, even their cheese is full of holes, so you can't expect too much from the rest of the culture . . .

The Swiss have the closest manifestation of direct democracy on the planet. All citizens have to spend a large component of their time dealing with all the laws that have to be passed. (Kind of sounds like that *soviet* stuff described above don't it?) And there is a much larger percentage of folks who serve in some sort of elected office. Like almost all of them. I won't say it's a chaotic system, but it's definitely a time-demanding system that most of the planet is not willing to ascribe to. That's why most of the planet is a multiparty state/representative democracy.

This is exactly the same as a direct democracy in terms of the government working for the people. But, instead of all of us voting on every damn thing, we just vote for a few people and say, "You guys go decide. We will elect you into positions of power, knowing that you are here for our good. If you piss us off, or you do something wrong, we will un-vote you by voting for somebody else." That's the way it works, but the main term here is "representative." That is, one person is going to represent our county, or district, or state, and we're giving him/her the power to decide what's best for us. Does that make sense? It should, it's not that complicated.

On a side note: Multiparty states and representative democracy are all the rage on the planet right now. It is the government option of choice for most. And one that is growing. In the last twenty years, since the demise of the Soviet Union, this is the one that all the cool kids do. It is the most accepted, and the most perpetuated by the UN, and by big states like the United States and European countries. This one is heading up in the numbers column. Most of the planet is in this category already.

Before we go on to the other ones, I want to point out another thing under this representative democracy description. How could direct democracy and representative democracy be right next to communism on the political spectrum? This is confusing, and we've already pointed out why the term communism is so confusing. So if we are not leftists here, then why are the two right beside each other on the left side of the spectrum? People in the US don't consider themselves to be leftists, but indeed, if you look at the whole spectrum, you are. That is, you're for the people, and that's more liberal, to the left. Liberate the people, freedom for the people, everything's for the people. In that sense, communism (on paper) is right beside democracy. There's just slightly different takes on how to go about getting power in the hands of the people. It's confusing, because communism has never worked. But in theory, it's all about people, just like democracy is. Now it gets a little simpler, as we're going to start heading to the right with one-party states.

ONE-PARTY STATES

One-party states are exactly what they imply. Something that looks like elections happen from time to time. Sometimes there are things that look like choices on the ballot. But there's only one real political party that always seems to win. There's only one political party that seems to be in charge. Some of these are in a transition zone from what used to be called communism, like China. Some of them are bordering on dictatorship, like Egypt, but have been wise enough to keep in the good graces of the West by putting on the democracy window dressing. That is, they do have parliaments, and they do have groups of people come together who make laws, but it's pretty much only one group of people in charge, or one political party that's in charge. In other words, you can go vote at the polls, but there's only one group of folks that you vote for. Egypt would be another great example of a category that was not a former Communist state but who has a president;

Hosni and Hu: The only ones to vote for.

they've had elections for thirty years; and the same guy has won every single time. Is he that popular? Do people love him that much? Well, perhaps, but maybe it's because he's the only person on the ballot. So, even though he's a staunch ally of the United States, and we say, "Hey, that's kinda democracy." Hey, we know that it's "kinda not." It's a one-party state.

Now one-party states have the illusion of choice; some of them might have some choices for some of the legislature/parliamentary sections, but it's really one group of folks that kind of have most of the power. They do some things for the people—they are not necessarily completely top-down hard-core, but they are indeed not democracies. It perhaps would only take a nudge to get them there though. As opposed to theocracy.

THEOCRACY

We are holy, and we are in charge.

Now we're getting to real hard-core rightist politics. Here's where the pyramid now has tipped, and indeed there are some people who rule the states, and they do it for their interest in what they consider the right way to do things with little to no input from the people. This will get worse as we progress rightward.

Theocracy is fairly straightforward. It's an *ocracy*, "ruled by," *theo*, "religion." Some sort of religion controls the state, and our best examples would be Iran and Vatican City. These are states which are not secular. There is no division between the church and the state; in fact, it is one singular unit. The church *is* the state. The person at the top—which in other places we would call the king, or the president, or the head cheese—is a religious person in a theocracy. Like the Pope: he is the head of the Catholic Church; he is also the head of that state. In Iran, you have the Ayatollah: the supreme religious leader. He is also the leader of the state; they are one in the same.

Now the Pope has been around for a while, hell, I don't know, like since biblical times I think. But the Iranian theocracy is something quite new on the world stage, and is a whole new take on how states should be managed. Indeed, most consider the Iranian Revolution of 1979 the last truly revolutionary idea of human history thus far. It's a big deal. The idea that a modern state can be recast and re-organized with religion as the central theme has not been tried lately. If ever. Yes, in the past we have had kings or queens or governments that are inherently tied to religion, or that even share power with religion, but this version of theocracy is totally unique in that ALL other power structures are subservient to the religion. It is a new idea . . .and one that has not totally figured itself out yet, even in the Iranian example. But the concept is finding fertile ground in many Islamic countries around the globe.

As you might expect within these states, religious law or biblical law, or religious text law is the state's law. This is of particular significance for Muslim states, as there are lots of folks around the planet in Muslim countries who would like to see their countries become theocracies. In doing so, they want to enact religious law as their state law. The Muslim manifestation of this is something called **sharia.** Sharia law is Koranic law: the laws and punishments described in the Islamic holy text, the Koran. The big problem with this, and why I'm pointing this out in this section, is because this is becoming a world issue. There are very few states in the world that have just Muslim people in them, or just *any* ethnic group, or just *any* religious group. So to adopt the religious law as state law means to enforce that religious law on people who are not of that religion. We'll look at this in more detail when we look at the Middle East and sub-Saharan Africa, as this is a particular problem in Nigeria and Sudan. But we need to finish off our political systems. Let's go further right to . . .

MONARCHY

Royal goobers: A dying breed.

Now these are getting extremely easy. Monarchies are the royal families, who, by the blessing of God, are smarter and better than all the peasants within the country that they lead. Now this used to be all the rage in Europe; everybody loved their monarchs in Europe. In fact, those chip-eating, goober British still love their monarchs so much that they still have them there, hanging out, even though they have no real power. If you want to get into a good fight in Australia, just make fun of the Queen of England. For whatever reason, there is a strong attachment to this idea. An idea that the Plaid Avenger not only finds preposterous, but quite frankly, revolting. The concept that, at birth, someone is better than me and has the power by the blessing of God to rule me, I find repugnant.

We don't have to describe the system any further; it's simple. The original royal family touched by the divine hand of the creator and papal decree begat some sons and daughters, creating the kings and queens who are far superior to us mortals, so they get to rule until they beget more sons who beget more sons, and pretty soon, they're all begetting each other, and that's why half of them are insane anyway. And what is the power structure of the state? Why, it exists for the frolicking and pomp and circumstance of the crown-wearers of course! By your leave, your majesty? Yeah, I'll leave you something of great majesty—my plaid boot in your ass!

There is one important point to make about this government type: it was repudiation and disgust with monarchy that led to the creation of most of those systems to the left of it on our spectrum. The concept of "divine" rights reserved for this elite group of people, particularly the rights to rule the rest of us, became so repugnant to so many on the planet that it became the catalyst for revolutionary thinking—thinking that created a lot of the other government types that we just talked about. Democracy (as we know it today), communism, Marxism, socialism, and probably a handful of other –isms on the left side came about because people were so pissed off and tired of the monarchy system which dominated Europe at the time.

Can anyone think of any examples of this? Oh, how about the USA? Yeah, they had a revolution and kicked those tea-sipping suckers out. And later on, the Frenchies, who outright killed the royals during their French Revolution, took their fight one bloody step further than we did! Lenin and his commie crew assassinated the royal family as part of the Communist Revolution too. Wrap your head around this idea in particular: that many of the alternate systems of government around the world today are the rebellious progeny of former monarchies. Now before we go any further, let's point out that democracy is an ancient concept; Socrates and the other philosophizing Greeks came up with this stuff long ago. However, democracy in its modern form, in its modern manifestation on the planet, was a result of aversion to monarchy. As was communism. But as top-down, and as goofball a concept as monarchy is, there are some other political systems that leave a worst taste in the Plaid Avenger's mouth, like military governments.

MILITARY GOVERNMENTS

Military governments are exactly what they say they are. They are governments run by people with guns. Now every country on the planet has a military . . . or something that looks extremely similar to a military. Maybe called a self-defense force, or an emergency reserve, or a ground self-defense force, or a national guard—places like Japan and

Costa Rica don't have an "official" military. But whatever name it goes by, the military in most states is subservient to the central government. That is, it's there for national defense, maybe even to internally put down revolts, but it works for, or at the request of, the government. Typically the head of the state is also the ultimate commander of the military, but is not active militarily. Typically.

However, in states run by military government, the military has actually superseded the political leaders. Often a small group of military elites takes over effective, real control of the government (directly or indirectly) by military coup. The best examples of this on the planet today are places like Burma, Pakistan, and perhaps even Libya. In those states, folks who are from a military background, or are still active in the military, have wiped out the government for whatever reasons—maybe the government was corrupt, maybe as a move for national security—and they now control the government. Does this mean they control everything and everyone at gunpoint? Not necessarily, but the military is the true power in any country.

My guns are bigger than the politicians!

I know this is confusing. People in the United States might say, "No, not here" but just ask yourself this, if the entire military of the United States wanted to take over the United States, could they? Well, obviously, but we have laws and stuff in place here that we all, including the military, respect. Their role is to serve, and to uphold the law. In other parts of the world, that's gotten a little fuzzy. Governments are taken over by military dictatorships. The government may continue to run as a functional entity, and we would say, "Hey, they've got a senate or legislature; they have courts," but the real power is from a small group of people, and if it's a singular person, we typically refer to them as a military dictator. If it's a group of military people, we would typically refer to them as a **junta.** There are several of these around the world that are still quite active today. Of particular note in current events in Burma, and a more crooked pot of scum and villainy you won't find anywhere else in the world. Those junta jackasses have been killing folks outright for years, and more recently refused to let the international community even come in to help out after the typhoon that killed thousands back in the summer. Other folks like Muammar Quadafy, the leader of Libya, may look like kindly old gentlemen, but check out his job resumé. Yep. He's only ever had one job, as leader of the military, and then later he picked up the 'leader of the country' title. That makes it a military government. Now when military governments get particularly nasty, they can turn quickly into dictatorships.

DICTATORSHIP

Saddam and Mugabe: They held all the cards!

Dictators are typically, but not always, started as military governments, where the military has taken over for whatever reason. But then a central strong figure rises from the crop, and sometimes through cults of personality, sometimes through brute force, becomes the sole leader of the country. A true dictator exists when all decision making occurs at this one individual's whim.

He has the final say on all laws, all actions, all everything. The state apparatus functions only through him. For example, Hitler said "I am the state," and he meant it! He decided if they were going to invade another country, or what the tax system would look like, or what rights individuals had. Again, it's usually implemented by force of the military, but that's not the defining feature—it's the singular person holding all the cards that sets it apart. It can be military, or it could be religious; these lines get fuzzy. We can say the Ayatollah kind of looks like a religious dictator, and perhaps that's kind of true. But even he has a group of religious folks who work for him that have to come to a consensus on certain things. That does not exist in a true dictatorship, where a single guy has all the power.

The best example of this in the modern world was Saddam Hussein, currently residing somewhere in hell. He was a single dude insulated by a cult of personality around him who built up and protected his power through use of force. But there are other active ones, like the president of Zimbabwe, Robert Mugabe. Mugabe—and again, all dictators are not active military, although he started as a military guy—was a rebel leader who helped fight off the colonial powers, helped liberate his country into independence, and originally was a hero. He was elected, and assumed elected power, and then over the years and decades, he consolidated that power and just couldn't seem to get enough of it. After 30 years, he holds all the cards. One man, with all the power; that's a dictatorship. He has refused to give up power, as is often the case in these scenarios, particularly in Africa. Power seems to ultimately corrupt, and the longer you hold on to it, the greater the hunger for it. Kind of like crack. Or "the one true ring" that Bilbo Baggins found. But I digress. Damn hobbits always get me off track . . .

The point here is that dictators can come from a variety of backgrounds, often military, but not necessarily. We might have the tendency to look at Castro as a dictator. And this leads to some questions about a dictator vs. a fascist.

FASCISM

I am the State!

As has already been reflected in the extreme left, anarchy doesn't exist anywhere. Fascism doesn't really exist in today's world either. And what separates fascism from dictatorship? A very thin line I suppose. What the Plaid Avenger calls the manifestation of "true fascism" is that it *is* kind of a true dictatorship, but it's a dictatorship that's not necessarily perpetuated by the use of force. In other words, it's typically a cult of personality. It is a dictator—it is one person with all the cards—but one who has been put there because people like him so much. He's put there by popular mandate.

This is where your best examples are Hitler and Mussolini, perhaps the only real examples in modern history. While we consider most of their dictatorial actions pretty bad in hind sight, at the time, they were very popular. They were rulers of the military, but they did not need the military to maintain control. Nor to gain power originally. Hitler certainly was the leader of the military, and certainly using that military knocked the living crap out of Europe. But, in his rise to power, he did not hold the Germans under the sway of the gun and say, "I want you to agree to all these policies." Most people just said, "We think you're great, do whatever you want, this is awesome." And then Hitler got his ass kicked and that was pretty much that.

Let's face it. Fascism blows on every level. On the one hand you have a generally charismatic leader who is a few fruit loops short of a complete breakfast who rises to power by mesmerizing the hell out of some needy folks who are only looking for a solution to their miserable lives. On the other hand you have a large population of people who more or less blindly allow their government to get away with ultimately controlling their lives while destroying the lives of others. What a bunch of assholes.

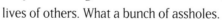

ANOTHER PLAID AVENGER INSIDE TIP: Neither Hitler nor Stalin drank alcohol. Both were teetotalers in societies well-known for their drinking habits. Think about it. Have a drink.

SO WHO IS WHAT, AND WHERE?

Check out the map in Figure 3.4 of current political systems around the globe. Can we detect any patterns? Any problems? Regional variation? As you can see, we have some dominant political systems with some variations on theme region to region.

Look at the Americas. Really all of North America is staunchly democratic with a well-established government. Europe is also staunchly democratic with well-established governments—even the ones that still have kings and queens hanging around. South America too, staunchly, long-term democratic. Mexico's in the democratic column; Australia; of course. Oh, look over at South Asia. They've got a real mixed bag; India is the largest democratic nation on the planet. Bangladesh is fairly democratic as well. Pakistan, as we said earlier, does have something that looks like elections—but there's still a military dictatorship in charge. Places like Japan also still have a queen and king, but they are democratic. And don't forget about Turkey, easily the most die-hard democracy on the planet that happens to be totally composed of followers of Islam . . . hmmmm . . . interesting.

New or newly established democracies on the planet are found in Eastern Europe and Russia. Since the fall of the Soviet Union, they've embraced democracy, but they are still what we call in transition, only about ten years old. Most of Africa you see, both in the Middle Eastern sections and sub-Saharan Africa, is kind of in the democracy column, but they are kind of new too. And if we want to summarize the rest of sub-Saharan Africa, there's a little bit of everything going on down there. There are some chaotic states, some military dictatorships, some new democracies, and a couple of old democracies; it's quite the patchwork quilt. The Middle East is characterized by a patchwork quilt of a different flavor, which is that they have most of the theocracies and true monarchies on the planet. Iran is a theocracy, but Saudi Arabia, Yemen, and Morocco have some true old-school kings and queens stuff still in charge of the place.

FIGURE 3.4 POLITICAL SYSTEMS OF THE WORLD

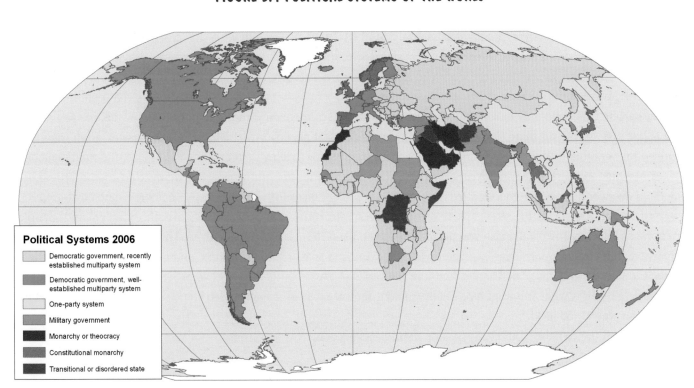

Political Systems 2006

- Democratic government, recently established multiparty system
- Democratic government, well-established multiparty system
- One-party system
- Military government
- Monarchy or theocracy
- Constitutional monarchy
- Transitional or disordered state

We get to Central Asia to find a real crapshoot. Some states have put up the new democracy façade, but it's too new and too close to call which way they are going. One of the themes we'll talk about in Central Asia is that they're kind of leaning back towards one-party states. Folks are getting in charge there and hemming up power and staying in control. So there are tentative democracies in some parts of Central Asia, but they may be leaning towards tentative something else. Of course we get around to places like Southeast Asia, a mixed bag; they've got a little bit of everything. Some places are staunchly democratic, like the Philippines. Some places are staunchly not, like Burma, a military dictatorship, and then there's every place in between. We've got some commies in there too. You've got a little bit of everything in Southeast Asia.

And of course, the giant East Asia, where we have China, which is definitely a one-party state. Again, I know that the label of "Communist China," is confusing to a lot of people because well, yeah, politically they have a party called the Communist Party, and that is the one party that is in charge. But they are not an economically communist state—therefore it's better classified as a one-party state. North Korea is definitely a distinct crazy wacko one-party/dictator state (perhaps better described as a one-psycho state), and South Korea is just the opposite, a staunchly democratic region. That's just a quick summary of what's going on politically in the world. We'll go into more detail about this in each of our regions.

A FINAL WORD ON THE STATE OF STATES

A few general points to consider across the planet here in the dawn of the 21st century:

The number of states is actually growing. That's number one to consider. Why is that? The bigger entities are breaking down to smaller ones. Smaller entities perhaps better fit the people within, (e.g., the demise of the Soviet Union, the breakdown of Yugoslavia). The best example of all is the division of Czechoslovakia into a Czech state and a Slovak state.

The other main trend to consider is the demise of communism on the global sphere, and the movement away from dictatorships and one-party states to democracies. That is, there is a growing trend of democratization across the planet, something the leaders of the United States are very happy about and promote, of course. You can see this particularly in places like Eastern Europe—the Ukrainian Revolution of late, the Georgian Revolution even more recently, respectively referred to as the "Orange" and "Rose" Revolutions. Afghanistan and Iraq too? Well, I suppose they are heading towards a democracy. Even if it has to be implemented at gunpoint.

And a minor trend that you should also be aware of: the Iranian experiment with Theocracy is both new to the world stage, and being exported abroad. Meaning, other states with large Islamic populations may be gravitating towards this system of government. I should say the *people* in those states are interested in some form of theocracy, but certainly not the current governments of those states who like the power structure that has them in the driver's seat right now, thank you very much. One need only look to an extreme manifestation of theocracy, the Taliban of Afghanistan, to see that this idea is not just an Iranian thing. There are also numerous political parties in virtually all Muslim states, from Nigeria to Egypt to Saudi Arabia to Pakistan to Indonesia, which are pushing for a ruling system along the lines of the Iranian model.

So the number of states is on the rise, the number of democracies are on the rise. But we need to know a little more. The Plaid Avenger has put together a little high school yearbook of faces for you to identify, memorize, and be able to recognize if you pass them on the street. These are good people to know—not because they are necessarily "good" people, but because knowing them will make you personally "oh so good" as a savvy global citizen. This yearbook is certainly not exhaustive, but contains particular faces that will be movers and shakers, news-makers, and deal-breakers in the year to come. Know them well, my plaid friends, and join the ranks of those "in the know." I've provided the names and places. You figure out who is who, and what type of government they are part of. I've provided some superlatives as clues to help you on your way. Good luck!

You simply got to know your heads of state to be globally cool . . .

THE PLAID AVENGER WORLD YEARBOOK

Names	Places	Government Types
Kim Jong-il	Iran	Established Democracy
Benedict XVI	Australia	Young Democracy
Abdullah bin Abdul Aziz Al Saud	Russia	One-Party State
Angela Merkel	Chile	Theocracy
Hu Jintao	Argentina	Monarchy
Recep Erdoğan	Zimbabwe	Dictator
Hosni Mubarak	Israel	Anarchy
Gordon Brown	Afghanistan	Communism
George Bush	North Korea	Fascism
Dr. Manmohan Singh	Vatican City	
Lula da Silva	Saudi Arabia	
Hugo Chavez	Germany	
Yasuo Fukuda	China	
Nicolas Sarkozy	Turkey	
Yuliya Tymoshenko	Egypt	
Viktor Yushchenko	United Kingdom	
Mahmoud Ahmadinejad	United States	
Kevin Rudd	India	
Vladimir Putin	Brazil	
Michelle Bachelet	Venezuela	
Cristina Fernández	Japan	
Robert Mugabe	France	
Ehud Olmert	Ukraine	
Hamid Karzai		

Most Likely to Fahrevergnügen

Chancellor _____

State: _____

Type of Gov't: _____

Chinese-iest

President _____

State: _____

Type of Gov't: _____

Most Likely to Never Lose an Election

President _____

State: _____

Type of Gov't: _____

Frumpiest

Prime Minister _____

State: _____

Type of Gov't: _____

The Other, Other White Meat

Prime Minister _____

State: _____

Type of Gov't: _____

Most Likely to Invade

President _____

State: _____

Type of Gov't: _____

Best Turban Wrap

Prime Minister _____

State: _____

Type of Gov't: _____

Cleanest Linens

King _____

State: _____

Type of Gov't: _____

Most Likely to Lambada

President _____

State: _____

Type of Gov't: _____

Leaning-est Leftest & Most Winning Smile

President _____

State: _____

Type of Gov't: _____

Most Likely to Run Screaming from a Large Lizard Creature Who was Awakened from Its Underwater Slumber

Prime Minister _____

State: _____

Type of Gov't: _____

Most Likely to Surrender

President _____

State: _____

Type of Gov't: _____

Insane-ist

"Dear Leader" _____

State: _____

Type of Gov't: _____

Most Holiest Roliest

Bishop of Rome _____

State: _____

Type of Gov't: _____

Most Likely to Be Poisoned

President _____

State: _____

Type of Gov't: _____

Most Likely to Eat Vegemite, Crikey!

Prime Minister _____

State: _____

Type of Gov't: _____

Most Likely to Stroke a Nuclear Missile in an Inappropriate Way, If He Had One

President _____

State: _____

Type of Gov't: _____

Baddest Ass

Prime Minister _____

State: _____

Type of Gov't: _____

Hottest President

President _____

State: _____

Type of Gov't: _____

Hottest Prime Minister

Prime Minister _____

State: _____

Type of Gov't: _____

2008 World Prom Queen

President _____

State: _____

Type of Gov't: _____

Most Kosher

President _____

State: _____

Type of Gov't: _____

Biggest Bastard

Prime Minister _____

State: _____

Type of Gov't: _____

Most Likely to Not Survive Until the Next Edition of This Book

President _____

State: _____

Type of Gov't: _____

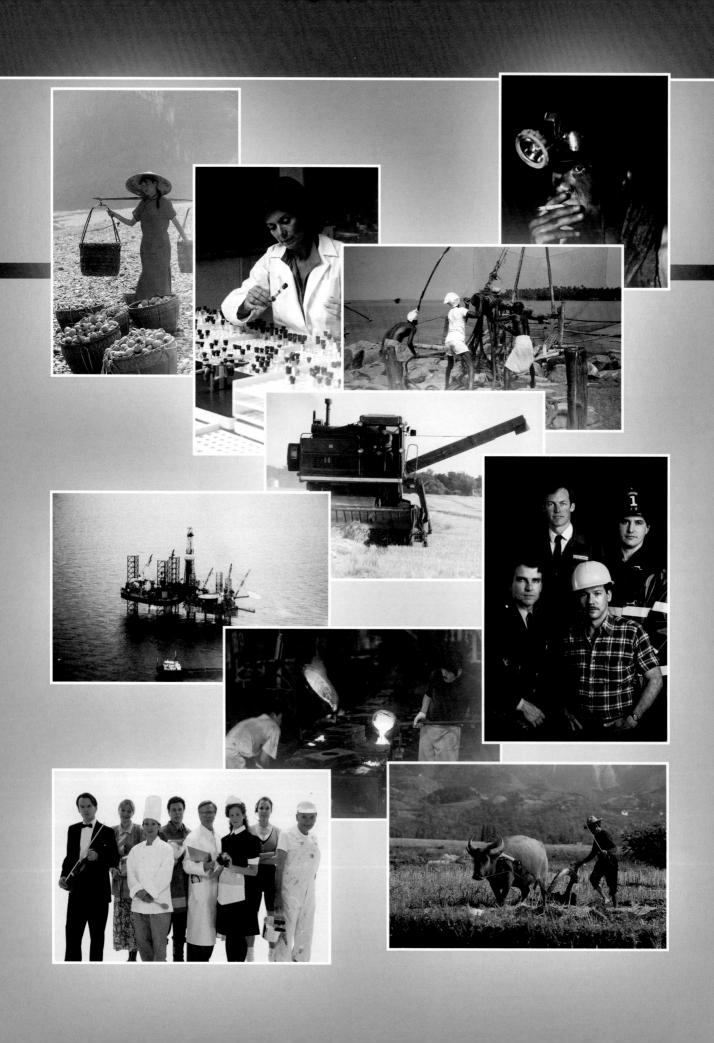

The Plaid World Economy

4

OK we talked about people on the planet, where they are, how many there are, how they procreate. We then looked where people live, the state, and how they are ruled within that state. Now let's look at what people do. People all like to eat. People like to buy clothes. People like to buy cars. People like to buy shit for the kids. People like to buy shit for themselves. For all this shit people want to buy on the planet, they have to have money to do it. So how do people make money in the world? Of course we don't want to look at each individual person; we want to look at the entire state. How does the state make money? What is going on in the global economy? Let's talk turkey about world economic systems shall we?

ORGANIZATION OF ECONOMIES: HOW THEY SHAKE THEIR MONEY-MAKER

Now to start, we have to look at the overall organization of the economy within each state, and subsequently each region. We are going to revisit a theme we talked about last chapter which is: the left versus the right. There's a left and a right in political systems and there's left and right in terms of social idealism; there's also a left and right spectrum when it comes to economies. So what does it mean in the economic context when the media refers to the left versus right?

THE LEFT VERSUS THE RIGHT . . . ECON-STYLE

Often, you see terms such as communism versus capitalism related to the economic spectrum and indeed that's a good place to start. Think about the Cold War. Not only was it the "free" democracies versus the "evil" communist in terms of politics, but was also defined as "free market" capitalism versus communist "command economy."

Communism

Socialism

Capitalism

When we talked about the left versus the right politically, we said things like communism was a system that was all about the individual where their state was functioning in a capacity to serve the individual: the state exists only to serve the people. The opposite, right side of that spectrum was exemplified by a person or small group of people at the top of the government that had all the power and the state worked for them. We can kind of look at this similarly on the economic spectrum by discussing what systems exist and on what sides.

TYPES OF ECONOMIES

COMMUNISM

We'll start on the extreme left just like the last chapter, which makes sense since communism is at once a political system and an economic system all rolled into one. In the economic sense, communism refers to a society where everything in the state is owned, possessed, controlled and operated by the government. What? I thought you just said that the left was all about the people having all the power? I know this is confusing as hell, but dig this: the government in a true communist society simply controls all these things . . . in the name of the people. The commie interpretation is that all the people in the state *are* the state, and thus are the true owners of everything. The government is simply composed of a small group of people that are passing all the stuff out to you, as you need it, because it's your stuff. Bottom line: all stuff is public stuff; no private ownership of anything allowed.

What stuff are we talking about here? All the goods, all of the services, all of the resources, all the factories, and all the means of production. Everything. Under resources, it's pretty obvious: all the oil, all the wheat, all the coal, all the gold, all the forest, all the land—which is an important one. Means of production include all the factories and processing plants, all the plants that make cars, and tanks, and refrigerators, and light bulbs. Everything is owned and controlled by the state.

Again, the state is doing this for the people; all the people truly own all the stuff. People, people, people. Why do I keep reiterating that the people own all this stuff in a communist system? Because it don't fucking work, never has, never will. It's a farce; it's just an abstract idea on paper that this is the way that it should work. As we already referenced in the last chapter, communism has never manifested itself truly in this way—in fact, it has never even come close. Every attempt at it has gone awry. A small group of folks has gotten in charge in order to make the transition to this type of society but it has never worked, because money and power ultimately (and sometimes quickly) corrupt the small group of people in charge.

In addition, an entire economy—of even the smallest state—has way too many variables to try to control through a central administration, and winds up being more complicated than any small group can handle. The Russian description of this experience was **command economy,** and you can see just from the words themselves, that the government attempted to control and thus command all aspects of everything. A tall order for even the smartest and least corrupt.

So corruption and complication have combined to make pure communism pretty much an abject failure everywhere it has been attempted. So true, pure economic communism is, on paper, possession of everything by everyone. In the real world, it's nonexistent.

Confusing commie points:

→ Communism is both a political and economic term because it combines politics and economics into one system in which ownership of all property is communal, and there is not supposed to be a central government.

→ You may think, and correctly so, that Russian communism's political and economic power was very concentrated in the hands of few. This was supposed to be a temporary position while they "fixed" the economy to a true communist utopia. As you know now, they never got it right.

→ But even in today's world you hear references to "Communist China," "Communist Cuba" or even "Communist Vietnam." Make no mistakes about it my plaid friends, these countries' economies are full-on capitalist in nature. Their political leadership may still be called communist, but not their economies.

CAPITALISM

Let's head right to the other extreme. On the other side of the spectrum is something of which we are much more familiar: capitalism. In capitalist society, all the resources, all the stuff, all the oil, all the land, all the fish, all the gold, all the crap and all the means of production, all the factories, all the car plants, all the refrigerators are all owned by private individuals. **Private ownership** is the key here in a purely capitalist society.

Where did this system come from? Capitalism is an amazingly popular and resilient system, mostly because it happens quite naturally. Humans naturally gravitate towards marking off territory and claiming stuff. There is also an inherent agreement that the harder you work and the more risks you take, the more money you should accrue, or at least deserve to accrue. Everybody takes care of themselves, and in doing so, the economy takes care of itself too. What this equates to over time is ownership by the few—which reinforces why these systems are on opposite sides of the spectrum. In a communist society everybody owns everything; in a capitalist one, just a percentage of the population owns things.

Hard-core capitalists would argue for free trade, for free markets, and for minimal government intervention. "Let the market forces run their course" is a mantra of the capitalist. However, in a purely capitalist system in which the government plays no role, it would pretty much be every man for himself. Dog eat dog world. Only the strong, smart, and/or rich survive. Wealth would continue to be further and further concentrated into fewer and fewer hands. And that would eventually equate to large segments of the society as destitute, impoverished, uneducated, and perhaps even unemployed. Is that a society that anyone wants? Probably not. Thus . . .

Just like communism, where does true capitalism exist? Nowhere. We live in a predominately capitalist world and capitalism is a popular system on the planet right now. But where does a purely capitalist like a pure communist state exist? Not anywhere because virtually every place on the planet is in the middle. What is in the middle? Socialism. That's next.

Confusing capitalist points:

→ We think that all the rich countries, and many of the poor, are pure capitalist societies. Pure capitalism is an extreme in which the central government of the state plays absolutely no part in the economy. This is not true anywhere on the planet, not even in the US which is resoundingly the biggest proponent of capitalist expression on the globe.

→ Even hard-core capitalist countries end up having antimonopoly laws for big businesses. Why? Because if businesses and capitalist entities are extremely successful, they will keep getting bigger and bigger and absorbing other businesses until their power becomes unchecked, and uncheckable. Isn't that what capitalism is all about? Indeed. But no state wants to become second fiddle to a corporation.

→ We like to think of the capitalist system as the "best" or most equal or even the most catering towards individual rights because everyone has an equal opportunity to own the stuff. However, having the same opportunity does not make for equal, or even fair, distribution of stuff. In the end, capitalism will concentrate wealth into fewer hands—many would say this is appropriately based on how smart you are, level of skill, your hard work, etc. Others say that concentration of wealth perpetuates stagnation in the masses, as their opportunities to access that wealth diminish. What do you think?

SOCIALISM

Now I know some of you ardent conservatives are saying to yourselves right now, "Blasphemy! There is no such thing as socialism in the US. We're not socialists here in this country; that's a bad word! They're just a shade off of those damn commies!" But I'm here to tell you that when we're looking at things economically on the planet, virtually everybody is somewhere in the socialist sphere. Having said that, there is a broad range of what it means to be socialist and it goes all the way from close to the extreme left to close to the extreme right. In other words, that's where everybody really is: in a shade of socialism. And there are many, many shades. They all have the root of the word in their interpretation: *social*. In other words, they look out for, or have some role in, the societies over which they rule; societies made up of people.

So what is socialism? You might have figured this out already. It's somewhere between the extremes. That is the government (i.e., the state), owns some stuff and controls some stuff, maybe some lands, maybe some industries, maybe some of the resources, maybe some oil. At the same time, private interests or private individuals own some stuff too: some oil, some factories, some lands, some things, and indeed, that's pretty much where the world is. Like it or not, that's kind of the way it is. So let's kind of flush this out in a little more detail.

Why would the state want to control any of this economic stuff? Short answer: to provide services for its peoples. Even the most ardent capitalist would agree that the state should provide things like an army to defend the country and maybe road systems or postal systems to facilitate economic growth. Others in a society think that the state should do a whole lot more, like provide social security, welfare systems, and unemployment checks, maybe even health care. Different states provide different amounts of these things.

In either case, how is the state going to pay for these things? The answer: by way of resource/industry control or taxation or some combination of both. Some states are very heavy-handed in this approach, perhaps controlling the most lucrative industry in its entirety, like in the state operated oil industries of Saudi Arabia or Venezuela. Other states like the US make some money off resources (mostly by selling the rights to drill to private companies) and some money off taxation. Other states, like Sweden, tax the living hell out of everybody to make money. Different states have different approaches to making money. Look at the graphic below to see what I'm talking about.

Confusing Socialist points:

→ Socialism comes in many packages; you may see references to democratic socialism, or mixed systems which are prevalent in Western Europe and increasingly prevalent in Latin America.

→ Socialism can refer to heavy state ownership and control of some industries—South American model. Socialism can also refer to states that generate revenue by heavy taxation in order to provide lots of services to citizens—the European model.

→ The term is often misused by the conservative right in our country who confuse regulation of certain aspects of the economy with government ownership of business—you will see this when any laws are passed which limit big businesses in any way; those on the right will say we are drifting into Socialism. You may also have heard "socialism" used when government tried to start regulating health care industries a few years back. Oh, and that health care issue is going to be hot again soon . . . so watch out for the socialist mudslinging to break out again. And watch the film *Sicko* to understand these systems even more.

So let's look at this spectrum from left to right again in terms of some active interpretations of this socialist sphere because really the entire planet is somewhere in here—albeit in varying degrees.

If we think of all-the-way-left commies like Lenin, we see the attempted manifestation of true communism. He wanted the state to control everything in order to provide all stuff and all services to all the people all the time. He died. Didn't work out so well in the long-term. Or the short-term. Or really any term in between.

Castro is the modern-day Leninist attempt at communism. In Cuba's case, the state does control quite a bit, all of the resources in Cuba are owned supposedly by the people and are administered and controlled by the government for the people. But it's not working out so well, and there is a large underground free-market/black-market economy at work to supplement the services and stuff that is supposed to be supplied by the government, but is not—because they're broke.

King Abdullah and Hugo Chavez are slightly more to the right. Neither embraces communism, and indeed there are a lot of private businesses and private ownership in their countries. However, in both cases, the state controls the extremely lucrative

Extreme Left, State Control . . .

oil industries and uses the profits generated from oil to provide all sorts of services to their people. Saudi Arabia happens to be a little bit better at it right this second, and everything from health care to education is provided to its citizens. Hugo is trying, and he openly embraces socialism full-on as the way to success for his country, but his rhetoric is bigger than his actions thus far. However, he is widely supported by the poor people because of this same propaganda, which promises more stuff to the masses.

We can go a little bit further to the right and we get perhaps a lot of European states like Sweden, France, and Norway that—while they don't control a lot of resources outright—heavily tax luxury items like cars in order to raise revenue to supply stuff to their citizens. So in Sweden, (I'm picking on Sweden in particular because everybody likes those boxy Swedish cars, the Volvos) almost no one can own a Volvo because the government taxes the living shit out of them. Why do they do this? It's considered a luxury good like alcohol or mink furs. They heavily tax those items to raise revenue, because they supply some serious services to their citizens. When a woman has a baby in Sweden, she gets like two years off—PAID—maternity leave. Two damn years? Paid? Damn. In the US, women get like two hours off after having a child. Then it's "Okay, it's out. Get cleaned up, and get back to work! And by the way, those sheets you messed up, yeah, we're gonna have to get five hundred bucks from ya for those. Thanks bunches."

Next we see Vlad "the man" Putin from Russia. What? Russia? They were the center of the commie sphere! How can they be right of center now? Because they fully embraced the capitalist way after the collapse of the USSR, and they did it with such a vengeance that it became a "wild west" of capitalism. Most things went into private ownership, and the government got so broke that it could not provide all those services that it once did. As a result, Russia has since re-taken control of its lucrative oil industry once more . . . leaning back towards the left side of the spectrum. More on that later. This is the classic example of how the world as a whole is firmly capitalist in outlook, even if the individual states exhibit varying characteristics of socialism. China is in this category as well—in a big transition from all state controlled to privately controlled industry and services.

Now we're on familiar ground. The US is certainly much closer to the purely capitalist camp, but through limited resource control and taxation does provide a lot of services to the people. Quite a bit actually . . . but not as much as many European states or even Canada, which has free health care. None of the government activities of the developed countries would be considered resource reallocation, as maybe we would define activities in Venezuela or Cuba, but a lot of stuff is provided to the citizens nonetheless.

It is always up for debate in the US between Republicans and Democrats as to how many of these services the government should supply. In fact, it's one of the main dividing lines between these two parties. Republicans are considered favoring big business because they support free market, free trade, and privatization of perhaps all government services. Democrats are typically associated with wanting the government to provide these services, and maybe even more (remember talk of government provided health care under Bill Clinton?). You may have heard reference to this lately as President Bush wants to privatize pension funds, which are currently government controlled and distributed. As is the Alaskan Wildlife refuge which has oil that we may want.

And that's why we see our good friend Prime Minister Fukuda of Japan even further to the right than George Bush; Japan is privatizing even more of their government than the US is right now. They just sold their postal system to a private business last year. The less stuff in government hands, the closer you get to pure capitalism.

. . . to the Right, Private Control

Adam Smith rounds out our line-up on the extreme capitalist right, and he is here intentionally. Because as I've already pointed out, pure capitalism doesn't exist anywhere. And Mr. Smith is long since dead, so he doesn't exist anywhere either. No state on the planet does nothing for its people—because that's actually a really good way to get your ass thrown out of office, chucked off the throne, and/or guillotined.

WHY SO MANY SYSTEMS?

Speaking of getting your ass chucked off the throne, where did these systems come from? Just like the concentration of political power in the hands of a few was the undoing of monarchy in Europe, there is the same type of impetus in the economic sys-

Industrialization: Rise of the Machines.

tems. This largely arose because of the Industrial Revolution. The Industrial Revolution, which occurred in the 17th, 18th, and 19th century European experience, enabled a vast concentration of wealth in the hands of the few industrialists—the factory owners—and simultaneously pathetic circumstances for the peasants, the peons—the factory workers.

During this societal evolution, there were not many laws; in fact, they were nonexistent for things like child labor or workplace safety or minimum wages. The industrialists were all for the 195 hour work week—hey, that sounds good. How about we only pay people a dime a day? That sounds good too! Five-year-olds working in the factory? Why not? Got to give the little people something to do!

So what you had was unregulated growth and crappy working conditions that really tested the limits of what societies would tolerate. This really pissed off lots of folks and got them thinking about possible alternative systems to unregulated capitalism. Marx and Engels, and then Lenin and others, thought "Hey, this is unfair. These few factory owners have concentrated wealth and power. And we are powerless." This sentiment was not unlike the active aversion felt by peoples ruled under monarchies at the time as well. Result? Marxism, communism, socialism, and perhaps a few more –isms I don't even know about, were created to offer other options. Alternative economic systems evolved to offer alternatives to the unchecked power of capitalism—just like alternative government types evolved to counter unchecked power of monarchy at the time. And now, strangely enough, we have come full-circle. Whereas many of these systems originally evolved to check concentration of power and wealth in state systems, the states are now looked to by many to help counter wealth and power which has accumulated somewhere else . . . where would that be?

Corporations are a significant thing to consider if for no other reason then they've kind of replaced governments as the true holders of real power on the planet. You have to understand this; governments were seen as holding all the real power 200 years ago giving way to revolutions to unseat or redistribute that power (e.g., see American Revolution, French Revolution, Russian Revolution, etc.). In today's world, multinational corporations are seen as the real powers on the planet and thus we've had a kind of move from protesting against a government or saying "Hey this government is unfair, we should change it or do

What Is the Deal with . . . MultiNational Corporations?

An executive with Dow Chemical recently said, "I have long dreamed of buying an island owned by no nation and of establishing the World Headquarters of the Dow Company on the truly neutral ground of such an island, beholden to no nation or society." Such is the story of multinational corporations. For most of history, the world economy has been controlled by nation-states. They made the rules, set taxes, and imposed regulations and corporations had to follow them. This is changing.

In today's world of globalization, multinationals have become the primary actors in the world economy. Free trade agreements are reducing the barriers for companies to operate in other countries and the global economy is becoming more interdependent. Many countries want multinational corporations to do business within their borders because they boost the local economy, bring jobs, and pay taxes. Therefore, countries, and even regions of the world, compete with each other to attract multinational corporations by offering tax breaks, lax environmental or labor standards, and improved infrastructure. Multinational corporations may have their headquarters in one country, but they do business in multiple countries of their choosing. In this way, the multinationals now make the rules.

Multinational corporations, which include Exxon, Microsoft, Pepsi, and Nintendo, have become very powerful and some of them have higher revenues than poor countries. However, they have their critics too. Nationalists and patriots are suspicious of them because they think that all they care about is making money (corporations would never do that!) and taking advantage of the host country. Antiglobalization protestors claim that the great power the multinationals wield is forcing countries to bend over backwards to please them by doing things like looking the other way when they ruin the environment or take advantage of poor people. There have been arguments that multinationals ruin local culture (so you won't be able to tell Cairo from Tokyo in a few years) and that they destroy local businesses because they just can't compete with the big multinationals. Either way, the multinationals are taking over and you better watch out.

Fun Fact: Some people consider the Dutch East India Company, founded in 1602, to be the first multinational corporation in the world.

something about it" to "Hey this multinational corporation has all the power; they've got more money than our government does and they work outside the laws of our government because they're operating in maybe ten or twelve different countries."

When you see protests against multinational corporations, or outcry against entities like the WTO, you are seeing a manifestation that true power is not held by singular governments anymore. These protestors feel that the new oppressing force on the planet is not any particular state or government, but these powerful economic entities. In their opinion, real threats to human rights and human pursuit of happiness are made primarily by corporations. And now it appears that these multinational corporations are bigger, badder and with more money than most states on the planet.

The result? Folks are turning to state governments to counter the unchecked power of multinational corporations. Confusingly enough, the liberal movement started as anti–big government, and now in most countries is credited with being very pro–big government. Part of that answer lies in how the world has changed in the last couple hundred years; 200 years ago, governments were the primary sources of all power, with economic entities like corporations running a very distant second. Is that how it is in today's world? Not hardly. The multinational and even just the national companies in our world have become the major powers, with governments running a close second. In this atmosphere, the liberal attitude has shifted from "liberating" people from an oppressive government to attempting to "liberate" them from the economic powers of today's world. They attempt to do this by using the powers of government to counter those of big business.

NATIONALISM VERSUS PRIVATIZATION

We need to further define a couple of terms that we've been tossing around here while describing all of these economic systems. You will see these terms frequently, and they often cause consternation for folks on either side of the economic spectrum. These forces in action have oftentimes been the cause of public unrest, of strained international relations, and have even been the impetus for invading countries or assassinating leaders. What's the big deal?

Nationalization is the state acquisition and operation of businesses previously owned and operated by private individuals or corporations. It is usually done in the name of social and economic equality, often as part of communist or socialist doctrine. Nationalization of foreign owned property, like the Suez Canal by Egypt in 1958 or the copper mining industry by Chile in 1971, typically attempts to end foreign control of an industry or the economy and poses complex problems for international law.

In other words, the state assumes control of an industry, kicks out owners/operators, and starts taking the profits to the state bank account. This seriously pisses off the corporations, who in turn usually get their home government to kick up a fuss, take the case to an international arbitrator like the WTO, embargo the nationalizing state, or maybe even invade the country outright to get their shit back. Sound preposterous? It's happened plenty in the last hundred years. France and Great Britain invaded Egypt to try to regain the Suez Canal, and the US has destabilized or overthrown whole governments in Chile, Guatemala and Cuba to satisfy pressures by corporations who fell victim to nationalization.

As you might have guessed already, **privatization** is just the opposite. Return of businesses to private ownership after they have been the property of the state is the process of privatizing. Since the collapse of the USSR, Russia and all of its former areas of control have been in a mad scramble to privatize industries. But they are not alone. India and China are fertilized fields for mass privatizations, and the trend is still occurring in the developed world too. Western European countries and Japan, who just privatized their postal service, continue to push more government operations to the private business sphere. In the US, the term has often been broadly applied to the practice of outsourcing the management of public schools, prisons, airports, sanitation services, and a variety of other government-owned institutions. Sometimes this contracting of services does not entail the outright sale of the industry to private hands.

Why the popular theme of privatization in the world? The popular argument is that government-run business is like a monopoly—and lack of competition makes the business not-so-productive and noncompetitive and wasteful, and maybe even ripe for corruption. That is certainly a valid point. The other reality is that bigger and bigger corporations have much more leverage than ever before in the past to put pressure on states to privatize. Who funds lobbying groups to persuade congressmen to privatize? Who has money to fund big studies that show that government operations are wasteful? Who would have the money to buy the senator a Ferrari for his teenage daughter's graduation present? And then who would be wealthy enough to bid on the sale of government resources and services that were being auctioned off? Um. . . maybe massively rich multinational corporations? You can call the Plaid Avenger jaded, you can even call him a leftist, but he is merely a realist. It's the way the world works.

Privatization is the growing theme in the 21st century, but nationalization is far from extinct. Hardcore capitalists and businessmen and multinational corporations across the planet still shudder when they hear the word. Five years ago I would have said that this idea and this concept were completely dead and that you wouldn't see this happening much anymore. However, it is making a slight resurgence particularly in the left-leaning South American region—I should say left-leaning Latin America because it rolls off the tongue much more glibly. You'll also see some of this happening perhaps in Africa in the very near future, but I digress.

TYPES OF ECONOMIC ACTIVITY

No matter what the type of economy or how far to the left or right in the socialist world they may be or even if things are being nationalized or privatized, people on the ground are always doing something to make this thing called an economy go forward. What is it those guys are doing?

I'm not talking about economic structure at the state scale. I'm talking about what people do on the ground. In real life. What the hell do you do? You chop down damn trees for a living or do you make toothpicks? You raise kids? What do you do that makes money? I can certainly think of all the unsavory things that people do on the planet to make money because I've participated on both sides of the trade myself. Now we're on familiar ground here, and this chapter gets exceptionally easy because we can really classify all economic activity that happens in the world into four distinct types of activity.

Why are we doing this? Just so we can call out people and see what level they're on? To point and laugh? Haha—your mama sells crack for a living in the service sector. No! We want to identify these things because it's important to understand what different states are doing and how many people are dedicated to certain activities within the state. This in turn tells us a lot about how the economy operates, why some places are richer than others, and how this is currently changing in different regions around the globe. And it is oh, so simple too. They all go in order and it is even numerical. Let us proceed with speed: Primary.

Primary economic activities is as simple as it gets. Literally. This level includes anything and everything that involves natural resource extraction from the earth. Just taking stuff from momma earth and then selling it is a primary activity. The list is actually short:

→ Agriculture production: Cucumbers, acorns, squash, cocoa leaves—I don't care what it is; it's a primary economic activity if it's just simple agriculture.

→ Timbering/logging: Chop down a tree and take it. That's extraction of a raw commodity.

→ Mining: Oil, coal, gold, diamonds . . . mining of everything. That's all simple extraction. Just pull it out of the ground and give it to me.

→ Fishing: Yep, just taking a damn fish out of the water. That's a primary economic activity. Even if you use dynamite to do it.

Pretty straightforward, pretty simple stuff. Resource extraction is the key. And that is primary. Now the point to take home with you here, particularly when you hear things like gold or oil, you think: "oooooweee . . . that shit is worth a lot of money!" Here is what the Plaid Avenger wants you to know: No it really ain't.

Virtually all primary activities aren't worth dog shit in the long term. How can I say that? Oil is worth a lot of money isn't it? Well, it's critical for everything; it's used for everything, it's . . . worth less per gallon than homogenized milk. And that isn't worth much either, is it? And speaking of milk, what are all agricultural products worth per pound? Per boatload? How about wood? Quick question: would you rather have a business that grew oranges, or made orange juice concentrate? Why? Because one makes more money than the other due to processing of the product, which leads us to . . .

Secondary economic activities involve the processing of everything you got from the primary economic activities. All secondary activity consists of somehow manipulating, altering, refining, making better, doing something to the shit you got from the primary activities—that is, the raw materials are modified in some way. And here's the main point: modified in such a way so it is worth more money.

You are adding value and that is something that will continue to happen as you go up this chain of economic activities. As I've suggested earlier, products of primary activity are not worth much. You can cut down a tree, and a tree lying down on the forest floor is worth something, but not a lot. How about if we take that tree, rip off the bark, cut it into planks and then further cut them into boards. Now that's worth a lot more! Contractors and construction people will pay for boards, not for a damn tree.

So processing something of a big quantity to a smaller quantity is simple processing, but it still adds value. Then there is also refining. If we take oil out of the ground, it doesn't go straight in your gas tank. It has to be processed. It has to be cleaned up. So taking the oil out of the ground is our primary activity, processing it at a refinery is a secondary activity that adds a lot more value. Further manipulate it into gasoline and its worth quite a bit more.

This can include a vast array of activities, which you don't often think about. Simple things like cleaning up coffee beans or roasting coffee beans. Are roasted coffee beans worth more than raw coffee beans? Indeed they are. How about mud? Mud? Mud is just mud—but form it into squares, let it dry out, and now you have bricks. You can't sell mud but you can sell bricks. You've processed it; you've added value. Processing of any raw material counts—including taking a fish and chopping out its guts. Is a gutless fish worth more than a fish with guts? Indeed it is. Ask anybody who wants to cook a fish. So processing is the main component of secondary activities. And the main thing to consider is that we're adding value to that raw commodity.

Now let's get on with it; let's get to tertiary level activities. **Tertiary level activities** are also known as service sector activities so stage three includes all services on the planet. Perhaps we're going to take some of the raw commodities, or even some finished commodities, and do something with them, maybe move them around, further manipulate them, or sell them—provide a service of some sort.

The service sector is what most of us in the developed world are used to. What most of us have done for a living; you really got to go out of your way to find agriculturalists or lumberjacks or people who work in mills anymore in the rich countries. But a service sector job? Yeah, we've all done those.

Every hamburger that gets fried, every surgery that gets performed, every used car that gets sold, every fire that gets put out—someone has provided a service. Even simple transportation is a service. Truck drivers are an excellent example of this: taking raw commodities from one place and simply moving to another place. I'm sorry, what have we done here? We've added value to the commodity! A bunch of lumber sitting in the middle of Saskatchewan Canada don't do a damn thing for us here in the United States—but if you put it on trucks and move it here, well now you've added the value to it; we can use it; it's more accessible.

But that's just one division of the service sector. We tend to think of everything from construction to police to doctors to teachers to army people, navy people, air force people, marine people as all providing a service. Perhaps the biggest one you think of is sales—service people at McDonalds, at the mall, at Wal-Mart, cashiers, wait staff; all these people are providing a service to you. They are moving around stuff from the first two activity levels and are getting it to customers and/or are increasing the value in some way, shape, or form.

Again, this process entails a ton of different activities, but its main feature is its tendency to increase the overall value of stuff from stages one and two in some discernable manner. Reconsider our hamburger: a cow that we killed in primary activity terms is ground into hamburger during secondary activity—worth more than the cow to be sure, but even raw hamburger is not valuable. Now take it to a restaurant and provide some services in the form of a cook and then maybe a maitre d' that seats you at the table and maybe a waiter or waitress that brings you that hamburger. Now you've provided a bunch of services and

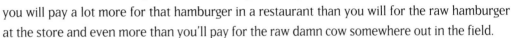

you will pay a lot more for that hamburger in a restaurant than you will for the raw hamburger at the store and even more than you'll pay for the raw damn cow somewhere out in the field.

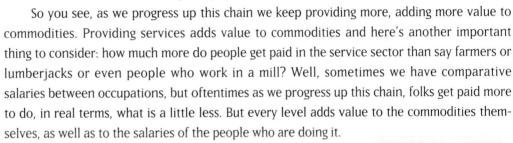

So you see, as we progress up this chain we keep providing more, adding more value to commodities. Providing services adds value to commodities and here's another important thing to consider: how much more do people get paid in the service sector than say farmers or lumberjacks or even people who work in a mill? Well, sometimes we have comparative salaries between occupations, but oftentimes as we progress up this chain, folks get paid more to do, in real terms, what is a little less. But every level adds value to the commodities themselves, as well as to the salaries of the people who are doing it.

So what's left? **Quaternary sector** is kind of a new one. Some analysts and economists don't even recognize this one yet, due mostly to the fact that these types of jobs have not been on the planet for very long, and don't constitute a big percentage of the labor force. But they are on the rise, and do

tell us some important things about the societies in which they occur. Quaternary sector provides something new. Not a natural resource, nor a processed commodity, and not really a service either. In essence, the quaternary sector deals with the creation and manipulation of intangibles—and the main intangible that I am thinking of here is information.

In the technologically advanced countries, an increasing number of people aren't dealing with hamburgers or trees or oil or services so much anymore as they are with the idea of information for information's sake. Computer programming, researchers, lab technicians, even astronauts are all in the realm of data creation, but don't necessarily "provide" a service to anyone. The results of their work may lead to a commodity that is mass produced, but their work in and of itself is neither a commodity nor a service.

And to a certain extent you can even say stock market people are in the quaternary sector because they are not really producing anything. Perhaps they are providing a service but it's more likely that they are manipulating information and moving abstract things around to create or add value to them (i.e., stocks).

So it's a fuzzy one to be sure but the reason I like to point it out is because we can make some easy assumptions about any country that has folks working in this sector. It has to be developed, advanced, and rich if you have a significant presence of quaternary sector jobs filled in your state. No two ways around it. And how much do those folks get paid? Sweet-ass bank, that's what. And what are those products worth? Genetic code, computer programs, cures for diseases . . . are you kidding me? That's real money!

If you can critically examine what economic activities that different countries and regions focus on, you can go a long way to understanding why rich countries are rich, why poor countries are poor, and how the global economy is working. This insight, or should I say sight beyond sight, gives you the inside scoop on the real mechanics of money flow in the world. What? You don't have the sight beyond sight yet? Better call in Lion-O and proceed directly to. . . .

I WANT TO GO UP THE FOOD CHAIN DAMMIT . . .
SECTOR EVOLUTION

We can look at any state on the planet, just in terms of the what economic activity, to get a fuller picture of what's going on, how rich they really are, and indeed, what their future holds. It's not only about how much money they've got and how much money they are going to make but also what's going on in their society, how developed or developing they are, and lots of other things that we can typically tie to other demographic and cultural factors. And it's easy. Check it:

FIGURE 4.1 ECONOMIC SECTOR RATIOS

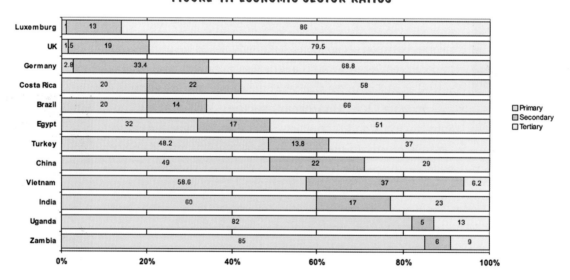

As you can see in the above graphic, the percentage of people within each state who work in each of these levels of economic activity tells us volumes about what's happening. We can define some obvious patterns between developed and developing countries, as well as explain anomalies to these patterns. First, the trends:

The fully developed countries, that is the richer countries in the world, have a much greater percentage of their workforce in the tertiary/service sectors than in primary and secondary sectors. Check out Luxembourg, the UK, and Germany on the top of the chart. In fact, primary industries in the developed world account for almost nothing, but that should make sense to you now. Advanced technology and machinery in these countries equates to small percentages of folks needed to grow all the food and mine all the coal.

In the US, just 2 percent of the population is farmers, yet they supply the other 98 percent with food, and even export tons of food on top of that. They are all the way thru the demographic transition; one big tractor in the US operated by one guy can do the work of 1,000 small farmers in Africa—hell, maybe more like the work of 10,000.

Secondary/manufacturing sector jobs are continuing to decrease in the developed world due primarily to the cost of labor. Developed countries have labor unions and health benefits and minimum wage laws; all of which serve to increase the cost of labor. Developing countries typically have none of these things; thus labor is cheap. Manufacturing jobs of virtually all things—cars, toasters, toys, luggage, computers—have been migrating from developed countries to developing ones to take advantage of this cheaper labor. What does that leave for everyone to do? Service sector employment in an area emphasizing skilled labor coupled with an increasing commodity value. Good money for most. And of course some of the folks in these societies have the know-how and opportunity to create and manipulate information, leading the world in quaternary level activities. So in developed regions there is:

→ hardly anyone in the primary sectors,

→ typically less than a quarter in the secondary processing sector,

→ a majority of the workforce in the service sector,

→ and a significant number of folks in the high-end quaternary sector.

Just the reverse is happening in the developing countries. To point out these major differences, let's start with some of the countries that are the least developed . . . and subsequently are the poorest parts of the planet. Check out the bottom brackets filled by the African countries. They are overwhelmingly primary industry based, very limited secondary and service sector employment; quaternary is out of the question. What can we say about a place that is almost exclusively agriculture or fishing or mining based? What are those products really worth? As pointed out earlier, not much. So in the least-developed regions:

→ most folks are in primary—most of them are farmers,

→ less than a quarter are in manufacturing—sometime much less than that,

→ Even fewer are in the service sector—none in quaternary.

Most states on the planet are somewhere in between. The trends do seem to indicate that the more developed a place becomes, the more tertiary and secondary will be gained at the expense of the primary sector. More service, more manufacturing, fewer farmers. End game: more money. And we can see this reflected in the chart above. Costa Rica and Brazil are diversified across sectors more in tune with developed countries, and are doing pretty well. We wouldn't think of those countries as impoverished or undeveloped. India and Vietnam are hustling and transforming too, but they are still overwhelmingly agricultural based societies, and as such, are not making the big bank money yet—not per capita anyway. China and Turkey are stable, prosperous societies that are perhaps the most balanced across the board in economic activities. A Plaid Avenger inside tip: this balance and diversity will probably serve both these countries well in the future, and you may see other countries try to emulate this approach as opposed to stacking up solely in the tertiary category. Just a hypothesis. But I'm usually right. China has actually stated that they want to keep this diversity in order to maintain their competitive edge in manufacturing.

Confucius say: Keep farmer. Keep miners. Keep low wage to keep manufacturing sector; make China strong.

He could be onto something. . . .

And now, to look at an anomaly. What's the deal with Egypt up there? Looks pretty balanced, perhaps even more developed than Turkey or China. Are they really approaching full development as their economic activity breakdown suggests? Probably not. We have to look at the real world in this case to decipher the truth; Egypt has a low percentage of folks in primary sector not because it's an evolved economy but because they don't have a lot of agricultural land to farm! It's a desert! Except along the Nile, of course. And they have some oil to mine, but not very much, and it just doesn't create many jobs anyway. So low primary activities. Why high service sector then? One of the moneymakers for Egypt is tourism. You know, go see the pyramids. How much money are those tourism jobs worth? Again, not too much. So we can make sense out of these economic activities on a case by case basis when some of these countries buck our trends.

But the trends do make sense. And they do seem to support the concepts outlined in the Demographic Transition Model from Chapter 2. Most states are working towards increasing manufacturing and service sectors, and lessening dependence on primary sector, because that makes them more money. Currently, most of the value added to

Confucius say: Show me the money!

primary commodities happens in the developed world—to primary products shipped to them from the developing world. You should be able to see how this puts the poorer countries at a "permanent disadvantage"—they export low value stuff and have to import high value stuff. That's why the more successful countries in the 21st century are trying to catch up, not by producing even more cheap stuff, but by changing percentages in their economic activities sectors. China and India are changing fast and will be making big bucks. Saudi Arabia and Equatorial Guinea are making big bucks on primary sector stuff (oil) but not changing or diversifying internally. Who is going to win in the long term?

SO WHAT THE HELL IS THIS GDP STUFF?

So how does what all these folks do for a living in all these different states in the world affect real wealth—that is, real money and real dollars. That something is called GDP. What does that stand for? **GDP** is Gross Domestic Product. You may have also heard of GNP, or Gross National Product. What's the difference between the two? Are you ready for this? Nothing; they are two terms which mean the same thing. GDP has been growing in popularity and GNP has been falling out of use. Okay, so what do they mean?

GDP is simply all the goods and all the services within any state that are created and sold in that year. What do I mean by all the goods and all the services? Well, everything. Every damn thing that is bought and sold. Every transaction in terms of a final sale. Every hamburger that's sold, every car that's sold, every service that's provided, every employee salary at McDonalds, all of it. All of it added all together for the year is the GDP.

You do have to put this in context of the *final sale of the commodity* and what that means. For GDP, we only count the final sale and not all the transactions that led up to that final sale. Example: a car. A car gets sold on a lot for $20,000. That $20,000 dollars car transaction is the final sale because it is going to a consumer, who will then "consume" it. That $20,000 dollars goes into the total for GNP for that year. Now the reason we say only the final sale counts is because you can't sell things twice or three times or five times in the case of commodity chains anywhere in the world. The car has tires on it when the guy sold it off the lot. Well those tires were made somewhere, and then sold to a distributor, who then sold them to a retailer, and then the retailer maybe sold them to a car manufacturer and that's like three separate transactions, but you wouldn't count those other transactions because then you would be counting the same tires three times within one year. Only the last sale counts.

However, the car salesman's salary, the distributor's salary, the assembly-line worker's salary—all these services are a part of GDP for the year. So its final sale and all worker salaries go into this equation. It doesn't matter if twenty people were involved in the movement, creation and distribution of that car; all their salaries go into GDP.

So GDP, now we know what it is, but what can we say about patterns of GDP on the planet? Keep your world regions in mind when analyzing the following map.

If we look at the GDP planetary totals, we see that the heavy-weights who make the most damn money on the planet are represented by the developed world, with the United States economy weighing in at number one in the world (for now). Second in line, Japan has the number two economy on the planet. The third is Germany. And they all have GDP that total in the trillion-dollar range. That is a million million, or is it a billion million? I can't remember; its a one with a hell-load of zeros behind it. Over a trillion dollars per year.

But this is where the lines are drawn and we have to stop making comparisons about what we consider to be the developed and developing world based on just GDP. Mainly because the number four economy on the planet makes things interesting: China has just surpassed France and the UK to take that honored position, which I'm sure is really pissing off my Euro-trash friends. Is China developed? Most would say not, but we will get to this in the next chapter. They sure are making bank, though.

We see that most of the western European states are still in the high GDP category, and most of Africa and Asia are in the low GDP category, with Latin America, South Asia, and East Asia falling somewhere in between.

But I do want to point out a couple things as we see these totals around the planet. Maybe you are thinking "Wow, the rich countries—they are really, really rich. And the poor countries, they really suck ass. They don't make squat. I guess

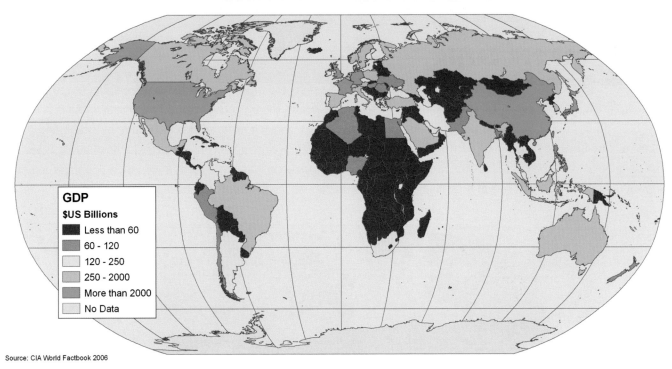

GDP
$US Billions
Less than 60
60 - 120
120 - 250
250 - 2000
More than 2000
No Data

Source: CIA World Factbook 2006

everybody's sitting around there not making any money. They're not providing any goods or services. They suck." Reality check: we have to throw in a disclaimer here. When examining GDP totals, in relations to a state's actual wealth we have to consider what is not included in GDP. (Check out the little green box Yo!)

I'd like to point out one example in particular. If we look at Columbia on the map above, we see that they are on one of the lower levels of GDP on the planet. Were you to include the cocaine economy, they would instantaneously be in the top ten nations on the planet for GDP. So don't undervalue the stuff that's not being counted.

What Is Not Included in GDP?

We said all the goods and all the transactions of all the goods and all the services are included in GDP—so that's everything isn't it? What would this not include?

First, think of some things that don't have monetary value in an exchange sense, but are indeed actually work. This list would include housework, child rearing, any labor done in the home, food grown for home consumption, food gathering, food preparation, firewood gathering, the list goes on. Why would I point this out? Because that's what most of the people on the planet are doing. Every single day. Day in, day out. None of these activities are included in GDP.

Second: anything that the government doesn't know about. Any transaction that occurs between folks under the table. This can refer to anything as innocent as a flea market or a yard sale to items or services traded, bartered or sold between people that is untaxed and therefore not included in the tally. But this also includes anything illegal—stuff the government prohibits and therefore wouldn't be able to tax or know about, including all illicit narcotic production and trade, all moonshining, gunrunning, and human trafficking. All of these activities, which do generate large amounts of wealth, are not included in GDP.

I bring this up because when we look at the poorest ass places on the planet, they're actually working pretty goddamn hard—but none of the stuff they do actually counts in the totals. GDP is a Western-derived definition of wealth, a Western-measured definition of wealth, and simply does not always adequately reflect reality. What do I mean by this? Well, when we look at Africa, it looks like nothing's going on there but indeed, let's face the facts; a whole hell of a lot of work goes on there to keep that place going; it's just not measured. What else is not included?

So in summary, anything that's done at home, for home, anything that happens between friends, any type of barter transactions, and any illegal, illicit activities are not counted as part of GDP. That would radically change the map of what's going on here. There's one more thing to consider and that is the comparison between GDP and GDP per capita.

GDP PER CAPITA

Total GDP we covered earlier. **GDP per capita** is simply the total GNP divided by the population total for the state. In other words, it tries to approximate how much wealth there is per person in the society; this is perhaps a much better indicator of how the average Joe is doing in the world. Looking at these two maps side by side offers a contrasting picture of what's happening on the planet in terms of levels of wealth and economic activity. As to be expected, the most developed countries maintain themselves in the highest brackets, and the most undeveloped countries maintain themselves in the lowest brackets of both maps. But look what happens to some interesting places in between . . .

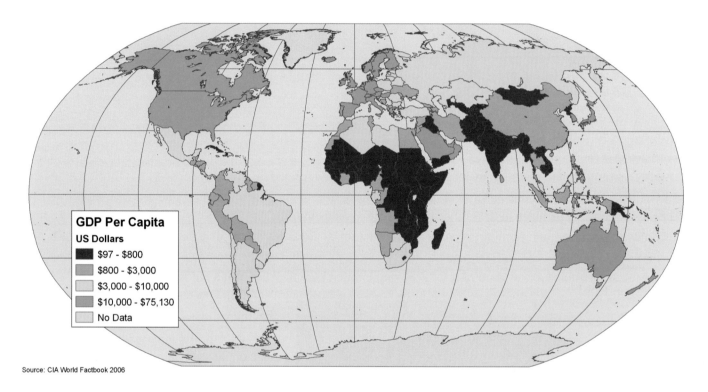

Source: CIA World Factbook 2006

If we look at total activity, that is the total GDP map on the right, we see total wealth as a singular number that a society or state produces. All these numbers look really big and wow, would you look at that? China and India are right up there with the developed countries! So is Saudi Arabia! Sweet! They're making bank money! They're not doing too bad, right? Brazil, Argentina, they're doing pretty good too. Everyone in Saudi Arabia is rich, aren't they? Um . . . how do I put this delicately for my Arab friends? . . . Does a chicken have lips? How do I know everyone there is not rich?

Well, let's check out a more realistic interpretation in the GDP per capita. What you see is a bit of a shake-down. India and China in particular have gone from the top classes of total GDP, to the bottom classes of GDP per capita, a significant shift when broken down to the individual level. Why does this happen? Well, because they have big populations, and they're producing lots and lots of valuable stuff, *but* broken down to an individual level, it ain't really that much. **GDP per capita** is a much better gauge of what's happening in the society in terms of how well the place is really doing. A trillion dollars doesn't really make as much impact if everybody in the society is only getting a buck each.

This high GDP, low GDP per capita scenario possibly could be a very equal society, but unfortunately it never happens that way . . . at least not on this damn planet. The reality is a concentration of wealth in certain businesses and certain sectors and certain hands, with most people not really cutting much of a piece of the pie. This comparison becomes a much better measure of wealth disparity, and as such, is a much better indicator of how this society or state is really doing.

Now sometimes these measures can be skewed radically. In other words, even if a state has a huge number in terms of GDP, and perhaps even when a state has a big number in the GDP per capita category, we still may not be getting the real picture. And I'll pick on a few states in particular here. Places like Equatorial Guinea, Saudi Arabia, even Oman; what's happening in these places? High total GDP, high GDP per capita. Are they really so rich? Are they fully developed like the other rich, developed countries?

I think you already know the answers to these questions. Something don't add up. Equatorial Guinea, a rich place? Look how much money per person! On the books, they make $50,000 GDP per capita. That makes them one of the world leaders in that category . . . oh, except for the fact that most folks are starving to death under a thieving dictator. Indeed, the majority possess squat and a handful of folks own virtually everything. Wealth disparity is massive, but the figures remain high because of a double whammy; the GDP total is absolutely massive, and the total population is low which equates to an exceptionally high GDP per capita, too.

That's when you have to take the sector breakdown of labor in conjunction with GDP and GDP per capita to get a real sense of what's happening in these states. And the real deal that's happening is that these societies have high numbers based on one single thing: the export of oil. They export tons and tons and tons of oil which means they make tons and tons and tons of money, a big number. Even if you divide by the population, it is still a decent number but all of the wealth is, in reality, in the hands of very, very few people.

So Equatorial Guinea is a particularly nasty case where none of these numbers mean crap because most of the people here are impoverished beyond belief. Saudi Arabia, Oman, Iran, and many other OPEC countries fall into similar situations. So you have to consider other things—looking at the economic sector breakdown of a place in conjunction with its GDP per capita gives us a good sense of what's going on. And a good sense of development and standards of living.

SHOW ME THE MONEY!

In summary, what people do around the planet and how the economy of the state is structured, in large part, determines how well or how poorly, the state is doing—and will be doing in the near future.

We have to look at several more factors to determine the true level of development of a place. Numbers aren't always enough, but we can look around the planet and see some obvious trends. Some of the obvious ones we've already pointed out:

→ The developed countries and regions are richer, have high GNP as well as high GDP per capita, and have more employment in service sector and quaternary sector activities than primary and secondary ones. North America, Western Europe, Japan, Australia

→ The developing countries and regions typically have lower GNP as well as lower GDP per capita. However, in some circumstances, even when GDP total is high, the GDP per capita will still come out on the lower end of the spectrum.

→ The developing countries and regions typically have more people employed in the primary and secondary activities than tertiary and quaternary. Sub-Saharan Africa, the Middle East, Central Asia, Central America, the Caribbean

→ The states and regions that are developing the fastest are changing this equation more successfully than other states who are still heavily reliant on primary activities. South America, East Asia, Turkey

→ Some states and regions are currently lagging in GDP not due to economic activity structure, but because of turbulence attributed to shifting economic systems. They are slowly rebounding. Russia and Eastern Europe

So a diverse mix of what's going on economically in the world. Know these factors and features and what people are doing around the world to get a better sense of what's happening in today's world and which way the states are heading. Who has got the money? Who will have the money? Who is developed? Who is developing?

Developed or developing? Hey, that's our next topic . . .

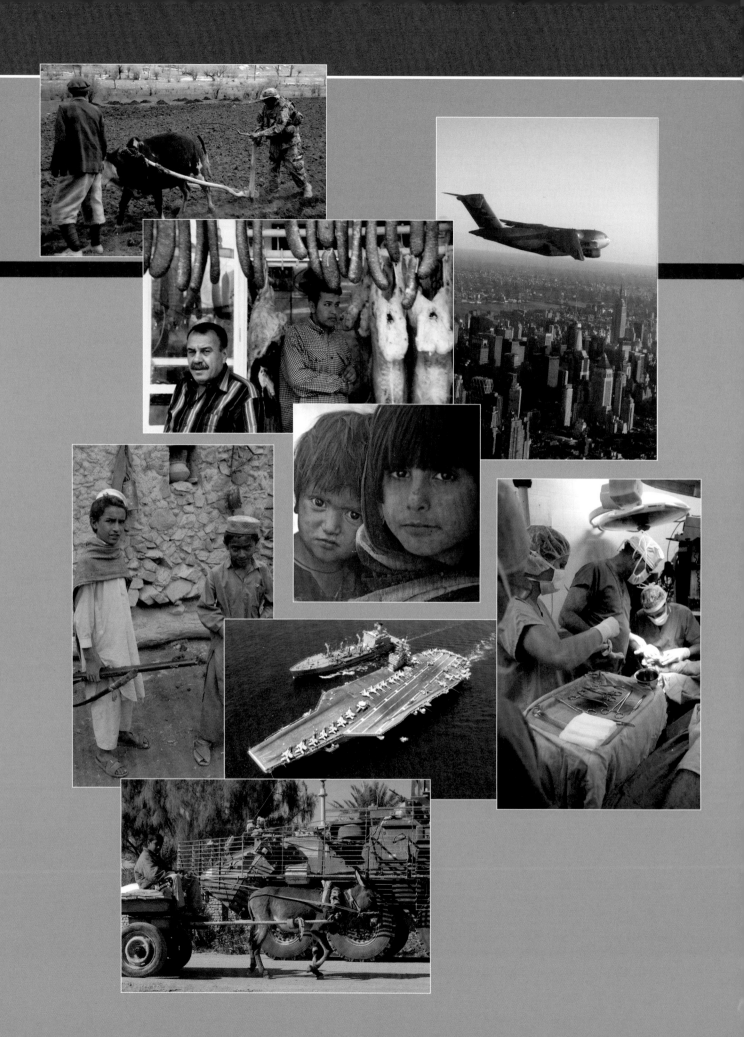

Developed or Developing?

5

RICH -ass places. Poor-ass places. Some states are really well-off, and a whole lot more are struggling day to day to make ends meet. Why are some countries/regions rich, and others poor? As this manual has pointed out, it is not simply a matter of size of the country or the resources it contains. Reality, as always, is much more complicated than that. Before we can even identify traits of these developmental differences around the globe, we should first sort out some basic definitions and terms. Have you ever wondered . . .

IF THERE IS A THIRD WORLD, WHERE ARE WORLDS ONE AND TWO?

Let's run over some common words and descriptors often tossed around to describe the state of states—that is, how well-off they are, or inversely, how close to being in the shithouse they are.

A **developed country** is one that we would consider first and foremost . . . rich! Most texts, news articles and really smart people somehow always forget to just speak the plain damn truth and call a spade a spade. They will describe lots of different variables that account for why a state is rich, without ever outright just saying it. Dammit! The developed countries are the rich ones! Admit it! Have you heard of a fully developed country that's flat broke? It's possible, but not common.

Developed also carries the connotation that these countries are matured, at the end of the cycle, and therefore stable. I think that's a very good way to put it. But what cycle are we talking about? We'll get to that in a bit. You might also hear developed countries called: *industrialized countries, more economically developed countries* (MEDC), *fully developed countries,* or even *the First World.*

A **developing country** on the other hand, is perhaps not so rich. However, it may not necessarily be totally poor either, indicated by such measures as GDP and GDP per capita. Most of the planet would be in this category (both numbers of states as well as numbers of people) and, as such, there is tremendous range in the spectrum of "developing-ness." Some states are close to being fully developed, some are desperately poor and stagnant or perhaps not really "developing" at all.

Perhaps developing countries are best described as all the regions that are obviously not fully developed. Is that a nebulous enough description? Yes, but it kind of works. The operative word here is developing, which means that these countries are in transition, are changing, are—we assume—developing into something newer, better, and richer. No state is actively trying to undevelop are they?

Developing country synonyms include: *less-developed countries* (LDCs), *least economically developed countries* (LEDCs), *underdeveloped nations, undeveloped nations,* and the most popular term that everyone recognizes: *the Third World.*

The Third World. What a hilarious term. A term everyone recognizes and uses, but no one knows what it really means. And it really doesn't mean anything anymore. Here's the real deal. During the Cold War, there were two opposing camps: Team 1 was the capitalist democracies lead by the US aka "The West," Team 2 was the communist countries lead by the USSR aka "The Soviet Bloc." They became known, respectively, as the First World and the Second World. All the other countries were encouraged to join one of these teams, and many did—or at least would allow themselves to be associated with Team 1 or Team 2.

However, there were a group of holdouts who refused to side up. They wanted nothing to do with the Cold War nonsense, and identified themselves as nonaligned. India, Egypt, Ethiopia, and Yugoslavia led this movement of nonalignment. I point them out by name because their status then, as now, has a lot to do with how the meaning of the term evolved. Many other similar states joined this movement, and as you might imagine, the characteristics of their poorer, less-developed economies became an identifying mark . . . a mark that still sticks today. There is no more Cold War, and there are no more First and Second Worlds, but somehow the Third World is still out there batting. Can someone please tell them the game is over?

SO WHAT DOES IT REALLY *MEAN* TO BE DEVELOPED . . . OR DEVELOPING?

So what are some common measures of this richness? People in a developed state typically enjoy a high standard of living—i.e., life is good. Well-fed, healthy children, bills paid, access to health care, good housing, good environment, and there's even some leisure time to party. Yeah, that sounds about right. And developing? Those folks are probably not eating as much as they should, maybe not getting access to health care, maybe not having clean water or electricity, and leisure time is otherwise known as "too sick to work."

But we can do even better than that. Let's look systematically at some categories of human life to better compare and contrast the standards of living on our planet.

So what do these terms mean? What's the difference?

A DIAGRAM OF DIFFERING DEGREES OF DEVELOPMENT TO DIGEST . . .

Below is a brief outline of some of the contributing factors of current levels of development on the wider world. This list is not exhaustive, as we have not included historic factors that have influenced current state of affairs, or physical resources that these regions possess. Again, the purpose of this review is to get you to think about the big picture in these places we are labeling as developed versus those that are developing—if we can understand the mechanics of what is going on in these places, we can better understand the present and better predict the future.

TECHNOLOGICALLY SPEAKING . . .

The developed state has the highest levels of technology across the board. I'm not just talking about computers here either. Agriculturally, they can grow more food with less people. One big tractor can do the work of hundreds of humans. Industrially, they can produce more and better stuff with machines that typically displace workers as well. Machines do the work; people run the machines. The newest and coolest stuff is devel-

Nukes are high-tech!

oped in the developed world. Infrastructure like roads, bridges, buildings, and communications are at the highest quality levels. Emergency and medical services provide lightning response and insane possibilities of keeping people alive. You can reattach an arm? No way! Meanwhile, Grand Theft Auto IV offers mind boggling graphics to thousands of glassy eyed users.

The developing state does not have all of these technological advances, and some states may have little to none of these things. Agriculture and industry are still labor intensive, and typically not as productive. Infrastructure is not as good; roads and communication systems may be lacking. Buildings and sewer systems and electric grids may be not as safe or efficient as possible. They may possibly be at minimum standards, which means they don't function as well, or for as long. Life saving technologies and services map operate at less than favorable standards. There is no 911. You will lose the arm.

INDUSTRIALLY SPEAKING . . .

The developed state uses more machine labor than human labor. As such, they have higher labor productivity which means one human can do a shitload of work. One guy on a tractor can plow a thousand acres. One guy in a semi can move twenty tons of cargo a thousand miles in a day. Because of this, the developed world is much higher in energy consumption per person; just think of all the energy you use in one day for electricity in your home, at the office, driving your car around, making skinny, half caff, sugar free, mocha lattes. In addition, most of the energy produced in the developed world is based on fossil fuels. As a result, there is a high fossil fuel dependency in this world.

The developing world can have great variation in the amount of machine versus human labor is employed. In places where development is low there is a greater percentage of human labor involved, therby reducing the rate of productivity in total work done. How many humans does it take to plow that same thousand acres? And how much longer does it take them? Just using elbow grease, the energy consumption per person is significantly lower. Even the type of fuel used changes in the developing world; fossil fuels are too costly, so less efficient fuel sources like coal, wood, and even dried dung are used more often. There's a plus side: a lower dependency on fossil fuels, and dried shit is cheap. However, those fuels are not very efficient in terms of energy output and are fairly polluting.

ECONOMICALLY SPEAKING . . .

In the developed state, higher technology and industrial capacity equate to increased labor productivity, which in turn equates to higher salaries. The economy is more diversified. There are more desirable types of labor, more choices of occupations, of typically safer types of labor. You can get a job just using your brain. What a novel idea. More of the economy is focused in the service sector, with some in the quaternary sector as well. Primary and secondary jobs are available, but are not the primary earners of GDP, which is high in the developed state.

More importantly, GDP per capita is high too. Corporate earnings are higher. The developed state produces value-added products which makes them more expensive. Processed goods and high-skilled services are apparent: computers, cars, lawyers, investment bankers. Exported high value goods equate to a **positive trade balance** for the state; it sells more stuff than it buys every year. It has a surplus at the bank. All of these factors lead to increased investments that are funneled back into the economy and infrastructure, perpetuating the positive cycle.

In the developing state, lower labor productivity usually leads to limited options for everyone economically. Most of the economy is focused in the primary and secondary sectors. Lots of agriculture and basic manufacturing exists, which produces goods of less value. Harder labor, and laxer environmental and safety laws mean more unhealthy/dangerous working conditions.

Lower salaries, lower corporate earnings, and a special twist—many of the companies operating in the developing states are foreign multinationals, so most profit exits the state and goes back to the multinationals' country of origin. Low value goods are exported, high value goods imported, resulting in an overall **negative trade balance.** Put it all together and it spells out a lower investment in the infrastructure and economy, less personal wealth, less GDP usually, and less GDP per capita almost always—although we have seen some exceptions to this rule as well.

SOCIALLY SPEAKING . . .

In the developed state people make decent money. There is a significant middle class—more often than not, they are the majority of the population. Those folks have higher salaries, which equates to more disposable income, which equates to higher consumption rates of everything and higher rates of saving. It also means people can invest in their own future, as well as provide better health care and education to the next generation. That is crucial. Literacy rates are high. They have higher mobility and social safety nets, like welfare, which increase risk-taking and increase opportunities. You can risk quitting your job to start a new business or go back to school without your family starving to death. This increases your opportunities for employment and income-making potential.

Also in the developed world, population growth rates are stable or only slightly growing. The population pyramid is a column, or inverted. The biggest cohorts are the working/providing groups of people. Fertility rates hover around 2.1, and fewer children per person means higher investment in each child. Usually in education—each generation gets smarter, richer, better, and more cognizant of the Plaid Avenger's World.

We aren't fully so developed. This sucks.

In the developing state, the poor people outnumber the rich ones—sometimes radically so. There may be a middle class, but it is not the majority. General Plaid Rule of Thumb: the smaller the middle class, the poorer the state, and vice-versa. Less expendable income means less food on the table, less overall consumption, less investment in the future genera-tion, less education, and generally lower literacy rates. Lack of social safety nets leads to less risk-taking, fewer opportunities in employment, and in life. And to brighten the picture, popu-lation growth rates are higher, meaning the population is get-ting bigger. We know that this can have considerable variation within the scope of development as well—and is perhaps one of the best indicators as to how far down the path of development a state is: the lower the growth rate, typically the more developed they are. Very high growth rates invariably point to the lesser-developed states. Population pyramids in the developing states are a true pyramid shape, with the biggest cohorts being children under the age of 15: the dependent class. In the least developed states, each new generation gets larger, poorer, less educated, and more stuck.

AND HOW'S YOUR HEALTH?

In the developed state, people are pretty damn healthy overall. Increased education, increased access to health care, and increased public hygiene equate to decreased infant mortality, increased longevity, and decreased susceptibility to epi-

Poorer people eat more grains and veggies. The richer you get, the shittier your diet!

poor   rich

PLAID AVENGER SURE-FIRE WEIGHT LOSS PROGRAM: Move to a Developing Country

demic outbreaks. You will live longer in the developed world, but what will it eventually get you? Due to changes in work types, increased consumption, and wider variety of dietary choices, a distinct health shift occurs as a state becomes fully developed. People become more sedentary as they use their brains instead of their brawn to work. They have stress from using their brains too much. People overconsume in caloric intake. In diet, they move from whole grains and fruits and vegetables to processed foods with a radical increase in sugars, fats, and meat. Result? Around 75 percent of people in a developed world die from diseases of the circulatory system (heart disease, stroke) and cancers.

In the developing world people are not as healthy. Less education, less access to health care, poor public sanitation and hygiene, and even little or no access to immunizations equate to high infant mortality and lower life expectancy. Epidemics can be catastrophic. Diets consist of basic grains and fruits and vegetables, which is really good, but their caloric intake may not be sufficient for optimal health. Result? 50 to 60 percent of the people will die of an infectious or parasitic disease, or in childbirth. The infectious diseases are easily preventable and curable.

GOVERNMENTALLY SPEAKING . . .

In the developed states, democracy is the undisputed champion. All the fully developed states on the planet are democracies. The political/economic structure may have varying degrees of socialist policy, but all are staunchly democratic. These systems are more dynamic, more open to change, and prove it by rotating out leadership in a timely and regulated manner. Developed states are politically stable, leading to stable economies which actively participate in global trade and investment. This stability is one of the primary reasons that international investment is typically higher in developed countries: because your money and your investment are safe in a stable environment.

In the developing world, most other types of governments can be found. Military dictatorship, theocracy, monarchy, one-party states, and chaotic states abound. It should be noted that most developing states are indeed democracies, but usually not well-established with long track records. Why is this important to note? These are systems (other than the newer democracies) that are more static, or closed to change—some exhibit no change at all. The more closed a system is, the more opportunity arises for corruption. This creates an unstable situation in the long term as underlying tensions and forces usually manifest themselves in violent upheaval, civil war, or outright implosion of the state. Unstable governments can often lead to unstable economies, and unstable economies are not where international investors put their money. These states are often insular, protecting their industries or economic interest above all, which discourages global trade and investment.

MILITARILY SPEAKING . . .

There's one last category that most folks don't really look at to assess development status, but the Plaid Avenger does lots of things that other folks don't. I think it's a keen insight into what's happening in the society . . .

In the developed world, military technology is at the maximum. Nuclear capabilities are either possessed or easily acquired. Like in industry, most manual labor is done with machines. Soldiers operate big

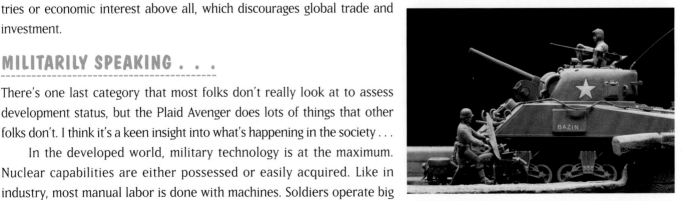

machines and their "death-wielding labor productivity" is very high. Developed states prefer to use their military technology as opposed to large numbers of humans on the ground. Casualties on all fronts are minimized at all costs. A major final point: while total expenditures on the military may be high, in a developed state this expenditure is a fairly low percentage of their GDP.

In the developing state, military technology can be high, but typically is not. Some states, like India, Pakistan, and China, have nuclear capability, but they are pretty much alone in the developing world in this respect. Lots of other states may want it, but will have to try and buy it as they lack the infrastructure to develop it. In developing countries, manpower is still the primary component of the military, and most real action will be dudes on foot, firing guns. China has the largest free-standing army on the planet right now. The last major point: while total expenditures on military expenses may be lower in the developing world, it's a fairly high percentage of GDP and/or the government's budget. Yep. You got it. The less money a state has, the more it usually spends on guns.

PLAID AVENGER RULE OF THUMB AS TO WHETHER OR NOT A PLACE IS DEVELOPED OR DEVELOPING . . .

You won't find this theory in a textbook anywhere, besides this one, because it's a Plaid Avenger original. Lots of different states have lots of the developed world features, but still don't seem to be in the fully developed category.

Pakistan has advanced weaponry and nuclear bombs, but is not fully developed. India has nuclear bombs and is a well-established democracy, but is not fully developed. Saudi Arabia has a huge GDP and free health care, but is not fully developed. China is getting rich as Midas, has high technology, has nuclear bombs, a stable population growth rate, and even a diversified economy, but even they don't seem to be in the fully developed column yet. So what makes the Plaid Avenger difference?

For me, it's all about how the average Joe is doing. How are *most* people doing in the society? How much health care or good jobs or education do the *majority* of folks have access to? What is the real GDP per capita of the *bulk* of the workers? It kind of gets back to that theme I've hit you with about the middle class. There will always be a small percentage of excessively rich folks, and there will always be a lot of poor folks. But how are folks doing in the *middle?* Any country can have any amount of any of the factors listed above, but if it's not accessible to the majority of folks, then I classify the state as still developing. The fully developed states are always marked by the *majority* of people doing well and having access to all of those great things.

MILITARY EXPENDITURES AS A PERCENT OF TOTAL GDP
(THIS IS NOT AN EXHAUSTIVE LIST)

Country	Percent
North Korea	23%
Oman	13%
Qatar	10%
Saudi Arabia	10%
Iraq	9%
Jordan	9%
Israel	7.5%
Yemen	6.6%
Armenia	6.5%
Eritrea	6.3%
Burundi	5.9%
Syria	5.9%
Angola	5.7%
Mauritania	5.5%
Kuwait	5.3%
El Salvador	5%
Morocco	5%
Bosnia	4.5%
China	4.3%
United States	4%
Russia	3.9%
France	2.6%
United Kingdom	2.4%

Make sense? That's why places like India and China may be booming economically right now, and their populations are indeed getting richer overall . . . but *most* people in India still live on a buck or two a day. And *most* of a billion is a lot of damn heads. India may have lots and lots of trappings of the developed world, but how can you call them fully developed when half a billion people don't have access to health care, or lack a proper diet?

My answer: I don't.

FIGURE 5.1 MAP HDI

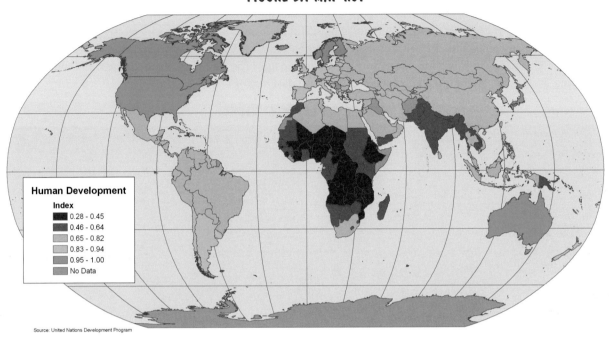

HDI: A UN TAKE ON HOW FOLKS ARE DOING

And the good folks at the UN feel the same way, I think. Here is their take on things:

The **UN Human Development Index (HDI)** is some sort of complex mathematical formula that takes into account poverty, literacy rates, education, life expectancy, fertility rates, and a host of other factors for states. It has become a standard means of measuring overall human well-being. The index was developed in 1990 by a Pakistani economist, which gives it more credibility in the Plaid Avenger's book, and is used by the United Nations Development Program in its annual Human Development Report.

As you can see from the map, the closer you are to a perfect score of 1, the better off the humans are in that state. Take what you like from the map, but I just wanted to point out a few trends. Obviously, the developed, richer countries stand out near the top of the spectrum in North America, Europe, Australia and Japan. South America is not in bad shape by this measure, especially the southern states on the continent. Eastern Europe and Russia have slipped; they probably used to be in higher brackets, but factors such as life expectancy in some of these places has plummeted, as has their HDI. China and some parts of the Middle East and Southeast Asia come next, perhaps rising in the ranks. All of South Asia—India included—are pretty far down the scale. Sub-Saharan Africa pulls up the lower ranks, as we might have predicted.

THE WORLD AT NIGHT: A PLAID AVENGER TAKE ON HOW THE WORLD IS DOING

There's a final image to consider. It can show you a lot about the levels of development on the planet. Plus, it's just so damn cool.

From the Visible Earth: A catalogue of NASA images and animations of our home planet:

This image of earth's city lights was created with data from the Defense Meteorological Satellite Program (DMSP) Operational Linescan System (OLS). Originally designed to view clouds by moonlight, the OLS is also used to map the locations of permanent lights on the earth's surface.

The brightest areas of the earth are the most urbanized, but not necessarily the most populated. (Compare western Europe with China and India.) Cities tend to grow along coastlines and transportation networks. Even without the underlying map, the outlines of many continents would still be visible. The United States interstate highway system appears as a lattice connecting the brighter dots of city centers. In Russia, the Trans-Siberian railroad is a thin line stretching from Moscow through the center of Asia to Vladivostok. The Nile River, from the Aswan Dam to the Mediterranean Sea, is another bright thread through an otherwise dark region.

FIGURE 5.2 EARTH AT NIGHT

Even more than 100 years after the invention of the electric light, some regions remain thinly populated and unlit. Antarctica is entirely dark. The interior jungles of Africa and South America are mostly dark, but lights are beginning to appear there. Deserts in Africa, Arabia, Australia, Mongolia, and the United States are poorly lit as well (except along the coast), along with the boreal forests of Canada and Russia, and the great mountains of the Himalayas.

Credit: Data courtesy Marc Imhoff of NASA GSFC and Christopher Elvidge of NOAA NGDC.

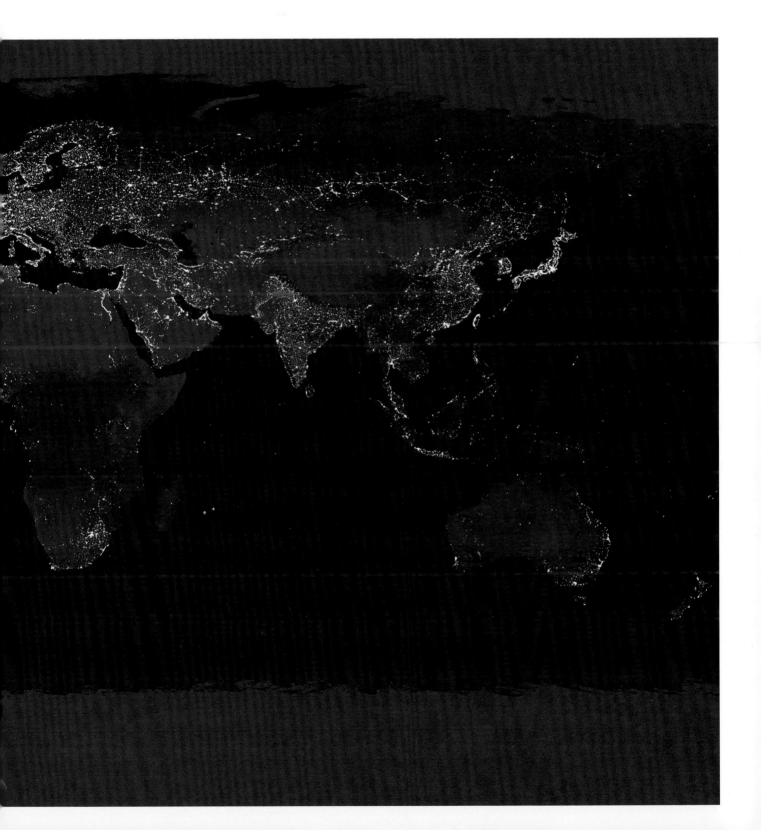

So what can you see? Can you find your hometown? Yeah sure, if your hometown happens to be Moscow. This is what the earth looks like at night. The patterns of light highlight particularly developed *or* populated areas of the earth's surface; sometimes both, but not always. The seaboards of Europe, the eastern US, and Japan are as defined as it gets. What a coincidence; they are all developed regions with high levels of infrastructure and energy use. But, India is lit up pretty well too—due more to raw numbers of people than true levels of development. Hell if everyone in India just held up a candle, you would be able to see it from Pluto. China is somewhere in between; lots of people, getting close to fully developed—but all in the eastern side. Western China is lights out!

Other particularly dark areas include central parts of South America, Africa, Asia, and Australia. Which dark areas are due to lack of population, which are due to significant physical features (like deserts), and which ones are due to lack of development (which means less infrastructure, less electricity, less lights)? All these answers, and more, will be uncovered as you proceed through this book.

TELL US PLAID AVENGER: WHO IS DEVELOPED? WHO IS DEVELOPING? WHO IS DISORGANIZED? WHO IS DAMN NEAR DECEASED?

I'm so glad you asked fellow world-watchers. So many textbooks and news sources and academics simply lack the spine to actually point things out for what they are. But you know that I've got balls-a-plenty, and I'll tell you the shades of developmental plaid that I view the world in. Consider the following map, as created by yours truly:

Here's what the UN has to say about them:

> There is no established convention for the designation of "developed" and "developing" countries or areas in the United Nations system. In common practice, Japan in Asia, Canada and the United States in northern America, Australia and New Zealand in Oceania and Europe are considered "developed" regions or areas. In international trade statistics, the Southern African Customs Union is also treated as developed region and Israel as a developed country; countries emerging from the former Yugoslavia are treated as developing countries; and countries of eastern Europe and the former USSR countries in Europe are not included under either developed or developing regions.

Here's the Plaid interpretation:

FIGURE 5.3 PLAID AVENGER'S LEVELS OF DEVELOPMENT

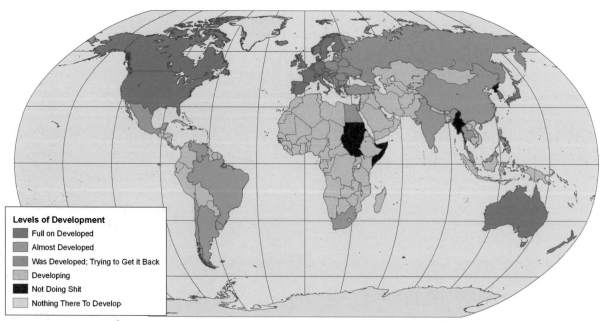

Levels of Development
- Full on Developed
- Almost Developed
- Was Developed; Trying to Get it Back
- Developing
- Not Doing Shit
- Nothing There To Develop

Full-on Developed: The easy category. We've beaten these guys down enough this chapter. North American region (US and Canada), Western Europe region, Australia/New Zealand region, and Japan are the pedal to the metal, full-on fully developed regions/countries. And one wildcard from Southeast Asia: Singapore. Fully developed. No doubts.

Almost developed: This can be a bit tricky, but you can handle it given all you have learned in this chapter. Many South American countries are getting close, as is Mexico. Mexico wavers back and forth—sometimes closer to full development, sometimes falling back to developing status. Check it year to year to see how it's doing.

South Africa, Egypt, and Turkey are beating down the door of full development as well. They have most of the features, but their GDP per capita is still fairly low in comparison to other developed places. China is booming; and Macau, Hong Kong, and Taiwan are already considered developed, and are being reintegrated back into China proper. They, however, have a way to go to close the wealth disparity gap. India is booming too, but with a much longer way to go, and a much bigger gap to close. The Philippines, Thailand, and Malaysia are our best Asian examples that are rounding out those countries getting close to developed status.

Was developed, trying to get it back: Eastern Europe and Russia are the only players in this category. And a distinct category it is. We don't really consider any place becoming "undeveloped," particularly when those places are nuclear powers and former world superpowers. However, the economic and political meltdown caused by the dissolution of the USSR has left many of these countries with GDP numbers and life expectancy numbers more similar to impoverished African nations than European states. But they have the know-how, they have the technology . . . and like the six-million-dollar-man . . . they can rebuild it. The Plaid Avenger is assuming that they will: go for it commies!

Developing: This category still includes a whole lot of countries with a whole lot of people. Comprising big areas of sub-Saharan Africa, the Middle East, Central Asia, South Asia, Southeast Asia and South America, there can be tremendous variability on how far down the path of development they are. Or aren't.

Despite their high per capita GDP, places like Brunei and the Middle Eastern states of Bahrain, Kuwait, Oman, Qatar, Saudi Arabia, and the UAE are generally not considered developed countries because their economies depend overwhelmingly on oil production and export. However, some of these countries, especially Bahrain, have begun to diversify their economies and democratize. Similarly, the Bahamas, Barbados, Antigua and Barbuda, Trinidad and Tobago, and Saint Kitts and Nevis enjoy a high per capita GDP, but these economies depend overwhelmingly on the tourist industry.

Many other countries—particularly in sub-Saharan Africa, Central Asia, Central America, the Caribbean, and Southeast Asia—have a patchy record of development at best. Most indicators of progress discussed in this chapter would be on the lower end of the development spectrum. Many have a hell of a long way to go, and are not currently traveling that fast on the footpath.

Not doing anything category is comprised of countries with long-term civil wars, large-scale breakdown of rule of law, or leaders who are totally insane. All could be described as nondevelopment-oriented economies or just outright chaotic systems. You may also see them referred to as "failed states." Best examples: Haiti, Somalia, Sudan, Burma, and North Korea. Zimbabwe may be joining them soon if Mugabe continues his dictator antics.

I'M DEVELOPMENTALLY SPENT . . .

There it is. That's the Plaid round-up. Hope you now understand the true differences in what is going on in the world in terms of levels of development, and that you have a better handle on how the world will be changing in the coming decades. I know I do.

International Organizations

6

AND now we get to a chapter that's not really a chapter. There are no great explanations or models or theories on how the world is working. This chapter consists of brief explanations of some entities that fall outside, or rather across, state boundaries—global players in a global age. We call them *supranationalist* organizations. Above and beyond the national level, these organizations play an increasingly important role in what is happening across our planet. But who are they? Where did they come from? How are we supposed to know this shit? I don't know friends. If the Plaid Avenger doesn't tell you these things, who will?

Supranationalist organizations are groups of states working together to achieve a common, or outlined, objective. This is another fairly new concept in human history, as states or nations have spent most of their time doing the inverse—beating the hell out of each other or undercutting each other at every available opportunity. So why do countries now work together? The Plaid sees order in the universe; we can classify cooperation into three main classes: economic, defensive, and cultural.

I'll introduce you to the more important and happening entities here, but by no means is the list exhaustive. This chapter will also serve as a functioning reference for you as you progress through the rest of the manual; come back often to refresh your memory when you see these acronyms appear in the regional chapters.

ECONOMIC ENTITIES—SHOW ME THE MONEY

Money. Who doesn't want it? Not any of the states of the world, that's for sure. A great way to make more money, if you are a country, is to make some trade deals with other countries. I'll buy all my bananas from you, if you buy all of your wheat from me—sound good? On top of that, I won't put an import tax on your bananas, but if any other countries try to sell bananas here, I'll tax the hell out of them. Deal? This is the essence of *trade blocks* which are, as you might have guessed, quite a bit more powerful than the individual countries that are in them. Here are a couple of the big ones, along with some future big ones.

Many economists believe that "free trade" between countries increases efficiency and is beneficial for everybody involved. For this reason, both The United States and the European Union are trying their hardest to promote "trade blocs" or "free trade zones" with neighboring countries so that they can improve their economies. Even countries in Latin America, Africa and Asia have caught the bug.

However, there is a tug-of-war going on. Independent nation-states naturally want to protect their economies, so they are reluctant to sign up for free trade when they think that their industries will not be competitive. For example, if Chinese shoe companies make cheaper and better shoes than French shoe companies, France is not going to want free trade in shoes with China. Everybody in France will obviously want to buy Chinese shoes and French shoe companies will go out of business. Historically, the cheaper products are hit with a *tariff,* an import tax, which subsequently makes the price of the product more expensive, and thus the local products can compete better.

Many times, poor countries accuse rich countries of trying to take advantage of them using free trade agreements. These poor countries argue that free trade isn't beneficial for both sides; it's only beneficial for the industrialized country, because their companies are more competitive. Furthermore, they accuse developed countries of cheating, and point to agricultural *subsidies* in these rich countries as an example. Farmers in Europe and America produce shit tons of food using lots of big equipment and fertilizers, thus their costs are high and subsequently the food they make costs more. Farmers in poor countries don't use that expensive stuff and have cheaper labor, therefore their food should cost much less, giving them a competitive advantage in the world market. However, the rich farmers still "win" on the international market because Europe and America give their farmers huge subsidies to offset the higher costs of production they face. So Uncle Sam gives American farmers money just to be farmers, and the farmers can turn around and sell their food for cheaper prices and still make money. You dig? And if you dig a lot, maybe you should become a farmer.

Poor countries argue that the only reason that rich countries became rich in the first place is by protecting their domestic industries using things like tariffs and not signing up for free trade agreements. Also, it can be argued that fully developed rich ass companies from rich countries are so technologically superior that they have a competitive advantage that can never be overcome . . . meaning that the less developed states will always be stuck buying finished goods and selling primary level commodities, thus always losing money. But free trade usually does mean more trade, so the less developed countries do stand to sell much more oil or lima beans or flip-flops or beef lips. So poorer countries are torn as to whether or not it is in their best interest to join these trade blocks with the fully developed states.

Perhaps it's on these grounds that we are seeing many new trade blocks springing up that are comprised solely of states in developing status, with no "rich kids" invited to the party. It certainly is the reason for the foot-dragging with the FTAA, but once again, I have gotten ahead of the story. . . .

Check out these economic entities that you will be hearing a hell of a lot more about, as they will play an increasingly larger role in the way the global economy operates:

NAFTA

Members: United States, Mexico, and Canada

Summary: NAFTA, which stands for North American Free Trade Agreement, is a free trade agreement between the United States, Mexico, and Canada. This agreement is meant to gradually eliminate all duties and tariffs between these three countries. However, the three nations are resisting lowering barriers that would hurt their economies. For example, the United States and Canada have been bickering because the United States imposes a duty on Canadian lumber that goes to the United States. The Canadians are accusing the Americans of not sticking to the treaty and are considering imposing duties on American goods to retaliate.

NAFTA has been very controversial in other ways. Generally, transnational corporations support it because lower tariffs mean higher profits for them. Labor unions in the United States and Canada have opposed it because they believe that jobs will go from the United States and Canada to Mexico because of lower wages there. They were mostly correct. Also, farmers in Mexico oppose it because agricultural subsidies in the United States have forced them to lower the prices on their goods. There has even been an increase in illegal immigration from Mexico to the United States because Mexican farmers have gone bankrupt.

Fun Plaid Fact: Chapter II of the NAFTA treaty allows private corporations to sue federal governments in the NAFTA region if they feel like that government is adversely affecting their investments.

DR-CAFTA

Members: United States, Costa Rica, El Salvador, Guatemala, Honduras, Nicaragua Dominican Republic. Currently, the US Administration is pushing hard to get Columbia and Panama into this club as well.

Summary: DR-CAFTA stands for Dominican Republic—Central America Free Trade Agreement and is an international treaty to increase free trade. It was ratified by the Senate of the United States in 2005. Like NAFTA, its goal is to privatize public services, eliminate barriers to investment, protect intellectual property rights, and eliminate tariffs between the participating nations. Many people see DR-CAFTA as a stepping stone to the larger, more ambitious, FTAA (Free Trade Agreement of the Americas).

The controversy regarding DR-CAFTA is very much like the controversy regarding NAFTA. Many people are concerned about America losing jobs to poorer countries where the minimum wage is lower and environmental laws are more lax. Also, some people are concerned that regional trade blocs like DR-CAFTA undermine the project of creating a worldwide free trade zone using organizations like the WTO.

Fun Plaid Fact: Many Washington insiders see DR-CAFTA as a way of reducing the influence of China in Central America.

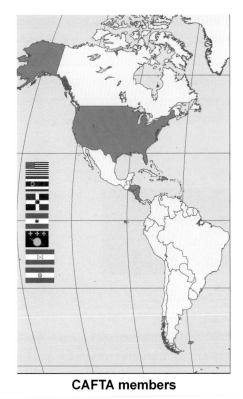

CAFTA members

FTAA

Members: *PROPOSED* All of the nations in North and South America except Cuba. Cause we hate commies. Damn commies.

Summary: The FTAA, which stands for Free Trade Area of the Americas, is a proposed agreement to end trade barriers between all of the countries in North and South America. It hasn't been ratified yet, because there are some issues that need to be worked out by the participating countries. The developed (rich) countries, such as the United States, want more free trade and increased intellectual property rights and the developing (poor) countries, such as Brazil, want an end to US/Canadian agricultural subsidies and more free trade in agricultural goods.

The key issue here for poor countries is agricultural subsidies. Farmers in the United States (and rich countries generally) produce agricultural goods at a higher price than poor countries do. However, to keep their goods cheap (and thus competitive on the world market) the government of the United States pays their farmers subsidies. These subsidies make developing countries very angry because they believe subsidies give American farmers an unfair advantage. For this reason, some Latin American leaders have stalled the agreement. Venezuelan President Hugo Chavez has called the agreement "a tool of imperialism" and has proposed an alternative agreement called the Bolivarian Alternative for the Americas.

Proposed FTAA members

For rich countries, the issue is intellectual property rights, which is best exemplified by copyright laws. Poor countries sometimes oppose these rights because they believe that if they are enacted, they will stifle scientific research in Latin America and widen the gap between the rich and poor countries in the Americas.

It should be noted, as of this writing in 2008, that this tentative agreement has been totally stalled by the leftist alliance of Castro, Chavez, and the new Bolivian president Evo Morales. The "leftward swing" of Latin America, that we'll talk about in a later chapter, has seriously squashed the Bush administration's agenda on this issue.

Fun Plaid Fact: The only country that would not be included in the FTAA is Cuba, because the United States has an economic embargo that prohibits all trade with its communist regime. For this reason, Cuba has already joined the Bolivarian Alternative for the Americas.

EU

Members: Belgium, Bulgaria, France, Germany, Italy, Luxembourg, The Netherlands, Denmark, Ireland, United Kingdom, Greece, Portugal, Spain, Austria, Finland, Sweden, Cyprus, Czech Republic, Estonia, Hungary, Latvia, Lithuania, Malta, Poland, Romania, Slovakia, Slovenia

Summary: For years, European philosophers and political observers have realized that the best way to ensure peace on the European continent *and* to increase trade is to politically and economically integrate the nations. After the destruction and loss of life caused by World War II, European nations finally began to slowly increase interdependence, by small steps. They started by integrating their coal and steel industries in the ECSC (European Coal and Steel Community). Currently, the European Union, which has 27 member states, has a common market, a common currency for all of Europe (the euro), a European Commission, a European Parliament, and a European

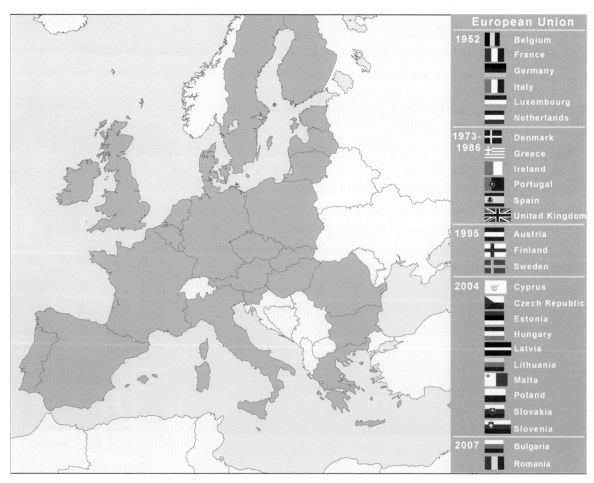

Court of Justice. The nations of the EU have also negotiated treaties to have common agricultural, fisheries, and security policies. Unlike other free trade agreements, the European Union covers many areas other than free trade.

This is the most evolved supranationalist organization the world has ever seen—perhaps a "United States of Europe." Free movement of people across international borders of the member states makes it unique in the trade block category. Of greater importance are an evolving EU armed force, a single environmental policy, and increasing a single foreign policy voice. That is a very big deal!

However, there has been some resistance within European countries to integration. Some countries, like Norway and Switzerland, have refused to join and others, like the United Kingdom, have refused to fully adopt the euro. Also, in 2005, a constitution for the European Union was rejected by French and Dutch voters, putting the future of European integration into question. Many Europeans simply don't care about the European Union and others see it as a secretive, undemocratic organization that is taking away power from their home countries. Some of the richer countries in Europe are afraid that adding nations with weaker economies will take away money from them and give it to the poor.

But make no bones about it, the EU is still expanding. And fast. It has been absorbing more and more of Eastern Europe; the most recent inductees being Romania and Bulgaria. The next likely candidates are Croatia, Bosnia, Macedonia, Albania, Ukraine and Turkey. Russia is usually invited to big talks as kind of an associate member already. Not everybody likes it, but the EU makes Europe a player in the world economy and world political terms. Divided, they are not much. United, Europe still has a big voice.

MERCOSUR

Members: Brazil, Argentina, Uruguay, Paraguay, with the newest addition: Venezuela!

Associate Members: Bolivia, Chile, Colombia, Ecuador, Peru

Summary: MERCOSUR is a free trade agreement between several South American countries that was created in 1991 by the Treaty of Asuncion. Like other free trade agreements, its purpose is to promote free trade and the fluid movement of goods, peoples, and currency between the member countries. Venezuela was accepted as a member in 2006, much to the glee of anti-FTAA and US-basher Hugo Chavez. But he is not alone. Many people see MERCOSUR as a counterweight to other global economic powers such as the European Union and the United States.

MERCOSUR faces several challenges. For one, its countries are generally much poorer than those of the United States and Europe. Its GDP is only 1/12 of the United States, standing at 1 trillion dollars. MERCOSUR was also greatly weakened as a result of the collapse of Argentina's economy in 2002. In addition, two of its biggest members, Brazil and Argentina, have been locked in trade disputes. However, keep an eye on this one as leftist events unfold in Latin America. It could become a viable force.

MERCOSUR (MERCOSUL)

Member states
Associate members

Fun Plaid Fact: MERCOSUR means Mercado Común del Sur, which means Southern Common Market in Spanish.

PLAID ALERT!
Holy shit, keep your eyes on this one too. This very well could turn into the largest, richest, baddest ass block on the planet in your lifetime. Booming economies in most member states, with more growth in the future. Bigger deal than that: China, South Korea, Japan and India as 'associates'? Are you kidding me? That's like over half of the entire planet's population under one economic umbrella. Watch out! They are going to be hot!

ASEAN

Members: Brunei, Cambodia, Indonesia, Laos, Malaysia, Myanmar, Philippines, Singapore, Thailand, Vietnam

Summary: ASEAN, which stands for Association of Southeast Asian Nations, is a free trade bloc of Southeast Asian countries. Like the European Union, ASEAN is more than just a free-trade zone; it also aims for political, cultural, and economic integration. It was formed in 1967 as a show of solidarity against expansion of Communist Vietnam and insurgency within their own borders. During that time, many countries around Vietnam were going communist and capitalist governments were extremely worried that communism might infect them as well. However, Vietnam has joined ASEAN since then.

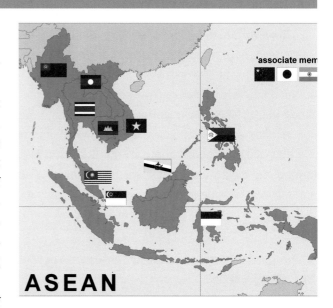

ASEAN

ASEAN is significant because of the heterogenous nature of its constituent countries. ASEAN countries are culturally diverse, including Muslims, Buddhists, and other religions. Governments in ASEAN range from democracy to autocracy. The economies of ASEAN countries are also very diverse, but they mainly focus on electronics, oil, and wood.

These guys are increasingly modeling themselves after the EU experiment too. Even though they remain much more nationalistic than the European countries, the ASEAN group has much bigger goals than to simply be trade block. A common electric grid across the member countries has been proposed; an 'open-sky' arrangement is soon taking effect (free movement of all aircraft among member states); and common environmental policies are being adopted across the region.

Fun Fact: During annual ASEAN meetings, the three ASEAN Dialogue Partners (China, Japan, and South Korea) meet with ASEAN leaders. India hangs with the cool kids now too.

APEC

Members: Australia, Brunei, Canada, Indonesia, Japan, Korea, Malaysia, New Zealand, Philippines, Singapore, Thailand, United States, China, Taiwan, Mexico, Papua New Guinea, Chile, Peru, Russia, Vietnam—pretty much all the guys with Pacific coastline.

Summary: The Asia-Pacific Economic Cooperation trade bloc is a group of Pacific Rim countries that meets with the aim of improving economic and political ties. Like most free-trade blocs, the goal of APEC is to eventually reduce tariffs to nothing. Also, like many free trade agreements, agricultural subsidies have become a point of controversy. The leaders of all APEC countries meet annually in a summit called "APEC Economic Leaders' Meeting" which meets in a different location every year. The first of these meetings was in 1993 and was organized by American president Bill Clinton.

The countries in APEC are responsible for the production of about 80 percent of the world's computer and high tech components. The countries in the Pacific Rim are also significant because the population in these countries is increasing dramatically. This trade bloc will possibly become a huge force in the global economy in the near future.

OECD

Members: Austria, Belgium, Canada, Denmark, France, Germany, Greece, Iceland, Ireland, Italy, Luxembourg, Netherlands, Norway, Portugal, Spain, Sweden, Switzerland, Turkey, United Kingdom, United States, Japan, Finland, Australia, New Zealand, Mexico, Czech Republic, Hungary, South Korea, Poland, Slovakia

Summary: The Organisation for Economic Co-operation and Development (OECD) is an international organization of countries that accept the principles of democracy and free markets. After World War II, when Europe was in ruins, the United States gave European countries aid in the form of the Marshall Plan to improve the economy of Europe and ensure that European countries remain democracies. The Organisation for European Economic Co-operation (OEEC) was formed in 1948 to help administer the Marshall Plan. In 1961, membership was extended to non-European countries and renamed the OECD.

Like many trade agreements, the purpose of the OECD is to promote free trade, economic development, and coordinate policies. The OECD also does a lot of research on trade, environment, agriculture, technology, taxation, and other areas. Since the OECD publishes its research, it has become one of the world's best sources for information and statistics about the world.

Fun Plaid Fact: The Republic of China (Taiwan) has observer status on two OECD committees, but since many countries do not recognize Taiwan as an independent country, it is not a formal member.

DEFENSE

Why should countries get together defensively? If they are all on the same team, then they won't fight—right? Well, that's the emphasis of the UN. But perhaps more pertinent are regional defense blocks that have cropped up between countries throughout history. Their thinking is more along the lines of: "I'll help you if you get attacked by an outsider, if you help me if I'm attacked by an outsider." If this sounds like trivial schoolyard thinking, don't laugh; the basis for World War I was a whole host of such pacts between European countries—once one country

was attacked, virtually every other country was immediately pulled in as a consequence of defense agreements. Here are the big three that are pertinent in today's world—even though one of them is now gone.

THE UNITED NATIONS

UN Secretary General Ban Ki-Moon

Members: All the sovereign states in the world except Vatican City. There are currently 192 of them. Even the Swiss finally joined a couple of years ago.

The United Nations, or UN, was founded in 1945 as a successor to the League of Nations. Like the League, the goal of the UN is to maintain global peace. Unlike the League, no major world wars have happened on the UN's watch. This is not to say that the United Nations has achieved global peace. In fact, UN "peacekeepers" have been on hand to witness some of the most egregious violations of human rights in recent history.

The UN is made up of several bodies, the most important of which is the Security Council (see Security Council section). The second most important body in the UN is the General Assembly where each of the 191 member nations has a representative and a vote. The General Assembly has produced gems such as the *Universal Declaration of Human Rights* and the lesser known *International Convention on the Protection of the Rights of All Migrant Workers and Members of Their Families.* The General Assembly is clearly the home of utopian thinkers, but, not of any real international power. This leaves the United States free to ignore everything that the General Assembly says, without even having to waste the time vetoing it.

The UN also includes hundreds of subagencies that you've heard of before, such as the World Health Organization (WHO) or UNICEF. The WHO is in charge of coordinating efforts in international public health. UNICEF (The United Nation's Children Fund) provides health, educational, and structural assistance to children in developing nations. Both agencies are supported by member nations and private donors. UNICEF also receives millions of pennies collected each year by children on Halloween.

Critics often charge the UN with being ineffective. This is largely true, but the United Nations was never really intended to be a global government. The best way to view the UN is a forum in which nations can communicate and work together. The UN is ill-equipped to punish any strong member for violations. If a member is especially naughty, a strongly worded UN resolution might recommend voluntary diplomatic or economic sanctions. Perhaps after World War III, the United Nations will be once again renamed and given stronger international authority.

THE REAL POWER AT THE UN: THE UN PERMANENT SECURITY COUNCIL

Members: US, UK, Russia, China, and France

The Security Council is composed of five permanent members (the United States, the United Kingdom, Russia, China, and France) and ten other elected members serving rotating two year terms. The Security Council is charged with responding to threats to peace and acts of aggression. Basically, for anything to get done, the Security Council has to do it. But, things rarely get done because each of the five permanent members has the power to veto and prevent any resolution that they do not like. A single veto from any one of the permanent members kills the resolution  on the spot. This group of rag-tag veto-wielding pranksters is currently the ultimate source in interpreting international law. Most of the Cold War saw little to no consensus on anything, as Team US/UK faced off against Team Russia/China. Whatever one team tried to push, the other team generally would veto. The Frenchies vetoed according to mood and lighting of the room.

The other ten rotating members of the Council do not have veto power, but are often used as a coalition building tool to get things done. During the build-up to the current war in Iraq, the US worked very hard to get as many members of the Council as possible to back the resolution to invade Iraq, knowing full well that China and Russia would veto it. This was a strategic move to show some sort of broad support for the war, even though the US accepted up front that the resolution would not be passed.

There is currently speculation that new members may be added to the UN Security Council. The prime candidates are Germany and Japan. The United States supports their candidacies; maybe because we have over 270,000 military personnel (including dependents of military) in Germany and Japan combined. There is also talk of including Brazil or India, or even more remotely, an "Islamic member" or an "African member." But seriously, what incentive does the Security Council have to dilute their powers? Remember all five would have to agree to let a new member in, so while the United States would certainly support the incorporation of Japan, China would be more likely to tell Japan to go piss up a rope. However, the four most likely members (Japan, Germany, Brazil, and India) have released a joint statement saying that they will all support the others entries. The best argument for enlargement is that Japan and Germany are the second and third largest contributors to the UN general fund, and thus deserve more power. Regardless, don't count on the Security Council getting any bigger unless shit starts going down, which it will, sooner or later.

NATO

Members: Bulgaria, Estonia, Latvia, Lithuania, Romania, Slovakia, Slovenia, The United States of America, France, The United Kingdom, Iceland, Spain, Portugal, Germany, Italy, Belgium, Switzerland, Luxembourg, Finland, Poland, the Czech Republic, Hungary, Greece, Turkey, Norway, the Netherlands, Denmark, and Canada

NATO, which stands for the North Atlantic Treaty Organization, is a military alliance between certain European countries, Canada, and America. It was originally created in 1949 to serve as a barrier to a possible attack from the Soviet Union (which never occurred). The most important part of NATO is Article V of the NATO Treaty, which states, *"The Parties agree that an armed attack against one or more of them in Europe or North America shall be considered an attack against them all. . . ."* This is called a mutual defense clause and basically means that the United States must treat an attack on Latvia the same as it would treat an attack on Tennessee.

Although NATO is a multilateral organization, the United States is clearly the captain of the ship. As a rule, US troops are never under the command of a foreign general. NEVER. Because of this, NATO troops (mainly American) are ALWAYS under American command. The United States also uses NATO countries to base its own troops and station nuclear weapons. Many historians blame the United States for provoking the Cuban Missile Crisis, saying that the Russians only wanted to put nukes in Cuba because the United States had recently stationed nukes in Turkey (a NATO nation).

Since the Cold War, NATO has been looking for a new role in the world. Many of the former Soviet republics have since been admitted to NATO (which, by the way, really pisses off Russia). NATO expansion was promoted as an expansion of democracy and freedom into Eastern Europe. More likely, it was to make sure Russia would never be able to regain the territory. NATO has also been increasingly active in international police work (although there is no real justification for this in the NATO Treaty). NATO forces were heavily involved in the Bosnia conflict in 1994 and the Yugoslavia conflict in 1999 (in reality these were just American troops under a multinational flag). After September 11th, NATO has also become involved in the anti-terrorism game, even invoking Article V for the first time with regard to Afghanistan. Remember, the war in Afghanistan is a NATO mission, not a US mission. But let's be honest here; the US does most of the heavy lifting, as usual.

NATO Secretary General Jaap de Hoop Scheffer. Don't make him angry. You wouldn't like NATO when he's angry.

Fun Plaid Fact: The only country in NATO without a military force is Iceland. The Icelandic Defense Force is an American military contingent stationed permanently on the island.

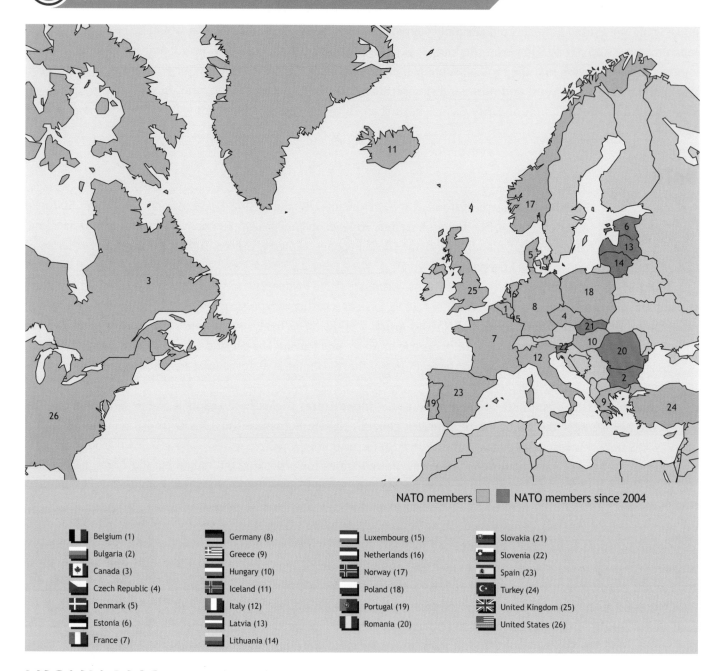

NATO members ☐ ■ NATO members since 2004

Belgium (1)	Germany (8)	Luxembourg (15)	Slovakia (21)
Bulgaria (2)	Greece (9)	Netherlands (16)	Slovenia (22)
Canada (3)	Hungary (10)	Norway (17)	Spain (23)
Czech Republic (4)	Iceland (11)	Poland (18)	Turkey (24)
Denmark (5)	Italy (12)	Portugal (19)	United Kingdom (25)
Estonia (6)	Latvia (13)	Romania (20)	United States (26)
France (7)	Lithuania (14)		

WARSAW PACT—DEFUNCT!

PAST-Members: Soviet Union (club president), Albania (until 1968), Bulgaria, Czechoslovakia, East Germany (1956–1990), Hungary, Poland, and Romania.

The Warsaw Pact, or if you prefer the more Orwellian Soviet name—the "Treaty of Friendship, Co-operation and Mutual Assistance," was the alliance formed by the Soviet Union to counter the perceived threat of NATO. The Warsaw Pact was established in 1955 (six years after NATO) and lasted *officially* until 1991 (two years post-Berlin Wall). Much like the Bizarro-Superman to the United State's real Superman, the Warsaw Pact never had the teeth or the organizational strength of NATO. Perhaps this is because many of the members actually hated the dominance of the Soviet Union. Two countries, Hungary (1956) and Czechoslovakia (1961), tried to assert political independence and were subsequently crushed by Soviet military forces in exercises that would make Tiananmen Square look like an after school special.

The main idea behind the Warsaw Pact was mutual protection. If the United States attempted to invade any of the Warsaw members, it would guarantee a Soviet response. In this way, the Warsaw countries acted like a tripwire against the expansion of Western-style capitalism and democracy, firmly establishing the location of the Iron Curtain. Shortly after the Cold War, most Warsaw countries either ceased to exist or defected to NATO.

Fun Plaid Fact: The Soviet Union despised American acronyms. Instead of taking the first letter from each word, the Soviets preferred taking the entire first sound. For example, Communist International was "Comintern."

CULTURAL ORGANIZATIONS

Some supranationalist organizations form out of a desire to keep a cultural coherence with like countries, or to promote certain aspects of their culture among their member states. In other words, monetary gain is not the driving force behind the organization, although economics usually sneaks in there as well. Here are three very different such organizations to compare and contrast.

ARAB LEAGUE

Members: Egypt, Iraq, Jordan, Lebanon, Saudi Arabia, Syria, Yemen, Libya, Sudan, Morocco, Tunisia, Kuwait, Algeria, United Arab Emirates, Bahrain, Qatar, Oman, Mauritania, Somalia, Palestine, Djibouti, Comoros

The Arab League is an organization designed to strengthen ties among member states, coordinate their policies, and promote their common interests. The league is involved in various political, economic, cultural, and social programs, including literacy campaigns and programs dealing with labor issues. The common bond between the countries in the Arab League is that they speak a common language, Arabic, and practice a common religion, Islam. The Charter of the Arab League also forbids member states from resorting to force against each other. In many ways, the Arab League can be seen, like the OAS, as a regional UN. It was formed in 1945.

However, the Arab League is better known for their lack of coherence and in-fighting more so than any unifying activities they have had so far to date. In fact, Libyan leader Moammar Gadhafi threatened to withdraw from the League in 2002, because of "Arab incapacity" in resolving the crises between the United States and Iraq and the Israeli-Palestinian conflict. If the Arab League ever gets its act together, it could be a powerful force in the world. Right now, it is not.

Fun Fact: Egypt was suspended from the Arab League from 1979 to 1989 for signing a peace treaty with Israel.

Let's get this Arab party started!

OAS

Members: Argentina, Bolivia, Brazil, Chile, Colombia, Costa Rica, Cuba, Dominican Republic, Ecuador, El Salvador, Guatemala, Haiti, Honduras, Mexico, Nicaragua, Panama, Paraguay, Peru, United States, Uruguay, Venezuela, Barbados, Trinidad and Tobago, Jamaica, Grenada, Suriname, Dominica, Saint Lucia, Antigua and Barbuda, Saint Vincent and the Grenadines, Bahamas, Saint Kitts and Nevis, Canada, Belize, Guyana

Summary: The OAS, which stands for Organization of American States, is an international organization headquartered in Washington, DC. According to Article 1 of its Charter, the goal of the member nations in creating the OAS was "to achieve an order of peace and justice, to promote their solidarity, to strengthen their collaboration, and to defend their sovereignty, their territorial integrity, and their independence." Other goals include economic growth, democracy, security, the eradication of poverty, and a means to resolve disputes. Historically, the first meeting to promote solidarity and cooperation was held in 1889 and was called the First International Conference of American States. Since then, the OAS has grown, through a number of small steps, to become the organization it is today.

Unlike free-trade blocs, the OAS encompasses many areas other than just trade. For example, it oversees elections in all of its member countries—of particular note, they declared the last election in Peru as illegal, and the last election in Mexico as the first verifiably legal. However, it has been criticized as a means for America to control the countries in Latin America. For example, when America wanted Cuba kicked out, the organization quickly did so. However, the many dictatorships that America has supported have remained within the OAS.

Fun Plaid Fact: Even though Cuba is a member state, the current regime is denied the right of representation and attendance at meetings and of participation in activities.

AU: AFRICAN UNION

Members: Algeria, Angola, Benin, Botswana, Burkina Faso, Burundi, Cameroon, Cape Verde, Central African Republic, Chad, Comoros, Democratic Republic of the Congo, Republic of the Congo, Côte d'Ivoire, Djibouti, Egypt, Equatorial Guinea, Eritrea, Ethiopia, Gabon, Gambia, Ghana, Guinea, Guinea-Bissau, Kenya, Lesotho, Liberia, Libya, Madagascar, Malawi, Mali, Mauritius, Mozambique, Namibia, Niger, Nigeria, Rwanda

Suspended Members: Mauritania

Summary: The Organization of African Unity was established in 1963 at Addis Ababa, Ethiopia, by 37 independent African nations to promote unity and development; defend the sovereignty and territorial integrity of members; eradicate all forms of colonialism and promote international cooperation. This organization changed its name to the African Union in 2002. Institutionally, the AU is very much like the EU, with a parliament, a commission, a court of justice, and a chairmanship which rotates between the member countries. The AU is also beginning to deploy peacekeepers, and it is planning to send 2500 soldiers to the Darfur region of the Sudan. Every country in Africa is a member of the AU except for Morocco, which withdrew in 1985. Also, Mauritania was suspended in 2005 after a coup d'etat occurred and a military government took power. The new government has promised to hold elections within two years, but many observers are doubtful that it will.

African military problems to be increasingly solved by African troops. How novel!

There are many problems facing Africa such as civil wars, disease, undemocratic regimes, and poverty. However, the biggest problem facing the AU is the spread of HIV (the virus that leads to AIDS) on the African continent. It is expected that millions of people will die in the coming years, and these events will probably destabilize the African continent. The AU has many challenges to face in the coming years.

Fun Fact: The idea of an African Union (separate from the OAU) came from Muammar al-Gadhafi who wanted to see a "United States of Africa." He was sick of developments in the Arab world and publicly gave up on being an Arab.

"Up yours Arab League. I'm African now!"

INTERNATIONAL ODDBALLS

In addition to these, other entities have been formed at the international level for specific functions as well as for the supposed good of all humanity. Many of these organizations are frequently in the news, so I feel a brief intro to them is merited. Haven't you ever wondered who the heck is the G7, the G8, the IMF, the World Bank, or the WTO, and what is an NGO?

G-7 GROUP OF SEVEN

Members: Canada, France, Germany, Italy, Japan, UK, and the USA

The Group of Seven (or G-7) is the country club of international relations. It's a place where the richest industrialized nations go to talk about being rich, form strategies for staying rich, and—like any other country club—figure out how to keep everyone else poor. The leaders from G-7 countries meet each year for a summit. The summits are often widely protested for reasons such as global warming, poverty in Africa, unfair trade policies, unfair medical patent laws, and basically, for a general sense of arrogance. Protesters mark your calendars, the summit returns to the USA in 2012 (location TBD).

The origins of the G-8 are with the G-6 (G-8 minus Russia and Canada), which formed out of the *Library Group,* and formed because rich countries were pissed about the 1973 oil crisis. Canada joined the group in 1976 making it the G-7. In 1991, Russia was given a special membership creating the P-8 or G-7+1, which in 1998 was rechristened the G-8. However, the original G-7 still meets annually to discuss financial issues (Russia is not invited). There is also a meeting of the G-8 ministers with leaders from Brazil, China, India, Mexico, and South Africa which is typically called the G-8+5. If you are confused, please reference the following practice math problem.

G-8 GROUP OF EIGHT

Members: G-7 plus Russia

Same as above, with Russia in attendance. Russia is still a nuclear power, still the largest territorial state on the planet, and perhaps most significantly a major energy resource provider to the world—especially to the G-7 countries. They have to invite the big boy to the party every now and again, or the big boy might get too pissed and go play with China. The G-7 doesn't want that. They need their energy!

WTO

WORLD TRADE ORGANIZATION
ORGANISATION MONDIALE DU COMMERCE
ORGANIZACIÓN MUNDIAL DEL COMERCIO

Dudes In Club—150 total members

Dudes Observing the Club—Iran, Iraq, Sudan, Vietnam, Vatican City . . .

Dudes NOT In the Club—Palestine, Somalia, North Korea . . .

The World Trade Organization (WTO) is an international, multilateral organization that makes the rules for the global trading system and resolves disputes between its member states. The stated mission of the WTO is to increase trade by promoting lower trade barriers and providing a platform for the negotiation of trade. In principle, each member of the WTO is a privileged trading partner with every other member. This means that if one member gives another a special deal, he's got to give it to everyone else too—like in elementary school if you were caught with candy.

Things that make the WTO sigh in delight are "open markets," "tariff reductions," and "long walks on the beach at sunset." The WTO is basically the application of capitalism on a global scale. The key idea is that competition creates efficiency and growth. *Any* country should be able to sell *any* thing it can, *any* where it wants, at *any* price that *any* one will pay. The WTO can boast some successes in growing international trade, but these have also been accompanied by increased wealth disparity between rich and poor nations AND between the rich and poor within nations.

Formally established in 1995, the WTO is structured around about 30 different trade agreements, which have the status of international legal texts. Member countries must ratify all WTO agreements to join the club. Many of the agreements are highly criticized including the Agreement on Agriculture, which reduces tariffs hurting small farms in developing countries. One of the most famous antiglobalization protests occurred around the 1999 WTO meeting in Seattle. Also, the Man loves the WTO.

Fun Plaid Fact—The Kingdom of Tonga became the 150th member in 2005. The oldest animal ever recorded, a tortoise named Tu'i Malila, died in Tonga in 1965. Okay, this has nothing to do with the WTO, but turtles are cool.

IMF

Members: Everyone. Seriously. Okay, you got me, except North Korea, Cuba, Liechtenstein, Andorra, Monaco, Tuvalu and Nauru.

The primary responsibility of the International Monetary Fund (IMF) is to monitor the global financial system. The IMF works at stabilizing currency exchange rates. Doing this, they provide security to overseas investors and help promote international trade. The IMF's policies are also aimed at reducing the phenomenon of "boom and bust," where economies grow rapidly, then stagnate, then grow rapidly, then stagnate, then grow rapidly, et cetera. The main tool of the IMF is "financial assistance" (aka loans), which they provide to countries with "balance of payment problems" (aka big time debt). As a condition of the loans, the IMF mandates "structural adjustment programs." These programs are designed to turn a cash profit, allowing the borrowing country to repay its debt to the IMF. Here is a short glossary of "structural adjustment" terms and how they are interpreted by the locals:

IMF sez . . .	Locals sez it means . . .
Austerity	cutting social programs
User Fees	charging for stuff like education and health care and water
Resource Extraction	selling stuff out of the ground that rich countries want
Privatization	selling state owned stuff to rich companies (usually foreigners)
Deregulation	removing domestic control over stuff
Trade liberalization	allowing foreigners to open sweatshops and exporting stuff made in sweatshops

Much like the WTO and World Bank, the IMF is often congratulated for growth in the global trade and production and simultaneously scorned for increasing the poverty gaps within countries and between countries.

THE WORLD BANK

Similar to its Bretton Wood's sister, the IMF, the mission of the World Bank (actually the World Bank Group) is to encourage and safeguard international investment. All the while, the World Bank attempts to help reduce poverty and spawn economic development. The World Bank works primarily with "developing countries" helping them develop in a Westerly fashion. Also, like the IMF, the World Bank loans are contingent on adopting "structural adjustments." While the IMF deals primarily with currency stabilization, the World Bank is primarily like a real bank, loaning countries money for very specific development projects like a hydropower plant or a disease-eradication program.

Currently, the World Bank is headed by the never controversial Paul Wolfowitz (who ironically succeeded James Wolfensohn both at the IMF and in the Washington DC phonebook under W). Wolfowitz has stated that he will continue to reach out to developing countries much in the same way he helped the Department of Defense reach out during his tenure at the Pentagon. Unlike the IMF, which is headquartered in Switzerland, the World Bank Group is headquartered in Washington, DC.

It should be noted that the World Bank is breaking new ground on the redefinition of the sovereignty issue that we covered in chapter 3. Due to government corruption in many states, particularly Africa, the World Bank is now putting further stipulations and oversight on all the loans it makes to countries. They are going in and making sure that the money they give a country to build an AIDS clinic doesn't end up getting used to buy weaponry for the state. The Plaid Avenger is proud as punch at such a bold move, but many states are hopping mad that this type of intense oversight, which is now mandatory before the Bank hands over any money, violates their sovereignty. I'm with the World Bank on this one. Tough shit, sovereign states. If you want the jack, prove it's going to be used responsibly.

Watch for this issue to gain world attention soon. As of this writing, it's causing consternation in Chad as we speak . . .

NGOS

NGOs are Nongovernmental Organizations. These are basically every organization that is not directly affiliated with the government, from Amnesty International to Greenpeace. We are talking about the growing number of highly influential international groups that are playing an ever important role in transnational politics. These groups transcend borders and unite common interests. NGOs are set up to represent a diverse array of special interests (environmental protection, human rights, et cetera). Here are a few examples of influential NGOs:

→ Human Rights Watch—With a budget of ~$20 million a year, this NGO aims to document violations of international humanitarian law by sponsoring fact-finding research. HRW recently waged a successful campaign against the use of land-mines (which the U.S. government opposed).

→ Freedom House—This NGO supports research for democracy promotion. Also, each year FH ranks countries on a scale from "Free" to "Not Free." Luckily, as of 2006, the United States is still "Free."

→ Greenpeace—As the name suggests, this NGO hopes to achieve greenness using peaceful means. Greenpeace is also the only NGO to own a ship *(The Rainbow Warrior)* that the French government intentionally sunk. Funny story actually, google it and find out.

→ Amnesty International—This NGO is committed to protecting the human rights enshrined in the Universal Declaration of Human Rights.

→ International Red Cross (and Red Crescent)—The sole function of the Red Cross is to protect the life and dignity of victims in armed conflict. The Red Cross is independent, neutral, and all that other crap. They help anyone and everyone.

We will discuss some of these NGOs in more detail in later chapters. Party on.

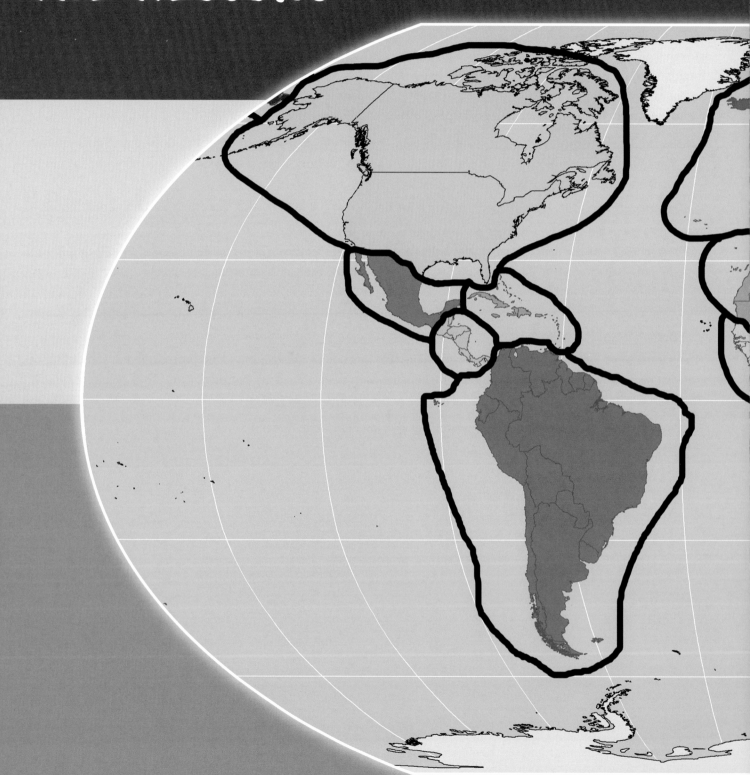

PART TWO
THE REGIONS

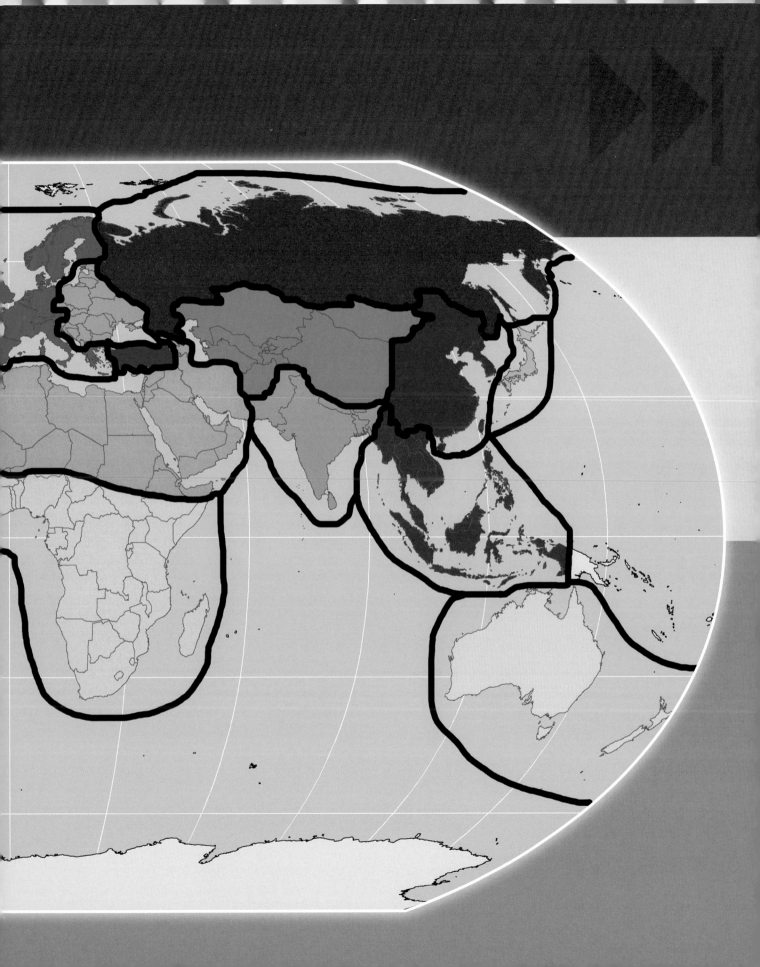

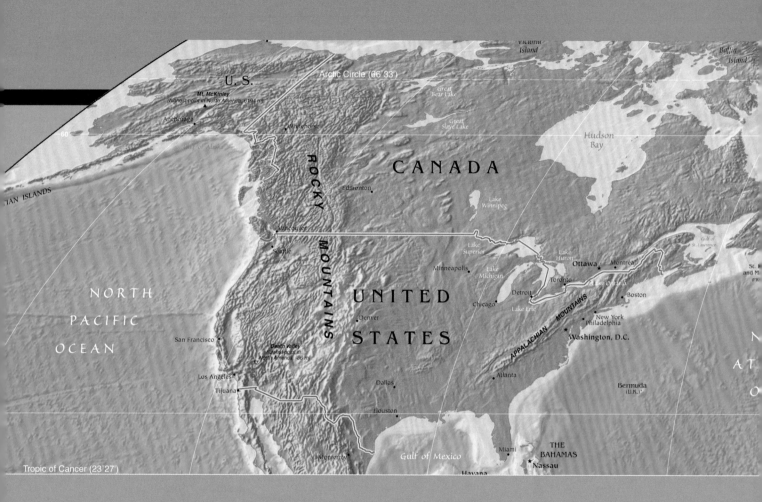

CHAPTER OUTLINE

North America

OK, now that we've discussed all the preliminary stuff, we can get to the real meat and potatoes, and let's start with the biggest meat and potato eaters—the North American region.

This region consists of two major countries: the United States and their redheaded stepchild to the north, Canada. But damn, what an incredible impact on the rest of the world this region makes. Of course I'm referring mostly to the powerhouse of the planet, the United States of America. For most of the following discussion, I'll be talking about the United States, but always keep in mind that our chilly Canadian cohorts are generally on board for all things North American, even our foreign policy. And so is their population; 90% of Canadians live within 100 miles of the US/Canadian borders. Hell, I'm not even sure why it's a separate country at all sometimes. I think the only real difference between these states is the bacon. But I digress . . .

The Canadian

2 shots Canadian Whiskey
1 shot Red Bull energy drink
1 Tbsp maple syrup

Fill a rocks glass with ice. Drizzle the maple syrup over the ice. Add in Canadian Whiskey and top with Red Bull energy drink. One quick stir and you are ready to go. Pre-game with a Moosehead lager if needed.

WHY IS THIS A REGION?

Why is this a region at all? We learned earlier what exactly a region is. A region takes up space, which North America has. A region must also have some borders, which may be fuzzy. The region's borders are actually very clear cut; it's everything north of the US-Mexican border. Also necessary for a region is homogeneity. It must have some traits that are roughly the same throughout the region in order to unify the countries.

This is one of the most homogenous regions on the planet due to several main characteristics. It has a high standard of living; it is one of the wealthiest regions in the world. If we head south of the border, we see that Mexico is distinctly different economically, which is one reason why it is not included in this region.

Another factor is language. There is, for the most part, a single language that dominates. Although there are many people who speak Spanish in the US—and of course there are also those wacky French Canadians—primarily both countries are English-speaking. Canada and the US also share historical/cultural backgrounds. Both countries were British colonies at one time. This cultural baggage, which includes religion and the aforementioned trait of language, also solidifies these two countries into a region. The fact that the US and Canada are the oldest and most stable democracies is also important. Human rights, the belief in individual freedoms, and similar governmental structures also make this a solid region.

THE GREATEST REGION ON EARTH!

Wow, that's a bold claim that the Plaid Avenger's making. Why would I suggest that the United States and Canada combined into our North American Region would be the greatest on the planet? Well that does come with some caveats, of course. The greatest at many things, and simultaneously the not-so-greatest at others. Two sides of a very particular coin here in the

Canadian lights not too far from the border.

21st century world. So let's just kind of talk about what the hell I'm getting at here. We'll start with "the greatest."

+THE RICHEST

Why would I say that the United States and Canada is the greatest region on earth? Well, for starters: they're the richest. There's no getting around that. And my plaid friends, I think you all accept this, as do most, that the United States is the richest country on the planet. We forget their Canadian cohorts to the north, though. The Canucks are pretty well off too in terms of per capita GDP. Why and in what respect are they together two of the richest countries on the planet? Let's kind of break this down.

PHYSICAL RESOURCES

One: physical resources. These two countries are the second and fourth largest countries on the planet in term of size. Lots of land to move around in; lots of space to grow in. Space/Land is a valuable commodity in and of itself for future potential growth of a country, and both these big boys got it. Big countries that contain shit-tons of natural resources . . . and I mean everything across the board. These countries produce tremendous amounts of food, be it grain or grape or bananas or corn or any damn thing else. They have tremendous amounts of water resources. H_2O is an oft overlooked resource when people think about how rich a place is, but hey, you've got to face it friends; if you ain't got no water, you ain't got nothing. So, lots of food and lots of water . . . but also lots of the other natural resources. North America is virtually saturated with resources. It has almost every type of resource possible. Coal, oil, tobacco, lumber, copper, steel, gold, fertile croplands, and almost anything else. You use it, you want it, North America has got it.

PHYSICAL DISTANCE

This North American region also has a strategic advantage in that it is far from other places. Now, what's so special about that? Why would that make them rich? If for no other reason, you have to consider the fact that while the US and Canada have been involved in virtually every major world conflict of the last century, the fights have never occurred on their own soil. To my recollection, Pearl Harbor and the 9/11 attacks are the only times that anyone for a century has even made it to North American shores for a strike. While those were horrific events to be sure, they were pinpricks in comparison to the larger wars of which they were a component. Having two great oceans separate this region from the rest of the planet is a big plus, indeed.

Specific example: After World War II, Europe is destroyed. China is decimated. Parts of Russia blasted. Japan completely leveled. And the US/Canada? Sitting pretty man, virtually untouched. Besides Pearl Harbor, not shit happened on the soil of this region during those wartime eras.

Also consider 'terrorism' in the modern world: for those with malicious intent, it is very difficult to get to North America from other parts of the world, the attacks of 9/11 not withstanding. That was a really big deal in the North American region. People just couldn't believe it. Folks around the rest of the world are used to bombings, terrorist attacks, uprisings, but it's very unique in the North American Region, it just doesn't happen. Terrorist attacks have/do occur in Europe, Asia, the Middle East, and across Africa all the time. But not in North America. Which is why after 9/11, everybody was like "Oh my god! Holy shit! The world is coming to an end!" when quite frankly things like that happen all over the world all of the time.

Now why do they happen in other places and not here? Distance! Because people that may be upset with the United States and Canada are very far away. This is not a place that is easy to get to if you're a disgruntled Afghan. You can hate the US all you want but you're not going to get there to do anything about it unless you are well-funded and organized . . . which rules out most of the people on the planet.

The US and Canada have chosen to get involved in world affairs when it suits them. Very few other places have this convenience. The result? Untouched for virtually all global wars and global confrontations of the last 200 years, and even now in the 21st, they have a wide safety buffer from the rest of the world's problems. Their distance is a key feature.

EVOLUTION OF AN ECONOMIC POWERHOUSE

Why else rich? This region has had 200 years of continuous growth. That's not something that any other region can brag about. Any of them! Look through the rest of this damn book. There is no other place on the planet that has essentially gotten richer decade after decade, century after century, like the US and Canada have for 200 years straight. Now what am I talking about?

Well the formation of these countries in these regions, of course, goes back to the colonial era when all the British and Spaniards and the Frenchies were all coming over here and staking claims with the thirteen original colonies and from this nice little nest egg of an area where they proceeded to invest heavily into infrastructure and to developing industries. It was a beautiful little place to get a 'start-up' country going, a nice little fixer-upper.

The physical geography of the region ties in here because of the Appalachian Mountains. European settlers were all over the few hundred miles of land from the shores of the Atlantic to the mountains, the location of the 13 colonies. This became a perfect little incubator for the embryonic US. It set the colonies away from Amerindians who were on one side. The protection that the mountains provided allowed the locals to gain control of the region, and build up resources and population which in turn set up the right conditions for westward expansion when the time was right.

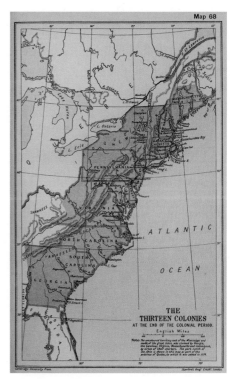

This is where distance begins to tie in to the history of the US. As the colonies began to develop their own ideas about government, freedom, and self sufficiency, they figured out that they didn't need their bullshit European monarchs overseeing them anymore.

So during a little thing called the American Revolution, though the British had superior firepower and superior numbers, the distance was still too much to effectively fight a prolonged war. Distance helped win the war, and also kept foreign powers at bay while the fledgling US strengthened itself in the early years.

So the yoke is off, and the US is out of the blocks, running. Economically, a boom begins. It has continued to this very second. No other country in the history of the world has had such a large amount of growth continuously sustained for 200 years. This place has gone steadily upwards since its inception.

So at that point, forward, that's the inception of the United States and Canada to a lesser extent, from that point forward, 200 years ago, the United

The east coast womb.

States grows westward, as does Canada. Grows westward, in effect adding more resources, adding more water, more fields to grow more food, more coal, more oil, more gold. Expanding all the way to the west coast of the continent, you have essentially 100 years of continuous physical and economic growth; gaining more stuff, more resources, more land. Manifest Destiny at its best. And Mo' money, mo' money, mo' money. Running out of land or opportunity in Virginia? Then move to Indiana or Saskatchewan and then on to California or the Yukon!

So does this mean economic expansion now stops? Nope! It's just going to take a new direction. This is in the late 1800's, early 1900s, when the American Industrial Revolution begins to kick in. Luckily, the Americans had witnessed a similar revolution in Britain almost a hundred years earlier, when they were the top dog.

Now, the Americans take all the best things from the European industrial revolution, and eliminate all the worst. So while Europe was very destructive during theirs, the Americans were able to avoid a lot of the pitfalls, and go straight for the goods. The US shifted from an *agricultural* based economy to an *industrial* one. After the land grab and resource grab, they exploded industrially.

"You all have little girly economies"

And by the way, a Plaid Avenger note, if you broke off California from the rest of the continental US, and made it its own sovereign state, it would have the 8th largest economy on the entire planet. And Gov. Arnold Schwarzenegger himself would be the 18th largest landmass.

In the 1960's and 1970's there was another change. When other countries also begin to industrialize, they could produce things cheaper than the US could—due primarily to their cheaper labor costs. Things like car production, textile production, and steel production shifted to developing countries. So is this the end of American economic expansion? Again, the answer is 'hell no.' The US once again shifted gears and changed to a *service sector economy* with an emphasis on *technology*. You know: computers and shit. Mo' money. Nowadays, the next wave of transformation has the US as a leader of the *information age* . . . in which the economic focus is on manipulation and creation of computer programs and new medical breakthroughs and patenting DNA codes. Instead of making cars and textiles, the US now produces information as one of its key resources. This region is truly the first to undergo this technological transformation. Mo' money.

So, long story short, 200 years of growth in various ways, either increasing land or resources, then increasing to an industrial capacity, and then increasing into the service sector, and now transforming the world as the leader of the technological/information age. Of course you have the Great Depression in there, we don't want to forget that little tidbit, but that was a real blemish on a basically 200 year perfect record of economic growth. Even now, here at the outset of the 21st century, the North American region has the biggest total GDP on the planet, with no close second. If money talks, then this region has a lot to say.

The Boilermaker

1 shot Kentucky Bourbon

1 cold beer

This is an old-school drink that is awesome for stumping bartenders—because it's so damn easy. It also demonstrates a great economic point about the US. The drink is named for blue-collar workers who would order a shot and a beer after their shift. Blue-collar as in steel, textile, and automobile production workers. Oh, and boilermakers too. Why don't young bartenders know the drink? Because secondary economic activities have largely disappeared from the US; thus, boilers are made elsewhere. Most of those jobs are gone, and the culture surrounding them is gone too. I always order the Boilermaker to honor those manufacturing sector folks that made the US great.

USA GDP =

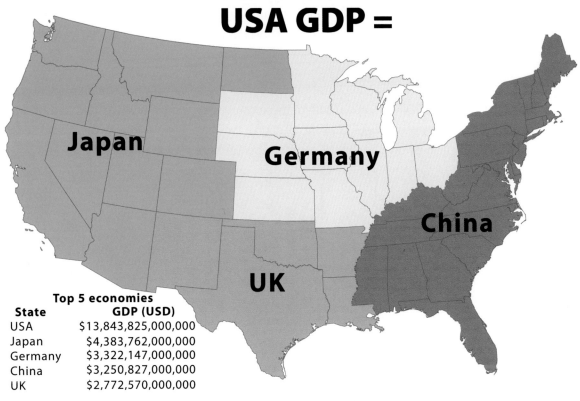

Japan

Germany

China

UK

Top 5 economies

State	GDP (USD)
USA	$13,843,825,000,000
Japan	$4,383,762,000,000
Germany	$3,322,147,000,000
China	$3,250,827,000,000
UK	$2,772,570,000,000

BIRTHPLACE OF IDEAS; TECHNOLOGY TITAN

But back to the subject. Why this is the greatest and the richest region on earth? It's got to do with what we just talked about a second ago. This is a birthplace of ideas. The North American region is the place that came up with things like the telephone, the computer, the internet (specifically, of course, it was Al Gore, but we'll say it was the region in general). This is the region that has freedoms to do lots of things and grow industrially and technologically, and it comes up with all kinds of new crazy great stuff. It has the highest levels of technology because of this always pushing forward on the fore-front. Japan makes cool stuff cooler, and China is growing fast, and India is becoming a software hub . . . but you still have to look at the core of where are the forefronts of science and engineering and computer stuff being pushed forward, and North America is still the top dog. But the competition is getting tougher.

However, since World War II, the United States has been not only an industrial leader but the leader on the forefront of science and technology in all capacities. The internet, the computer, the telephone, the microwave, nuclear bombs, put a damn man on the moon? Yep: this region did it.

That is one of the things that makes the US really rich, and people come from around the world to invest here, to go to school here, to do all these things because this is the place to do it in. Alright? And it's got the highest levels of technology too—across the board from science stuff, math stuff, computer stuff, nuclear capabilities, military stuff, right on up to

the upcoming space race. The US, because it's the leader of technology, is still the only country that has made it to the moon. It will be joined soon by China, but that's for another chapter.

BIG REGION; SMALL POP

Why else rich, though? To finish off this rich section, this North American region actually has a fairly small population given its size and this equates to very high GDP per capita. Both of these countries are fully industrialized, fully developed, fully rich as shit, and there's not that many people here. Now this of course may be argued by folks in the United States right this second who have problems with immigration: "We've got too many people here! Wah wah wah!" Whatever!

The original (and equally unsuccessful) Anti-Immigration Faction

There's only about 310 million people in the United States, Canada has about 30 million; of course it's the biggest population that they have ever had in its history. About 340 million people total across, again, two of the biggest countries on earth. There's a lot of space in this place and not really that many people in it, relatively speaking. There's tremendous room for growth, but even if growth does not occur, you're looking at tons of resources, a huge economy, both in the US and Canada, that's divided up amongst not that many folks on the global stage. If you're looking out at China, they've got a billion and a half; India is working on 1.2 billion; Sub-Saharan Africa has three-quarters of a billion; and even rich-ass Europe has over half a billion. And the North American region? Ha! A fraction of that! Quite frankly a fraction, especially given the space.

So, lots of space, lots of room, and lots of stuff per person, and that's what makes them fairly well off. The United States does have the biggest GDP total on the planet. Canada is in the top ten as well and both countries have some of the highest GDP's per capitas, and that's not likely to change anytime soon. Yes, China is growing fast, India's growing fast. Neither will ever have the amount of richness per person that the United States and Canada enjoy right this second . . . if ever.

+THE STRONGEST

Okay, so we just talked about why North America is the richest. Now let's talk about why it's the strongest.

MILITARY POWERHOUSE

The North Americans are the strongest and best-est when it comes to military stuff. Again, you can talk about whether you like the US or not, you can talk about whether you agree with its policies or not, but that's of no consequence to the Plaid Avenger. I'm just trying to explain to you people why this is one of the richest regions on the globe, or the greatest region on the globe. Militarily speaking, you cannot dispute that the US has the strongest single military power on the planet. And this is not by size, by the way. Yes, size does matter, but in this case the Americans don't have the largest standing military (meaning boots on the ground.) China holds that top slot with 2.5 million folks in their mili-

tary, but the United States and Canada don't need to have the largest amount of people in the military because technologically speaking, of course, we all know they are the best.

The North American region has the most weapons per capita on the planet. And we're not just talking about handguns: we're talking about shotguns right on up to intercontinental ballistic missiles, tanks, and warships. The United States has the most aircraft carriers on the planet and this is a very real projection of power. Militarily speaking, there is no one to compete with the United States. Not even Russia, the United States' old Cold War adversary. In terms of military spending, no one else is even in the US ballpark. Yearly military expenditures for the US now top half a trillion dollars. Wow. That's ten times what China spends, and roughly half the world total. So there is no contest when it comes to who's the strongest, or who's the most technologically advanced military on the planet. That's the North American region, particularly the United States.

PROJECTION OF POWER ABROAD

However, it's not just numbers and budgets. It's also about the ability for the Americans to project this power abroad. This is what makes them the strongest. Aircraft carriers are a great item to consider. With an aircraft carrier, you can push your power to all points on the globe, and this is what the United States is perhaps better at than anyone on the planet right this second and perhaps even throughout history. Yes, the British had their fleet that did a pretty damn good job, and the Spaniards had their Armada before that. But that was centuries ago and the United States has the technological capacity to annihilate so many more humans than the British did that it can't even really be compared to today's world. With a carrier, you can essentially 'move' your country anywhere in the world on the water to set up an island to launch a strike. That is some serious global power. Fan fact: the US has 12 aircraft carriers . . . which is more than the rest of the planet COMBINED!

Country	Military Expenditures 2008 (US$)
United States	$583,283,000,000
EU Total	$311,920,000,000
France	$74,690,470,000
United Kingdom	$68,911,000,000
China	$59,000,000,000
Germany	$45,930,000,000
Japan	$41,750,000,000
Russia	$40,000,000,000
Italy	$32,600,000,000
Saudi Arabia	$31,050,000,000
South Korea	$28,940,000,000
India	$26,500,000,000
World Total	$1,200,000,000,000

The American region is the absolute best at moving troops, people, guns, and missiles anywhere on the planet and that is real power. One need look no further than current conflicts the American region is involved in: the ones going on in Afghanistan and Iraq which are on the other side of the planet from the region itself.

And if you start to look at American military stationed abroad, it's mind boggling. The US has active troops, that is dudes and dudettes with guns, in about fifty countries. That's astounding if you think about that. That you would have military people stationed all over the planet, even in countries where there is not an active conflict, is quite amazing and a real projection of power. This region is certainly the most powerful when you consider the current active conflicts, current military deployments, and consider that the United States is a natural leader of NATO (check back to chapter 6 if you don't

know what that is). The Plaid Avenger argues NATO is easily the most successful defensive organization of all time in history. I stand by that claim. And the United States is at the core of it.

The United States has the most intercontinental ballistic missiles, the most nuclear missiles, and, as suggested earlier, is the only country to have been to the moon, and really, I won't say dominates space, but has the strongest presence in space as well. If we also factor in that the US is a big, big proponent of some sort of anti-missile defense shield, which will certainly, if it ever comes to fruition, which I seriously doubt, but if it ever does, make the United States even more powerful. And we do have to think back to the Ronald Reagan era when he wanted to put lasers in space to shoot down other countries' missiles. This again is a real projection of how great the US is to 1) even consider such a plan and 2) put resources toward actually making it happen. I keep harping on space because that is the next frontier and the US is promising to have a moon base and perhaps a missile defense shield in space, and lots of other things in space as well. Well again, that just takes tremendous resources, and you've got to be great to pull off shit like that.

And by the way, I keep saying the United States, but Canada is right beside the US in every single conflict that it has ever been in. All of them. Not one, not a couple, not one 100 years ago, not one now, in all of them Canada has been there. So we can logically speak of this as a singular North American venture.

MULTINATIONAL CORPORATIONS

Why else the strongest? Think about North American corporations in the world, both US and Canadian. These are some of the biggest, richest entities on the planet. I'm speaking of multinational corporations which operate globally . . . but every multinational corporation has to have a home base somewhere and for many of these, this base is North America. Of the top 2000 hugest corporations on the planet right now, over one-third call North America home (that is down from over half a decade ago). Exxon, Wal-Mart, General Motors: these are some of the richest entities on the planet and with that wealth comes power. These folks have a lot of power to do things they want to do in other parts of the world.

Consider an entity like Exxon. Yeah, it's just a company. It's not a government; it doesn't have political power like the US. Well . . . yes and no. Exxon makes a quadrillion dollars a year and if it wants to look for oil in Namibia, it is going to get what it wants, regardless of Namibian opinion. I mean let's face it, the company makes ten

2008 TOP SALES OF MULTINATIONAL COMPANIES

Company	Home Base	Sales
Wal-Mart Stores	USA	378.00 Billion
ExxonMobil	USA	358.60 Billion
Royal Dutch Shell	Netherlands	355.78 Billion
BP	UK	281.03 Billion
Chevron	USA	203.97 Billion
Toyota Motor	Japan	203.80 Billion
Total	France	199.74 Billion
ING Group	Netherlands	197.93 Billion
General Motors	USA	181.12 Billion
General Electric	USA	172.74 Billion
Ford Motor	USA	172.46 Billion
ConocoPhillips	USA	171.50 Billion
Citigroup	USA	159.23 Billion

From Special Report: The World's Biggest Companies, edited by Scott DeCarlo 04.02.08, Forbes.com

million times more money than the country of Namibia and with that money comes tremendous weight to throw around. Whether through open economic pressure or illegal backroom bribery of officials, huge corporations can get their way.

Some of these North American companies are the biggest in the world, some of the richest in the world, and many are getting richer and more powerful by the day. At this writing, Exxon just captured a world record by earning the highest profits in a single economic quarter ever, in the history of the universe . . . thank $150 a barrel for oil for that one! Folks are starting to openly debate about, "are multinational corporations even stronger than governments?" and the answer already is: of course. The uber-rich corporations are already stronger and more powerful than small countries and weak governments. There's no doubt about that, and that's a situation that's likely to increase in the future. To restate: a lot of those countries are US or Canadian in origin. But let's shift to another topic, and the final subsection of why this region is the greatest.

+THE FREE-EST

OLD MAN DEMOCRACY

Both the United States and Canada are two of the oldest democracies on the planet. This is an entire region that prides itself in a somewhat egalitarian light, that everybody is equal regardless of race, sex, creed, religion, anything else and everyone has an equal voice. That is kind of one of the cornerstones of this entire region. They are the free-est. Yes, there are the places in Europe. Yes, there are other folks around the world that have democracies, but the North American ones have been around pretty much the longest and been doing it the most successfully for the longest stretch. In fact, these countries, mostly the US (sorry Canada, I have to poke a little fun at you) were so determined about democracy that they had a little revolution and kicked all of the little European assholes out. They said: "Hey, well Europeans, that's cool, we're glad you came here and set up shop for us, sent us some immigrants, set up some industries, but you guys can all go home now because you're not being fair enough to us. "

Maybe you heard of it: the American Revolution. Now why am I making fun of the Canadians? Well, because they kissed the queen's ass for quite a bit longer, like another hundred or so years, before they kind of threw off the yoke of

Piss off Brits! And take your tea with you!

the British Commonwealth motherhood. But even during their Queen-kiss-up years, Canada was pretty much into the democracy thing too. So to restate, North America is the home of two of the oldest, strongest, longest lasting democracies on the planet.

In fact, these guys have really set the trend for everyone else. You can look at Europe and say that they are also rich, developed democracies with a long track record too. Yeah, that's true, dudes. But starting when? Was it before the American Revolution or after? That's right, it was after. The American experience was kind of the impetus for the French Revolution and the French Revolution then begat other revolutions across Europe, which eventually led to all of them becoming something closer to democracy. So if you look at it as a chain of events, the Americans really kind of started things up. Washington, Jefferson and Franklin kick ass! Nice job guys!

FOCUS ON INDIVIDUAL LIBERTIES

Why else the free-est? A focus on individual liberties is also a cornerstone of this region from its inception, and this is something quite distinct from democracy itself. Democracy is a ruling system in which the people have a say in who's ruling them. But on top of that, civil rights and individual liberties are extremely important to this region. And again, maybe this is confusing to you but I just want to point this out: there are other democracies in the world, pseudo-democracies or real democracies, where they don't have this focus on individual liberties as much.

Places like Egypt or other parliamentary systems in the Middle East are kind of a democracy. They vote; they elect people. But there is nothing in their constitution that says that they believe every single person is exactly equal, and the

state is there to protect their individual rights. Or look at Iran which has a semi-democracy. People vote, and in fact their voter turn-out shames most US election participation. They do elect many of their leaders . . . but they definitely don't have the focus on individual liberties. The government still controls ultimately what people can read, what people can say, the way people dress. But perhaps making comparisons to Iran or Egypt is too extreme because they aren't developed and rich like the US. Okay, how about Singapore or Russia? Rich and developed as hell, but done so at the expense of individual liberties; they are tightly controlled democracies where too much individual expression may be detrimental to your business.

"We come for individual freedoms . . . and native babes"

Really only in the North American region, they first and foremost say "Yes. We're having a democracy, but also it's based on individuals having liberties." And by the way, if you think about how the United States came to be, it's because people were fleeing from places that weren't giving them true liberty. You know, those Pilgrim cats who went to Plymouth Rock were fleeing religious persecution back in Europe. They wanted more freedoms to individually do their own thing here in North America and that's how the thirteen original colonies started, and quite frankly, it's still going on today. People flock from around the world to head to the North American region! The US and Canada, man. Because they know when they get there they have individual liberties to live the way they want to. Again, yes this is definitely true in Europe, but this is not the fact or the case across the entire planet even in established democracies.

Of course, I'm not suggesting all these liberties have been there since the beginning. Freedom of thought, religion, and speech were there early on. I'm not downgrading Martin Luther King Jr.'s work by any stretch of the imagination: civil rights and liberties regarding race and sex did have to be fought for most recently. And the US not only now sets the world standard for freedoms, but continues to be on the front lines of battles over civil liberties/rights: look at the fight for gay rights or the rights of an unborn child for examples of how passionate this region gets about individual liberty.

And the reason this is because the North Americans, quite frankly, don't give a shit. Hahahahahahahaha! Say what?

PERSONALLY THEY DON'T GIVE A SHIT

This region doesn't give a shit about you individually. Now that sounds a little backwards. What does this mean exactly? We can make fun of North America for being a region of imperial power, of gun-loving nuts, of isolationism. But if you get there—when you are actually in house—it's really freakin' cool. North Americans just generally don't give a shit who you are or where you are from on a personal basis. They are laid back. Do whatever! It's cool. Just don't ruin any of my shit. This is a phenomenally great component of North American society.

If you look around the planet, the history of human society around the world, we have a pretty consistent record of kicking the living shit out of each other. Why do we do this? It has a lot to do with intolerance of the differences between people. Sometimes we kill each other over resources or land or whatever. However, conflict mostly arises between people of different religions, different ethnicities, different colors, or different nationalities . . . and sometimes it escalates to some pretty nasty shit. Just think of the atrocities of Nazi Germany or the Rwandan genocide or the implosion of Yugoslavia. The list goes on and on.

This is a common theme across the planet, except for in North America. By no means are all Americans sitting around eating s'mores and singing 'Kumbayah' together. Of course there are people here who don't like other people, but this is at nearly the absolute minimum in the history of the world. Americans don't care where you're from, don't care

See? They even let Britney live there! Talk about not giving a shit!

what color you are, don't care how smart or stupid you are, don't care what god you pray to . . . Quite frankly, American tolerance towards their fellow man may be the best example the rest of the world should follow.

In real life in America, not giving a shit equates to everyone being pretty much equal. Some people call it a meritocracy, meaning you only advance by doing good stuff—by earning your way. Your position in society is not, or isn't supposed to be, based on your religion or skin color; they don't have organized ethnic or religious clashes. This region is actually a place that many people from around the world come to escape those very issues.

And let me kind of elaborate on why I'm saying this is a positive thing. Because in most other parts of the planet, and this is today's world, not historically, folks don't have the luxury of not giving a shit meaning that there is serious ethnic strife, religious strife, racial strife all around the world. And if you are in the minority, if you practice a religion that's not fashionable, if you're from the wrong ethnicity, the wrong club, you may not have equal rights at all. And even if the country pretends you do, you may be discriminated against on a daily basis, persecuted, not get the house loan, your kids might get beat up at school, you might get the shit kicked out of you yourself, you might be thrown out of the country or there could be some sort of ethnic genocide/civil war/religious purging which happens all the time across the planet.

Let me bring it back to you. That doesn't happen in North America because individuals are doing their own thing and they don't give a shit about the guy sitting next to them on the bus. They just don't and that's a very powerful thing. Again, I can't stress it enough: it's one of the reasons why folks from around the world say "Damn. If I could just make it to North America, then I truly am free. Nobody cares that I'm from a Hmong ethnicity. Nobody cares that I'm a Zoroastrian. Nobody cares if I tattoo my face, dye my hair blue, and watch Pauly Shore movies. I can do what I want to when I get to those shores" and by and large, that is true and that is one of its real benefits. It is one of the free-est places on the planet. Okay, maybe they should pass a law against Pauly Shore movies, but for now it is still protected behavior.

PLATFORM FOR SUCCESS

And what this sets up, essentially, is that the North American region is a kind of platform for success. Meaning people know that once they make it to North America, all other factors are equal. So you work hard, you pay your dues, you put your nose to the grindstone, then you can be successful. No, the streets aren't paved with gold in North America, as the old saying goes, but they are paved with opportunity because immigrants don't have to worry about any of that other shit that they'd have to worry about in their home countries. So the North American region is a real platform for success and that sets up something, a situation in the world, known as **brain drain**.

What's the Deal with . . . Brain Drain?

Any person given a free plane ticket from their 3rd world country to any other destination in the world will most likely choose the North American region.

The type of people that actually make it here are smart, educated people with options. Also, wealthy people, who want to become wealthier figure out ways to come to the North American region.

This is actually a problem, because the elites of other societies are leaving their native regions to come to wealthy regions to become successful. There are all sorts of political, religious, and economic reasons to flee native lands and set up shop in North America. When the political problems arise, people leave. When people are afraid of losing their assets or afraid of religious persecution, they will go to a place that accepts them and allows them to continue growing. For a hundred years, the destination of choice has been the US.

Brain Drain has been a fantastically successful concept in the development of North America. Whenever bad shit happens around the globe, the US and Canada stand to gain.

Political crackdown in Iran? Economic meltdown in Thailand? Religious persecution in Sudan? North America gains in refugee/immigrant populations.

For example, after World War II, the Russians took half of Germany's rocket scientists and America got the other half. That's why both the US and Russia started space programs. Brilliant inventors come here, and they use the US as a platform for success. There are other great platforms, but the US has been a very important one for the last 100 years.

This has a lot to do with immigration. People want to come here to express themselves. It has become a self-perpetuating cycle; the US is so rich and doing so well that people all over the globe want to come here with their ideas. People want to start businesses with the highest probability for success—and that is in the US. Success breeds success, and more people want to come. US success is a strong magnet in the world. Rich and poor folks alike find strong attraction to the North American region for all of its opportunities. It's an extremely competitive place, but it does seem to work for the vast majority of its inhabitants. Poverty numbers are very low; opportunities exist for even the most destitute.

If you live in an impoverished society, one with no welfare program or unemployment benefits, you cannot take risks. New things come about by taking risks, and environments like that do not enable people to take risks. America will take care of you if you or your idea fails. You can afford to work hard, save money, start your own business. No wonder people think the streets are paved with gold—golden opportunities, that is.

Another great thing about this region is its **hyper-mobility**. The size of the region allowed for the interstate system, developed by Eisenhower, whereas other countries that are smaller rely more heavily on public transportation. Folks can

We Like Ike! What's the Deal with . . . the Interstate System?

The formal name of the United States interstate system is the "Dwight D. Eisenhower National System of Interstate and Defense Highways". The US interstate system was created by the 1956 Federal-Aid Highway Act, which (as the name suggests) was championed by Ike Eisenhower. The US interstate system was built for both civilian and military purposes. Some of you might be thinking, "Yeah! One in every five miles of road must be straight so that military aircraft can land and take off on them!" Well, maybe. The true military aspects of the interstate system are primarily to facilitate troop movement and to allow for the evacuation of major cities in the event of nuclear war.

The civilian aspects of the Interstate Highway System have helped shape American culture in more ways than we can possibly imagine. Most US interstates pass through the center of cities, which allows people to live outside the city and commute in for work . . . which has played a huge role in the creation of US suburbs and urban sprawl. The highway system also gives the United States Federal Government power over State Governments. The US government can withhold interstate highway funds (huge amounts of money) from uncooperative state governments. The US government used this tactic to increase the national drinking age to 21 and to lower the blood alcohol level for intoxication to 0.08%. According to the Constitution, both of these issues should be decided by states. But, if they choose to disobey, they don't get their highway money.

Also, the US highway system allows high speed transportation of consumer products. This makes the prices of everything, from bananas to concrete, cheaper. I guess that's pretty important too. The result: the US is a car culture heavily reliant on fossil fuels for the movement of everything and for virtually all aspects of our lives. Americans are quite unique in this respect. It's also why they are the best drag racers in the world. Who else has NASCAR? And who more is worried that the price of oil is reaching $150/barrel?

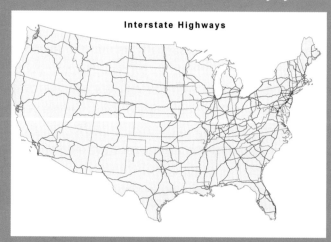

Interstate Highways

go anywhere, do anything; anytime they want. They even have 4 wheel drive vehicles to take them anyplace that doesn't even have a damn road to it.

Mobility allows people to take advantage of opportunity and expands peoples' choices. Any job, any opportunity, any time, any place. Not all other folks in other countries have this convenience. There is an exactly proportional relationship between mobility and choice. The more mobile you are, the more choices you have and the more successful the US is as a result.

Being in the North American region furnishes infinite choices and provides opportunity to take risks that is unprecedented anywhere else on the planet. If you have a great idea and you could have any choice of where to cast the dice to really make it work for you, it's a no-brainer for you to come to North America. It just makes sense. The odds are stacked in your favor. Not true in Europe for immigrants, not true in Asia or Africa as a whole—but particularly true in North America.

CORE OF 'TEAM WEST'

To wrap up this free-est section, all of these factors put together are what make the North American region the true core of what I will continue to refer to as 'Team West.' This is a concept we'll come back to later in the book. But essentially North America, along with Western and Eastern Europe, and even Australia, form a common block of ideology that sets them apart from other cultures in the world. Hell, you know what? Let's throw Japan in there too. Even though they're way out in 'the east', they more closely follow the western tradition.

And what are the identifiable traits of this team? As exemplified by North America, 'Team West' has a basis in the western civilization tradition that values democracy in their governments, a focus on individual rights in their societies, and are strident free-market capitalists when it comes to their economies. This team consists of regions/states that are fully developed, largely rich, technologically superior, and focused on service sector/information age types of employment. Other attributes include rampant materialism, an obsession with pop culture, and un-proportional power and leverage over the rest of the globe...but those are more negative attributes.

Oh! Wait! How appropriate, 'cause it's time to get negative on the team leader right about now . . .

THE WORST-EST PART OF BEING THE GREATEST

Okay, now we're going to shift gears, we're going to flip the coin, we're going to see the underbelly of the Greatest Region on Earth. Now that I've told you about how awesome it is and why it's the greatest and the leader in terms of richness and power and freeness, let's look at why it's perhaps not so great. What's the worst part of being the greatest region? And you know what? It's an easy schemata because we're just going to follow the same outline we did before. We'll start with number one.

-THE RICHEST

Wait a minute! I thought I just said that being rich was great? Yeah, hell, everybody thinks being rich is great, but the bad side of being the richest region on the planet is that US and Canadian policies, of course, favor their own companies.

UNSPORTSMANLIKE CORPORATE CONDUCT

In other words, they take care of their own. Well why wouldn't they? Every country in every region probably makes the same decisions. That is that, the US foreign policy favors intervention into another country or manipulating the World Trade Organization or some sort of other pressures on other countries in order to help their own multinational corporations. Yep. It happens. Now again, I ain't making fun of anybody. I'm trying to get you to understand why other folks around the world may have discontent about the US power and this is one of them in that yes, all countries would look out over their own multinational corporations.

However, the United States and Canada have some of the biggest, richest multinational corporations in the world and simultaneously, the US and Canada are two of the richest countries in the world. Therefore, it's almost a set of unprecedented power players that have really never occurred before—that the richest country can help out the richest multinational corporation. This gives those corporations quite a bit of leverage and power in the world. Power to do what? Well, most free-marketers would say to do what business does: go out and acquire resources, produce products, and sell those products. That's true. That's fine. But they also have a lot of power to screw with other people or governments too, if they so choose. They have the power to ignore other countries' environmental regulations or to at least bend the rules to favor themselves as frequently as possible. And there is no way that a local company in a less-developed country could possibly compete with a Wal-Mart or an Exxon, so these big boys can pretty much take what they want, when they want it.

This does present a problem. It is a situation where there is a fairly lopsided trade balance around the world where multinational corporations have the power to take a lot more from poor countries and give a lot less back. It's just simply the way it is. It's not good. It's not bad. In my book, that's just the way it is. So US/Canadian policy favors their corporations, which are excessively rich already. And again, this helps them perhaps take advantage of other countries. Also, the North American's global policy typically ignores the rest of the globe to maintain its own richness. Now again, let me put in a disclaimer: every country does that. China certainly is going to try to favor Chinese policy. The Frenchies look out after France. But the North Americans are so powerful and so rich, that here in the dawn of the 21st century, their attitudes towards the globe are now looked upon with some animosity by others on the planet.

SELECTIVE SELF-SERVING SELF-RIGHTEOUSNESS

Let me give you some examples, and there are many to choose from. The idea of 'free trade' may be the most blaring example of North America not practicing what it preaches. The US and Canada are fervent supporters of this concept, which essentially equates to trade based on the unrestricted international exchange of goods. This means no tariffs (taxes) should be levied on other countries' goods that are coming into your country, and no 'helping out' industries within your country to make their goods more competitive than imported goods. North America regularly touts, praises, and leads the charge for 'free trade' to the rest of the planet. The US in particular wants a free trade area for the entire western hemisphere (FTAA, see chapter 13) and it pushes hard to beat down the countries of Latin America to support the idea. Also, the US is the unrivaled leader in bringing up lawsuits against other countries at the WTO for infractions of the world trade rules.

Your taxes already paid for it, so eat it, dammit!

Unfortunately . . . the US and Canada regularly cheat on free trade all the time! Both countries support agricultural subsidies for their farmers, which essentially equates to paying your farmers money every year in order to make them more profitable . . . so farmers can charge less money for the food they produce, making it cheaper than food imports from Africa or Asia. Both countries also fairly regularly slap tariffs on imported steel or imported textiles in order to kiss the ass of political lobby groups and voting constituencies at home . . . especially in election years. Go figure!

Just one other example of this selective support on issues: US policy on global warming. Yes it's changing right this second here in the year 2008, but it has taken a long time for the US to come around. Most of the other countries on the planet for a decade or two have been saying: "Hey! This warming is a global thing, part of a global commons, and we need to look after the globe by all working together to reduce CO_2." The US and Canada have basically been very frank by saying "No, we're not doing shit. We refuse to do shit because it's going to hurt our companies. It's going to hurt our richness. We don't want to change our consumption patterns. We don't want to change how much money we have, and therefore, we don't give a shit about reducing CO_2 emissions. So all the rest of you countries, go do whatever you want. We're going to keep doing our own thing."

It's also important to point out that North America as a region is the highest user of world resources per capita. Meaning, folks in the US and Canada use more oil per person, use more food per person, use more plastic per person, use more everything per person than any other folks on the planet. Now again . . . whatever! It's a free market economy and people can do whatever the hell they want to, right? But other folks on the planet, and there are quite a few of them, kind of look at this as "Dudes. You guys are really selfish. You use the most, but you don't want to help out with any global problems." So being the richest has come at some cost here lately. Mostly at a cost to the reputation of the region, which is increasingly not seen as a real world leader on world issues.

-THE STRONGEST

Hey, what's wrong with being the strongest? Somebody's got to be the strongest, right? Well when it comes to North America, and I'll pick on the United States mostly right here, there is a perceived or real threat of US imperialism by many folks across the planet. That is, as I suggested earlier, the US is the undisputed, strongest country on the planet; and because of this people think: "Damn . . .they are unstoppable!" The US is so powerful, it appears that it could do anything it wanted to. You know what? Quite frankly, that's true. If the US wants to bomb Uzbekistan tomorrow, it can and it has the capacity to do it, and current events have shown that sometimes it does.

So it is a very real consideration that people around the world say "Oh my gosh. The US scares me. They have absolute power. Nobody could stop them if they want to do something" and that is true. Who would stop them? Russia? China? The UN? Ha! Give me a break! The UN . . . that's a good one.

We need look no further than the current Iraq war where most folks around the world said "Hey! We think it's a bad idea." Most countries of the UN said "No, we're not going along with that. We're not doing it." And the US said, "Well, we're doing it anyway." Again, I'm not making fun of them. Hold the phone folks. I'm not trashing the Iraq war or the Bush administration. I'm just saying, think about the perceived light of imperialism that most folks around the world now view the United States bathed in. It does cause more than a bit of consternation and concern for both enemies and friends of North America alike.

DOESN'T PLAY WELL WITH OTHERS

The current Iraq war is worthy of further consideration for a moment more. This story gets at a larger point . . .

There is a particular disdain of the United Nations by the US. Let me put it more bluntly: the US as a whole totally hates the UN. Why? Because the US is so powerful and resourceful on its own, that the only thing the UN does for it is to get in the way of US objectives. Does that make sense? The US has a certain opinion about things in the world, and it wants to act on its opinion to fulfill its own self-interests. Many in America would argue that indeed this is exactly the job of their government: to look out for their own self-interests, and the rest of the world be damned. Since the US *can* do anything it wants, it *should* do anything it wants to benefit itself. Following this train of thought, what exactly is the point of 'asking' the UN for permission, for advice, or for any damn thing else?

You almost can't blame it either. The US did save Western Europe's ass from Hitler without asking permission from anybody. But other folks don't like this unchecked influence, even if it is supposed to be for good. This is something that people in the US just don't get. They don't get it because they see themselves as good. "We are the good guys! We help people! We helped the poor Frenchies and Brits in World War II! We saved the Koreans and Kuwaitis and Kurds! We have always helped to defeat bad guys around the planet!"

By and large, that is true. The US seems to be fighting the good fight, but that's not the perception around the world, particularly in this day and age. Again, back in World War II, everybody understood that the Germans were the bad guys, and recognized the US as fighting the good fight. But in the current

US Nuclear Hit List still in play

'War on Terror', the enemies and objectives are not so well-defined. This unchecked ability of the United States to make all the judgment calls on all these issues bothers lots and lots of folks.

Another example involves nukes. Even though the Cold War is now over, and the US is busy fighting terrorism and not communism, the United States still maintains the **nuclear hit list option**. What is that? During the Cold War, all of the countries that had nuclear capabilities had lists of who they would blow up first. So number one on the US list was of course Russia, then maybe China 'cause they are commie, then maybe France just for good measure, etc. All countries with nuclear capabilities had these lists during the Cold War.

Recently, most countries have said, "Now that the Cold War is over, we'll get rid of the hit list and start to disarm our nuclear warheads. We're not going to point them at anybody." So all the countries got together, particularly Russia, and said "Hey let's all do this! It'll be a good thing!" The United States pretty much said, "You guys are so cute! You should do that! But, no thanks; we are going to hang on to our nuclear hit list option."

So at a time when many states want to ratchet down the nuclear issue, the US stands alone in its opinion . . . and that has increasingly been the case for the last two decades. The US maintains its hit list; is not a full player in UN procedures; and openly refuses to sign treaties that the vast majority of countries in the world support. Things like the 'Law of the Sea' which defines territorial rights of the ocean, the Kyoto Protocol to reduce greenhouse gases, or even legislation banning the production of land-mines . . . in all of these circumstances and many more, the US stands virtually alone in its non-participation.

Is the Plaid Avenger trying to indoctrinate you into thinking the US is bad, or too powerful, or too pompous? Nope. I'm trying to educate you on perhaps why the US has a bit of a bad rap on the world stage right now. Sometimes standing alone is a sign of strength; sometimes it is a sign of selfish stubbornness. You have to decide for yourself, as will the rest of the world.

POWERFUL POWER PROJECTIONS

The overwhelming strength of North America has also brought a sense of helplessness and outright fear to some parts of the globe. Specifically, the US has a basically open, identifiable, and some folks would say scary projection of real power as evidenced by the active wars in Iraq, in Afghanistan, and possibly in Iran next. And these active wars are possible, and proceed rapidly, because of the active US military presence around the globe. Whether for good or bad, it's not a judgment call here, there are North Americans with guns all over the planet.

More often than not, you see US soldiers more than you see any other country's soldiers. You can see UN soldiers, NATO soldiers, and EU soldiers sometimes, but those are groups, associations of countries, not single countries like the US. US soldiers are the only ones from a specific country that you can find all over the planet. This military

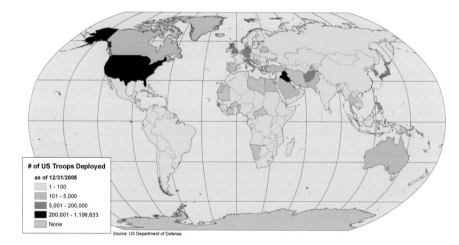

Active US Military World Wide

presence is perceived as unchecked strategic military power. In a very real sense, you can't find Chinese soldiers in Iraq, or Afghanistan, or in the United States. Can you even conceive of having foreign soldiers on US soil? The thought is almost comical. Other countries accept that there are US troops around the world, on foreign soil in Europe, Asia, South America, just about everywhere. It is reality elsewhere, but it is inconceivable in North America.

There are no other countries that have that type of real power evidenced around the entire planet. Not just the active wars, but in deployment of troops. Factor in the largest nuclear arsenal on the planet, the most sophisticated and largest air force, and more aircraft carriers than the rest of the world combined, and you have the basis for other countries soiling themselves at the thought of US intervention.

CULTURAL IMPERIALISM

Finally under the strongest category is something that you probably have never thought of before critically: cultural imperialism. With no doubt, North America is the most successful (if you can call it that) at this thing called cultural imperialism. Now whether the US and Canada are true imperial powers is debatable. However, it isn't really up for debate that the culture of the US is the most successful thing being spread around the planet. Well what am I talking about here?

We just discussed power-driven imperialism, including an actual military presence, so what is this cultural imperialism thing? Imperialism usually means that people step in with guns and take over saying, "We are an imperial power; your shit is now ours." Think about Darth Vader, and the imperial storm troopers. They are taking over and ruling by force.

However, cultural imperialism is much more subtle. There are no guns, there is no iron-fisted dark lord, and there are no storm troopers. Sorry, Darth. Cultural imperialism simply means that people begin adopting your culture. Think about pop cul-

American secret weapon of imperialism: cheerleaders!

ture. This is the one that most often springs to mind. People around the world from France to South Korea to Australia to South Africa like watching crappy American movies, listening to crappy American pop songs, and watching ridiculously crappy TV shows like American Idol. Think about the title: it's 'American' Idol and it's watched and *idolized* by people all over the planet! How sick is that shit?

So cultural imperialism is much more subtle, because nobody has a gun to anybody's head telling them to do this or that; people just like it for some strange reason. There have been millions of movies made in America that have been exported to every other country on the planet, so many of which you'll never see because they suck so bad that nobody in this country will watch them . . .
but people in other countries will, just because they're American. People are attracted to that successful vibrant American pop culture. So you can go to Tibet and watch 'Titanic,' you can go to Russia and listen to Run DMC (sorry, the Plaid Avenger's old school), you can go to Burma and see an episode of Baywatch.

But a lot of countries in today's world are passing laws to try to limit the amount of American pop culture that enters their countries. France is a good example, because every few years they attempt to ban the importation of American-made films. It never lasts long, but they try. In places like Bhutan, they have refused to have the Internet because they don't want any cultural influence from other places; they claim it destroys their own culture.

So this is a perceived threat to unique cultures and pop culture is the main component of cultural imperialism that you know of, but here's one that is much more intriguing to the Plaid Avenger . . .

America's fifth column: Team Ocean

Cultural imperialism from an *ideological* standpoint is much more important to acknowledge, especially considering how world events are going down right this second. I'm talking about the ideologies of capitalism and democracy being spread. As you know from current events I hope, unless you have been living under a rock, the United States has an active military presence in Iraq and Afghanistan and perhaps will occupy some other places in the very near future. They don't necessarily import Britney Spears at the end of a gun, but what is happening is that they are heavily influencing the societies to become like the US in terms of adopting democracy, individual liberties, and capitalist culture.

IT'S UP TO YOU

PROTECT THE
NATION'S HONOR
— ENLIST NOW —
ASSOCIATED MOTION PICTURE ADVERTISERS

Don't let Lady Liberty get bent over!

The capitalist part is not that difficult, since every country makes money in some way or another on capitalism. The democracy part is the one that some people in the world tend to have a problem with. These are ideas which Uncle Sam does push across the planet, and quite openly. The US says "Hey! We're going into Iraq because we want a democracy here. We're going to help them have a democracy. We're going to manipulate or push or try our best to get other countries to embrace capitalism because it benefits us and we think it benefits the world and we're going to try to get everyone to do it." And indeed the US and Canada in most of their endeavors say "Yes and we believe that all people are equal and that we think individual rights and civil liberties should be the norm across the planet."

Again, this is not something that's up for dispute. You can see this every day when the US government says "Hey! We think China has horrific human rights abuses and we're going to complain about it at the UN." The US may complain about the Chinese treatment of the Tibetans and say that their human rights suck. That is essentially saying "We believe that our system is right and yours is wrong" and that's something to consider.

Let the Plaid Avenger go on record stating that yes, I uphold the idea of democracy in the world and I think human rights are the most basic necessity for every human being on earth. I'm a bit biased since I'm from this region. I have this ideal myself. However, not everyone in the world does, and I'm willing to recognize that. I may not accept it, but I at least recognize that another point of view exists.

The US planting democracy seeds in the Middle East is of great consequence in today's world. It's the reason that your tax dollars are going to support troops who will continue to prop up governments and establish democracies in places that have no history or background in such cultural phenomena. Make no bones about it; lots of folks in the Middle East and other places in the world have no experience with democracy and don't necessarily want it. They do, however, feel as if the world power, i.e. the United States, may be pushing them towards it.

And I don't think it's an exaggeration to describe it as 'pushing them toward it'. I think that's a fair assessment. And quite frankly, it's up to you as American citizens and ultimately as world citizens to decide if that's kosher. However, I just want you to understand that democracy is a major part of your culture that you accept as right and good and proper. Other folks in other places may not share that sentiment. Food for thought.

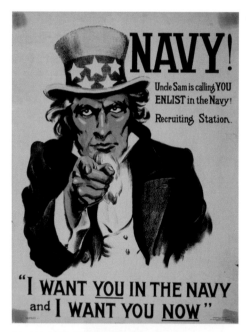

NAVY!
Uncle Sam is calling YOU
ENLIST in the Navy!
Recruiting Station.

"I WANT YOU IN THE NAVY
and I WANT YOU NOW"

Source of the Village People song.

-THE FREE-EST

What would be the worst part about being the free-est? The first thing I want to point out is the freedom to be clueless. North Americans as a whole, and we do have to pick on the Americans more than the Canadians in this respect, are completely clueless about what's going on in the world.

FREE TO BE CLUELESS

Most Americans have no idea where Tibet even is on a map much less what the hell human rights abuses are happening there. And it is part of the North American society in that yes, they're semi-isolated as I suggested. They're far away from other regions therefore they're not as heavily impacted, even in this global interconnected world. North Americans focus on their own thing. I won't call them isolationists, but they have a tendency to focus on themselves at the cost of simply just not caring about the rest of the world.

To kind of sum this up: internationally, they don't give a shit.

It seems bizarre for the Plaid Avenger to say because this entire chapter so far has been spent explaining how the US is a central key player, deeply involved in the world's political and economic systems. But by and large, American citizens don't give a shit about other countries. Many around the world would say that American politicians, whose job it is to give a shit about foreign affairs, don't give a shit either.

As the Plaid Avenger has traveled around the planet and talked to lots of folks everywhere, a common theme reveals itself: many people perceive America as an unchecked power, and around the world people feel that America doesn't give a shit about them. Perhaps they are too small or not enough like the United States, or they have no economic resources that the United States cares about . . . and so their perception is that the United States doesn't give a shit about them. Perhaps they're right.

In this interconnected and globalized world where everyone knows everything all the time, citizens of the United States, by and large, know the least about what's going on in the world. If that's a radical statement to you, then open your eyes.

You heard the man! "Have you got your Hoe?"

If people in Sudan can get to the Internet, they know everything that's happening in the world and they pay attention to what's happening in global movements of ideas and people. Of course, they especially know the details of the relationship between the US and Sudan, and what the UN Security Council is doing about Sudan. If you ask anyone in the United States, they won't have an utter clue. Sudan? Security Council? Huh? Is *American Idol* on yet?

That bothers a lot of people around the world. "Wow, this is the richest group of people who have the most influence on the entire planet, and they don't give a shit because they don't know. How could they not care enough to know, for instance, that this genocide is going on?" Well, isolation is a dual edged sword. We say the US is great because it has been isolated, but at the same time, that allows its people to be lazy. The general US population does not know what's going on, and that really burns people's asses around the planet simply because citizens of the United States have so much power individually. They could easily change some things if they wanted to, but they don't because either they don't know and/or they don't care.

EXPORTER OF FREENESS . . . BY FORCE

As I suggested just above, this region is also a huge exporter of democracy and capitalism and individual civil liberties and rights . . . at least the concepts of them. Now that sounds like a pretty good deal, and quite frankly the Plaid Avenger is all about individual liberties and justice so I'm all for it. Let's get this game on! Mostly the North American region exports these themes in its literature, in its ideas, in its technology, and in its pop culture. However, we can't overlook the fact that sometimes these good ideas (democracy, capitalism, and individual rights) are also exported by force if necessary. That can be a little problematic.

Yes, it's awesome that you want people to have a democracy. Perhaps not so awesome that you go there and kill them in order to make them one. Current events are playing out right this second to determine how successful forced democracy is going to work out in the Middle East. And it don't look too good so far for the forces of freedom. In terms of freedom, can it be forced upon a society? Can it be given . . . or can it only be earned? We shall see; unfortunately, at the expense of many lives.

So North America is the free-est, with lofty and admirable goals for others. But being blinded by ambition has led to a big fat negative for North America which leads us to the next theme . . .

HUBRIS AND HYPOCRISY

Now for some of you reading this book, don't even write me letters saying that the Plaid Avenger is some blatant tree-hugging bunny kissing liberal wannabe commie who's just making fun of the US. I'm not, alright? I'm trying to get you to understand what the hell is going on!

It is problematic around the globe right this second that the United States and Canada say "Hey! We're all about democracy. We're all about individuals. We're egalitarian. We think democracy is great." They do. I truly believe that. However, when you have things like the Abu Ghraib prison scandal in Iraq as well as increasing civilian death counts there, when you have people being held in Guantanamo Bay without individual rights forever . . . well, you start to get a bad rap. The world, not the Plaid Avenger, is looking upon this saying, "Wait a minute. You guys are talking this mean game about equality and democracy, but you're not even doing it yourselves." So given current events, in the modern context in the 21st century, there's a bit of a problem with being the free-est when you're not living up to it.

Well, maybe not in the Middle East . . .

'FREENESS ENVY'

And finally, there might be something going on that I like to call "freeness envy." Oh man. Am I good or what? Freeness Envy . . . ha! And that is something that other cultures don't necessarily dig. Freeness in the United States/Canadian definition. What am I talking about here? The North America region is all about the freeness, man. Equality, democracy, freedom of speech, religion, choice, peace, love, dirty hippies, whatever. It's all about equal rights. Everybody's equal. Everybody's cool. Yeah man, pass the greenery Snoop Dogg . . . . oops, I digress . . .

Point is, don't assume that the rest of the world holds these ideals as highly as the North Americans do. Let me give you some examples. The Saudi Arabian government and most of the Saudi Arabian population is not necessarily in favor of equal rights for women. Sorry guys. I'm not making fun of my Saudi friends but the idea that women are completely equal in all aspects doesn't really play there. And even if you want to argue that point, that's fine. Let's go with something else like gay people. You know, in North America, everybody's equal. Be as gay as you want to be. That don't play in Africa, man. In Sub-Saharan Africa, and parts of the Caribbean, those folks are persecuted heavily and most folks in those societies would say "No. We ain't about them people being as free as we are." You can go around the world and look at different societies (and this is the people I'm talking about here, not just the governments) and lots of folks would say "No, we're not about that type of freedom." China ain't really into freedom of press. Caribbean ain't really into freedom for gay rights. The Vatican ain't really into freedom of choice. The Middle East may not be really into sexual equality or freedom to draw cartoons.

So a little 'freeness envy' may be happening around the globe. Now again, the Plaid Avenger is all about individual liberties, so I am a big proponent of it. But even I, when I go into other cultures, don't assume that everybody around the entire planet wants democracy. Well, I think they should have it, but that don't mean they all want it. And yes, I think that all women should be equal, because in the Plaid Avenger's world, all women are equal in my eyes. But I don't assume that all cultures necessarily accept that either and you have to keep this in context.

Freeness Envy, huh? Great term.

UNCLE SAM WRAP-UP

Alright, let's wrap this thing up. We've looked at the good side of the greatness of North America. We've looked at the negative side of

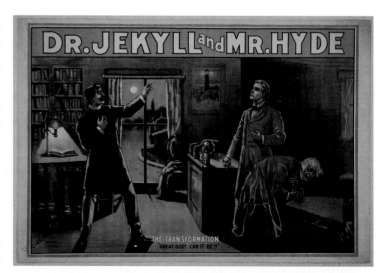

Dr. Uncle Sammy . . . or Mr. Cheney?

the greatness of North America. Yes, Uncle Sam is really a bi-polar fellow here lately. Sammy, my man, has a real Jekyll/Hyde complex going down.

You know Dr. Sammy Jekyll, the good doctor. He's out there doing good, fighting the good fight, standing up for the impoverished, the folks that don't have democracy or with no rights. Yes, Uncle Sam does quite a bit and even though he's taken a bad rap in today's world, the United States and Canada continue to be the biggest foreign aid donors, biggest funders of the UN, and do a hell of a lot for the planet. Even though sometimes they're a bit heavy handed about it, they think they're doing it for good reasons and who's to dispute that?

But there is of course, the seedier Mr. Hyde that comes out every now and again and sometimes this region does bad things abroad in the world . . . even when done supposedly for a good cause. However there are other times that this region is quite openly selfish in terms of looking out after its own interests. And since it's the most powerful region, it can do it in the most aggressive manner across the globe. Again, no judgement call here. That's just the way it is. The US and Canada are going to look out

Nice Uncle Sammy always picking up the ladies . . .

after their own corporate and economic interests. And if that means telling people to kiss their ass on the Kyoto Protocol, then that's what they're going to do and that's typically what they've done.

Uncle Sammy you are scaring me!

The bigger issue to think about is we are in the midst of big changes in the world power structure, and that is going to most greatly affect the North American region more than any other. Why? Because Uncle Sam has been used to being the sole super-power for 20 or 30 years now. Ever since the USSR went away, and Uncle Sammy won the Cold War, the North American region has been uncontested for power on the planet. It has the most political military, and economic power as I pointed out earlier.

But times are a-changing Sammy: China and India are on the rise, the EU has tight-ened up as a unit, Russia is back and bolder than ever, and other international players like Iran, Team Arab, and the Latin Leftists are all making regional impacts on the balance of power as well. The planet is morphing into a multi-polar world, a place with more than one superpower. This isn't up for debate nor a future prediction. This is happening now. The world of the future is a place where the US is not the only primary actor making global decisions. The question then becomes, how is Sammy going to deal with this new world, this up-and-coming, changing world that is our planet, right now in the 21st century?

Will Sammy go lightly into this world? Will he see the changes that are coming and work with other big powers and other big countries to get the job done and still push his own agenda? Or is it going to be more of a rougher road where the United States has a tough time giving up its top slot and is perhaps bound and deter-mined to have its way at all costs? This could result in potential conflict, potential war, potential stonewalling economically or in other things, or becoming isolationist and just putting up a big wall and looking inward to try to focus on itself only.

That is the big question. The $20,000 question that no one has the answer to yet because only time will tell. But this is a region of greatness and the US/Cana-dian team is not going to go away anytime soon . . . meaning it's going to main-tain its powerful position as a major player in planetary affairs for some time to come. No doubts about that. But will it be a bigger force for good or more of an internally-looking isolationist state? Only time will tell.

As the insightful Uncle Ben once told Peter Parker: "With great power comes great responsibility." Good advice for Spiderman. And probably for North America as well.

What next Sammy?

Western Europe

WORLD MAKER, SHAKER, AND BREAKER

Ok, what the hell's that supposed to mean? Well just this—while the United States and the North American region in general may enjoy prominent status in today's world, it's Western Europe that really has shaped and make-ed the current cultural, social, economic, and political world in which we live today. They've been at it for about 500 years longer than the U.S. was, and have been a tremendous impact worldwide in determining what's happening right now.

Let's face it—English is an international language not because of America, but because of the British, and their influence. Soccer is the world sport, not American football, for the same reasons. When we look at today's world, Western Europe may not be the world leader anymore, but it certainly was the maker and shaker. What about the breaker?

Well as you know, Western Europeans spent a lotta time in the last thousand years, and particularly the last hundred, beating the living shit out of each other. WWI, WWII. . . need I say more?! But today's world is very much different for Western Europe for it is united as never before—making, and shaking, without breaking, in the 21st century. Let's get to it!

WHO IS IN THE REGION . . . AND WHY?

Everybody knows and understands that Western Europe is a region. It is the western side of the Eurasian landmass. But being a Plaid Avenger world region is not solely based on just the physical geography, so what is it that makes this a homogenous region? We need to back up before we ask that question and ask who, what, and where is this region? What states? All the western European states? So which ones are those? All those cool ones that we take vacations to and go visit. Places like Norway, Sweden, Iceland, UK, Ireland, Germany, Belgium, Luxembourg, Switzerland, Austria, France, Spain, Portugal, Italy, Greece. Oh, wait, and Greece . . . Greece? But it's on the eastern side of Europe . . .

Look at the map here on the opposing page. All of those that are connected somehow are all Western Europe, but Greece is disconnected; it's over on the side by itself. But indeed, I think all of us would say, "Yes of course. That is definitely part of Western Europe." And that gets at the heart of what it is to be Western Europe, of what it is to be in this region, and the homogeneous traits therein.

What characteristics do these countries share that categorize them as a region? What could possibly be the same about all of these countries?

What we have is a set of extremely distinct nation states. In fact, all of these countries are exceptionally different from one another. When we look back at the US and Canada we said they share a common culture and language and background. When we get over to Western Europe, we have Spain; there's Spanish people who speak their own language and have their own culture, Spanish everything. Go next door and there's France; there are French people there and they speak French, and in Germany there are German dudes and they speak German. All of these things bring to mind extremely distinct cultures. The Germans eat sausages; the French drink wine. The Germans attack and the Frenchies surrender. Backgrounds and histories are all very different. On top of all that, Western Europe is a collection of states that vary in size: big states like France and Germany, and micro states like Luxembourg and Andorra.

However, there are a whole lot of homogeneous things about this region even though they have radical differences in backgrounds, histories, cultures, food, and drink. That last one is why the Plaid Avenger loves Europe: the great diversity of drinks.

But there is a bunch of stuff that is quite the same. Most of our culture here in the North American region is based on cultures from Western Europe, not Eastern Europe or Russia, but predominantly Western European backgrounds. So what are the similarities?

"Western civilization" is one. These are the places that created the big ideas on which our lives are based. I'm talking about the big things here: things like philosophies, legal systems, economic systems, medical practices, writing systems, and particularly religions. Christianity may have been created in the Middle East, but Western Europe became the cradle of Christianity and all its subsects. Europe expands and grows the religion into a global movement.

As it did for so many other ideas. This is why Greece is thrown into the fray; it's the birthplace of all the Western philosophies. People like Socrates, Plato, and all those dudes from Greece that affected history in a major way. Ideas of democracy and western medicine even have their origins in Western Europe. All of the "-isms" that you learned in high school, political/economic systems like socialism, Marxism, communism, and capitalism manifested themselves in Western European countries. These countries have shaped the way we think about life and how we want to live it.

There are great cultural differences between these separate and distinct nation-states that make up the birthplace of western civilization, but *they are united in their ideologies.* Another uniting factor in this region is that it is a rich place. The quality of life is similar to North America, even exceeding that quality of life in some places. It is a very interconnected place and is very urban like the United States. There are high levels of technology, high levels of consumption, and high GDP overall. Compared to the rest of the world, this is a pretty well-off place. Considering the combination of quality of life and its ideological background as the birthplace of Western civilization, Western Europe is a distinct and homogenous region in and of itself.

The EU

1 **glass red Bordeaux wine, from France**

1 **shot Jagermeister herbal liqueur from Germany**

1 **tumbler of Glenfiddich Scotch whiskey from the UK**

1 **glass Pinot Grigio white wine from Italy**

1 **shot Absolut vodka from Sweden**

1 **Chimay Grande Reserve from Belgium**

1 **shot ouzo from Greece**

1 **snifter of sherry from southern Spain**

1 **Guinness Draught beer from Ireland**

1 **glass port from Portugal**

Line up one drink with one seat around a very large table that seats 10. Each person gets one drink. Congratulations. You are now representing the EU. To complete the circle, you must go and find out the appropriate toast in the language of the drink you have. Skoal! (That's Scandinavian)

Jesus, Socrates, Marx, Descartes . . . bearded dudes of note in Western Civilization.

PHYSICALLY

What can we say about this place physically? The Plaid Avenger doesn't want to spend too much time talking about the physical aspects of this region, but when it comes to Western Europe and its profound impact on the planet, we have to consider the physical geography for just a minute. This is a group of countries on the western end of the Eurasian continent. For those of you that heard Europe is a separate continent, that's *poppycock!* It's not a distinct continent in terms of geology or any other "-ology." It's just the western peninsula of the great Eurasian landmass.

It's a snobbish European thing to suggest that it ever was a stand-alone continent. They were making themselves distinct from the rest of the people on the Eurasian continent, perhaps putting themselves a notch or two above the rest, but we will get to that momentarily. So what we have is a group of countries on the western edge of the Eurasian landmass that have a couple different distinct things about them that have made it a region of major power players in today's world. They actually have not been around as long as Chinese society or Indian society, and especially not Mesopotamia for that matter; the Middle East has been around way longer than Europe. So how did they get into a position of dominance in the last 500 years?

In terms of physical geography you need to know, Western Europe is an interconnected place . . . look at the map. Water, water everywhere. Think of water's effect on trade and commerce. River systems, which go through every inch of Western Europe, interconnect economies. This makes trading very fluid, pun intended. Not only is Western Europe permeated by river systems, but water is all around it too. We know Western Europe has peninsulas, but if you look at it, you can see that it is a peninsula itself. It is a peninsula of peninsulas. That is: if it's not an island like the United Kingdom or Ireland or Iceland, then it's a peninsula. Look at the Scandinavian Peninsula, the Iberian Peninsula, the Italian peninsula. There is water surrounding all of them. You're never far from water in Western Europe.

What does this have to do with the Plaid Avenger History you need to know? It's this closeness and association with water that propelled Europe into the limelight 500 years ago. Virtually all of the countries in this region were once maritime powers, or at least maritime explorers. This makes these Western Europeans some serious seagoing folk. We think about guys from Italy, Spain, Portugal, and Britain, even the Vikings of Scandinavia, going out and poking into the rest of the world. People did this in other parts of the world too, but the Western Europeans took it to the next level by taking over the entire globe with a passion and speed unrivaled in history.

Another physical consideration about Western Europe is that while it's very far north (most of it is north of the US-Canadian border) it has an extremely moderate climate because of something called the **Gulf Stream.** This is a warm water current which forms in the tropical areas in the Gulf of Mexico, Caribbean Sea, and Atlantic Ocean. It actually sweeps up the eastern seaboard of the United States and flows very far north, next to Ireland and the United Kingdom, all the way to the top of the Scandinavian peninsula around Sweden and Norway.

With water all around acting as a climate modifier, what we have is a place

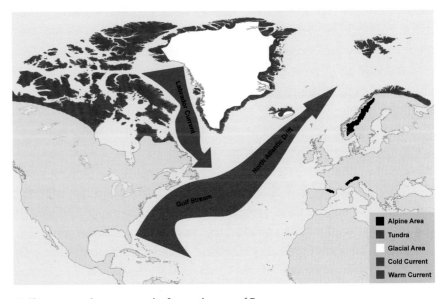

Gulf Stream moderates even the far north areas of Europe.

that is much warmer in the winter and a little cooler in the summer than other places at equal latitudes. As we move into the continent towards Eastern Europe and Russia, we are going to see the places at the same latitudes get quite a bit colder. Western Europe is pretty moderate. What's so great about that? As we saw in America, a well-watered, moderate climate is conducive to human settlement and population growth. While a few thousand years ago nobody was hanging out in Western Europe, in the last couple thousand it has become increasingly populated, and has become one of the cores of population on the planet because, physically speaking, the situation is right.

PLAID AVENGER'S HISTORY OF WESTERN EUROPE

We don't need to waste too much time talking about European history as you have probably already had a thousand classes on it in during your scholastic career, but the Plaid Avenger can summarize the last couple thousand years for you very quickly. The big pluses: the agricultural revolution (they learn to produce a lot of food), the age of colonization (they learn to take over the world and get a lot of stuff) and the industrial revolution (they learn to invent machines to make a lot more stuff). Put it all together, and it's a rich region.

It should be noted for the record that the transformation of this region into the dominant world leader is really only a product of the last 500 years. Yes, I know the Greek and Roman Empires were really hip in their day . . . but they were also very local . . . and then they went away and Europe was completely ass-backward until the Renaissance. The region was NOT a global leader, and it was NOT a global force, prior to 1500AD. Other civilizations around the globe made Western Europe look like a backwater of buffoons. And it was.

But then those Europeans got savvy after their Dark Ages. They learned about sailing and navigation and shipbuilding from Muslim traders. They learned about the global trade network from Asian merchants. They learned about gunpowder from the Chinese. The Europeans took all this information and applied it in new and exciting ways which subsequently made them masters of the seas, masters of the global economy, and master kick-asses militarily. China made fireworks with their gunpowder. Europeans made guns. You can figure out the rest from there . . .

So if these guys were taking over the world by storm, then what were the negatives? In a word: competition. All these different ethnic groups, religious groups, and different nationalistic groups have spent a whole lot of time in the last couple centuries beating the living hell out of each other. You have probably heard of war after war after war that you had to memorize in high school; all of them occurred on European soil. The last couple of biggies were the World Wars of the 20th century, but of course there were hundreds of other confrontations before those.

Virtually all of these contests were based on competition between these European states for more power, more money and more influence on both the European and the world stage. The states of this region, as a whole, have spent a good deal of their time figuring out how to out-maneuver, out-flank, and generally beat up their nation-state neighbors. Why is that? How did it get to be this way? How has it radically changed in the last 50 years? These are the important questions that you need to consider. The whole concept of a nation-state was formed in Western Europe. How did the concept of a nation-state form here if they have spent all this time whipping ass?

There are groups of people identifying themselves as distinct cultures, like the French, the Italians, the Swiss. Those terms mean something to us. It means something to them too. The idea that you would have a distinct group of people and that you would outline a political area in which you reside is a Western European phenomenon, just like all the -isms and philosophies we talked about. Unique, competitive cultures sitting side-by-side in the little chessboard of Europe. Yep. That's how conflict started.

I should also reiterate that there are people who begat people who begat people to make Western Europe one of the most populous regions on the planet, especially in the last 500 years. People are all over Europe. The coastlines and river systems are packed to the point that Europe as a whole is about half the size of the United States with about twice the population. We talked about the North American region having tons of space that fostered the evolution of the automobile, interstate system, suburbs, and individual transport systems; Europe is the reverse. You don't have all that space. You have double the population in half the space. We can see the physical manifestation of this with public transportation. People use trains and buses; not everybody owns vehicles there. It's quite a different society just from the standpoint of land and how little of it there is.

I said something about colonies a second ago, which has everything to do with everything. You already know from the Plaid History that the North American region is the number 1 region in terms of military, economy, wealth, and all that stuff. But that only came about in the last 100 years. Who used to be there? Western Europe did, and they had their day in the sun for a good 500 years. From Columbus right on down until about World War I, Western European countries had the tiger by the tail and controlled most of the world.

Land and latitude comparison: US & Europe.

What does the Plaid Avenger mean by "controlled most of the world?" You mean like cultural imperialism from the United States? No. I mean *direct imperial control.* Because of the physical geography we talked about, Western Europe was full of maritime nations, and because of the certain situation at that time in their history, they started going out and exploring the world. Their technology increased and surpassed the technology available in other places on the planet. Thus, their exploration potential increased.

These guys, at the exact right time in history, go out and bump into the New World. They take over all the New World. They colonize it; this small group of countries actually take it. They say, "Hey, look! North America! That's ours! South America! We'll take that too! Divvy that up between Spain and Portugal! North America we'll divvy that up between the French and the British!" That's not all. Throughout the last 500 years, a tiny handful of states from Western Europe have controlled the rest of the planet.

As you can see from the graphic to the right, eight nations (UK, Germany, France, Spain, Portugal, Italy, Netherlands, and Belgium) controlled all the countries in pink. This is a massive territorial holding. Again the Plaid Avenger is trying to get you to understand how it is that Western Europe has some of the richest countries in the world right now. Look at this chart again. For 500 years these guys siphoned the material wealth off the rest of the planet.

Let's think about a place like the Netherlands. There isn't shit there my friends. It's flat. They grow tulips! How are they, of all countries, one of the richest in the world?

Colonial masters of disaster!

You have to understand this much about history: it's because they controlled massive territorial holdings, many of which were exclusively economically exploited colonies. The Dutch just siphoned off wealth.

Think about the Spanish Armada, which controlled all of South America, Mexico, Central America, and the Caribbean. They brought back gold and silver bouillon . . . the booty! It was all there in the New World, my friends. What did the Spaniards do with it? Did they dig it up in Mexico and redistribute to the natives? Hell no! They took all that shiny shit and brought it back to Western Europe. All of it. Meanwhile, the British were busy bringing back all the tobacco they could smoke up, as much cotton as they could weave into fabric, and as much rum as they could pull out of the Caribbean and disperse to their sailors.

All of this stuff occurred to the benefit of these Western European countries. This is not the case with Eastern Europe. You do not see Eastern European or Russian colonies in the world. There is a small enclave in Western Europe of material wealth, which controlled the rest of the planet. This is significant to note, to learn, to learn to love. It has been largely overlooked in textbooks, for whatever reason. All of the world's wealth went floating back to a small group of countries. That may sound pretty negative. Maybe it is. I think if I were somewhere in sub-Saharan Africa and had been a colonial holding for the last 500 years, which left me and my people poor as hell while those countries are rich as shit, I might be a little bitter. Fortunately, the Plaid Avenger grew up in the United States where we kicked those assholes out before they exploited us for too long. The United States is in a much different situation than many other ex-colonies in the world.

But let's not beat up our European brothers anymore right now. Let's think about some of their other impacts on the world. What are the other things to consider when we look at the Western European region that had such a tremendous influence on the planet? What's the number 1 sport in India? Cricket. Brazil? Soccer. What language do they speak in Pakistan? What language do they speak in Chile? What religion do they follow in Mexico? What are the religious practices in the Philippines? What types of government do all the countries of the world follow? What are the major philosophies that most people in Africa ascribe to? These questions all have answers of Western European origin.

All the types of government in place across the globe, many modes of thought, major religions, major languages were all spread throughout the world via the conquests of Western Europe. People in Brazil speak Portuguese because it used to be a colony of Portugal. A lot of people in India speak English because the British used to colonize those dudes. All sorts of little things including dietary habits, holidays, and particularly the world's sports that people love for unknown reasons have their origins in Western Europe.

Why are significant portions of the populations of North America, South America, and Australia white? In addition to the movement of ideas and culture, you also have the mass movement of peoples. You have English and French and German and Italian and Irish and Scottish enclaves all over the damn planet. As a result of this movement, nearly all of European thought and culture is accepted as part of today's world culture all over the globe. You need to know the good and the bad. Why is Western Europe rich? It has something to do with them exploiting the rest of the world. Why can you communicate using English all over the world? Same reason.

If you are a pilot that flies between countries you must speak English. It's an international standard. Why? It's not because America is so great, but because Western Europe, Britain in particular, has had so much influence on the planet over the last 500 years. America was just the heir to the throne of global power and influence that was created by the period of Western European colonial imperialism.

This colonial period is really the most important in European history, probably in world history. It led to the amalgamation of wealth that essentially made Western Europe the rulers of the world. We can debate whether the United States is an imperial power, but there's no debate about Western Europe. They were a hegemonic imperial power that controlled the entire known world and amassed incredible wealth from it. They don't have that position anymore of course. The US has that #1 slot. What are some of the reasons for this? One, they lost their colonial holdings; and two, they have run out of land. They cannot continually expand as the United States has done over the last 200 years. They don't have any more resources because they have been using those resources for generations upon generations. So Europe is like a geriatric version of the US. It ran out of its room to grow and is a young buck no longer.

THE BEGINNING OF THE END: THE 20th CENTURY

That's enough history to set the stage. Western Europe is not number 1 today. Why is that? It is still very rich. It still has a lot of influence in the world, though what we are seeing in the 21st century is that European power is actually on the decline. How did it go from top banana to just another in the bunch? Europeans may not like to hear the Plaid Avenger say that, but it's true. They are slipping. They have a very unique solution on how to stop that slip, by the way, and we'll discuss that in the last part of this chapter. But back to the slip . . . wait a minute. Banana slip. Damn am I good or what? But I digress . . .

As we already pointed out, they were on top of the world for quite a while, but the 20th century was unkind to not only Western Europe but Europe as a whole. Just as America is exploding onto the world scene, Europe decides to beat the living hell out of itself for 50 years solid—and does a damn good job of it. These nation-states with their independent cultures and separate identities smash themselves not once but twice in World Wars I and II. The Cold War settles in after that, and that doesn't help matters at all. The same 100 years that Europe is destroying itself, it is losing its colonial holdings. They had already lost America long ago, but in the 19th and 20th centuries they lost all the rest. Canada goes away, South America goes away, a lot of Africa goes away, Australia goes away. And the few colonies that they retain to the bitter end are giving those Europeans nothing but a headache too: India for the British, French Indochina for the French, the Middle East for everybody. These places break out into independence wars, civil disobedience, and catastrophe in general. So little by little as we approach the modern era the Europeans lose these territories that for a long time gave them their wealth accumulation and serious competitive edge.

Massive WWII Destruction in Europe.

As the Plaid Avenger suggested already, America has continuously expanded economically because of its incredible amount of resources and territory. You have that with the Western European powers as well, but this reverses in the last 100 years. They lose all their territory. They lose the unfettered access to the resources of those places too. This reversal of fortunes is happening at the same time they were beating the living hell out of each other in wars, destroying their entire infrastructure. Make no bones about it: World War II was the most destructive thing that could have happened to any region as a whole. There was total devastation across the entire continent. Factories, roads, and bridges were entirely wiped out. Again this plays back into why America is so great . . . because none of this shit happened in America.

So, the first half of the 20th century was not kind to Europe. It lost colonies and destroyed themselves to the point of collapse. At the end of this destruction, people woke up and realized they needed to do something different. They couldn't continue to beat each other up. Some very wise people figured out that Western Europe couldn't compete on the world stage anymore. These thinkers dreamt up a new way to get back into the game. What they thought up was something entirely new . . .

THE EU

THE RISE OF THE EU

The EU is the salvation of Western Europe and the only real reason it is still a global player, period. What do I mean by that? Well, after the destruction of World War II some smart dudes (incredibly, they were French) say, "We've got to stop killing each other. We need to economically integrate ourselves so that we are not competing with each other anymore."

They thought that part of the problem was that the Germans hate the French and the French hate the British and the British hate everybody because they are in competition with each other. And they were right. The Western Europeans were once the masters of the universe, but those days are gone. To continue to compete with each other, just within the continent, was disastrous as they already found out. So they said "We should work together, we can all get a little bit richer if we all try and work together better. Let's start rebuilding from WWII by pooling our coal and steel industries . . ."

And that's how the EU started. Everybody needs coal and steel to rebuild stuff, and all of Western Europe had to be rebuilt. The smart guys who thought this up knew it was going to evolve into something else. They said, "We'll do this as a start, and it will tie us to each other so much that we won't be able to afford to attack each other. If we make this into a common industry Germany won't be able to attack France because it would be hurting its own economic needs." You can't beat up the people you're actively trading with because you will lose their trade. It was an interdependence that they formed in the coal and steel industries, but they wanted to make it something else. They wanted it to reach farther.

This is where we have the real rise of supranationalism in Europe following WWII. The EU grows and it says, "Well let's not stop here; let's continue to make things more and more solid as every day passes so we can't compete anymore. We are so far behind now; we are so wiped out. America is totally whipping our ass, and we lost our colonies. How can we effectively compete on the world stage?" The answer was to expand the coal and steel thing into a free trade zone thing—a free trade block.

What does this have to do with world trade? Can Belgium compete with the United States' economy? No. Can Italy? No. How about Ireland? Not a chance, they are all drunk on Guinness. How about Germany, the number 3

What's the Deal with . . . Coal and Steel?
In 1951, six European countries—France, Belgium, West Germany, Italy, the Netherlands, and Luxembourg—signed the Treaty of Paris establishing the European Coal and Steel Community (ECSC). The ECSC created a common market, free of trade barriers, for steel and coal. These two commodities were especially important, because both were key resources for industrialization and rebuilding after WWII. Trading coal and steel freely was the first move to quell European power rivalries by establishing this economic unity and interdependence. The ECSC is often credited with creating a community between former World War II enemies. In fact, the European Union can directly trace it roots to the ECSC. The ECSC member countries soon after established the European Economic Community, which was renamed the European Community; this became the first (and most important) "pillar" of the European Union in 1992.

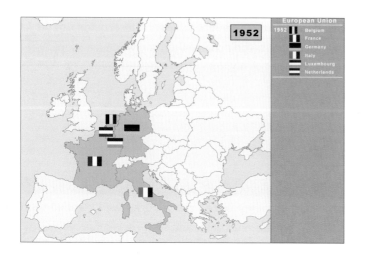

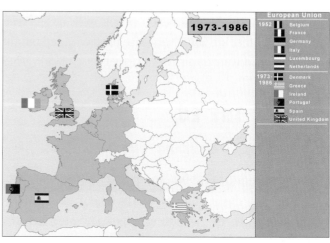

economy on the planet, can they compete? Nope. Bidding on a contract or trying to make some sort of international tie or trade tie with another country, the United States will win every time. So these countries got together and said, "Wait a minute! What if we all act under a common umbrella? Can all of our countries together as a unit effectively compete against the United States?" Yes, and they can compete with lots of other trade blocks around the world too.

So the EU evolved into a **trade block,** and (as you read about in Chapter 6) trade blocks are all about decreasing tariffs and taxes between states to encourage trade. The French say, "Hey Germany, we won't tax your sausages if you don't tax our wine!" So they all agree not to tax each other's stuff and therefore, people can afford to buy more of it. People buy more, people sell more. Mo' money. Once that got going and they've gotten back on their feet during the last 50 years, the EU expanded into something that the world has never seen. That's why I am going to spend the rest of this chapter just talking about what's so cool about the EU.

WHAT'S SO COOL ABOUT THE EU?

Why is it of such great significance? Thanks to the EU, Europe is turning from a bunch of nation-states that competed with each other for a thousand years into the **United States of Europe.** What does that mean? The independent sovereign nation-states of Europe are becoming much more like substates of the United States than independent countries, in terms of free movement of peoples and elimination of borders. Borders are still there, but they don't really mean anything. If you walked in a straight line across Europe twenty years ago, you would get your passport checked twenty different times according to how many countries you went into and out of.

That policy is largely disappearing. In fact, the number 1 thing for you to remember about what's different from the EU and all other trade blocks, or even supranationalist organizations around the planet, is the *free movement of peoples*. Nowhere else on the planet do you have a coalition of countries in which the people in your country can move anywhere within all the countries of the club without having their passport checked. This free movement of people is a big, big deal. A 2008 note: This free movement of people is being seriously re-evaluated right now, especially for the most recent EU inductees, but it is still a critical and revolutionary idea within a trade block.

Compare this to NAFTA, the free trade union between the US, Canada, and Mexico. Do we have a free movement of people? Hell no! You can go back and forth between Canada and the US and they will check your passport, but you can't just do anything you want. Can you move back and forth from Mexico to the United States? Oh, hell no! The US has a huge wall that they are in fact trying to make bigger. So the unique factor about the EU is free movement of people. Because of

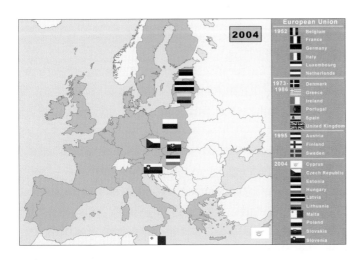

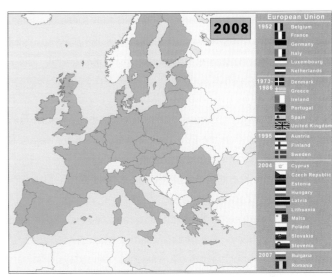

this fact, they have to have a common law system as well. They are building a common judicial system, and a common legislative system. Thus, the EU is becoming a United States of Europe.

Before I go any further, does everybody in Europe think this is the most awesome idea ever, with everybody standing around the campfire singing Kumbaya? Oh, hell no again. Political leaders think a United States of Europe would be totally sweet, particularly leaders whose countries participated in the wars. Businesses and a lot of other people like the idea too. However not everybody does, and the reason for the animosity lies in that cultural imperialism thing that we talked about in the last chapter.

What does that have to do with the EU? People in Italy are Italians and they have their Italian heritage. A lot of the Frenchies are fiercely defensive of French culture. Those damn Brits will defend the Queen and teatime with their lives. Because EU dudes are nation-states with independent cultures, there are lots of folks within them that see the EU as a threat to the survival of their culture. Sometimes you'll see a McDonalds restaurant being set on fire in protest of the EU. You can interpret any sort of anticonglomeration or antihomogenization attack on a multinational organization as a protest against the EU. The anti-EU opposition is losing the battle, but they are there. They will tell you, "This EU thing sucks! I don't want to be in the United States of Europe! I want to be Italian!" . . . or Swiss, or whatever the hell they are.

So the EU is definitely continuing despite the small amount of dissent, but where's it going? Well, it's got a common defense system, which is a huge stride. Each country, for the most part, has its own little army, but the EU also has a common defense army. You can hear about the EU forces being sent into places like Yugoslavia, or EU forces being requested in Iraq. The idea of a unified army for these countries is a massive change in a region that has spent a thousand years beating itself up. They now have a common defense force, which pretty much eliminates the possibility of any future conflict. You can't fight wars with each other if you have the same army.

POWER STRUGGLES AND THE STRUCTURE OF EUROPE

The EU is growing because most member countries think that for their organization to compete better on the world stage, their numbers need to be higher. Those members think the EU should become bigger. The bigger the club, the more world power it has, and the more power they have as individual countries. That is the common perception in the EU, so they are expanding into Eastern Europe. This means places like Poland, the Czech Republic, and Latvia are now in the EU. Places as far east as Ukraine may be members of the EU soon. This bad-ass block is expanding eastward, unifying Europe more than it's ever been.

This has set up some internal power struggles within the EU. There is something the Plaid Avenger calls **Europe's Continental Divide of Power.** These internal struggles for power within the EU have a lot to do with how the system is set up. It's a lot like the United States in that there is a legislature, a judiciary system, and something similar to a House of Representatives in which each nation-state has a say according to the size of its population. The EU also has something like a Senate, in which each nation-state has a single representative. We can obviously tell who has the power by looking at populations. So who's got the power? Big surprise: France and Germany. They're the big power players in population and economics within Europe, so they have much more say in what the EU does. A lot of smaller states within the EU say "Hey wait a minute, we are not getting as much of a voice! This is unfair! We don't like this! I'm Liechtenstein dammit! Hear me roar!"

> Here in the Plaid Avenger's book, we have been talking about Western Europe and Eastern Europe in separate chapters, but in another five or ten years there may be no difference; it may just be Europe. We will save the remaining differences for the next chapter but for now we will leave it at that.

While the French and the Germans have battled each other throughout history, they are actually a team now. And what a team! It's the **Franco-German Alliance,** if you want to have some really cool terminology to throw around at dinner parties. These guys are also on the continent, so I call them **the continentals.** Germany is the number 3 economy on the planet, and France is number 6. This makes them a huge power core of the EU. These two states, while they have historically agreed on nothing, pretty much agree on everything nowadays. They are big pro-EU states quite frankly because they are power players in it. A lot of the EU's smaller states complain that if France and Germany don't like a proposal or idea, then it's not going to hap-

SIDE BY SIDE -
BRITANNIA!

Britain's Day Dec. 7th 1918
MASS MEETING

pen. There is definitely some truth in that. If France and Germany are against an idea, it can get stymied easily. This causes a true power divide between big states and small states.

The EU's number 2 power core is the UK. Perhaps you never thought of the UK this way, but it is kind of distinct from the rest of Europe. "Say what? Plaid Avenger, I thought you just said the UK was *part* of Western Europe?" It is physically; it's there off the coast of the Eurasian continent, and all of its history is European history. However, the British have, for quite some time, been elitist. Snobbish. Tea-sippers, with the pinky in the air. Remember the old British blue-blooded aristocracy—the same ones who still think the Queen is the shit. A bit of snobbery remains, and the British have seen themselves as distinct from the rest of Europe proper throughout history.

As I said before, the British were the predecessors to American power on the planet. They were on the world throne for a very long time. But not anymore. Here's a Plaid Avenger interpretation; the attitude of the British is that they are still number 1. They would still very much like to be the singular world power. And if you *can't* be the world power, what should you do? *Hang out* with the world power! If you're not the biggest kid on the block, *hang out* with the biggest kid on the block and make him your buddy. So the British actually have much more in common with, and are much more eager to hang out with, the United States in world politics than they are with the Franco-German alliance on their own continent, in their own trade block.

So big states and small states argue over constitutional power structures and representation. And the 'older' EU states argue with the 'newest' EU states over immigration policies. And the Franco-German axis may argue with the British over economic and foreign policy. But . . . the times are a'changin' on this front as well . . . which brings us to:

WESTERN EUROPE NOW

Western Europe's going through some fairly radical changes here in the dawn of the 21st century. The first that's already been alluded to, and that's the EU. It's regeneration. It's the butterfly coming out of the chrysalis as a brand new creature that is really flying high in more ways than one. So let's elaborate a bit more on the EU in today's world, because it really has become the face of Western Europe and Europe as a whole, led by Western Europe, though.

The EU, if taken as a singular entity, is the largest economy on the planet. It has the largest GDP. Yes, indeed, a Gross Domestic Product bigger than that of even the United States. Now again, that's putting all the member countries of the EU together into a single block, but that's of course, what they are. And although it perhaps started as trade, perhaps morphed a little bit into politics, it is something entirely new on the world landscape. And it's becoming more powerful every day.

So what's so new? What am I talking about here? Well, the EU has been working hard to frame a constitution for itself. An endeavor which has not met with ultimate success—so far. But it's quite important to consider, if for nothing else, that when it does get passed eventually, and it will, it's going to dawn an entire new age for Europe. It really will lay the foundations of Europe being the United States of Europe. A different beast altogether than anything that has come before in continental Europe. And they're doing a whole lot of things to cement this idea that this is a very different beast.

A constitution, and also a unified judicial system which is becoming stronger every day. They have unified, singular environmental policies. Of course they've already unified their monetary system. The borders between the original EU states are fairly solvent, meaning you can move around within them—free movement of people. We've already talked about that. With the introduction of lots of new states in Eastern Europe, from Eastern Europe, the free movement of people is changing a bit, but we'll get to that in just a second.

The thing I want to finish on, relating to the EU and its future in the world, is that it also has a common defense. And this appears to be growing rapidly here very recently, as well. They want to have a defense structure—essentially an army—an EU army, that behaves and acts independently of the United States and even of NATO, of which most EU countries are a member.

And to finish, the big point, is foreign policy. Increasingly, and this is bizarre, the EU is more and more speaking with a single voice when it comes to foreign policy. That's important because here lately, the EU foreign policy line does not agree with, or contradicts, the US foreign policy line. And this is, again quite important to understand what's going on in the world. Meaning that the EU, a singular entity, puts out political statements about its attitude about things that are happening on the planet. It's not always completely unified, but the fact that they are doing it is what's important. Maybe a few examples are warranted here.

When Robert Mugabe's trashing Zimbabwe here lately, the EU steps forward with a statement and says, "We do not condone this behavior. We are going to have sanctions against Zimbabwe." That we being the entire EU. We're seeing that increasingly the EU is acting as a singular entity to make statements about, say, Chinese human rights, or other issues that are occurring around the planet. This, combined with this singular EU national defense, are the most important points that are being developed rapidly here at the dawn of the 21st century, and are what's making the EU a real political, as well as economic, force in the world.

Again, why would they do this? Just like with the economic stuff. No singular European nation can compete with the US or increasingly can even compete with China, or Japan, or many other places in the world. So they got together, and as a singular economic unit, they can compete quite well as one of the biggest economic units on the planet.

And now the same thing has happened with politics. They realize that, yes, while Great Britain has a big voice in the world, by itself it can't do as much. And certainly Belgium can't. And hell, there's no way in hell Poland can. But as a singular unit, politically their voice is much, much stronger. But they don't agree on everything . . .

PROBLEMS: IMMIGRATION AND CULTURE FRICTION

But Western Europe also has some big problems ahead of it. And the main BIG issue that it's currently confronted with is people. What? Why are people a problem? People are a dual-edged sword in Western Europe because the populations of most Western European countries are stagnant (which means they're not growing), or they're actually declining—they're getting smaller. Therefore, to keep their economies going, moving forward and growing, you have to have people. You have to have people filling jobs—working on farms, working in restaurants, washing dishes, putting down the beds at the hotels. So Western Europe with its declining local populations, has had to rely on immigration from other regions in order to fill those jobs. So it has to happen. That's a fact. But how is it happening?

We talked about distance being one of the United States' great physical attributes; it is far away from most other places in the world, and only borders one other distinctly different region. On the other side of the spectrum, Europe is very close to every place else. Western Europe can almost be considered the epicenter of every place nearby, in that it is infused with people from Eastern Europe, Russia, the Middle East, Africa, and pretty much anybody else that can very easily get to Europe proper. Europe, like the US, is extremely rich. The Middle East, and Africa, and Russia could be put in the poorer column. Maybe even the *extremely* poor column. This results in a great movement, a great migration wave, of people that are hitting Europe, and causing tremendous problems. Europe has generally welcomed them, but it is reaching a kind of critical breaking point now.

The French in particular have always had a sort of an open-door immigration policy with all of the citizens of its former colonies, particularly in Africa. "You were French citizens when you were a colony, so we are going to consider you French citizens if you want to come here." Well that's all fine and dandy, except that the French state is now going broke! A more lefty, socialist state which provides a lot of government benefits is starting to feel the economic strain as its population continues to swell with Arab and African immigrants. In addition, *collisions of culture* are starting to ferment.

CULTURE FRICTION

Cultural collision—what does that mean? That sounds a bit strong. Perhaps cultural friction is better. A lot of folks are getting quite worried across Europe right now, that they're losing their Europe-ness. That perhaps the Belgians are losing their Belgian-ness, that the French are losing their French-ness. Why? Because the larger and larger numbers of immigrants from other places are bringing their cultures and languages and religions into the European homeland . . . and in more deeply integrated ways than ever in the past. Let's consider this for just a moment more.

A big debacle in worldwide news in September of 2005 was the Danish cartoon of the prophet Mohammad that originated in Western Europe. Why was *that* such a big deal? Because so many immigrants are of Middle Eastern Muslim and African Muslim background, both of which constitute growing percentages of the population in Western Europe. But cartoons are only the tip of the iceberg when contemplating the current European friction with Muslim culture . . .

Now why would I pick on those folks in particular? Well, what these both black African and Arab Middle Easterner's that are of Muslim religion have brought to Europe is a whole new kind of layer of different culture into the European experience. There are mosques being built all over Europe. There are folks who dress differently being incorporated into Europe. And there are folks with different ideas about, say, individual liberties and rights that are being incorporated all over Europe. Liberties like the value of freedom of speech to draw a cartoon of a religious figure.

Result? An anti-immigration backlash has started to creep into European society. There has been a rise of more ultra-conservative rightist political factions across Europe—in places like Austria, Germany, and even France in particular. Those political parties are gaining popularity by saying, "We're losing our Austrian-ness, we're losing our German-ness. And we wanna kick out all the foreigners or at least limit them coming in to prevent this."

Legislation has been passed in Switzerland and in Austria banning the construction of new mosques. In France, laws banning Muslim headscarves have been passed, and the Dutch are debating about banning the burka altogether. Speaking of the Dutch, some radical from the Netherlands now has 24-hour a day protection for life since he released an anti-Islamic film this year . . . mostly as an ultra-rightist political stunt. A stunt which resulted in Muslim countries around the world boycotting Dutch goods. Starting to see the problem here?

To make a long story short, Western Europe is torn right now. Its governments (being part of 'Team West', the core of Western Civ) say, "Hey, we protect individual rights to do crazy stuff like offending Muslims by drawing a cartoon of the prophet Mohammed," however, they also have larger and larger Muslim constituencies, which is causing real conflict and clash in different parts of Europe who find offense in some of these things.

This cultural friction is not limited to the Muslims either. Let me give you another example, and we'll even stick with our Dutch wooden-shoe-wearing-tulip-growing friends. The Netherlands is also having problems with Catholic Christians from Poland! What?? What the hell is that all about? Well the Netherlands is . . . I won't say an atheist state . . . but it's not really a fervently religious

Burka high fashion not hip in Holland

group of folks. In fact, most of Western Europe is fairly blasé when it comes to attending church or being very religious . . . but the Poles sure are! Staunch Catholics, that bunch! As lots of Polish folks have migrated to western Europe seeking better economic conditions, their numbers are starting to tip the balance on societal views of everything from drug use to abortion rights

And that's a good topic to pick on. Of course Catholic Poles are staunchly anti-abortion. Well, the Netherlands is known as being staunchly whatever-the-hell-you-wanna-do! "Hey, we have a Red Light District—go have a hooker! It's all legal. Smoke some hemp! We don't give a shit! You wanna have an abortion? Hell, have three." Well wait a minute now. Now you have a big constituency of Catholic Poles who are in there saying, "No, we don't agree with that." And the Dutch government has to consider these things. So the Dutch may be losing their 'Dutch-ness' to Catholic Poles now as well as Muslims from North Africa. At least that is the perception of some.

IMMIGRATION

One last point on the whole immigration, cultural friction issue that you should be aware of is that immigration is not equal across all of Western Europe, and that means immigration problems are not equal across all of Western Europe. I just wanted to point out this spatial feature of who's the most pissed off or most concerned about immigration within the greater EU. As might be evident, the closer a state is to, say, North Africa or the Middle East, the more concerned it is with immigration, because that's the most used and easiest traveled avenue to get into Europe.

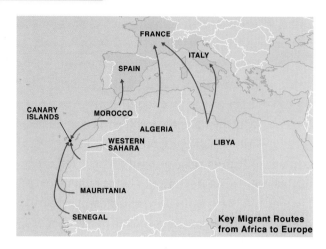

Meaning, if you want to migrate from North Africa to Western Europe, you go through the countries that are closest to you, namely Spain, Italy, and Southern France. And, as fate would have it, the countries that are most concerned with immigration, most worried about it, raise up the most fuss about it at the EU, are: Spain, Italy, and France. Surprise! The further that European countries are from other world regions, the less likely they are to be complaining about any immigration problems, because the less likely they are to have any. Again, let's start with the evident . . . Norway, Sweden, Finland—these places are *far* away. Hell, they're a lot colder, too. Who the hell wants to go from North Africa to Finland? And Iceland? Don't even get me started! Like those guys would ever have an immigration problem. Even Leif Ericson hauled ass out of there.

So you should be aware of this, that there's also internal tribulations when the EU gets together and meets. Because states like France and Spain say "Hey, we have a real immigration problem and we need to pass more stringent, strict laws to control this." And other places say, "Well, no we don't really think it's that big an issue." It has become enough here in 2008 that the EU is now working on a singular, collective immigration policy for the entire block. Look for it to be passed by 2009, and I'm willing to wager it's going to make getting into Europe a lot more difficult for potential immigrants.

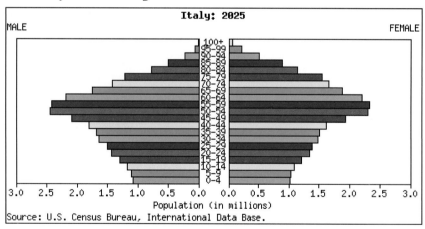

Bye-bye Italians! Hello immigrants!

Of course, the complicating factor here is that Europe is *dependent* on at least some immigration. European population dynamics, as we discussed in Chapter 2, indicate that population is declining in Western Europe. In Italy the population is declining because people aren't having enough babies. In Sweden the population is going down perhaps due to too much porn watching.

Now lots of folks are saying, "Isn't that good? Less people means more stuff for the people there, right?" Not necessarily . . . who's going to work at the factories that prop up the country's GDP? Who's going to make money for the economy? Who's going to work in the service sector? Population is completely stable or declining in all of these countries in Western Europe, which means they actually need immigrants to come in and keep things moving forward economically. And that's the rub. They cannot possibly stop immigration, and at the same time, it's causing tremendous conflicts both culturally and with the movement of jobs and people. *This is Western Europe's biggest problem.* Think I'm making it up? The conflict over the anti-Muslim film in Holland, the rise of skinhead movements in Germany, and even anti-Semitic crime in France have all been major headlines in the last year.

NEW FACES, NEW DIRECTIONS

Okay, to sum up and finish up our tour, we just need to talk about the power structure of what's happening in Western Europe right now as new folks have arrived: not the immigrants, but the fresh faces on the political scene. Leadership has rolled over all across Europe in the last year, but let's just focus on the folks that make the biggest impact worldwide, and for the US in particular. The people: our main man Gordon Brown, Prime Minister of the United Kingdom; Angela Merkel, the Chancellor of Germany; and to round out the trilogy, French President Nicolas Sarkozy. Why do I want for you to know these folks? Cause I want you to understand what the hell's going on in Europe and how it's changing rapidly.

Sammy needs you baby!

First, the way it was: As we have previously discussed, the US and the UK are tight allies, and the UK has typically, in the last hundred years, gone along with all things the US desires, more so than they have with the folks in their own neighborhood, namely the rest of continental Europe. You could see this highlighted at its best most recently as the US was ramping up for the current Iraq War, and came to the EU and said, "Hey, we're all buddies, we're all in NATO, hey EU countries help us out. Support us for our Iraq invasion." The British, of course, said, "Absolutely we're lap dogs of the US foreign policy, we'll do anything you want. Yes sir, yes ma'am, sure thing Uncle Sam."

However the Franco-German alliance said, "No, absolutely not. We're not on board with that policy at all." And indeed most of the rest of Western Europe went along with the Franco-German alliance on that. That's very typical of the way things have been for the last 10 to 20 years . . . hell maybe more like 50 years. Yes, the Europeans *in general* are US allies and friends, but when it comes to global issues and foreign policy, the US has only been able to rely on the UK year in and year out. And it could generally count on the Frenchies to oppose it year in and year out. But this equation is changing . . . we can pretty much put that relationship on its head here in 2008. What do I mean?

UK first: Gordon Brown took over from Tony Blair last year. Tony Blair was a total US lap dog on all foreign policy, right on up to and including the current Iraq war. That pooch would sit up and beg anytime a US president asked. But he's gone now. Now to Gordon Brown aka 'Brown Sugar'—he's a Scot, so he probably wears a kilt in his off hours, and he's much more resolute and much more independent than Tony Blair was. Brown ain't no beagle.

Of course he is still a huge US ally. No getting around that. But Gordon is much more reserved and he is making the UK much more independent on the foreign policy front than the Blair government did. How can we see this? As soon as Brown got into office, he started pulling back troops from Iraq. Great Britain under Gordon Brown has said, "Yes we're going to withdraw all our troops from Iraq and fairly soon," and it has already begun, much to the chagrin of the US. So, yes they're still an ally, but not as staunch and certainly not going to be on board for everything the United States wants.

Now let's shift to the continent: France and Germany—the biggest states, populations, and economies in the EU. So, together they form a significant power center, and again, to restate, one that is typically not always in agreement with all things British . . . or American. And what of our Franco-German friends? Strangely enough, they have completely flip-flopped too!

Gordon 'Brown Sugar'

'New-School' Nick Sarkozy

Both Angela Merkel and Nicolas Sarkozy, the leaders of Germany and France respectively, took over for folks who were more liberal, more on the 'left' spectrum of things. Both of them are more conservative and closer to the 'right' side of the spectrum. As such, both have become much stronger advocates of the United States in world affairs. Okay, strong may be too powerful a descriptor for Merkel, but not strong enough for Sarkozy! Nicolas Sarkozy has already visited and partied with George Bush two or three times. He has been throwin' down with the Bushies, ever since he came to office last year. Merkel doesn't like Bush personally (dudes, google 'Bush-Merkel back rub' to see what I mean), but Germany is now a much greater friend of the United States, as is France.

The proof? Both countries, the French in particular, have recently pledged more troops to the US-led NATO endeavor in Afghanistan. As soon as Sarkozy came into office, he said, "No, no, I'm gonna help out the US-led NATO endeavor in Afghanistan. We're gonna dedicate more French troops." But hold the phone: Sarkozy is also calling for French participation in Iraq via the UN. Wow. That's crazy! Cause as I already suggested earlier, France and Germany refused to even support the initial endeavor into Iraq.

It's a full turnaround—Nicolas being very assertive on the foreign policy stage. He is trying to bring France back into the limelight of world affairs. He wants to get France back into the command leadership of NATO too. And he is talking about making new French army bases around the world, to perhaps even mimic the US, but certainly going to be much more proactive in world affairs than any of his predecessors since World War II. Hell, since before World War II, cause even those people didn't do shit for world affairs in France, they just surrendered.

As for Angela, nobody is taking the Teutonic titan of a Chancellor for granted either. Merkel has had much success in the last couple of years swinging the Germans back to the conservative side of the spectrum. Her predecessor Chancellor Gerhard Schroeder was much more liberal, much more anti-US, and probably a much heavier drinker than Angela . . . although I would like to see a direct competition to settle the score on that count. Anyway, Germany's first woman leader has strengthened their economy, pulled in the reigns of immigration, and become a serious force in world affairs in her own right as well. When she talks, people listen. Merkel is more of a supporter of US policy, although not enough to get involved in the Iraq thing, as most Germans on the street are still vehemently opposed to it. But do remember this, my plaid friends: increasingly Germany has been invited to sit in on the workings of the UN Permanent Security Council. So even though it does not have an official vote, the German voice is becoming of greater significance on the world political stage by affecting UN policy decisions.

She's Merkel-icious!!!

So big changes going on. New faces, new directions. These leaders taken collectively carry a lot of weight in Europe, and in fact their countries together are often referred to as the *EU-3*. All three of these leaders are much more comfortable with the US, and cozier with each other too. Am I suggesting this is some big love fest between these three? Some ménage à trois, to coin the Sarkozy phrase? Absolutely not. They're still competitive to a certain degree, but these three countries and these three leaders are friendlier to each other than any of their predecessors of the recent past. And, as I've suggested in the prior section, all three of these folks are for a stronger EU. They are all for a stronger defense system within the EU. And they are all three for a singular foreign policy voice of the EU. Again, they all know that they're gonna disagree on certain points, but they are a more pro-EU group to strengthen their hand both within Europe, but also within the wider world.

SUMMARY—WESTERN EUROPE

Increasingly, Western Europe and Eastern Europe are simply becoming Europe. However, we can still tease out enough stuff in today's world to make some finishing remarks about this Western Europe region. It is one of the richest regions in the world. It is one of the most politically powerful regions in the world. Along with the United States, it is the foundation stone of Team West: one of the most important economic, political, and hell, even cultural forces on the planet. Team West—not to be underestimated. And while the US certainly leads Team West in the world today, Western Europe is where Team West started. Thus the term—Western Europe . . . Team West, go figure!

It does have some new faces, some new attitudes, but of course the main big theme in today's world is the EU becoming somewhat of a United States of Europe. What that means for the future in terms of not just a Constitution, but defense and foreign policy, are important points to consider. And following that with these new faces in today's world, we're seeing a Western Europe that is being increasingly supportive of the United States, but still quite independent in its own right.

And the EU is still growing. Mostly so that Western Europe, Europeans in general, continue to hold the top slots of economic and political power on the planet. This is a situation not likely to go away, even with Western European problems of cultural friction and immigration that it is dealing with here at the dawn of the 21st century. A rich-ass place, becoming more multi-ethnic, multi-linguistic, multi-religious as every day passes, that will continue to be a major power center in Team West and in the world.

CHAPTER OUTLINE

Eastern Europe

9

THE BOOKENDED REGION

We just wrapped up Western Europe. We now know of its extremely rich and multifaceted world influence. And we are aware of how it destroyed itself in the 20th century. Let's move on to Eastern Europe. It has slightly different physical geography, slightly different cultural geography, and it's a place that has been radically different from Western Europe in the past. But things are changing . . .

Eastern Europe is the *bookended* region, as the Plaid Avenger refers to it, and bookended in a variety of ways. The bookend reference means there is something in the middle being held up, propped up, or pinched between two bigger sides. And in this respect, physically, Eastern Europe is between the giant Russia to its east, and those Western European states to its west. (Western Europe—the region we just covered.) Ideologically, it's also in the pinch in the middle. And Eastern Europe has been a buffer zone between these two same giants—Russian culture to the East, Western European ideas to its west. And because of this, it has essentially been the battleground between these two teams, and therefore a fuse to the powderkeg of big conflicts. Where did the major transgressions of the 20th century start? World War I, World War II, the Cold War? Yep . . . all got launched in Eastern Europe.

This region had been marked for a very long time by **devolution**, or shattering apart; big political entities breaking down into smaller units. This region is also distinct because it has been a **buffer zone** and a **battleground of ideologies** throughout the 20th century. It was a buffer between Russia and Western Europe, and as such, was a battleground for the Cold War. Commies in Russia thought one way; dude-ocracies in Western Europe thought another way; and everyone in Eastern Europe was caught in the middle. The book getting squished by the bookends.

On top of that, we're going to see that there are a lot of historical influences that have permeated Eastern Europe proper, making it extremely diverse in every aspect you can think of: linguistically, ideologically, religiously, ethnically, culturally . . . It's all here. This diversity is one of the reasons Eastern Europe has historically yanked itself in lots of different directions and shattered apart. That's why it's a region, and just one of the many reasons why it's distinct from surrounding regions. Russia is Russia, Western Europe is Western Europe, and Eastern Europe is something in-between right now.

But that was then and this is now. If you want a key word, a single word that keeps coming up in the discussion of Eastern Europe, the Plaid Avenger has one: **transition**. This is a region in transition. Of course, every place on the planet is changing and moving around, but this is an entire region in which just about all facets of life are on the shift: with an obvious place they came from, and with an obvious place they're going to. All the states in this part of the world are going through this process of transition. What sort of transition, Plaid man? A transition from what to what? We'll talk about that in more detail as we go along.

THE PHYSICAL MIDDLE GROUND

When we think of Eastern Europe as I just suggested, we think of that region that's sandwiched between two other world regions. But if we just look at it physically, just physically for a minute, it's also kind of a buffer zone in a very natural sense, in a variety of different ways.

CLIMATE

The temperature and precipitation patterns of Eastern Europe are more **continental** in character than areas to its west. Being further and further away from the Atlantic Ocean, and particularly its most moderating Gulf Stream effect, makes these states more prone to increased temperature disparity: that is, it can get much cooler in the winters and perhaps even more hotter in the summers. As we progress further into the continent and away from large bodies of water, this continentality effect becomes even more pronounced. We'll see this played out to the extreme when we get into Russia, deep in the continent's interior, where it's way colder still. Nothing is quite like Russia, where the only thing that's not frozen is the vodka. The Plaid Avenger's beard done froze up in that place multiple times on secret subversive missions. And when we think of the inverse, we think about the coastlines of Western Europe. We think of a more moderated climate. It's not too bad there; it rarely freezes, even in places as far north as Great Britain.

Eastern Europe is in between, in that it's not quite as bad, not quite as extreme as Russia but not quite as moderated as the West. As you progress from Western Europe inward, into the continent, you get more continentality—meaning less moderation, more temperature extremes during the year, and certainly cooler, if not downright colder, in the wintertime. So climatically, they're in a zone of transition, as well, from the West to Russia. But don't let me mislead you: this place does have some nice climates, and in fact some areas are exceptionally rich in natural resources and soils. In fact, Eastern Europe actually produces a lot of food. The Ukraine has classically been one of the breadbaskets of all of Europe, and it continues to be. So there is a lot going on here physically, but it's just not quite as pleasant, not quite as moderated as its Western European counterpart.

LAND SITUATION

But the bigger, physical feature to consider with Eastern Europe is that big sections of these countries are landlocked. When we think of Western Europe, we think of maritime powers—'cause all of them have sea access, all of them have coastlines, and, therefore, they all have big navies/armadas, and they're all big traders and were all big colonizers. Not so much so for the Eastern European . . . if at all. Yes, there is some coastline along the Black Sea for some countries like Bulgaria and Romania. Yes, some of them have Med access like Albania and Croatia. And yes, some have Baltic Sea frontage like Poland and Estonia. But none of these states in what we're considering Eastern Europe were ever big maritime powers, and they're still not. Unlike their Western European counterparts, none of these states were big colonial forces in the world. They didn't have the advantages we talked about in Western Europe of sapping off the resources and riches of the planet by controlling vast areas outside of Europe proper. Eastern Europe is quite distinctive in that history answers us quite clearly when we ask, "Why are they poorer?" Answer: They were never maritime powers!

CULTURE CLUB SANDWICHED

But the last big physical thing to consider is that they were physically in the middle of some very big powers, that have very different cultures. What do I mean by this? Well, Eastern Europeans have their own culture, obviously. There are Polish people there and therewith Polish history and Polish culture. And there are Ukrainian people there with their own Ukrainian history and culture. But those folks are sandwiched between entities that have *bigger* histories, *bigger* cultures, and are *bigger* powers. And by bigger, don't misinterpret, I'm not talking about "bigger is better." In some cases that's

Order up! Who wanted the Turkey, Polish sausage with Russian dressing on rye?

true, but I'm just suggesting here that they're *bigger* in terms of having more of an impact within their regions . . . but also beyond their regions as well. A main one to consider is Mother Russia: a very distinct culture, language, religion, and ideology that by its very size and strength has dominated areas close to its Moscow core.

But they're not the only ones. 'Team West' and its cultures influenced the region, as has North Africa. You also have the former Ottoman Turk Empire down south. And, the Ottoman Empire is long since gone but Turkey took its place, and so there's a Turkish culture that abuts them. An important part of that Turkish culture is the fact that they are Muslim, and the Ottomans brought Islam into the region in general. And that's important to note, by the way, because perhaps unlike any other world region or other part of the world, you have a variety of world religions that come together in one place. Albeit, not always on friendly terms. You do have Islam which did penetrate into Christian Europe via Eastern Europe. But even before you get to that, you have to think about the divisions of Christianity. Of course, there's Old School Christianity that got divided into Eastern Orthodox; hey, that's in Eastern Europe. That then got divided into Catholicism; hey, that's in Eastern Europe, too. And then Catholicism was further branched into Protestantism, and that's in Eastern Europe as well.

So kind of a quick summary here. Eastern Europe in the middle of major world cultures—Russian versus Western versus, say, Arab Islamic. Also, it's the middle ground of major world religions—Christianity, Judaism, Islam, and all the divisions of Christianity itself, as well. These divisions all coming together—different ethnicities, different people, different religions, different cultures, different histories—has served to play out within Eastern Europe, more often than not, as a battlefield of all these differences. This leads us to the concept of Eastern Europe as, not just a battleground, but a shatter belt . . . a zone of breaking down, breaking apart bigger entities to smaller and smaller ones. But perhaps I'm getting ahead of myself. Before we get to this idea of a shatter belt and a breaking down, aka **devolution** (another great word), let's back up the history boat for just a second and take these things one at a time as they proceeded throughout history.

IDEOLOGICAL MIDDLE GROUND

As pointed out above, Eastern Europe is in the middle of lots of different cultures, different religions, and different ethnicities who have battled it out across the plains of Eastern Europe over the centuries. And I'm not going to bore you with all the details; we don't need to get into a lot of this stuff. I'll just set the stage so you understand the modern era, how some of these outside influences came to cohabitate within this region over time, and why perhaps it's still causing some conflicts today.

HISTORICALLY
TEAM WEST VS. RUSSIA VS. THE OTTOMANS
Historically speaking, and I'm only going back a few hundred years, Eastern Europe was kind of a battleground of big empires. We have some of the Team Western players like the Austrian empire, the Prussian empire (which is going to evolve into the Germans), the Russians, and the Ottoman Empire. Four big entities which virtually controlled all of what we consider now Eastern Europe. Just so you know the Russians and the Ottomans

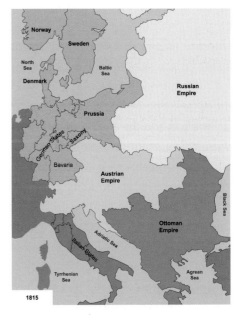

1815: Four main players.

1915: Good bye Ottoman Empire!

fought it out for long periods of time vying for control of these territories. The Russians and the Austrians did the same thing, as did the Prussians and the Russians.

And these empires have radically different cultures as well, in things like language, ethnicity, economies, politics, and religions. Differences which sow the seeds of conflict for generations. Consider only the religious differences for a moment more. The Germans and Austrians were mostly Protestants and Catholics; the Russians were staunchly Christian Orthodox; the Ottomans were Islamic. They are all vying for cultural and political influence in this region. Are you starting to get a sense of the confluence of conflicting ideas in this area? Empires trying to expand, fighting each other, in this fringe zone we're going to call Eastern Europe, as we get a little further along.

Now that's the background set-up. We need to get into the modern era, and in the modern era there are some major devolutions that occur. Evolution has the connotation of growth, of building into something bigger and more complex. **Devolution** is just the opposite: a term that simply means breaking down—devolving into smaller, simpler pieces. So devolution in a political sense involves a big empire or a big country breaking down into smaller countries; that's a real big theme for Eastern Europe historically and perhaps even into today's world.

WORLD WAR I

The starting phase of devolution in the modern era, was with the Ottoman Empire. The Ottoman Empire, which is a Turkish-Islamic empire, introduced Islam into southeastern Europe. Places like Bosnia, Albania, and Kosovo are still predominately Muslim today as a result of the cultural influences that the Ottomans brought in. You have to remember, the Ottomans were actually knocking on the door of Austria for a very long time in a bid to expand their empire into Europe proper, but they were weakened considerably and on the brink of collapse by the time the 20th century rolled around. Let's fast forward: this declining empire most unwisely allied themselves with the Germans during the lead up to World War I (you can read more about that in the chapter on Turkey). But the Germans lost that war, which resulted in the carving up of the Ottoman territory too. So by 1915, there is no such thing as the Ottoman Empire. It's subdivided, as you see in the map into a variety of new states already—places like Romania, Yugoslavia, and Bulgaria.

The Austria-Hungarian Empire, which kind of started World War I (or at least the assassination of their leader Franz Ferdinand started it off)—they kinda lose the war too, and the Austria-Hungarian Empire is the next shatter zone. Ottomans shatter first, then the Austria-Hungarian Empire shatters next, which creates a bunch more countries—individual entities which declare independence.

And we also have to point out that Russia was pulled into World War I, and got the living shit kicked out of it by the Germans. World War I is just so hilarious. Everybody declared war on everybody simultaneously. We have multiple fronts of people fighting and then losing. So the Russians get pulled into it, while dissent and revolution are fomenting back home by the way, and they proceed to lose horribly on the battle front. The result of which is that when our main Commie friend, Vlad "the Man" Lenin comes to power in Russia in 1917, he essentially says, "Hey, we want

1919: Good bye Austro-Hungarians!

out! We're out of World War I. We surrender. Germany can have all the territory that we have ceded thus far. They can have it. Take it! We're done!" And this was actually a very popular policy back home in Russia, which was on its way to becoming the USSR.

Even after the Russian withdrawal, Germany kind of didn't really win the war either and therefore they lose that Russian territory as well as some of their own. The result of which is a bunch new countries that pop up around 1920—places like Estonia, Latvia, Lithuania, Poland, even parts of Ukraine. They all declare independence. They're in this middle zone, again, this Eastern European middle zone between these major battling powers. A whole bunch of new countries pop up then, but they ain't gonna last . . .

Good bye Germans!

WORLD WAR II

Because, of course, Russia then becomes the Soviet Union under Lenin's tutelage, and, as the USSR grew in power, they wanted their Eastern European territories back. That brings us up to World War II, because the Germans are still over there hopping mad under Hitler and they want more territory back as well. Under 'der Fuehrer,' they decide to have a re-conquest of Eastern Europe and, what the hell, they'll take over Western Europe too. To ensure they could pull this off, Hitler got together with Stalin (what a fun party that must have been) and together these two signed what is called the **Pact of Non-Aggression**. Basically, Hitler says, "Uhh, okay, I'm gonna take over the world, but hey Stalin, you seem cool enough to me. We're both, uh, kinda fucking nuts, so, yeah, we won't attack you as long as you don't get in the way of us wiping out Western Europe. And we know you want some of these Eastern European territories back, so you can have those and we'll take everything else." Stalin, in all his wisdom, says, "Yeah, that sounds cool to me. Cheers!"

However, about halfway through the war, Hitler reneges. Why? Oh, that's right: he's fucking nuts! He decides to attack the Soviet Union, pulling them into the war. You know the end of the story: Since Hitler attacked the USSR, the Soviet Union sides up with the US and Western Europe to beat the hell out of the Nazis. And during this Nazi smack-down, the Soviet Union sweeps in from the

East, the US and allies sweep in from the West, and the Nazi smack-down finishes up with everyone high-five-ing right square in the middle of Eastern Europe.

Amazingly, if you look at the line where the Allies met, it's right in the middle of what we call Europe today. The troops met and high-fived each other when they finished killing all the damn Germans, or at least the completely crazy ones who continued to fight, then that was it. World War II was over. Peace! Peace out!

Well, kind of. It was great, for all of five minutes, before it becomes a face-off, again, but of new players . . .

THE COLD WAR

So after the success of the allied powers with the Soviet Union at the end of World War II, you essentially have what happens for the next 60 years—this ideological face-off. Now you've got the Soviets controlling Eastern Europe, where they swept in and

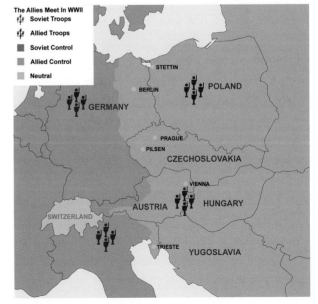

As Borat would say: 'Aaah-High-Five' in Europe.

cleaned out the Nazis, and the West who have swept in from the West and cleaned out the rest of the Nazis. Although they were playing for the same side during World War II, where they met became the new face-off of major powers. And this is more familiar ground we're getting into—the modern era. You, of course, know that this is the Commie world squaring off against Team West—the freedom-loving democratic capitalists in Western Europe. But how did this go down? How did this happen since they were all allies during the War?

SOVIETS TAKE OVER

Well, as I suggested, we had the Soviets, who were buddies of Team West at the time and helped wipe out the German threat. When it was over the Soviets said: "Well, you know what, you guys over in Western Europe are kind of crazy. We keep getting invaded by you. This Hitler guy was just the most recent one; the German Kaiser Wilhelm before that, and even Napoleon did it before him! You people are nuts!"

A PLAID AVENGER TIP ON WHAT NOT TO DO: Tip number 1—Never invade Russia. No one has ever successfully invaded Russia. Everyone who invades Russia loses. Always. Period. Napolean. Yep. Hitler. Yep. They sucked at it. And if megalomaniacs can't pull it off, who can?

So the Soviets said, "Hey, you know what you guys, crazy people over in Western Europe keep invading us . . . so we're going to stay here in Eastern Europe, for a couple of different reasons." One: they wanted to reclaim a lot of these territories they lost in World War I. That is Estonia, Latvia, Lithuania, parts of Poland and Ukraine were pulled back into Mother Russia—the Soviet Union. Two: Russia very openly said, "We're going to stay in Eastern Europe to create a buffer zone so that there are no further intrusions from the West." Now the way this turned into essentially a Soviet takeover to make this Soviet buffer zone, but it was done in such a way that it wasn't as imperialistic-looking as it truly was.

Here's how they did it. Just as the Americans, French and British hung around Western Europe to help with reconstruction, the Soviets claimed followed the same playbook by chilling out in Eastern Europe to mop up and clean up too. The Soviet official line was: "Okay, we're here helping out. We'll stay in Poland. We'll stay in Estonia. We're going to stay here in Hungary. We're going to help clean things up. We're going to help rebuild just like you guys are going to do in the West. And ya know what? We'll even help them run elections. This'll be great!" And lo and behold, every Soviet-overseen election that occurred in Eastern Europe resulted in a landslide victory for Communist candidates. What a surprise! Go figure. The Communist party just went through the roof of popularity!

Now was any of this real? I don't know . . . perhaps. Hell, I wasn't there. I was busy deep undercover protecting the Champagne stocks in the underground vaults of France. But in the east, the Russians really were liberators of many of these places during the war, so perhaps there was some sympathy, some empathy, and some popularity of communism at the time. But certainly not as much as would have swept a tide of elections across all of these countries. So, basically what I'm saying is, this was all farce. Soviets held up these elections and said, "Well, they all elected Soviet leaders, they all elected Communist leaders, so they're just under our umbrella now. We're just here helping out. Isn't that great?" It was, indeed, a Soviet takeover to create this Soviet buffer zone.

Folks in the Western European realm, and the US too, were exceptionally unhappy about these developments. Maybe you younger generations today might think, "Why didn't they just go in and get the Commies then? Get those damn commies outta there?" You have to remember that they were the allies during World War II; they were on our team, and we could not have won without them. And World War II had just finished too. Nobody wanted to fight a new war. Nobody wanted to then declare war on the USSR and have to do all that shit all over again.

So no one was really that happy about what the Soviets were doing, but they kind of happened anyway. This happened when Team West was busy rebuilding the west—rebuilding and restructuring: laying the foundations for the EU to rebuild Western Europe. It happened when the eastern side was being rebuilt and reoccupied by the Soviet Union. Where these two teams met during the war, of course, became the division between these two forces . . . and is where something called the Iron Curtain then fell. See map below for Iron Curtain.

Now when all this action was going down, all of those countries in Eastern Europe fell into one of a couple different categories that I want you to be familiar with. First, some of this territory of Eastern Europe was simply absorbed back into the Soviet Union and became part of other entities. Simply just went away. Parts of Poland were simply worked back into the Lithuania SSR and the Ukrainian SSR. So *absorption* was one option. But what the hell is an SSR?

Ah! That's the second option: some of these briefly independent states became *republics* of the USSR. See, USSR stands for the Union of Soviet Socialist *Republics*. Kind of like states of the United States of America, like Wis-

What's the Deal with . . . the "Iron Curtain"?

In 1946, British Prime Minister Winston Churchill delivered his "Sinews of Peace" address in Fulton, Missouri. The most famous excerpt:

From Stettin in the Baltic to Trieste in the Adriatic an 'iron curtain' has descended across the Continent. Behind that line lie all the capitals of the ancient states of Central and Eastern Europe. Warsaw, Berlin, Prague, Vienna, Budapest, Belgrade, Bucharest and Sofia; all these famous cities and the populations around them lie in what I must call the Soviet sphere, and all are subject, in one form or another, not only to Soviet influence but to a very high and in some cases increasing measure of control from Moscow.

This speech introduced the term "iron curtain" to refer to the border between democratic and communist (soviet controlled) states. Because of this—and because most Americans have no clue what a "sinew" is—Churchill's address is commonly called the "Iron Curtain Speech."

The "Iron Curtain Speech" was received extremely well by President Harry Truman, but much of the American public was skeptical. Throughout the speech Churchill's tone was very aggressive towards the Soviet Union. Many Americans and Europeans felt that this was unnecessary and that peaceful coexistence could be achieved. The United States had recently considered the USSR an ally. In fact, Stalin, whom the American press had dubbed "Uncle Joe" to boost his popularity during WWII, was probably the most pissed about the speech, feeling he was betrayed by his allies. The "Iron Curtain Speech," besides coining an important Cold War term, set the tone for the next 50 years of US-Russian relations (which is ironic considering it was given by a damn Brit).

Iron Curtain. But which side was Iron Maiden on?

consin is a political component of the USA. Some of these entities in Eastern Europe actually went from being an independent sovereign state, to becoming a republic of the USSR. I'm thinking specifically of Moldova, Estonia, Latvia, and Lithuania. They ceased to be sovereign states, and became a part of the USSR.

The third and final possibility, and perhaps the most important option, was that some of these sovereign states actually retained their sovereign state status but became *Soviet satellites*. Mainly, I'm thinking of Poland, Romania, Bulgaria, Hungary, Czechoslovakia, and East Germany. These were countries. They were sovereign states. They had a seat at the UN. However, they didn't really have control over their own countries, and everybody knew it. Everybody knew the Soviets were pulling the strings of the Polish government, of the

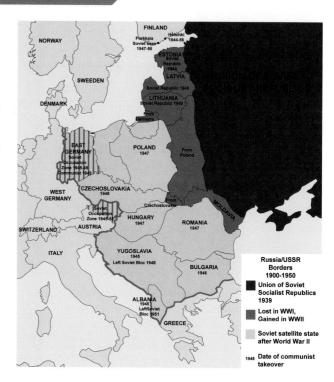

Romanian government, of the Czech government. Everybody knew it. They did have seats at the UN, they were supposedly sovereign states, but the Soviet Union really did control them, because the USSR had their patsy commie officials running the show in the governments of these places. Does that make sense?

That's the scenario as it was for about fifty years during the Cold War. The Soviets either controlled directly or indirectly (due to their massive influence) over every place that is now called Eastern Europe. Team West was on the other side of the curtain: the democracies, the free market capitalist economies that were supported by the US. Those are your two teams during the Cold War. Eastern Europe was close enough to see all the fancy shit going on in the democratic countries, while they were getting paid visits by the KGB to make sure they still loved being Commies. Of course now you see how Eastern Europe is a battleground in the middle of this most recent ideological game.

MARSHALL REJECTED

The other term I want you to think about as well, or at least understand and know, is that the Soviet satellite states did not accept the **Marshall Plan:** a US-sponsored program of aid, loans, and material support to rebuild Europe. The United States, in its infinite wisdom, said, "You guys are screwed over there! The whole damn continent's blown up!" Some smart folks in the United States government said, "We should help them out." In particular, Secretary of State George Marshall said, "Look, we gotta help these dudes out . . . We need to get them back on their feet, because if we don't, (1) their economy will get worse, collapse and then turn into complete chaos, and (2) if we don't help Western Europe out, the Soviets—who we are already worried about—are right next door. The Soviets will sweep all the way through if we don't do

something!" Probably a fair statement. That Marshall was a smart cookie.

More on the M-Plan: this aid package was offered to all of Europe. The US went to every single one of these countries and said, "Here, we'll give you a shit ton of money to help you out with industrial capacity and infrastructure to get you back on your feet economically." It was even offered to the Soviet Union. The countries in yellow text on the map accepted the Marshall Plan and took the aid, the sweet cash. Can you see what's happening here? Lo and behold, these are the richest countries in Europe right now. The countries in white refused the Marshall Plan, and those are the poorer countries of Europe right now. So while we certainly can't pin everything in the modern era on a singular aid package from the US, it certainly had its impacts back in the day.

If you look at this map of who accepted the Marshall Plan and who didn't, you'll see our same Iron Curtain division between Eastern and Western Europe again demonstrated perfectly. So we know that one reason why Eastern Europe is poor is because the Soviet Union eventually lost the Cold War . . . mostly because their economy sucked so bad. The second reason is they were stymied out of the gate because they were influenced by Russia to decline the Marshall Plan.

We've already talked about what a Soviet satellite was, and the Soviet influence in Eastern Europe. Make no bones about it; Poland would have probably loved the Marshall Plan. The citizens of the Czech Republic would have loved the Marshall Plan too, but they were under Soviet influence, and they were talked into declining it. Maybe there was stricter coercion than just talk going on. Who knows? That's why Eastern Europe is, generally speaking, poorer than Western Europe even today.

NATO VS. THE WARSAW PACT

But back to the story. Once those Soviet states and Soviet puppet states did not accept the Marshall Plan, the writing is really on the wall at this point. The lines are drawn. The Iron Curtain has fallen, and this is most evident by this nice Cold War relic map shown below of the formation of NATO versus the Warsaw Pact. Now NATO, you know all about NATO, is still around. And NATO was formed by the US and all of those Western European states who were looking over at the USSR and Eastern Europe saying, "Oh, we feel threatened by them. They might invade us. They might come and kill us.

Therefore, we're going to form up NATO, which says if any of you people attack any Western European state, the US is going to come to our aide—all the NATO countries will come to their aide." That's why NATO was formed, on one side of that Iron Curtain.

The USSR, not to be outdone, said, "Oh yeah? You guys have your own NATO club? Fine! We have our own club, too. We're calling it the Warsaw Pact." And the **Warsaw Pact**, was essentially an anti-NATO device based on the same premise that an attack on one constituted an attack on all. Of course everyone knows its bunk, since the participating countries were simply puppets of the USSR anyway. But the Soviets say, "Oh, no, no, no. Everybody's free around here. So we asked Poland if they wanted to join, and they said yes. We asked Romania, and they said yes too." The goofball Soviets even went out of their way to name it the Warsaw Pact to try and demonstrate that it was the Poles who had thought it up. Yeah right.

So what you have is kind of an entrenchment of ideas—NATO on one side, Warsaw Pact on the other. Free western democracies on one side, the Communist Commies on the other. And, again, why am I talking about this in detail? Because that's what Eastern Europe has been through for the last 60 years. Now you know the end of the story, though. It ain't going to last for too much longer as we approach the modern era . . . .

This is a sweet Cold War relic!

THE THAWING

So what's happening today? What we've had since around 1988 is that the Soviet Union began to **devolve**. There's that word again! The Soviet Union fully collapses in 1990. They finally figure out, "We can't do it anymore. We give up." During this entire Cold War, the Soviets kept insisting that the Eastern European states were voluntarily part of their sphere of influence, and specifically told the states themselves: "If you guys don't want to be part of the Soviet Union, just have a vote and we'll let you out." Basically that was a bluff. But occasionally the peoples some of these countries would take them up on it, and have street demonstrations and stuff like that. Every time that happened, the Soviet Union sent in the tanks and shut it all down. The Soviets were lying their asses off. They'd say, "No, really, you guys are sovereign states. Really!" wink wink, nudge nudge.

As 1989 approached, when the Soviet Union started to collapse, this notion creeps back up again. You may have heard of this Gorbachev guy. He's floating around saying, "The Soviet Union's in trouble for lots of different reasons. However, if you guys over in Poland want self-determination, maybe we'll *think* about letting you guys go again. If you really want self-determination, go ahead and have yourselves a vote." This caused an explosion. Once a little bit of the leash was let out, everybody ran. What you had was an instantaneous devolution, where Eastern Europe pulled away as rapidly as possible from the Soviet Union. You see here in this independence dates map is that the USSR, a single political entity, had turned into fifteen different countries virtually overnight.

INDEPENDENCE DATES POST-USSR

Free at last!

Czechoslovakia, Poland, Hungary and lots of other places said "Hell yeah! The Soviet Union is going to let us out! Good, we vote to be out, we're out! We're truly sovereign again, we're free!" Places like Estonia, Latvia, and Lithuania said, "We want out too!" Romania, Bulgaria, Ukraine, "We're out!" Everyone wants out. But it didn't stop there! Even after all these states are out, places like Czechoslovakia said, "Uhh, we're already out, and we want to devolve further into the Czech Republic and Slovakia for lots of different reasons." (see **What's the Deal with . . . the Velvet Revolution?** box below) There is another, separate wave of devolution in what was Yugoslavia, which all occurs roughly the same time, but for different reasons, but we will get to that later . . .

FLIGHT OF FANCY

But this flight from Soviet influence didn't end with declarations of independence. Oh no! That was just the beginning of their run for the border! Let's take a closer look at three states in particular that set the trend for what was to happen next: Poland, Czechoslovakia, and Hungary. These three states crystallize all of the stuff we've been talking about. During the Soviet occupation and the era of Soviet influence, every time the Soviets bluffed about possible independence, people in these three countries took to the streets to challenge it. As you can see from the map, the biggest street protests and riots in the last 45 years of the Cold War era took place in Poland, the Czech Republic, and Hungary. These countries were never entirely happy with being under Soviet influence. In fact, after World War II, they initially were like, "Yay! We're free! We can be just like Western Europe now!" But it's hard to be free when the Soviets set up a puppet government for you.

Now, guess which three countries pushed to get out immediately after the devolution process began in the early 1990's? Guess which three countries wanted in NATO immediately? Guess which three countries petitioned to be in the EU immediately? That's right kids! It's the same three countries: Poland, Czech Republic, and Hungary. As soon as it was possible, they immediately voted themselves out of Soviet influence. They were the first out of the blocks. But that wasn't enough for them. The peoples within these countries had been so pissed off being under the Soviet yoke for over 50 years that they wanted to ensure that it didn't happen again. So all three countries immediately petitioned to join NATO.

Hotspots of Uprising

We talked about NATO in previous chapters, so you know what the impacts of being a NATO member are. They wanted to become NATO members immediately to ensure no further Russian influence. I say again, *ensuring no further Russian influence*. These guys did not want to be anywhere near the Soviets; they wanted to be a part of Western Europe as fast as they could run to it! You know that NATO Article 5 says "Hey, anybody that's in our club gets attacked, then we take that as an act of war against all of us." So Poland, Czech Republic, and Hungary said, "Sweet! We're in the NATO club! Russia can't touch us. We're like the UK, France . . . hell, we might as well be Canada! Russia can't do shit to us!" That was exactly the case. All these countries also immediately petitioned to get into the EU. Eastern Europe, being under Soviet sway, was just as broke as the Soviets. They had not done well during the Cold War. So they started with a blank slate in the early 90's - broke, ideologically bankrupt, embracing the west, embracing NATO, wanting out of Soviet influence, and particularly wanting into the EU as quickly as possible for the sake of their economies.

RE-ALIGNMENT WHILE RUSSIA IS WEAK

As you probably already picked up from some of the details in this chapter, we are in an era of transition for this Eastern Europe region. And now it becomes quite obvious what they are transitioning from and to—from that Soviet era of occupation and control, they are mostly realigning and transitioning to become adopted into the capitalist democracies of the west. Now this happened at a brisk pace after 1991 when the Soviet Union officially voted itself out of existence, and the entity broke from one huge power into fifteen sovereign states, as already pointed out.

We also already pointed out, many of the states, Czech Republic, Hungary, and Poland, were quick to embrace the West; Estonia, Latvia, and Lithuania were right on their heels, by the way. Because, as you now have learned in this chapter, they used to be independent sovereign states in between World War I and the end of World War II, but then were reabsorbed by the Soviets. Those guys were always chaffing under Soviet rule, so Estonia, Latvia, and Lithuania were the second round of states that jumped ship into the arms of the West. Many others have since followed. All of this realignment and transitioning of these countries of Eastern Europe was occurring right after the Soviet crash . . . quite frankly, when Russia (and Russia became a new county, as well, at this time) was excessively weak. I mean, they just lost the Cold War, and they mostly lost the Cold War because they were freaking broke. You'll read more about that in the next chapter. So their economy was shit, their power structure is shattered, and their government is in chaos. It was precisely in this period of Russian weakness that so many of these Eastern European countries just *ran* to the west.

And this transition, of course, happened in a couple of distinct ways by some distinct entities we've talked about many, many, many times already in this great text. Number one was the EU—the European Union. Most, if not all, of these countries *immediately* applied for EU entry status. Many of them were soon granted it. As you can see by the maps below, there has been a progressive wave of Eastern European countries entering the EU since the very beginning of their "freedom" from Soviet domination.

As already suggested, Hungary, Poland, and the Czech Republic were the first three that jumped in. They were

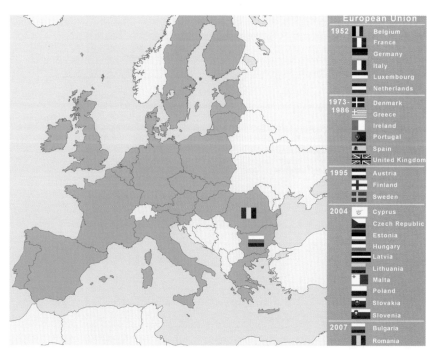

What's the Deal with . . . the Velvet Revolution?

What the hell's up with Czechoslovakia? Why did it split into two, the Czech Republic and Slovakia? . . . Slovakia? Were there two different ethnic groups that wanted their own self-determination and their own countries? Not really. While there are ethnic Slovaks and ethnic Czechs, neither group had much of an idea that a partition was even occurring. They couldn't have cared less. There was no animosity between these ethnic groups. So what's the deal? Why did they do it if there wasn't a problem? Why did they split?

They split because the western side of Czechoslovakia, where the Czech Republic is now, was much more like the West. It bordered Germany; it had the industrialized sector, and was richer, with a higher GNP. Slovakia, the eastern side of the state, was much more Russian/Soviet influenced. It was poorer and more agricultural. Folks in the Czech Republic, as the Soviet Union was collapsing, said, "Hey, we want to get into the EU. Help us out Plaid Avenger! What should we do?"

I said, "Well, let's look at this strategically. To get into the EU, your economy has to be decent and it has to be stable. As a whole, your economy is neither. But if you were to lop off the poor bastards on the eastern side of your state, your GNP per capita would go up! All your averages would go way up!" Indeed that's exactly what happened. People in what is now the Czech Republic said, "Hey, we'd be better off on our own without Slovakia dragging us down!" So Czechoslovakia underwent a transition called **The Velvet Revolution.** This revolution was like velvet, nice and smooth. There were no shots fired. From the stroke of a pen, one country became two.

Where did it go?

followed by a whole host of countries that jumped in by 2004, and the fun's not over yet. Romania and Bulgaria just entered in 2007, and there are multiple potential candidates. Most of the countries that constituted the prior Yugoslavia have asked for entry. And it's quite important to note that the Ukraine, a huge country and a former part of Russia historically, has applied multiple times and debates within the country are determining just how hard and fast they should push for EU entry. We'll come back to the Ukraine in a bit.

But perhaps the most telling tale to tell about the push for the EU in Eastern Europe is Czechoslovakia, a country that used to be one, that's now two—another shattering within Eastern Europe—simply to get into the European Union. That sounds bizarre—you've got to bust up your country just to join a supranationalist organization! Indeed it is a bit bizarre, and you should know why, when, and where that happened. It was called the Velvet Revolution.

That brings us to the other avenue for the 'Team West love embrace' by these newly independent Eastern European countries in the 1990s, and that was NATO. No surprises here. In fact, you can essentially look at the story told by those maps of EU entry and see that the NATO entry tells the same story. As already suggested, Czech Republic, Hungary, and Poland were quick to escape the Soviets and jump under the NATO security blanket. Estonia, Latvia, and Lithuania right on their heels—just like with the EU. And many of the other countries who joined the EU are also now NATO members.

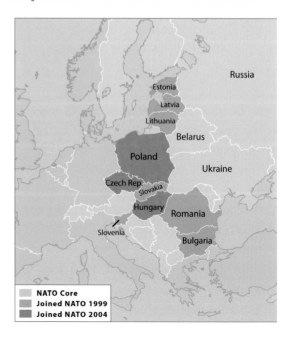

This has been miffing Russia a bit as they have watched the continued eastward expansion of these western clubs to their Russian borders. And that, my friends, is worthy of an entire new section . . . .

RE-INVIGORATED RUSSIA CAUSING NEW CONSTERNATIONS

Okay, so what's all that about? Well, this eastward expansion of western institutions, like EU and NATO, is now being slowed, stalled, or stopped . . . depending upon your point of view. What am I talking about? Hey, I'm talking about Russia, man. These guys are back. As I already pointed out, all of these Eastern European countries hauled ass for the west when Russia was weak—right after the Soviet Union crashed, when Russia was down and out, when they were poor, when they were politically bankrupt. But that time has passed. They're back and they're flexing their muscles in more ways than one. And by that I am thinking specifically of Vladimir Putin. Have you seen this dude topless? Watch out, the man is a menace! But seriously . . . okay seriously he is ripped . . . Russia as a great power is back on the world stage, and is no longer allowing encroachment into their arena of influence. We can look at some current events to underscore this Russian resurgence.

ISSUE 1: UKRAINE YEARNING: THE ORANGE REVOLUTION

Similar to the Velvet Revolution we talked about in Czechoslovakia, but the result wasn't a division of a country, rather it was struggle for control of a country. While the Velvet Revolution occurred fifteen years ago, the Orange one, in Ukraine, just happened in 2004-2005. Russia has exerted influence and/or control over the Ukraine off and on throughout most of its history. Russian influence is very strong in areas physically closer to it, like eastern Ukraine which shares a border with

them. A couple of years ago, the Ukraine had a big move towards true democracy. The scenario included two dudes. One's name was Victor Yushchenko: the pro-democracy, pro-EU, pro-

Bush behind Victor Y. while Victor Y. is backed by Putin. Y ask Y?

NATO candidate. A real poster child for the west. The EU supported him, and the United States thought he was awesome. They loved this dude!

His opponent, one Victor Yanukovych: an old-schooler, very conservative, more Russian influenced, and in fact, he's the candidate that Vladimir Putin from Russia came over and campaigned for. To try to help lock up the election before it even was held, the KGB even unsuccessfully poisoned Yushchenko! (See box: Yushchenko's Face) Damn! Talk about a street fight!

How hilarious is this? I can almost hear the boxing announcer: "In the red, white and blue trunks, fighting for Team West, hailing from western Ukraine, it's Victor Yush! And his opponent, in the red trunks, representing the red Russians, from eastern Ukraine, its Victor Yanu!" Hahahaha dudes, could you make this shit up? Victor vs. Victor . . . I wonder who will be the victor?

Why's the Plaid Avenger bringing up this election in Ukraine of all places? Because it exemplifies what's still happening in Eastern Europe, which is this battle between the West and Russia; it's a battle that's not so much for control but for *influence* within this region. Russia still pours lots of money into this area, and still

The Ukrainian

1 oz. Stoli vodka

2 oz. Grand Marnier orange liqueur

1 oz. Sunkist orange soda

Combine all ingredients in shaker. One quick shake and then strain into a shooter glass. The vodka represents Russian influence, the Grand Marnier represents Western European influence, and the soda represents a splash of US interest. It's a revolution in a glass!

What's the Deal with . . . Yushchenko's Face? Seriously, that thing is scary!

How the hell did this handsome man become so damn ugly? Did he live for a hundred years? Did he almost burn to death in a fire? Did his peanut allergies act up after dinner at a Thai restaurant? Nope, the poor son-of-a-bitch just ran for president in Ukraine. Viktor Yushchenko ran a campaign to western-ize Ukraine, including joining NATO. His main

Before   After

rival, Viktor Yanukovych, instead favored closer relations with Russia. Yushchenko was the victim of a giant mud-slinging campaign by Yanukovych, but more significantly, he was also the victim of *massive dioxin poisoning*. After people started noticing Yushchenko's face beginning to look more and more like the surface of the moon, he went to the Free University in Amsterdam for testing. The blood test revealed the second highest level of dioxide ever recorded in a living human being. Oh yeah, dioxide is the preferred poison of the Russian KGB. Although everyone pretty much knows that the KGB was behind the poisoning, no one has been able to prove it. After the election, Ukrainian officials announced that Yanukovych was victorious, even though exit polls suggested Yushchenko had won by a large margin. After days of protest, a re-vote was ordered by the Ukrainian Supreme Court. Yushchenko won the re-vote in what has become known as the Orange Revolution. So, Yushchenko became president and lived happily ever after. Actually, his face is still royally screwed and he will probably die well before old age. But as the Plaid Avenger always says, "You win some, you lose some, and sometimes you become horribly disfigured thanks to the Russian secret service."

likes to think of it as within Russia's sphere of influence. When this election went down, the pro-Russian candidate won, and everyone in the world said it was a fraudulent election. There were massive street protests, and this ultimately turned into the **Orange Revolution**. So much heat got put on the Ukrainian government, they threw out the election results, they re-ran it, and then the pro-western Yushchenko won. Now we can see this as part of an ongoing battle for influence in the Ukraine, which is representative of the broader battle for influence in the region as w hole.

So the Russian candidate was downed because the pro-western candidate won—down, but not out. In the Post-Orange Revolution Ukraine, there are still a lot of pro-Russian people. There's a pro-Russian political party, and indeed in March of 2006 the same party is gained enough seats to win back control of the Congress. The Plaid Avenger knows that those in the US think democracy's great, that the good guys won, and that's that. Not so! This is still a battle for control. It's not over! Most other countries have gone the way of the west, but it's definitely not over yet.

We can see this shit still going on in today's world, friends, because since the pro-Russian guy's party won the last round of elections, they got to choose the Prime Minister position. And guess who they picked? If you said Victor Yanukovych, you are right! So here in 2008, we're in this wack-ass situation where the President of Ukraine is a pro-Western, pro-EU guy, and the Prime Minister of Ukraine is a pro-Russia, wants-to-hook-up-with-Russians guy. Are you kidding me? In the same country? Dudes, this revolution ain't over yet.

ISSUE 2: RUSSIAN PETRO POWER

Now by this, I mean that Russia possesses vast amounts of natural gas and oil, something we will cover in more detail in the next chapter. For now know this: Russia provides something on the order of about one-third of all European demands for energy. That's a lot, dudes. By Europe, I mean Eastern and Western Europe depend on Russia for about one-third of its energy needs. So what's that got to do with current events? What's that got to do with a reinvigorated Russia? Just this: they got petro power now too. To reassert their strength and influence in Eastern Europe, they are playing the fuel card. Meaning, when those Eastern European states get a little too uppity, when they do things Russia doesn't like, (like, if the Ukraine says they want to join NATO) Russia says, "Ho, ho, ho. Hold on there comrades. You get

Caption: Russia keeps laying the pipe . . .

your oil from us. You piss us off—and the price of your heating fuel might double overnight. You piss us off a lot—and you get no oil. You dig that? It gets cold there in the winter too, don't it? How do you like them apples?"

Does this sound like fiction? It shouldn't my friends; it's already been occurring. Russia has raised prices at various points in the last couple years to essentially punish states that are doing stuff that they don't want them to do. They did it to Ukraine and Belarus in 1994 and again in 2006 when they doubled the prices to their Belarusian brothers. They completely dried up shipments to Latvia in 2004-06 to pressure the Latvians into a port deal. Most recently, the Russians shut down a section of pipeline that supplied a Lithuanian refinery under the guise that the infrastructure was just too old and needed to be replaced. I'm sure that was totally unrelated to the fact that Lithuania was threatening to veto an EU-Russian economic past. Total coincidence, I'm sure.

So, here we are in 2008 with the price of oil at $150 bucks a barrel, which could not please Russia more. Yes, they get rich off of it, but more importantly it has given them political power due to the economic leverage that controlling that commodity brings. Russia is like the crack dealer to Eastern Europe in particular: they've got the stuff that those Europeans need. If you piss off the dealer, you might not get your energy fix. That's not a situation the Eastern Europeans are happy about. The Russian influence is back. But that's not all that Russia is doing to flex its muscles in this region . . .

ISSUE 3: NYET! TO NUKE SHIELD

Another thing that's extremely topical—and we haven't seen the end of this story yet either—is the proposed missile defense shield system that is being pushed hard by the United States to be implemented specifically in the Eastern European countries that are NATO members. Specifically right this second, we are talking about the Czech Republic and Poland. This is seriously pissing off the Russians.

Maybe I should back up—what is this *missile defense shield* nonsense about? This is a concept the United States has been toying with for 60 odd years. It has never really come to fruition. But the idea is, you set up a bunch of missiles and a radar system which can detect if any missiles are coming into Europe. Then, you launch your missile to blow up the incoming missile before it lands. Again, it's never worked; out of perhaps ten million tests maybe they've done it once successfully, but that's not the point of this rant right this second.

It's the fact that these new NATO members in Eastern Europe have said, "Uhh, okay, yeah we still kind of kiss the US's ass, so alright we'll do it." At the most recent NATO summit which occurred in February of 2008, all the NATO countries—all of them—agreed to go forward with the US plan for the missile defense shield. And just to kind of wrap this up, Russia is seriously *pissed* off about it. They have been

Early version of European Missile Defense Shield.

pounding their fists on the table, saying, "Nyet, this shit is not going down. This is seriously aggravating us and we are going to use economic leverage and political leverage to intimidate the Eastern European countries that are going along with this."

What do they mean by that? Well, they've already made the fuel threat. And when the Ukraine said they wanted to join NATO, Russia said, "Yeah, that's fine. You join NATO and we will re-target nuclear missiles at you." This is something that Russia has also promised to do to any of the states that jump into the missile defense shield program. So this is serious shit, man. And, again, this story is still ongoing. The United States says, "Hey, look Russia. Come on dudes. The Cold War's over. We're not enemies anymore. This is mostly a defense system against . . . Iran, ooh Iran. Yeah. Iran's going to send a missile somewhere, so this is about that. Or other terrorists might bomb our NATO allies."

But Russia says (and you've got to empathize with them a little bit here) "Uh, yeah right. Come on. NATO's been encroaching to Russian borders for the last ten years. Now you're putting up this big-ass missile defense system. It's an obvious attempt to neutralize or marginalize Russian power in this region and in the world."

The Plaid Avenger's take on this mess is that the United States is probably telling the truth, but Russia sees it in a very different light . . . and, again, I always try to empathize. Not sympathize, not agree with, but empathize. The Russians do have a long history of being screwed with by folks over in Western Europe, from Napoleon, to Hitler, right on up through the 1980 US hockey team's miracle victory over the Soviets at the Winter Olympics. So in no way, shape,

Russians still pissed about that game . . .

or form, or any time soon, are they going to be okay with an encroaching military technology that is set up on their borders. And they're really pissed off about it. Vlad 'the man' Putin has been saying, "No, we're going to do everything we can in our power to make sure that does not happen, including veiled threats about missiles and open threats about energy issues." As always, sucks to be in the middle of the mess, but Eastern Europe seems to have a historical niche for it.

ISSUE 4: YUGO-SLOB-IAN MESS: KOSOVO CHAOS

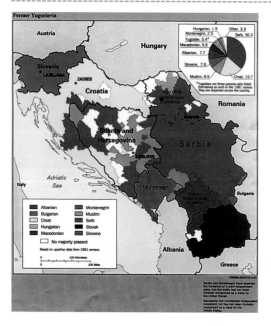

Finally, for the current events underlying what's happening in Eastern Europe with this reinvigorated Russia, comes the latest chapter in the disintegration of what was Yugoslavia. I've intentionally kept the mess out of the chapter up until this point because it's just a damn debacle that muddies the Eastern European waters a little too much to tackle it up front. But now that you understand the rest of the region, I am confident that you can now figure out this confounding coalition of convoluted crap with the greatest of ease. Well, we at least have to give it the old college try, since events here are once more crystallizing the fight between the West and the East. Let's do it.

The Plaid said earlier that Yugoslavia was different than the Soviet Union. Let's revisit them so you'll understand what's happening in today's former-Yugoslavia. They were never part of the Soviet umbrella. They were commies, but not Soviet. It was a communist state under the tutelage of **Marshall Joseph Tito**. 'Marshall' is really just a nicer sounding title than

Tito double vision: Josip or Jackson?

'oppressive dictator extraordinaire.' The Plaid Avenger suggested earlier, as we were talking about the historical background of this region, perhaps no other singular country has more different ethnicities and religions and cultures as did the former Yugoslavia. Emphasis on *did*.

They had Slovenes there, Croats, Bosnians, Herzegovenians, Serbians, Montenegrins; I don't even know what half these damn terms mean! On top of that, you have Christian Serbs, Muslim Serbs, also Christian Bosnians, a group that encompasses Orthodox and Catholic Bosnians, Muslim Bosnians . . . It's confusing as shit! It was a multi-ethnic, mutli-religious, multi-media mess.

So why has there only been serious conflict and devolution there in the past ten years? It's all because of Joseph Tito; not the Tito of the Jackson family, the other Tito, the dictator. Tito was a strong-armed dictator, like Stalin and lots of other folks in the communist realm. When ethnic or religious tension reared its ugly head in what was Yugoslavia, he sent in the army and crushed any uprising or disturbance with the iron boot. Through force, Tito held together this state full of all these different ethnicities and religions. Tito was the only reason it didn't devolve years ago. However, he died in 1980. Since Yugoslavia was essentially a military state, it was able to perpetuate itself for about another decade, until it fell apart under Slobodan Milosevic.

Look at the time frame and do the math . . . Tito

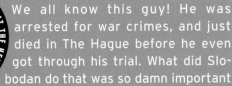 **What's the Deal with Slobodan?**

We all know this guy! He was arrested for war crimes, and just died in The Hague before he even got through his trial. What did Slobodan do that was so damn important that the Plaid Avenger has to tell you about it? We know from Chapter 3 that the ultimate test of sovereignty is that you can kill citizens in your own country with no international repercussions. The government can do anything it wants to in its country if they are a sovereign state; it's their right.

"I'm dead, and I'm still pissed off"

So what's the deal with Slobodan? He's another strong-armed guy like his predecessor pal Tito. Except when he comes to power, his state is disintegrating. He helped perpetuate the conflict that led to the breakdown of Yugoslavia. During that period, he essentially allows genocide to occur. He's an Orthodox Serb, which was the majority ethnic and religious group. He allows the Serbian people to start picking on and beating the hell out of the ethnic Albanian-Muslim minorities in the Kosovo region, which were perhaps petitioning for independence. He not only allows violence; he promotes it.

This starts to spiral out of control in the early 1990s to the point that people in the outside world—particularly Billy-boy Clinton from the United States and lots of folks from the UN—began debating the limits of sovereignty. The rest you know from our talk on sovereignty back in Chapter 3. After the US/NATO intervention, Slobodan is eventually arrested for war crimes and died while on trial in 2006. He made it onto our "Bastards of the Region" list because of his genocidal policies. Oddly enough, when his body was brought back to Yugoslavia, lots of people were cheering him. He's considered a war criminal by most of the world, yet lots of Serbs have him held up as a hero. That's typically a bad sign. We'll talk more about that later.

died in 1980; it held on for about ten years. That brings us to about 1990: the same time that all the other parts of Eastern Europe were devolving, splitting, splintering, fracturing, shattering into separate countries because of the implosion of the USSR. It all hit the fan in Yugoslavia as well. Without the strong-armed dictator there, it finally collapses. It goes into full-on civil war, with all of these groups that I've just suggested, and probably thirty more, all fighting it out for separate pieces of territory. Long story short, Eastern Europe in the last 15 years saw the USSR devolve from one entity to fifteen sovereign states, Czechoslovakia devolve from one country to two, Yugoslavia devolve from one country to five in the

1990's. In 2006, Montenegro became #6. And the fat lady has not sung yet my friends, which brings us up to current events . . .

So as you can see, the Yugoslavians have had kind of their own tale that's a bit separate from the USSR, but of course related, and that brings us full circle to today's world. And the shattering may not be over yet! Slippery #7 may be on its way . . . but this time it won't be without a fight. Kosovo may be the next to go. It is being widely disputed in today's world. In February of 2008, Kosovo declared independence. Immediately, a bunch of Western European states and the US recognized their independence, which, of course, *infuriated* both Yugoslavia and Russia. Russia is very much not happy about this. NOTE: Not all Western European states recognized Kosovo, and therefore the EU as a singular entity did not recognize it either. The big boys like the UK and France did, but many other minor European powers did not, for reasons we shall get to in a minute.

So, we have this situation that, again, crystallizes this new power struggle within Eastern Europe that's related to the old power struggle. Russian influence versus Western influence. The Russians, their historic ally Serbia (that is, what's left of Yugoslavia), and other entities around the world say, "You can't recognize Kosovo. That's bullshit. You guys were promising all along not to." Because, of course, the United States and NATO intervened in Kosovo, kicked out Slobodan, and protected the Kosovars. But they always claimed that they were merely preventing genocide, and not carving out a new state. So now Russia argues, "Hey, all along when you guys did that intervention thing, you said that you weren't setting up a new state, that you weren't going to let them have independence, that you were just going to stop the civil war, and basically you're all full of shit."

Russia is not alone on this issue either. China as well as many European countries have refused to support Kosovar independence because they think it sets a bad precedent. If there's one small, little group of people that are pissed off at a country and you're going to allow them to declare independence . . . then, damn, there's going to be a whole lot more shattering going on and not just in Eastern Europe. You're setting a precedent for other folks to do it around the world. Russia don't want the Chechans declaring independence; China don't want Tibetans declaring independence either. And it's interesting to note that places like Spain did not support Kosovo independence because they say, "Hey look, we have a small group of radicals who want an independent Basque country, so no way. There's no way we're going to support that, because then the Basque people will say, 'Well, hell, we're going to be independent too.'" So you see how complicated this issue has become.

But back to point: this is all about Russian influence here. And the Russians are supporting their old Serb allies, saying, "No, this is bullshit. We ain't recognizing Kosovo and nobody else should either." And the West is saying, "Oh, but, ya know, they want to be a democracy, and peace-loving and all that stuff. So we are going to support 'em." Yep. Eastern Europe right back in the middle again. I guess old habits die hard in the end.

But the point of this last section is that Russia is back. They are re-flexing their muscles. They are reasserting influence, not control, but influence over their old Eastern European sphere of influence, and the West is still pushing in as well.

CONCLUSION: THE TRANSITION IS ALMOST FINISHED!?

So a new era, a new time, and it seems like the Eastern European transition is almost done. Most of these states have joined the western block institutions, with perhaps just a few more to go. Most countries are in the EU. Most are in NATO. They are Europe now. Most are part of Team West. Most.

But Eastern Europe has historically been in a vice and perhaps it may be ready to explode again. This region does have a strange history of being under the influence of these greater powers to its east and its west, thus why I started the chapter calling it bookended. But somehow, Eastern Europe is the one that sparks all the trouble between the sides. Seriously, think about it. Go back to World War I. It was started in what is now Yugoslavia, when Archduke Franz Ferdinand (it's not just a band) was assassinated there by some Serbian radical. World War II started when Hitler invaded Poland. Then the Cold War battle lines were drawn in Eastern Europe, with most of the missiles either deployed on it, or pointed at it.

Why list all these transgressions again? To stress a not-so-obvious point: all major conflicts of the last century were sparked in this bookended region. Hmmm . . . that certainly is food for thought, isn't it? Major players seem to get sucked into confrontation over this swath of land between Russia and Western Europe. Sucked in, and then life really sucks for all involved.

Eastern Europe today . . . at least for now.

The disintegration of Yugoslavia also started here in Eastern Europe—go figure, because it's located there—and it's not done yet. That's why I bring up this Kosovo situation, which is once again pitting an east versus west, a Russia versus Team West. The Kosovo situation is promising to polarize these sides unlike really anything else that's going on here at the dawn of the 21st century. I know what you're thinking: "Hahahahaha what a load of shit, like a major war is going to start over some insignificant little hole in the wall like Kosovo?" Yeah you're probably right. My bad. How stupid am I being? I mean, the odds of that happening are about as likely as a global war being started over the assassination of an unknown Austrian Archduke while motor-cading through Belgrade. Ummm . . . oops. Bad example.

The question is, when will these people quit? How many more subdivisions can occur? How much more shattering before it's over? And, quite frankly, the answer is perhaps never, because it's outside forces which seem to promote, antagonize, and continue to push in this battleground buffer zone that we call Eastern Europe. But that's all for now. We keep talking about Russia being involved as one of the players in this battleground of ideologies in Eastern Europe, so perhaps we should now turn our attention to the Bear. Oh Vlad . . . are you out there . . .

Russia

THE BEAR IS BACK

Russia is the largest country on the planet. They were the Cold War adversary of the US; you know, the bad guys. We refer to Russia as the Bear, and this wild woolly bear seems to change focus and direction every semester that passes just as a wild bear hunts in the woods. I'm scared! Not really, but it is a region that is in transition, much like Eastern Europe, and in this regard it is changing every day. However, unlike Eastern Europe which has a very distinct direction of change, Russia is what the Plaid Avenger calls a fence-straddler— that is, it is playing the field in terms of who it does business with, who it has a political alliance with, and with whom it will throw in its future.

Russia has been a distinct culture, a world power player, a part of the Soviet Union, and a major shaper of world history and events of the 20th century. But in today's world, it doesn't have as much significance as it once did. It has experienced tremendous political and economic upheavals and can almost be considered behind the times here in the 21st century. How did this region go from a global power to a globally broken basket-case? And more importantly for our understanding of today's world, how is it successfully getting back into the game? All of these things and more, we will explore as we tell the story of the Bear.

One big bear. US/Russia size comparison.

HAIR OF THE BEAR

We always start our regional tour with a break down of what's happening in the physical world. When we think of Russia, several words typically come to mind: big, cold, and vodka. And there's some truth in this. Russia is a cold place. Russia is a big place. And those Russians do love their vodka, as does the Plaid Avenger when consuming a Bloody Mary. Big. Cold. Vodka. Check please!

Russia is the largest state on the planet, twice as big as Canada, the second largest. Does size matter? Do I even need to ask? Of course it does! Size matters in most aspects of life. This huge country crosses 11 time zones, spanning almost half of the globe. When the sun is setting on one side of Russia, it is rising on the other side! Just think of all the problems associated with infrastructure and communications in a state this big. Think of all the problems associated with just trying to keep all of your people within your country aware of what's going on at any given second, much less having to move things around in it, like military equipment.

Help! I've fallen in Siberia and I can't get up!

Don't even try to think about having to defend its vast borders. Your head will explode. Russia has a top slot in terms of how many different countries it borders, which I believe is now 14. But it's not all bad. This massive territory contains loads of stuff—what stuff? All kinds of stuff: oil and gold, coal and trees, water and uranium and lots and lots of land. And what do lots of people do with lots of land? They typically can grow lots of food, but that's not always the case in Russia because of its second physical feature—it's cold.

Maybe that's why the bear has such a thick coat. Virtually all of Russia lies north of the latitude of the US-Canadian border. This high latitude equates to the cooler climates found on our planet and indeed some of Russia lies north of the Arctic Circle which means most of its northern coast remains frozen year round. To compound matters, Russia lies at the heart of the Eurasian continent and because of this fact, has perhaps the greatest extremes of continentality expressed by its extreme temperature ranges, both season to season and also day to day. There are some parts of Russia in which the temperature within a 24-hour period may have changed 100 degrees—that is, it could be 60 degrees Fahrenheit at 3:00 in the afternoon and 12 hours later it might be −40 degrees Fahrenheit. That's extreme. Maybe this tough climate has something to do with Russian attitudes, their outlook on life in general. A

Siberia! The Spring Break destination of the Soviets!

tough place with a tough history which brings us to our last physical descriptor: vodka.

Russia is the greatest consumer of vodka on the planet. Both in terms of total quantity and per capita consumption, no one can touch the Russians when it comes to drinking vodka. I would like to think that we here in the United States could take back that top slot from the Russkies. We beat them in the Cold War . . . we should be able to take them in the beverage war eventually. But there is much work to do on this front, and we all have to do our part. Hang on while I mix a White Russian. Ok, sorry, I'm back. Perhaps it's the bleak and challenging climate that makes the Russian life so hard and vodka consumption a necessity to deal with the challenge. Perhaps this is why vodka is such an integral part of Russian history. Did someone say Russian history?

FROM CUB TO GRIZZLY

So how did the Russian state get to be the largest country on the planet? How did it get so much stuff? Where did these guys come from? What does it mean to be Russian? The "original Russians" were actually Swedish Vikings who moved into the area around modern day Moscow to Kiev, probably around 1200 to 1000 B.C.E. Thus Russians look European and share many of their cultural traits.

HISTORIC GROWTH

Looking at the maps across the bottom of the page, we can see that Russia, in 1300, was more like a kingdom than an empire, and indeed it was not a huge territory. It was a small enclave of folks that called themselves ethnically Russian but were politically subservient to the real power brokers of that era: the Mongols. **The Golden Horde** was a political subunit of the Mongol Empire that controlled parts of Russia and Eastern Europe at the time. It was not until 1480, under the leadership of Ivan the 3rd, aka **Ivan the Great,** that Russia stood up to the Mongols, threw off the yoke of Mongol oppression, and began its growth into the land juggernaut we know today.

Ivan unites his people, kicks some Mongol ass, and expands the empire. His son, Ivan the 4th, aka **Ivan the Terrible,** continues this trend by feeding the Bear and expanding the empire further. Ivan the Terrible earned his name by having an incredibly nasty temper, eventually murdering his son and heir apparent with an iron rod. Nice guy. Good family man. Should have drunk more vodka.

Soon after the Ivans created this empire called Russia, an imperial family line is put into place that lasted uninterrupted up until the 20th century. These are the Romanovs, to whom you've probably heard references before. I'm not going to go into great detail on all of them, but just to put a few into perspective, let's list some of the more famous names. **Peter the Great** pops up around 1700 and is known for many things, notably creating and building the town of St. Petersburg . . . I wonder where he got the name.

Why is this significant? Because it shows what Peter was all about, and that was embracing Europe. Even back then, Russia lagged significantly behind its European counterparts in terms of industrialization, technology, military, and economy. Peter was all about catching the Bear up. St. Petersburg was often called "a window to the West" because the city

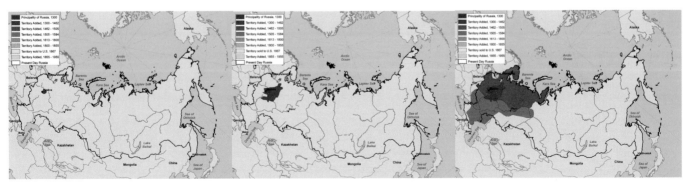

Russia 1300   Russia 1462   Russia 1584

embraced Western technology and architecture and there was a real sense that it was opening Russia to interaction with the rest of Europe. Here's another example of how Russia is tied historically to the West: the term "Czar" in Russia was taken from the Roman Empire's "Caesar." In addition, Moscow was often referred to as 'the third Rome' throughout history, as it viewed itself as the protector of true Christianity, in its distinctive Eastern Orthodox tradition. (Rome #1 was Rome; after the Roman Empire collapsed, then Rome #2 was Constantinople; after the Byzantine Empire crashed, then Rome #3 was Moscow). So Russia has embraced and associated itself with the West in many ways over the years, although in most cases, it lagged behind.

Peter expanded the empire in all directions. This brings us to an interesting component of the Russian Empire's growth, which is: Why expand? Many historians have speculated that there has been an inherent drive to expand the state in an effort to gain coastline. All major European nations with world dominance during this era had a lot of coastline and were maritime powers. Because of Russia's position on the continent, it is conceivable that most of its growth occurred in part to open up the coast in order to become a world power as well. This is speculative to be sure, but it does make some common sense.

One resource that's certainly driven Russian continental expansion was **fur.** Given the climate of this part of the world and the way people dressed, it certainly is the case that fur trading—that is stripping the exterior of live animals and making coats out of it—was the main economic engine behind the continued growth of the land empire. Cold climate = animals with lots of fur = animals we want to kill for their fur = fur coats worth lots of money = more land = more furry animals to continue driving the economy. And speaking of continued land growth, we come to another familiar name in history, **Catherine the Great.** She radically

Russian ambassador dealing with Napolean.

expanded the empire across the continent, was a familiar face in European politics, and helped propel the Russian state into serious power player status on the continent during the 1760s and 1770s.

The last face to consider during our old school Russian tour is that of **Napoleon.** Wait a minute! He's not Russian! True, but he did invade Russia in 1812 in one of the many great blunders in history. Napoleon was doing pretty well conquering Europe until he invaded Russia. Here's a little Plaid Avenger tip from me to you: don't invade Russia. Don't ever invade Russia. No one has ever successfully invaded Russia. As Napoleon found out (and later, Hitler), it's easy to get *into* Russia, but it's impossible to get *out*. As the French forces advanced to Moscow and eventually took over the city, they did so in the middle of a horrifically cold Russian winter, and because of their dwindling supplies were forced to retreat. They were attacked continuously on their way out. Bad call, Napoleon. Damn short dead dude.

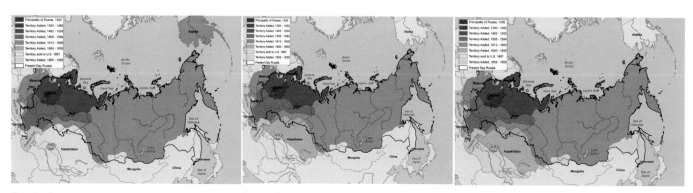

Russia 1800   Russia 1867   Russia 1955

Ivan the Great: Mangled the Mongolians

Ivan the Terrible: Skewered his son

Peter the Great: Wanted to be Western

Catherine the Great: had sex with horses?

I bring this up to reiterate a common theme in Russian history: Russia always seems to come out stronger at the end of extreme turmoil. After Napoleon's invasion, it comes out sitting pretty as the world's largest territorial empire. We will see this theme again after World War II.

SERF'S UP DUDES!

I've painted a pretty picture with lots of faces and names that you've heard before, but don't let me suggest that life and times in Russian history were good. Mostly they really sucked, for the lower classes in particular. During the imperial reign I've described thus far, life was fine for the royal court, but life as a commoner was brutal. We have a kind of a feudal system in Russia for most of its history. Serfdom in this country really turns into something more equivalent to slavery than traditional serfdom. What we're talking about here is a typical feudal structure where there is a lord who owns the land and under him, the mass of people in the country are tied to that land. As such, they have no rights to hold landed notes, no human rights, and they basically are workers or slaves of the land-holder. In combination with the fantastic climate of Russia, one can see how living here for most folks has not been a fun time. Chronic food shortages and mass starvations were common occurrences as particularly brutal winters, bad crop harvests, and repressive taxation systems kept the peasants in a perpetual state of shitiness.

So why talk about the plight of Russian peasantry? Because the dissatisfaction among a vast majority is soon going to culminate in a revolution; a revolution the likes of which the world has never seen. And it wasn't like the aristocracy didn't see it coming either.

In an attempt to placate the masses, Tsar Alexander II passed the sweeping Emancipation Reform of 1861 which was supposed to end this miserable peasant situation. WTF? Emancipation didn't occur until 1861? Damn! That's late in the game! That's the same year that the US started their Civil War in order to emancipate slaves! Unfortunately for Russia, this proclamation on paper didn't amount to much in real life, and the crappy peasant existence continued. By the turn of the century, freed slaves in the US had more rights than supposedly freed peasants in Russia. Not to mention that the vast majority of Europe as a whole had long since abolished both slavery and feudalism.

As we progress towards the year 1900, many Russian folks are still essentially slaves of the land. This is at a time when the rest of Europe is industrializing and getting more connected. Europe is having political revolutions, which are going to create states that emphasize equality for individuals, even the lowest classes. And folks in Russia know what's going on in the rest of Europe. They hear about the French Revolution and Britain's change to a constitutional monarchy. If you look at a political map of Europe's changes over time, you'll see that things start in the West, and these changes take a long time to make their way to Russia. Indeed, economic and political revolution comes there last. But when it does come, it comes big.

As changes are enacted in Europe, as common folk in Europe are getting more and more rights and perhaps even more and more wealth, Russia is stagnant. Russia is falling behind yet again. Dissatisfaction is also on the rise, and things in the 20th century make it quite a bumpy ride for the Russian Bear, particularly for its royal line.

RUSSIAN PEASANTS   4157-10

Dimitri! Where is the party at dude? You gots' all the ladies!

THE BEAR TAKES A BEATING

The 20th century, taken as a whole, has not been kind to Russia. It starts the century on a downward slide. As Russia falls farther and farther behind the times and as popular dissent increases, the imperial government does the worst thing possible: it loses a war. One of the things that will keep peasants in line is the concept of a strong central government, even though it may not be popular or even good. Citizens want a government that can protect them from foreign powers, protect them from invasion or destruction from somebody else. So even though the monarchy may not be popular, at least they maintain a strong military presence to guard their citizens and territory. When they fail to do that, full failure of the state is usually not far behind . . . and Japan provides the first kink in the aromor of the Romanov line.

GODZILLA ATTACKS

In 1905 the Japanese declare war on Russia. The Japanese, having risen in power for the last 50 years up to this point, begin encroaching on Russian lands in the east. This comes to a head when the Japanese take over part of mainland Asia claimed by Russia. **Czar Nicholas II** deems it necessary to go to war to reclaim this land and to put the Japanese in their place. Easier said than done. So the Russians send their entire fleet from Europe to take on the Japanese in the Sea of Japan. After this extensive voyage, the Russian fleet arrives to be beaten down by the Japanese fleet in a matter of minutes. It is the most one-sided naval battle in history. The entire Russian fleet is obliterated. Back home in Moscow, popular dissent turns into popular hatred after this stunning defeat. The **Russo-Japanese War** was costly and unpopular and served to really get people thinking about replacing the monarchy with a whole new system altogether. But the fun has just begun . . .

Back home in Russia, the peasants and workers alike have had about enough. Later in this same year of 1905, a general strike is enacted empire-wide to protest the slow pace of reform and general discontent with the aristocratic assholes. The system is broke, and the people know it. This protest is met with an iron fist by the government, and things turn nasty, fast. This 1905 Russian Revolution is best remembered for the legendary 'Bloody Sunday' massacre where cross-toting, hymn singing protesters were slaughtered by government troops as they marched to the Tsar's Winter Palace. Brutal! The Romanovs had restored order . . . but not for much longer . . .

"The Monk made me do it!"

WORLD WAR I

The Russo-Japanese War may have been damaging and unpopular, but at least it was far away. However the next phase of fun happens closer to home when Archduke Ferdinand of Austria gets assassinated in what will become Yugoslavia. This is the spark that ignites World War I and everybody declares war on each other. Russia has diplomatic ties with Serbia, who gets pulled into the war immediately, so the Ruskies have to jump in as well. As we just pointed out, this comes on the heels of a loss to the Japanese on the other side of the Russian empire. From the onset, World War I is extremely unpopular because people at home are saying: "Hey you already lost to the Japanese! Life here is sucking! Things are going down hill fast and now we are in a war? Nobody even knows what the hell we are in it for! Serbia? Serbia who? What the hell are you thinking?"

World War I was fought on Russia's front doorstep, and for three long years there is a catastrophic death toll on the Russian side. The Germans make huge gains into Russian territory and end up snapping up large parts of the front. Meanwhile back at the bear cave, popular dissent is growing wildly, fueled in part by the shenanigans of yet another famous Russian, Rasputin. 'The Mad Monk' as he is referred to by many Russians was a shaman/con-man who worked himself and his magic into the inner circles of aristocratic power . . . including being a direct advisor to the royal family themselves. In point of fact, Tsar Nicolas II was strongly advised by Rasputin to personally lead the charge on the front lines of WWI . . . even though everybody knew the good old Nick was not up for the challenge. Chaos then ensues both on the war front, but more importantly, back home too.

My death started WWI. Sorry!

My death made the Revolution irreversible. Sorry!

My death launched Stalin into Power. Sorry!

I'm still not dead. Someone get me the hell out of this coffin!

I don't need to get too much more into World War I history after this because the Russians don't have a lot to do with it. They get about halfway through it and internal dissent within Russia is reaching an all time high. The Bear reeks of revolt.

THAT'S REVOLTING!
COMMIES TAKE COMMAND

The revolt occurs in February of 1917 and Czar Nicholas II abdicates. In other words, shit is hitting the fan so bad that when the Czar, who had been out fighting in the bat-

"Let's redistribute some damn wealth, people!"

tlefield during World War I, comes back he finds that his people are in open revolt. He abdicates, putting his brother on the throne. Faster than you can say "I hereby resign from the throne" his brother abdicates too. Who is going to take over now? There is a temporary government that is set up, but in terms of who is really going to take the power, nobody can tell yet.

On October 25, 1917, this culminates into an event that people all over the world know, **the Bolshevik or Communist revolution,** led by our good friend, Vladimir Lenin. Communism is not something that everybody in Russia is just jumping up and down about. In fact most people had never even heard of it. Marx and Engels wrote about the concept in Germany and Austria; they weren't Russians. Lenin was a revolutionary even in his youth, and came in contact with a lot of these ideals during his youth and college years. His older brother, who was executed because of his socialist activism, also influenced him. Lenin became a lawyer, but was eventually exiled to Siberia because of his radical revolutionary activities.

In Siberia he wrote and published a lot of socialist literature, and became a prominent figure in the revolutionary movement. He eventually fled to Finland, and then Switzerland. While there, Lenin made appearances and speeches to other socialist groups in Europe. When the open revolt in Russia started to happen, Vladimir and other revolutionaries got on a train and headed back into Russia after a long absence from their homeland. Once Lenin

What's the Deal with . . . Rasputin?

The biography of Grigori Rasputin (aka the Mad Monk) is often fortified with folklore, which is fine by the Plaid Avenger because the folklore that surrounds Rasputin is hilarious. What is clear is that Rasputin prac-

Big City Russian Pimpin'

ticed some sort of Christian-like religion and gained favor with Czar Nicholas II by helping to medically treat his son through prayer. The Russian Orthodox Church didn't like Rasputin—mainly because churches never like competing ideology, but also because Rasputin loved sinning. Much of this sinning involved prostitutes.

During World War I, Rasputin advised Czar Nicholas II to seize command of the Russian military. This turned out poorly for two reasons: (1) Czar Nicholas II wasn't a good army commander and (2) while Czar was away, Rasputin gained considerable control of the Russian government and helped screw up the Russian economy. Needless to say, a lot of people were not happy with him. In December of 1916, a group set out to assassinate the Mad Monk. First, they attempted to poison him. The would-be-assassins loaded two bottles of wine with poison, which Rasputin drank in their entirety. The assassins waited and waited, but Rasputin continued to display lively behavior. So in a panic, they shot him point-blank in the back. When they came back later to deal with the body, Rasputin jumped up, briefly strangled his attempted killer, and then took off running. The group of assassins gave chase, shot Rasputin AGAIN—this time in the head with a large caliber bullet, and then beat the shit out of him with both blunt and sharp objects. Finally, they wrapped his body in a carpet and threw it off a bridge into the Neva River. But, the river was frozen over, so Rasputin's body just smashed into the layer of ice. The assassins climbed down to the frozen river and broke the ice under Rasputin so his body would sink into the water. They eventually succeeded and Rasputin disappeared into the freezing depths. Three days later, authorities found Rasputin's body and performed an autopsy. The autopsy revealed that Rasputin had died from drowning and, in fact, his arms were frozen in a position that suggested he died while trying to claw his way through the ice and out of the river.

Damn. That cat was a freaky-freak. And his lives ran out. Maybe . . .

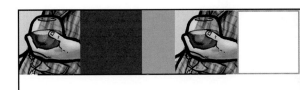

Russian Civil War Mixers

Red Russian

2 oz. Stoli vodka

1 oz. Chambord black raspberry liqueur

1 oz. Red Bull energy drink

Pour vodka and Chambord over ice cubes in a rocks glass. Fill with Red Bull and serve. You are a commie.

White Russian

2 oz. Stoli vodka

1 oz. Kahlúa liqueur

1 oz. light cream

Pour vodka and Kahlua over ice cubes in a rocks glass. Fill with light cream and serve. You are a loyalist.

returned, he became a prominent figure in the Bolshevik party and leader of the Soviet revolution.

One of his ideas that gained popular support was not necessarily that communism was the greatest thing ever, but that, "We need to get the hell out of World War I!" He received popular support for his Soviet ideas because monarchy, peasantry, and Russian life in general sucked. The power structure was completely unfair. What also gained popularity was the promise to get Russia out of the war in exchange for the support of his cause. Long story short, the Communist revolution became an internal power struggle, and the Bolsheviks came out on top. "Bolshevik" means "majority," but in reality, the movement was anything but a majority. The Bolsheviks had many political rivals in the struggle to control Russia. This was a very small group of people who enacted this revolution and took over the whole nation.

True to their word, as soon as the Bolsheviks took over the government at the end of 1917, they immediately bailed out of the war. They agreed to let the Germans have any invaded territory and signed a peace treaty. As you can see from this map, there were huge territorial losses as a result of this. The Russians lost territories that later became Estonia, Latvia, Lithuania, Moldova, and large parts of Poland. I am telling you this specifically because it is going to become Russian territory again after World War II.

Now as I just suggested, not everybody in Russia immediately embraced communism. In fact, there were many holdouts. As you might expect, there were conservative people in the aristocracy and the military who thought that the monarchy, the old established way, should return and things should revert back to the way they were.

As soon as the Bolsheviks took power, one of the first things Lenin did was put the entire royal family under house arrest. Shortly thereafter, a civil war broke out and from 1918 to about 1920 there was open fighting throughout the country. The Russian Civil War was fought between the new party in charge, the Communists, and the old conservative holdouts and much of the military. The parties who fought the Russian Civil War referred to it as "the Reds versus the Whites." Obviously, the Reds were the communists and the Whites, the loyalists. The Red Russians versus the White Russians!

So again our story here is that the 20th century is not very kind to Russia. It had a disastrous World War I and then an internal revolution which turned into a

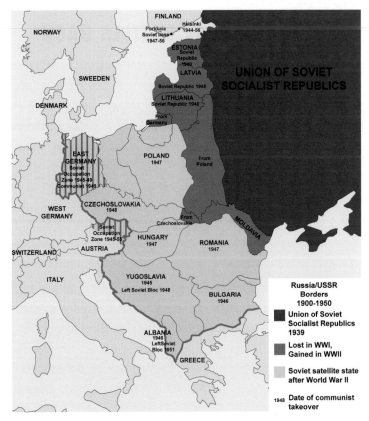

Check out the Russian losses in WWI.

civil war. The civil war is eventually put down. By the way, once the civil war broke out, Lenin ordered the assassination of the entire royal family. Why did Lenin do this? I thought he was a nice commie. The reason Lenin did this was because he believed that in order to succeed, Communist Russia had to sever all ties with the past. "You people are fighting for a monarchy? You want to restore an imperial royal line? Well, we will fix that! They can't rule a damn thing if they're all dead!"

This made the statement that no matter who wins the war, there will be no return to monarchy because there are no more monarchs. The Romanov line ends with the assassination of Nicholas II, his wife, and five children including little Anastasia, who bit the bullet as well. The civil war is finished by 1920, and the Communists now have power over the government and the country. Unfortunately, fate was still not smiling on Mother Russia, as the country years saw back to back famines in 1921–23 as the result of horrific winter weather . . . like the weather is even good in the good years?

What's the Deal with . . . Anastasia?
Anastasia was born the Grand Duchess of Russia in 1901. When the Bolsheviks took power in Russia, Anastasia's entire family was executed because of their links to the Romanov dynasty. However, legend is that Anastasia and her brother Alexei might have survived

Dead? Yep.

the execution. This legend is supported by the fact that Anastasia and Alexei were not buried in the family grave. Several women came forward in the 20th Century claiming to be Anastasia, but guess what: she's dead. Regardless of the intrigue and the great Disney movie, The Plaid Avenger is certain that Anastasia died of lead poisoning with the rest of her family. Lead poisoning induced by bullets. Lots of bullets.

However, by the mid-1920's the worst seemed to be over and it was time to get that commie transition on!

THE BEAR BATTLES BACK

The next event of great significance is in 1924 when Vlad "the Man" Lenin dies. Now for those vehement anti-communists, that was a day of celebration, but for Russians, it was not a day of celebration because Lenin was the founder of the party, a rallying post, a popular leader of the communist movement in Russia. He had the grand designs about where society was going, the ideal of equality where everyone shared the wealth, and the whole utopian society thing. So why is his death titanic? Well, because after he died, who was going to succeed him? The answer is Joseph Stalin.

STYLIN' WITH STALIN

From 1924 to 1953, Joseph Stalin, one of the biggest bastards history has ever known, is in power of what is now being called the USSR: the Union of Soviet Socialist Republics. The post–civil war title for Russia.

Stalin's ascension to power is tricky for several reasons. One: he is crazy. After he gains power, he is psychotic and becomes more psychotic as every year of his reign passes. He consolidates all power to the center under himself, basically as a dictator, and that's what he was. He set up the secret police that so many people know about, the KGB, who sent out spies amongst the people, and conducted assassinations of all political rivals, their families, their cats, their dogs, and their neighbors. Anyone who spoke ill of Joseph Stalin ended up in a grave with a tombstone over his head. No, I take that back. They ended up in a mass grave with dirt over their heads. He was a nasty guy in a tough place in an extremely ass-kicking century for Russian history. Our story is not over yet kids, the fun is still not done!

Before I go any further, I should say there is always a bright side to every individual. Smokin' Joe Stalin's bright side was that part of the commie plan was to consolidate agricultural lands and speed industrialization. The reds wanted to catch the country up with the rest of the modern world economically, technologically, and militarily. And as much as I hate to admit it, that is exactly what occurs during the Stalin era.

Essentially Stalin oversaw a 'crash course' of modernaization, industrialization, and collectivization. These hugely ambitious goals could not have been aceived just by planning though: the Russian people themselves have to be given a large share of the credit to have pulled this off. Perhaps Stalin's biggest contribution to these gains was not just organization and planning, but he somehow instilled a die-hard sense of uber-patriotic nationalism in the people that made for explosive societal gains. Specifically, the Russian people were convinced to work harder, work longer, make more out of less, consume less, and totally bust ass for the country, not for themselves.

Of course, Joe used all sorts of coercion and open force to achieve these aims when necessary. And again, he was nuts. But if we are going to credit Stalin with anything besides being the biggest bastard of the 20th century, we can credit him with the Soviet infrastructure moving forward at break neck speed, and they do indeed catch up in a matter of a few of decades. I mean, hell, they did create the atomic bomb shortly after the US did, and even beat the US into space with the launch of the Sputnik satellite. Fifty years earlier they were all beet farmers. Now that is some fast progress!

THE BEAR ENTERS WORLD WAR II

By World War II, the USSR is starting to be a major world force. Before the war begins in 1939, Joseph Stalin and Adolph Hitler meet and sign a nonaggression pact. The meeting went down like this, brought to you Plaid Avenger style . . . Germany says, "We are going to take over the world, but here's the deal: we won't attack you as long as you don't attack us." Smokin' Joe Stalin, in all of his wisdom, said, "Ok, go ahead and take over Western Europe and the rest of the world. That sounds good to us. They were always kind of bothersome anyway . . . and ok. We won't attack you as long as you don't attack us. Deal!" So in 1939 Russia and Germany signed a nonaggression pact. The war officially kicks off in 1941 when Germany attacks everybody. Hitler later makes the fantastically dumb-ass mistake (after taking over most of Europe) of reneging on the nonaggression pact. In other words, he attacks the USSR anyway.

As discussed before about Napoleon, one of the greatest historical blunders for anybody is to invade

Stalin
Biggest Bastard Ever

FDR
American Hero

Churchill
British Hero

Joseph Stalin: Biggest Bastard of the 20th Century
Unfortunately, the award for "Biggest Bastard" is highly competitive. I mean, you got Hitler, Pol Pot, Mussolini, Idi Amin, Pinochet, Margaret Thatcher, and many more. But the Plaid Avenger is fairly certain that Joe Stalin is the biggest ass of them all. Stalin was one of the Bolshevik leaders who brought communism to Russia in 1918. When Vladimir Lenin, who was the original leader of the Bolsheviks, unexpectedly died in 1924, Stalin slowly assumed power. In 1936, Stalin initiated "The Great Purge" which lasted for two years. During this time, "dissenters" were shipped off to Gulag labor camps and often executed. Most "dissenters" were actually just normal folks who had been wrongly accused by other normal folks who were being tortured at a Gulag labor camp. As you can see, this was a self-perpetuating cycle. If everyone had to sell out eight friends to stop getting tortured, and each friend had to sell out eight friends, pretty soon you would have a hellton of political "dissenters." It's like an incredibly violent email pyramid scam. Anyway, "The Great Purge" resulted in the death of approximately 20 million Russians.

While "The Great Purge" was probably Stalin's sentinel work of bastard-dom, it was far from his last. Stalin organized a giant farm collectivization which left millions homeless and millions more hungry. He also continued purging dissenters until he died in 1953. Historians estimate over 45 million Russians died directly from Stalin's actions (this figure does not include the estimated 20 million Russians that died during WWII). What a psychotic asshole.

Lining up for daily vodka ration . . .
of 3 liters.

Russia. No one's ever done it successfully, and Hitler is one in a long line of idiots who tried. After he attacks the USSR, the USSR is then obliged to defend itself and is pulled into World War II. This is of great importance: the USSR is the real winner of the war in Europe. Once the Germans declare war on the United States, who joins the rest of the Allies, it becomes the Germans versus the world. The Germans are really in a pinch now as they are attacked on all flanks, the Allies on one side and the Russians on the other. Now, while I am certainly not going to devalue the role of the Allies in the west, Russia really takes out a lot of Germans and causes them to divert resources and men to the Russian front, which is the reason why World War II was won by the good guys.

Had the Russo-German nonaggression pact been upheld by Germany, it would be hard to tell what the map of Europe would look like today. It certainly wouldn't look like it does now, because the Russian death toll was astronomical. There were almost 9 million Russian military deaths, and at least 20 million civilian casualties. 29 million people total! Take 29 and multiply it by a thousand, then take that and multiply it by another thousand! The Plaid's not trying to insult your intelligence. I just want you to take a second and think about how many folks died in this thing.

This was some of the most brutal fighting on the entire continent. The Russian front is bloody, it's nasty, it's deadly, and when all is said and done, the Russians beat the shit out of Germany. It is part of the main reason the Germans had to surrender in the end. I really want to stress the Russian losses. 29 million killed. We think about just the US's role in World War II, which was great by the way, but the US suffered maybe half a million to Russia's nearly 30 million deaths! So, as a result of WWII, Russia experienced a titanic loss and made a major impact on the European theater of war. Of course the war ends in 1945, the end of which sets up the scenario for the next 50 years . . .

IS IT GETTING CHILLY IN HERE? THE COLD WAR

At the conclusion of the war the Allies come in from the west and the Russians are mopping up in the east and they meet halfway through Europe. They all do high fives. They split Germany in half. Hitler is dead in the bunker, and we have a line where the Allies meet after the war. The Allies were the United States, Britain, France, and the USSR. That's right! Smokin' Joe Stalin was on our team! Where the two forces met, as you see on this map, is halfway through Europe. **The Iron Curtain.**

What does this mean? Well the Russians have come in as a mop-up campaign and after the war was over and everyone finished celebrating, the Soviets said, "Maybe we will just stay here for a little while. We'll make sure everything has settled down. We'll help rebuild this side of Europe." Of course the United States, under the **Marshall Plan,** was building up Western Europe. The Soviets were playing kind of the same role in Eastern Europe. Both parties occupied Germany to make sure it wouldn't start up trouble again—thus we had an East Germany and a West Germany, which reflected events happening in Europe as a whole.

In their effort to do this, the Soviets were pretty sinister. Under Soviet tutelage, elections were held all over, in places like Poland, Czechoslovakia, Hungary, Yugoslavia, and parts of Austria. And we all know the outcome . . . lo and behold, the Communist party won resounding victories in every single place they held a vote! Everyone in the West knew this was a farce, but

The metallic drapes were drawn.

nobody wanted to start another war. Remember they were allies, and they helped defeat the Germans together. The United States just wanted to get the hell out of there. They were not about to start a new war with Russia. The Western governments hesitantly went along with these newly voted communist states.

This sets up a scenario where puppet governments replace the previous governments. There's a term for this you should already know called **soviet satellites.** Some examples were sovereign states like Poland, Czech Republic, and Hungary that actually had seats at the UN—but everybody knew that the Soviets had the real control. These were puppet governments, to give the illusion of being expressive governments of their people. The situation simply evolved into Soviet occupation and control at this point. One of the reasons Western Europe and the United States allowed this to happen is that the Soviets very adeptly pointed out that they were staying in these Eastern European nations to make them a buffer zone because countries in Western Europe historically kept attacking them. That was true (e.g., see Napoleon, see Hitler).

These Eastern European states behind the curtain, that end up being Soviet satellites, are actually parts of the territory that the Soviets had lost at the end of WWI. So the Soviets regain that loss. I like to point this out because it plays into what is happening in today's world. Whole countries that were sovereign states for a while between World War I and World War II, like Estonia, Latvia, Lithuania, Belarus, and the Ukraine, were totally reabsorbed by the Soviet Empire. These places had declared independence after World War I and then they suddenly found themselves no longer sovereign states but republics or substates of the Soviet Union. That's why the map of Eastern Europe changed so rapidly. Places came and went as sovereign states were reabsorbed.

COMMIE ECON 101

The first half of the 20th century was fairly repressive, brutal, chaotic, and completely violent for Russia, but things stabilized during the Cold War. We have already set the stage in Europe for East versus West, which is going to turn into a global phenomenon that has shaped virtually every aspect of every region that we talk about in this book. So what's the deal with the USSR as full-fledged commies after World War II?

As I have suggested previously, they had massive growth during Stalin's regime. He dies shortly after World War II, but a lot of the industrialization which was radically successful under him continues on. Many of the programs, while oppressive and brutal, make the state a stronger world power. Indeed, it is the rise of the USSR which creates the bipolar world that defines the Cold War. Stalin does a lot, gets them up in the big leagues, and then checks out. He brings about massive industrialization particularly in the weapons sector, which continues after his death.

What happens under the Soviet experiment post–World War II? What do they do? What does it look like there? What do they make? What do they produce? How is that going to be part of their eventual undoing? During the Soviet era one of the primary goals, even under Lenin, was that they had to catch up industrially. They did this by centralizing everything. That's what communism is known for. The state runs everything, all aspects of politics (of course that's easy, it's what all governments do), but also all aspects of the economy (and that's typically not what the governments do). But that is the communist way—full political and economical control of the entire country.

This is called **central economic planning,** and it entails the government's approval of where every 7-11 is, where every ounce of grain is grown, where railroad tracks are laid down, where coal will be mined, where whole cities will be built to support something like an automotive industry. Every single aspect of life that we take for granted in a capitalist system is controlled in the Soviet sphere. This is done very early in the Soviet Empire to accomplish specific goals, one of which is called **forced collectivization.** Russia had been a peasant society, land based, rural, farmers digging around in the dirt, for hundreds of years. It can't do that shit in the 20th century if it is going to catch up and become a world power; it needs to get people off the land and into the cities. Why the cities? To work in the big factories that are industrializing and creating stuff.

Tanks for the memories, commies!

So goal number one is forced collectivization. Pool all the land together, because it now belongs to the state. "You used to have rights to it and a deed on it, Dimitri, and maybe you used to grow tomatoes on it, but those days are gone now, comrade! You've got two options: go to a city or get in a collective, government regulated, growing commune." See these are words we know now. The state is going to control all the land and agricultural production because the state can have one huge tractor that can do the work of 1,000 men, and it can have pesticides and fertilizers, which can make huge monoculture crops. This new system can produce tons more food, and indeed this is exactly what it does. And it does it with fewer dudes. Whereas 1,000 dudes had to farm a piece of land before, now just 10 can get the job done. 990 dudes can head to the city to accomplish the next goal: **rapid industrialization.**

To achieve rapid industrialization, the Soviet government needed to get everybody in and around the city into big factories. What are the factories going to produce? All of the things the West has that the Soviets need to catch up on. Things like tanks, petrochemicals, big guns, rifles, maybe some big fur coats every now and again because it's cold there, aircraft carriers, missiles, bulldozers, heavy machinery, etc. The question you need to ask yourself at the same time is: what are they not making? The big difference between the communist expression and the capitalist expression in the 20th century comes down to this question. The answer is that the Soviets don't make the items that normal people buy. Instead they make huge stuff that only countries use. Like I told you earlier, the Soviet system stresses more work and *less consumption* by the individual so that the state can become stronger.

You have to remember, the Soviet way is not focused on individual citizens or individual rights. The Soviet government doesn't care about personal expression or fashion statements or if you like building model airplanes. For them, the Soviet Union was an awesome state and an awesome idea and its citizens should all be ardent nationalists and do everything for their state. By and large people were pretty cool with that, at least most of them were, because to not be cool with that meant the KGB would run you down in the middle of the night and shoot you. So people accept it. Lots of them even like it.

So what doesn't get produced in the Soviet economy? Consumer goods like cool clothes, sunglasses, lawn chairs, microwave ovens, refrigerators, independent-use vehicles. Anything that you'd go to a mall to buy today did not exist in the Soviet world. Knick-knacks did not serve the greater goal of the government, which was to catch up with the capitalists. That's just the way it was.

Now, as much as the Plaid Avenger likes to make fun of knick-knacks and other crap you don't need, it plays a role in why the Soviet Union unravels after a while. But that's for the next section. They do indeed catch up and they do become a world power under this system. One of the other things the Soviets can do with the big things like tractors and bulldozers and weapons is to export them abroad. These are items that the Soviet Union is still known for. If you look at what country is the biggest weapons manufacturer in today's world, it's still Russia. Example: the Russian made AK-47 is easily the most popular and most widely distributed rifle on the planet.

Russia also exported a lot of this stuff at cut rates to other countries around the world. Why would you export a bunch of missiles to Cuba? Oh that's right, for the Cuban Missile crisis to be kicked off. You also want to send around machinery and petrochemicals and similar items that you produce to make money and recoup costs, but more importantly, to promote your influence in the world. That is what the Cold War was all about: coaxing other countries to join your side by providing them with things they really need, building bridges, selling them weapons and chemicals, and maybe even lending money. Anything to get people on your side. The United States and the Soviet Union both do this all over the place.

Only in a few places does this battle of ideology turn hot and people start shooting at each other. Two places of note where this occurs are in Korea, resulting in the Korean War and in Vietnam, resulting in the Vietnam War. We might even go as far to say as this also happens in Central America for all the Central American wars during which both these two giants funnel in weapons so that the locals can fight it out between their opposing ideologies. The commies versus the capitalists in all these places is really what the wars are all about, and the two giants fund their respective sides.

CATASTROPHIC COMMIE IMPLOSION

So how does the Cold War end for the Soviets? We want to get into modern day. Why am I suggesting that knick-knacks on the shelf may have been the saving grace of the United States when all is said and done?

RUBLE RUPTURE

Well, because the thing that happens to the Soviet Union from the 1960s through the 1980s, when it gets really bad, is that it simply overextends itself. The United States and Western Europe's economies are based on producing everything. They build big weapons like the Soviets; they had petrochemicals, machines, and also had all those consumer goods.

When you have stuff that individual citizens can buy and sell, you don't have to solely rely on bulldozers. How many bulldozers can you sell in one season? How many missiles? So the US system ends up championing in the end because people buy knick-knacks all the damn time. People like to buy refrigerators and new cars and blow dryers and pet rocks. We also buy and sell bulldozers and missiles. So the long story short is we get richer; they get poorer.

Buy now! These things are flying off the shelves!

So yes, their economy sucked ass because it was based on flawed principles and was focused on items that eventually make it unsustainable. But there were other reasons these guys were going broke too. Namely, they liked to give lots of money and support to their commie allies worldwide. During this expansion of Soviet influence across the planet, they really start to overextend themselves. They are giving stuff to Angola and the Congo in Africa; they are buying sugar from Cuba that they don't even need just so Cuba will be their ally, and they are lending money to places in Southeast Asia. By the 1980s, they are going broke while their economy is stumbling too.

Another ruble-draining effort was being stupid enough to get involved in a war in Afghanistan. Geez! Who would be dumb enough to get bogged down in an unwinnable war in Afghanistan? Oh . . . ummm . . . sorry US and NATO . . . I forgot about current events for a second. You guys should have really learned more from the Soviet experience, which was a . . .

AFGHAN BODY SLAM

But let's go into it in a little bit more detail on this mess, because it does play into current events more than most want to admit. Ever since the USSR had come into existence, it had crept further and further into control of Central Asia. eventually absorbing all of those -stan countries and making them into Soviet republics. All except one: Afghanistan. The USSR stays very cozy with the leadership of the country though, and gives them lots of foreign aid to endure that they stay under the commie sphere of influence.

However, there are other forces within Afghanistan that don't like the Soviets, and for that matter don't like their own leaders either. A group of Muslim fighters we'll call the mujahideen decide to wage a war to overthrow the Afghan government. The government fears a greater coup is at hand, so it invites the USSR to invade them to help out. Sounds good so far, huh? Yeah right. This is a huge freakin mistake for the Soviets . . .

In 1979 the Soviets invade Afghanistan, and start a decade-long war which will serve to demoralize and humiliate them. Remember, this is during the Cold War, so the US CIA (under orders from the government) funnels in shit tons of weapons and training to the mujahideen to keep the Soviets pinned down. And it works like a charm. In fact, it works too good! After the mujahideen eventually repel the Soviets, they then proceed to have a civil war, and the winners of that civil war become the Taliban. Damn . . . any of this starting to ring a bell yet? The Taliban are buddies with and shelter al-Queda, and after 9/11, the US declares war on both groups. And now the US finds itself fighting against forces it helped arm and train back in the 70's. Oops.

But that is a tale for another time; back to our soviet story. The Soviet/Afghan campaign of 1979-89 is a titanically devastating war for Russia which I compare to the Vietnam War for America. This active conflict in Afghanistan starts to siphon away resources at a rapid rate. At the end of ten years of fighting, many Russian lives have been lost, many Russian rubles have been spent, and all for nothing as they are forced to walk away from the whole damn mess with their tail between their legs. Check out an awesome new flick which shows how this went down: *Charlie Wilson's War* starring Tom Hanks. And it has an ass shot of Hanks too. Double bonus.

THE GREAT COMMUNICATOR SAYS: "I HATE COMMIES"

Once the 1980s roll around, we have to introduce a new component: the Reagan Factor. Ronald Reagan is the most hilarious president ever in the Plaid Avenger's opinion, and is certainly one of the reasons for the demise of the USSR. He is often credited as being the entire reason, which is preposterous, but his administration does a lot to accelerate the processes that are in play regarding Russia's economic decline. The drive for military buildup during the Cold War was all fine and dandy when the Soviet Union was expanding and growing industrially and economically, but this starts to take its toll on them in the stagnant 1970s and 1980s. The Americans would develop a new type of missile, so the Russians would also develop a similar one in order to stay competitive. Then the Americans would build a new type of tank, so the Russians would then build one. It's a "keeping up with the Jones" sort of situation. You have to be as cool as your neighbors by having the same stuff, the newest and coolest stuff. That had been happening since the 1950s. The Space Race is a classic example of that competitiveness. Then in the 1980s: enter Ronald Reagan.

"I hate commies."

Ron hates commies. If you are going to learn one thing about Ron, it's that Ron hates commies. He hated commies when he was a Hollywood actor and ratted out a bunch of other actors as communists during the McCarthy hearings. He hated commies when he was the governor of California, and he really hated commies when he became the president of the United States. He hated them so much that he was willing to send money and arms to anybody on the planet under the guise that they were fighting commies. So Ron Reagan hates commies. Have I made that clear yet? When he came in power in 1980, he had to deal with domestic issues because the US economy sucked, but one of the primary things that he and his administration did very early on is accelerate military spending. This was a very clever move because it did a couple of things at one time: (1) It helped the American economy by creating jobs building more bombs and shit, and (2) Reagan knows that the Soviets are trying to keep up militarily, so he is making them spend more money too.

This spending craze happens during the entire decade of the 1980s, just as internal dissent becomes more prevalent within the Soviet Union. Rioting breaks out in places like Czechoslovakia, Poland, and Hungary, and as the economy continues to worsen in the Soviet Union, people begin to starve to death. The US media showed scenes of people in long bread lines in the Soviet Union. These guys weren't just broke; they were going hungry at the same time they were spending millions, if not billions, on weaponry to keep up with the US. It was a crafty move that pays off huge dividends for the US. When the final Soviet leader comes to power, Communist Party Secretary General Mikhail Gorbachev, he inherited a state that was broke and riddled with holes. Mikhail comes to power and he knows his administration is screwed. The comrades can continue to lie to themselves and use the KGB to scare the hell out of everyone so they don't utter it out loud, but the people at the top know that the party is over.

20TH CENTURY COMMIE COUNTDOWN

Lenin: 20th century premier commie and snappy dresser.

Stalin: 20th century premier bastard with a serious 'stache.

Krushchev: Placed missiles in Cuba. Nice job laughing boy.

Brezhnev: Patented the "Unibrow," kin to Herman Munster.

Andropov: He "dropped ovv" after only 16 months in office.

Chernenko: Not to be outdone, he croaked after only 13 months.

Gorbachev: "Damn, this place is falling apart."

HOLY GLASNOST THIS IS DRIVING ME MAD . . . PASS THE SALT, PERESTROIKA

What Mikhail does is enact three things. Two of them are words you should know. One is **glasnost,** which means "openness." The second is **perestroika,** which means "restructuring." The third thing he did was try and limit military funding. Glasnost meant Gorbachev was tired of the secrecy of the Soviet government. He didn't want to lie to people anymore, and he wanted to stop the KGB from terrorizing people. He wanted citizens to be more open with the government so it could improve. Places in Eastern Europe such as Poland, who wanted their own votes and no longer wanted to be a part of the Soviet Union, were let out. Under perestroika, Gorbachev knew they had to restructure the economy and reel in military spending. They also needed to cut off subsidies to countries they could not afford to prop up anymore. This all leads to number three: not being able to spend money on the military anymore.

This third enactment leads to the **SALT,** first in the early 1970s and then again late in the decade. The **Strategic Arms Limitation Talks** were about curbing weapons production—not stopping weapons production altogether, not getting rid of weapons—just slowing down the speed at which they were being made. What you have to understand about the Cold War is that if humans survive for another 1000 years, it will be looked on with hilarity and humor because the whole reason that we haven't killed each other yet is because there are so many bombs on the planet between the Soviets and the USA. There was a principle that basically sustained our life on earth, known as **MAD. MAD** stood for **Mutually Assured Destruction,** which essentially meant if anybody lobs a bomb, then the other side will throw a bomb in which case both sides will throw all their bombs and everyone will die. Who is going to do that? MAD is the most hilarious thing ever in human history, because it stopped us from attacking each other, but it made us continue to make more bombs. We were already to the point where we'd annihilate each other off the face of the planet, but we kept making better bombs. The US would say, "We have 1000 bombs that can each destroy 5 countries at once!" So the Soviet Union would build 1001. That's where you get into these astronomical numbers of bombs, a bomb for every damn person on the planet. Why? I can't really answer that, because it makes no sense.

But I digress. I get a little agitated thinking about MAD; how fitting. So back to our story: this equates to Gorbachev realizing that they have to stop doing this. During the SALT talks, they agreed, "Ok let's not build this type or class of bomb anymore, or build half as many as you were going to and we will build half as many. Also, how about we eliminate this type of submarine, and you guys eliminate that type of submarine." When these talks started, there was some capitulation, but for the really big thing, Gorbachev would say, "Let's not build these big intercontinental ballistic missiles," but Reagan, because he hates commies so much, builds more of those missiles because he knows the Soviets are going broke. Indeed, not only does he *not* agree to weapons elimination, but accelerates production and builds more. In the same year Reagan appeared in front of the US Congress during the State of the Union address and said that the USSR was an "evil empire" and that we must do everything in our power to combat evil. He is really throwing all the cards down on the table here, what a huge bluff in the global game of poker. It's hilarious, but indeed that's exactly what did it.

Here is the bluff that won the game: Somebody made mention to Reagan of how cool it would be if we put missiles in space and when the Soviets shot nuclear weapons at anyone, we could shoot their bombs out of the sky with our space missiles. This missile system would be a space laser to shoot out bombs and was called **SDI,** the Strategic Defense Initiative, given the nickname **Star Wars.** The Plaid Avenger is convinced this whole concept evolved at a cocktail party with some dudes who had way too many drinks.

When this idea came out it was merely that: an idea. Then some people started throwing around some funds for this idea, which was most likely sketched on a cocktail napkin. Somehow Reagan got his hands on this cocktail napkin and started to circulate it around. Has anybody heard about this Star Wars thing? It sounds pretty good. When news of this gets to Gorbachev in the Soviet Union, the comrades said, "Oh shit! They are going to have an orbiting missile defense system! In space! We are going to have to spend millions and billions of research dollars to figure out how to get one of these too and we are already broke. We can't do it!"

THE END

So Gorbachev goes to Reagan and says, "We will stop making these bombs, guns, and tanks, just don't do this Star Wars thing!" Reagan, in all of his wisdom, said, "Sorry, we can't; it is already built. We are too far along and can't stop now." This was a complete line of bull. There was nothing in space. Nothing was even tested. This huge bluff pays off because Gorbachev decides to throw up his hands and say, "Well that's it then; we can't keep up. If we can't have a missile defense that means you guys win. You could nuke us so we quit. MAD is over and so are we!" This is when the USSR really falls down, around 1988 to 1989.

Several things collide here. The Soviet economy is in trouble, they've overextended themselves with their propaganda around the world and with Soviet aid in other countries. They have had this war in Afghanistan with active fighting for 10 years, from 1979 to 1989, which was

"We're not MAD anymore; we're broke!"

proving to be disastrous. It takes a huge toll in not only millions of dollars of equipment, but also the death of 25,000 Russian soldiers. When all is said and done, they haven't done anything there for 10 years. They still don't control Afghanistan, so they have to walk out of it. Glasnost and Perestroika are starting to be interpreted literally by Eastern Europeans and the Soviet people themselves, who are now calling for revolution and independence. In 1989 the Soviet Union has to throw in the towel. "Poland you want out? Go ahead. Estonia, Latvia, Lithuania, you want out? I guess you guys are out too. Central Asian republics, you guys are out too." It all disintegrates in very short order, and all those countries declare independence.

Fifteen new sovereign states emerge from the ashes of the USSR. The strings of the Soviet satellites' puppet governments are cut. The map gets redrawn in one fell swoop. In 1990 they adopted economic and democratic reforms into what is left of the USSR, which becomes the United Federation of Russia. In 1991 Boris Yeltzin is elected president of Russia. He recognizes the independence of all the countries that had declared it. In that same year, the newly formed Congress votes for the official and permanent dissolution of the USSR. It is no more and from 1991 forward, it will be called Russia.

RADICAL RUSSIAN TRANSITION

So by the 1990's the commie threat is gone, the USSR is dismembered, so everybody should be happy and gay and frolicking, right? Well no, everything still sucks for Russia. It has gotten a lot better in the last few years, but we are going to carry it forward from 1991 when all this becomes official in today's world. That first decade of post-soviet independence for the Ruskies sucks as bad as the decade before it. The pain of a radical transition has to be suffered through as they approach the 21st century. What kind of transition, and what kind of pain?

ECONOMY TAKES A DUMP

As we pointed out during the final decades of the Soviet Union, their economy was in bad shape, and changing their name doesn't change the facts. Now it's the Russian economy that sucks. Their industries are still in Cold War mindset and only produce big stuff like tanks and missiles that don't have much use in today's world. You can still sell such items, but not nearly enough to rebuild an economy. They have had tremendous problems with shifting their entire industrial sector to more capitalist-centered stuff, normal consumer goods. Capitalism was still a new concept for them, and they are still breaking in their capitalist cowboy boots. So the transition from commie to capitalist was full of pitfalls and road bumps and full-on collisions which made for an extremely rocky economic road to recovery.

The Bear gets skinned.

On top of that, Russia had lost its international status. They used to be 'the other world power' but in the 1990's nobody would give them the time of day, much less a bank loan. Again, this has changed in the last couple years, but right after 1991 no one was willing to help Russia. Russia used to be a somebody, but now it's a nobody. It's also important to note that the USSR went from a singular sovereign entity to 15. It lost tremendous amounts of territory. Those other 14 countries that aren't Russia are plots of land that it no longer owns. Land itself isn't valuable, but there's the agriculture produced on that land, the mineral and energy resources under it, and the people as a workforce. Those are the basic foundations of economies. This scenario is a tremendous blow to the Russian economy, an economy that was already hurting.

On top of this you have to think about the Soviet era during which the Soviets used a lot of resources from these countries. For example, most of the food production for the Soviet Union came from the Ukraine and Kazakhstan, which became separate countries. A lot of oil and natural gas came from Central Asia, and not only is Russia no longer profiting from these resources, now it has to buy them back. It is a double-edged sword with both edges towards Russia. They are getting sliced and diced. Finally, most of the nuclear and weapons stockpiles were in what are now the Ukraine and Belarus, and there are a lot of expensive complications involved in destroying and/or relocating these weapons.

Now the second problem with the economy is the influence of organized crime: the Russian Mafia. Organized crime is easy because it is everywhere. Crime is everywhere, so organized crime is everywhere too. It is really strong in Russia. In fact if you have ever seen adventure movies or international crime dramas, there is always a Russian mafia somewhere. They have always had a presence, even back in the days of communism when they created the Russian black market, which moved untaxed alcohol, weapons, and hardcore drugs. Indeed they are still doing a tremendous job trafficking drugs and weapons internationally. They're also trafficking people. Yes, I did say people. A lot of the Russian mafia deals with the movement of women and children for sexual exploitation purposes. It's a fairly nasty business, but I guess that's what mafias do.

During the confusion and transformation of the Russian economy in the 1990's, these illegal criminal elements had a complete field day. The Soviet system was fairly corrupt internally to begin with, and that was perpetuated under free market capitalism where there are not a lot of rules. In addition, the government was broke and couldn't pay federal employees such as the military and police. In such circumstances, corruption becomes endemic and easy to do at all levels. People do what they have to do to stay alive. The influence of organized crime is a major function of what is happening even in today's Russia. Vladimir Putin himself came to power on a platform of being tough on crime, and in fact, nobody would be elected who is not.

This powerful criminal element in Russia not only stymies local business, but has negatively influenced international investment as well. But the open and outright blue-collar criminals were not alone in the 1990's: **a new dimension of** white-collar crime arose to give the underworld a run for their money (ha! Pun intended!): **the Oligarchs**.

OLIGARCHS OVER-DO IT

The oligarchs are white-collar criminals who, during this transition period of communism to democracy and capitalism in the 1990s, worked for the government or had insider ties with the government and bought whole industries and businesses under the table before they would go to auction. In communism everything is owned by the state—all the oil, land, timber, energy production, everything. In capitalism, individuals own everything and the state owns virtually nothing. So when a government goes from communism to capitalism, it starts selling everything. Ideally, this process would allow any individual the opportunity to buy former state industries at fair market prices. However, in Russia, this did not happen and most purchases were made by government insiders at rock bottom prices.

Here's an example: Yukos was Russia's oil company, a government owned oil company that was going to privatize. If you knew some government officials when it was going up for sale and could get the price, and you knew people who worked at a bank, here is what you would do. You find out the day before the sale occurs and go to your friend at the bank and say, "Lend me half a billion dollars," with the promise that you will personally give him 100 million. He smiles and you take the check for 500 million bucks from the bank over to the natural resources department to your buddy who is overseeing the sale of the oil company. You hand him the check for 500 million; he stamps it sold and hands you the deed to the oil company. You and your conspirators walk out together the next day as owners of this oil company, and sell it for 2 or 3 billion dollars, its true value,

Top Five Russian Oligarchs			
Who?	What did he steal from the people?	How Much? (USD)	Where Now?
Roman Abramovich	Oil (Sibneft)	$14.7 Billion	In England, owns big-time soccer team: Chelsea FC. Owns four giant yachts and is building a fifth.
Vladimir Lisin	Aluminum and Steel	$7 Billion	Most likely sleeping in a pile of hundred dollar bills
Viktor Vekselberg	Oil (Tyuman)	$6.1 Billion	Buying Faberge Eggs, seriously, he digs them
Oleg Deripaska	Aluminum (RusAl)	$5.8 Billion	Hanging out with good friend Vlad "the Bad" Putin
Mikhail Fridman	Conglomeration of Valuable Shit (Alfa)	$5.8 Billion	Lost much of his wealth in Russian tort suit—for stealing from the people, probably not enough evidence for criminal case

and you bank the rest. You go back and settle up your loan for 500 million with your banking friend and you split the rest. Some dudes in Russia actually got away with this and came to be known as the Oligarchs. This is a savvy big business tactic in the wild west of capitalism where there are no rules. These guys became ultra-millionaires and billionaires overnight.

Now what is the big deal with this? What's the problem? The Russian people got screwed, that's what. You have state owned resources whose sale should have contributed to the economic growth of an entire country, which instead got turned into a billion dollars in a Swiss bank account under one man's name overnight. It's been a legal transaction apparently and whatever multinational company bought it will go in and start producing oil so there will be jobs and such, but you have had a massive loss to the government.

In his rise to power, Vlad "the Bad" Putin brought some of these crooks to justice—including Yukos head Mikhail Khodorkovsky (formerly the second richest Russian)—although his motivation for doing so is questionable. It is likely a move designed to consolidate power more than a move to achieve justice.

Another platform in Vladimir Putin's campaign was, "I'm going after those Oligarch sons of bitches too! Going after crime and those chumps that robbed the Russian people!" That is one of the reasons he's such a popular leader. He is seen as a strong anticrime, progovernment force to be reckoned with. He's backed it up too, because the owner of Yukos is now sitting in jail. As a result, Putin has helped Russia stabilize itself a little more.

PURGIN POPULATION

Another issue that is extremely problematic for Russia is the population itself. What's happening to the people in Russia? Russia's population is one of the classic examples, if not the classic example, of a population in decline: negative fertility rates and dropping birth rates. The population total is declining with only about 150 million people in Russia and this number keeps getting smaller every year. People have been leaving in droves, which doesn't do much for Russia's economy. You need working people to keep things moving. A lot of things are going on that can account for Russia's demographic decline. It is hard to pinpoint a single factor, but nevertheless, the population is shrinking. And the shrinkage is just the start of problems . . .

If we looked at some of the social indicators for what's happening in Russia, you would swear that you were looking at an African nation. The life expectancy for males is around 47 years, a little more than half that of the United States. You might guess this life expectancy for sub-Saharan Africa or Central Asia, but you typically would not think of

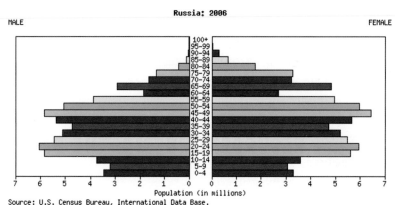

Source: U.S. Census Bureau, International Data Base.

Numbers are going down.

Russia. Several things may be contributing to Russia's decline. One is *lack of health care.* Because of the collapse of the economy and the corruption associated with it, health care has become a huge issue. Access to good health care is almost nonexistent, but again this may be changing. People aren't as healthy as they should be and don't have access to certain operations or preventive care. Drinking an average of 30 liters of vodka a year probably isn't helping matters either. Other unhealthy attributes include . . .

ENVIRONMENT ENDANGERED

In its rapid industrialization, forced collectivization, and striving to catch up with the West to be a global power phase, the Soviet system completely ignored the environment. There was no limit to the amount of toxic spilling and dumping, or atomic weapons' testing. Anything the Soviets could do to get ahead was done with the thought that once they won, they'd go back and clean everything up. Oops, they lost! So it's all still sitting there. Parts of the Kara Sea glow green sometimes from all of the accumulated toxic waste that was dumped into the river systems. And be sure to check out the Aral Sea as soon as you can . . . because it is disappearing due to mis-use and pollution during the soviet era. There are no less than 50 sites in Russia with pollution of catastrophic proportions. Don't forget to include all of the old nuclear weapons silos that are sitting around, deteriorating. There is impending disaster on an environmental scale here just based on past pollutions and degrading weapons. Russia has dealt with this huge problem during the last 15 years, with some international help from the United States and several others.

STOLEN SPHERE OF INFLUENCE: THE REALIGNMENT

The last thing you should be aware of in Russia right now is that a lot of its exterritories and exstates in its sphere of influence have now disappeared under radical realignment—much to the chagrin of Russia because it still sees itself as a world player. What am I talking about? Eastern Europe is now desperately trying to become Western Europe by realigning with the West. So Russia is losing its sphere of influence all over the place, though it's desperately trying to hold on. It is still actively courting Central Asia politically because there is a lot of oil and natural gas there. Of course they are also courting China and want to keep good strategic ties there. It is really losing influence over Eastern Europe, and what's happening now only rubs it in their face.

That NATO stuff we talked about last chapter is still troubling the Russians. Something quite radical, that would have been unthinkable a decade ago, has happened. Places like Poland, Hungary, and the Czech Republic joined NATO very quickly after they declared independence in 1991, mostly to ensure no further Russian influence. The next wave of folks was 2004 when Estonia, Latvia, Lithuania, Romania, and Bulgaria joined NATO: places that were once firmly in Soviet control. Russia now finds that its former territories, which it sometimes harshly subjugated, are now sovereign political entities that want nothing to do with it. They are NATO members and could theoretically have NATO weaponry pointed at Russia. This is a big loss of status and influence for Russia. Think about this in an abstract context. The Baltic States go from being owned by Russia, to ten years later being sovereign states with weapons pointed at Russia. That's a fairly big change. But the scales are starting to tip back to the Russian side . . .

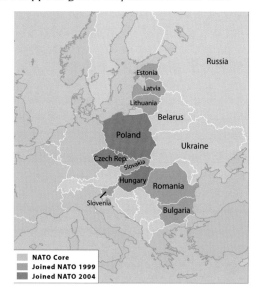

NATO Core
Joined NATO 1999
Joined NATO 2004

RESURGENT RUSSIA: THE BADASSES ARE BACK!

But watch out! Things continue to change fairly rapidly for Russia, and it is the understatement of the century to say that things are looking up. Yes, I've talked about how crappy its economy has been. Yes, I've told you all about its people problems, its environmental problems, its crime problems, its international status problems. But what a difference one man can make . . . and the Russian man of the century is with no doubt Vladimir Putin. Putin, along with petroleum, has brought the Russians from the brink of the abyss back to world power status in less than a decade. There are a few other factors at play here as well that are serving to bring the Russian region back to a starring role on the world stage. Let's wrap up this chapter looking at this incredible reversal of Russian fortune.

"I can snap your neck with my bare hand. Enjoy your dinner."

PRES TO PRIME: PUTIN POWER!!!

Holy crap this guy is unstoppable! So rarely in life can you truly credit a single individual with changing the course of history but, for better or for worse, that is an apt description for our main man Vlad. It's no wonder that Time magazine voted him Man of the Year for 2007—he really has made that big of a difference in his country, and in the world. Vladimir Putin is also easily the baddest-ass leader on the planet: as a former KGB agent and judo blackbelt, he could handily whip the ass of any elected official on this side of the Milky Way. And the people love him! Putin held 60 to 80% approval ratings his entire 8 years in office . . . and just stepped down as President with closer to 90% love from the Russians. Hell, Stalin would have killed for that kind of popular support . . . . oh, wait a minute . . . he did kill to get that kind of support . . . but I digress. Why all the love?

Putin is only the 2nd president Russia has now had, and was the hand-picked successor to Boris Yeltsin, a fairly popular leader in his own right. In his eight year run from 2000-2008, Vladimir oversaw the stabilization of the economic transition process that had thrown Russia into chaos for its first decade. He was tough on the oligarchs, and tough on crime, which helped stimulate international investment. He also took a fairly pro-active government role in helping Russian businesses, especially those businesses dealing with petroleum and natural gas. More on that in a minute. GDP has grown six-fold, and propelled Russia from the 22nd largest economy up to the number ten slot. The economy grew 6-8% on average every year he was in office. Investment grew, industry grew, agricultural output grew, construction grew, salaries have grown . . . pretty much every economic indicator you could look at has gone up during his tenure.

President? Prime Mininster? It's all Putin to me!

Unlike most world leaders, Putin has been very savvy with this cash flow too. He paid off all Russian debts. Imagine that: Russian National Debt = 0. Damn. That's whack. Putin also has stashed billions, if not trillions, in a Russian 'rainy day fund' that is set aside for any future hard times. How refreshing! Most leaders usually stash that extra cash in their personal Swiss bank accounts. No wonder Russians love him!

However, the love is not just based on economics. Vladimir Putin has re-instilled a great sense of nationalism to his citizens as well. After the demise of the USSR, Russia was a second rate power, with even less prestige, that was really at the mercy

Back off NATO! Putin is protectin' his hood!

of international business and banking and stronger world powers like the US, the EU, and NATO. Russia pretty much just had to go with the flow, even when events were inherently against their own national interest . . . like the growth of NATO for example. But watch out! Putin has brought them politically back to a position of strength. He plays hardball in international affairs now, and has re-invigorated a Russian national pride that has long laid dormant.

Of course this has come at a cost: Putin has achieved a lot of this by consolidating power around his position, by controlling a lot of state industries, by cracking down on freedom of the press and free speech, and by manipulating power structures of the government. In fact, he just stepped down from the Presidency in May 2008, and stepped immediately into the Prime Minister position the same day . . . maintaining a lot of command and control of the system simultaneously. That crafty fox! He is increasingly reviled and even hated by 'Team West' because people see him as leaning back towards totalitarianism, but also because he increasingly clashes with western foreign policy on the international stage.

So Putin power is not to be underestimated. And since he can hold the Prime Minister position indefinitely, he will be around for some time to come. The Russians love his ass for making them strong, and making them rich . . . so let's look at some specifics of how he has pulled this off and the implications for the future . . .

PETRO POWER!!

Now Putin is a bad ass. On that point we are clear. However, we do have to at least partially (if not fully) credit his great success in turning the Bear around on this one single commodity: petroleum. Dudes! Russia has made total bank on oil and natural gas in the last decade. To understand the importance of oil for Russia, one need only consider this: when the USSR crashed in 1991, the price of a barrel of oil was about $10; in 2008 the price of a barrel of oil is approaching $150. And my friends, you should know this: Russia has a shit-ton of oil!!! Look at the map! You do the math!

Increasingly, Russia has also reeled in all control of the petro industries to the state as well. Meaning that they did privatize a lot of those industries back in the 1990's, but they have been busy **nationalizing** a lot of them back since 2000.

Russian Oil and Natural Gas at a Glance

Oil	2006	Natural Gas	2006
Oil reserves	80 billion barrels	Gas reserves	48 trillion cubic meters
Oil reserves, as percentage of world	7 percent	Gas reserves, as percentage of world	26 percent
Saudi Arabian reserves	264 billion barrels	Iranian reserves	28 trillion cubic meters
US reserves	30 billion barrels	US reserves	6 trillion cubic meters
Oil production	10 million barrels per day	Gas production	612 billion cubic meters
Oil production, as percentage of world	12 percent	Gas production, as percentage of world	21 percent
US oil production	7 million barrels per day	US gas production	524 billion cubic meters
Oil exports	7 million barrels per day	Gas exports	263 billion cubic meters
Oil exporter, rank	2	Gas exporter, rank	1
Oil exports, to US	370,000 barrels per day	Gas exports, to Europe	151 billion cubic meters

Remember those terms from Chapter 4? Russia sure does. It now has controlling interest in virtually all the oil and natural gas businesses in the country . . . which of course means even more of the profits swing back directly to the state.

To reiterate a few points from this chapter and the last: oil is power for Russia. Not only have they paid off their foreign debt with oil money, they have re-invested that oil money back into their economy, and also set up their rainy day fund with oil dollars too. Since the Russians supply 1/3 of European energy demand, this gives them all sorts of economic and political leverage over their Eurasian neighbors. Piss off Russia, and you might not have heating oil next winter. But the Europeans aren't the only ones who need oil. Look eastward and you see Japan and China both vying for petro resources too, so Russia is really sitting pretty right now. Energy master of the continent!

GLOBAL WARMING? NO SWEAT!

And I just can't get out of this section without referencing the global warming situation. While the rest of the planet may be wringing their hands in a collective tizzy about rising temperatures, melting polar ice caps, and rising sea levels, let me assure you that Russia is not sweating the situation at all. Ha! Not sweating the warming . . . am I good or what?

Seriously though, think of the strategic benefits that are being bestowed upon Russia as the thermometer continues to creep upward every year. Russia has forever been a land empire due to its lack of accessible and navigable coastlines. Additionally, almost all of its river systems empty into the ice-locked Arctic Ocean, making them essentially useless for transportation and exporting commodities. But just wait! As the permanent ice cap covering the North Pole disappears . . . Russia will become more open to the world like never before in recorded human history!

You may not be paying attention to any of this shit, but the Ruskies sure are. In preparations for its ice-free northern coastlines of the future, Russia is staking a claim to the entire Arctic sea east of the North Pole. No, seriously, I'm not making this up. The race for the Arctic has begun! And Russia stands to be the biggest beneficiary as well. Not only will it open up their territory for greater sea access, greater land access, and greater export power, but it is widely believed that there are massive oil reserves in the Arctic basin as well; reserves which will become accessible once the ice is gone. Damn! Russia is all about the global warming! Let's get this party started! No, actually let's end it with. . . .

GEOPOLITICAL JUMP START

"Yes comrades, the North Pole is ours now. Bye-bye Santa!"

So you got your Putin, and you got your petroleum, and you add to that a huge dose of nationalistic pride. Bake for 20 minutes, and you end up with an extremely resurgent and resilient Russia on the world political table. These guys are playa's once again. Their huge economy, their huge oil reserves, and their huge potential for the future is fast becoming the envy of the world. And they can afford to play the fence when suitors come calling. What do I mean by that?

Well, Russia has been invited to become a strategic partner state of the EU . . . not a full-fledged member, mind you, but a partner. Europe realizes that the Russian economy and Russian energy is such an integral part of their own lives, that to not have Russia at the table for major decisions would be folly. So Russia has a real impact on some EU policy. The same can be said of NATO. While Russia is not a member, the group realizes that almost all major decision-making should involve the Russians since they play such an increasingly important role in Eurasian affairs. Russia is typically invited to major NATO summits now. So why doesn't Russia just join the EU and NATO fully?

Because the Russians are forging economic and strategic political ties to their east as well, mostly with China. They are at a historical east/west pivot point right now and they are straddling the fence about which relationships to make or break. I think they're being extremely savvy and are going to avoid taking sides in anything. Could Russia join the EU? It's already a strategic partner of the EU. I bet it will be invited to join as a full-fledged member, but I also bet it will decline.

Why? It is also strategic partners with China, the other huge ass economy on the other side of the continent. Russia will not be stymied economically by joining a club that can possibly limit their economic options. The Bear is also still a major player in Central Asia—an area with tons of natural gas and oil that has to be moved out of Central Asia to the rest of the world that wants it. That oil and natural gas usually moves out through Russian territory, supplying most of the fuel for Eastern and Western Europe, in addition to increasingly supplying fuel for Japan, China and India.

Without getting too far ahead of the story, let me also go ahead and reference a serious international entity of the future that you probably have not even heard of yet: the SCO. Flip ahead to the Central Asia chapter to get the full run-down on this group, but just let me tease you for now by telling you this much. The SCO is going to be a bizarre cross between an Asian version of NATO and a Russian version of OPEC. And my friends, Russia has every intention of being the leader of this grand experiment. Stalin would be proud . . .

GHOST OF STALIN RETURNS

Which is a good jumping off point. Well, I guess any mention of Joseph Stalin is a good point to get the hell out of Dodge. I want to leave you with this: the memory of Smokin' Joe Stalin is actually being softened in today's Russia, and that is a very telling sign of what's happening in the society. Some folks in Russia are looking back with pride at what most of us consider one of the biggest bastards in history. Why? This vibrant and growing economy, this resurgent world role, and this overall restored sense of Russian greatness has not been felt since the Stalin era . . . and quite frankly the Russians are quite proud to be Russian again.

WRESTLING FOR WEALTH.

Team west taught the Russians too well!

Add in trillions of petro dollars, increasing empire due to global warming, and a renewed sense of global political power, and you got yourself one kick-ass region that will be shaping world events of the future. Growl! The Bear is back!

THE BATTLE FOR TOKYO IS ON . . .

Japan

KONNICHIWA!! Welcome to the islands! And a most unique set of islands they are . . . so unique in fact that we will classify Japan not just as an independent state, but as an entirely unique region of the world as well. One of the classic mistakes that all textbooks make, and that a lot of people in the West make, is overgeneralizing Asia. They look at this place and say, "Oh well, you know it's just Asian people there and six of one, half dozen of the other. Japanese, Chinese, Koreans . . . whatever." This couldn't be further from the truth when we are talking about Japan and mainland Asia. Japan has an extremely distinct culture from all the countries around it (as do the Chinese, the Koreans, the Vietnamese, etc.), but unlike the others, Japan has followed a more 'western' trajectory in the last century that has set them quite apart from even their closest neighbors. They are the most 'western' of the 'eastern' cultures. Huh? Hang on We'll get to that in a bit.

But just know this for now we are coming up on the Clash of the Titans of the 21st Century: The Clash of the Asian Titans. The titans are of course Japan and China, two states with huge economies, two states shaping global events, and two states with a long history of animosity between them.

One of the most critical relationships that will be affecting 21st century events is how these two Asian giants will deal with each other as China rises to full superpower status. But I am getting ahead of the story as usual. Let's get some background on Japan itself, then look at its evolution into the modern era, and then we will finish with that all important relationship with China. Ready? Then Godzilla game on!

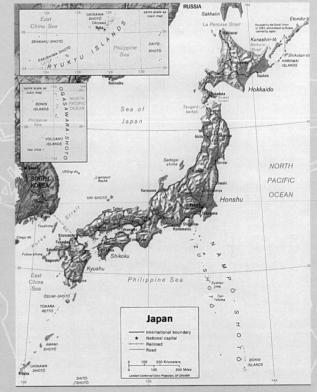

Japan/US: size and latitude comparison.

PHYSICAL

Japan is a group of four main islands: Hokkaido, Honshu, Shikoku, and Kyushu, from north to south. Japan was created by three or four different tectonic plates coming together in this area. Because of this, Japan is volcanic in origin. Another feature that goes along with this is its mountainous terrain. There are very few flatlands, and this equates to very little agricultural land. Due to plate tectonics, Japan is also earthquake prone. We've heard this before and we've seen some titanic earthquake events in the last hundred years in Japan. It is a cyclical thing and it will not go away anytime soon. It is not a question of *if* Japan is going to be hit by another major earthquake; it's only a matter of *when*.

Why should you care about this? Well, Tokyo's stock exchange and pretty much Japan as a whole, holds tremendous amounts of foreign investment, foreign currency, and bank reserves on the planet. When the day comes that a major earthquake shuts them down, depending on the scale of the disaster itself, it could plunge the entire world into recession almost instantaneously. If it is a tremendously bad earthquake, it could plunge the world into a depression in the long term. It's another instance of globalization at its worst in that a big hit here from the physical world could equate to disaster for the entire planet. But the Plaid Avenger doesn't want to scare anybody; it's just a matter of when so we'll see how it goes.

Ahhh! Most honorable Mt. Fuji!

"Honey, I think this section of the interstate is closed"

The other physical thing to consider with Japan is climate. Climatologically speaking, this is an easy one for the Plaid to describe to you because you could superimpose Japan, keeping latitude constant, on to the eastern seaboard of the United States. As you can see, latitude and size being held constant in this image, the climate of Japan is identical to the eastern seaboard of the United States. Hokkaido is around the upstate New York, Buffalo area and they get a lot of snow up there. Southern Honshu, as well as Shikoku and Kyushu, reach down into the southern United States and indeed there are actually smaller islands that go down to what would be tropical Florida. Every place else is similar to some place else in between. For instance, Tokyo is roughly the latitude of Washington, DC. These two regions, though on opposite sides of the planet, have very similar climates.

One disclaimer here is that Japan is an island nation. As an island, it is surrounded by water, and water is a major modifier of climate. As such, it has a similar climate to the east coast of the United States, though somewhat moderated due to the influence of the surrounding water.

Cherry blossom festivals in Tokyo and Washington DC. Can you tell which is which?

Lastly, physically speaking, Japan is lacking in natural resources. I just suggested that Japan is mostly mountainous, which means it does not have a lot of agricultural resources. The Japanese have found ways throughout the centuries of getting around that by terracing rice paddies and fishing. There is still no way it can supply itself with its own food needs at this point due to its lack of agricultural resources, and lack of arable land. More importantly, it lacks just about everything else too.

Japan is a real conundrum in that it is the second largest economy on the planet that, at the same time, lacks virtually everything that most countries with powerhouse economies have. Japan has to import most of its metals, ores, and virtually all of its energy resources. Japan is entirely dependent on the rest of the planet for all of these things. That has something to do with its history, which goes. . .

SAMURAI TO JACK

So what about natural resources, Plaid Avenger? Well, not having any has something to do with Japan in the modern world. I'm going to go through the early history of Japan in fairly short order to point out one thing in particular: In terms of unique Asian cultures and unique ethnic groups, Japan is really a laggard. It's the latecomer. It's the last one to show up on the world scene.

Chinese civilization has been around for 5,000 years. The Koreans have been around for 3,000–4,000 years. Lots of people from Central Asia and Southeast Asia, like the Thais, the Vietnamese, and other ethnic groups with distinct cultures, have been around for a while. If you search hard, you will find that Japan's culture cannot really be called a distinct culture until about 1400–1500 years ago, and even at that point, it's not anything closing in on what we consider a nation-state.

Japan started as a small group of folks that migrated from mainland China and through the Korean Peninsula over the course of the previous thousand years. They don't become a unique entity themselves until comparatively late in the Common Era. The Plaid Avenger points this out not because I'm that concerned about you learning the history of every place in the world, but because this history plays into the modern world. In what way?

Virtually all of Japanese society is borrowed from other societies. All of the writing systems, all of the religious systems, all of the philosophical systems: all have roots over in mainland Asia. However, if you read Japanese literature or

government propaganda over the last 100 years, it's all reversed. The Japanese are fiercely proud of their independence and their distinct culture, so given that they have been a powerhouse over the past 50 years, they have rewritten history to make it look like as if they were there first and everybody else gleaned stuff from them. This couldn't be further from the truth.

So what we have is this group of folks that start up in 500–700 CE, and it is only at this point that they form into something vaguely resembling a state. They start to have a head of state, a prince. They start a royal/imperial line, which actually stays in place to the current day. For those of you saying, "What? They still have a royal family there?" Yes, there is still an Emperor of Japan and there is still an Empress of Japan. They have the longest standing monarchy/royal family in world history, and it continues. You can trace it back to

Move over UK! Japan has inbred snobs too!

600–700 CE, same family, same dudes. The faces change, but the DNA remains the same. It is very much like Great Britain and its constitutional monarchy—the idea of royals hanging out. They don't have any real power but they are still there.

So let's get back to history. We can fast forward very quickly because Japan turns into, for the next thousand years, something very similar to a feudal state in medieval Europe. That is, there is the Emperor on top, there are Dukes underneath him, there are Lords underneath the Dukes, and eventually, we get to the peasants that are essentially tied to the lands that are controlled by the Lords. There are different names and faces in Japan. They are Asians, not Europeans. They have bad-ass Samurai outfits and swords, instead of long shafts and jousts but it's all essentially the same bullshit on opposite sides of Eurasia.

The peasants live on the lands and are essentially owned by the Lords, who pay tribute to the Dukes, who of course have one master, the Emperor. The easy reference is to what we call **Shoguns,** essentially militaristic governors which are the Dukes and the Lords. Just like in Europe, they compete for lands and ownership of things to gain political influence. They all still recognize the Emperor as the main dude, but they all fight for places right below him on the totem pole.

Why is this so great? Well nothing is really great about it, unless you're the Emperor. He allows this feudal system to continue because as all of his subordinates are fighting each other, no one is ever actually threatening him. That's the point. The kings of Europe did this shit too. The point of feudalism is to keep people beating the hell out of each other so they can't mess with you too much. This becomes standard operating procedure in Japan fairly early on, and it continues for most of Japanese history, which begins pretty late in the Asian game.

We can tie some dates to this age of the Shogun, this kind of really entrenched take on the feudal system. From around 1000 to 1580 CE, they have multiple competing shogunates all vying for power and influence. After 1580, one group rises to the top. They are called the Tokugawa Shogunate. The Tokugawa Shogunate pretty much unify the whole country under their single command from about 1600 to 1800. A single Duke or Lord from this line of shoguns becomes so powerful that they actually stop all the infighting. Japan has a period of stability and peace where everybody is under the same blanket because those Tokugawa guys are such bad-asses. Here's the big thing: they unify the whole country; they unite all the smaller armies battling each other into a singular army, but most importantly, they plunge the whole country into global isolation.

What do you mean, Plaid Avenger? Well, these guys are tough. You've seen the movies! You've seen these guys; they are total bad-asses. They're so bad-ass that they repelled a Mongol invasion in 1274—no one else pulled that off! They have

their own little world going on and they are not interested at all in the outside world. They cut ties with everybody—not that they ever had a lot of contact. Historically speaking, they had always been a subservient state, or **tribute state** to the Chinese, though the Chinese never took them over physically. Japan

knew that China was the big power, and it therefore kept itself on the fringe. This has all been fine and dandy throughout history. The Japanese have escaped takeover by all other entities. . .

But what is happening in the rest of the world from 1600 to 1800? Europe is colonizing the world, is taking over other big parts of the planet and seeing the beginnings of its industrialization period. You have a foreign influence that is making its way over to the Far East, even into Japan. With industrialization occurring, these European guys have better weapons, better ships, and better navigation. By the 1800s, Europe virtually controls three-quarters of the planet and finally gets to Japan. Europeans started making in-roads to establish trade with Japan.

During the Tokugawa Shogunate in 1600–1800, missionaries had started showing up at Japan's doorstep. The Shogunate was like, "What are you peddling? What are you trying to convert us to? Really? Christianity? That sounds great . . . and now we'll chop your head off! Get the hell out of our country! We are not interested in your shit. We are isolating ourselves! We are the Shoguns, we are the Samurais, we are THE bad-asses! We don't need your stuff, so go away! If you don't go away when we tell you to, then we'll kill you!" That was the way it went for a good long time, but it was only going to be perpetuated for so long.

We know this story already. This story is told again and again when we go through the rest of the regions on the planet. As Europe's technology and military hardware became more advanced they could only be put off for so long. Through its self-isolation, Japan gets behind the times technologically. It comes to the realization that it can't compete with the rest of the outside world. The Japanese are still fighting with swords, fighting dudes with guns. So their isolated world comes to a quick halt. The Plaid Avenger is not big on dates, but this is a good one to note: 1853. This is not long ago. In 1853, a dude named Commodore Matthew Perry shows up on the scene. Commodore Perry wants to open up trade so he pulls his ironclad battleship into Tokyo Harbor and comes ashore. He says, "Let's meet with the local head-honchos, these Samurai guys with their swords." Perry says, "Hey, we want to establish trade."

For the previous 250 years, the Shogunate answered that with, "Get your ass back on your ship and get out of here or we'll chop your head off!" Perry was like, "Hold on, fellows, hold on. Take a look out in the harbor. Do you see that? That's an ironclad vessel. See those things poking out of it? Those are cannons. We can blow the living hell out of you and all of your people right now and you are completely defenseless." Remember, these Samurai fight mostly with swords. Now they are stacked up against modern military hardware. The Samurai figure out pretty quickly that this is going to be a one-sided affair. So in one fell swoop, in 1853, Commodore Matthew Perry forcibly opened up trade with Japan. They kind of say, "Oh, yeah, those guns probably do better than our swords. We probably are not going to be able to survive this."

What the . . .? Commodore Perry, stop this Sumo madness!

Commodore Perry, official Japan-opener

It is important to note which country the Commodore is from: the United States of America. It's actually the United States that forcibly opens up trade in Japan and not a colonizing power. It is historically significant that it was *not* the Europeans who went over to Japan to take it over but the Americans who went over there to establish a trade relationship. This is the beginning of one of the most amazing occurrences in modern history, as far as the Plaid Avenger is concerned.

When a country is confronted with an outside world in which they are severely behind, they can take one of two roads. All other regions faced this exact same choice as the onslaught of European colonization of the world occurred. Road One: "We can fight it out! Let's try to kick them out! Let's have protests and shoot guns at them and do whatever we have to do to kick out the European powers!" Most countries went that way. Road Two, which only the Japanese seem to have found, says "Let's embrace the West! Let's do it way better than they do!" This precipitates a fascinating time in *world* history, not just Japanese history. This is what makes the difference between Japan and China in today's world. This is the crossroads. The Plaid Avenger is telling you, it's rare that you can say, "This is a definitive turning point . . . everything is different after this!" The Plaid Avenger is telling you: **this is it.**

MEIJI

Meiji Makeover: Rickshaw to Railways

In 1868, the Japanese decide to undergo something now referred to as **The Meiji Restoration,** named for the Emperor at the time, the Head Honcho Meiji as he came to power. He is known as being a fairly savvy guy, but it was probably the collaborative effort of his counselors and the people around him that, once they saw the world unfold around them, understood how far ahead the Europeans and the Americans were. They made this radical decision, saying, "Wipe the slate clean. Let's redo everything, EVERYTHING, in light of what we know about the outside world." So then they embarked on this fantastic restoration.

They sent what would be the equivalent of college students, learned men, as well as government workers, all over the planet. They sent thousands of them to Europe, to America, to the Middle East, everywhere there were centers of learning, centers of technology, centers of industry. Their mission was to find out every single thing they could. They not only learned stuff at universities and through businesses, they brought stuff back. They brought back military hardware, guns, tanks, whole steam engines, railroad equipment. They shipped it back to Japan, and teams of smart dudes would rip the stuff apart to figure out each individual component. They started the individual industries to make the pieces, the wheels, steam engines, and everything else on their own, from the ground up. This was a massive innovation, rejuvenation, a catching-up period, for technology in particular, but also for government and military.

The Japanese did this fantastically well. Think about what Japan does today. It's still like this, isn't it? They don't really make anything . . . they make everything better! They started this tradition way back during the Meiji Restoration. They are reverse engineers and efficiency experts. They did this in very short order, in around ten years. In two or three decades, they catch up from a lifetime of technological stagnation. It's insane! It's crazy! It's the Meiji Restoration!

At the same time, they modified a lot of things internally. You can see great movies about this, such as *The Last Samurai* with Tom Cruise, that little freak. Scientology aside, it's a pretty decent movie. The film shows the extremely turbulent times in Japan when everything changed. Not just the technology stuff we talked about, that's easy enough. The social restructuring is the big thing. They actually got rid of the Samurai. They reinvented their society in the likeness of Western Europe and America. They banned the Samurai, which is what *The Last Samurai* is all

about. They wanted to rid themselves of the old ways. They said, "No, we're going to rejuvenate! This is the restoration! We are doing everything to catch our military up, which means we're getting rid of the old Shogun ways. We're going to consolidate into a bureaucratic government, just like all these other places. We're going to restructure our banking system. We're going to redo EVERYTHING!" And they did it, in the image of the West.

This is why Japan is a very Western looking nation as opposed to its neighbors. The Meiji Restoration is the critical turning point in history. Japan became Western-like. Every place else in Asia did not. Japan currently has the number two economy in the world. Every place else in Asia isn't even close, with the exception of China (number four), who has stepped up in the last few decades. But watch out! South Korea just broke into the top ten as well. Damn. This region has three economies in the top ten. That is a fact worth remembering.

TERRIBLE LIZARD

Back to the story. The Meiji Restoration is the complete, inside-out do-over of Japanese society on all levels, and it is extremely successful. Like I already suggested, they pretty much catch up within a few decades. Japan goes from the 1850s, where the Samurais are in charge and fighting dudes with swords, to 1895 when, having been a subservient vassal state of China for their entire history, they attack China. Why? Because once the beast is awakening, it is hungry! The beast must be fed! What does it want? Resources! And the Japanese adopt another very western concept in order to get these resources: imperialism!

GODZILLA IS BORN

In 1895, during the Sino-Japanese War, the Japanese go into parts of modern-day Korea and Manchuria and start conquering. They attack China, its colossal powerhouse neighbor, *and they win*. In 1905, ten years later, they attack Russia, the largest state on the planet, *and they win*.

What are they doing this for? They are taking parts of Russian territory on the east coast of Asia. The Russians send their entire naval fleet around to sink the Japanese fleet because they are like, "Hey, we're Russia, we've been around for like 500 years. We're bad-asses! We're the biggest state in the world! We're European; we know what's going on." They send their entire fleet around the entire continent, and it was sunk in 5 minutes. To put this in perspective: 40 years earlier, the Japanese were fighting with swords. They just sunk the entire Russian fleet in 1905 in 5 minutes, the biggest one-sided naval defeat in all of history! The **Battle of Tsushima** was an embarrassment for the Russians, and established the arrival of Japan in the modern world. Japan goes on to advance further into Korea and in 1910 it took over all of modern-day Korea. In 1917, it annexed more of Russia, while the Russians were busy in their communist revolution.

> ### The Godzilla
>
> **1** shot Japanese sake
>
> **1** shot Midori Japanese melon liqueur
>
> **Combine ingredients in a shaker with crushed ice. Shake, strain and serve into shooter glass. Is one part old-school Japan, one part new-school Japan. It will awaken your inner monster from its slumber!**

Minute 1: battle begun. Minute 5: no Russians alive.

Now we can stop for a second and ask, "What are they doing all this for? Why are they taking all this land, inciting fights with their neighbors?" This gets back to what I was talking about in the physical section. This place has no resources. To become a world power, you need resources. To build railroad cars and tanks and airplanes and industries, you need resources. To build an army, you need resources. So what Japan does, as it starts to come into power, is acquire resources. Take them from other places. Take over lands. Japan becomes really the only Asian colonizing power in modern history. They are the only Asian imperial power in the Western European sense of the word (i.e., by forcibly taking over other parts of the world). Once the beast is awakened, he must feed. An insatiable hunger develops which inevitably leads to . . .

GODZILLA ATTACKS!

With Japan's acquisition of all this territory and all these resources in mainland Asia, you might say, "Oh that's enough. You've got enough now, Japan." But once Godzilla is awake, he's not going back to sleep very easily! The Japanese continue to meet

with success after success. In 1914, before World War I was over, Japan strategically joined the Allies against Germany, though they played no real part in the war. As a result of their maneuver, they gained control of German territories in China Proper and German-controlled islands in the Pacific. So without doing anything, they gain more territory at the end of World War I. We already said they started to pull out more pieces of Russia during Russia's civil war. After Russia got the hell beaten out of them in World War One, the Japanese took over some more of their territory in the interim period.

In 1931, the Japanese pretty much take over all of what is now Manchuria, the entire Northeastern part of China, and during the rest of the 1930s, they establish more footholds in China and virtually every other Southeast Asian nation. In each new place, they set up shops and military camps.

In this period between World War I and World War II, all the Europeans were worried about themselves. No one is paying much attention to Japan, except The United States. The United States was very worried about Japanese movement and the growth of their Empire. Even before the war was officially launched, there was animosity between these two powerhouses, Japan and the United States.

The United States, being an antiimperial and anticolonial force, was looking over the Pacific and saying, "That doesn't look good. How could this end well? This isn't good for us or anybody!" Indeed, they were right. A lot of folks were like "Whoa, we're really surprised that Japan attacked Pearl Harbor." Nothing could be further from the truth. These countries may not have declared war at the time, but they weren't on friendly terms. In fact, the United States already had an oil embargo against Japan. That's one of the reasons Japan said it attacked the United States. Let's get to this attack . . .

In 1941, the Empire continues to expand, taking over mainland China and places in Southeast Asia such as Vietnam, Cambodia, Laos, Thailand, Burma, Indonesia. Japan continues to expand its Pacific Island holdings as well. In 1941, it got so big that it decided to attack the United States over in Hawaii. Why didn't it attack mainland United States? That's anybody's guess. In hindsight, it may have been a better idea, but who knows why any of this occurred? What if the Japanese had not

attacked the United States? Maybe the United States wouldn't have done anything to them and there would still be a huge Japanese Empire in what is China today. It's hard to tell.

The Plaid Avenger's take on Pearl Harbor is that it was a warning signal. Japan was setting up a fence around its territory. Japan wasn't trying to take Hawaii over; it was establishing where the fence was. The Japanese were saying, "Okay America, you're a powerhouse; we're a powerhouse now too. We can bomb you in Hawaii so don't come on our side of the fence. This stuff over here, this is ours. This is our imperial holding over here, so just stay on your side." Japan apparently didn't reckon that would be a failure. So we know the ultimate end to this. Maybe we've talked about World War II too much already in this book. But in the official war years, 1940–1945, Japan invaded every other nation in Southeast Asia and the Pacific.

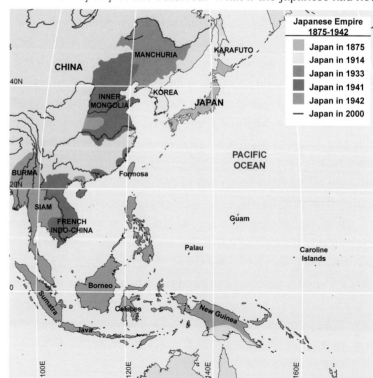

Here's a little known fact that the Plaid Avenger wants you to understand and know: Japan also had designs to invade India and Australia. When I said they had designs, I don't mean some sketches on a cocktail napkin. We're talking about war plans; they had their little Risk board marked with the movements of soldiers, and their troops were in place for this to become reality. It was only a matter of time. They already had small landing parties in Australia, who were camping and scoping things out on reconnaissance.

The other concrete item that still exists in the world today as evidence of Japan's dream to take over all of Asia is the Burma Railway, nicknamed "Death Railway" because 16,000 Allied POWs (mostly British, Australian, Dutch, and American) and over 100,000 Asian laborers died making it. It is the subject of a movie, *The Bridge on the River Kwai*. The laborers were forced to build this railroad system as a supply line for the planned Japanese invasion of India. It ran from Thailand, through Burma, right up to the Indian border.

ANIMOSITY IN ASIA

In these ambitious Japanese plans lies a few more details we should flush out in order to understand today's world a little better. How was it that such a small state with a small army ended up rolling over all of Asia in the first place?

Before all the war crimes and atrocities, Japanese forces were often welcomed to intervene in internal affairs of many of these places. The Japanese Army in the 1930s didn't have to fight tooth and nail to take over many of these countries. Why? By and large, the Japanese came in under something called **The Greater East Asia Co-Prosperity Sphere.** The Japanese used this concept to say, "Hey, we're not here to take over; we're here to free you from your Western European colonizers! These guys are assholes! They're whiteys! Look at us! We look like you, man; we're Asians! We are here to liberate

The Asian Liberators?

you!" So, Japan was often welcomed, particularly by French Indochina, where Vietnam, Laos and Cambodia are today.

Japan goes into these places and do indeed throw off the yoke of European colonialism. Yes indeed . . . but they simply replace the colonizers, without any real liberation effort. It was all a big sham. This made a lot of folks within Asia pretty pissed off because the Japanese ended up being, during the war years, very brutal. The Plaid Avenger can tell you, war is hell, war is brutal, war sucks for everybody involved. Everybody knows that nowadays. However, the Japanese in WWII had a particularly nasty style of warfare and the war crimes and atrocities that were committed against a whole hell of a lot of Asian people by the Japanese has not been, and will not be, forgotten.

A horrific example is the Rape of Nanking in China from 1937 to 1938 where the Japanese took over a city with millions of people, and since they didn't really feel like having a prison camp, they just killed everybody. They just took their bayonets and chopped people's heads off. They lined people up in a row so one bullet would go through more than one of them. For several weeks, the Japanese just slaughtered everybody. This is something the Chinese will never forget. It is still mentioned in popular context, in terms of why we should hate the Japanese. See inset box: Japanese War Atrocities.

Let's not forget about our friends in the middle, the Koreans. Many still hate the Japanese with a passion as well. Japan took over and extracted all of the resources out of Korean mines. How did they do that? They enslaved the Koreans! The whole country essentially became a work camp for Japan. Everyone in Korea was also forced to change their names to Japanese names. Every single person in the country! This was an incredibly difficult time for the Koreans. And trust me, they have not forgotten about it.

The occupation was also pretty nasty for the Chinese and the Koreans, in that some of the worst documented use of biological warfare took place. The Japanese said, "Let's poison a water supply in a town of 5 million and see how long it takes to kill everybody!" Here's one of the Plaid Avenger's personal antifavorites, "Let's get a bunch of plague-infested

What's the Deal with . . . Japanese War Atrocities?

Bataan Death March

Approximately 75,000 Filipino and US soldiers, commanded by Major General Edward P. King, Jr., formally surrendered to the Japanese under General Masaharu Homma, on April 9, 1942, which forced Japan to accept emaciated captives outnumbering its army. Captives were forced to make a weeklong journey, beginning the next day, about 160 kilometers to the north, to Camp O'Donnell, a prison camp. Most of the distance was done marching, a smaller distance was a ride packed into railroad cars. Prisoners of war were beaten randomly, and then were denied food and water for several days. The Japanese tortured them until death. Those who fell behind were executed through various means: shot, beheaded, or bayoneted. Over 10,000 of the 75,000 POWs died. Check out the old-school films *Bataan* (1943) and *Back to Bataan* (1945) with John Wayne.

Bridge on the River Kwai

Great freaking movie. You have to check it out. Based loosely on these real life events: In 1943 the Japanese used POWs to build a railroad across Burma (this is against the Geneva Convention on treatment of prisoners). This was part of a project to link existing Thai and Burmese railway lines to create a route from Bangkok, Thailand to Rangoon, Burma (now Myanmar) to support the Japanese occupation of Burma. The railway was going to be a critical connection and supply line for the planned invasion of India. About 100,000 conscripted Asian laborers and 16,000 prisoners of war died on the whole project. Damn. And Obi Wan Kenobi is in the movie too. That helps.

The Rape of Nanking

The Nanking Massacre, commonly known as **The Rape of Nanking,** refers to the most infamous of the war crimes committed by the Japanese military during World War II—acts carried out by Japanese troops in and around Nanjing (then known in English as Nanking), China, after it fell to the Imperial Japanese Army on December 13, 1937. The duration of the massacre is not clearly defined, although the period of carnage lasted well into the next six weeks, until early February 1938.

During the occupation of Nanjing, the Japanese army committed numerous atrocities, such as rape, looting, arson, and the execution of prisoners of war and civilians. Although the executions began under the pretext of eliminating Chinese soldiers disguised as civilians, a large number of innocent men were wrongfully identified as enemy combatants and killed. A large number of women and children were also killed as rape and murder became more widespread. Final toll: 10,000 to 80,000 raped; 5,000 to 20,000 slaughtered.

Want to know why there is animosity between the Chinese and Japanese to this day? Look no further.

---

rats, put them in a bomber, and drop them over the countryside to see how the disease progresses through the country!" They also did some other "little" things like mustard-gassing whole towns . . . this was pretty nasty business.

Now you know why many Asian countries view Japan with extreme suspicion, apprehension, and/or outright hate. The Chinese government and some other governments still want more **war retributions:** monetary payments from the Japanese for the atrocities they committed during World War II.

The Plaid Avenger had to elaborate on this animosity that exists to this day between Japan and many other Asian countries, particularly China and Korea . . . because it continues to play a part of politics in today's world. Every year when the Japanese educational systems releases their history textbooks for the K-12 schools, Korean and Chinese people protest. Huh? WTF? Why would Koreans care about what school kids in Tokyo read? Just this: the Japanese textbooks continue to gloss completely over the war years, thus marginalizing all the bad stuff that was perpetrated on the other Asians groups. War crimes, biological warfare, and Japanese sex slave operations in Korea are all conveniently missing from the history books in Japan, and that really pisses off a lot of folks.

This animosity also bubbles to the surface whenever the Japanese prime minister visits a war shrine located in Tokyo: The Yasukuni Shrine. Why do you need to know this? It will continue to be a point of friction between these two countries who will be the two big power players of the 21st century. It's good to know why they hate each other and this is a great example. The shrine commemorates all of the Japanese soldiers who died fighting for, or in service of, the Emperor, no matter what the circumstances.

So you have to know about these bad things in order to 'get' the attitudes that these countries and their peoples have about each other. From the Japanese standpoint, you need to think about how big this goal of dominating Asia proper really was. From the Asian standpoint, think about how far the Japanese demonstrated that they were willing to go to achieve it. This isn't a trivial thing. This gets into why Japan is viewed with suspicion, animosity and sometimes hatred by parts of Asia to this day. The Plaid Avenger started off this chapter by saying China vs. Japan, Japan vs. China for a reason. These are places that do not like each other at all.

Now, I'm sure you think that all this stuff is ancient history and that it really doesn't affect today's world at all. Oh contraire my friends. There hasn't been an official heads of state meeting between China and Japan for almost a decade because of the Yasukuni War Shrine stuff. Trade deals have been blocked between the countries when tensions rise. Lawsuits between the countries on war reparations are still active. Is that real enough for you? But let's go ahead and get past the war years and bring it on home into the modern era . . .

I don't think America was happy about Pearl Harbor. Do you?

GODZILLA IS DEAD

After the Germans are defeated in Europe, Uncle Sam then turns all his attention to finishing the job in the Pacific theater of war. And it was brutal. Island by island, enclave by enclave, the Japanese are beaten back by the Americans, but at a horrific cost of human lives on both sides. The US was suing Japan for total, unconditional surrender, and that was something that was just not going to come at an easy price.

What's the Deal with . . . the Yasukuni Shrine?
Yasukuni Shrine (literally "peaceful nation shrine") is a controversial Shinto shrine located in Tokyo that is dedicated to the spirits of soldiers who died fighting on behalf of the Japanese emperor.

So what's the problem? Every country honors its war dead, don't they? The Yasukuni Shrine also honors a total of 1,068 convicted Japanese war criminals, including 14 executed Class A war criminals, a fact that has engendered protests in a number of neighboring countries who believe their presence indicates a failure on the part of Japan to fully atone for its military past. President Koizumi regularly visits the shrine, which serves to seriously piss off China and South Korea . . . and perhaps even North Korea, but who knows since they are totally whack-ass insane.

It's the equivalent of the Germans visiting a war shrine to pay respects to Hitler and the other Nazi war dead. Sound extreme? Yep. I call 'em like I see 'em.

Yasukuni

To finish up, we know in August 1945—Hiroshima and Nagasaki go boom. The other part of World War II history, which is mostly unknown yet crucial, is the fact that the US had been firebombing the living shit out of the entire country for months leading up to the actual dropping of the atomic bomb from the Enola Gay. After the second bomb, the Emperor gives the unconditional surrender, and for the first (and only) time in its entire history, Japan is not only defeated, but occupied.

Nagasaki go boom.   The aftermath.

Japan, much like Europe after World War II, is totaled. The two cities that the atomic bombs dropped on were gone, but the rest of Japan was leveled as well. There was nothing; it was utter destruction. This is important to note before we go on. Before we get to the rebirth, the rejuvenation of Godzilla!

AFTER THE FIRE

After World War II, it's another fascinating time because—just like the Meiji Restoration—the Japanese do it again. It's unfathomable. Their country has been smashed, destroyed, and occupied by a foreign power. The United States, led by MacArthur, is in effective control of the entire government and they set about redoing it again, in a more democratic fashion. MacArthur and his team wrote them a new constitution, fashioned them a new society, and set about helping them rebuild so that Japan could become a strong, stable US ally in the area.

MacArthur: Japanese breaker, taker, and re-maker

So the Japanese are again faced with the same two paths. "What should we do . . . should we take Option 1: resist the foreign invaders or bide our time and wait for them to leave, should we have some underground resistance movement? Or Option 2: should we embrace them, do everything they say and do it better?" Of course, they go with Option 2 again. They have another major restoration, but this one has no name. It's just a 'do over' of everything this time, completely under United States guidance. They go from a monarchy to a constitutional monarchy, which is basically a fair equivalent of a democracy in today's world. In fact, it is exactly like American democracy except they pay tribute to a royal line, just like the British. Hmmmm . . . that sets me to thinking. There are quite a few other British-Japanese similarities you should be aware of . . .

One side note of note: The Japanese themselves added a clause to their new constitution which banned them from establishing a military. Apparently they felt so bad about their wartime activities that they wanted to completely eliminate any possibility that they would repeat their mistake in the future. McArthur and crew were adamantly *against* this clause, but Japan insisted. Why would McArthur not want this? Well, the old General was pretty savvy: he was already looking over at China as a potential Cold War adversary, and he wanted Japan to be the counter-balance to that growing commie threat. However, instead of getting a militaristic Japan under US direction, he got a pacificist Japan that needed US protection. This sets up the situation which still exists today: the US is the primary protector of Japan should any outside force attack it.

So the Japanese embrace capitalism, democracy, re-industrialization and rebuilding of their society with a passion under the tutelage of the US. Uncle Sam gives them billions of Yankee dollars to achieve this goal; much like an Asian version of the Marshall Plan. However, one big difference is that the US stuck around to oversee the rebuilding and restructuring of Japan . . . particularly because they had assumed a 'big brother' role since Japan had officially banned itself from possessing a military of its own. This is one of the main reasons that these two countries are still tight when it comes to foreign policy issues.

United Kingdom and Japan: Siamese Twins?
Why are the two countries similar? **Number One:** Island nation, **Number Two:** Off the coast of Eurasia, flanking opposite sides of the continent. **Number Three:** Kind of stand-offish from their neighborhood international organizations: Great Britain is distant from the EU, Japan is distant from ASEAN and other Asian groups. **Number Four:** Lapdogs for US foreign policy; they do pretty much whatever the US tells them to do. The UK does it because they love us; Japan because they owe us and we are still their defenders. No one will attack them because the United States is their military.

Queen of England

Emperor Hirohito

Gordon Brown

Fukada

USA's loyal pets . . . oops, I mean allies.

One final thing about the military issue: think of the big bonus and boon to Japanese society due to not having to invest in a military. Most of the countries in the world have to provide for self-defense. They have to spend at least *some* money on it. Not so in Japan . . .

ECONOMY NOW

. . . and this is one of the reasons, among many others, why Japan is so rich today. They've had big brother United States there. They have had the luxury of investing every ounce of capital straight into the infrastructure to make themselves better and better and better. Let's make a list of why Japan has the number two economy in the world today:

→ **Number One:** They have not *had* to invest in any military expenditures for 60 years now.

→ **Number Two:** They have enjoyed US influence and economic ties with the number one economy in the world for the last 60 years.

→ **Number Three:** Just like BASF, the Japanese don't make anything . . . they make everything better. They are a value-adding society. So while they never invented the automobile, the computer, the video game, television, or cell phones, they make all those things better. They continue to add value in the high spectrum of things, bringing us to

→ **Number Four:** They are almost completely technology and service sector oriented, and they are very good at it. They're so good at it that they run **positive trade balances** with every other country in the world with whom they trade. They make more money on the sale of the stuff they make than they spend on the stuff they buy. They are always in the plus. I will come back to the list.

What else is going on with Japan? It's role of Japan in Asia is very similar to the United States' role in our part of the world. While there is some animosity between Japan and some other Asian countries because of the past, it is still looked to as an economic leader. The United States is the number one powerhouse and Japan is number two and both these countries are looked to as leaders. Just like when the United States' economy takes a turn for the worse, places like South America and Caribbean follow suit, when Japan's economy takes a dive, all the surrounding economies in Korea, Taiwan, and Indonesia do too, because there is so much trade from one country to the next. So in this respect, Japan is to Asia what America is to the Western Hemisphere.

We can draw a few more parallels to the United States. Japan is an extremely rich society, so it is industrialized and fully urbanized which means labor is really expensive, just like in the United States. You cannot get cheap labor in Japan. Like the United States, Japan has minimum wage laws and generally high labor costs. So what? What is the parallel here, Plaid Avenger? This high cost of labor has caused jobs and industries to move out of Japan, just as they have in the United States.

Just like all the car manufacturing companies that were once in the United States are all in Mexico or other nearby places with cheap labor, Japan's service sector jobs have been moving to places like China, Korea, and Indonesia. Corporations make more money if they manufacture things where labor is cheap. Back in the 1994 US presidential election, Ross Perot was hearing "a big sucking sound" as jobs were moving to Mexico at the onset of NAFTA. The same deal is happening in Japan as businesses move towards cheap labor taking all those jobs with them. So while Japanese corporations might still be the biggest moneymakers on Japanese cars, most of them aren't making them in Japan anymore; they are made in all points south: China, Indonesia, Vietnam, and so on.

POPULATION NOW

So how do they differ from the United States? For starters, the total population of Japan is around 126 million. That is actually quite a few folks on a handful of islands, that is mostly covered with mountains and forests. Japan is overwhelmingly urbanized, post-industrialized, and sanitized. They have some of the highest living standards, highest levels of technology, and highest GDP per capitas on the planet. Sounds good so far! However, the population of Japan is shrinking. This is a double whammy. People are

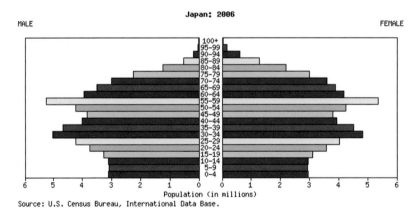

Source: U.S. Census Bureau, International Data Base.

Like the Russians, it's going down.

increasingly coming up short on the 2.1 child **replacement level,** which you remember from Chapter 2. So every year, the population of Japan, while still stable, gets slightly smaller. What does this have to do with anything? You need workers in the factories to make stuff, to make money, so that the economy will benefit. If you don't have workers, employers have to go somewhere else. And boy, have they ever! They can't even *maintain* the technology and service sectors there at this point in time because the population is getting smaller. But wait, it gets compounded even further!

As I suggested earlier, the Japanese are extremely, fiercely, culturally independent and ethnically distinct. They're *Japanese,* not Chinese and not Korean. Everybody else in the neighborhood would agree with that statement. By the way, this is not a racist slant by The Plaid Avenger. Both Japanese and Korean societies are purely Japanese or Korean. This is even more true in Korea, the most ethnically pure place on the Earth. It's easy to take the census in Korea because there is only one damn box to check: the Korean one. In Japan, 99 percent of the population is Japanese. They actively discourage immigration there. When you visit there, you will have a great time but if you move there permanently don't expect too many people to be very friendly, particularly if you are a few shades away from Asian. This may sound blunt, but racist or not, the Plaid Avenger is telling you how it is around the world.

This is not a place that is embracing a lot of people from around the planet. That might be all fine and dandy with them but as I suggested, their work force is going down, birth rates are falling. This is a shrinking population. In the United States, people are not having that many kids but immigrants come

"Yes Plaid Avenger, I need your help to increase Japanese population . . ."

from other parts of the world to fill those work spots and keep the economy growing. Japan is coming to a critical juncture at which they need to figure out what the hell to do. These trends cannot go on indefinitely. They are actually pulling people out of retirement to keep things floating. I've heard these folks referred to as the *Silver Hair League.* People continue to work into their 70s . . . and beyond! Hey Granny Fu, get your ass back to work!

Not only is the declining population affecting the workforce, but it also has impacts on the consumption side of the economy too. Many car manufacturers and other retail businesses are re-focusing their sales to accommodate consumers in other parts of Asia. What's the point of having a Honda dealership in Tokyo where everybody already has a car, and the population (and therefore consumer base) is shrinking? Better to invest in India or China or Vietnam where consumers are plentiful, getting richer, and are growing. This is affecting development of new products line as well; Honda and Toyota are introducing new lines in India that cost less than $2500 per vehicle! Sweet!

The Japanese government is really struggling with this issue right now. They need workers, they need a tax base to draw from, and they need their economy to stay vibrant so they can maintain their great standards of living. Unfortunately, people don't want to have big families . . . and they also don't really want to change their extremely restrictive immigration policy either. Something's gotta give though. Don't be surprised to hear about the government either promoting people to get busy in the bedroom, or 're-educating' their population to be more accepting of foreigners.

MILITARY NOW

If it looks like a military, and smells like a military. . . .

Another thing to consider in modern Japan is the fate of the **Japanese Self-Defense Force.** What's this all about? As I suggested to you, after World War II, under MacArthur, the Japanese signed away their desire and ability to have an active military. Like the Germans, the Japanese conceded that they screwed up so bad and that they were going to be peace-loving people now. So their current 'national Self-Defense Force' is exactly that: the equivalent of the US National Guard that serves as an emergency 911 for the whole country in times of national disaster/national emergency, or, theoretically, to repel any attack on the nation from foreign powers.

It is important to note that it is implicit in their charter that they do not possess any powers to pro-actively attack anybody . . . meaning, they have absolutely no offensive role, no offensive tactics, no offense, period. No troops abroad, no missions abroad, no action abroad. Only self-defense of the state. It's the 'home team' in every sense of the phrase. You do have people wearing helmets and camouflage outfits, sometimes with guns, on ships and in tanks and airplanes and helicopters . . . I mean, it sure as hell looks like a military. But their only function is helping out when natural disasters like earthquakes strike.

The reason that the role of this Self-Defense Force was so specifically defined was because right after World War II, everyone in the neighborhood was scared shitless that the Japanese might re-militarize and start its imperial rampage all over again. Apparently Japan was scared of this too, and that's why they neutered themselves. But everyone was willing to accept a Self-Defense Force. That's no prob. So end of story, right? Well . . .

This force has been evolving rapidly into something that looks more and more like an army here lately. Important to note is that this only came to the attention of China and the world a few years ago. How'd they find out? In the last five years, since the US invasion of Iraq, Japan has volunteered its "troops" to go and support the US in Iraq. This was done primarily as a show of support for their US buddies; to be a part of the 'Coalition of the Willing.' In reality: all they were doing was refueling and resupplying US navel vessels out in the Indian Ocean, but its the thought that counts. The United States may say, "Oh that's a good thing; they're our ally and they owe it to us." But this is taken with great apprehension by other Asian nations, particularly China, who has reinforced the notion that if Japan says it doesn't have an army, it shouldn't. They say, "How is a Self-Defense Force defending Japan in Iraq?" The rest of Asia has concluded that this has morphed into something different. The fact that Japan has sent its Self-Defense Force abroad challenges the definition of self-defense. You send armies abroad, not self-defense forces. This has changed the whole equation.

With no uncertainty, the Plaid Avenger wants you to know this for sure: While many Asian nations may be apprehensive about the Japanese Force, there is a country on this planet that wants Japan to throw the antiwar clause out of its constitution altogether and get busy rearming. I wonder who that could be? The United States is practically *demanding* that they remove it. Why would the United States want this? The United States wants to use Japan as a countering force to the rise of China in Asia. It's a checkmate. In this respect, Japan's role is very much like Great Britain.

Sounds strange but that's what it is. That's why the Japanese Self-Defense Force is a big issue. The Plaid knows that anytime this issue is even hinted at, China gets extremely pissed that Japan is morphing its self-defense force into an army, almost as pissed as China gets when any Japanese prime minister visits that war shrines we talked about earlier.

One more point on the Japanese changing their constitution for their military: There are several states in the world that the UN is considering allowing on the UN permanent Security Council. Japan is one of the candidates to be on this council and the US is its biggest sponsor. The US is all in favor of Japan being on the UN permanent Security Council. Gosh I wonder why? Maybe because Japan will do everything the US says. China is flipping out because it is vehemently opposed to this.

Here's the funny thing about it: The US has told Japan, more or less, that it will not support its candidacy until Japan gets a military. If it gets one, it would be no surprise if it was to develop nuclear capacity within days. Japan

already knows how to produce nuclear power. It is feasible that if it gets a military, it would be the next declared nuclear power in the world. That is exactly what the US wants: to have a nuclear station off the coast of Eurasia to be on our team. Again, this is a check and checkmate situation for the US. It is using Japan to keep checks and balances against the rise of Chinese power.

Along with the Chinese checkmate, the US would very much like Japan to reassert itself militarily for much more practical reasons too:

1. The US military has become over-committed, over-stretched and over-used in other parts of the world, and they simply can't keep tens of thousands of troops hanging out in Japan and South Korea indefinitely. Redeployment of troops is already underway.

2. If Japan gets its army back, then they could actually help out the US in all of its current active conflicts. I'm sure the United States would welcome the change from being their protector to being a joint partner in military activities. The US would warmly welcome any permanent addition to their 'Coalition of the Willing' in the War on Terror.

3. If Japan re-arms, especially in the nuclear capacity, then the US could let them deal with the North Korean freaks more effectively. Japan was always the only legitimate possible target of a North Korean attack anyway.

So back in 1945, Japan decided that they weren't going to have the military anymore, so they couldn't get into any more trouble. Unfortunately for Japan, trouble has found them. The status and activities of their Self-Defense Force has them in a pinch between their pro-military, US ally and their anti-military Asian neighbors. Anchors away my samurai friends! Troubled waters ahead!

FOREIGN POLICY NOW

Which brings us to the last, and appropriately so since all that Self-Defense Force talk is intimately related to Japanese diplomacy in the modern era. As I have suggested earlier and often in this chapter, relations between Japan and its neighbors have been tense to say the least since the war years. Downright hostile might be a better description at times. Every

Koizumi to Fukada shift: Hater to player!

year when the school books are released and every time a high-ranking official hits up the Yasukuni Shrine, the Chinese and Koreans get severely steamed and relations get further strained. Japanese troops sent abroad to support the US is just more fuel for the fire . . .

But wait kids! Things are looking up right this second! Japan's current mindset is that perhaps they should do more to appease the neighborhood. They want to be a good neighbor. Perhaps they should call in Fred Rogers for advice. You know what? They don't even need Mr. Rogers' input right now, because they are making positive moves on their own which are working fairly well. After a decade of hard-line politics from the former Japanese Prime Minister Junichiro Koizumi, a regular Yasukuni visitor, the current administration has taken a much more conciliatory stance towards their Chinese cohorts. What gives?

The current Prime Minister of Japan Yasuo Fukuda understands that the future of the planet is one that features China as a major player. Japan cannot afford to piss off the economic giant that China is becoming: both exports and imports are increasing dramatically between these two super-states, and no one wants to jeopardize that. (This is true for Korea too . . . it will soon be the 10th largest economy on the planet.) Since Japan pissed off everyone during their imperial period, China increasingly has the upper hand as the future economic and political leader of the wider Asian region. Japan cannot risk entirely isolating itself amongst its Asian 'hood.

In light of that, Japan has been opening up to more local dialogue. In May of 2008, President Hu Jintao paid an official state visit to Fukuda in Japan . . . where Hu displayed not only his savvy statecraft, but also his wicked serve in a round of ping-pong against some of the local superstars. (Is there really such a thing as a ping-pong superstar?) This was the first official heads-of-state meeting between the two countries in a decade. That is a big deal! On top of that, Japan just sent a shit-ton of foreign aid and expert teams of search and rescue folks to aid the Chinese in their Sichuan earthquake disaster. The take-home lesson: there is currently a big thaw in Sino-Japanese relations that will likely be the trend of the future.

And what of their US big brother? Well, the balancing act continues. There is actually a large percentage of popular opinion in Japan that favors keeping the anti-military clause in the constitution, and this same group is adamantly opposed to the Self-Defense Force being abroad too. In February of 2008, the Japanese Diet (the equivalent of Congress) refused to fund the Force's mission of re-supplying US ships for the War on Terror. This was a big blow to not only the US, but also to Prime Minister Fukuda himself and his political party who really had egg on their faces for not being able to help their old ally. Funding has since resumed, but the political outcome is still unclear. The future status of the Force is far from resolved, as is Japan's direction in future foreign policy.

SAYONARA!

With no doubts we can say that Japan will have considerable impact on world affairs for some time to come. As an economic leader in the world and in its neighborhood, it has set the example that other Asian economies are rapidly living up to. That role as an economic powerhouse will hold for a while longer . . . and it has company coming to dinner too! Japan is the number 2 economy. China is the number 4 economy and soon will be number 3, South Korea is number 11 soon to be number 10. Wow. Three top ten economies all within spitting distance of each other. This 'hood is hot!

But Japan is also staunchly in the western camp as well, and one need look no further than the spill-over in commercial and popular culture to see how intimately ties they are to the west. Ninjas, karate, **Atari**, judo, manga, sushi bars, sake shots, Panasonic, Nintendo, **Sony**, Honda, Toyota, Kawasaki, Speed Racer, Samurai Jack, Tamagotchi, Totorro, Akira, the Matrix, Kill Bill, and the godforsaken Pokeman Shit, man, there was a damn Pikachu blimp floating in the last Macy's Thanksgiving Day parade right beside Snoopy for pete's sake. Japan not only adopted western institutions and technologies, but has the unique ability to morph the east and west traditions together to come out with interesting products that appeal to consumers in both cultures. They do it like no other.

As they improve relations in Asia, and continue their strong relations with the US, the EU, and other rich entities on the planet, Japan will certainly have a unique perspective on the events of 21st century. A shaper of the global economy, of global politics, and most importantly global culture, our Pokeman playing friends have a critical role to play.

If we can just get them to un-invent karaoke. . . .

一條治郎忠槙
能光守教種

Don't be fooled by the dress: he is a bad-ass

CHAPTER OUTLINE

Australia and New Zealand

G'DAY MATES!!!

So we're heading south from Japan to our friends in the Australia and New Zealand region. When the Plaid Avenger is traveling around the world and can't make it back home to America, I just stop off in Australia, or as I like to call it, the **Mini-America of the southern hemisphere**. America for short. If you ever want to piss off people from Australia, just pass that along. It infuriates them for some reason. They tell the Plaid Avenger that they're distinctly Australian and unique in their own way. Yeah right! You dudes and dudettes are exactly the same as us, just a European and American 20th century cultural amalgamation rip-off!

The Plaid Avenger is always straight shooting, so I am not going to lie to you; this region is not one of tremendous significance on the world stage. But like Japan, it does play its part to effect current events. Its primary role right now is as a platform of European culture and US foreign policy in the southern hemisphere. But even that is changing quickly here lately as the mates from 'down under' are shifting their political and economic focus to be more in tune with their Asian 'hood. But I am getting ahead of myself. Let's first focus our attention on the physical traits of the region.

LET'S GO FOR A WALKABOUT!

Physically, Australia and New Zealand are two island countries, even though Australia is classified as a continent. If you look at it, it's really just a big island. They are two islands of extremes. In Australia, the vast majority of the interior is desert and steppe. It's very similar to the American Midwest. There's a bunch of cattle ranching going on; it's

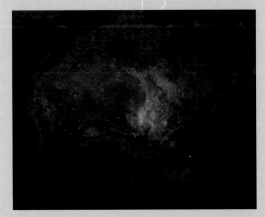
Area comparison.

Lights out in the middle!

the Outback after all. But there aren't too many people there. In fact, a massive percentage of the interior of Australia, being so dry, has caused a primarily coastal settlement pattern. Everybody's hanging out on the coast and the vast majority of Australia's population is located on these coastal margins, particularly the southeastern coastal margin.

As you can see from the lights at night, virtually everybody is on the east coast of Australia. Before we go any further let me begin pointing out the parallels between Australia and America. Here is one outlined for you on the map: population primarily in coastal areas, particularly the eastern seaboard. In New Zealand we have the same pattern, but for different reasons. New Zealand, much like Japan, is a mountainous country. In fact, Japan and New Zealand are almost identical. They are both island nations, made of several different islands, and both are on the borders of major continental plates: both volcanic in origin, so the interior of the country is very mountainous. The terrain makes it a no-brainer for most people to live on the coast. Especially those damn hobbits which seem to be over-running the country here lately. Gandalf . . . help us!

Climatically speaking, these two countries are opposites. New Zealand is cooler and wetter, with a climate more like the Pacific Northwest section of the US, or even like the UK. Australia has some Mediterranean style climates on the southern coastlines, and even a little tropic savanna-type areas in the north, but the interior is largely steppe and desert. Dry ass area with limited rainfall, few trees, and scrub and short grass vegetation. **What** are those **climates** good for? **Cattle and sheep production. There is a lot of grazing action going on in Australia.** Big exports of wool, lamb, and beef.

One last physical note: what Australia lacks in climatically, it more than makes up for in physical resources. They have tons of coal, iron, copper, opal, zinc, and uranium. Put that together with the agricultural commodities, and you have a serious export base to work with. Think about that for a second . . . what types of countries mainly export primary products?

Hold that thought, we'll be back to it soon enough.

AMERICA JUNIOR

Why does the Plaid refer to this region as the mini-America of the south? Where do many people from America, who like to travel abroad, want to go? Australia! Why? Because it's just like home! People want to see the same shit as in the US, want to eat the same shit as in the US, want to talk the same language as in the US, because they are more comfortable in that setting. But it's far enough away that you think you're actually being adventurous! There's actually something to the idea of Australia just being a transplanted southern piece of America or Europe, but just 'down under.' Down under the equator that is.

Australia is quite unique in the southern hemisphere of this planet for a few reasons. For one, it's the only region in the southern hemisphere that is habitated primarily by white people. It's also the only region south of the equator that is totally rich and developed. It has standards of living and material wealth on par with that of Western Europe, Japan, and the US, and no other region south of the equator can say that. So the standard of living thing is another reason why Australia is the Mini-America of the south. But oh, there's so much more . . .

BACKGROUND

Why is Australia white? Why, because it was colonized by whities of course! Both the US and Australia were originally British **convict colonies.** In the UK back in the day, in the 1600's and 1700's, one of the subsidiary purposes of Britain's colonies was to get rid of the British criminals. Britain was getting overpopulated, and laws were very strict. The historical anecdote that explains this fairly well is the establishment of the **baker's dozen.** The baker's dozen is 13 instead of 12. Why? There was actually a law that stated if a baker shorted you a donut, he could be put in jail. So the baker's dozen was born. Throw in an extra one, cause who the hell wants to go to jail over a donut?

So this was a pretty legally strict society where lots of people got tossed into jail for sometimes menial offenses. Among the options given to convicts were the gallows or a boat ride to a colony. Guess which one people chose? So you know there is a criminal element to America's background, and the same goes for Australia. Here's the funny part: the British used to ship their convicts to their American colony, so when did they start shipping them to Australia? Right around the 1780's. Why is that? Well, in 1776 America had a revolution, so we kicked those British prisoner-exporting ass-holes out, eliminating their felon-absorbing resource. So the British, who were floating around the world, figured out that they had claimed a huge chunk of shit down in the southern hemisphere. There's a place to send convicts! So Australia was established in 1788 as a convict colony because the British couldn't send them to America anymore.

SOCIETAL STRUCTURE

How is Australia like America? Let me count the ways . . . If we look at virtually any facet of life in this part of the world we can look at America and see that it's pretty much the same. Let's just start listing them off, shall we? Australia consists of a highly **urbanized** society. There are roughly identical urbanization rates between Australia and the US. This point is of significance because everybody has the opposite impression about Australia. Everybody thinks they're all about the Outback, the Crocodile Hunter, and Crocodile Dundee. There are all these wild and crazy guys down there! Make no bones about it; if you go down and ask any Australian how much time they spend in the Outback, "You've got to be kidding me, mate" is a likely response.

Why is that? Because the Outback sucks. It's crazy that anybody would want to go to the Outback. It's got all kinds of crazy shit in it, spiders that will jump onto your face, the top ten poisonous snakes in the world . . . nobody wants to go out in "the bush." It is a classic mythology of Australia. It sounds cool, makes them seem all brave and manly, but nobody hangs out in the interior of Australia. Most people hang out in cities, in suburbs, which you are all probably familiar with. They are all content to stay the hell out of the Outback, and have the nice little picket fence around their manicured suburban lawns. There is no difference between the levels of urbanization in the US and Australia.

That is due to the **standard of living.** This is a very rich place. Per capita, it is on par with the US and Western Europe and any other rich place. Standards of living, levels of technology, material wealth: there's no difference. People live there just like they live here, and have all of the same creature comforts. This reiterates why nobody is out in the wild, because rich people go and see the wild when they're on vacation, and then they get the hell out of there because the wild sucks.

And one of the reasons that they have a high standard of living is that there are not a whole lot of them there to have to split the resources among. Australia and New Zealand populations are extremely low: there is only about 23 million folks across this entire region. Most major metropolitan areas of the world have more people than that. And just look at the population pyramid! As stable as

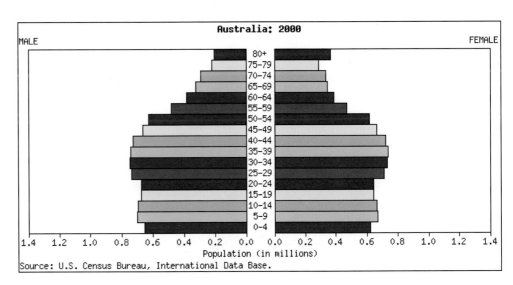

Australia: 2000

MALE   FEMALE

80+
75-79
70-74
65-69
60-64
55-59
50-54
45-49
40-44
35-39
30-34
25-29
20-24
15-19
10-14
5-9
0-4

1.4 1.2 1.0 0.8 0.6 0.4 0.2 0.0 0.0 0.2 0.4 0.6 0.8 1.0 1.2 1.4
Population (in millions)
Source: U.S. Census Bureau, International Data Base.

stable gets. Only through immigration will the population of the region increase, kind of like . . . ummm . . . the US. But there's more!

Australia also has similar dietary habits, which ties back in with standards of living. They are big meat consumers, just like in the US. The only big difference is that the Americans like to slay the cows and eat the hamburgers, but the Australians are all about lamb.

Lambs! How cute.

And . . . how delicious!

They love the chops. They are also big beer and wine drinkers, like the US. In most places that were colonized by Western Europeans, the beer and wine tradition still exists. Australia is one of the booming wine regions now, soon to be the number one wine exporter on the planet. Of course many of you don't drink wine yet, but you do drink beer. What kind of beer do you think of when you think of Australia? That's right, Foster's!

Perhaps the Plaid Avenger is getting too shallow, talking about standards of living and beer and meat consumption. What other parallels are there?

This may just seem like a funny side note, but this may play a part in why the two nations are so similar today. Both countries have a criminal background, a criminal profile . . . remember they started as convict colonies. How has that played into today's society? This is a stretch, but stay with me folks. What do people like to do in both of these societies? We've already pointed out the beer drinking thing, which seems like a nice criminal element. Both beer drinking societies, both like to party. What else do they like to do while consuming alcoholic beverages? I don't know . . . watch brutal sports? Yes! The Americans have their football, Australians have rugby. And the Aussies are even more hardcore than the US: they take the pads off and beat the hell out of each other while everyone who isn't playing drinks beer and watches.

On a more serious note, each country has a rugged, individualistic archetypal character. The Americans have the Marlboro man, a lone, rugged warrior out on the plains, wrangling cows and looking out for coyotes. So that's part of the common symbology, the perception of what it is to be an American. He embodies individualistic pride. They've got the same stuff down in Australia except they wrangle crocs and look out for dingoes. Do these types of characters represent the majority of either place? Hell no. But these characters are popular symbols in this society. There really aren't these archetypal figures anywhere else in the world. It may be partially due to the fact that both places have **large expanses of land** with **low population density.** They have frontiers, and there has to be the rugged individual to go explore those frontiers.

Here's another similarity between Australia and the US: the settling convicts exterminated nearly the entirety of their respective native populations. There is a history of repression of native peoples in both places. In the US, it was the Native Americans, the Amerindians. In Australia they had the Aborigines. Both of those peoples suffered immensely in the onslaught of British colonization in exactly the same ways. In fact, it was particularly bad in Australia.

American Cowboy
See the difference?

Australian Cowboy

In Tasmania, the island off of the south coast of Australia, there were some indigenous people called the Tasmanians who were openly hunted during a period of the settlement of Australia. The government essentially said, "Hey settlers, want some free land? Go down to Tasmania! And if the natives give you any trouble, don't feel bad about killing them." So it became a sport to go out and hunt the indigenous Tasmanians. This was done so efficiently that they killed every one to the last man, woman, and child. That's the criminal background manifesting itself in one of the nastier ways in history.

Another historical consideration of why both societies evolved out this frontiersman mythology has to do with how the both countries grew. Both started on the eastern seaboard of a large uncharted land mass, and proceeded to expand and conquer the continents in a continuous westward expansion. Interesting, isn't it? Australia even underwent a western 'Gold Rush' at almost the exact same time as the famous Californian rush of the same name, but with one slight difference: theirs was more profitable!

So brutal sports, slaughter of indigenous populations, mostly white, cowboy image, and an affinity for beer all play into this criminal background in Australia, and this is why the Plaid Avenger refers to it as the Mini-America of the south.

Put all these historical, physical, and cultural factors together and you are starting to get a sense of why the Plaid Avenger draws so many parallels between the US and Australians regions. But you don't have to take my word for it! There is proof a'plenty that these two states have a tight relationship: let's just take a look at their foreign policies for a minute . . .

AWESOME ALLY

When it comes to 'Team West' foreign policy, one could not find a better friend than those Aussie mates. They have been there year in and year out for their western allies, for every single international conflict and conflagration. But we can be even more specific: first, Australia has always supported every endeavor of the old British motherland, and then later came on board for all things American too. This bunch really sticks together.

And I'm not talking about supporting them on paper, or in a UN vote, or economically. I'm talking about Aus-

The 'Roo Brigade will always be ready to serve freedom!

tralians participating side by side with their English-speaking brothers-in-arms in World War 1, World War 2, the Korean War, the Vietnam War, the Cold War, the War on Terror, which has spawned the two newest Aussie supported wars: the campaign in Afghanistan and the war in Iraq. Every conflict. Every time. They are there for the West. Check out one of Mel Gibson's first starring roles in a movie named Gallipoli; it shows Aussie troops fighting the Turks in WWI.

Now, being a small country with a small population, the numbers of Australian forces that have participated in these conflicts is not a huge number. But it's the thought that counts. Especially when the thought is a bunch of dudes with sub-machine guns. But I digress . . . Point is, that they have regularly been looked to as a vote of support for western ideology worldwide; most currently counting themselves as one of the 'Coalition of the Willing' in the lead up to the Iraq War. They are the only folks south of the equator you can say that about.

So historically strong are the Australian/American ties that the Plaid Avenger counts them among the three most reliable, solid platforms of US foreign policy in the world. The UK, Japan, and Australia can pretty much be counted on to support US endeavors, almost with no questions asked. In the past, this essentially made these countries the US's bitches in terms of foreign policy. But times do change . . .

While I stand by the description of Australia as a loyal ally of the US, modern times have forced them to be more pragmatic. And sometimes being a loyal ally has to be pulled back due to popular opinion. Most Australians were opposed to the

US-led invasion of Iraq, and the government did take a popularity hit for its staunch participation. It perhaps was part of the reason that the old government just got thrown out in the most recent elections. Time to introduce you to someone new:

In a sign of the times, the newest Prime Minister Kevin Rudd has already announced Australian troop withdrawal from Iraq. He is the equivalent of a Democrat in the American political spectrum, and a fairly liberal one at that, that came into office in December 2007. Rudd also immediately signed the Kyoto Protocol on limiting greenhouse gas emission: an international treaty that both the US and Australia had jointly been stonewalling. So suddenly it seems that the US is standing alone a bit more on the international stage. But don't be fooled by this slight change in support: Australia is still a big component of US and Team West foreign policy, and will stand by their boys for some time to come.

Prime Minister Kevin Rudd: "Sorry US, but we are getting the hell out . . ."

A WORD ON THEIR WEIRD WAY TO WEALTH

This is where things get a bit trickier, so the Plaid Avenger is going to have to sort a few things out for you. We've made it expressly clear that the US is the powerhouse economy of the planet, but China, at number four, is catching up. Japan is at the number two slot and Germany's at number three. Where's Australia? It's in 15th place. In terms of total GNP, how rich is this place? Not very. However, in levels of material wealth per person, they're not in bad shape. How could this be? How could they have a standard of living that's identical to ours? They just sit around drinking beer and grilling shrimps on the **barbie.** That's a pretty good life. How can they be that way if they're not in the top ten economies? It is a strange circumstance, and perhaps a unique circumstance to Australia, that when we think of features that make it the most unique, it's not an exceptionally wealthy place as a total.

Australian number one export. Money!

What do they produce? What do they really do? What do you buy from there? Do they make computers? Cars? Linens? VCRs? Software? Video games? I don't think so. What have you ever bought that said "Made in Australia"? Here's the quick answer: didgeridoos and boomerangs. That's not much of an export economy to put them among some of the wealthiest countries in the world. Well, that's not what has made them wealthy.

Australia is perhaps the only country in the fully developed world that has gotten rich from the export of *primary products.* That's pretty much what they do. Remember that primary products are things extracted from the earth like coal, oil, minerals, diamonds, uranium, wool, cattle, and meat. What is all this stuff worth? When it comes right down to it, it's not worth too much. They are a bunch of unprocessed materials. So how can the Aussies be rich if they are doing stuff that poor countries do? It's because there's nobody there. The population is so small. There are only 20 million people in the entire country, and it's the size of the US. They export so many goods because of the resource-rich land, and the wealth generated from that is spread between so few that they are rich overall.

"Avenger? Agent Aussie here. We need help diversifying my portfolio . . ."

Don't let the Plaid Avenger lead you too far astray. If you look at the numbers, over 60% of the workforce is in the service sector. But who are they serving? Pretty much just themselves.

No seriously, no sexual innuendo implied. They work in malls and mailrooms and telemarketing centers. They produce computers and cars, but the manufacturing facilities are owned and operated by multinational companies, and the products are only built to be consumed in Australia. In other words, they make Apple computers there, because people there want Apple computers. They are not exported out of Australia. There are no cars or refrigerators exported from Australia. And that's because they are too busy making serious bank on exports of primary commodities. Their internal economy has enough juice to keep them going and growing, but it is a matter of low population and lots of primary resource wealth that makes for such high GDP per capita. They are the only place on the planet that I know of that has gotten away with that. Bottom line is this: they may have 65% of the people in the service sector, but they make 65% of their total GDP on exports of primary products.

You'll often see information about sheep and lamb being a huge export to places like the Middle East, since they consume more lamb than they do things like beef and chicken. You'll also see information about the coal and oil that Australia has being exported to places like China and Japan, both of which are hungry for those things. Australia also just signed a uranium deal with China on April 4, 2006, to export raw uranium to be processed and used. No other "rich" country on the planet is exporting raw commodities at this scale. Everybody else processes things because that's where the money is. So it's fascinating that their primary source of income is from raw products. They are definitely the economic black sheep of the world.

PACIFIC SHIFT

What is in Australia's future? To answer that we might ask ourselves what's changing . . . because while we've been saying that this is the mini-America of the south, things are definitely on the move. And in many ways . . . changing.

ECONOMICALLY

As China is increasing in world power and wealth and requiring more resources, Australia is reorienting its economic focus to nearby countries in Asia—instead of trading primarily with other white English-speaking countries like the US and Great

Mmmmm . . . throw him on the barbie . . .

Britain. In the past, these whiteys were the primary trading partners with Australia. Seriously, what a pain in the ass it is to ship exports that far. It's a long commute for meetings and it's difficult to maintain trading relationships with their white, English-speaking allies. What a joke. That's on the other side of the planet! Nothing, other than fine Australian wine, can be shipped economically all the way across the world anymore. Don't take my word for it; check back to the inset box on Foster's Lager to see where it's made . . . and why.

Also, consider what impact longitude has on trade relationships. If you are at the same longitude, you are in the same time zone. So now, Australia is doing business in real time, during their business day, instead of having to deal with the massive time difference between it and other trading partners like the US and Europe. It's a tremendous complication to be awake when your trading partners are asleep.

So they have reoriented their trade relationships to more local areas like China and Japan. "Why continue trading with the white people that look like us, when we can make a hell of a lot more money trading with the yellow people that don't look like us?" Money talks and bullshit walks. This is the way it is.

Bottom line: Aussie economic future lies in Asia. So, over the next few years, look for the portion of Australia exports of raw goods to Asian countries to increase, and dramatically. And raw material exports are not the only thing on the menu my friends. Many Australian businesses, like so many others across the planet, are moving manufacturing facilities as well as research/developments operations to Asian locations to take advantage of both cheap labor and the large local talent pool. Damn. I suppose the future of the Jr. continent may be as a giant national park serving tourists from around the world serving shrimp and Foster's on tap. Besides primary product production, what the hell else will they be doing?

Even more so than America, Australia's future is tied closely with Asia. Asia is a booming region on the planet, a place where a lot of things are going on economically, and Australia is right there to help them along and make some profit at the same time. As we will see in the Mexico chapter, it is good to be next to a gigantic economic engine, and Australia's proximity to China, who will be the largest consumer of raw goods on the planet in the coming century, will enable them to turn huge profits. **Prime Minister John Howard** of Australia has been quoted in the past about Australia refocusing their efforts and economy to better compliment China's rising power. He has himself called Australia "an anchor of stability" in this region. He has also said, "When we think about the world, we inevitably think of a world where China will play a much larger role." That's a real quote from the man, not a Plaid Avenger paraphrasing.

Former Prime Minister Howard: "How can we as Australians kiss China's ass more?"

POLITICALLY

Let's stay with Former Prime Minister John Howard for just a minute more so I can explain to you how Australia's role in the vicinity is changing politically as well. To do this, I must elaborate on the most hilarious 'story of the sheriff' which ruffled many feather a few years ago. It goes a little something like this:

Well, several years ago, President Bush *complimented* Former Prime Minister Howard during a press release by referring to Australia's status as the "sheriff of Asia." What the hell is that supposed to mean? Most Asian countries interpreted this as "the white dudes in the area are in charge," that the long arm of the US law is being stretched through Australia to keep them down. So this seriously pissed off all of Australia's neighbors. Malaysia, which is a hilarious state in its own right, nearly declared war over it. To paraphrase the Malaysian prime minister, "Think that bullshit all you want, but if you ever set foot on our damn soil we will declare war on you instantaneously, no matter what the US says about it."

Even John Howard was a little miffed. He was probably thinking: "Thanks for the compliment, but try not to ever say anything about me in public again." This is a problem especially since Australia is reorienting itself toward Asia. These are the guys they are trying to buddy up with! The last thing they need is negativity about their foreign policy ties to the US. They still want to be allied with the US, but they don't want to be throwing it in people's faces. So this is a big stress factor for Australia in their part of the world.

The Plaid suggested in an earlier chapter that Europeans are slightly apprehensive to support US foreign policy, as there is a more likely possibility of terrorist threats due to their proximity to the Middle East. Australia is in the same boat. They're closer to other regions that may be slightly hostile to the US foreign policy. Australia is right there beside Southeast Asia, parts of which are known hotspots for extremism and terrorism. The Plaid Avenger isn't making fun of his Muslim friends, but there are some seriously extreme fundamentalist Muslims in this area; even my Muslim friends would concur. Terrorist cells are known to exist in lots of places in Southeast Asia (e.g., see Indonesia, the Philippines, or Malaysia).

This is why John Howard was quick to offer a modification of Bush's comment, because there is a real threat nearby. The US is far enough away to be safe from imminent threat; it's harder for terrorists to make it to the US. But it's not hard for them to make it from Southeast Asia to Australia. Because Australia is seen as the face of American foreign policy in the area it is very surprising that Australia has not seen any terrorist activity on their soil already. However, there have been several foiled terrorist plots in recent history and this situation is not likely to let up anytime soon. The Aussies remain ever vigilant.

Bush was quoted as saying that he doesn't think of Australia as a deputy sheriff, "but as a full sheriff." In fact, Australia does supply soldiers in most UN activities in the countries surrounding them. In many cases, they are actually doing patrols and peacekeeping directly for the UN in places like the Solomon Islands, Indonesia, and other hotspots where the UN needs to send soldiers. So the idea of them as sheriff does have some weight, and is going to cause them some problems in the future. Many countries in the 'hood remain perpetually pissed that the whities are on their soil at all, even as peacekeepers.

To end this rant, know this: this is changing fast too. The new Prime Minister Kevin Rudd is a bit more liberal and conciliatory than his conservative Howard predecessor, and he has already made moves to soften the Australian image in this part of the world. As I suggested above, he has decided to pull Aussie troops from Iraq, and seems to be much more engaged with local Asian countries' leaders to head-off any friction that might arise due to Australian presence, as UN representatives or otherwise. Given his liberal nature, I suppose it's no surprise what he did during his first month in office, but that has to be in the next section . . .

DEMOGRAPHICALLY

Because Australia is doing a lot of business with China, Japan, Indonesia, etc, they will become more like those countries culturally. This is changing very rapidly just in the modern era, because quite frankly it was not allowed to happen any earlier. How so Plaid?

At the expense of pissing off my Aussie brothers, I will have to tell you that a racist streak has run through the society since its inception—a bad habit that they probably inherited from the Brits. Perhaps racist is too harsh, but certainly they had a superiority complex when it came to other peoples in their neighborhood. The Australian's treatment of the Aboriginals was pretty damn bad from the get go, mostly treating them as third rate citizens at best. There was also an official state policy from 1870 to 1970 which made it perfectly legal for the state to take Aboriginal children from their parents to re-educate and civilize them in white families. Ewww. These folks are now refereed to as the 'Stolen Generation.'

But I guess that is better than what the Aussie's did to the Tasmanians . . . which was to kill them all in an open hunting season. Damn. That sucks. On top of that, Australia had a 'white-only' immigration policy in place for most of its history. What? Yeah, I'm afraid it's true. If you were of European or American background, then you had an open door to the country; the door was firmly shut for Asians of any stripe. Pretty nasty business.

To be fair to our friends down under, they have made great strides in the last few decades to make amends. Much has been done to alleviate the impoverished plight of many Aboriginal communities, and even more has been done to overcome the negative attitude and stereotypes of the group. In fact, Australia picked an Aboriginal woman to carry the flag into the

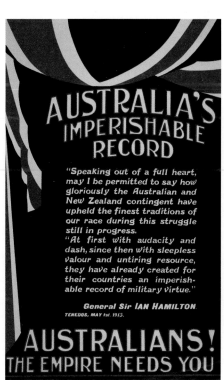

Dude, does this really say 'finest traditions of our race'? Ew.

Aborigines: Not held in high regard.

DISTRIBUTING SHIP CARGO OF STANDARD BUGGIES COAST OF AUSTRALIA

What is this madness? . . . No wonder Rudd apologized.

introductory ceremonies for the 2000 Olympics. And that brings me back to what Prime Minister Kevin Rudd did his first month in office: in February 2008 he made an official government apology to the Aborigines for all past reprehensible deeds of the Australian government, specifically citing the Stolen Generation. This was big news, and perhaps a critical turning point for the society.

Back to the story: Since 1976, when their historically strict immigration laws became more relaxed, the country's Asian population has increased. Surprise, surprise. More

people that are close by, from regions adjacent to Australia, are coming there because it is a rich place where there is more opportunity to succeed than there may be in their home countries. Again, it's America Jr.! All of the poorer people nearby want to get there so they can set up shop. Australia may not be full-on encouraging it, but at least they are allowing it. They are changing direction, changing focus, and becoming more Asian. When you visit Sydney now, you can bump into a very vibrant and growing Chinatown for the first time in forever. And the changes are occurring nation-wide.

Who else have we talked about that is becoming more Asian due to increasing immigration from Asian states? Oh, that's right: America Sr.!

NO WORRIES

This is a region that plays a dual role as a US foreign policy anchor and as an economic player with China. This might put them in a tricky position, but a position perhaps enviable by nearby countries. They have a lot of natural resources and stable population growth. There is still the terrorist threat, however, and about that, we'll just have to see how they balance their security against their economic interest.

Australia would like to be a power broker between China and the US. This is promising; they have far fewer complications to worry about when dealing with China, as opposed to Japan, which has loads of emotional baggage. Japan may be a little more abrasive than Australia when dealing with Asian relations in general, and this gets the Aussies ahead.

The Down Under

- 8 oz. Australian shiraz red wine
- 8 oz. New Zealand sauvignon blanc white wine
- 1 can Foster's Lager
- 1 lb. shrimp
- 12 oz. filet mignon

Start drinking the New Zealand wine while you do the following: fire up the barbie, marinade the steak and shrimp in half a can of Foster's Lager with teriyaki sauce and salt and pepper added to taste. Grill the shrimp lightly, leave the steak on for 2 minutes more. Finish the white wine while eating the shrimp, and savor the Australian shiraz with the steak. Use the remaining half can of Foster's lager to extinguish the barbeque grill coals: you don't really want to drink a can that big by yourself . . . unless you

So Australia is going to have a leg up dealing with China and all the other Asian economic giants, because of proximity as well as the fact that they don't carry a lot of the cultural baggage. What do I mean by that? They haven't pissed anyone off. They haven't invaded anyone. They never colonized anyone. They are pretty antiseptic all the way around. That is a big plus in today's world—particularly for any state wanting to get in on the action in Asia, which is of course everyone.

Uncle Sam's little brother down south is still a staunch ally of the US, but luckily they remain just distant enough to dodge a lot of the negative press associated with such a role. Of course, the Aussies are distancing themselves slightly from US foreign policy right this second . . . but damn, who isn't? Australia is a pretty chill place all the way around: politically, economically, socially. That's why we like to go vacation there, because Australia is a laid back sort of place. Throw a shrimp on the barbie, have a beer, and enjoy the prosperous future, America Junior.

What's the Deal with . . . Foster's Lager in that big-ass can?

Those manly Australians are huge beer drinkers; they're so bad-ass they have to drink right out of a huge oil-can. Huge beer for huge people!

That's the common perception anyway. What type of beer is it? It's plain old American lager, which is why it sells so well here.

But where is Foster's lager actually produced? From Australia, right? Nope. Try Canada . . . because it's cheaper to produce the beer close to where it is going to be consumed. Why isn't it made in the US then? Well, then they can't put the word "IMPORTED" on the label to make you think it came from Australia. Think I'm joking? Check it out yourself. You'll find that The Plaid Avenger never leads you astray on alcohol. That's just not cool. But grabbing a big-ass cool oil can of Foster's is primo.

CHAPTER OUTLINE

Latin America

13

A SINGLE REGION?

Latin America is a region with a question mark after it. The Plaid Avenger has never really considered it a region in the past, mainly because a regional definition involves some sort of homogeneous singular trait that you can apply to the geographic space in question. I've said for years this place is too big. You can't apply singular homogeneous traits across all of Latin America because it encompasses everything from the south of the US-Mexican border all the way to Tierra del Fuego, the tip of South America which is almost in the damn Antarctic. It's too damn big. You can't see any singular thing that applies across all of those regions!

What's the Deal with . . . the Latins in Mexico?

What happened was this freaky-freak Napoleon III (not Napoleon the short, dead dude we all know, but one of his later kin) sent over this other French dude named Maximilian to sit on the Mexican throne in a feeble effort to reestablish France's presence in the New World in 1862. The French were actually invited to do this by an elite rightist core of Mexican aristocracy who wanted to dismantle the leftist movements occurring in what was independent, sovereign Mexico at the time. So this French dude Maximilian is in charge, and when he was out scouting around he was like, "What the hell? We're French, we're not even Spanish. What rallying point can we possibly use to generate empathy that we should be in charge here?"

Maximiliam being executed.

What our brilliant French brethren came up with was that the Spanish, Portuguese, and the French languages are all linguistically tied. They are all part of the Romance, or Latin derived languages. So in a fit of what must have been desperation at the time, Napoleon III told ole Maxi to say, "Look I'm the French guy here in Mexico, but we are all brothers under the Latin language, so we're all family here in Latin America." Again, a totally bogus, politically made-up term, but somehow it stuck. The Mexicans deposed Maximilian's ass fairly quickly, but the term stayed—in fact, kicking out the French is what the Cinco de Mayo holiday is all about; its not Mexican Independence Day.

So that is what's Latin about Latin America. How bizarre. Now we associate "Latin" with scantily clad women shaking their booties to Ricky Martin songs. Caesar would be proud.

Cinco de Mayo Festivities.

At least you weren't able to in the past. What the Plaid Avenger has now realized is that, indeed, there are a lot of traits that can be recognized across the whole of Latin America. We're going to look at some of those traits in this kind of pre-chapter to the subregions of Latin America.

WHAT IS LATIN AMERICA?

Latin America is a *hilarious* term because it doesn't mean jack. It's a term that everybody understands, everybody gets, you know where it is, but it's based on a word that is completely and utterly meaningless: Latin. Do all of these people speak Latin south of our border? Hell no. Latin is a damn dead language. Nobody on the planet speaks that Caesar-ized stuff anymore. In fact, there are really only two predominate languages spoken: Spanish and Portuguese.

So how did we get this term Latin America: are they all of Latin or Greek ancestry? Hell no, obviously not. As with many things on the planet, we can blame the French.

Geographically, the term means everything south of the US border. That's common knowledge across the planet. Mexico, which we teased out for obvious reasons earlier, is not part of the US/Canadian region. There are too many differences including its Latin-based language, but levels of development, poverty, and lots of different issues distinguish Mexico from the United States. One reason Mexico is thrown in with Latin America is that there are a lot of similarities across countries south of the US/Mexican border. Before we get to those similarities, let's identify frequently referenced regions in this part of the planet.

LATIN LOCATIONS

There are a few terms that The Plaid wants you to know before we get into these subsequent chapters. These definitions will help us understand a lot of terminology used on the global stage. For starters, the term 'Latin America' encompasses every single damn country south of the US border, in the entire western hemisphere. Easy enough. The commonalities of this huge swath will be covered in the remainder of this chapter. Subsequent chapters will deal with more concise and homogeneous parts of this great whole.

SOUTH AMERICA

The first one is easy enough. South America is both a continent and a region. The South American continent is that other big-ass continent in our hemisphere. That one is pretty solid. It starts with Colombia and then east to Venezuela, Guyana, Suriname, French Guyana, down south to Brazil. South of Colombia is Ecuador, Peru, Chile, Bolivia, Paraguay, Uruguay, and Argentina. In between South America proper and the United States is a broad region that is defined as **Middle America.** Maybe that's easy enough to understand too. It's everything in the middle of the US and South America. We're not going to spend a lot of time with this, but we're going to look at three subdivisions of Middle America, the stuff in the middle.

MIDDLE AMERICA

So the term Middle America is everything between the US and the South American continent. It's a fairly generic definition that usually only gets play in high school and college level textbooks anymore, but I suppose it doesn't hurt to know the reference when you see it pop up. For this magnificent treatise of learning, I will further break this area down to more

 +  +  =

manageable and meaningful sub regions, described below. Study the Middle America map equation above to be carto-graphically clever.

MEXICO

The first subdivision is Mexico. Mexico is a country, a state in its own right, but it's also radically different from all the states around it including the US, and it's also different from the Central American states and the Caribbean countries too. So Mexico is its own subregion that we're going to define in the next chapter. In respect to size, resources, economy, population and level of development, Mexico stands alone from all its neighbors.

THE CARIBBEAN

The Caribbean is a group of island states that comprise the Greater Antilles and the Lesser Antilles. The Caribbean, when we think about it, calls to mind a distinct culture in terms of . . . everything. Cuisine, language, stuff they drink, how they party . . . its all different. Caribbean means something to us, and it means something that's different than Mexico. Mexico is not Caribbean; Caribbean is not Mexico. We all understand that. We go to a Caribbean restaurant or a Mexican restaurant, but we never really see the two put together. (Note to self: that might be a good idea. Instead of Tex-Mex cuisine, how about Car-Mex cuisine . . . or is that a lip balm?) The island nations in the Caribbean Sea, south of the United States, are a distinct subdivision.

CENTRAL AMERICA

The last one is Central America. This is the one that causes the most confusion for younger students of the world. It is everything between Mexico and South America, noninclusive. Mexico and South America are the bookends. There are seven distinct countries in what is widely accepted as Central America: Belize, Guatemala, El Salvador, Honduras, Nicaragua, Costa Rica, and Panama.

So we've got a bunch of Americas here, and Central America is quite distinct in that it has nothing to do with Mexico, the Caribbean, or even South America. It has a lot going on, particularly in terms of the violence that we will talk about in much more detail when we get to the Central America chapter. But it's a distinct place, a bunch of small states that bridge both North and South America, but all are quite distinct in all other aspects.

South America plus the three regions of Middle America: Mexico, Central America, and the Caribbean: that's Latin America all the way around. Now that we know where it is and where the definition comes from, let's talk a little bit more about what it is to *be* Latin America. What are the homogeneous traits in terms of how we can define this region?

WHAT IS LATIN ABOUT LATIN AMERICA?

COMMON CULTURE

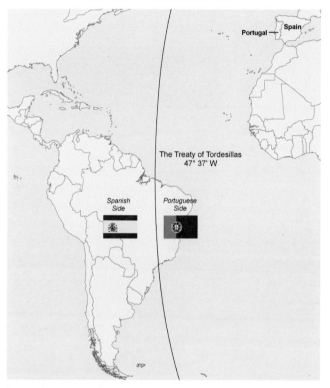

Portugal got screwed.

We can see some distinct things to point out so we don't have to keep repeating ourselves in subsequent chapters. Number one is culture. There is a common culture south of the US/Mexican border, be it in the Caribbean, Central America, Chile, Argentina, or Brazil; there are some things that do remain the same. One of the kind-of-the-same-stuff things that we already pointed out is language. While Latin America is a joke term in and of itself, they do primarily speak Spanish and really the only other big language is Portuguese.

How did this come about? Easy enough. It came about because of colonial endeavors in this region that date as far back as 1492 when Columbus sailed the ocean blue, came over here and bumped into the Caribbean. After Columbus's great discovery, the big naval powers at the time, Spain and Portugal, started floating over here in fairly short order as well. (Great Britain didn't come along until later. It wasn't as big of a naval power as the Spanish at the time and so it was a late-comer. It therefore had to head north for colonial expansion which is why it gets the leftovers—North America.)

But let's get back to our story here. Why do we have these two main languages, Spanish and Portuguese? Columbus came over in 1492. Two years later a fairly important event occurred, which I want you to understand and know about: **The Treaty of Tordesillas.** The Treaty of Tordesillas occurred in 1494 when these European countries are bumping into the New World, colonizing, taking over, and staking claim to places. Of course there is friction between the countries. They have been beating the hell out of each other for hundreds of years at home anyway, now they are just taking the fight abroad. Much of the friction was between Portugal and Spain, two of the main colonizing powers in this part of the world. There was claim

staking, and there were people getting pissed off about what country owned what. Both these countries, being predominantly Catholic (which is another common cultural tie we'll see more about in just a second), would listen to the papa, the **Pope,** the main man in the Vatican. So the Pope says, "Hey guys, come on now, we're all civilized colonial imperial masters here, let's all get on the same page, get around the same table here, let's work together! We don't need to fight! You're good Catholic boys, so do what daddy says. Papa is going to draw a line for you." The line happened to be 45 degrees western longitude. The Pope says, "Ok, we're going to settle this fair and square. Just draw a line on the map and everything on one side we'll give to the Spanish and everything on the other side we'll give to the Portuguese. Now you guys be good!"

Pope responsible for Tordesillas . . . and Catholicism in Latin Lands

As you can see from the map, the Portuguese look like they got screwed pretty damn good on this deal. They only got the tip of what is now known as Brazil. Why is this? Did the Pope just want to shaft the Portuguese? No. This is during early exploration in 1494, only a few years after Columbus got there. They don't know what's there yet. They're just bumping around the coastline; and have no comprehension about how big the continent is . . . neither North nor South America quite frankly. So what they thought was a good deal was based on known circumstances at the time, which really wasn't much. As we all now know, this is a pretty big place. South America is the fourth largest continent on the planet. As discovery continued and the true scope of the land's magnitude unfolded, the Portuguese did pick up what is now modern day Brazil. Its boundaries natu-

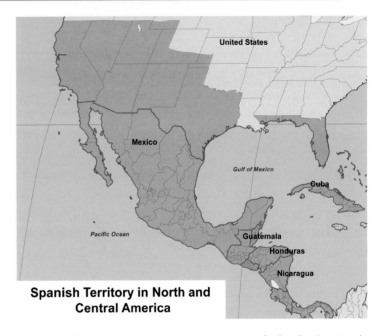

Spanish Territory in North and Central America

rally fell back to the Andes, a nice, easily defined natural border. And this same treaty is the cornerstone of why the Spaniards end up controlling so much of the New World—like all the rest of it outside Brazil.

First of all, they controlled Mexico. We think of the Mexico of today as down south, but Mexico in its days as part of the Spanish Empire included all of western North America as well. It was everything that's now California up to Washington State, to Utah, to New Mexico, to Texas. Spanish territory also included Mexico proper, all of Central America, most of the Caribbean, Florida, and all the way down the western seaboard of South America proper. That is why today these territories are Spanish speaking. I guess in today's world the Spanish-speaking territories might even include California, Florida, New Mexico, and Arizona, but that's a separate issue in immigration that we'll get to later.

This all means that those old colonial ties formed this common culture that's still in place today. It's a common culture primarily based on language, but also one other thing I mentioned earlier: Catholicism. Two primarily Catholic countries colonized virtually all of South America. You can still see the deep, deep-seated Catholicism throughout Latin America today. There are no countries in Latin America that are *not* Catholic. Now when The Plaid travels down there he can see some freaky-freaky crap that doesn't look like Catholicism. You can see some stuff down there that could make the Pope soil his robes, no doubt. You'd be like, "That's not Catholicism! What is this voodoo shit? What are people doing with voodoo dolls and holding up bloody chickens saying Hail Marys?" Then there's this crazy stuff that's going on down in Brazil; they have these big parties that don't look like traditional Catholicism: the 'Carnival'. But what you have is indeed the basis of Catholicism mixed in within indigenous culture, local culture, and imported African culture.

We're going to see in a little bit that a theme of South America and the Caribbean is the importation of folks from Africa. So Catholicism reaches across Latin America. It's all over the place; you can't miss it, but sometimes it's morphed into something that looks a bit strange to the white dudes in Europe who light candles and incense and stuff like that. So culture is our number one element of "What is Latin about Latin America."

Latins love the Savior.

URBANIZATION

Urbanization is a primary feature that is consistent across every place in Latin America, and I do mean *every place.* I've never even thought about this until recently, but this region is one of the most urbanized on the planet. Now when we usually think of urbanization, we think of it as that most people don't live in the countryside; most people live in cities. We typically associate this with fully developed countries like the US, Canada, and Western Europe. That's where you *typically* have people who are all jammed in the cities, and hardly anyone out in the country. For some reasons that we will get into in a minute, Latin America is more urbanized than even fully developed places. This means everyone in virtually all of these countries is jammed into something called an **urban area,** typically a very big city.

Latins packed into the cities.

On average, upwards of 80–85 percent, sometimes upwards of 90 percent, of the population of a Latin American country is located in just a few major cities. This is highlighted best by Mexico City, which will probably soon be the world's most populated city with well over 30 million inhabitants—a full one-third of the total population.

Why do people go to the city? It is suggested that in the developed world people go to the city for all the reasons we already talked about back in Chapter 2. That's where jobs are. Jobs are concentrated in urban areas. People want to go to urban areas because there's health care, doctors, clean water, sewer systems, electricity, movie theaters, good restaurants. The reason everybody wants to move to a big city or urban area is because there is good stuff there. The standard of living is higher and that's where your jobs are.

Is that true of Latin America? In most cases, not. It is a kind of conundrum in Latin America. In most urbanized places in the Latin world, all of the **pull factors** that we just mentioned—the good things that pull people to the city—are simply not available for the masses that come. So there is the *perception* that all these great things are in the city and the *perception* that all these jobs are in and around the city, but it is simply not true for most folks who end up going to the city.

Now those are the pull factors, but there are also some **push factors,** or the not-so-good things that push people from rural areas to the city. One of the main push factors, a major theme across Latin America that we'll discuss at length, is **landlessness.** Because most people do not have access to land, or resources on the land, they are pushed away from it. Owning no land in title or having no serious claim to the land is just another reason to go to the city. So there are a lot of pull and push factors that make Latin America one of the most urbanized places on the planet . . . and still growing.

Squatters got squat.

One last note: An interesting phenomenon in Latin American cities that most Americans don't get is that they are set up in a kind of "economically reversed" scenario from the way we live. What the hell am I talking about? Well in America, what's found deep in the inner city? In fact, what is the connotation of the term "inner city"? I'll tell you what it connotes: slums, projects, poverty, ghettos. That's not where people want to be. As a result most people who have money don't live in the inner city in America. They've got money, so what do they do? They move *away* from the city and into the "burbs," which we talked about back in the North America chapter.

In Latin America the situation is just the reverse. The city center is still the prime real estate, so the rich people concentrate themselves and their businesses in the true city center. So where do all these impoverished masses go that I have been suggesting flood into the cities? They make a ring around it. They get as close to the city as they can, usually in ramshackle, shanty-like town dwellings they put together out of corrugated-cardboard and any damn other thing they can pull out of a landfill. These shantytowns get very big and grow into almost permanent fixtures in rings around the cities. Whole shantytowns are a phenomenon that's very easy to spot in any major Latin American city. Just drive straight into or out of the city and notice how the poverty line fluctuates one way or the other. It's a distinct characteristic that has something to do with urbanization. It also has something to do with . . .

WEALTH DISPARITY/LANDLESSNESS

Perhaps there is no other region that we will talk about in this book or that you can go visit on the planet that has wealth disparity as extreme as Latin America. What is **wealth disparity?** Disparity is the difference between highest and the lowest, the difference between the greatest and the least. In terms of wealth, no place in the world is like Latin America in that so few people have so much of the wealth. I'm just going to guess-timate some numbers here. These are Plaid Avenger Figures that vary from country to country, but on average the extreme amounts of wealth are held by the upper 5 percent of the population. The richest 5 percent typically own something like 80 percent of all the shit. That's all the land, all

Times haven't changed much economically.

What's the Deal with . . . Landlessness in Brazil?

Unofficial stats in Brazil refer to 1.6 percent of the landowners control roughly half (46.8 percent) of the land on which crops could be grown. Just 3 percent of the population owns two-thirds of all arable lands. The Brazilian constitution requires that land serve a social function. [Article 5, Section XXIII.] As such, the constitution requires the Brazilian government "expropriate for the purpose of agrarian reform, rural property that is not performing its social function." [Article 184.]

This is a big deal for everybody. It concerns politicians, business people, and the landless poor. In Brazil they have a law on the books that basically says, "if you can successfully squat on a piece of land, cultivate it, and make it produce something for one year then you have a legal stake to it. You can take it! It's yours! Here's the deed in your name!" You may say, "Hey, that sounds like a pretty good policy," and maybe it is.

However, the scenario develops a lot of squatter settlements: large groups of people who are squatting on owned land that is typically owned by some rich businessperson or some rich urban dweller who is not out there in the countryside. If they find out that people are squatting on their land, they send in henchmen to go clear them out. When the landless poor fight back or try to continue their stay on the land to finish out the year so they can have legal claim to it, the situation can turn violent.

This situation has also led to the formation of the Landless Worker's Movement, or in Portuguese Movimento dos Trabalhadores Rurais Sem Terra (MST). This is the largest social movement in Latin America with an estimated 1.5 million landless members organized in 23 out of 27 states. And they can get violent too.

This is still an issue that is alive today in Brazil and all across Latin America where hired gunmen are going and literally cleaning out villages and killing everybody on site. Because it is private property, the owners, ranchers, and other types of folks can just say "This is legally mine and these people wouldn't leave, so I killed them." So this is a very hot issue. How hot? Brazil's current President Lula da Silva promised land reform and government action on the urban poor issue, which he is currently trying to make good on. And the poor are putting his feet to the fire . . .

Get on it Lula!

the factories, all the businesses, everything. Well maybe you think that's not too bad—perhaps that's the way it is in America too. Not really. Because the other part of the equation is that 95 percent of people have got to split up that other 20% of the stuff. Of course there is always a significant, or at least partial, middle class; some people have got to own some stuff, but there's always a significant majority of people in these countries that own nothing. No title to their land, no title to their house, no other economic means except their labor to sell. That is a kind of common feature across Latin America from Mexico down to the tip of Tierra del Fuego, and is particularly nasty in Brazil and lots of other places where people kill each other over land.

The George Washington of America: Simon Bolivar.

Which brings us to the issue of **landlessness.** Because of this lopsided scenario of so few people owning so much, including the land, people can't stake a claim to anything. In such societies where people don't have anything, their options are very limited. Mostly they go to cities as already suggested. They can also try to work on someone else's land without their consent. This is a very unstable situation because the owner can show up at any time and kick them off. This is a particularly resonate issue in Brazil where landlessness has turned into an occupational hazard.

This problem of wealth disparity and landlessness is a common theme across Latin America, and a pervasive theme throughout history. You can look at the history of any country from independence (these movements in Latin America began in the 1820s–30s) and onward. This dude named Simón Bolívar headed up many of these egalitarian independence movements, and is viewed historically as the George Washington of Latin America. Wealth disparity/ economic equality was one of his central themes to rally folks to fight. But the issue wasn't resolved at state inception, and has plagued Latin America ever since. Just one example for now: The Mexican Revolution in 1910 was fought over land. Too many people got pissed off about landlessness, so they had a revolution. One of the core parts of their new constitution included equal rights for people and access to land. All politicians of any stripe have had to deal with this issue historically, and still do today.

So Poncho Villa and his crew were fighting in the Mexican revolution for land reform. But even 100 years later former Mexican President Vicente Fox, who by all definitions is conservative and could be compared to George Bush in political stance, had to run on a platform based on land reform. If you're going to run for office at all in Mexico you have to address the land issue. The main opposition party in Mexico is called the PRI. It's a land reform party; go figure. It was founded to redistribute land and work out ways to give people access to land. We already referred to Lula in Brazil (see page 223)—he got into office as a land reformer. We're also talking about people like Hugo Chavez in Venezuela who are all about equal economic rights in a country with increasing wealth disparity, and other historic figures like Castro, who had his Cuban revolution to basically reclaim land and businesses from the rich and redistribute them to the poor in an old-school communist-style revolution. This issue of wealth disparity and landlessness is a prevalent theme whether you are in Brazil, Mexico, Cuba, or Chile.

Pancho, Fox, Lula, Castro and Hugo: Brothers for Land Reform?

IN-'DOCTRINE'-ATION: A HISTORY OF US INVOLVEMENT

The Plaid has talked to many folks from Mexico all the way down to Argentina, and can tell you with no reservation that people respect the United States. Nobody hates any specific person in the United States, but taken as a whole, Latin America's historical relationship with the US in today's world is largely seen as a negative. Now that may seem like a bold statement, and certainly there are those that still support US policies, but I can tell you who those people are. They are the rich people in Latin America. If life is good you've got no reason to have qualms with the United States. But unfortunately, as we've already pointed out, that's not the majority by any stretch. Most people see the United States with a bit of an imperial taint, or in a bit of a **hegemonic** light. Certainly, given the US's involvement in virtually every country in Latin America, it's not hard to see why they have kind of a bad taste in their mouth when it comes to historical intervention by the US.

"Don't mess in our hemisphere, bitches!"

So what is The Plaid referring to? You've got to know this shit. It still applies in today's world. The number one thing you've got to remember from the US's history of influence is **The Monroe Doctrine.** It's this dumb-ass antiquated 200-year-old statement that was made in 1823 by President James Monroe. It was a foreign policy statement that said pretty much *(Disclaimer: Plaid Avenger Interpretation)*, "If any European power messes in any place in this hemisphere, the US will consider it an act of aggression against the United States." In essence, if Spain were to go try to retake Mexico or Chile, if the Portuguese were to try to retake Brazil, if the British try to take back Jamaica—the US will consider it an attack on US soil. Hell, it doesn't even have to be a full-on takeover; any intervention at all will be considered an act of aggression. "If you mess with anyone down there we will consider it as you screwing with us." It's extremely similar to NATO article 5 in saying, "if anybody here gets messed with, it's an attack on all of us."

Now why the hell would we say that? It seems kind of silly. I mean in 1823 what sort of position is James Monroe in? This is a new country that has only been around about 30 or 40 years. It's only expanded *slightly* over the 13 original colonies and is certainly not a world power. We did a great job shooting the British from behind trees, but other than that we're not capable of fighting anybody. We can take care of our own soil but we are not up for fighting anybody else on foreign soil. This was largely a toothless threat. So maybe you are thinking: "Why is The Plaid Avenger telling us that this is important?" Here's why: This statement became a cornerstone that remains relevant in US/Latin America policy TO THIS DAY.

Uncle Sam ready to whip some European ass back in the day.

It didn't mean anything at the time when Monroe said it, but it has come to mean *everything*. Ok, why did Monroe make it at that particular time in 1823? Mexico has declared independence in 1820. The Central Americas seceded out and most of the South American countries are declaring independence at or around this time. It was seen largely as a supportive gesture. We think it's a good idea, "Yes, kick all the Spanish and other colonial powers out. We just did it in America so we will encourage everyone else to do it. We're the good guys and we're helping the other good guys, so it's all good!" Again, it was largely toothless and didn't mean anything at the time. We literally could not take on the Spanish Armada at that time. Forget about it. No contest.

But the Monroe Doctrine leads to a bunch of other things, such as the **Roosevelt Corollary.** The Roosevelt Corollary was issued in 1904, about a hundred years later, and at that point the US is quite a bit more powerful than it was during Monroe's tenure. The US was also under a very powerful president at the time, President "Rough Rider" Teddy Roosevelt. What was Teddy known for? What was one of his most popular sayings during that time? "Speak softly and carry a big stick." Indeed that saying can be applied directly to what becomes known as the **Roosevelt Corollary,** which is the foreign policy towards Latin America at the time. Teddy said, "Well I like the Monroe Doctrine's policy that if anyone messes around in our backyard we'll consider it an act of aggression against us. That's good, but let's take it a step further. If there is any flagrant wrongdoing by a Latin American state *ITSELF* then the US has the right to intervene."

"Speak softly, and carry a big stick. And a can of whup ass."

In other words, if any Latin American countries south of our border attack each other we have the right to intervene. Better than that, if they just screw up internally we're giving ourselves the right to intervene as well. This has serious repercussions for what sovereignty meant at the time. Of course I can't go back in time to hear their exact thoughts, but there is no doubt that it was not held in high esteem by Latin American states that were considered sovereign at that time.

In other words, you had the United States saying, "Sure you guys are sovereign as long as we agree with your sovereignty. Otherwise, we give ourselves the right to intervene." This became kind of a big deal because Teddy was carrying that big stick and he was not afraid to smack people, or entire Latin American countries, down with it. Under Roosevelt's corollary, we gave ourselves the right to internally intervene in Latin American affairs, which led to more of a bright spot in US/Latin American relations under the Good Neighbor Policy.

That's right, its FDR.

The **Good Neighbor Policy** was a popular name for foreign policy at the time of the next Roosevelt, Franklin D., in the 1930s. In a marked departure from the heavy-handed foreign policies up to this point, FDR said, "You know, we're good guys, we're your buddies. We don't need to come down there and beat you with a big stick. My fifth cousin Teddy was a funny guy, but we don't really need to be that heavy-handed. We'll throw out that Roosevelt Corollary and we'll just be here to help if any leader needs us."

Now that sounds pretty good and certainly it was an improvement over the Roosevelt Corollary, but under the Good Neighbor Policy we had a scenario where US troops were sent down at the request of "leaders" that sometimes could also be referred to as, oh I don't know . . . let's call them *military dictators* . . . who happened to be touting US foreign policy at the time. So even though it sounds better, there are still slight implications that perhaps it's not completely on the up and up. That brings us to the last part of the US's history of involvement.

COLD WAR EFFECTS . . .

After WWII we have the Cold War on. The Cold War has already been referred to several times in this book, and a lot of people think, "Ah I'm tired of fucking history; I don't need to know any of this stuff," but you can't understand the world unless you understand the historical and political movements of at least the last hundred years. Nothing has affected the world more than the Cold War and its politics. Even Latin America was affected.

We might think of Latin America and say, "What? There was no hot war down there, much less a cold war! There are no Commies down there; there's no nothing." Not so! Latin America was actually quite radically impacted by the Cold War because of US anticommunist policies that were applied across the planet. That's the reason we got involved in Vietnam, Korea, and damn near everything else that was active at the time including Cold War activities like supporting leaders' questionable character just as long as they didn't associate with the Soviets. This became of great consequence in Latin America.

Now when we think of the Cold War and Latin America the first thing that pops into mind is Cuba and Fidel: that flagrant flaming Commie that the US still hates to this day. There have been lots of repercussions between the US and Cuba, (i.e. why Cuba's pretty impoverished today), but all of the other countries were impacted as well. Some of them had much more violence with a much greater death toll than Cuba ever did.

What I'm talking about is a renewed distrust of the US as a result of its Cold War activities. The American government was so rabidly anticommunist that any movement towards the political left by any Latin American country was almost viewed as a hostile act. And so it became ingrained in US foreign policy for the last 50–60 years that it was absolutely intolerable for anybody to be left leaning.

If you think back to our chapter on global politics and governments, not every single system on the left is Commie—but all forms of socialism were viewed as being a slippery slope. The US government believed that any form of socialism, however mild, would lead to communism or would lead to an opening for the USSR to make inroads. It really was battled at any cost. No cost was too high; no moral too low to violate in order to ensure that Latin America stayed firmly in the US's backyard of influence.

Now that we've gone through the grandiose two paragraphs about what the hell was going on, we can get into some specifics.

Sole Western Hemisphere Commie.

What did the US do in this all-out barrage to stop communism in Latin America? Be forewarned: This is going to hurt for the uninitiated. It's a little hard for many proud Americans to hear, but we did some pretty nasty shit, quite frankly. While we are the champion of democracy on the planet, at the time of the Cold War, the USSR was seen as such a threat that we said, "Well, we're all about democracy, and it would be great if we had democracies there, but we can't allow anybody to go near the left. So it would be better to support someone on the extreme right as opposed to anybody that might be even the slightest bit Commie."

What this equated to was US support for people who might be considered brutal dictators, at worst, and elitist dudes of questionable ethics and character, at best. During the Reagan years in the 1980s, the threat of communist infiltration by arms sales in places like Nicaragua was interpreted as an immediate hostile threat. In response, support for dictators was sometimes pitched to the US Congress as basically, "We're about to get freakin' *invaded* by the Commies. They're going to get into Central America and they're going to sweep through Mexico and then they'll be knocking down Texas's door!"

Stuff that in hindsight we find preposterous. To be fair to the Reaganites and their ilk, we do have to consider that at the time, the Soviets were as aggressive as the US was, had as many nukes as the US did, and had previously tried to hide missiles in Cuba. At least that was the argument. There was a very real fear of global domination by the Soviets.

So you can listen to speeches by Henry Kissinger and the like that say, "You young people just don't understand that we had to do these horrible things because if we didn't you'd all be wearing red right now." The Plaid Avenger is not here to speak on whether that's true or not because I'd be wearing plaid no matter if it were commie plaid or otherwise. But what this equated to in the Reagan era was not only supporting extreme dictatorships but also plots to overthrow—and sometimes assassinate—democratically elected leaders. This also equated to supporting extremist rightist factions and rebel groups. Nicaragua comes to mind, as does Guatemala and El Salvador. So we supported *anybody* as long as they weren't left leaning and weren't socialists and didn't support any of that shit, especially communism.

A lot of these groups ended up slaughtering thousands, and tens of thousands of their own people. Many just ended up as bands of guerillas running around the countryside slaughtering folks. It's pretty nasty business. The end result of all these anticommunist policies in Latin America, particularly Central America, was civil war. These excessively destructive civil wars were supported in part by movements of US funds or arms or funds for arms. One of the more famous ones is the Iran/Contra scandal, during the Reagan era, where arms and guns were floated into Nicaragua in support of antileftist movements to overthrow the democratically elected leftist regime, which we'll discuss more in the Central America chapter.

All these things together in terms of US intervention or involvement in Latin American affairs bring up a term that's often used for Latin America, **the US's backyard.** You'll see this term used even in modern political science magazines and international news. It really summarizes the way the US has felt about Latin America, which is, "It's not really our house, but it's our backyard. We're not really cleaning it up or taking care of it *unless* someone starts coming around and messing around in it." The US doesn't want anybody messing around in its backyard; that's why it's been heavy-handed at times throughout history.

DRUGS

Oh yeah, I almost forgot about drugs! That is the hot new thing with US intervention in Latin America. The Cold War is over. We don't really have a Good Neighbor Pol-

Coke-a-dope! Just say 'no'!

What Is the Deal with . . . Plan Colombia?

Plan Colombia is a program supported by the United States to eradicate coca production in Colombia. It may sound good, but Plan Colombia has become extremely controversial for several reasons. For one, although the coca plant is used to manufacture cocaine, it has also been used by indigenous peoples in the area for thousands of years for health reasons. Many of these people depend on coca to make a living. Furthermore, some of the methods that the United States uses to eradicate coca, such as aerial fumigation and the application of deadly fungi, pose severe health problems for people exposed to it.

Plan Colombia is also controversial because Colombia is undergoing a civil war right now. Many people claim that the goal of Plan Colombia isn't really to stop drugs, but to help the Colombian government fight the Marxist rebel group FARC, which gains much of its funding through the drug trade. When Plan Colombia was first introduced by the president of Colombia in 1998, its main focus was to make peace with the rebels and revitalize the economy of Colombia. However, policymakers from the United States revised it and the focus became more about military aid to fight the rebels and the elimination of drug trafficking. Human rights organizations are indignant at Plan Colombia because they see it as a way of strengthening right-wing paramilitary groups in Colombia who are committing atrocities against peasants who are speaking out for equal rights and economic reform.

It's your tax dollars, so you should know: the US government has spent close to four billion dollars on Plan Colombia since the year 2000. In 2006 it has been reported that coca production has actually increased in the last three years. Hmmmmm . . . I'm no mathematician, but something don't add up here. . . .

Fun Plaid Fact: After Plan Colombia was revised by the Americans, the first formal draft was written in English and a version in Spanish wasn't created until months after the English copy was available. In related news, many Colombians have accused Colombian pop-star Shakira of being a language sellout for releasing an album in English.

icy or Roosevelt Corollary going on. Nobody is invading (that we know of) and we're not going to do anything about it if they invade each other. BUT the current and active deal with US Intervention in Latin America is all centered on **drugs.** What the Plaid Avenger already knows from personal travels is that Latin America produces the bulk of the world's cocaine . . . and the United States *consumes* the bulk of the world's cocaine.

This creates a situation where the US government, armed with an antidrug policy that it named "The War on Drugs," facilitates or makes it an imperative for us to intervene in other countries to stop drug production all over the world. Now the Plaid won't get into a big debate about the pure insanity of such an endeavor. I'll leave that to you students of the world to figure out if that's a good method to stop drug use or not, but certainly it is the US policy: "We don't really care so much that people are hooked on drugs up here; we just want to make sure they don't produce them down there." That will somehow solve the problem? Yeah, good luck with that one . . .

This brings up one particular aspect of US foreign policy today called **Plan Colombia.**

US direct intervention right now is mostly focused on Colombia, Ecuador, Peru, and Bolivia: the big drug producing and exporting countries. Plan Colombia, in particular, has equated to around 4 billion tax dollars in an effort to stop Colombia from producing drugs. Money well spent! Some governments, like Colombia, go along with US policy. However some others, like Bolivia, are increasingly not. That brings us to a related topic . . .

LEFTWARD LEANING

This is the most fun, exciting, new, and current part of "What's Latin about Latin America." Through a combination of virtually all the above reasons that Latin America is Latin, this notion is the one that pulls it all together. As we've already cited, particularly during the Cold War era, the US was very troubled by and directly intervened in leftist or left-leaning countries in Latin America. God forbid they embrace some sort of socialism and certainly not communism. But nonetheless, some people went left anyway. Castro springs to mind. Cuba has been communist and certainly in the "lefty" column for this entire time.

But by and large, he has been alone in the hemisphere until very recently. What we've seen in the last decade—perhaps because of the wealth disparity or landlessness or poverty in Latin America—is a general bad taste in Latino mouths about the US's history of intervention. This has really culminated in a lot of countries heading back towards the left column. One that springs to mind is Venezuela in South America. A rabidly left country (some might even say it's already communist), Venezuela boasts a new brand of socialism that strives for social equality and redistribution of wealth to a limited degree through social programs. But even its leader is not alone. President Evo Morales of Bolivia has recently joined the ranks of hard-core leftist, and has been busy nationalizing industries and moving his country in a fully socialist direction. The US government can look at Castro, Chavez, and Morales and hate them. They are easy men for the US to hate because they send the hate right back.

But it's not just the bold and brash loud-mouths in Latin America who are embracing the left. Brazil has a left-leaning president as well. Last year Argentina elected a left-leaning government. Chile just elected its first female president, and she's left leaning. Ecuador, Nicaragua, Haiti, and Peru have headed that way too. As you can see from the map on page 230, the future of Latin America does seem to be in the left-leaning categories. Let's explore why that is.

Why is the left progressing and gaining popularity? Many people in the world are starting to look at Latin America as a singular entity (one of the reasons I decided to do this chapter) that perhaps may become a new axis of power on the planet. What the hell am I talking about? Well, as a group of disparate countries that didn't have a lot of common economic or political goals, now they do. And as they have this leftward move, we can look at this entire region as representing that single ideology. There is no other region like that on the planet at this second. We can look at most of the planet which has progressively over the last 50–100 years been going toward something that's more on the right, more strictly capitalist, democratic systems. While certainly these are all democracies down there, they are going more left in terms of social and cultural issues, becoming much more openly liberal. In other words, the overwhelming focus in Latin America is to remedy the very wealth disparity that we talked about earlier.

Why is this happening here? Doesn't everyone want social justice and equality for people across the planet? Well yeah, lots of people do. But as I already suggested, this is the place on the planet that has the greatest wealth disparity. The landless, impoverished masses make this a perfect lab setting for this kind of experiment to evolve. Why is it here? Why is it right now? You have to understand that when you have any state, country, or place where most people are incredibly poor, you are asking for a revolution. When most people have nothing to live for, no stake in the land, no claims—it's all fine as long as the majority, who has the power and wealth, can keep them down. But when it becomes too lopsided, it becomes tougher and tougher for the elite to keep a lid on it, and things will eventually boil over.

So societies like this are always on the brink of revolution (see Mexican Revolution, Communist Revolution, Bolivarian Revolution), and they are rocketing back to that point today. It is because of this inequality that people are voting for the left, voting for parties whose *primary goal* is to alleviate wealth disparity. They want to make things more equal. They are striving to improve infrastructure like roads and schools as part of their primary goal. I'm not saying that this isn't a goal of the other parties, but this is the *primary goal* of leftist parties.

The primary leftist agenda involves things like human rights, investment in education and healthcare, and equal access to land for the impoverished masses. That is the main unspoken priority and that is why the leftist agenda is so popular. In democratic countries, where nobody has jack shit to their name, the leftist candidates are extremely appealing because they are telling the people, "Hey we are trying to make this better for you or more equal for you." Thus it should not be a radical surprise that there is a big movement towards the left across the region that has the greatest wealth disparity on the planet. That's why people are voting for the leftist candidates.

Why are they not voting anymore for the rightist candidates? It's got a lot to do with the US's historic involvement and where we are in today's world. These are all established democracies, and in the 21st century, it is increasingly hard for a military dictatorship or for a government supported by an exterior government like the US, to hold power because issues are getting clearer and fewer people are being influenced to vote against their interests. The blatant corruption is getting easier to identify, so it's very difficult for extreme rightists to hold power anymore.

2008 Political Positions

■ Far left
■ Left leaning
■ *Center right*

Just look at all that leaning!!!

What's the Deal with . . . the US Hatred of Venezuela?

Why does the US despise Hugo Chavez so much?

Venezuela has the means to produce over 3 billion barrels of oil per day, 60 percent of which is bought by the United States. Using this revenue, Venezuela has started to pick up some serious military might in recent years. President Hugo Chavez has worked hard to secure arms deals with countries such as Brazil, China, Russia, and Spain.

Take these newly acquired MiG jets, attack helicopters, AK-47s and Scud Missiles, put them into the hands of two million well-trained Venezuelans and you've got yourself one hell of an adversary. While Venezuela may not have this strength right now, these are the plans being set in motion by Chavez, convinced of a coming invasion by the United States.

Number One on the US HATE List

Now why in the world would Chavez believe that the big bad US is going to march into little Venezuela? Maybe it was the name-calling by Condolezza Rice when she accused Venezuela of being a "side kick" to Iran. Perhaps Chavez was offended when Donald Rumsfeld compared him to Hitler. Or maybe Chavez took it personally when evangelist Pat Robertson called for his assassination. In any case, Chavez certainly became suspicious of his neighbors to the north after the US refused to denounce an unconstitutionally, and extremely undemocratic, coup which would overthrow his democratically elected ass, even though it only lasted a few days. Virtually all countries denounced the coup within hours, but the US stayed mysteriously quiet. Damn they hate his ass!

The US continues to criticize the policies of democratically elected Chavez as being "undemocratic," and he is pissed. He vows to cut every drop of oil exports and to mount an all-out guerilla war should the US step foot in Venezuela. And, given the current administration's doctrine of preemption, a simple cry of "terrorist!" could drive hundreds of thousands of US troops to South America. Sound crazy? Yeah, I guess. But that's probably what people in Afghanistan and Iraq thought too.

But hang on! Don't be misled by the Avenger's rap on this dude . . . I'm not promoting the pronouncements of this proud peacock. He is certainly leftist, certainly socialist, and certainly legally democratically elected . . . but that doesn't mean he is doing a particularly good job. The dude apparently enjoys the international limelight he gets bashing the US slightly more than he enjoys actually getting anything done back home. While billions have been made off of oil revenues in his tenure as president, Hugo has not been so successful at actually rebuilding his economy or pulling the masses out of poverty. He won't be around too much longer . . .

LOSING THE LATINS: US UNDONE

AKA: Why the US is *really, really* worried about this . . . The US is troubled by this leftist lean because it is largely seen across the planet as "The US has screwed up their foreign policy so bad that they have lost control and influence in their own backyard," which may be an extreme statement. But it is a fair statement to make nonetheless. Part of the reason they have done that, and part of the reason rightist regimes have lost power, is that they have been perhaps a little too heavy-handed over time. Most of the US involvement and incursions into the region were for reasons previously mentioned, such as anticommunist intervention, but even through the Cold War and to current day, another reason for US involvement is to protect US economic interests. This is seen as extremely problematic for locals, who are as poor as hell.

So a lot of times when the US has invaded places like Nicaragua or Belize, or helped assassinate a democratically elected leader in Chile, it was because of this fear that in lefty/commie countries a redistribution of land and resources was going to occur—you remember: **nationalization.** That was unacceptable to the US, largely because there were US corporations down there and "Hey, that land you poor people are taking is US property!" This was argued during the Cold War era and in fact this was argued about Chile. A company said "Hey! US government! You can't let commies take over Chile. They will **nationalize** our company (which means the commies will take it over and make the profit), and this is US property." A lot of US involvement has been due to protecting these US corporate interests. We'll examine this more in future chapters.

AND THE NEW KID IN TOWN . . .

The perception of US involvement as self-serving, coupled with massive wealth disparity, in part explains why much of Latin America is going to the left. A lot of leftist candidates, particularly Chavez, Castro, and Evo Morales in Bolivia are saying, "We're not even pretending to do the neoliberal capitalist policies. To be a free market with free and open trade works for the United States, and it looks good on paper, but it isn't working for us."

A lot of these leaders are saying, "We're not anti-US, we're just anti-free trade." The current President of Bolivia says, "We've done it. We've tried to do free trade, and we're still poor as shit! We won't do it anymore! We're not going to give priority to American corporations and we're not going to give tax breaks to American anything!" Why is that? Because there's a new kid in town that many countries may give incentives to: China. It is making huge inroads into Latin America right now. That's another reason America fears a loss of influence in Latin America.

And to be honest, you can't really blame the Latins for taking advantage of the Chinese interest in their region. The Chinese are courting countries around the world, making sweet trade deals with them, in order to feed their economy's ever-increasing hunger for natural resources. And Chinese foreign trade/ foreign aid deals are even sweeter because they come with no strings attached . . . unlike deals from the US. On top of that (and this is critical), in the last decade the Chinese President Hu Jintao and/or Chinese Premier Wen Jiabao have personally visited virtually every single Latin state, and multiple times, on multiple visits, in multiple years. US President Bush has only managed to head south of the border twice in the last 8 years. Starting to get the picture here?

About people on the political right: I don't want to suggest that they just want to make money and they don't give a damn about people; that's not the case. Even these people on the opposite side of the spectrum (real anti-socialist) would argue, "No,

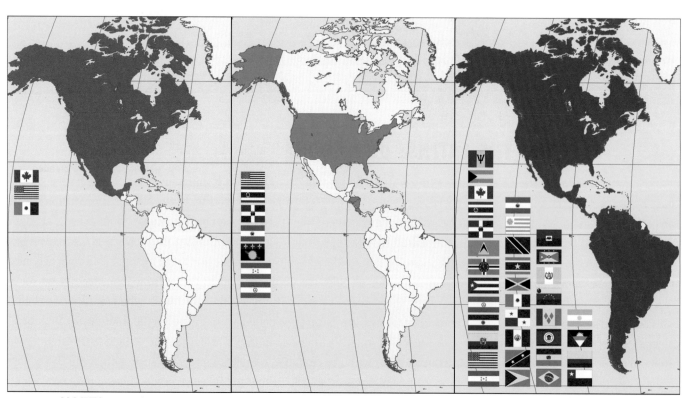

NAFTA members   **CAFTA members**   **Proposed FTAA members**

we want to make these countries richer too. We want their citizens to have more stuff and not be poor, but we don't think social programs are the way to do it. We think the way to make people richer in Brazil and Colombia and Mexico is to have free trade." Free trade is the typical conservative approach on how to alleviate poverty. I don't want to deify anyone that is socialist because there are people on the other side who want good things too. They just don't think leftist methods will work, "You can't just give them a welfare check! That's not going to solve anything! Then nobody will be rich! What we need is free trade." Thus . . .

The **Free Trade Area of the Americas** (FTAA) already is and will be a hot issue for this hemisphere over the next decade. It's going to be a rallying point for antiglobalization as well as globalization powers. There are going to be big revolts over it; there are going to be heavy stones thrown over it. It's already a big, big deal that's just going to get bigger as the adversaries of capitalism (and/or the US) use it as fodder for their fire.

I bring this up because free-traders say "Oh we want Brazilians to be happy too, but the way to accomplish that is a free trade union." **NAFTA** is a free-trade union between Canada, Mexico, and the United States. CAFTA is an ever-growing free trade area between the US and a handful of Caribbean and Central American countries, with the inevitable goal of being the FTAA. The **FTAA** is a proposed free-trade area of every single country in the Americas. The United States, of course having an edge in all of this, is a big fan and proponent of the FTAA. It thinks the FTAA will make it richer, for one, but it also thinks it will help to reestablish influence in the Latin American region as a leader of the FTAA. Anti-US, antiglobalization forces and leftist politicians in Latin America say "No. We've been playing that shit-game for a hundred years and we're still poor. We don't like it. We don't buy it."

We shall see how the battle for free trade pans out in the coming decades.

Chapter closer: These pervasive themes are not only historical, but play into today's Latin America. Now let's take a look into some of Latin America's subregions to provide more specific details so you can understand how each one works into today's and tomorrow's world.

My Latin Lover

1 oz Cruzan Coconut flavored rum

1 oz Cruzan Banana flavored rum

3 oz pineapple juice

1 oz Coco Lopez cream of coconut

1 oz raspberry juice

1 oz cream

1 scoop ice

Combine all ingredients in a blender until smooth consistency. Rim a hurricane glass with grenadine and coconut shavings, and pour in the mixture. Serve. Think of Maximilian, and France's great legacy in the America's. That should make you smile.

"Oh, Plaid Avenger . . . please love my latin-ness . . ."

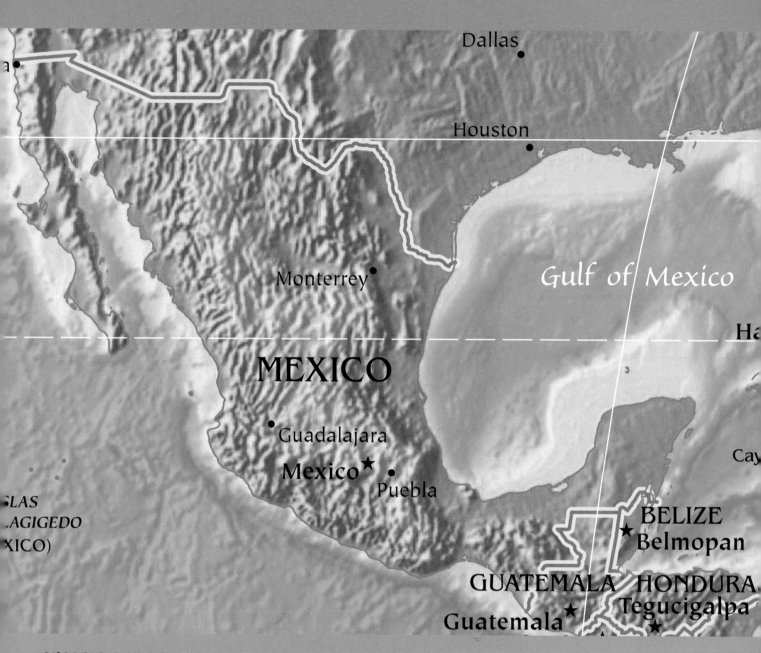

Dallas

Houston

Gulf of Mexico

Monterrey

MEXICO

Guadalajara

Mexico ★

Puebla

SLAS
AGIGEDO
XICO)

Cay

BELIZE
Belmopan

GUATEMALA HONDURA

Tegucigalpa

Guatemala

CHAPTER OUTLINE

Mexico

MEXICO!

The centerpiece; the central holding; the command center of the Spanish empire while it was conquering the New World. As such, it was a regional power center, and a resource center, with a significant population and a more than significant native civilization. When we hear about all the gold and silver bullion that was heading back to the Old World on Spanish ships, Mexico is primarily where all this stuff came from. So for a variety of reasons, Mexico has been the center of things in Latin America as the launching pad of Spanish expeditions. But that was then, and this is now.

'NEW' MEXICO?

When we think about the term Middle America, which I gave to you in the last chapter, Mexico holds roughly 75 percent of Middle America's land. It's a big place, which by the way, used to be a lot bigger. And it also has roughly 60 percent of Middle America's population, so by any account, it's the real powerhouse of Middle America. It is the giant among the smaller countries in the neighborhood. On another note, we can distinguish between Mexico and all of the other countries of Middle America and even South America, because it shares a border with the US. Being next to the colossus of the US, which is of course the one power on the planet militarily and economically, opens Mexico up to a lot more opportunities than its Middle American neighbors. It's in "The Good Neighborhood" so to speak. In this chapter we'll go back and look at how it got to this point.

¿Qué? . . .

Perhaps an appropriate title for this chapter would be, **Mexico: The *Next* Developed Region.** One of the distinguishing characteristics that caused us to tease Mexico out of the North American region is that it's not like Canada and America in levels of development. A point that I will try to make and that I want you to know and understand before you finish reading this chapter is that Mexico should be rich! It should be wealthy! It should be in the "fully developed country" category for lots and lots and lots of different reasons! It's still the powerhouse of Middle America population-wise, even economics-wise, but it's not on par with the US and Canada. The Plaid Avenger here is suggesting that perhaps it should be. We need to figure out why.

PHYSICAL

Speaking physically for Mexico, this is an interesting country because it's got two major mountain chains running through it from north to south that are a continuation of the Rockies from the US, except in Mexico they call them the

Sierra Madres. We have the Sierra Madres **Orien-tales,** and the Sierra Madres **Occidentales,** which of course are to the east and west, respectively. If we look at Mexico as an entire entity, it's kind of mountainous. Mountains are all over the place. These mountain ranges run down both of the east and west coasts, making the entire central plain of Mexico essentially a plateau, or uplifted plains region. It's around 2000 m above sea level.

When Hernándo Cortés was conquering Mexico back in the 1800s, even he had a quick description of the Mexican terrain. When he went back to Europe, someone asked him, "Hernándo, what's Mexico like? What's the New World like? What's New Spain like?" And Cortés said, "Oh I can show you!" And he grabbed a sheet of paper and crumbled it up, smashed it up,

Muy mountainous!

threw it on the ground and said, "There you go, that's Mexico right there!" Mountainous terrain, all the way through from north to south, and a central plain which raises everything up right in the middle. This is important to note because Mexico City, with about 20 million people in it, is one of the highest capitals on the planet. It is about 10,000 ft. elevation, in between valleys. We're not talking about Andes style, or Himalayan style with huge mountains; it's all on an elevated plateau.

¡HOT TAMALE! MEXICAN CLIMATE

We know a little about Mexican climate . . . it's connected to the US down there at Arizona and New Mexico, so it's all desert right? When we think of our old friend Speedy Gonzales from Bugs Bunny cartoons we think of desert and steppe: dry territory. Well, that's a bit of a mis-nomer, a dab of misinformation, because only the north is dry desert. The Sonora Desert creeps down into Mexico into the Chihuahua Desert which is part of the same system. It is a dry place in the interior, but as you progress south, you get into some semi-tropical areas, and by the time you get to the Mexican-Guatemalan border in the south, it's full-on tropical rain forest. As you progress from the north part of Mexico to the South, you go up in elevation onto this high plateau, and it gets wet-ter. You go from dry climates to tropical wet climates. So there is quite a bit of diversity within Mexico's physical systems and that sets the stage for us to talk about Mexico's timeline.

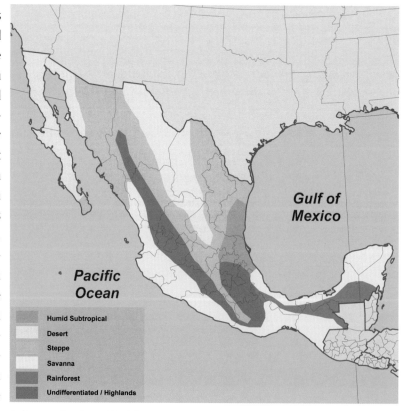

A diverse climate; not just desert.

MEXICO IN HISTORY . . . WATCH OUT FOR MONTEZUMA! AND HIS REVENGE!

The Plaid's got just a few things for you to consider as we are trying to figure out the Mexico of today and why it's important and how it's different from every place else . . . we've already pointed out that it has been a centerpiece, a rallying point, a base of command for the growth of the Spanish Empire in the New World. Let's go back even further than that!

What is completely different about Mexico versus really every place else in the New World of 500 years ago? It's different because we've had not just a *few* folks hanging out here, and not just *big groups* of folks hanging out here, but full-on *civilizations* hanging out here for at least a couple thousand years! When the Europeans—some of these are British, some French, but mostly Spanish in this part of the New World—bump into most parts of the New World 500 something years ago, it's virtually uninhabited. Around this time, if you go to places in North America, there's almost nobody here. I may have pointed this out to you when we talked about the US and Canada's evolution, but there were maybe 2 million Native Americans hanging out in all of North America when Columbus arrived. There were maybe 4 or 5 million indigenous people in all of South America when the Spaniards arrived. That's not a lot of folks for such a big area. But when you get into Mexico, everything is different. The conquistadors came face to face

with upwards of 20 million inhabitants in what is now modern-day Mexico! We know these folks as the Aztec civilization. This group of folks had been hanging out for a while, and they weren't even the original folks here.

The conquistadors came upon a full-fledged civilization that had a huge urban area, temple complexes, complex religious and social systems that had been in place for a thousand years. A little known fact is that Mexico City—what we consider Mexico City today—when the Spanish arrived, was by far the largest city the Europeans had ever seen. Let me clarify that:

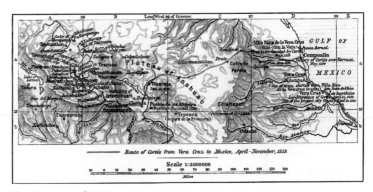

The Conquest of Mexico 1519–1521.

not simply the largest city they had seen in the New World; the biggest city they'd ever seen in their lives, period. Twenty million people in and around a singular city was unheard of at the time, even in Europe. It would dwarf any European city-state at the time. There were lots and lots of folks in Mexico, not a lot of folks outside of Mexico. It was what we call a true cultural hearth.

ONE OF THE MAIN DIFFERENCES BETWEEN MEXICO AND THE REST OF LATIN AMERICA. WHO WENT WHERE? WHO COLONIZED WHAT?

Spanish exploration. Cortés wanted all the gold and riches and took his small group of people, around 200–300 soldiers, and conquered millions. Cortés and the Spanish were after the **Imperial G Trifecta: Gold, Glory, and God.** They beat a quick path to the trifecta and were radically successful because within only two years, a handful of Spaniards overthrow the entire Aztec civilization. How the hell did 200 or 300 Spanish dudes manage that? Well for one, Cortés was very good at rallying the locals to his cause to help defeat the Aztecs. Many of the locals hated the Aztecs much more than the innocent whities that had just shown up on their shores. Oops. Big mistake there.

But there are three more things for you to know . . . firepower, horses, and the Spaniards biggest ally: DISEASE! The Spaniards and Portuguese brought measles and smallpox and mumps, which entirely wiped out native populations. Most natives in Latin America were never even in contact with the white man. They died from European originated disease to which they had no biological resistance. Long story short, disease enables the Spanish and the Portuguese to take over the New World in short order.

RAPID-FIRE PATH TO INDEPENDENCE

→ Most of Latin America was built up by Spaniards purely to be one massive extractive colony.

→ American independence was the fuse for Mexican independence.

→ The Mexicans got pissed enough to fight for their freedom in 1821.

→ Shortly after declaring independence, Central America secedes from Mexican union.

→ In 1836, Texas secedes from Mexican union. You can see that Texas then was even bigger than Texas now. This act started the Mexican-American War.

  → Texas declared independence before they were accepted into the US, and were considered an independent state.

  → It's still in the Texas constitution to be able to opt out of the US if they want. Legally. I'm all for it.

→ The Mexican-American War lasted from 1846–1848, and resulted in Mexico losing roughly two-thirds of its original territory. This is how the US acquired California, Arizona, Nevada, Utah, New Mexico, and Colorado.

→ In 1853, the US tried to buy more territory from Mexico. Mexico refused but the US government strong-armed them into it. This resulted in the Gadsden Purchase.

The sum total of all this territorial loss really pisses Mexico off, but they can't really do anything about it. They develop an inferiority complex because of it. They're all bent out of shape because historically, they can't compete. And maybe this inferiority complex has got something to do with why Mexico is not better off in today's world. Because quite frankly . . .

**Mexico Gains Independence
From Spain -1820**

**Independence of the United
Provinces of Central America - 1823**

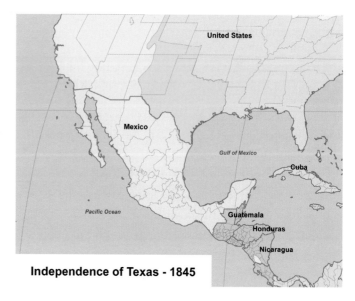

Independence of Texas - 1845

**Mexican Cession to U.S.
Following War - 1848**

Gadsden Purchase - 1853.

Present Day Mexico.

MEXICO SHOULD BE RICH . . .

It really should. There are not too many places in the world where you can look at the country as a whole and say, "Wow, you should be doing a lot better than you are, you've got a lot of things going for you." But you can in Mexico. It is a state fully in the developing realm, no one would argue with that. As the Plaid has said before, that's one of the main differences between Mexico and the US. The US is extremely developed, extremely rich; Mexico is not. But it should be. Why should Mexico be a developed country? We can look at a few main factors you should consider, know and understand. The first of these is:

RELATIVE LOCATION

What do I mean by that? I simply mean where it is situated on the planet, in terms of everything that's around it. If you could magically place a parcel of land anywhere that you wanted to, you could put it anywhere, would you put it at the North Pole? No way. South Pole? Probably not. Middle of Russia? No. Central Africa? No. If you were wise, you'd probably stick it right where Mexico is, because it will be next door to and have a shared border with the US: the one economy on the planet. You would want to be situated next to the world's economic nucleus, the powerhouse of the US, the insatiable market that can consume everything that the Mexican market produces.

LOCATION AND ECONOMY: ¡MAKING LOS PESOS!

Everybody would like to be neighbors and close trading partners with the largest economy on the planet. Everything Mexico makes, including all the vegetables consumed during the winter in this part of the world, all the mineral resources, every product manufactured using their cheap labor, EVERYTHING! Everything that Mexico produces can be sold in the US. Everything can be exported to the US; TVs, VCRs, automobiles, countless other manufactured goods available in stores everywhere, waiting to be consumed by the giant American market, are made in Mexico. That's the best position in the world to be in! It should be exceptionally rich.

It all comes from south of the border, baby!

You have to remember that Mexico's a member of NAFTA (the North American Free Trade Agreement) along with them, the US, and Canada. US: one economy on the planet. Canada: One trading partner with the US. Mexico: two trading partner with the US. NUMBER 2! How can they not be rich? It's incredible! Almost astounding! It flies in the face of every-thing that would be expected, everything that makes sense, to be trading partners with the biggest be-yatch with the most money on the planet and not be rich yourself!

Almost all of the things that are produced in Mexico end up in the US, and that's one of the reasons why so many businesses have relocated to Mexico. Car manufacturing, TV manufacturing, really all major-market products, are com-piled and assembled in Mexico and end up in the US. They are adding value to a product, which means they should be get-ting something out of that. It's much better than just producing vegetables, which we have already pointed out that they do. But the main commodity of significance produced in Mexico, though they can never produce enough of it, is oil.

Oil is one of the main things Mexico produces, and it's also what the US is the biggest consumer of. In other words, no matter how much Mexico produces, every single fluid ounce of it is *already* sold to the US. It's a guaranteed market. That's a really, really big deal. So the economic nucleus to the north is of extreme importance in regard to why Mexico should be rich.

Consider stuff that's hard to deliver, hard to sell . . . things like drugs. It takes serious planning and coordination of efforts to move and sell drugs. But Mexico does it! Very well, I might add. Why is Mexico a huge producer and trafficker of drugs? It's obviously because America consumes copious amounts of drugs. So even something that's illegal, that you can get thrown in jail for, that you can get shot at and killed for . . . even this stuff moves from Mexico into the US in huge volume every single day. So Mexico should be rich solely off what it can do under the table for its northern neighbor.

Slightly more challenging imports.

LOCATION AND MILITARY: ¡DON'T MESS WITH ME, ESE!

Not only is Mexico in the perfect location geographically to really reap the benefits of an economic powerhouse, but on top of that, its geography also provides a military advantage. What does the Plaid Avenger mean by this? Mexico has not had to invest in a military for decades. Most countries on the planet have to defend their territory: they have to buy tanks, develop serious weaponry, and do a lot of expensive things that take money away from developing infrastructure in other ways. Mexico's relative location has again given it the prime spot because it doesn't have to do any of that shit. Why? It's not a member of NATO because it doesn't have to be. Mexico is not a military power because it doesn't have to be. Why? The US is sitting right there, who in the hell is going to invade or attack Mexico? Nobody. Not even Russia at the height of the Cold War considered invading Mexico. Would China do it? Not a chance.

Even though Mexico is not protected by any specific treaty, nobody is going to mess around in the US's backyard. Think back to the Monroe Doctrine: touch the backyard and your ass is grass. It's just not going to happen. Not spending millions on a military is a tremendous boon for the Mexican economy. They could take that money and do something else with it. For some reason they haven't quite gotten there, which we will get back to in a second.

Relative location is key. There is no better one on the planet. Mexico and Canada are in the catbird seats. Canada has advanced, but Mexico has not. Being a NAFTA member with close ties to the economic powerhouse of the world, and already benefiting from its relationship with the US in terms of defense, Mexico should be rolling in the pesos.

¡RECURSOS! = RESOURCES!

The second major reason why Mexico should be rich: it is resource rich. It has tremendous amounts of everything. I already pointed out agriculture, and that it has guaranteed markets for its agricultural products in the US. Bananas, avocados, other fruits and vegetables come up from Mexico. We already talked about primary products and how they're not worth as much as others. Mexico's primary products are no exception. That's why relative location is important, because they pretty much have a guaranteed market for their agricultural products. Mexico also has things like tin, copper, iron, lead, zinc, magnesium, the list goes on and on, and they can sell every bit of it to manufacturers in the US. Guaranteed. The US can't get enough of that stuff. The one resource of particular consequence, referred to earlier, is oil. A brief word about oil . . .

Mexico is not a *major* producer of oil on the planet, but it is in our neighborhood. What's so great about that? Main reason why it's so great: the US is the biggest consumer of oil on the planet, both in terms of total volume and per capita. What better resource to have right beside the US than the one resource it uses the most? But it's a dual-edged sword. Why? It has been a blessing because there's a guaranteed market for it in the US, every drop they produce can be sold, but it's been a curse because of the history lesson to follow . . .

1973 OIL EMBARGO

This is a major event in US history, even world history, because it has shaped economic and political relationships between the US and several different countries. Since we'll discuss it in more detail later, I'm going to keep this pretty simple. The US supported Israel in the Yom Kippur War in 1973. All of the Arab nations got seriously pissed off as a result, and they decided (since they are the lion's share of the members of OPEC) to enact an embargo against the US and Western Europe. They stop selling oil to the US. The spigot gets turned off.

We'll use some hypothetical prices to easily demonstrate how this affected the US and Mexico. Let's say oil was 10 dollars a barrel before the embargo. In a matter of weeks it skyrockets to 40 dollars a barrel. Prices quadruple almost overnight, causing tremendous shortages. You probably don't remember this, but your parents might remember, and your grandparents certainly do. The shortages resulted in rationing, which was a huge deal. Unprecedented.

So how does this relate back to Mexico? Mexico had oil, mostly offshore, but it wasn't worth a lot. It was of lower quality than Middle Eastern oil. There was much more refining that had to be done to Mexico's oil. So Saudi Arabia can suck its oil out of the ground with a straw, dump it into a barrel, and let it go for 10 bucks. But Mexico had to pull it out of the ground, clean it up, filter it, process it a bit, ultimately costing it, let's say, about 15 dollars a barrel just to get it out the door. So with these hypothetical prices, it is losing 5 bucks per barrel. Needless to say, Mexico wasn't in a rush to lose money quenching the US's thirst, so it wasn't a big oil producer. However, when the price of oil blows up to 40 dollars a barrel—now there's a profit of 25 bucks on the oil that our friend Pepe just refined for 15! It's worth it now!

At this point, Mexico develops its oil industry as fast as it can and, go figure, the US would like to see another source of non-Arab oil pop up. So the US lends Mexico millions and millions of dollars to invest in its oil industry's infrastructure to grease the wheels, and everything looks peachy for a couple years . . . until oil prices stabilize. After the embargo ends and the price of oil drops back down, Mexico is still producing, but not nearly at the profit margin when it was 40 dollars a barrel. Having diminishing profits and millions in loans to pay back to the US results in a big economic crunch for Mexico—which came to a head about 15 years ago during the Clinton administration when Mexico was essentially going broke. So, oil is a mixed blessing, it has been good overall, but it put Mexico in tremendous short-term debt, from which it is still trying to recover.

Mexico is resource rich and can provide tons of raw materials. It also adds value to a lot of these things and sends them over in the form of TVs and cars, which are gobbled up in the US, their guaranteed market. And it has got one huge bonus for being next to the largest oil-consuming nation on the planet. Oil! So Mexico *should* be rich . . .

MEXICO SHOULD BE RICH . . . BUT THEY'RE NOT!

Why? What has happened? They have some prime real estate with great situation on the globe in terms of economic and military support, and they've got tons of resources . . . so what's the problem?

ANOTHER PLAID AVENGER INSIDE TIP: Every time the price of oil goes higher on the planet, watch the US's president go and visit three different countries to discuss increasing oil production. The first is Mexico. The president will go down and get it to produce more, which will help resaturate the market and bring prices down. He'll also visit Norway and Russia. These are three big oil producing and exporting countries that are non-OPEC members. This means that they are not tied to the rules and regulations that govern prices or limits of production. They don't care, and the US loves them for it.

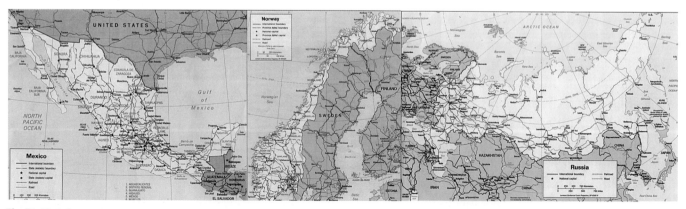

The Big Non-Opec 3.

NUMBER ONE ¡LA GENTE!

They have too many people. You know about the demographic transition; you know what a developed country looks like. Take a look at Mexico's pyramid and you see something much more like Africa, Central Asia, and the Middle East. This is a population that is still *exploding*. It's a perfect pyramid; there's a high fertility rate, and people still have lots and lots of

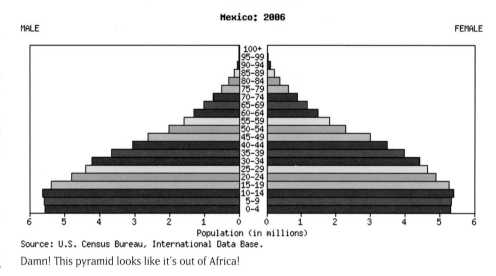

Mexico: 2006

MALE   FEMALE

Population (in millions)

Source: U.S. Census Bureau, International Data Base.

Damn! This pyramid looks like it's out of Africa!

kids. So while Mexico's economy has expanded and diversified and it has actually gotten richer, it has also added way more people. So when you look at total amounts of economic gain in terms of GDP, it's grown. But the people have grown more, at a way higher rate than their economy. As a result, their per capita numbers have gone down. This is still a place that we consider kind of poor.

This seems to be currently tapering off, stabilizing somewhat. But it has a long way to go. The current population is about 110 million. That is a huge number. It is the population leader in Middle America and a population that is almost exactly one-third of the US. This is funny, because it's about one-third of the land size of the US. However, the economy is not even 1/300 of the US economy! That's where they've fallen down. So people are a big problem, and as The Plaid pointed out when we talked about Latin America, this is a place with massive amounts of urbanization. Most people live in the city. There is a draw, the idea that you are going to get a job in the city, which is often not the case.

Mexico City is now one of the largest cities on the planet, population-wise. It will probably approach the number one spot in the next 5–10 years. There just aren't enough jobs for all those folks there. So there are burgeoning urban populations, and on top of that, there is one other place where the Mexican population is increasing. Where? Along its border with the US. This leads to the number two reason why Mexico is not rich . . .

NUMBER TWO ¡MAQUILADORAS!

Maquiladoras are towns along the Mexico side of its border with the US, built around factories that are owned by foreign companies. There are some that have been there for a while, but many new border towns started popping up steadily after NAFTA was set up. NAFTA allows free movement of capital and business across the borders of its constituent states. So the companies build factories just over the border to take advantage of cheap Mexican labor. Many unemployed Mexicans flock to these towns for jobs.

In the last 20 years the situation has developed such that companies in the US, or another place, manufacture the individual parts, ship them to their maquiladoras just across the border where Mexicans working for less money assemble the parts into the retail version of whatever product the company sells. It allows the companies to pay some guy a nickel an hour or whatever to put your TV or your car or your stereo or your car stereo together. The labor is so cheap that it makes it worthwhile for the company to import the raw materials to make the parts and ship the parts down to be assembled in Mexico, and then ship the finished product all over the US to be sold at a huge profit. They can afford to ship the same shit three times! Just for comparison, in 2000 the American minimum wage was about $5.25 per hour; the Mexican minimum wage was $3.50 *per day!*

This scenario is another dual-edged sword for Mexico, like oil. Lots of folks down there would say, "Hey, don't complain; they're creating jobs and that's a good thing. We had nothing before, but now at least we have jobs, even though they don't pay shit." Many other folks would also point out the obvious; not only are the workers in the maquiladoras getting paid jack, but all the true value of the product is made by taking advantage of the impoverished Mexicans working for wages so small they're practically slaves. From the Plaid Perspective, there is something to be said for both sides of the argument.

Know maquilladoras. Even though their growth has slowed, they still contain a large concentration of the Mexican population. The other big chunk of the Mexican population, as mentioned, is in Mexico City proper where the population is around 20 million and growing. This growth is based on the hope that people have that they will find jobs. And here's the real kicker: even though these "sweatshops" may suck, the loss of them may suck more. As labor becomes cheaper in China and Asia altogether, companies are starting to move out of Mexico because the labor is too expensive. Too expensive? Damn, that's wrong!

NUMBER THREE ¡VIVA LA TIERRA!

Here's one thing that we already know occurs all across Latin America, and it's the number three reason why Mexico is not rich: **wealth disparity and landlessness.** This means that the top tier of citizens, the elite, own a disproportionate amount of the land. A very small percentage of the people own virtually everything. This means that the great majority of people own nothing, not even the land they live on. Landlessness is a big issue across Latin America as a whole, and Mexico is a great example of why this is.

Mexico's history is replete with the important issue of

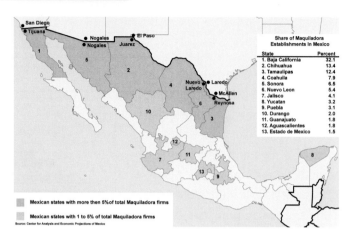

Share of Maquiladora Establishments in Mexico	
State	Percent
1. Baja California	32.1
2. Chihuahua	13.4
3. Tamaulipas	12.4
4. Coahuila	7.9
5. Sonora	6.5
6. Nuevo Leon	5.4
7. Jalisco	4.1
8. Yucatan	3.2
9. Puebla	3.1
10. Durango	2.0
11. Guanajuato	1.8
12. Aguascalientes	1.8
13. Estado de Mexico	1.5

Mexican states with more then 5%of total Maquiladora firms

Mexican states with 1 to 5% of total Maquiladora firms

Source: Center for Analysis and Economic Projections of Mexico

SOME MAQUILADORAS COMPANIES YOU MAY KNOW

- 3 Day Blinds
- 20th Century Plastics
- Acer Peripherals
- Bali Company, Inc.
- Bayer Corp./Medsep
- BMW
- Canon Business Machines
- Casio Manufacturing
- Chrysler
- Daewoo
- Eastman Kodak/Verbatim
- Eberhard-Faber
- Eli Lilly Corporation
- Ericsson
- Fisher Price
- Ford
- Foster Grant Corporation
- General Electric Company
- JVC
- GM
- Hasbro
- Hewlett Packard
- Hitachi Home Electronics

- Honda
- Honeywell, Inc.
- Hughes Aircraft
- Hyundai Precision America
- IBM
- Matsushita
- Mattel
- Maxell Corporation
- Mercedes Benz
- Mitsubishi Electronics Corp.
- Motorola
- Nissan
- Philips
- Pioneer Speakers
- Samsonite Corporation
- Samsung
- Sanyo North America
- Sony Electronics
- Tiffany
- Toshiba
- VW
- Xerox
- Zenith

land reform. What am I talking about here? Just in the last 100 years, we have something called the **Mexican Revolution.** It seems like every major country has some sort of revolution. We talked about the Communist Revolution in Russia, the Meiji Restoration in Japan.

Mexico had its revolution in 1910. What was it about? It was about human rights and lots of other things, but its central concern was over land. When wealth disparity gets large enough, where wealth and power are concentrated in the hands of the few, the political system becomes unstable. When this happens people typically get pissed off until revolution rears its ugly head. The tinder keg gets lit and they're off. The two revolutionary leaders you see pictured here are classic examples of what happened in Mexico when wealth accumulated too much into too few hands. In the north, there was Pancho Villa, who was a rebel/revolutionary leader, essentially a bandit type with sort of a bad reputation. He took up arms against the government as things became too corrupt and land was controlled by too few in the early 20th century.

Pancho Villa (with his men).

Villa's counterpart in the south was Emilio Zapata. A poor farmer, good all around guy, a charismatic hero, Zapata takes up the cause and gets the word out to people that the government is screwing them over. "Look at us amigos, we are poor as hell, none of us have land! We need to overthrow the government and make this a better place!" So there are two guys on both geographical extremes of Mexico, who ended up overthrowing the government. The central point is that it was all over land, all about the issue of landlessness. Zapata was a real foundation of this, since he was a farmer himself. It wasn't a political thing where he wanted to rule or be president; he just wanted land for everyone so they could all support themselves and each other. He wanted it to be fairly distributed. Why is this important? Land is *still* a major theme in Mexican government and politics today.

How did land ownership in prerevolution Mexican society get so topheavy? Under the Aztec system, society was strictly hierarchical, a sort of military dictatorship almost. All the power was concentrated around the top. The head Aztec honcho basically owns and controls everything; all land and all wealth is subject to his will. It is an ancient tradition. When the conquistadors arrive, under Cortés' leadership, they have an easy time taking over because they just lop off Montezuma's head and replace him with themselves at the top. The system doesn't get altered much when it changes hands from the indigenous rulers to the Spanish. Even when Mexico has its revolution

Emilio Zapata.

and kicks out the Spanish, they had an oligarchic system where there were a few ex-Spaniards that had control and maintained power over large amounts of the country. So the wealthy hang on to all their resources and the poor get nothing. This arrangement stays in place until the revolution.

The Mexican Revolution was a pretty big deal. It happened in 1910, and when it was successful, they wrote such an awesome constitution that almost shamed the US's. It was an extremely thorough document all about human rights, access to land, and many other important issues. But in many ways, this has been an unrealized dream in Mexico because some of the great stuff in the constitution never really came to be. It's a far-reaching document, and its promises are still being pursued in today's world.

Like I said, this land thing is not just a historical remnant. All political parties in Mexico today have to deal with the land issue. You can't get away from it. Both ends of the political spectrum in Mexico use land reform as a major element of their campaign platforms. Even though strides have been made, land is still a major concern in Mexican politics.

¡REBELS!

There are still rebels, and they are still pissed about land reform. They are fighting actively for the same shit as 100 years ago. General Marcos leads the Zapatistas, named after Emilio Zapata. These guys are in the southern Mexican state of Chiapas, which is in the tropical jungle highlands near the border of Guatemala. This revolutionary movement has been going on for two decades. What are these dudes still fighting for? You guessed it! Land Reform!

Interesting to note, the Zapatistas are one of *the* first, if not the first, revolutionary movement to have an official website: Zapatistarevolution.com. This link is actually a website posted by a trial lawyer in Texas who is sympathetic to the Zapatista cause, and who visited with them during a trip to Mexico. He wrote a fictionalized novel based on the facts of a 1994 Zapatista uprising. The site isn't maintained by the Zapatistas themselves, though a lot of their plight is described on it. They are a truly unique rebel/terrorist organization in this respect—the first online rebels.

So we know Mexico is not rich for a few key reasons: wealth disparity, land issues, the dual-edged sword of oil, the mixed blessing of maquileladoras, and population dynamics. What about their future?

¡EL FUTURO DE MEXICO!

The Plaid Avenger used to say that things are liberalizing, opening up, that perhaps NAFTA is going to be further entrenched and that Mexico will become a truer part of the North American region in terms of movement of people and economic activity. That was the case up until the US's "War on Terror" began which has served to stymie movement between the US and Mexico, as they try to catch potential terrorists. It has recently been compounded even more as illegal immigration has become a hot button election issue in the US. The current political mood in the US right now is to build an even bigger wall between these countries/regions. One complication has arisen because of the fact that the US needs immigration, and everybody knows it. Business people in the US know this: They need immigration for economic growth to continue. Immigrants fill many service sector and manufacturing jobs that some Americans either won't or don't want to do.

Mexican President Filipe Calderon (and even his predecessor Vicente Fox) is the political party equivalent of a Republican in the US. As such, he has been a pretty staunch supporter of President Bush, agreeing with Bush on all policies minus one: immigration. Calderon and others have expressed many reservations at the idea of building a big ass wall between the countries. Mexico is more of the European frame of mind, which is essentially, "Aren't we in a free trade block? Aren't we allies? Aren't we friends? Why do we even have a fence at all?" Mexico is working towards further economic integration with the US, including a 'worker passport' system that would indeed allow for more open movement of folks across the entire continent. However, open trade borders that allow the free flow of goods and people can also allow the free flow of lots of other things . . . like drugs.

And holy hot tamale, be forewarned about this drug situation my friends!!! This is the hottest—and by far most serious—cause for concern for Mexico, the US, and everybody in between. Drugs, drug crime, and gang related crime, all of which have been infiltrating the border region, have simply exploded in the last several years. In the worst ways possi-

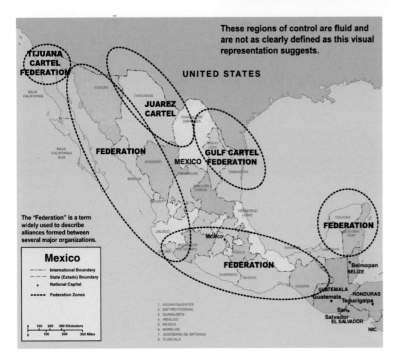

These regions of control are fluid and are not as clearly defined as this visual representation suggests.

The "Federation" is a term widely used to describe alliances formed between several major organizations.

Source: U.S. Drug Enforcement Administration, adapted by CRS (P. McGrath 3/2/2007)

ble too. The volume and value of all that coke, dope, and amphetamines crossing into the US through Mexico has become so damn huge that organized crime has taken over . . . but the competition is so fierce that multiple syndicates/gangs are fighting to the death in turf wars all up and down the border.

We're talking about some nasty shit here my friends. Gangland kidnappings and assassinations of Mexican police, politicians and even army soldiers. Whole villages of innocents being slaughtered in turf wars. Mass graves being found. Human heads being thrown into high school prom dances to terrorize towns. I wish I was exaggerating here. These criminal gangs have grown so powerful that they don't run from the police: they stand and fight them. And the army. And the DEA. The Mexican cartels of the 21st century are being compared to the old Colombian cartels of the 1980's in terms of power, wealth, organization and bloodlust. It is getting scary.

Go out and research it yourself to see the current situation, just know this for now: this insane gang violence being brought directly to the doorstep of the US will probably be the straw that breaks the camel's back. Add the new drug wars to the already festering illegal immigration issue, and you can easily predict that more calls will be made for a 'Great Wall of China' to be built on the border. President Calderon, being a conservative law-and-order guy himself, is working hard to fix this mess. He is working diligently alongside the US to restore order to the region. That means more cops, more army, more border patrol, more DEA involvement. Good luck to the boys in blue down on the border. They are going to need it.

Here at the onset of the 21st century, these two countries are strong allies by all standards, but are divided on the issue of the free movement of people between them. Will Mexico ever be fully developed? It is entirely possible once the population stabilizes, and its economy becomes a bit more robust, and they reclaim their northern territory form the criminal syndicates. However, new competition from elsewhere in the world is also threatening

Filipe fighting to fix border fiasco.

Mexico's dominance on cheap labor for US businesses. Like outsourcing from the US, Mexico has lost international business investment to East and Southeast Asia, who have even cheaper labor than Mexico can offer! What a twist they are in! As are all regions and states close to developed status, they typically get richer by offering cheap labor, which brings in investment dollars. Then, as Mexico becomes successful and richer, labor rates rise. This causes the businesses to pick up and move elsewhere. Damn! Caught in a vice on that one, due to the preeminent rise of the Asian economies and their huge, cheap labor pools. Well, at least Mexico will never be invaded by anyone. Oh, except the coke dealers. It appears that the Conquistadors have returned, albeit in a new and more lethal disguise.

The Come on Calderon!

1 shot Jose Cuervo tequila

1 lime wedge

1 bottle of Corona Extra beer

You do the math on this one. It's what I call the Mexican equivalent of the Boilermaker.

Central America

CENTRAL America is part of Middle America, as we've pointed out in an earlier chapter. It's an easily defined place, because it can be distinguished by just looking at political borders. It goes from the Mexican-Guatemalan border all the way down to the Panamanian-Columbian border and encompasses the countries of Guatemala, Belize, Honduras, El Salvador, Costa Rica, Nicaragua, and Panama: the Central American seven. The Plaid Avenger can best summarize this region, unlike any other region on the planet, in a single word: **VIOLENCE.** This is an incredibly violent arena, in pretty much every way imaginable.

Central America is a place that, while not that far from the economic powerhouse of the US, is one of the poorer regions on the planet. Poverty is of course one reason for all the violence, but not the only one. There is a lot going on here, but not a lot to be happy about, quite frankly. The Plaid Avenger is fairly sure that most people in Central America would agree. Why is it such a violent region?

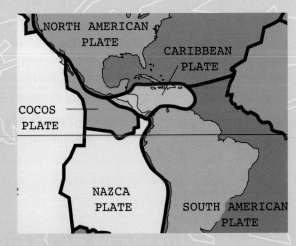

PHYSICALLY VIOLENT

To start, the physical world of Central America contains massive amounts of violence. If you look at a map of plate tectonics, you see several plates coming together in Central America causing a zone of geologic activity. The Cocos plate is ramming against the North American and Caribbean plates. It's actually getting shoved under the Caribbean plate, causing hell-load of volcanic and seismic activity all over the Central American isthmus. Earthquakes and volcanic activity abound. Central America has always been and probably will remain this way, for the rest of human history at least. We can project ahead and look at the Caribbean islands, and we can see that they have also been formed because of plate borders activity, but that's a story for the next chapter.

So the isthmus here is a really violent arena, simply considering its geology. Does that have anything to do with why it's poor? Or why it's a hotspot? It does! We like to think that the physical world doesn't affect people's lives too much, but as we have seen with the other regions we've talked about, that's simply not the case. It's hard for people and businesses to move, adapt, or build structures to

withstand frequent earthquakes and hurricanes. And these countries definitely don't have the resources to control the climate or the physical environment around them. The Plaid Position on Central America is that nature really rules the people here more than any other region we will look at. This cycle of physical violence from the natural world has shaped this region forever . . . and continues to!

Let's get to some specifics. Here's an interesting story about the Panama Canal, which was originally supposed to go through Nicaragua. Some senators from the US were planning to build a canal 100 years ago, but they didn't know where

just yet. Where is the US going to invest its money? Plans to build in Nicaragua were already drawn up, and they were nearly ready to mobilize. But some senator's business interest paid him off to lobby for their plans to go through Panama. It's tough to scrap plans that are in their final phases of development, but the senator pulled it off by using a postage stamp from Nicaragua with a picture of a volcano on it. He made copies and passed it around the senate, and said, "Check this out, chaps, we'd be fools to invest in a place full of volcanoes!" It's the Panama Canal now, not the Nicaraguan, thanks to a savvy, stamp-holding senator.

That may be just a cheese side story, but on top of the seismic and volcanic violence in this region, there is also the weather to contend with. The tropical climate of this region, bordering the Caribbean, is prone to hurricanes. There are violent, devastating weather systems that come through this region with regularity, every year, sometimes multiple times during a season.

Hey, Plaid Avenger, does that have anything to do with this region's poverty problem? Hell yes it does! How many financial investors think it's a good idea to build a multimillion dollar hotel or factory that may be completely destroyed in a hurricane or earthquake? Not too many. Nobody is that rich, or nobody who's that rich is that dumb. Very few companies would even try to go there. The outside world does not regularly invest anywhere in Central America precisely because of the physical world. Pretty much only fruit production companies are heavily invested here, because how much damage can your banana trees sustain during an earthquake? It's a pretty safe bet. The physical world complicates life here, and it will continue to do so.

VIOLENCE IN THE SOCIAL SPHERE

Central America is also a very violent arena from the standpoint of the people. Central America shares its ancient history with Mexico, so we won't go into that. It was part of Mexico during the colonial period through when Mexico became independent in 1821. In 1823, Central America seceded from Mexico and formed a union of independent states. In 1840, even their union started falling apart. In hindsight, perhaps seceding and splitting up even further wasn't the best thing for Central America to do. They are all very small countries now. And as the Plaid Avenger always says, "Size *does* matter!" Since they are small they don't really have any sort of big world role, nor do they have a lot of resources, individually. Perhaps they could have been wealthier and more prominent had they remained a union of states instead of splitting into many individual countries.

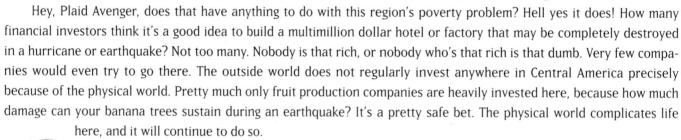

What we have had since the independence of all these countries is a spiraling cycle of violence that is by no means over. After seceding from Mexico, they split up into the individual countries we see today. Apparently, they were never wholly convinced by the revolutionary leaders trying to unite them all under a single umbrella. Too bad; to be a singular political entity may have helped them a lot in the long run. Instead, they end up being a bunch of small bananas, with limited resources and political power, in a much bigger world. Pun intended.

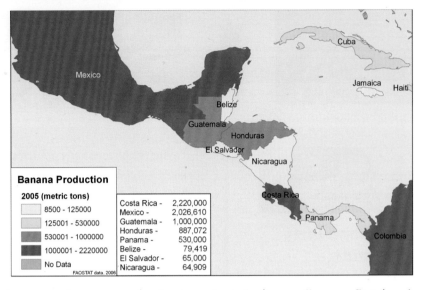

Banana Production

2005 (metric tons)

☐ 8500 - 125000	
☐ 125001 - 530000	
☐ 530001 - 1000000	
☐ 1000001 - 2220000	
☐ No Data	

Costa Rica -	2,220,000
Mexico -	2,026,610
Guatemala -	1,000,000
Honduras -	887,072
Panama -	530,000
Belize -	79,419
El Salvador -	65,000
Nicaragua -	64,909

FAOSTAT data, 2006

Bananas, fruit in general, became the main source for revenue (and not much at that) as well as conflict (much more than revenue). There were several attempts in the 1800s to unionize Central American fruit labor; it all pretty much ended with the union dudes dying in battle or getting executed later for political reasons. And the region becomes synonymous with a political term as well . . . **banana republics.** We'll get to this a little later when we talk about economic violence.

ECONOMIC VIOLENCE

In these places, and this even goes back into the 1820s when these guys were declaring independence, there were foreign multinational companies doing business there. It's not just a current phenomenon. A lot of the folks who still own the resources in Central America aren't even citizens of the countries themselves but are these exact same multinational companies. Gee, I wonder where these companies are from . . . You guessed right! Predominately the good ole US of A. You may be asking yourself, "What do these people make down in Central America that anybody wants?" Well, the bananas you had for breakfast probably came from there. Where do you think the coke you're going to snort later came from? Cocaine, coconuts, bananas, chocolate, most tropical fruits . . . all this is from somewhere south of the US-Mexican border. And a lot of it comes from Central America. This has been the case for a couple hundred years. Who brings all of these goods to America? The US companies that established the markets.

What's the Deal with . . . Banana Republics?

A "banana republic" is a small nation south of the border that is plagued by political corruption and is economically dependent on basic agricultural exports. The term was coined in reference to Honduras, which at the time was basically owned by US multinational fruit companies (see box: What's the Deal with . . . United Fruit Company). Although the terminology sounds cute, it is also highly disparaging—implying a backwardness that can only lend itself to producing fruit for rich Americans. Leadership typically consisted of a very small, wealthy, corrupt elite invariably topped off by an overbearing generalissimo type in a uniform covered with medals and badges. Even worse than being under the domination of such an oligarchy, "banana republics" were/are typically under the domination of US multinational organizations.

Some of our favorite tropical commodities.

Goddamn Dirty Bananas

2 oz. 99 Bananas banana
    schnapps

1 oz. Kahlua coffee liqueur

1 oz. Bacardi 151 Puerto
    Rican rum

1 oz. cream

Throw all ingredients in blender
with ice. High speed blend for
15 seconds. Pour into margarita
glass. Put a bunch of fake medals
from a cracker-jacks box on your
chest and pretend you are a
military dictator. Cheers
Generalissimo!

When impoverished countries start to have leftward leanings—leaning towards socialism or communism—one of the first things the people start asking themselves is, "Why does this American company own 100 percent of the banana market in our country? We produce all the bananas, and we don't get shit for them. This company takes them from here, where they were grown with our cheap labor, pays us a penny and gets a dollar for them in the US. We're getting screwed!" Case in point: United Fruit Company was so huge they controlled virtually all the fruit in Central America for about a hundred years.

There is a big part of the history of this region involving the US protecting its economic interests. So, in many of these countries, when they have a significant leftward lean, and they appear to be heading towards a socialist or communist revolution, one of the first things that the socialists that come into power will do is **nationalize** the industries. As I said before, this is essentially taking an asset that was held by a private multinational company, and saying, "Hey, we've been doing all the work, and you pay us jack and make a ton of profit. But this is *our* land! We're taking it back and we're going to nationalize it. Thanks for setting up shop, for setting up this oil platform, or copper mines, or whatever, thanks; we're going to take it from here and make more money for ourselves; you may now leave." This is nationalization. Corporations do not dig it.

Multinational companies live in mortal fear of this, since basically they get their stuff taken from them. As you can imagine, they have a point. They spent money on the investments there, they have stockholders, and they don't want their livelihoods taken away. They get bothered by this. History shows us that when a company fears that this may happen to them, or if it actually happens to them (and it has happened plenty), they go to the US government and say, "Hey, we're US citizens. Those are US investment dollars down there; that's US *property* down there! You need to help protect US property!" By and large, over the last 150 years, that's exactly what the US government has done, especially in Central America. So when a government like Nicaragua is taken over by popular uprising, and they want to nationalize the banana industry, suddenly, the US marines show up to save the day! For who? The US corporation is saved and the poor people who slave for it get to work another day for the man.

Some of you may stop reading this right now, because I'm just talking communist gibberish. That's fine. I can't please everybody, and I'm not going to lie. The Plaid won't just pretend things like this never happened. They are all part of the public record. Just because the history books you read back in the day didn't say them doesn't mean it never happened. There were several instances when the US military went down to quash uprisings and attempts at nationalization, dating back to the 1850s when it looked like some Panamanians would endanger the railroad down there, and maybe nationalize it. The US did not want this because

Whew! Low banana prices are saved again! Circa 1930's Nicaragua.

What's the Deal with . . . The United Fruit Company?

The United Fruit Company (UFCO) was an American corporation founded in 1899 that was dedicated to providing the American consumer with delicious and affordable bananas and pineapples. The United Fruit Company is also one of the best examples of capitalism gone awry. Throughout the 20th century, the United Fruit Company maintained a virtual monopoly on banana exportation to the United States. UFCO owned huge plantations in Columbia, Costa Rica, Cuba, Jamaica, Guatemala, Nicaragua, Panama, and Santo Domingo. They also owned 11 ships named "The Great White Fleet" and miles of railroads. United Fruit was the unofficial king of Latin America. And like most kings, United Fruit was a giant ass to its subjects.

The worst offenses by United Fruit occurred in Guatemala. As in many other countries, United Fruit owned or leased much of the farmable land in Guatemala. They also left a significant portion of their land barren (not producing fruit) just in case something happened to their good land. All this wasted farmable land started pissing off hungry people in Guatemala. In 1951, Guatemalans elected (in their first ever election with universal suffrage) Jacobo Arbenz Guzman who pledged land reform. Arbenz proposed redistributing some of the unused land to the large percentage of the population that was landless.

The United Fruit Company was royally pissed about Arbenz, so it launched a campaign to convince its friends in the US Government (Dwight Eisenhower, John Foster Dulles, etc.) that Arbenz was aligned with the Soviet Union. UFCO even went so far as to produce a video titled, "Why the Kremlin hates Bananas"—documenting UFCO's fight against Arbenz. The result of UFCO's propaganda and influence was Operation PBSUCCESS: a CIA covert operation designed to overthrow Guatemalan president Arbenz. The CIA trained and armed an ad-hoc "liberation army" and organized "strategic" air strikes on Guatemala City. The result of CIA action was years of oppression for Guatemalan citizens under a right-wing dictatorship that "saved the day" from the communist threat. On the bright side, Americans can, to this day, buy bananas for less than $0.50 a pound—thanks partially to Chiquita Brands International, which took over United Fruit in 1970. Thanks guys! You wacky bunch of bananas!

that railroad was a critical part of a much bigger shipping network between the east and west coasts of the US. The US sent troops several more times to protect the railroad and the Panama Canal.

You typically think of US military services as guarding the US, as protecting US citizens, but by and large in this part of the world they have done none of that. They have protected the private interests of US businessmen. A lot of folks, including the Plaid Avenger, speak out against this because it's basically whoring out the Army to protect some rich guy's stuff. That bothers me a little bit. It bothers people in Central America even more, because they are the ones who catch the bullets from the US military when this sort of shit goes down.

So there's a history of violence since their independence based on the physical world, and even the economic world. But that was then. This is now. But current events are not much kinder, because commie influence is going to serve to create more friction in the 20th century.

UNDER THE INFLUENCE . . .

We know that when people are "under the influence" they should be having a good time. Unfortunately for Central America, their time "under the influence" has been a little destructive. Understatement alert! It has been *incredibly* destructive to Central America, which has recently awoken from its haze thinking, "What the hell happened? How did I get so jacked up? I was just hanging out in the backyard and all of a sudden I'm awake and I feel like crap!" That's almost exactly what happened to Central America.

We already discussed the **US's Backyard** principle in the introduction to Latin America, and indeed the US has been *the* major influence in Central America's recent history. It has been under the US's influence technically since the **Monroe Doctrine** and **Roosevelt Corollary** days, but didn't really get messed with too much until a bunch of lefties got together down there during the Cold War years. So a bunch of lefties were hanging out in the backyard and ended up under the influence. Now they're emerging from it with some serious boo-boos.

In the Latin America overview, I touched on this a little. The US hates commies. The Cold War clearly shows that they just can't stand the commies. The US and Soviet Union were vying for influence all over the world, willing to sell arms or intervene covertly to get more people on their team. That's always part of the Cold War game, but perhaps no other region in the world has been so negatively affected by this face-off of ideologies than Central America.

How negative could it be? Central America saw some pretty nasty shit during the Cold War. Some of the political parties and presidents in Central America acquired leftward leaning administrations or liberalizing policies to try to pull their people out of poverty in the 1950s and 1960s. A lot of talk about nationalization of industries—and sometimes direct action—incited serious suspicion from big brother in the north. The US interpreted and treated all leftward leaning governments as the first step of an all-out communist invasion, and spent the last 40 years facilitating the interior destruction of these countries by any means necessary. Virtually all of Central America has been racked by civil war that has been promoted, if not initiated, by outside US forces that thought the leftward lean was just a little too commie for their backyard.

For those of you who are going to stop reading this because you think the Plaid Avenger is bashing the US, maybe you should. Maybe you do need to stop reading this. I am not going to pull any punches here. This is not a liberal rant. It's not a procommunist rant. This is a matter of public record. The recent history of Central America has been well documented, and even more information has been released as a result of the Freedom of Information Act. In various countries there was unabashed CIA involvement, primarily to incite civil war. It did anything it could to destabilize the countries it perceived as potential communist threats. The US is responsible for the funding, fueling, and arming of extreme-right rebel groups all over Central America whose sole purpose was to topple legitimately elected governments and keep certain US approved military dictators in power. A fairly current example should help illustrate this point . . .

That's the basic deal. There was some heavy-handed US activity in Nicaragua as a manifestation of the fear of commie takeover and because of its view of this area as US backyard territory. In places like Nicaragua, your tax dollars are still infused to help defeat the Sandinistas. They were a popular Communist Party led by Daniel Ortega in which the Reagan administration funneled away millions of dollars in an attempt to defeat. Reagan's tactics eventually worked, and the Sandinistas lost. By the way, I also brought this up because the same dude, Daniel Ortega, after 20 years, just won back the presidency again. Today. Now. And your US tax dollars are hard at work funding his opponent to make sure this doesn't happen next election already.

Ortega back in the socialist saddle in Nicaragua.

So this outside intervention from the US has really "been unhelpful" in Central American society, from the inside out, multiple times. This happened in Guatemala, Nicaragua, Honduras, and El Salvador. Those countries in particular have destroyed themselves 20 times over in the last forty years. They have been totally racked by civil war. There are always exceptions, of course, and Costa Rica is considered the most stable country in this region. I wonder why that is? Here's why: they got rid of their military 40 years ago! They saw the writing on the wall in all the other countries around them, and they actually disbanded their own military.

Panama also looks semistable now. It avoided having civil wars due to a string of military dictatorships that ended up running the show for most of the violent Cold War period. The US government propped up one dictator there named Manuel Noriega, a drug lord and former CIA employee, who's now in a Miami prison for drug trafficking.

What's the Deal with . . . the Iran-Contra Scandal?

Even though Nicaraguan dictator Anastasio Somoza had been in control of Nicaragua for 50 years and had been a staunch ally of America, a leftist rebel group called the Sandanistas overthrew him in 1979 and established a new government headed by Daniel Ortega. Protecting its old friends, America helped Somoza and his generals escape Nicaragua safely. Since the Sandanistas were beginning to drift towards the Soviet Union and Cuba and were Marxist-Leninists, America started organizing old Somoza National Gaurdsmen, disaffected peasants who didn't support the Sandanistas and others, into an army called the Contras. The Contras were armed and trained by Americans and operated in Honduras. Since the Sandanistas had a huge army, the Contras could not fight them in a head-on war, so they focused on attacking soft targets like schools, factories, etc. to make people realize that supporting the Sandanistas would only cause disaster.

I was just following orders!

By 1986, Americans were sick of supporting the Contras so Congress passed a law prohibiting aid to the Contras. Since people in the Reagan administration were bent on destroying communists, they hatched up a plan where they would illegally sell arms (specifically antitank missiles) to Iran and use that money to illegally fund the Contras. This plan was known as the Iran-Contra scandal, which became the biggest political scandal of the 1980s. Iran was desperate for weapons because it was fighting Iraq in the Iran-Iraq war and Americans thought that if we sold the Iranians arms, they would release American hostages in Lebanon held by Hezbollah. The problem was that Iran was an avowed enemy of the United States, and its government was the largest state sponsor of terrorism in the world. Furthermore, America was already selling arms to Iraq to use on Iran. Both sides of the plan were illegal and the plan was exposed in 1986, and some members of the Reagan administration were indicted, but nobody went to jail.

Fast forward to 2008. Iran is now building nuclear weapons and perhaps becoming a menace to the world. Just like then, Iran is run by religious fanatics. The Contras and the Sandanistas signed a peace treaty in the 1980s and Daniel Ortega won back the presidency last year. So he is President of Nicaragua again, after serving from 1979 to 1990. Iran is back in the spotlight too . . . and lo and behold, the President of Iran has already met with Ortega a couple of times in order to beef up their relationship. The US is not a happy boy right now.

Fun fact: A member of the Reagan administration named Oliver North (America's favorite traitor) was indicted for the Iran Contra scandal and also for lying about it. Ollie claimed that he had only been following orders, but according to the Uniform Code of Military Justice, it is a soldier's duty to disobey illegal orders.

Fun Fact Matching Game: Match the name of the *current* high-ranking Bush Administration official to his Iran-Contra Affair criminal input:

1. John Poindexter, Information Awareness Office Director
2. John Negroponte, National Intelligence Director
3. Elliott Abrams, Special Assistant to the President and Senior Director of the National Security Council for Near East and North African Affairs

   A. Found guilty of multiple felony counts for defrauding the government, lying to Congress, obstruction of justice, the alteration and destruction of evidence, and conspiracy.
   B. Introduced American mercenaries to Honduran army contacts for additional weapons and support, and laundered aid to Contras through Honduran government to which he was ambassador from 1981 to 1985.
   C. Entered guilty plea when charged with unlawfully withholding information from Congress.

Answers: 1A, 2B, 3C

So while we have this overall leftward lean in Central America, it was countered by US support for rightist politicians and outright military dictatorships. This set the precedent for this region's continual violence. The people have been politically divided and usually brutally suppressed in terms of human rights, individual rights, and other political freedoms that are commonplace in civilized societies. The current effects of this turbulent and violent past cannot be understated.

CONTINUED CYCLE OF VIOLENCE

So what is still fueling this violence if the Cold War is over? Well, it's not so easy to just set up shop again when such harsh dividing lines were drawn for so long. There was so much human suffering and loss of life and so much political division that recovery will be equally long and hard. For at least 100 years, poverty has been endemic to this region. It's a poor place, the poorest region in the western hemisphere actually. With the possible exception of Costa Rica, there is anywhere from 60 to 80 percent of the population below poverty level. That's A LOT. There is a huge, intense wealth dis-

Where Is Manuel Now? A Brief History of Manuel Noriega

A former CIA spook, a former leader of Panama, a former prisoner in Miami, Florida—but where is Manuel now? OK, so he's in a hospital, but it is still a pretty nutzo story . . .

Manuel Noriega was a career soldier—having received training in Panama and at the School of the Americas in the United States. By 1983, Noriega was the de facto ruler of Panama. Noriega may have played a role in the 1968 military coup in Panama, but the details are uncertain. What is fairly clear is that Manuel Noriega was on the CIA payroll from the early 1970s to 1988. During this time, Noriega was a favorite of US diplomats. When the Shah of Iran—Mohammad Reza Pahlavi—was overthrown in the Islamic Revolution, the United States convinced Noriega to offer him amnesty in Panama. He even helped the United States funnel money to right-wing guerilla movements in El Salvador and Nicaragua.

And Manuel: the US imprisoned him

Over the years, the United States began to see through Noriega's kleptocratic and narcotic ways. By 1989, official Panama/United States relations were at a low. US diplomats and soldiers were being harassed by Panamanian officials. After one US soldier was killed leaving a restaurant, President George H. W. Bush launched Operation Just Cause—a military invasion of Panama. During the invasion, Noriega fled but was eventually captured in the Vatican embassy in Panama. Noriega was brought back to the United States and tried on drug and racketeering charges. In 1992, Noriega was sentenced to 40 years in US prison. In 2004, he suffered a minor stroke and was transferred to a Miami hospital.

What a resume: Military. CIA. President of a country. Drug Trafficker. US prisoner.

parity in this region. Many of these states have assessed that it's gotten worse, even since the end of most of their civil wars in the last decade. So even though the violence has toned itself down, it's still hard to get the countries going economically. The people are putting together new governments and are trying to get things back on track. Like we said before, these governments tend to lean to the left.

Why do Central American countries have leftward leanings in the first place? This is something we talked about that applies to all of Latin America. Remember? Any place on the planet where you have endemic poverty, where most people are ridiculously poor, they tend to gravitate towards leftist political and economic systems. Why is that? Because it makes complete common sense. Socialism and die-hard communism are based on the redistribution of wealth. Pretty much everywhere in the world there are at least some socially influenced national programs like welfare and such that come from taxing the population, and then redistribute additional benefits to people in need. Then you have full-on communism, which ideally takes all the wealth and distributes it equally. Most places on the planet are someplace in between.

Now, in places where most people have nothing, which system are they going to choose? Free-market capitalism, where it's every man for himself, or communism, where everybody gets a share of the total? Obviously, if you have jack shit, you'd support a system that can give you something. That's why there is a leftward leaning in Central America. It's the 60 to 80 percent poverty rate! Of course the majority of voters there will lean way left, and favor socialism or communism!

Am I defending these people? Not really. I'm not really interested in promoting communism, or any other—ism. I just want you to understand the mindset in impoverished countries. When you don't have shit, you want to get shit. Plus if you are politically oppressed and have no political voice, what are you supposed to do about it? Eventually this type of situation caps itself in some sort of revolution or outright civil war. Indeed, that's what has happened and continues to happen. Leftward leaning politicians and parties gained popular support. In a region where 2–5 percent of the people own everything, and the other 95–98 percent split up whatever's left, it's no wonder that social programs are widely supported. For the most part, people have no title to land, no real home, no nothing, and they vote left because they can't possibly get poorer.

So this is part of the history of Central America, but it's not over. There are many companies in the region, and not all are owned by the US anymore, that have inordinate amounts of rights beyond what even humans have. By that I mean that there are some plantation-style economic establishments where people are essentially slaves. Where the people who own the banana companies have hired men with rifles standing by to make sure workers are picking bananas fast enough. This sounds incredible, but it has become the way it is. There are no labor unions, no real labor rights. Protection of companies' interests over those of the individual people—with an infusion of US interest usually to support rightist regimes—conflict continues to this day in Central America.

We usually think of the US as the good guys, who go out and fight for peoples' human rights, and individual rights, for democracy all over the world. Unfortunately, we don't really have any of that on our track record where Central America is concerned. Quite frankly, the US has been more interested in supporting strong, central leaders, who will maintain economic stability at any cost; the hope is that they will make sure that stuff will not be nationalized so the private investments aren't compromised. As such, they will even support military dictatorships that will suppress the local population who may be trying to rise up and fight for a revolution. Probably a damn commie revolution—yet another reason to squash it.

But the times are a changing. The Cold War is indeed over, and fighting the communist threat in Central America doesn't hold a lot of water. The United States now has a new tactic in order to ensure economic growth and stability for itself—and the region as well. That tactic is free trade blocks. As we previously discussed, the FTAA is a US-supported attempt at a hemispheric-wide trade block. One that has fizzled as of late. But things are still going forward on this front in Central America. Thank CAFTA.

To be fair, many politicians and businessmen truly believe that free trade is the real solution to poverty in Central America. Who the hell am I to claim righteousness? Perhaps they are right. President Bush has said that free trade, "will advance peace and prosperity" in the region. In this vein of thinking, free trade = movement of capital = more businesses = more

What's the Deal with . . . CAFTA?

CAFTA stands for Central America Free Trade Agreement and is an international treaty to increase free trade. It was ratified by the Senate of the United States in 2005. Like NAFTA, its goal is to privatize public services, eliminate barriers to investment, protect intellectual property rights, and eliminate tariffs between the participating nations. Many people see DR-CAFTA as a stepping stone to the larger, more ambitious, FTAA (Free Trade Agreement of the Americas).

The controversy regarding DR-CAFTA is very much like the controversy regarding NAFTA. Many people are concerned about America losing jobs to poorer countries where the minimum wage is lower and environmental laws are more lax. Also, some people are concerned that regional trade blocs like DR-CAFTA undermine the project of creating a worldwide free trade zone using organizations like the WTO.

CAFTA members

jobs = more money to these depressed economies. Also, creation of jobs in the poor places means people won't have to immigrate to the US to get a job. Sure, that might work. However, most people believe it will just help them get ripped off more: just more crappy jobs, not worth much money, which is not real economic development and diversity. Free trade is not widely supported in these countries by the general population, but widely supported by their administrations—as witnessed by CAFTA being signed.

LEGACY OF THE CIVIL WARS

What Central America is known for now, aside from Costa Rica being a major destination for ecotourism, is narcotics production, its transfer and trafficking. A lot of crack, dope, smack, amphetamines, and whatever else is produced in South and Central America, have to go through Central America to get to their ultimate destination: the US. What is a by-product of this? GANGS!

Currently, several Central American countries, along with Mexico, have actually signed a pact and accord to combat gang violence. What the hell is that all about? Independent sovereign states have to form a coalition to fight organized gang crime? YES! This is a big deal. Why is this? Gosh, I don't know . . . long history of civil war, divided society, oppressed societies, tremendous wealth disparity, people are freakin' poor as shit, poor governments, corrupt governments, and there are drugs everywhere. Put that all together in a stew and what do you come up with? GANG CONTROL!

During the civil wars in Guatemala, Honduras, Nicaragua, and especially El Salvador, lots of people hauled ass, as you might imagine. This resulted in an enormous refugee population that emigrated to the US. There were also tremendous amounts of people that tried to get the hell out of Central America to the US just to find work. During the last 30 years, during all the oppression, violence, and civil war, lots of folks who made it to places like LA, Santa Fe, even as far north as San Francisco, were poor and uneducated. This lovely combo makes some people gravitate towards crime. Over the years, this has evolved into a syndicate of criminal activities, with ties back to Central America, and now they are importing people just for this criminal activity. It's a mafia now.

Central American gangs are a problem all across North America, from Central America into the US proper. They have gained a lot of strength. Since they have no options, the poor kids gravitate towards gang membership—the same reasons people join gangs in inner cities in the US. This same phenomenon is happening in Central America, so the popularity of being in a gang and joining this organized crime movement has gotten so out of control that the governments can't even handle things in their own countries. That's why you have this effort now, signed by Mexico, Guatemala, and Belize, to basically work together to combat organized crime in and among their countries, as well as to combat movement to the US.

On the same lines, Mexico is under a big squeeze because so many people, not just gangs, want to get to the US. Work immigrants want to

What's the Deal with . . . MS-13 and Maras? How did they get here? People from El Salvador, Honduras and other Central American countries escaped during the 1970s to the United States of America. These people were running away from the civil wars that struck the countries of Central America, particularly El Salvador. Disaffected and disenfranchised refugee youth in the LA area gravitated toward gang life. Almost all maras members display radical tattoos on their bodies as a sign of their affiliation to their gang.

MS-13 is a gang based in Los Angeles with roots in El Salvador and operations throughout Central America. Many experts believe MS-13 and other maras have spread and benefited from the US policy of deporting criminals to their country of origin, allowing maras members to recruit new members abroad. MS-13 has recently been in the news for activities in Northern Virginia and Maryland. Maras are involved with everything from drug trafficking to petty crimes.

Maras are gangs originally from Central America, including MS-13 and Sombra Negra.

as well. They aren't really refugees anymore; they just want to emigrate from a shithole to the land of milk and honey. How are they going to do that? Well they aren't swimming, so they have to go on foot, across borders. The same way that Mexicans get across the border into the US, Central Americans have to go all the way through Mexico to get to the US. So Mexico has become a funnel; it's even funnel shaped, a throughway to the US. It has to deal with all these people who are even poorer than its own people coming through its territory, sometimes not making it to the US and staying in Mexico, putting even more stress on the ailing Mexican economy.

So now there are organized criminals and gangs running drugs through Mexican territory. Mexico's in a real pinch because the US wants to build a larger fence, to fortify the borders even more to keep immigrants out, and more are still coming in from Central America. One side of Mexico is being dammed up, and the other is still open for the free movement of people. The US has put pressure on Mexico to stop anybody from coming to the US, while its population is growing from people just trying to pass through its territory.

IS THERE A LIGHT AT THE END OF THIS TUNNEL?

I'm looking, but it's such a faint glimmer. So many factors are working together to keep this place hurting. At least the civil wars are officially over, but Central America remains replete with latent violence. This is a violent arena, due to tremendous wealth disparity perpetuated, and in some cases accelerated, by the US's role. In our Central American backyard, US intervention has typically been a negative thing.

Economically, all of the countries we're talking about are highly dependent on the US economy. What is it that they produce there that is shipped to the US? Primary goods. Products that aren't worth shit. Pretty much all they have to offer is worth nothing. Absolutely nothing in terms of big business and the businesses that are there, are typically owned by foreign companies anyway. That's why poverty is endemic to this region. Primary economic activities: it's all they've got, and it ain't worth much.

The price of bananas hasn't changed in 100 years. It has only crept up because of standard inflation/cost of living. Adjusted for cost of living, bananas cost the exact same as they did 100 years ago. And think, you can go into the grocery store and buy them for *40 cents a pound*. That's after they have been cultivated, fertilized, pruned, picked, packaged, and then delivered a few *thousand* miles to get to you. How the hell is that even possible? What are the people getting per pound in Nicaragua? Approximately jack is the Avenger's calculation!

Politically, the civil wars of the 1960s, fueled by wealth disparity and anticommunist fervor, have yet to abate the damage done to these societies. Releaning to the left for many of the countries in Central America will certainly cause more friction with the US. Immigration is also a hot button issue between the US and all of Latin America; an issue that Central America will probably not come out winning, no matter what the eventual solution may be. Growth of the **maras** is another current event that will not be going away anytime soon, and is radically affecting the region, and the US, and everyone in between: the reach of these Central American maras is now up to Seattle in the west, and Baltimore on the east coast.

This cycle of violence, the endemic poverty, which has propagated even more violence due to gangs, is why the Plaid Avenger really calls this a violent arena. Central America has been a place of open warfare within states, between states, it has been a Cold War battlefield, a corporate battlefield, and now that the gang violence is skyrocketing, it's a drug and crime battlefield. This is not likely to go away anytime soon.

But don't get me wrong. It's an awesome place to party. The people in Central America are incredibly resilient, and continue to push forward in spite of all the chips being stacked against them. Get down there. Check it out. But please remember this Plaid Avenger Tip: Just say "no" to gang tattoos.

Havana

★

CUBA

ayman Is.
(U.K.)

JAMAICA
Kingston ★

Port-au-
Prince

Navassa
Island
(U.S.)

HAITI

Turks and
Caicos Islands
(U.K.)

DOMINICAN
REPUBLIC

Santo
Domingo

Milwaukee Deep
(deepest point of the
Atlantic Ocean, -8605 m)

British Virgin
Islands
(U.K.)

Puerto
Rico
(U.S.)

Anguilla (U.K.)

ST. KITTS AND NEVIS

ANTIGUA AND BARE

Guadeloupe (FR.)

Montserrat
(U.K.)

DOMINICA

Caribbean Sea

AS

RAGUA

San José

Aruba
(NETH.)

Neth. Antilles
(NETH.)

Maracaibo

Caracas

ST. VINCENT AND
THE GRENADINES

Martinique (FR.)
ST. LUCIA

BARBADOS

GRENADA
Port-of-Spain
TRINIDAD AND
TOBAGO

The Caribbean

REGGAE and calypso music. Voodoo religion and Carnival. Rum. Pirates. Banana daiquiris on sunny beaches washed by that beautiful blue Caribbean Sea. A tropical paradise for those that visit; a tropical hellhole for those washing the dishes at the hotel you stay at. Caribbean color, Caribbean music, Caribbean-style shrimp platter at Red Lobster. The Caribbean is just too distinct to be included as part of any other region in Latin America. Yes, it is also considered a "US backyard." Yes, it is also endemically poor. However, the culture, history, and current events of the Caribbean all combine to make this place different.

PHYSICAL

Like Central America, the Caribbean is a violent arena from a climatic and geological standpoint. The islands of the Caribbean, as you can see from this plate tectonic map, are on the edge of a trench between two plates that are being pushed together. So a lot of the islands are volcanic in origin, but not all of them. The big islands are also referred to as the **Greater Antilles:** the islands of Cuba, Jamaica, Haiti/Dominican Republic, and Puerto Rico. They are not volcanic in origin, but are old parts of the larger plates and are quite stable, geologically speaking. However, the arc of smaller islands that form the chain known as the **Lesser Antilles** are the result of contact at plate boundaries which in this circumstance, results in volcanic activity. Some are still active, volcanically and seismically.

Though the larger islands are more stable geologically, they and the smaller islands both have to deal with the climatic instability of the region. *The Caribbean is the hurricane zone of all hurricane zones!* There may be big typhoons in the Pacific, and the US may get hit by a few big-ass hurricanes every now and then, but no place has them like the Caribbean. No matter where hurricanes end up in the regions near the Atlantic, most of them go through this region first. And due to the small size of the islands, hurricanes have a devastating impact almost every time. We are talking about storm systems that can completely cover an entire country. In places like the US and Mexico, the hurricanes may hit the coast, or travel a little bit into the mainland, but they are not destroying all areas of the country simultaneously. The Caribbean is a place that is, physically speaking, an incredibly violent arena.

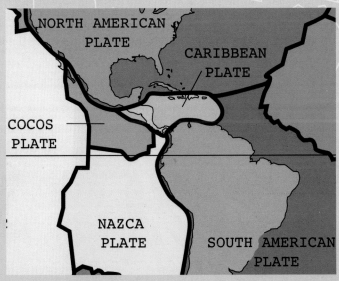
Caribbean plate tectonics: active arena.

Another consideration is that it is a tropical region. It is a very hot and humid place. However, large bodies of water always act as moderators of temperature and thus it's always a little nicer right along the coast. Where everybody lives. And where everybody visits. Which ties into another distinct quality of the Caribbean: tourism is the biggest GDP earner on pretty much every single island nation. That's why everybody comes here to party. Everyone flocks to the nice tropical beaches, because that's where the nice warm water is. The entire region is tropical—it's located in the tropics! The tropical temperatures also play a part in warming the water of an important Atlantic physical feature: the Gulf Stream—a warm ocean current originating here and flowing as far north as Russia, moderating climate its entire journey. Ever wonder why it never snows in England, even though it is very far north? Gulf Stream effect is the answer. It originates in these parts.

WHAT ELSE IS GOING ON THERE?

The simplest way to highlight the cultural distinctness of this region, Plaid Avenger style, is by talking about the five S's: Sun, Sand, Sex, Sin . . . which is why people come here. The Bahamas, Jamaica, the Virgin Islands, Barbados . . . what comes to mind? Party! You know that's right! Let's get it on, Caribbean-style! Bronzed bodies basking on baked beaches. Their economy is largely based on tourism. So what's the fifth S? SUGAR, which we'll get to shortly.

So tourism is a main component, if not the major component of the Caribbean's GDP. In some Caribbean islands, tourism accounts for more than half of the entire GDP each year—in some places it's even higher than that! Half of the entire state's economy is due to one single industry. That's a lot. As such, so much of the wealth of the region is dependent on other people, from other countries hanging out there and spending their money. This of course sounds good—bring them on!—but there are some negatives, maybe more than the positives . . .

SUN, SAND, SEX, SIN: TOURISM IN THE CARIBBEAN

We can start out by asking: what is tourism really worth to the Caribbean? The Plaid Avenger's take is that it's a **primary economic activity.** You are essentially just selling the land as a resource, not unlike drilling for oil in it or cutting trees off of it. All you are doing is letting people come look at the land. As a primary commodity, it's not really worth that much, economically speaking.

Fun, fun . . .

fun . . .

and rum!

On top of that, there is quite a bit of variability in tourism. If there is a bad economic year somewhere else, it can affect how much money they make off of tourists. A bad hurricane can affect tourism negatively too. People won't come from all over to hang out on an utterly devastated beach. Tourism fluctuates to both extremes very quickly. It is very unstable; it's definitely not something that you would want as your economy's anchor. But it unfortunately is for many nations in the Caribbean region.

So, what do the locals actually get out of selling their beach? Do they line up and have all the tourists give them a dollar each? Not hardly. Typically what happens is a multinational corporation from somewhere else, like the US, Great Britain, or Germany, comes and builds a big-ass hotel on a nice stretch of beach. Those corporations are also the ones getting the $300 a night for the tourists to stay there. They also get the $8 that a tourist pays for a mai tai at the hotel bar. The McDonalds and TGIFs and Olive Gardens that spring up around the hotels are also foreign-owned.

So for the people actually living there—the locals in Jamaica or Grenada or The Virgin Islands—tourism equates to low-paying, minimum wage jobs. The local is the guy who serves the $8 mai tai, the guy who opens the door, does the dishes, changes the sheets, and flips the burgers at Mickey D's. Those aren't really the most enviable jobs, and we all know inherently what those jobs are worth. It can be argued that tourism is a complete sham for the locals, and that all the money made there doesn't stay in the country to do any good. The locals are working the crappy jobs while all the money being made there is exported to another country via the multinational company that owns the hotel or casino or swanky bar there. I've seen statistics indicating that for every dollar spent in the Caribbean, less than a dime actually stays in the country. I can't prove it, but I believe it.

Country/Territory	Contribution of Tourism Economy to GDP (2002) Percent of GDP
Anguilla	58
Antigua and Barbuda	72
Aruba	47
Bahamas	46
Barbados	37
Bermuda	26
British Virgin Islands	85
Cayman Islands	31
Cuba	11
Dominica	22
Dominican Republic	18
Grenada	23
Guadeloupe	33
Jamaica	27
Martinique	10
St. Kitts and Nevis	25
St. Lucia	51
St. Vincent and the Grenadines	29
Virgin Islands (U.S.)	42

Tourism: major big deal to this region.

Others would argue that those may be shit jobs, but they are jobs, period. What would the locals do without those jobs? Wouldn't they be poorer than they are now? Both are valid points, but just remember next time you visit the multi-million dollar hotels, that the locals are not the ones partying and having a good time. They're mopping up because you drank too much.

So for the most part, it is "Awesome Vacation Land" for us, where we can party, do whatever we want to do, hang out in the sun, walk on the sand, have lots of great sex, and live in sin. The sin part is one to pay attention to as we later consider Cuba. One of the reasons that Cuba went communist when they had their revolution was because of the sin part. People saw Cuba as a tropical island paradise that became infiltrated by American mafia, and became a playground for other rich and famous Americans from the late 1800s all the way up to the 1950s. It was essentially the Sodom and Gomorrah of the tropics. People would flock down there for their vacations and take advantage of all the legal drugs, gambling, prostitution, and alcohol, whatever. Just thinking about it, the Plaid Avenger salivates, anxiously awaiting the return of those good old days . . .

Though that sounds absurd, this is actually how much of the Caribbean region is viewed, as a place for sin and all around partying. This is one of the reasons why Fidel and his boys kicked everybody out of there. So tourism is a dual-edged sword that, overall, may not be the greatest of impacts on the Caribbean.

WHEN THE US GETS A SNIFFLE, THE CARIBBEAN GETS A COLD

What does this post-nasal drip reference mean? Since we are considering the economic make-up of the region, it's important to point out this economic relationship. This saying has way more than a grain of truth in it; it is a fact. And what it's saying is this: If anything bad happens in the economic colossus of the US, there is a ripple effect that gets magnified down south. The Caribbean gets it first and worst. No matter how small the fluctuation is in the US, it can heavily influence the entire economy of this region.

The tourism industry is a perfect example of this, since it relies heavily on people traveling to spend time and money there. When there is a bad economic year in the US, people are less likely to go on vacation, because people can't afford it. If you need to make money, you're not going to take off from work and spend thousands of dollars on a Caribbean vacation. If there is an economic depression in the US, the Caribbean is trashed. Economically devastated immediately. This ripple effect reaches into all aspects of life down there. Even the 9/11 terrorist attacks in 2001 precipitated a drastic reduction in Caribbean tourism. People were afraid to fly on planes, and overnight, the Caribbean economy got dumped. Into the next year, there were still repercussions from the decrease in tourism due to 9/11. This single event, that didn't even affect the American economy that much, *destroyed* the Caribbean economy. Even something as trivial as an increase in airfare to these places can affect the economy negatively.

Another way that the Caribbean is reliant on our economy is through something called **remittances.** This term can be applied not only in the Caribbean,

"Welcome back to the islands Mr. Avenger. Can I get you the usual?"

Not likely to be visiting the resorts anytime soon.

Plaid Sex on the Beach

1 oz	Malibu coconut flavored rum
1 oz	Chambord raspberry liqueur
1/2 oz	peach schnapps
1 1/2 oz	pineapple juice
1 splash	grenadine syrup
1 oz	whipped cream

Pour the Chambord liqueur, Malibu rum, peach schnapps, pineapple juice and grenadine into a cocktail shaker half-filled with ice cubes. Add the whipped cream, and shake vigorously until frothy. Pour into a small highball glass or equivalent, and serve. What happens after that is up to you . . .

but across Latin America as a whole. Many people come from other countries—like Mexico and virtually every Caribbean country—to the US to work. These people work primarily in the agricultural sector, but there are also people who move to cities like New York and work low-paying jobs there. Some even start their own businesses. New York is a good example, because there is a huge Jamaican population there. These people are not necessarily immigrants, though some of them are. Many come here just to work, since the job outlook might not be very good in their respective countries.

"I've got something you can remit!"

So what does that have to do with this term, remittance? A remittance refers to money sent back home to the families of those people who have come to the US to work. So Jamaicans, or Puerto Ricans, or Barbadians come here to work, and send part or most of their paychecks back home to support their families.

Why bring this up while talking about the Caribbean region? Remittances comprise a significant component of the GDP of many Caribbean countries. Think about that. In 2004, the remittance market for Latin America as a whole exceeded $40 billion. In some Caribbean countries, 5–10% of the economy may depend on getting money sent from people working in the US and other places. If this activity were stopped, if guest workers could no longer send money home to their families, there would be an immediate economic impact on the economies of this region. The Plaid Avenger is not being a bleeding heart here, these are just the facts. To stop guest workers would mean immediate, instantaneous negative repercussions south of our borders. The sniffle becomes the cold—perhaps pneumonia for some of these small states.

THE FIFTH S: SUGAR

The role of sugar in the Caribbean cannot be understated. When the New World was being settled by the colonial powers, primarily the Spanish and even the British, there was one single commodity that had an enormous impact on the historical development of the Caribbean. This of course is the processing of sugar.

Sugar's an interesting tale that not many people know about for whatever reason. By the 20th century, sugar had become so entrenched in the Western diet that it's no wonder the average person nowadays really doesn't know how or when sugar became popular. We only know that sugar is a huge, prominent part of our diets. We think it has been around forever. Everybody since the beginning of time has consumed an average of 152 pounds of sugar per year just like we do now, right? Hell no.

Sugar is still big business.

This consumption of sugar is a new phenomenon. Sugar was originally from Southeast Asia. It is a type of grass, never planted and processed in volume anywhere. It moved from Asia to India to Africa, but not until it gets to the Caribbean did it become a mass produced cash crop. The Spanish had small sugar plantations on the Madeira Islands, which were a way station between Spain and the New World. As they were looking for gold and silver in the New World, they also looked into what crops could be grown there.

When they brought sugar to the New World, it exploded. Sugarcane was brought into an environment in which it goes gangbusters. It can be grown so fast, sometimes two or three times a year, so cheaply and in such abundance that it catches the eye of those Spaniards. Up until this point in history, the "sweet tooth" was pretty

Sugar as high as an elephant's eye.

much unheard of. Sugar was a scarce commodity. Nobody in Europe had sugar. Cane sugar in tea, cookies, crumpets, was unheard of 500 years ago. Nobody knew what the hell it even was; it was only a plaything of the rich and famous. Its appeal is analogous to that of cocaine: An incredibly valuable commodity imported from a far away tropical location. But the Caribbean changes all that. By providing this commodity en masse, the Caribbean is the single region that changes the dietary consumption of the entire planet for the next 500 years. But it also changes the Caribbean quite a bit.

Sugar is an extremely labor intensive commodity. Today, it is still mostly done by hand, planted and harvested by hand, with knives and baskets. During the colonial era, people couldn't get enough of it. That's the case even today. It was processed a variety of ways, into the table sugar that we are familiar with, but that also led to by-products like molasses, which can be made into rum. Even by-products and leftovers from the sugar making process were used to make other products. This essentially diversified sugar into a ton of different commodities, all of which make good money.

Rum was almost as big a hit as sugar was. It was gangbusters part two in the colonies and in Europe, so much so that British sailors even got a rum ration during much of this era. They are paid in rum . . . the Plaid Avenger should really have been an old scallywag. Yo ho ho and a bottle of rum.

MO' MONEY

Sugar was a big business, a big deal. The point I am trying to make about sugar's impact on the Caribbean is this: When it became popular, everyone wanted to plant it everywhere; it was the crack cocaine of its day. It's awesome; it gets great prices. People will pay anything for it. You can make a shitload of money on it. However, as I suggested, it is very labor intensive. The plantation owners need lots of labor, and cheap labor is preferable. Cheap labor? How about free labor?

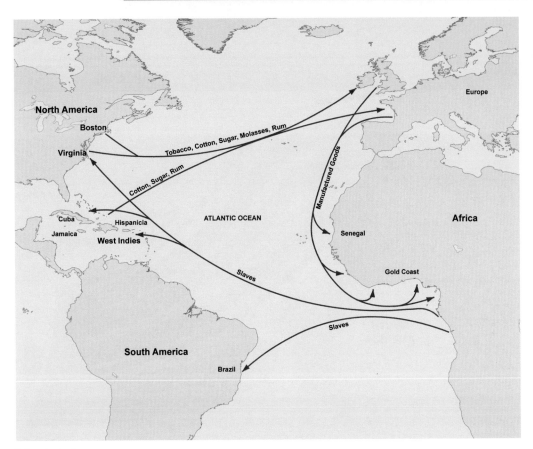

Triangle trade.

Guess what that means? That's right: slaves. "Hey guys, let's enslave the local population! It's the perfect solution!" They tried. But most of the natives, as I pointed out in the Mexican section, died of European imported disease. It virtually wiped out everyone in the Caribbean before they even saw white dudes. The few that were left over got worked to death in very short order. So basically, the colonizers virtually wiped out the native populations of the Caribbean islands to the man.

So the colonizers were on the lookout. "We need more labor. Where are we going to get them?" You already know the story. They find out that they can bring people over from Africa. This sets up what is called the **Triangle Trade.** There are several different routes one can take on the Triangle Trade, but the bottom line is: if you're going to sail about from one place to the other, you never want to sail the ship empty. It's a waste of time and a waste of resources. You always want to have something in your boat that you will trade or sell at the next place, and then pick up a load and go somewhere else. And the first leg of the triangle trade . . .

Let's say you're a British trader. What do you have in Great Britain? Well, you have finished goods. You've got guns, knives, swords, cigarettes, alcohol, woodworks, woven fabrics, a cute accent. See, all the places in the New World, they just have raw commodities that must be brought back and processed. You can process tobacco, process wood, process cane sugar, or take sugar and do something else with it. Turn that into rum, actually, just add value to it in any way you can so you can charge premium prices and keep yourself in business.

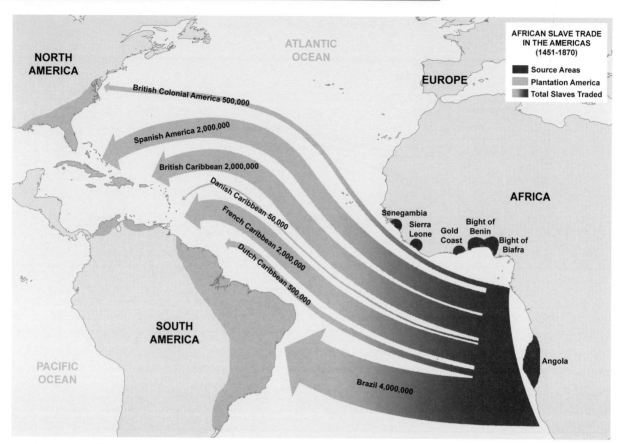

Massive human trafficking.

So you're in Britain and you load up your ship with finished goods; in this case, alcohol and guns—what a fantastic combination. So, you take your alcohol and guns, and float down to Africa. This is the first side of your triangle. What are you going to get in Africa? You're going to offload the liquor and guns and sell them to the local chiefs in exchange for what? Slaves. Fill the ship that you just emptied, fill every last nook and crevice with slaves. What are you going to do with those? Take them on the next leg of the trip to the Caribbean.

Now I am getting ahead of my story, because not all of the slaves went to the Caribbean. Some of these slaves are going directly to the east coast of South America, and very few will go to North America, proportionally speaking. However, millions go to the Caribbean. Millions and millions of black African slaves end up in the Caribbean. Why so many? Well, the Caribbean's population is not that big at the time, and there were a lot of sugar plantations that needed to be worked. Once millions of slaves had moved to these very small islands, why did the slave trade continue over such a long time? Why so long? Why didn't the slave traders or owners have the slaves propagate themselves?

Because sugar production is an extremely labor-intensive industry in a tropical location. It's HOT. It is hotter than hell in the Caribbean during the summertime. It is hot in those fields. It sucks. Not only that, but there's malaria. People died like there was no tomorrow. People were basically worked to death. A huge percentage of the slaves brought to the New World to work died within 2–3 years of their arrival. As you can see, this caused the need for continual replenishment. More slaves. Every year they needed more, because they kept dying off. I don't mean to underestimate figures; there were certainly large numbers of slaves brought to the United States. A significant proportion of today's population is of African-American descent. However, the numbers that went to the Caribbean dwarfed the total that came to North America proper. This is all solely because of the economic engine built around the sugar industry. The Plaid Avenger can't stress the impact of this trade enough.

Once you offload your slaves in the Caribbean or North America, what do you pick up then to take back home? All those raw commodities that they want back home. Fill your ships with sugar, tobacco, rum, wool. Take all that stuff back home and process it. That's all the shit that people want and it's cheap as hell. You've made money on every single leg of the journey. That's the Triangle Trade, which lasted for several hundred years. And lots of folks get really, really rich off of it, at a terrible cost in human lives, primarily African lives. Sugar can't be underestimated, or undervalued, in terms of its contributions to human suffering, economic growth, and its worldwide dietary impacts.

Am I telling you this long tale just so you can understand why people eat so much sugar in the world today? In part. But also think about the face of the Caribbean today. How would you describe Bob Marley? More generally, what does your average Jamaican look like? Even broader, why are many faces black in the Caribbean? Think of Jamaica. Think of Haiti. The Plaid Avenger is a straight up guy, I don't care if you think this is a racist comment. It's definitely not. They aren't white and they aren't Chinese, they are black, as are most of the populations of the Caribbean islands. Why? Because of the Triangle/Slave trade which so significantly impacted the demographics of this region.

The hell with sugar, I make reggae.

Many slaves also ended up in what is now Brazil, on the eastern coast of South America, which was another sugar production center in the New World. We can look at many countries in Latin America today, and you can see in the reflection exactly how much sugar they grew. The more sugar was grown in the country, the larger the black population presently is. So when we think of the Caribbean, we think of its population as mostly from African descent. That's absolutely true, and it's all because of sugar.

THE MELTING POT

The Caribbean is also a great place that I consider to be a great melting pot. We often think of the US as a melting pot, but the Caribbean is even better. There is such a singular and unique culture that emerges, on the individual islands and as a whole, from the numerous colonial powers that had colonies in the Caribbean.

As you can see, the Spanish, the British, the French, and the Dutch have colonies here. These colonial powers are in control of these islands. Some of the islands changed hands between these countries multiple times. This equates to European cultural influence on top of the indigenous culture of the surviving natives infused with the African culture brought along during the days of the Triangle Trade. Over time, this has created a very unique place on the planet, culturally speaking.

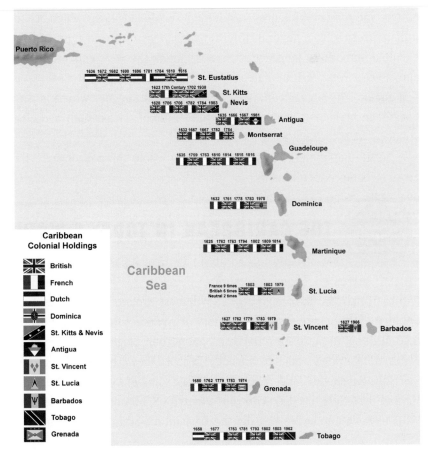

What Is the Deal with . . . Voodoo?

Voodoo (which can be spelled many different ways, including Vudu, Voudun, Vodun, etc.) is an animistic religion that began in West Africa many years ago and was transplanted to Haiti by way of slaves. Animism is a philosophy that believes that everything, even regular objects, has a soul and a spirit. Most Vodouisants believe in a single God that created the world. However, this God is distant and detached from the world so Vodouisants must turn to "mysteries," "saints," or "spirits" for help. Voodoo has many different traditions and these different traditions have slightly varying beliefs and worship different spirits. But on the whole, most Vodouisants believe in personal spirits, harmony with nature and the world, and the importance of family. Western pop-culture sometimes depicts voodoo as a bizarre religion that is all about zombies and sticking pins in dolls. In reality, these elements are very small and insignificant portions of the religion.

Fun Plaid Fact: Harvard ethnobotanist Wade Davis went to Haiti in 1982 and claimed the zombie tradition actually had some real basis in fact. Years ago, when voodoo priests had determined that somebody deserved to be punished, they would feed them pufferfish, whose toxic glands put people in a paralytic coma. After burying this person, they would dig them up a couple days later, and give them another dose of hallucinogenic drugs. This entire experience, including the drugs, the burial, and people's religious beliefs, were enough to actually convince people that they were really will-less zombies. Obviously, Davis's research has been questioned. Check out the film *The Serpent and the Rainbow* (1988) for Davis' screen adaptation. Pretty spooky!

Three continents have come together and crystallized in several ways. The first obvious one that we already talked about is race. Many different ethnicities have been combined, to come up with several unique ethnic cultures. Languages have also changed in the Caribbean. The way people talk is a mixture of colonial, native, and African influences, resulting in Creole languages which are formed by infusing terms from several different languages into one type of speech. For example, the official language of Haiti is Haitian Creole, a combination of French and several West African dialects. There are also the several music styles of the Caribbean. The biggest one we can think of is Reggae, which is a distinctly Caribbean style that has roots in other regional styles, such as Calypso. And voodoo—what the hell is that?

So the Caribbean is a combination of a whole shitload of stuff, from three different continents.

To hell with reggae, I grow ganja.

THE CARIBBEAN IN TODAY'S WORLD

We already talked about Central America, and the Caribbean shares the common feature of being in the **US's backyard.** Since the Monroe Doctrine, no foreign powers will mess around here; the US won't allow it. Especially today. So these countries don't need to spend money on a military or any other form of national defense, and many of them don't. This is definitely a good thing, because they are damn poor. Their biggest concern should be avoiding widespread devastation by hurricanes, not getting invaded by anybody, because they are under the protective umbrella of the US.

But that's a dual-edged sword, as I have said before, because being under the umbrella means more US intervention. Haiti in particular has been controlled by the US, off and on, several times in the last 100 years. The US military occupied Haiti from 1915 to 1934. Why did the US military occupy Haiti? Once fighting ended after the long Haitian Revolution period, they did fairly well until their national debt started to get out of control. This was fine for the American banks they owed, until the country became unstable and there was another revolutionary movement. Scared that they wouldn't make any of their money back, the banks pressured Woodrow Wilson, who sent in the troops. The occupying US forces improved Haiti's infrastructure while they were there, mostly by supervising forced labor chain gangs to improve old roads and build new ones.

We've supported some fairly brutal leaders in Haiti, as well as the Dominican Republic which was taken over by the US in 1965 after a rightist coup (whose connections to the US are unclear) had trouble completely overthrowing the leftist government there. The US went in to make sure that the leftists wouldn't regain control and turn it into "a second Cuba."

Which gets us to the biggest intervention that the US has had in the Caribbean, if not the world . . .

CUBA

A fifty-year-old economic and diplomatic embargo. Refusal to allow US citizens to visit the country. CIA sanctioned assassination attempts on the leader of the state, Fidel Castro. Why the hell does the US hate Cuba so much?

Historically, the United States and Cuba have had a very close relationship, especially because Cuba is only 90 miles away from Key West. The United States has dominated Cuban politics, intervening whenever it wasn't happy with the leadership, and basically treating Cuba like a vassal state. This relationship changed in 1959 when Fidel Castro and a band of revolutionaries seized power in Cuba and installed a communist regime. Since then, Cuba and America have had absolutely no diplomatic contact or official trade.

In the 1950s, Cuba, especially the capital city of Havana, was a playground for rich Americans. Flights left Miami every hour on the hour for an orgy of drugs, prostitution, and gambling that Havana had become famous for. Havana became a hangout for American mafiosos and many believed that Havana was going to become bigger than Las Vegas. (Check out *The Godfather, Part II* (1974) for insight.) Some Cubans were becoming rich, but a vast majority of them were still desperately poor and living in the countryside, and these peasants became distrustful of their corrupt government. To make matters worse, Cuba was controlled by an unelected dictator named Fulgencio Batista, who had somehow managed to anger everybody in Cuba from the landless poor to the middle and upper classes of society. Every time people tried to revolt against Batista's government, he responded violently and brutally, often executing those who were responsible. The time was ripe for somebody like Fidel Castro to come and seize power in Cuba.

The Cuban Revolution was an intense struggle. Castro and his army of around 100 men—including 20th century badass Che Guevera—sailed to Cuba on a rickety yacht named the Granma, but things turned sour when they landed and the Batista army quickly killed most of them. The remaining dozen or so soldiers went and hid out in the mountains, beginning a long guerrilla war from the Sierra Maestra mountains that quickly gained supporters around Cuba. After defeating Batista's forces several times, Batista left Cuba on January 1, 1959, and the rebels took power.

The Cuba Libre

2 oz Havana Club rum

2 oz Coca-Cola soft drink

1 lime wedge

Combine with ice in highball glass. Garnish with lime wedge. Sound like a rum and coke? It is! But with the lime wedge, it is transformed to the Libre. Was created just after the Spanish-American War when American soldiers were still hanging out in Cuba. Those Americans do love their Coke! They took the local rum, mixed in their imported soda, and toasted to a Free Cuba! A great drink, and so richly ironic that it still deserves praise.

At first, the United States supported the Cuban revolution because they thought that Castro was a liberal constitutionalist and nationalist and that he was good for Cuba. He ended corruption, gambling, prostitution, and expelled the American mafia who were living in Cuba. However, Castro quickly turned communist and took some steps that angered American officials. He began seeking ties with the Soviet Union (remember, this was during the Cold War!) and purging anticommunist people from his administration. He nationalized all foreign-owned property and even nationalized the land and property of many wealthy Cubans. For this reason, many rich Cubans, extremely angry at Castro, left Cuba and went to America. The largest exile group formed in Miami, which has become a famous base for anti-Castro activity.

Why does the United States hate Cuba? During the Cold War, it was a no-brainer. Cuba was a satellite state for Soviet Russia, and America was fighting a war against communism. In 1962 Americans became very uneasy when Castro let the Soviet Union point nuclear missiles at America from Cuban soil during the Cuban Missile Crisis. During this time, the United States made several attempts to assassinate Castro, even hiring Mafia members to do the job. It never worked. After the Soviet Union collapsed, Cuba became much poorer and desperate because its main supporter was gone. Many people thought that the time had come for America and Cuba to begin re-establishing relations.

Yet, Cuban and the US governments are still enemies, mainly because of Cuban exiles living in Miami. More than one million Cuban exiles live around Miami and these people hate Fidel Castro with a flaming passion. They had been living rich, comfortable lives in Cuba before the revolution, and the communist regime took everything they had away from them. They have become a huge lobbying force and very influential in American politics; their goal is to do everything they can to hurt the Cuban government and take Castro from power. So far, Castro is still in charge of Cuba and many people believe that the Cuban government will not change until he is dead.

What's the Deal with . . The Cuban Missile Crisis?

Many people consider the Cuban Missile Crisis as the closest America—and the world—has ever come to nuclear war. In 1962, during the Cold War, the Soviet Union deployed nuclear missiles in Cuba that were aimed at the United States. Part of the reason the Soviet Union wanted nuclear missiles so close to America was because America had deployed similar nuclear missiles in Turkey aimed at Soviet cities. After American spy airplanes revealed the existence of these missile sites, there was an intense debate in the White House about what America should do. Some people in the Kennedy administration favored a naval blockade of Cuba, while others insisted that America invade Cuba. The Kennedy administration decided on a blockade and it was later revealed that the Russians had short-range nuclear missiles that would have probably been used on American troops had they invaded.

MRBM LAUNCH SITE 1
SAN CRISTOBAL, CUBA
25 OCTOBER 1962

For several days, the situation was very tense between the United States and Russia. An American U-2 spy airplane was shot down over Cuba and another was shot down over Russia. After 12 days, Soviet Premier Nikita Khrushchev eventually decided to remove the missiles from Cuba and in return, America promised not to invade Cuba and also to remove the American missiles that were in Turkey. This crisis was widely seen as an embarrassment for the Soviet Union, and the Cubans felt betrayed because the situation was resolved between America and Russia, with Fidel Castro playing no part in the negotiations.

Fun Plaid Fact: The Cuban Missile Crisis led to the development of the "hotline," or the famous red telephone that Moscow and Washington could use to have direct communication in the case of another crisis.

The bat-phone to Moscow.

So . . . Cuba. They have been left-leaning, and they redistributed land and resources and wealth through nationalization . . . and the US can't stand that. They also had missiles pointing at us. And that's part of the animosity today, and why the US maintains its archaic embargo against them to this day. Those commies took all the rich peoples' stuff, US multinational corporation's stuff, and nationalized it. That whole deal with taking the world to the brink of nuclear war didn't help the situation either. To make matters worse, Castro just won't die either, despite all the best assassination attempts. So the US hates them, won't talk to them, and you Americans can't visit them. Until Castro dies, and then it's going to become Disneyland again!

Plaid update to the second edition: Fidel Castro had to step down as the President of Cuba due to his deteriorating health. However, the equation has still not changed much. His brother Raul took over, and is maintaining the old ways at

What Is the Deal with Che Guevara?

Why is Che the baddest ass revolutionary in the 20th century?

Che Guevara has become a symbol of youth rebellion for generations but most have no idea who he was or what he did. He has become a wildly popular pop-culture icon and a symbol for alternative culture, as well as becoming a symbol for communism and socialism. His images have been reproduced on a vast array of merchandise, such as T-shirts, posters, coffee mugs, and baseball caps. In Cuba, his face adorns billboards and the sides of government buildings.

Ernesto Guevara (Che is a nickname that means "buddy" or "pal") was born in Argentina and studied to become a physician. However, he took a year off of school and began traveling around Latin America on a motorcycle to witness first-hand the crushing poverty that many Latin Americans were enduring. These experiences helped turn him into a revolutionary and Marxist. He believed that revolution was the only way to obtain equality for the people so he began traveling to Latin American countries and helping out with Marxist revolutions, first in Guatemala and later in Cuba.

Around 1955, Che met Fidel Castro and agreed to join him in this battle against the Cuban dictator Fulgencio Batista. They sailed to Cuba in 1956 on a rickety yacht named the Granma and after a two-year war took over Cuba. Since Che was a Marxist, he was instrumental in persuading Castro to become communist. For his work in the revolution, Che was awarded some important positions in the Cuban government and wrote some books about guerrilla warfare right after the revolution. However, he could not sit still long. He soon left Cuba to encourage revolutions in other parts of the world including Congo and Bolivia. Che was eventually caught and assassinated by Bolivian forces, with assistance from the American CIA. They chopped off his hand so they could prove it was him.

While many people admired Che, others saw him as a dangerous lunatic. He has been accused of murdering and torturing thousands of people in Cuban prisons, as well as murdering peasants in guerrilla areas where he was fighting. Che has also been called an idiot and accused of being single-handedly responsible for the collapse of the Cuban economy, which had been one of the strongest in Latin America up to that point.

Che is famous for many reasons. For one, he was good-looking, charming, and got laid a lot, as opposed to most world leaders. Secondly, he was killed in the prime of his life fighting for his cause, so he has that whole Bob Marley-Jimi Hendrix-Buddy Holly dead rock star thing going. Thirdly, even though he came from a rich family and was trained as a physician, he dedicated his life to helping poor people around the world and often put his life on the line for his beliefs. For this reason, many people who disagreed with his communist beliefs still admired him for his self-sacrifice. Lastly, an important reason Che has become so famous is because of a really cool-looking photograph of him taken by Albert Korda in 1960 that has become a symbol for counterculture youth around the world.

least for now. You should know this: Raul is not quite so extreme as Fidel, and likely will start making moves to liberalize the economy, and perhaps even normalize relations with the US. But any big, bold changes will still have to wait until older brother kicks the bucket.

Before we leave the topic of Cuba, we should say a few words about one of the most recognizable pop icons of the 20th century whose claim to fame was the Cuban Revolution—but he was not Cuban himself! Who is Che?

CARIBBEAN TODAY . . .

Today the Caribbean is still under the US umbrella of defense except for Cuba, which we would like to un-defend, aka attack. As I already suggested, they are also heavily reliant on the US economy. This makes them particularly susceptible to economic fluctuations, which means they are unstable. And like all other places in Latin America, they have, as a general rule, a tremendous wealth disparity and tremendous poverty. Because what do they produce? Tourism, which isn't worth a lot, and sugar, which is worth even less.

This brings us to the two issues that do show how the Caribbean is trying to diversify their economy and bring in higher paying jobs: offshore banking and drug trafficking. Wow. I guess that's one way to diversity. Let's elaborate.

Perhaps due to their endemic poverty, or due to the fact that they are close to the US, two lucrative industries have popped up in the Caribbean. One of them is **narcotics trafficking,** and perhaps this also applies to other places in Middle and Latin America, but it's definitely big in the Caribbean too. They don't actually produce a lot of illegal narcotics there, but traffickers fly it there and end up launching off of these small islands in little clipper planes, or cigarette boats, and dumping the stuff off around the US coasts. Once it's on the coast, it can go anywhere else in the US, and you've got a large scale trafficking operation on your hands.

The US is of course not happy about this. Unfortunately for them, it's simple market forces at work. Capitalism at its fine-tuned best. Dig the facts: The US is the end-consumer of virtually all narcotics made in Latin America (okay, some of our European crack head friends get some too, but not that much). The Caribbean is very close to the US, and has lots of poor people in it willing to do anything to make ends meet. The ocean is a hard entity to control and monitor all the time. End result: the Caribbean is an excellent launching pad for drug-runners to get to the US. Always has been. Always will be. It's a growing sector in the region.

The second industry that has popped up is **offshore banking.** Lots of people now do offshore banking through an account in the Bahamas. Which is great! I guess. Isn't it? Why wouldn't people just put their money in a US bank?

If you have millions of dollars in the United States, you have to pay taxes on it. And if you happen to be doing anything that happens to be, say slightly illegal, then you might get punished for that. One good way to avoid being caught evading taxes, or dealing drugs or whatever, is to take your money outside the US. Banks are increasingly opening up in the Caribbean and they're operated essentially like Swiss bank accounts. There is a high degree of privacy, and since these are sovereign states, they don't have to reveal bank records if the United States asks for them. "We're a private bank in a sovereign state, and we don't have to show you our customers' records, thank you very much."

This happens even though the FBI, the CIA, or the IRS may know that the people who are putting their money in the bank are big drug dealers, or crooked businessmen in the US who are either scamming or just evading taxes, or mafia types trying to launder money. So in places like the Bahamas—because they are more stable economically than the others and not entirely poverty stricken—have become the Swiss of the Caribbean. And since it's not too far offshore, banking in the Caribbean is becoming much more popular. The bank is close enough to easily do business with, but just far enough to get away from those annoying taxes and laws in the US.

But let's not end on illegal activities. Let's end with someone we can all rally around:

What's the Deal with . . . Bob Marley?

Bob Marley, famous reggae singer and songwriter, was the ambassador of the Rastafari Movement to the Western world. Marley lived his life and created his music in the Rasta tradition. Rastafarianism is a religion that developed in Jamaica in the 1930s. Rastafarianism has also come to embody a cultural movement of racial equality and African heritage. Central to Rastafarianism is the belief that Haile Selassie I—former emperor of Ethiopia—is a reincarnate of God (or "Jah" in Rasta terminology). Rastas cite Old Testament prophecies to justify this belief. In fact—like Judaism, Islam, and Christianity—Rastafarianism is an Abrahamic religion. Many Rastas see themselves as true Israelites—the descendents of the 12 tribes of Israel.

Rastafarianism is a diverse religion. In fact, most Rastas reject the term Rastafarianism ("-isms create schisms") and prefer to call the Rastafari movement a "way of life."

However, there are several near universal symbols and traditions in Rastafarianism including:

The lion—the proud and noble ruler of the African savannas
Ethiopia—the home of Selassie I and a country that fiercely resisted European colonialism
Dreadlocks—a natural hairstyle at odds with European fashion, and
Ganja—the stuff they smoke.

There are over one-million Rastas in the world today including approximately ten-percent of the Jamaican population.

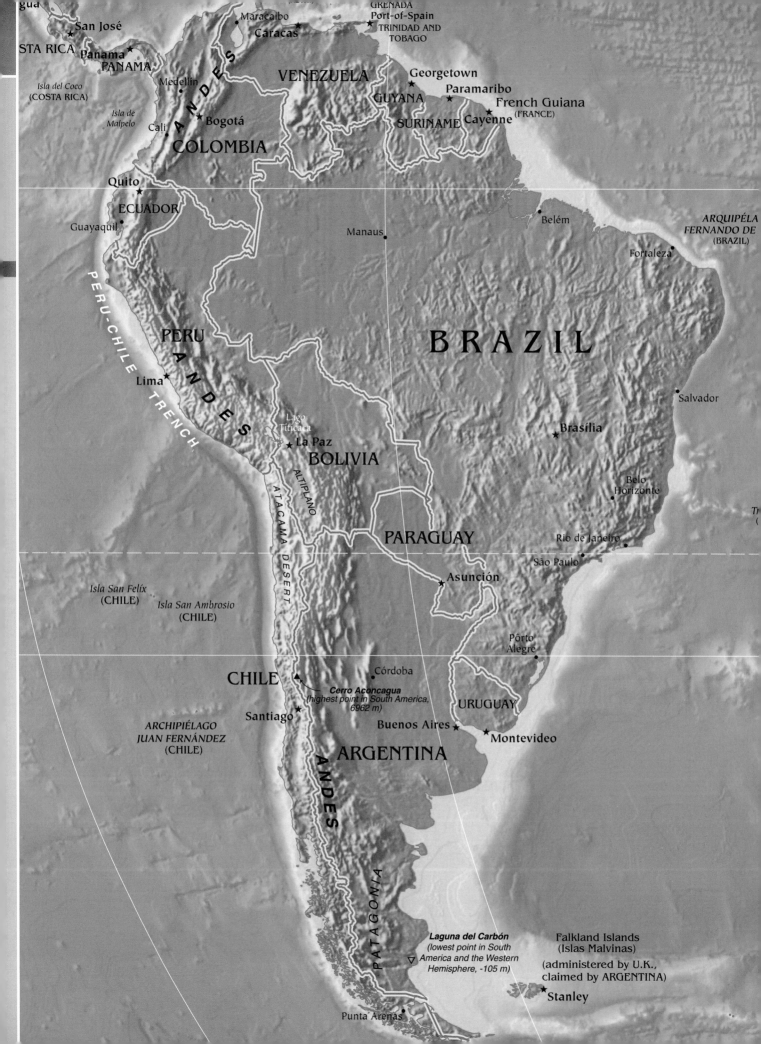

South America

ALRIGHT Plaid fans, it's time to get to our last subregion of Latin America, the region/continent of South America. Makes it nice and tidy. South America is the fourth largest continent on the planet. A continent comprised of 12 countries, and fairly good-sized countries for the most part, which separates them from the other subregions in Latin America, particularly in the Caribbean. Middle America is mostly dinky states but there are full grown countries in South America—including Brazil, which is the fifth largest country on the planet. So the Plaid always wants to ask the question: you have the United States of America up there in North America, why don't we have a United States of South America down here? Why are these distinct countries in South America not unified? I'm not sure. From all practical standpoints we should be looking at a much more unified entity down south of the border. But maybe that's where they are heading.

So why isn't there a US of South America? Many people would answer, "There are all these differences from country to country! Bolivia's got nothing in common with Peru or Chile or Argentina!" Many people would be wrong. What is it that's the same about these places? We already talked about a lot of these similarities back in the Latin America chapter. There's a common history here, a common colonial presence. Lots of commonalities with very few differences. Looking across the entire continent, there are only a couple major languages spoken. You really can't say that about any other continent besides North America. Portuguese spoken in Brazil, and Spanish spoken in the rest of South America along the western seaboard. So there's not even major difference in language. How about major differences in religion? Nope, they are all die-hard staunch Catholics, which we talked about in the Latin America chapter. So where are these differences? What's different here?

We have to look a little bit deeper into the histories of these places to find any differences whatsoever. Let's look at a couple of major entities. In precolonial history there's the **Inca Empire** down

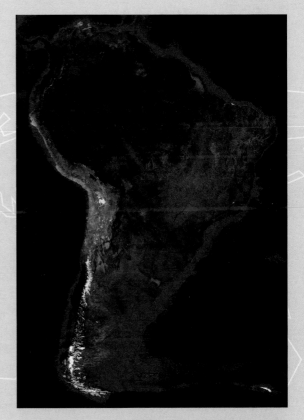

Machu Pichu Mucho!

here as opposed to the Aztec up in Mexico, but like the Aztec up in Mexico, the indigenous cultures were largely wiped out or denigrated fairly rapidly after the introduction of the European colonial masters. So even that's not a separating factor; that's not why there is no United States of South America. How about independence movements? Did they all get up and run with different independence movements led by different folks in different places? No—in fact one guy led the independence movement all across South America, the George Washington of South America, **Simón Bolívar.** During the 1810s and the 1820s he played a direct role in most of the independence movements in South America, and an indirect role in all the rest. So what is the difference? Why is this not the United States of South America?

The main man of South America.

PHYSICAL

Perhaps the main reason why we don't have a singular state in South America is because of the physical factors, specifically the terrain. If you look at the Rocky Mountain system up in North America, that's a pretty high range (highest peak at 14,000 ft., averaging in at about 10,000 ft.) but not enough to really separate things from east to west in the United States of America. It's a divider, but not a permanent divider. However, when we get down to South America, the Andes system running through the spine of South America is indeed a true divider, both culturally and physically. At roughly (highest 23,000 ft., 13,000 ft. average) 13,000 thousand feet high, it's a big divider. The Andes separate Chile, Ecuador, Peru, and Colombia from everywhere else, so there is not a lot of east-west movement or cultural interaction across the continent. We just talked about all these similarities that exist between these countries, and then there is this physical factor, which keeps things fairly divided.

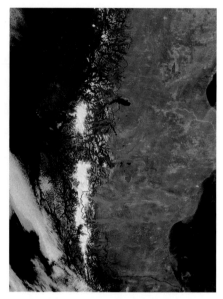

The Andes: major continental divider.

On top of that there are a couple of other physical factors to consider, one being a physical term I want you to know: **escarpment.** What is an escarpment? An escarpment is a very abrupt change in elevation right off the coast. It's a common physical feature in South America, and also Africa. One of the best examples of this is the Brazilian Highlands, and also the Guyana Highlands up north. The Brazilian Highlands are in the southeastern quadrant of Brazil, but lead all the way down to Argentina. The Guyana Highlands go all the way through into Colombia, Venezuela, Guyana, and the northern part of Brazil. This kind of abrupt change as you get off the coast means there's not a lot of coastal margin. A few miles inland, although it's not the Andes or high mountains or anything, there's a little jump of maybe a few hundred feet up to an elevated plateau.

Throughout history this has kept the interior hard to get to because throughout most of history, explorers or traders traveled on rivers through waterways to get into the interior of a continent. That's not the case in South America. Most of the places that have escarpments cause rivers to turn into waterfalls. Boats and waterfalls don't mix, so you'll have to figure out a new way in, conquistador! Unfortunately, your journey to the waterfall didn't really bring you in too far from the coast either. So it's been historically hard to enter and traverse the continent. The Andes on one side of South America and the highlands or escarpments on the other side of South America give travelers a double whammy of difficulty. And that's just the terrain!

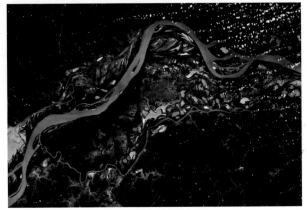

Remotely sensed Amazon—sweetness!

There's another difficult double whammy for any travelers, traders, and explorers, which is of course the climate and vegetation combo. When thinking of South America, the gut reaction that people have is rainforest, big rainforest, a bunch of damn monkeys running around in the rainforest! And in large part, that is true. The only river system that allows you to penetrate the continent at all is the Amazon River system. However, it's the one that coincides with the Amazon rainforest basin, meaning it's a damn jungle out there: the biggest continuous jungle in the world; the single largest acreage of rainforest on the planet. It's mostly throughout the northern part

of the continent, in Venezuela, Colombia, Guyana. Brazil holds the biggest chunk of the rainforest, about 60 percent of the total. There's also some in Bolivia, some in Ecuador, some in Suriname, some in Peru, but watch out, don't make the common mistake of thinking that all of South America is rainforest.

Keep in mind that South America is the 4th largest continent. The equator goes through the northern part of Brazil in the true tropical region. But South America spans all the way down to the tip of Tierra del Fuego, which is closing in on the Antarctic Circle. And there's almost every possible climate in between. In Argentina and Chile you will find midlatitude climates like humid continental, humid subtropical, with temperate forests very much like the eastern seaboard of the United States. The Pampas, the grasslands of Argentina, are very much like the Midwestern United States. You've got the Atacama—it ain't rained there in a hundred years—Desert in Peru and Chile. Over in Chile there is even an area or two with a Mediterranean-style climate. This huge latitudinal range means South America has got a bit of everything, a huge diversity of vegetation and climate. It's not all rainforest.

It's a combination of the tough terrain, the Andes, and the escarpments—manifesting themselves as the Brazilian Highlands and the Guyana Highlands—combined with thick jungle vegetation of the rainforest that has served for centuries to keep people out of the interior, making it very hard to traverse the continent. The interior is sparsely populated as you can see at our favorite Lights at Night image. And, there is not a lot of communication and interaction from east to west, which is probably the main reason why there is not a United States of South America.

SOCIALLY SPEAKING

We have already talked about a lot of social factors across Latin America. Problems like poverty, wealth disparity, high urbanization rates, and landlessness all appear in South America as well, and some of them manifest themselves in extreme ways. Is there anything different about South America? What's perhaps a little more unique about South American society in contrast to other places in Latin America?

South America is a true melting pot, and Brazil is really the center-piece of this. What's the Plaid Avenger talking about here? Well, like the Caribbean during the colonial period, there was a huge infusion of folks from Africa, who were slaves at the time. Brazil and the Caribbean were the two main destinations of African slaves back in the day. Between three and four million Africans ended up in Brazil, and five to eight million more in the Caribbean, as opposed to the half a million that went to all of the United States. We are talking about exponentially larger numbers of Africans, and it shows in the face of Brazil as well as in the culture.

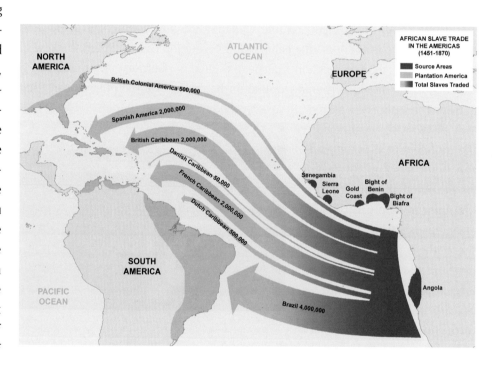

What does that equate to in today's world? There is a currently a significant African component in Brazil's culture as well as the rest of South America. Cultural input from the African continent added to the cultural fray in South America. What other continents are represented? We have the colonial masters themselves, The Portuguese and the Spanish. They have infused their culture into South America as well, through years of conquest and rule. Like the African flavor of Brazil, the European background is also very apparent in the way people look and speak, the music they create and holidays they observe. You can see extreme manifestations of the European influence in places like Argentina and Chile.

This is not widely known here in the US, but during the 19th and early 20th centuries there were huge infusions of Europeans to South America. We Americans tend to think of our country as the immigrant country, but not all of them came to the United States of North America. A bunch of them went down to South America too. In places like Argentina and Chile we see that there were significant numbers of Italians and Germans during this period of mass European immigration. Now we already mentioned the original colonial masters, the Spanish and Portuguese, but in places like Argentina and Chile even in the 21st century, you can run into the unusual phenomenon where entire villages speak only Italian or German.

The extreme manifestation of the Portuguese colonial heritage in Brazil is why their official language is Portuguese. The Spanish were everywhere else and that's why they speak Spanish in the rest of South America. So we have the African influence and we have the European influence. But there's one more: The indigenous influence. There were people hanging out in South America before the Spaniards and Portuguese got there. The Inca Empire was kicking ass down there for a while, as well as other small native groups that were spread all over, similar in structure to Amerindians in North America, but also distinct jungle-dwelling native cultures as well. Indigenous peoples make up a significant portion of South America's population still today, as opposed to some other places in Latin America.

Cortez & Pizzarro: Spanish bad-asses.

What am I talking about? South America being a big place and the Inca having a big Empire meant there were lots of folks already there. As we already pointed out, when the conquistadors got here, not only did they take over the hierarchical structure of the Inca Empire and the Aztec Empire of Mexico, but they brought with them diseases that pretty much wiped out a huge component of the native populations all across Latin America, and South America in particular. Most natives of South America died long before they saw a white Spanish or Portuguese dude. However, there are still a lot of descendants of the indigenous peoples here, particularly in Peru which had the highest concentration of indigenous peoples when the conquistadors arrived. That brings us to three main ethnic groups in the South American social mix, from three continents.

THE DARK SIDE

A theme that I didn't elaborate on in great detail in the Latin America chapter is the concept of racism in Latin America, because it manifests itself in a greater extreme in South America than it does in other places. Racism is a very real part of South American society, where it's worse than anywhere else in the Americas. So how is it more extreme here than everywhere else?

There is a direct correlation between how light your skin is and how well you are going to do in life, how easy life is going to be for you, how many times you might be arrested, or if you are going to get a bank loan. The lighter your skin is, the more doors are open to you. If you go into a bank to get a loan, you will probably get it if you have light skin. If your skin is very dark then you probably won't. If you're walking down a street somewhere in a bad part of town and the cops roll by, they are probably not going to bother you light skinned folk, but if you have dark skin you're more likely to get harassed. It's true that we have racism in the United States, as there is some amount of racism in every society across the planet; but it's nowhere as engrained as it is in South America. The Plaid Avenger will put money on that. You can ask folks on the street there all day long and nobody will disagree with that statement. It is a very real and very visible part of life.

Of course it's been outlawed; it's not legal at all, but it still exists. It's still the way it is. Here's why I brought it up at the end of talking about the indigenous factor: The only exception to the very strict hierarchy of color is the indigenous population. They are at the bottom rung, even though it's not a direct skin correlation. You can clearly see that the indigenous folks are not as dark skinned as say, someone with an obvious African heritage. But even though they aren't as dark, they have fewer rights and are looked upon as the lowest tier of society virtually everywhere in South America. If you look at a list of classes that are most impoverished, the indigenous will always be there at the top of that list. It's a hot button issue across all South America, and it's important because this manifests itself in today's world. Lots of these indigenous groups are fighting back for their rights. There was even a dude named Evo Morales of indigenous descent who just got elected to the presidency of Bolivia, the first indigenous president in South America since the Inca Empire. This is a very big step forward for the indigenous population.

So these are very real factors that I want you to be aware in order to comprehend what's going on and how the social world is slightly different in South America. But wait a minute! We're not done yet, because there is actually a fourth main ethnic group in South America. Along with the indigenous, the European, and the African influence, there's a visible Asian influence. Similar to the United States, there are folks that came across from Asia in the last 100 years. Perhaps not in numbers as large as those in the United States, but still significant and continuing to grow. I pointed out that the current president of Bolivia is of indigenous decent, but check out this recent president of Peru.

Evo Morales: 'I used to grow cocaine. Now I'm President. Go figure!'

Alberto Fujimori demonstrates this other element of the diversity in South American society. Here is a guy of direct Asian persuasion who ends up being the president of a South American country. We'll see later on that Asia is playing a larger role in South America: China being the forerunner of all this. Chinese influence is permeating the continent as more and more Asian and Chinese folks come in. The situation looks much like what is happening in the United States. So South America is a very diverse place with a lot going on, making it socially different; although, some aspects of its social hierarchy are not particularly nice.

'I used to be President. Now I'm under house arrest. Go figure!'

THE MAKING . . . AND UNMAKING . . . AND NOW REMAKING OF MERCOSUR

MERCOSUR (MERCOSUL)

- ☐ Member states
- ☐ Associate members

So what do people do in South America for money? What's their GDP? What's hot and happening? They've got themselves a trade bloc just like we have NAFTA up here. We need to talk about trade blocs for a little while. This is perhaps one of the reasons that most of the countries in this region are not in the fully developed category. What comes out of South America? What do they do down there?

They are all about primary products, as you might imagine. They're just like the rest of Latin America in that respect. We get a lot of raw materials from South America, like copper, iron, and tin. We already talked a lot throughout this book about what that means in terms of value. It doesn't equate to a whole lot. There is some industrialization there, but what cars have you gotten from South America? What computers? Do you know of any corporations that were founded in South America? It is increasing in today's world to be sure, but they certainly have not developed any fully industrialized societies for the last 100 years, like Western Europe or the United States, and therefore they are still seen as a provider of raw materials. Again that's kind of changing, but it's one of the reasons that they are not as rich as other parts of the world. So what does any of this have to do with MERCOSUR?

MERCOSUR is the local trading bloc of South America. You see that the current MERCOSUR states are Brazil, Paraguay, Uruguay, and Argentina, with Chile as an associate member. The newest inductee was Venezuela, and perhaps others will follow. Why just these states for now, and why isn't there a United States of South America? We can't we even have a single trade bloc of South America like NAFTA?

Well, we have talked a little bit about the physical differences, and those remanifest themselves here. Chile and Argentina are a classic example. Why are two countries that are next-door neighbors not big trading partners? The answer is the Andes. Why is Chile only an associate member of MERCOSUR? Because it actually trades more with the United States: because it's too hard to transport stuff over to Argentina, but it's quite easy to put stuff on a boat and float it up to the United States, which has more money to spend anyway. So that's one issue; the physical obstacles of the world do play a part in why this map looks the way it does.

Why are only the southern states of South America in this trading bloc? Physical barriers are one reason, but reality is the other. If you look at South America as a whole, as a pretty picture, it looks kind of like an ice cream cone. The Plaid Avenger wants you to remember that. South America is an ice cream cone, and if you were actually holding that ice cream cone, the cone part is Chile, Argentina, Paraguay, Uruguay, and southern Brazil. That's the cone; the ice cream is all up on top. Here's a term I want you to remember that will help you to understand what's going on in South America in terms of economic clout: **the southern cone.**

The reality of the South American continent is that most of the money is in the south. It's where the action is, where the economies are most developed. They're the places that are most industrialized, so they've got more to trade with each other; they have more in common. If you had to pick some place to go to in South America that was most like the United States, then you would probably pick Chile, Argentina, Paraguay, Uruguay, or Southern Brazil. Not northern Brazil, unless you want to take a ride on the gigantic mosquitoes and live in mortal fear of panther attacks. Southern Brazil is where you get that rich southern cone action.

The ice cream up top isn't even ice cream, really. It's just a big ball of cocaine. As you see in this graphic, there is an inverse relationship in which the biggest cocaine producing countries on the planet are the exact opposite of the MERCOSUR countries.

Coincidence? Probably not. It is a big deal. Why are these guys cocaine producers? Well, because the whole continent produces primary products, and one of the most profitable primary products to produce is something with a guaranteed market, with customers willing to pay whatever necessary. In short, cocaine or any other kind of drug is the way to profit from a primary product. Bananas don't get shit for money on the market, but cocaine gets a ton. Here's a fun fact: the street value of cocaine in America is somewhere around 35 billion dollars. You do the math and figure out why people make cocaine in South America. Colombia is the biggest cocaine state on the planet, but Peru, Bolivia, and Ecuador are not too far behind. It makes for a nice dividing line on the continent. We already said there's a physical dividing line, but this is kind of an economic dividing line as well. It has a lot to do with the current issues in South America—why things are the way they are.

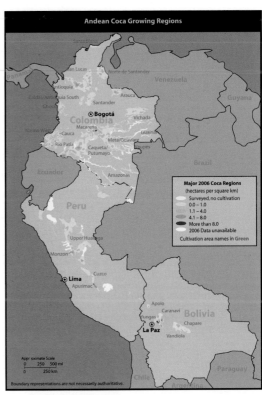

Let's get back on point. MERCOSUR, like so many other trading blocs around the planet, is set up to encourage trade between the countries so their economies will grow and propel them further. There's also a point of pride here. This is what the Plaid wants you to know about as far as what's happening in South America: the real leader of MERCOSUR, if not South America as a whole, is Brazil. Brazil is a big proponent of MERCOSUR. Why is this? Brazil sees itself largely as the United States sees itself in NAFTA: as The Man.

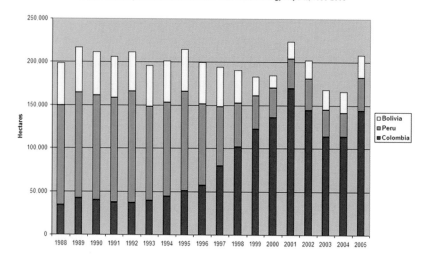

Andean Coca Cultivation
Source: State Department International Narcotics Control Strategy Reports, 1996-2005

There is really no questioning that the United States is the real nucleus of trade with Canada and Mexico. Likewise, Brazil sees itself as the real regional leader in South America. It is the biggest country, the most populous, and has the biggest GDP. In the self-defining role of regional leader, they really want to perpetuate MERCOSUR and make it successful. MERCOSUR's growth makes Brazil grow too, making its role in the world bigger, making South America a bigger and more prosperous, industrializing place.

So lots of countries in South America, particularly Brazil, are really keen on making MERCOSUR work. And there has really been a rallying effect around the group in the last several years, especially since Hugo Chavez had been beating the drum for his continent-wide 'socialist revolution' and economic independence from the US. Ten years ago I would have said, "It's doing okay, but it's starting to go downhill." Five years ago I would have said, "MERCOSUR is pretty much done, you can stick a fork in it," but my, my, my, how times change. What is the Plaid talking about here? They were done, but perhaps they are getting resurrected. How? Well about ten years ago some new idea called the FTAA sprouted up . . .

FTAA. ¿QUE? THE BATTLE OF TRADE BLOCKS IN SOUTH AMERICA?

What the hell is the FTAA? The FTAA stands for the **Free Trade Area of the Americas.** I really want you to know this stuff and understand it because it plays a big part in what's happening in South America right now. The FTAA is something that has changed radically and flip-flopped completely in the last decade. Over ten years ago the United States dreamt this up: a free trade area of all the Americas. This would be a free trade bloc like NAFTA, but for the entire Western hemisphere. How fantastic would that be? They held a meeting in 1994 in Miami. The heads of states for 34 democracies in the region, which of course excludes Cuba, all got together and decided to do a NAFTA sort of thing. "This would make a free trade area, lower tariffs, and eliminate subsidies to protect our own industries. This will be great and will encourage trade across the whole hemisphere. We will kick ass in the rest of the world!"

Why would the United States lead this off? They are already the richest in the world, why would they care? Much like the little lesson we learned back in Western Europe, the EU wants to expand to include more member states and to include more economic activity to make themselves bigger on the world stage in order to be a real competitor. So with this logic, the United States thinks ahead (something they don't do very often) and says, "Hey we are the biggest economy in the world, but that EU is growing over there, and look at China! We should probably grow too. Let's do this FTAA thing. We will make the largest free-trade bloc on the planet, and we will continue to lead the pack."

Not a bad idea. Ten years ago all countries were at least partially onboard, and many were avidly onboard saying, "That's awesome, lets do it!" Several countries were more hesitant, but everybody said that free trade sounded like a good idea. Free trade typically means investment, which typically means increasing industrialization and all of the rest of the good things

The Three Amigos: socialists smacking down the FTAA.

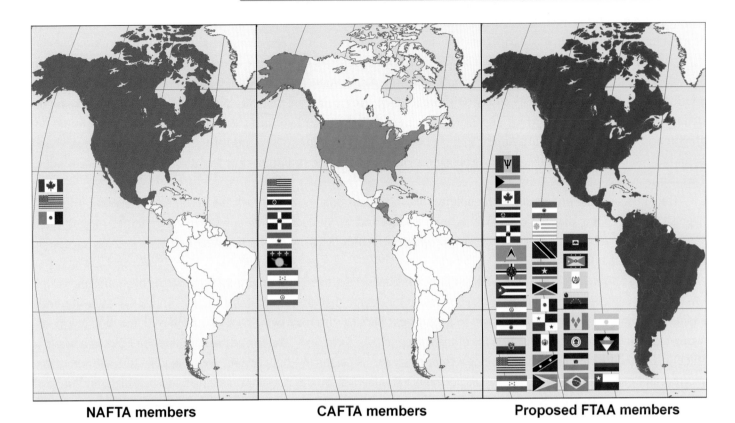

NAFTA members   **CAFTA members**   **Proposed FTAA members**

that encompass growth. Everybody was at least a little onboard, if not fully. Five years ago President Bush was really hot on this and was pushing hard saying, "Let's get ahead of schedule and start inking some of these trade agreements right now," in other words, "Let's get it on!" They set a target of 2010 for everybody to sign up.

Again this is basically like NAFTA, but for everybody. Unfortunately for the Bush administration and the FTAA as a whole, other cards entered the picture here, one of them being Hugo Chavez of Venezuela. Hugo, as you might imagine, is an ally of Fidel. When their powers combine, they are two leftists who consider the United States an imperial power and look at the proposed free-trade areas as a vehicle for the United States to get more of what it wants while screwing over more poor people in Latin America. That's not a Plaid Avenger call, just what Hugo and Fidel were thinking. And then Evo Morales, another hard-core leftist, just joined their ranks when he became President of Bolivia . . . so the leftist socialist, anti-free trade, anti-FTAA ranks have been swelling. This movement has now attracted more than just the extremists too . . .

Because more and more governments in Latin America are going to the left, this whole FTAA process has really been derailed. More and more folks have said that they are more hesitant about this now, and Brazil has already said, "Wait a minute, we have MERCOSUR already, let's grow this more." Brazil was opposed to FTAA from the get-go because it saw itself being removed from its role as the leader of South America. Brazil would just be another subservient state to the United States powerhouse in the FTAA schemata. Then we had Venezuela come onboard fully against it, and Fidel was already against it. In the last five years they have really turned this thing back around to the point now where just this last year Washington has kind of backed off on its push and said, "Ok we will give up on the whole FTAA thing for right this second. We are not going to try and shoot for the deadline that we were originally shooting for. Let's just do free-trade agreements with individual countries, and then make it an official group later."

This has manifested itself *just in the last few years* as something called CAFTA. We already have NAFTA, which is the North American Free Trade Agreement. Now we have CAFTA, which is the Caribbean Area Free Trade Agreement that involves five different countries in Central America and the Caribbean. We already talked about this in the Caribbean section, but basically CAFTA is somewhere between NAFTA and the FTAA. It is the United States saying, "Oh we are encountering too much opposition with the whole big deal right now so we will start doing smaller deals and eventually conglomerate them all into a big group." This is the deal with FTAA; this is where it stands right this second. It has fully reversed itself in the last 10 years in that the momentum it had back then is all but gone right now, but we can only wait and see where it goes.

I am not jumping on the communist bandwagon with the lefties down there and saying that the FTAA is all doom and gloom and that it's horrible. Most people from the North American standpoint (and many business leaders in South America and Latin America as a whole) would say, "Hey come on. The way out of poverty and the way to get richer is to encourage trade, which encourages business, which encourages job creation. So what you guys should do, all you poor saps down in South America, is support this. This is going to be good for you!" Again, it is very probusiness, but the conservative take is that probusiness plans will equate to better stuff for all of you once you get a job. This is one avenue towards growth.

The leftists on the other side of the political and economic spectrum approach the argument differently. They say, "No, we've been doing that for years. We've been trading and we've been selling our cheap commodities to the United States and we're still poor as hell! We've got the greatest wealth disparity on the damn planet! Why are you suggesting that continuing that is going to help us?"

The Plaid's not telling you what's going on or which side is right; there's never any right and wrong on stuff like this. You can't really prove either side. Those are two options up for debate that are causing some friction. That's the battle currently happening within the FTAA that I want you to know about because this may swing back and forth over the next few years. Again, individual leaders of countries, some of them even leftists, have said, "Well we're not sure that the FTAA as a whole is great or that the United States as a whole is a great entity for us personally, but certainly we would like to trade with them. We'll certainly sign a one-on-one free trade agreement with America." So this is again something that is not black and white. It is with Fidel and it is with Hugo, but it's not with most other countries. And this whole story about FTAA ties to . . .

LEFTWARD SWEEP

This is the real deal of what's happening in South America right now, and will have huge effects on how shit goes down there in the future. We've referred to politics across the region in the Latin America chapter and every chapter since, and it's the same deal here. There is indeed a movement towards left-leaning governments. Not communist governments, because nobody is going to call themselves a Communist besides good old Fidel, but they are governments that are openly embracing and encouraging socialist ideologies. And it is a more proactive socialism than anywhere else, even in Europe or the United States. We've talked about this before in various points in this book, this manual to understanding the world.

Pretty much every government is somewhere in the socialist category, even though we in the United States say we are hardcore capitalists. We say free trade is what we are all about. Yeah that's true; it's all good, but don't we have welfare systems and unemployment benefits? Sure, we have all those things. We look out for members of our society on some basic levels. The Latin American governments, particularly here in South America, are now saying, "Yes we are going even further down that road. We want to nationalize industries, like Venezuela which controls their oil industry." It's not a private affair; the state runs it, and they are saying that their interpretation of socialism is they can use that money to build better schools and roads and hospitals. Private investment may come and build a business, but the state is going to be very proactive in helping people more rather than less. I am not going to lie: its happening. Bolivia just nationalized their natural gas industry in May 2006.

The Plaid Avenger calls it like he sees it. This movement is gaining real momentum because of Chavez's success in Venezuela. His success has fueled his self-defined 21st century "revolution" in South America. What revolution?

Chavez is a guy who has totally embraced socialism. How has he been able to pull this off? The socialism thing is only working so well because his country produces a shit-load of oil, which we know is the crucial resource in today's world. The price of oil continues to go up, so every time you put five-dollar-a-gallon gasoline in your SUV, Hugo Chavez is being empowered. I am not making fun of the guy; I am not even making fun of oil companies. I don't give a shit. I just want you to understand what is going on.

In fact, I'm not so sure that we can say that his movement is even that successful there in Venezuela. Their economy outside of oil is pretty flimsy, and they have yet to make any big strides in infrastructure development or poverty eradication. Thus far, Hugo's bark is much louder than his bite . . . but boy oh boy can that dog bark. He has most successfully used all that oil wealth to make himself a loud voice on the global stage, making pledges of foreign aid to other countries and making speeches bashing the US . . . when perhaps his time would be better spent tending to business back home.

The main reason Hugo has been able to launch this socialist experiment is because his country is making shit-loads of money off of oil. Not all South American governments are in that category. He is meeting a lot of success, his country is getting rich, and he is investing a lot of that money in schools, satellite communications to make his country communications independent, building roads, building hospitals, and training medical folks. This is the fringe, the far leftist fringe of socialism. The state is doing all of this. Those are things that private businesses do in our country. He is afforded the luxury of meeting all of those needs because of oil, and he is being very successful at doing it right this second because oil gets such high returns. His success story has been carrying his message and inspiring a lot of Latin Americans. I am not advocating socialism or communism, but he is successful because of the oil, so what can you say?

I should tell you though, his popularity is on the wane here in 2008. Too much rhetoric, not enough results, and last year he lost a popular referendum to increase his socialist powers. Hugo's time in the sun may be running out, but the movements towards a more united South

What's the Deal with . . . the Bolivarian Revolution?

The **Bolivarian Revolution** is an ongoing mass social movement and political process started in Venezuela and most closely linked to its rabid leader, Hugo Chavez. Proponents of Bolivarianism trace its roots to an avowedly democratic socialist interpretation of the ideals of Simón Bolívar, an early 19th century Venezuelan and Latin American revolutionary leader (you know, the George Washington of Latin America) prominent in the South American Wars of Independence. He was the man. One of the main ideals of "Bolivarianism" is promoting the unification of Latin America into one country.

Simon in space?

So this push for MERCOSUR could be interpreted as a true beginning stage of perhaps an entire South American trade bloc, which is what Hugo Chavez and his Bolivarian revolution is all about. Simón Bolívar wanted a United States of South America. Hugo Chavez is using all of his power and oil money to try to reestablish this whole movement of a United States of South America, and the movements toward the unifying trade bloc seem to be working. And the satellite?

Keeping the revolution alive.

The Simón Bolívar satellite, so dubbed by Hugo, is due to be launched into space in August, 2008. Chavez earmarked a half a billion dollars and has Venezuela's top scientist working to put their first object in space, putting them officially in the "space big-boy club." The satellite will provide broadcast of Latin America news and entertainment, and be accessible to all in Latin America. Pretty interesting stuff. One last point of interest: Guess whose helping build it? If you said "the Chinese," proceed directly to GO and collect $200 from the bank.

America will probably continue, as we can see by the region-wide shift to the political/economic left here recently . . .

The leftward sweep that's been occurring in the last two years has virtually all the governments of South America now going towards the left, more openly embracing the socialist take on how the world should work. Places like Argentina. Chile just elected their first female President, who is left-center. Peru is in a run-off right now, and both the people in the run-off for the presidency are center left, which means they are going left as a whole. Brazil's Lula da Silva is left leaning. Hugo, we already talked about, so far left you can see him on your right. Ecuador is going left. We already talked about other places in Latin America, but this is a big trend; this is a big deal.

2008 Political Positions

MEXICO
CUBA
BELIZE
HONDURAS
GUATEMALA
EL SALVADOR
NICARAGUA
COSTA RICA
PANAMA
VENEZUELA
COLOMBIA
ECUADOR
ECUADOR
PERU
BRAZIL
BOLIVIA
PARAGUAY
CHILE
URUGUAY
ARGENTINA

- Far left
- Left leaning
- *Center right*

It's such a big deal that a lot of folks around the planet, including world watchers like the Plaid Avenger, are starting to see South America really gaining its own identity on the planet. Maybe for the first time. The region is doing something unique, and it is presenting an alternative to the traditional systems here in the 21st century. In the old world, you are either communist or capitalist and everybody sided up, and everybody in the middle was polarized to one side or the other. You had one or the other, and that's why you had a lot of US intervention and even Soviet intervention and influence in much of the world, including South America, Sub-Sahara Africa, and Southeast Asia. That's why the US fought the damn Korean and Vietnam Wars, a battle of ideology between communism and capitalism.

That world is gone now and Latin America, particularly South America, is filling the void with a new option. And it is a region, with the voice of a singular entity, that is taking this socialist approach openly and more extremely than any other place on the planet right this second. A lot of folks around the planet are looking at it and saying, "Hmmm . . . that's interesting. It is kind of a new axis of power so to speak, this leftward socialist axis of states". If MERCOSUR continues to strengthen, it will become the world's only 'socialist' trade block! Interesting indeed! So it's important to know about this if you're going to understand what's happening in the world.

Make no bones about it; Washington is not thrilled with this development. As has been pointed out already in the previous four chapters, Latin America as a whole has been historically viewed as the **backyard** of the United States. Now the backyard is increasingly slipping away from US control. "Under US control" is completely inaccurate, because it is not even "under US influence" anymore. Washington would not encourage all those policies of blatant socialist origin; it is not in the US's economic or political self-interest. There is a lot of concern and a lot of debate in American politics about "losing Latin America." The US has been focused on other parts of the world like the Middle East, and lo and behold, what used to be the US's subservient little stepchild of the south is now staunchly not.

And that's a big deal. That is why we are talking about world regions. This is a place that's drastically different then it was 50, 20, hell even 10 years ago. It is a very different place that the US now has to deal with on entirely different terms. So the leftward sweep can't be denied. Will it last? Nothing ever lasts, but it is here to stay for a little while at least. All of these leaders are new and they are getting elected in some cases by radically popular consensus. This movement is not to be underestimated. This movement is sometimes referenced in the United States as the **pink tide.** Pink referring to pinko commie.

A Lulu for Lula

1 1/2 oz cachaça

1 1/2 oz white rum

2 oz pineapple juice

3/4 oz coconut cream

3.4 oz cream

1/2 peeled mango

Blend ingredients together with crushed ice in a shaker or blender. Pour into a large highball glass over crushed ice, and serve. Cachaca is a leading brazilian liquor distilled from pure sugarcane juice. Toast to Brazil's leader. He looks so jolly.

EL EXTREMO

That brings us to the end of this chapter, and a few closing comments about South America as a whole. The leftward sweep: can't be denied, it's making a big impact. New axis of power? You decide. Loss of the United States' backyard? If not a

What's the Deal with Left vs Right in S. America?
A Summary:

1. Extreme left
2. US hates him
3. Democratically elected; won 60 percent of vote
4. US claims he is a threat to democracy and stability of the continent
5. US funds opposition parties to him, zero dollars given to government
6. Undeclared "leader" of leftist movement in South America
7. His country is massive oil producer; US buys most of the product

Hugo Chavez of Venezuela.

1. Extreme right
2. US loves him
3. Democratically elected; won 70 percent of the vote
4. US supports him as a close ally and a model of democracy
5. Through Plan Colombia, US has sent over 6 billion dollars to government
6. The only rightist leader in South America
7. Country is massive cocaine producer; US buys all of the product

Alvaro Uribe of Colombia.

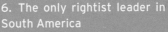

full loss, certainly trouble that the US is not prepared to deal with right now, manifesting itself in the leftward sweep and also the derailment of the FTAA. There is one other little side bar that we need to consider, and what the US is already extremely troubled over: the influence of China. We referenced this earlier and are now going to get back to it to finish off this chapter.

Hu's on first? Maybe heading for second base in South America . . .

China, as we will see when we talk about it several chapters from now, has a very savvy foreign policy in the world right now, as the Plaid Avenger sees it. Some would say they are very strategic in dealing with countries on a one-to-one basis to win them over, or as the US likes to say, "to win over their hearts and minds." China is doing it perhaps better than the United States right now. China is certainly more successful at winning the hearts and minds of the people in Latin America. What am I talking about? China is increasing its presence in South America. It is a minimal presence compared to the United States, as is their foreign investment in South America. But it's a presence that is strategically increasing, day to day.

President Hu Jintao of China and his Premier Wen Jiabao have paid official state visits to every South American country and some of them multiple times in the last decade. It is important to note that President Bush has only made it south of the border two times in the last eight years. President Hu has signed multiple trade and aid deals with everyone on the continent, particularly Venezuela for oil and energy resources, but also for agriculture commodities. The Chinese have an unquenchable thirst for raw materials, and are doing their best to get the hook-up from the Latin Americans. They really are on kind of a goodwill tour with South American countries; a lot of their investment comes with no strings attached, unlike the United States who usually hands them a whole ball of string.

This Chinese influence is currently nowhere near the levels of US involvement, investment, or trade, but it's increasing fast—leaving the US a little worried, and rightly so. Perhaps even more so because people like Hugo Chavez are encouraging it and saying they want to sell *all* their oil to China and not the United States. This is yet another thing to consider when you're trying to figure out what's happening in the world. There is Chinese influence, FTAA, and the leftward sweep; consider what all this stuff means for South America and the world as a whole.

How far will the Bolivarian Revolution reach? I wouldn't start buying ammunition to repel the pinko-commie horde just as yet. But it will certainly be an interesting time ahead for our hemisphere. . . .

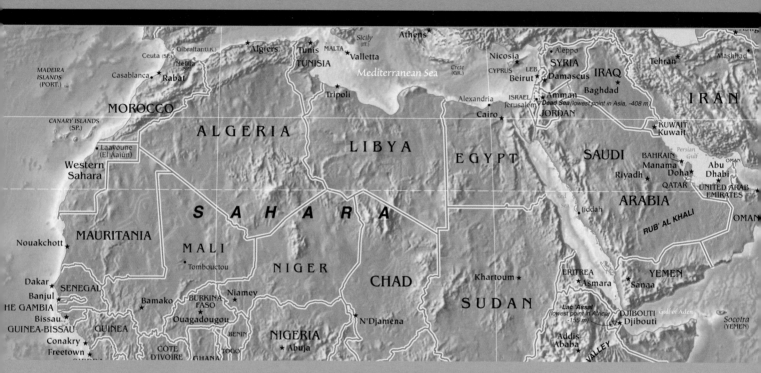

CHAPTER OUTLINE

Middle East and North Africa

18

ALRIGHT, we're in the Middle East now. The hot spot of the globe. The thorn in the US's giant side. Everybody's watching the Middle East. Will there ever be peace in the Middle East? Hell no, there won't be peace in the Middle East. How did it get to be such a pain in the ass anyway?

WHERE IS THE MIDDLE EAST?

I'm confused. Is the Middle East the center of the planet, the point from which everything emanates? Obviously not. So what's the Middle East in the middle of? Western Europeans defined the region with this term as you might expect during the Western

"Oh, hello again Mr. Avenger . . . can I get you the usual?

European colonial era. The Western Europeans, of course, are in the west and all of Asia is to their east. China is as far east of Europe as you can get—thus the phrase "Far East." So in between Europe and the Far East becomes . . . you guessed it: the Middle East. It's a term that everybody in the world recognizes today that is just a historic artifact from a bygone era. So there you go, students of global history and current events, that's where the Middle East is, it's the middle of the old British Empire's known and controlled world at the time, several hundred years ago.

Where's the Middle East in the terms of the Plaid Avenger's world regions? There's a classic section of the middle of the Middle East, and that is the Arabian Peninsula, consisting of Saudi Arabia, Yemen, and Oman. But we also add to this core area by including Jordan, Syria, Iraq, Iran, Lebanon, and Israel. These places we would all definitely agree are in the center—indeed, the middle—of the Middle East. Everybody accepts that; it's the Middle East. However, we are going to expand the region for our definition to include most of North Africa as well. Places like Egypt, Libya, Tunisia, Algeria, Morocco, are all obvious players in the Middle East which share some homogenous traits. But also places like the Western Sahara, Mauritania, Mali, Niger, Chad, part of Sudan, Ethiopia, Somalia . . . now we're starting to split hairs. There's kind of a fuzzy line somewhere in the middle of these countries. Everything north of and including the Sahara Desert in Africa is kind of the Middle East too. In addition, we could go into places like Turkmenistan, maybe Afghanistan.

We are in the 'Middle' . . . but middle of what?

For The Plaid's book, we're going put those in other regions. They have typically been included here, but we're going to hold off for now. Turkey has been defined as the Middle East too, but not in my world. So that's the core: North Africa and Southwestern Asia, from Iran in the east all the way to Morocco and Mauritania in the west, and everything in between. What's homogenous about all these places? What are the four big factors that are the same across all these territories? Are there some major exceptions to them?

There are four big factors that often come to mind when we think of the term "Middle East." We're going to look at those four characteristics. We're also going to look at the history of the Middle East, to see how it got to be the way it is, why it's so far behind, and its explosive potential in the very near future.

FOUR FAMILIAR FACES OF THE REGION

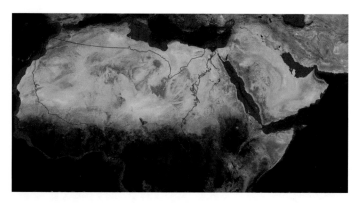

As always, we will start with some physical attributes of this place, and then get to some cultural factors too . . .

NUMBER ONE: IT IS DRY IN THE MIDDLE EAST

The physical world of the Middle East is obviously a very nice homogeneous trait to pick out. The first thing that pops up in your head when asked, "Hey what's the climate like in the Middle East?" It's *dry*. And indeed it is. It is mostly desert; the big Sahara Desert is plopped down in North Africa. It is the largest hot desert on the planet. The United States would fit nicely into the Sahara, as you can see.

But even outside of there, the Arabian Peninsula is mostly desert. We get into Iraq, we think of desert in the southern parts of that country as well. Outside of the true desert regions, we have a lot of steppe. Steppe is just like adding a little bit of water to the desert; there is some scrub vegetation, and that extends this dry region all the way to the borders that we have just defined. This is a dry place, though there are some exceptions.

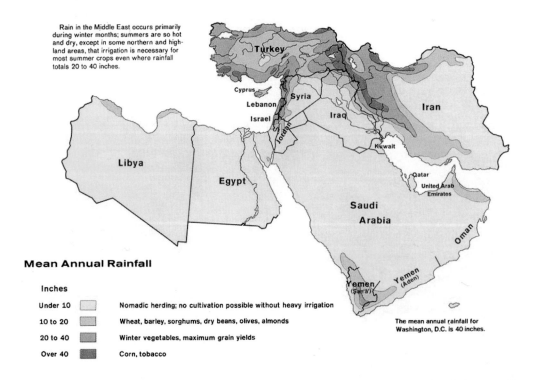

Rain in the Middle East occurs primarily during winter months; summers are so hot and dry, except in some northern and highland areas, that irrigation is necessary for most summer crops even where rainfall totals 20 to 40 inches.

Mean Annual Rainfall

Inches		
Under 10		Nomadic herding; no cultivation possible without heavy irrigation
10 to 20		Wheat, barley, sorghums, dry beans, olives, almonds
20 to 40		Winter vegetables, maximum grain yields
Over 40		Corn, tobacco

The mean annual rainfall for Washington, D.C. is 40 inches.

These exceptions are along the Mediterranean fringe, where there is a Mediterranean style climate. There are some narrow bands of nice climate around the Mediterranean that are well-watered enough for agriculture. You also have the Fertile Crescent, a classic area of biblical lore. The Fertile Crescent includes the Tigris and Euphrates river valleys, all the way over the Levant, which is now of course parts of Syria, Lebanon, and Israel. It's a fertile, well-hydrated place. The Tigris and Euphrates Rivers make up the old Mesopotamia river valley where western civilization actually started, and you can't have that without enough water. Let's add one more exception: Northern Iran. A lot of people don't know it, but believe it or not, up around the Caspian Sea, there are big plains of well-watered area. There are big grasslands that look like the Midwestern United States and can produce quite a bit of food. Even though Iran is mostly an elevated plateau and mostly dry, it has big areas that are well-watered. So those are the exceptions to the rule, but by and large, this is a huge area, and very much of it is very dry.

NUMBER TWO: THEY GOT OIL

The second homogeneous trait we think of when we consider the Middle East is *oil*. Indeed, this place does have some oil. If we look at proven reserves of oil on the planet, the Middle East has the lion's share. This is an equation that seems to be changing daily in the Plaid Avenger's world. As technology increases, the amount of extractable oil from different types of shales and tar sands changes according to extraction technology. And its getting better and

more efficient everyday. A a result, it appears that other countries have more oil than the Middle East right this second. Places like Venezuela, Canada, and Russia hold a lot in nontraditional oil reserves.

But for the sake of argument, let's just say for right this second, in today's world, Saudi Arabia is the giant in proven oil reserves. That means they could stick a straw in the ground and oil will come up—shitloads of it. Iran, Iraq, Kuwait, and the UAE have tons too. But here's the exception: As you get farther and farther away from the Persian Gulf Basin, which is the singular geological structure that all of these oil wells are tied into, the likelihood that you have lots of oil diminishes. As you go to the other side of Iran, into

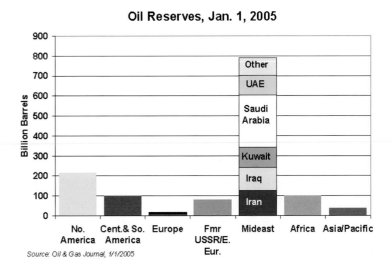

Central Asia, there's not a lot of oil there. As you go north out of Syria, into Turkey, there's not much there. South of Saudi Arabia, the far end of the peninsula, not too much down in Yemen, and indeed, when you cross into Africa, Egypt's got some, Libya's got some, Algeria some as well, but nowhere near the levels of what the Persian Gulf Basin does. As a general rule, the further from the Persian Gulf you are, the less oil you got.

Oil plays such a tremendous role in the world now, and the Middle East has so much of it. That's why this region is such a focal point of global events. The Plaid Avenger's writing this May of 2008, the price of oil has topped $130 a barrel, an all time high in all of human history. So we need to talk about oil a little bit more.

Petroleum use can be traced back to at least the 4th century AD when the Chinese literally began drilling for oil with bamboo pipes. The Chinese used this oil to light lamps and to produce salt by evaporating seawater. Petroleum was also utilized early in history by the Persian Empire (now Iran). However, petroleum use was slow to spread to the West. Instead of crude oil, most Western street lamps were lit using whale oil—which, as the name suggests, is harvested by crazy-asses in boats with spears. Whale oil was the primary source of artificial illumination and lubrication until American Edward Drake "discovered" oil in 1859 (sorry China!).

Jacked Up On Oil

2 oz. black sambuca Italian liqueur

4 oz. Arabic coffee

1 pinch of ground cardamom

Brew the coffee strong, to make it rich and black. Add sambuca and cardamom and give it a stir. No creamer allowed—this is high-test stuff.

The petroleum industry in the West began as a means to produce kerosene, which was used to fuel lamps. Enter: the automobile. Then gasoline became the most popular petroleum derivative. Gasoline was abundant and cheap for almost a hundred years. For much of this time, the United States was self-sufficient in oil production. Slowly though, America evolved into a car culture; advanced interstates were developed and everyone rich moved to the suburbs. The United States became highly dependent on foreign imports of oil. Even this wasn't that big of a problem, because the United States propped up dictators in almost every major oil exporting country. This all changed in 1973.

In 1973, the US and Western Europe support Israel in a war (explained below) against other Arab states. The result: the Arab states get pissed off. One country that was definitely pissed off was Iran. Iran and several Arab states decided to have an oil embargo. They understand their position of oil supremacy and they say, "Well, okay, since you helped out Israel, we're not going to sell you any more oil. How about them apples?" Indeed, in a matter of days, and certainly the course of a few weeks, the price of oil went up from about $3 to about $12 a barrel. It may not seem like much, but that's an instantaneous quadruple in price. Ask your parents or your grandparents about this deal—they probably remember. The result of this in the United States was **gas rationing.** You could only go to the gas station to fill up your car on even or odd numbered days, depending on the last digit of your license plate number. This was a big deal—it caused economic ripples around the world, damaging the economy of the US and those of the rest of the world. This was something that people remembered.

Even after the 1973 oil embargo ended, oil prices continued to climb. People realized that petroleum was a finite resource and that one day, it would run out. The future of petroleum production is open to debate. Most agree that the production capability has peaked in almost all non-OPEC nations (except Russia). Experts have continued to warn about the imminent peak in global oil production. But, the oil industry has such shady accounting practices that no one really knows how the hell much anyone else has, much less how much is left globally. There are also other methods to produce gasoline if crude prices become exorbitant. These include the gasification of coal or natural gas and extraction of shit like tar or other impurities. The Plaid Avenger endorses ethanol as an alternative fuel, mainly because it makes a great cocktail.

Technology will increase in order to find new ways to get to other sources of oil, and get it out of the ground cheaper. I'm telling you this story, in summary, because this is why OPEC's best interest is typically to keep oil prices very stable. Just the same way a crack dealer is with their product: keep it steady, keep it stable so you can keep them coming back. You don't want people to overdose and you don't want them to go dry and get cured of their addiction. You don't want to price yourself out of the market, and you don't want people to die. So to keep the oil price stable is in OPEC's best interest and that's exactly what they've been doing for years.

And not all OPEC countries are in the Middle East. As you can see from the map above, places like Nigeria, Venezuela, and

OPEC NET OIL EXPORT REVENUES AT A GLANCE

| Country | Nominal Dollars (Billions) | | |
	2005E	2006F	2007F
Algeria	$36.0	$41.6	$41.1
Iran	$46.6	$50.1	$46.5
Iraq	$23.4	$24.9	$23.7
Kuwait	$39.0	$44.1	$41.1
Libya	$28.3	$31.2	$29.9
Nigeria	$45.1	$52.7	$51.1
Qatar	$19.1	$23.3	$23.0
Saudi Arabia	$153.3	$162.0	$150.2
UAE	$45.6	$53.0	$52.2
Venezuela	$37.7	$39.4	$37.2
TOTAL	$473.1	$521.9	$495.2

Source: Energy Information Administration

High gas prices for you equals money in the bank for them. E = earned, F = forecast.

Indonesia are OPEC members. But they are all making serious jack as you can see on this chart . . . about 522 *billion* US dollars in 2006 alone. Just on oil.

When we think of oil in the Middle East, we invariably think of another thing, and that's OPEC. As you can see from the box, OPEC is a cartel whose sole reason for existence is to stabilize and control the price of oil. Many in the United States and the world abroad would say, "Oh, they are going to use that as a tool against us." But by and large, OPEC has be a stabilization force for the price of world oil. It is in their best interest in Saudi Arabia, and every other oil producing country, to keep the price stable, and they know it. Here's why . . .

What's the Deal with OPEC?

The Organization of the Petroleum Exporting Countries (OPEC) is an oil cartel designed to regulate the supply and therefore the price of crude oil in the global market. In the United States, cartels are prohibited by antitrust laws and are often called "monopolies." However, international cartels such as OPEC are both legal and successful. The goal of any cartel is to regulate the supply of a commodity (for OPEC, this is oil). By restricting the supply, a cartel is able to control the price of the commodity (again, for OPEC, this is oil). Cartels prevent the biggest producers from attempting to out-produce each other. If too much oil is being produced, prices drop and all oil producing countries are hurt. Oil is a finite commodity and OPEC sees its role as rationing the reserves to ensure constant supply for consumers and maximum profits for producers.

OPEC was founded in 1960 by the big five (Iraq, Iran, Kuwait, Saudi Arabia, and Venezuela) to protest against lowering prices. At this time, foreign owned oil companies (British Petroleum, Dutch Shell, etc.) were taking the lion's share of profits from oil production in the soon-to-be OPEC nations. Over the years, OPEC became more powerful and more unified (even playing a critical role in the 1973 US Oil Embargo). Currently, OPEC nations possess approximately 66 percent of the world's proven oil reserves and supply about 40 percent of the total oil production (including half of all the global oil exports). In other words, OPEC has the power to COMPLETELY shut down the global economy (although this would clearly hurt the member nations also).

However, there are several major oil producers who are not in OPEC. These suppliers—notably Russia, Canada, the United States, Mexico, China, and Norway—are able to fluctuate their production with increasing/decreasing demand. So, when oil prices are high, Russia (for example) cranks on the spigot and starts selling more oil at the inflated prices. When oil prices drop back down, Russia turns production back down. By doing this, Russia is able to capitalize on the market fluctuations of oil. OPEC countries, since they agree to limit their production, do not get to sell more oil when prices are high. This again, however, is the purpose of OPEC. If all oil producers could crank up production when prices were high, they all would. This would create a huge market surplus in crude oil and prices would instantly plummet. In this sense, Russia and other non-OPEC nations are free-riders on the OPEC regulatory system.

Top World Oil Producers, 2004* (OPEC members in italics)	
Country	Total Oil Production** (million barrels per day)
1) *Saudi Arabia*	10.37
2) Russia	9.27
3) United States	8.69
4) *Iran*	4.09
5) Mexico	3.83
6) China	3.62
7) Norway	3.18
8) Canada	3.14
9) *Venezuela*	2.86
10) *United Arab Emirates*	2.76
11) *Kuwait*	2.51
12) *Nigeria*	2.51
13) United Kingdom	2.08
13) *Iraq*	2.03

*Table includes all countries total oil production exceeding two million barrels per day in 2004.
**Total Oil Production includes crude oil, natural gas liquids, condensate, refinery gain, and other liquids.

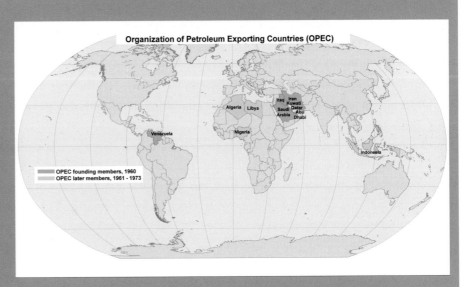

Organization of Petroleum Exporting Countries (OPEC)

OPEC founding members, 1960
OPEC later members, 1961 - 1973

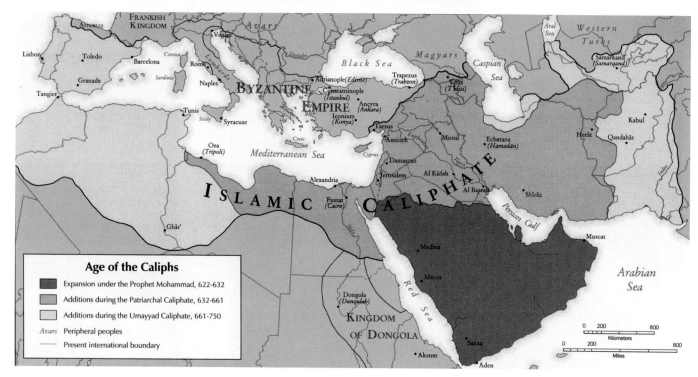

Age of the Caliphs

Expansion under the Prophet Mohammad, 622-632

Additions during the Patriarchal Caliphate, 632-661

Additions during the Umayyad Caliphate, 661-750

Avars Peripheral peoples

Present international boundary

From 600 AD onwards, Islam sweeps the region!

NUMBER THREE: THE MIDDLE EAST IS ISLAMIC

What else do we think of when we think of homogeneous traits of the Middle East? Perhaps this should be number one, but we definitely know that in the Middle East, they're overwhelmingly *Muslim*. Indeed the predominant religion is Islam across all of the countries that I've thrown into this region. We could push it on further; of course, we could say Central Asia is predominantly Muslim and Afghanistan and Pakistan, but those are different cultures. They are so culturally different from the Middle East that not even the fact that they're Muslim can make us include them in this chapter. How Islamic is the Middle East, and how'd they get to be that way?

I'm just going to summarize here. The movement of Islam started in this region, right in the middle of the Middle East, on the Saudi Arabian Peninsula. There you have Medina and Mecca, the two holiest cities of Islam, where the prophet Mohammad transcribed the holy book from Allah. Islam then expands outwards from this core in Saudi Arabia, in what can only be defined as an Arab/Islamic Empire. You may have never heard of that term before, but take it from The Plaid, it's a good way to put it. Saudi Arabia as you might expect is Arab, and because this is also an Islamic movement, I think it's a fair assessment to call the expansion of this political/religious entity the Arab/Islamic Empire.

After the death of the prophet Mohammed in 632 AD, you can see that they expanded outward across all of what's now North Africa, into what's modern day Turkey, Central Asia, and South Asia in very short order, in a matter of a few hundred years. That's how the empire grew.

Was everybody happy within the empire? Not exactly. There was some disagreement amongst Muslims about the faith, resulting in some subdivisions of Islam, the two main ones being Sunni and Shi'a. There's a third that not many know about called Sufi. But definitely check out where the major groups of Islam are located—especially the Shi'ites, as they are the minority sect of the religion. Most Muslims from virtually all parts of the world outside of Iran/Iraq are of the Sunni sect. Sunni is the vast majority.

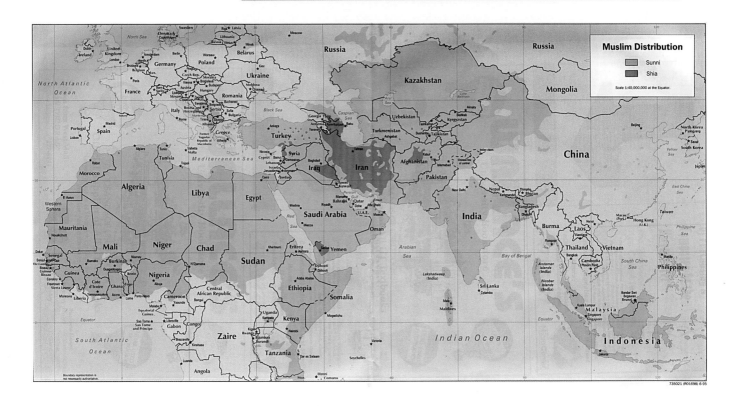

SUNNISM, SHI'ISM, AND WHY IRAQ IS SCREWED

When the prophet Muhammad died, Islam as a movement was left without a clearly identified successor/leader. The two major branches of Islam—Sunni and Shi'a—were formed in response to this dilemma. Sunni Muslims believe that Muhammad died with no intention of appointing a successor. Because of this, Sunni elites chose Muhammad's councilor and father-in-law Abu Bakr as the first Caliph (leader of Islam). There was a steady stream of Caliphs until the collapse of the Ottoman Empire in 1923 and there haven't been any since. Conversely, Shi'a Muslims believe that a dude named Ali, who was also Muhammad's cousin, was chosen by Muhammad (before his death) to lead Islam. Ali became the First Imam—roughly translated as "leader." Besides this, the differences between Shi'ism and Sunnism are minor.

The Iraq Sundae

Today, Sunnis make up approximately 85 percent of the world's Islamic population. Shi'as make up only 15 percent and are concentrated mainly in Iran (90 percent of population), Azerbaijan (75 percent of population), and Iraq (70 percent of population). This is highly important in Iraq today because the Sunni minority was in power under Saddam Hussein, even though his reign was highly secular. Since the United States crushed Saddam, the Shi'ites have a clear advantage in democratic politics. Much of the violence today in Iraq can be attributed to sectarian violence (i.e., Sunnis fighting Shi'ites) and is concentrated in the "Sunni Triangle" (where the minority Sunni population lives). Sunnis are afraid that if they lose power entirely, then the Shi'ites and Kurds (Kurds are typically Sunni, but represent an ethnic minority) will marginalize and/or discriminate against them.

Geographically, Iraq can be viewed as a tub of Neapolitan ice cream. The chocolate-flavored Kurds live up north. The strawberry-flavored Shi'ites live down south. And the vanilla-flavored Sunnis live in between. (Also there is a lot of uninhabitable desert [or dessert!] that doesn't neatly fit the Neapolitan ice cream model.) So why doesn't the country just split up into three smaller countries or at least into self-governing districts? Oil, oil, oil . . . and power politics. Most of the oil is in the Shi'a south, so if the country broke apart, the Sunnis and Kurds would be instantly poor. The international community is also afraid that Iran (Shi'a) and Saudi Arabia (Sunni), the strong neighbors of Iraq, would support their respective religious factions and cause a Balkans-style bloody-ass war. Also, there are Kurds in Turkey who want an independent state of Kurdistan. Basically, Iraq is a damn mess.

Iraq isn't the only place that has some Sunni-Shia friction . . . it is just the hotspot of current conflict which reflects this friction. In fact, we can back up and examine the entire region as having a bit of cultural clash based loosely on opposing teams of which can be defined, in part, by their Islamic sect differences. More on that later . . . first, let's get back to school. Cause school is cool!

Okay, here is a better map of the mess.

OLD SCHOOL OR NEW SCHOOL ISLAM?

The other thing to consider is, yes, most of the Middle East is Islamic, but how conservatively or how liberally do they interpret Islam? With any religion on the face of the planet you can have people who are real reactionaries, ultraconservative, or you can have people who are a little more, oh, how should I put it, free thinking, a little more open to change in the modern world. Of course most people are usually somewhere in between. I'm pointing this out because it makes a tremendous amount of difference in daily life, country to country. Even if the whole region is Islamic, there's extreme variation from one state to the next. Let me give you an example.

In Saudi Arabia, perhaps *the* most conservative state in terms of Islamic interpretation, there are lots of things that are completely accepted as part of common Islamic life which are different in other places. They strictly follow Sharia: the old-school Islamic code of law. They enforce legal and social restrictions for women, meaning women have to typically ask for permission to marry, travel, to drive, to leave the country, get a job, and go out in public. In Saudi Arabia there is also a strong tradition of capital and corporal punishment, meaning if you get convicted of a crime you can be killed, have your hands or feet amputated with a huge sword, or get whipped, depending on your crime. That's a pretty conservative interpretation.

In other parts of the Middle East like Tunisia, really none of those things apply. There may be some elements of Islamic law that you can see, like the Islamic dress code. Every place else is someplace in between. It's like labeling them all Christian, or all Catholic. Not all Catholics in the world are the same. Go look at some Catholics in Haiti who are doing voodoo versus Catholics in Italy who are really uptight. So there's a lot of variation in how liberal or conservative countries are within the Middle East.

Most of the Middle East is Islamic, and that's the end of that story . . . oh wait a minute! There's one exception, and it is a big, big, exception indeed. Every place in the Middle East is Islamic except Israel: the Jewish state of Israel. Boy is this a damn convoluted mess, and the Plaid Avenger's going to have to give this one a full page! But we will wait for the Team Play section to get to that. First, let's have a little fun identifying our Middle East Muslim leaders in a little game I like to call: 'Sunni, Shia, or Sikh?'

SUNNI, SHIA OR SIKH?

Instructions: Of the following world figures, tell me what state/group they lead and what type of Muslim they are. But watch out! A wild card Sikh has been thrown in to increase the challenge, and fun, of this game that is sweeping the nation!

Mahmoud Ahmadinejad
President of

_____

Sunni, Sha'i or Sikh

Hamid Karzai
President of

_____

Sunni, Sha'i or Sikh

Nuri al-Maliki
Prime Minister of

_____

Sunni, Sha'i or Sikh

Muammar al-Gaddafi
Colonel & Honorable
Leader of _____
Sunni, Sha'i or Sikh

Hosni Mubarak
President of

_____

Sunni, Sha'i or Sikh

Saddam Hussein
Ex-President of

_____

Sunni, Sha'i or Sikh

Recep Tayyip Erdogan
Prime Minister of

_____

Sunni, Sha'i or Sikh

Pervez Musharraf
President of

_____

Sunni, Sha'i or Sikh

Osama bin Laden
Leader of

_____

Sunni, Sha'i or Sikh

Manmohan Singh
Prime Minister of

_____

Sunni, Sha'i or Sikh

Abdullah Al Saud
King of

_____

Sunni, Sha'i or Sikh

Ali Khamenei
Ayatollah & Supreme
Leader of _____
Sunni, Sha'i or Sikh

NUMBER FOUR: PEACE IN THE MIDDLE EAST . . . ? ARE YOU ON CRACK?

Which leads us to the last homogenous trait which defines the Middle East and that fourth factor is . . . CONFLICT. The Middle East is a region defined by conflict. Now I've already said this about Central America, a pretty small region in between North and South America, and that does apply. Central America is a violent arena, but perhaps no other place on the planet right now, has so many current active conflicts: interstate conflicts (countries fighting countries), intrastate conflicts (people within a state fighting each other), and maybe the worst, foreign sponsored conflicts (US war in Iraq). This place is a mess, and here's the worst part: They aren't out of the woods yet. They've got a long 21st century of conflict ahead of them.

Old School Ottoman

"Oh gosh, Plaid Avenger, how could you make a projection like that? Aren't you just being negative? Couldn't things get better?" Quick answer: NO! They're not going to get any better not anytime soon! Not in my lifetime. Things may simmer down in a couple of places, but the region as a whole will be mired in conflict for some time to come and it could get fairly nasty before it's done, as if it's that clean right now. So what are we talking about here? Let's back up the oil tanker and start at the beginning. Why is this place mired with conflict? Well we just talked about Israel; let's take it further back than that, all the way back to WWI.

World War I saw the demise of the Ottoman Empire. We'll look into more detail of the Ottomans in the next regional chapter of Turkey. But for now just know this: The Ottoman Empire controlled what is now the classic Middle East, and expanded over a lot of North Africa, and indeed controlled territories in what's now Iran. However, they were an empire in decline coming into the modern area. The Ottomans were an old-school styled state going into the 20th century. They were way behind the technological times, their economy sucked, they still had a sultan on the throne, and this is when the world's coming into the 20th century. People in Europe really looked at the whole Ottoman Empire as a redheaded bastard stepchild that none of them even wanted to deal with. Nobody wanted to take the time to whip them, much less do anything else with them. So the Ottomans were pooling around for an ally, and leading into World War I, they were like, "Hey Britain, would you

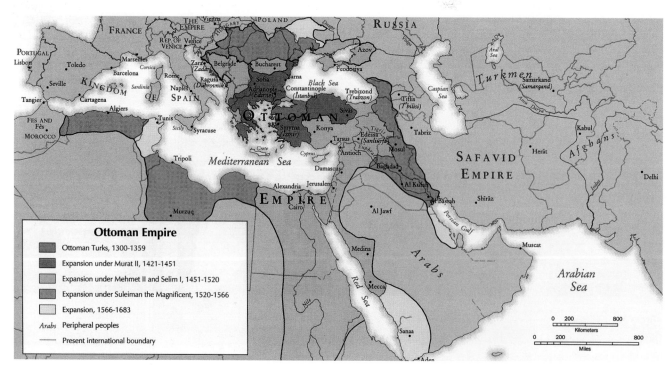

Ottomans: the last big Muslim Empire to dominate the Middle East.

be our friend? Hey France, would you be our friend? Somebody be our friend, because we're worried Russia's going to invade us!" The Ottomans have had several incursions with Russia at this point in history. Finally somebody said, "Ya, Junior, we'll be your fruend . . .," and that was the Germans.

Long story short, the Germans lost World War I and their ally, the Ottoman Empire, lost with them. Something happens here, which many historians would say is the critical reason why you have such tremendous conflict in the Middle East today. A guy wrote a book about it called *The Peace To End All Peace: The Fall of the Ottoman Empire and the Creation of the Modern Middle East* by (David Fromkin, 1989). Although a fairly dry read, if you can get through it you'll be like, "Oh, that's why." The title says it all; the peace process at the end of World War I subdivided the Ottoman Empire and drew arbitrary boundaries in such a way as to basically *ensure* that everybody would be pissed off at everybody else *forever!* Wow. I know it seems impossible since we're talking about something that happened 90 years ago.

Let's fast-forward to today's world. "Still looks pretty good, Jim. What do you think from your angle?" "Yep, they're still pretty pissed off at each other!" Again, it's not the entire reason; it's not the only thing going on here, but it is the start of the problems in the Middle East. What do I mean by arbitrary boundaries? Look at Egypt, that's a great one, someone drew the damn country with a T-square—they're not based on any natural or ethnic divisions. Somebody *drew* them. And that somebody was the winning powers at the end of World War I, mostly the British and the French. They subdivided up the old Ottoman Empire, saying, "Well you lost, you suck, and we want to make sure you don't come back and start a fight with us again, so we're going to parcel you out into smaller pieces. So let's see. Somebody get out a ruler. Okay, there's Iraq, good straight lines. Oh! Jordan, that's some good straight lines. Syria, yeah. Saudi Arabia, kind of an ethnic group there, we'll give you guys Saudi Arabia. Egypt, there's the T-square."

What you had at the end of this process was Turkey proper; in today's world the remnants of the core of the Ottoman Empire, which was technically left intact, and all the other countries were divided up as I explained. Most of these countries were not given outright independence. Some, like Saudi Arabia, were semi-independent even under the Ottomans. But most of them were put in a situation where they were called **mandates.** Primarily the British and the French, and some other players in there too, weren't so much the overlord, but more like the big brother of the new Middle Eastern countries. Egypt, Iraq,

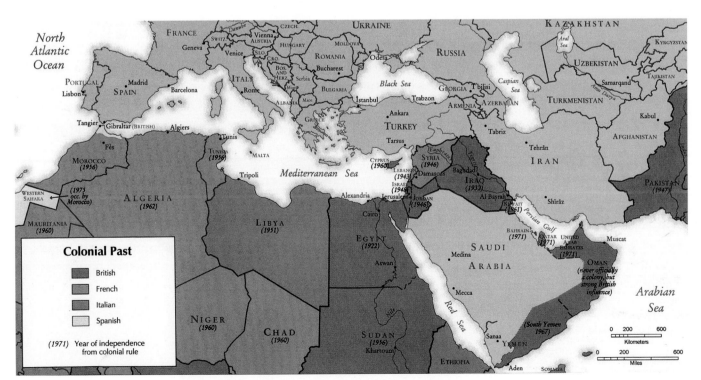

Europeans take over from the Ottomans; use of T-square is evident.

and Sudan were mandates of the British. Palestine and Transjordan at the time were a mandate of the British as well. Syria and Lebanon were mandates of the French.

Watch out for the pyramids!

In those cases, Big Brother basically said, "Here's what you need to do; we're going to put people in charge. We'll protect you militarily. But we'll basically run the show." I can tell you with certainty, after reading that book and others, that a lot of people in the Middle East were immediately incensed, outright pissed off, about this. In fact, places like Syria, a place that the US would like to bomb right now in today's world, *asked* the United States to take over their territory as a mandate. They *wanted* to be a mandate of the US. Wow, how bizarre is that. The United States, which participated in World War I, said, "Hell no, we don't want anything to do with that mess over there." Boy, don't they long for the good old days of the Middle East when the US didn't want to get involved. World War I is the launching pad for dissent in the Middle East. Let's take it up to World War II, shall we? The fun's not over yet!

Not only do we start with foreign influence and foreign dominance by the British and the French, we've got these artificial borders. It's incredibly similar to European colonialism, but not quite the same. In World War II the Middle East as a whole does not get too involved. There is some fighting on their soil, but by and large they stay out of it. The Germans do have their North African campaign (go look up The Desert Fox—what a bad-ass), so things get a little messy, but it's more of an influence thing and no one really sides up. The Allies say, "Hey, don't side up with the Germans, and we won't invade you." By and large, that's the way it went down.

However, it's when we get to the Cold War where things start to get tricky. The Cold War comes to the Middle East like it comes to every place on the planet, with the US and the Soviets vying for influence. The Soviets have been pushing for influence in places like Iran and Turkey for years at this point. So it does become a Cold War battleground for influence, which sets people against other people. The US supports questionable characters in any effort to make sure they don't have Soviet influence. One place in particular that springs to mind is Saudi Arabia, which is an entrenched monarchy. Totally not democratic, totally the antithesis of everything United States stands for. But that's the effect of Cold War; support anyone as long as they don't go commie. Saddam Hussein is another classic example of western forces supporting a total dictator simply so he wouldn't turn to the Russians . . . boy oh boy did we pick a winner on that one. Another one of particular note is some guy called The Shah of Iran, who was basically a dictator who the US supported for quite some time, again, just to counter Soviet influence. You can read about him a little later in the Team Persia section.

We're still under this banner of conflict, still in the Cold War era. But there were also internal wars in Sudan, Yemen, Lebanon, and Chad. And interstate wars between Sudan/Libya, Iraq/Kuwait, Eritrea/Ethiopia, and Iran/Iraq. And even international interventions into Somalia, Iraq, and Lebanon. Let's not forget the multiple Arab-Israel conflicts, which we'll get to momentarily.

You've got religious strife, ethnic strife, territorial border wars, and ideological wars all happening here in the last 50 years. Wars between states, wars within states, wars involving troops from outside the region altogether. It's a mess. This really gets at the heart of the world's perception of conflict in a lot of these countries. Western support of Israel, including its attempts to establish a peace process, manifestations of Islamic extremism, factional infighting between Sunni and Shi'ite, the war on terrorism; all these have now involved the outside world even more. The issue of Israel and the War on Terrorism in particular make this region unique on the planet because the globe is a player whether it wants to be or not.

Conflict is endemic; it has been and will be a defining feature of the Middle East.

WHY ARE THESE GUYS SO FAR BEHIND?

Now that we've looked at a bunch of homogeneous traits of why we define this area as a region (and some major exceptions), the Plaid wants to take a little step back in time again, but for a different reason. I'm not just going to look at conflict. Why is it that the Middle East is behind in the world? Yes, there are *some* countries that have *some* money. There are even some countries that look kind of rich, but let's call a spade a spade. There are a few countries that have a ton of oil, and really not much else going on. Looking at these countries demographically and economically in terms of economic diversity and standards of living for the average man; you will find that they are far behind on the development path. Like South America, this is a place of wealth disparity, where very few people own an excessive amount of resources. In this case, the rich people own oil resources. But the vast majority of folks have virtually nothing. This is compounded by the physical world, which makes it very hard to just go out and be a laborer or farmer. It's a desert! What are you going to do, farm sand? It's a pretty extreme environment and a place that's fairly far behind by any standards.

The Plaid's question is: Why is that? What has happened here? How is a region that is right beside the fully developed Europe so far behind? If we go back and look in our own neighborhood, we see that the United States is a fully developed country, and Mexico is not quite as developed. We already pointed that out, and it's absolutely true. But they're not as far behind as the Middle East is. How can a neighbor of a fully developed region be so far behind, in other words, how did the Middle East get left behind? Here's a brief run through of history that makes a whole lot of sense out of this region's condition.

It's a combination of several factors, which come together just about 500 years ago. Up until this point in history, the Ottomans were a pretty kick-ass empire. They're a powerhouse. The Ottomans kind of take over and run with the Arab/Islamic Empire, and continue the expansion. They are actually beating down Europe's door. The Ottoman Empire attacked Vienna, Austria on multiple occasions; that's how far they encroached into Europe proper. They were large and in charge. At this point in history, it was the Ottomans and the Middle East that had the highest centers of learning, some of the oldest universities. Most of the true breakthroughs in scientific technology (around the 1400s and 1500s) were in the Middle East, not Europe. This is where we reach a critical phase, because at the exact time that Europe is entering its Renaissance, when it starts to blossom around the 1500s, the Middle East starts to fall behind. Why is that? There are several main reasons.

REASON NUMBER ONE: PHYSICAL OVERLOAD

We've already defined the Middle East as a physically challenging place. It's dry, and as such, it's very easy to overfarm, overgraze, use too much water, and make even drier. And unlike Europe where people had not been hanging out there for very long, in the Middle East, you've had people hanging out . . . forever! The Middle East is the birthplace of western civilization. You've heard of Mesopotamia? All the biblical stuff you've ever heard of, you can look at the Jewish Torah, the Christian Bible, and the Islamic Koran. It's all in the Middle East. People have been here for a long time.

Western Civilization, that is people building cities, towns, craftsmen, agriculture, all of that happened in the Middle East, not Europe. It spread to Europe much, much later.

The reason I'm telling you this is because civilizations amount to thousands of years of people using stuff. From around 6,000 or 5,000 BCE, people have used trees, grown crops, mined minerals, and used water and other resources. For thousands of years! And dry climates are easy to abuse, so by 1500 CE the land is exhausted. Thousands of years of resource depletion take its toll, and the Middle East has simply run out of stuff, just as Europe *starts* to use its stuff. Think back to our North America chapter. One of the reasons that North America kicked so much ass is that Europe started running out of stuff when America opened up and started to use its stuff. There is a clear distinction between where people have hung out for thousands of years, and places that are untouched. And it has a lot to do with who's rich in the world today.

REASON NUMBER TWO: THE GOLDEN AGE OF ISLAM COMES TO AN END

Staring in 700 CE, there is this Golden Age where everything is awesome in the Middle East. There is continuous expansion of territory and wealth; they've got centers of higher learning, but it comes to a crashing halt in 1258 CE. How can we attach things to such a specific date? It's the date that another Empire intrudes into this one, and makes sure that everything comes to a screeching halt. The intruders are the Mongols from Central Asia. The rise of the mighty Mongol Empire, out of what is modern day Mongolia, spreads across China into Northern India, all through Central Asia, and all the way into the Middle East. This date is significant because 1258 is the year that the Mongols sack Baghdad, a center of Middle Eastern power, and *raze, or freakin totally demolish,* it to the ground. It's partly due to the rise of another region

The party is over . . .

during world history that this one starts to get behind. I've prepped you that the Ottomans are going to take over shortly and rise back up again, but this is a big blow to Middle Eastern expansion. The Mongols really knocked things out.

REASON NUMBER THREE: BYPASS

No, not heart surgery. They are physically bypassed on the planet. What am I talking about here? I've already told you that this place doesn't grow a lot of stuff. It's dry; it's not an agricultural epicenter, and nobody is really industrialized at this point in history, so what is it that these guys do? What big riches do they have? Gold? Copper? Anything? I've already given you the answer; it's dry and they've depleted all their resources. They don't have much.

So what's kept the Middle East going up until this point? The answer: trade. When you think of the Middle East, think of the term "Middle Man." What does a middle

CHRISTOPHER COLUMBUS
1492-1992

Damn bypassers!

man do? He buys something on one end, moves it to some place that needs it, and sells it for a profit. The Middle East has been classically "The Middle Man" of Eurasia, moving stuff from China and India to Europe and vice versa. Making money going both ways, they've been doing this for a good long time. Think about things like, I don't know, the Silk Road out of China. That stuff went through the Middle East. All the carpets, the fine silks, the whole spice trade . . . people think that the Plaid's joking them, but spices back in the day are like crack cocaine now. No price was too high and people would snort them up their nose and they could never get enough. Black pepper was the crack of its day, back in the 15th century; people loved it, and the Middle East was the dude that brought it to you.

So what's that convoluted long story got to do with the Middle East getting left behind? Because it just so happens here in the 1400s and 1500s that they get bypassed. Bypassed by whom? A couple of surly European lads, maybe you've heard of them. Christopher Columbus, who was trying to find a sea route to India. Gosh, why was Chris doing that? Oh that's right, I remember! Here's the impact for those of you who think this has nothing to do with the Middle East today. The combination of Christopher Columbus trying to head to India and

Bringin' in the Booty!

accidentally bumping into the *huge* New World (1492), and Vasco da Gama, who indeed finds a way to India by passing the Middle East and going around Africa (1498), is this a one-two punch. It essentially eliminates the need for the Middle East in the span of a *decade.* These guys figure out how to get what the Europeans want without paying "The Middle Man." Think about it. Overnight, your business is out of business.

Again, this is compounded by the fact that Columbus doesn't find India; he finds North *and* South America, and everything in between. He hits the jackpot, a literal goldmine. He's not getting the same old stuff from India or China or Indonesia; he bumps into a whole new source of stuff. And this stuff starts flowing back to the Old World in tremendous volume. I don't even have to tell you about *all* the things they shipped back, only two things. Silver and Gold. Think about all the silver and gold that the Spaniards pull out of Mexico and South America. They've got huge mines and a tremendous amount of wealth gets pulled back into Europe. Europe's getting richer and richer and richer, pulling new stuff in from the Americas and going straight to India, bypassing the Middle East. Getting bypassed, in combination with the general physical overload and the invasion of my main man Genghis from Central Asia, really takes its toll on the Middle East.

REASON NUMBER FOUR: OTTOMAN STAGNATION

But wait a minute Plaid, "How can we say that this is a period of decline in the Middle East when it coincides with the rise of the mighty Ottoman Empire?" Well, you're going to see this when you get to Turkey in the next chapter, but you can sum it up all in one word: booty. That's a word that the Plaid Avenger never minds throwing out. The Ottoman Empire's economy is largely based on expansion by acquiring wealth from areas that you're taking over. It's one of the reasons they were knocking on the door of Vienna, because under such an economic system, you have to continue to expand and take new areas over in order to get their wealth. This means that the Middle Eastern/Ottoman economy was fairly stagnant. That type of economy is artificial; it's not based on producing anything. This is ultimately their undoing. The Ottoman Empire: successful in appearance, bankrupt at the infrastructure level. When the expansion stops, they stop.

That's exactly what I was referring to earlier when I said the Ottoman Empire, going into the 20th century, had nothing. People in Europe are looking at this place and going, "How in the hell have they been sustained this long? Their economy is nothing but hot air!"

This really crystallizes in 1798 when Napoleon, the famous short dead dude from France, was a little bored. He had yet to start his takeover of Europe; he's just kicking around trying to get some practice in. So he says, "Hey, I'm going to take a boat load of guys over, and I don't know, take over Egypt." He goes across the Mediterranean to Egypt with a handful of guys, and everybody realizes in short order that this is a titanic event. Why? Well, Napoleon and his small army of men are radically outnumbered; they're in Ottoman territory, an empire that has made incursions into Europe

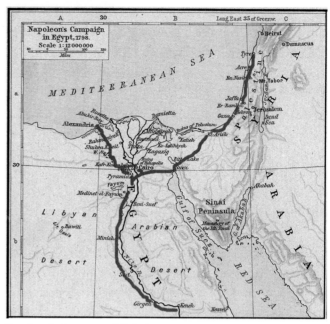

Napolean's Campaign of Kick-Ass.

and is apparently prosperous. Napoleon quickly figures out that they aren't really that badass. The Ottomans send out their baddest and bravest into battle to kick Napoleon out. They were called the Mamelukes, who were basically the marines of the Ottoman Empire. The Mamelukes come out swinging and Napoleon soundly stomps everyone's ass. Maybe you've heard reference to this tangentially: it is a common historical legend that Napoleon's troops knocked the nose off the Sphinx at this time, as well as taking the Rosetta stone.

I said this was a crystallizing, defining moment for history, and it is. Here's why: Napoleon looks around and says, "Wow, that's the best you guys got? Is this the Empire we've been afraid of? This is the Ottoman Empire, right? You guys are way behind! We just totally stomped you!" And this doesn't go unnoticed by the Ottomans, by the way. They were like, "What just happened there?" People started to assess their situation, "Oh, here we are with this artificial wealth, and we've been stagnant, and basically thought the Europeans were scumbags ever since the Crusades." Ever since the Crusades, the Middle East, and subsequently the Ottoman Empire, looked at Europeans as filthy bastards coming down into their holy land with no great technology, no great intervention, not really that smart or well-versed, not scholarly: basically European white trash. Then here they are, a few hundred years later, getting their asses handed to them by the same dudes.

In essence, the Ottoman Empire isolated itself and didn't care about the Europeans, because they thought they sucked. That's why they got behind. They failed to realize that the European technology had surpassed theirs during the Renaissance. Napoleon is the wake up call. Unfortunately it's not only the wake up call for the Ottomans, who realize, "Oh, we better catch up!" it's also a wake up call for Europeans to say, "Oh, look, we can totally whip those guys' asses. We should all get down there and get a piece of the pie." And that is precisely what happened. European contact for

The short, dead dude.

Another reason to hate the French: Nose Thieves

the Ottomans on their own soil becomes very quickly a European takeover. As I suggested, the next hundred years are a degenerative process for the Ottomans as they lose more and more real power, and by the time World War I is over, they get totally dismembered. Now we've caught the story back up, full circle. European contact turns into European takeover.

MIDDLE EAST . . . NOW

This is a place that has gone from pearls to protons (a Plaid Avenger saying) in just a few decades, and it's mostly because of oil. A hundred years ago polished pearls were one of the biggest exports out of the Arabian peninsula. Pearls collected by pearl divers. Pretty low technology stuff. Pretty low total GDP earner too. Now this place has some of the top technological institutes in the world, and some serious GDP earning potential. This place was far behind, in the grips of conflict, and for all practical purposes, would still be completely in the hole if not for the fact that it has ass-loads of one resource the world now needs more than anything else.

Just to catch you up on the story of oil we already started referencing some: In the early part of the 20th century, nobody really cared about oil. In 1900, oil was not used for much. But as the United States was industrializing, the automobile became a product that most people started using, and oil became very popular. From 1900 to the 1950s, oil became "Westernized" in Saudi Arabia. By that I mean that exploration and development of the oil industry was carried out by Western countries, not the locals. There are lots of companies, maybe you've heard of

TOP WORLD OIL NET EXPORTERS, 2004* (OPEC MEMBERS IN ITALICS)

	Country	Net Oil Exports (million barrels per day)
1	*Saudi Arabia*	8.73
2	Russia	6.67
3	Norway	2.91
4	*Iran*	2.55
5	*Venezuela*	2.36
6	*United Arab Emirates*	2.33
7	*Kuwait*	2.20
8	*Nigeria*	2.19
9	Mexico	1.80
10	*Algeria*	1.68
11	*Iraq*	1.48
12	*Libya*	1.34
13	Kazakhstan	1.06
14	*Qatar*	1.02

*Table includes all countries *with net exports exceeding 1 million barrels per day in 2004.*

some of them, Shell, BP (British Petroleum), and Exxon, that had scouts out all around the world in the early part of the 20th century. Lo and behold, they proclaim: "Wow, we think we've found a lot of oil in the Middle East."

Of note, Saudi Arabia originally gave all concessions to the United States, because several other European companies had already written off the peninsula, thinking there was nothing there. Enter a huge oil company in California, Standard Oil (So Cal) that said, "We think we've got a lead on something," to the monarchy of Saudi Arabia, and asked for concessions, which they received. Saudi Arabia said, "Make it 20/80. You guys take 80% if you find anything, give us 20%." Around a week later, the oil company said, "Oh, we just found the largest oil reserve the planet has ever seen." It's the main reserve that's still pumping today.

So basically, the oil was "Westernized" early on, as the Plaid Avenger calls it, meaning Western companies had been in there prospecting, developing it, extracting it, taking a lot of the wealth. No big deal. After all, they supplied all the labor and know-how. But in the 1950s–1960s, oil becomes "Arabized," meaning the states with the oil themselves start to play more of a role. Places like Saudi Arabia say, "Hey, wait a minute, this is *our* oil. Maybe it shouldn't be 20/80, more like 80/20 in our favor, so we'd like to interject, take over these jobs. Maybe you all could you train some of our people?" So a lot of these countries take over production outright, or at least play a bigger role in it.

For the most part, foreign companies acquiesced to these requests, and that is important to note because at this point—the 1950s—there is not a huge amount of animosity between Middle Eastern states and the West. In fact, the

US is largely seen as a positive force in the region, which brings me to an interesting historic event that underlines this fact. In 1956 there's something called the Suez Canal adventure. I point this out because this is probably the point at which the Middle Eastern countries viewed the United States most favorably, since we helped them out. After this point, support for Israel in the 1973 Yom Kippur War (which we've already referenced) triggered the 1973 Oil Embargo, which starts a downward slide of US/Middle Eastern relations—which may be at an all time low right now, today, the 21st century. We've already seen the amount of US influence in the region just from looking at conflicts in the last 40 years, and given current events, it's likely to get worse in the future.

How can they be really rich and also behind the times? The answer is oil, a mixed blessing here as it is everywhere in the world. Most Middle Eastern economies are still fairly stagnant, which is a big problem. They are not *diversified,* meaning their GDP's rely on this single resource. They don't have other jobs. If anything happens to oil—if an alternative energy source is found, if the price gets too high and people just stop buying it—the Middle East is going to be in serious trouble. Many of these countries are going to have a recession or a depression or a collapse overnight.

Several of these countries are doing something about this, particularly places like the United Arab Emirates (UAE) which is diversifying into computer technology. The UAE is now seen as a computer/technological

What's the Deal with the Suez Canal Adventure?

The Suez Canal, which opened to traffic in 1869, is one of the most important shipping lanes in the world. It connects the Mediterranean Sea to the Red Sea. Along with the American Transcontinental Railroad, the Suez Canal drastically decreased the time it took to ship goods internationally. Although built by France and Egypt, or more accurately by Egyptian slave labor, the British had de facto control over the canal as early as 1875.

The British maintain control of this vitally important sea route until 1956 when Egyptian leader Gamal Abdel Nassar decided to nationalize the canal. (Many parallels can be

Suez spells end of Middle Eastern colonialism.

drawn between Gamal Abdel Nassar and Saddam Hussein, including fluctuating support/hatred from the US/West). After flipping their shit for several days, the British and French came up with a plan to regain control of the canal—convince Israel to attack Egypt and *afterwards* offer to neutrally control the disputed territory, namely the Suez Canal. Israel was happy to comply and invaded Egypt on October 29, 1956. As per the agreement, British and French forces entered the Canal Zone to "separate the warring armies." Egypt responded by sinking every ship in the Canal.

The United States, after watching all this shit go down, was furious and worried that the British and French action would cause a Soviet military response. President Eisenhower pressured both the British and French to withdraw and publicly criticized Israel. A UN Commission took control of the Canal Zone. After the Suez Crisis, public opinion of the United States in the Arab world was at an all time high. Unfortunately, the US spent the next 50 years squandering this Arab street-cred with blatantly pro-Israel policies.

epicenter of the Middle East. There are some places that are going to do fine, but most states still aren't going to be in good shape in the very near future.

AND THE PEOPLE . . .

That brings us to some other problems in the Middle East today. They're having a population explosion. As you can see from population pyramids above, fertility rates and population growth are through the roof here. The Middle East does *not* have the world's biggest population total, but it's one of the fastest growing regions, period. They're adding people at a phenomenal rate. Why is that of particular concern or problem? Because they don't have that many jobs, and they don't have many physical resources.

Physical resources like what? What's the big deal? They've got lots of oil so they can buy everything else, right? There are a lot of resources they don't have. Simple ones, like *WATER*—you know, that stuff we humans need to stay alive. If you're going to have more people, you're going to need more of it. Well guess what? We've already pointed out this place is dry. Water is one resource they don't have, and they can't just make more. I guess you can process seawater, but boy that's an expensive operation. Unless they figure out how to drink oil, it's risky to grow so fast.

Limited resources and an exploding population typically spell disaster. This place has enough turmoil going on already and the Plaid Avenger's predicting it to get worse. In fact I'll go out on a limb here and say with all the current conflicts that are already happening in the Middle East, one that's not happening yet is almost guaranteed: the

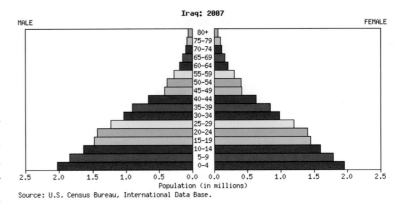

Source: U.S. Census Bureau, International Data Base.

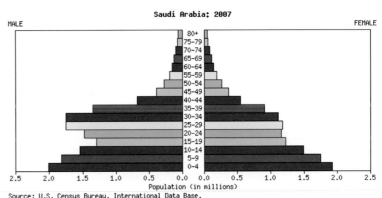

Source: U.S. Census Bureau, International Data Base.

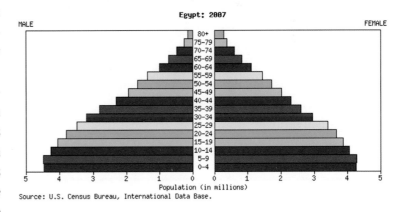

Source: U.S. Census Bureau, International Data Base.

battle over water. There will be interstate wars fought for this critical resource in the next 50 years. It's almost impossible that it will not happen. There are simply too many people being born, and not enough water for them all. Water has the potential for explosive conflict that's not even happening yet. As population is exploding, urbanization is exploding as well. The physical world in this area is simply too dry to support lots of folks. Most people have to be in the city, and there aren't enough resources or jobs in the city either.

Middle East governments usually to the right . . . but rarely in the right!

AND THEIR RULERS . . .

Let's compound the situation further, shall we, because it doesn't seem complicated enough. Let's look at some government types. What's a typical government type in the Middle East? Oh that's right! Theocracies, autocracies, monarchies, dictatorships . . . damn, all the rightist regime types are here! Power to the government! No power to the people!

Let's mix all these fun facts up in a bowl. Limited resources that are getting scarcer, undiversified economy, limited jobs becoming scarcer, way more people . . . top it all off with a nice layer of rightist regimes, which typically limit human rights and/or freedoms. Let's complicate it even further. Places like Saudi Arabia, that have a lot of money and see the explosion coming, are actually trying to appease their population by investing in education and welfare programs. But even that may be harmful.

What happens in a country like Saudi Arabia with a repressive regime and a bunch of people who are unemployed and highly educated? I got one . . . how about extremism and terrorism? Saudi Arabia is the true fighter of terrorism on the planet right now. We might be fighting a war on terrorism over there, but Saudi Arabia is the hardest working fighter of terrorism on the planet. No doubt in the Plaid Avenger's mind. Those guys are going to work every day, taking out suspected cells and blowing up stuff. There are lots of folks with nasty intentions in Saudi Arabia, mostly directed at their own government by the way, not America or any place else. Saudi Arabia is the hardest working antiterrorist group on the planet because of all those factors we just mixed together to make that big beautiful bomb-shaped cake. In the Saudi's antiterrorism league are also states like Egypt and Pakistan who have the same conditions that are ripe for extremist activity.

We can add in one more fun fact and that is, of course, foreign influence. We've already talked about foreign influence in history, but it doesn't seem like we've got enough going for this region yet to really, really and genuinely, piss people off. So let's bring in people from the other side of the planet, loaded to the teeth with guns. I don't know, but the Middle East doesn't seem like the vacation spot for the rich and famous right this second. But things may change. Wait a minute . . . no, I don't think so. Shit's only going to get worse, and probably fast.

DAMN, ARE WE DONE YET?

Yes. Well, for now. Of course, I haven't really even touched upon the hotbed of current conflict that defines this region. And this is conflict that while actually being played out within the region, has global repercussions that affect us all. The Israeli/Palestinain issue is a world issue. The US 'War on Terrorism' is a global phenomenon. The competition for the region's resources has planetary scope. That's why I decided to add a special section to this chapter just to tackle the thorny issues of exactly what forces are shaping and defining this region, and thus the world. It is an addendum of sorts . . . how quaint! An addendum! What supposedly scholarly book would be complete without an addendum?

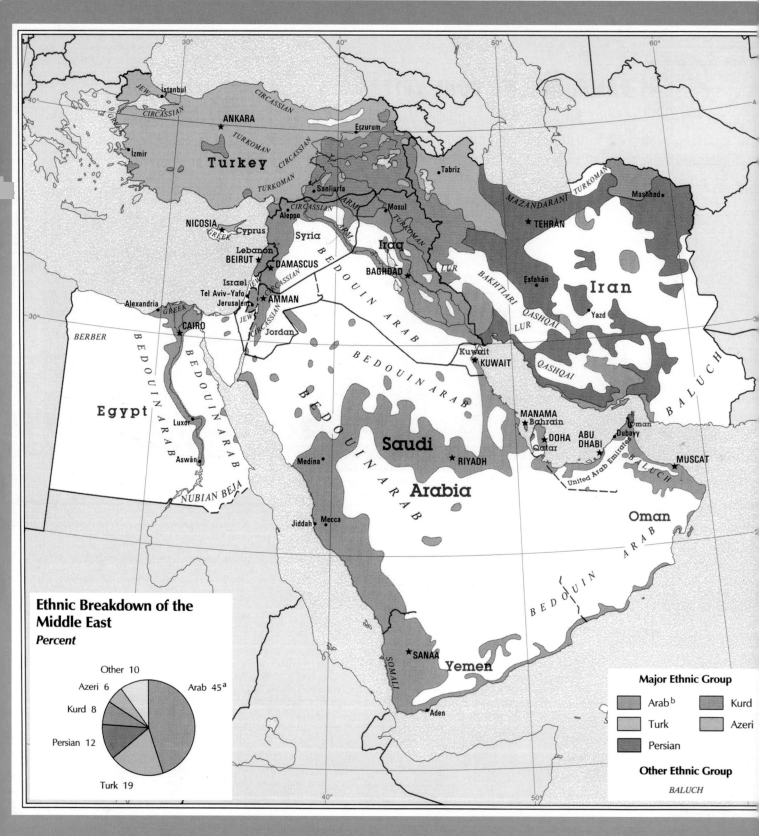

Ethnic Breakdown of the Middle East
Percent

Other 10
Azeri 6
Arab 45[a]
Kurd 8
Persian 12
Turk 19

Major Ethnic Group

- Arab[b]
- Turk
- Persian
- Kurd
- Azeri

Other Ethnic Group

BALUCH

CHAPTER OUTLINE

Addendum: The Competition for Control . . .

NOW for the last, and most complicated, component of understanding the Middle East mess in the modern context. Many (if not all) of the conflicts, trials, and tribulations that have been described so far in this chapter can be related to a much bigger competition that is occurring across this region . . . and that is a competition among big powers for influence, if not outright control, of the destiny of this troubled chunk of land.

This is a total Plaid Avenger assessment, and would be labeled by experts as completely unorthodox and overly-simplistic in its approach . . . which means it's probably exactly right! I admit right from the get-go that this approach does not do a thorough analysis of all the details and all of the complex inter-relationships that exists between these groups of folks; if you want to understand them better, then by all means use this text as a launching point for further research into this tangled web of geopolitical skullduggery. Wow! How often do you see the word skullduggery in a textbook? But I digress . . .

Here is what you need to know to know your Middle Eastern mess: there are many ethnic and religious and political differences among folks in this region which cause fractures and frictions . . . and almost all of these things are totally unrelated to input from the outside world. In other words, many players are vying for influence and control from within the Middle East itself . . . and moves from outside forces like the US, the EU, Russia, or even al-Queda simply accentuate/benefit/stymie the game being played internally. You dig what I'm saying so far?

Before you go any further, go back to the addendum opening page and examine the map for major ethnic distinctions within the Middle East, as they are the primary basis for the Team divisions.

The following is a list of distinct 'teams' that the Plaid Avenger feels are currently in this competition. Again, some of these teams are vying for influence, some are vying to control resources, some are vying to control major events, some are trying to outright control territory . . . and some are just trying to disrupt the other teams from winning. I will point out what makes each team distinct from the others, their motives, who they like, and who they hate. I will start with the easiest ones and continue to get further complicated as we go. You ready for this reality? Then let's do this:

TEAM TURK

Since we are starting with the easiest and least complicated, let me go ahead and reference the Turks. First and foremost this team's distinctive characteristic is its ethnicity . . . Turkey is full of Turks. Go figure. But Turks are not Arabs, nor Persians, nor 'Middle Easterners', whatever that means. The next chapter of this book deals with Turkey in much more detail, so I will keep it brief for now. As you will find out soon enough in the following pages, I do not count Turkey as a part of the Middle East region at all, so in a sense it's a bit of an outside entity itself . . .

Having said that, Turkey is in a very unique position to influence affairs in the Middle East in multiple ways. First, unlike any other outside entities, Turkey is overwhelmingly Muslim which makes them more culturally sensitive and sympathetic to all its Muslim Middle Eastern neighbors. But that is about where the similarities end.

Because unlike its regional neighbors to the south, Turkey is a staunchly secular society that maintains a strict separation between Islam and the state. Turkey is also a well-established democracy, is a founding member of the UN, is a founding member of NATO, is a possible future member of the EU, and has a well-established and strong, modern military. All those factors together make it much more western in outlook, and indeed Turkey is an ingrained part of most western institutions. Especially that NATO one: all operations in the Middle East utilize the Turkish corridor as an operating platform. Most NATO and UN operations in the region would be screwed without Turkish support. That gives Turkey a loud voice on all Middle Eastern matters.

That's why Team Turk is in a strong position to influence some Middle Eastern policies . . . especially ones that are advantageous to itself. Since the Turks are US/NATO allies, they typically work towards the goals agreed upon by those entities . . . to a point. Turkey openly refused to support the current US invasion of Iraq on the grounds that it could not be party to an illegal invasion of a fellow Muslim state. And recently, Turkey actually invaded Iraq itself to go after Kurdish terrorists, much to the chagrin of the US. That is important to note: Turkey has a large population of Kurds in its own territory, and thus has a vested interest in any/all Kurdish developments in the region. Stability of Iran and Iraq play prominently into the Kurd situation, and thus the Turkish response.

Other important considerations: Turkey controls the all-important headwaters to the Tigris and Euphrates river systems, which supply the critical resource to many countries to the south . . . meaning they have a very effective control measure should they ever decide to use it. Also, Turkey is hosting a summit between Israel and Syria here in summer 2008. This is a role that they will probably increasingly be playing: as mediator between other sparring Middle Eastern parties. Look for their role in any peace process to expand significantly in the future.

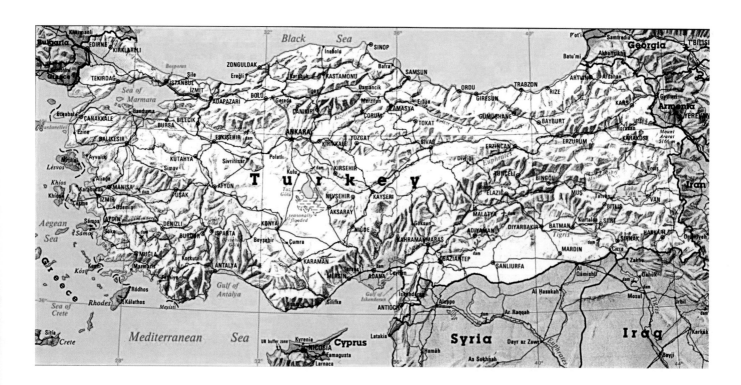

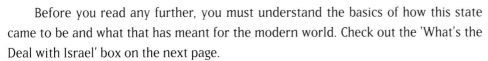 **TEAM HEBREW**

Onto the next team, and what a doozie this one has become! Team Hebrew consist of one state, and one state only, and it's the state that may be a central issue for tons of regional friction: Israel. Now I know what you may be thinking already: "What? How can this be the next easiest team to comprehend when it is the source of so much animosity and conflict?" Well, I'm glad you asked. While many folks believe the Israeli-Palestinian issue may be the source of all conflict across this region, their team's motives and motivations are actually quite easy to identify and understand.

Before you read any further, you must understand the basics of how this state came to be and what that has meant for the modern world. Check out the 'What's the Deal with Israel' box on the next page.

Okay, now that you are back, we can make some generalizations. All the neighboring Arab states have attacked Israel on multiple occasions ever since its inception, and Israel has pretty much won each of these wars . . . resulting in increased territory for Israel, and control of other areas that are not even part of the state. It also has resulted in the displacement of the ethnically Arab Palestinians, who are without a state of their own. Many of these Palestinian refugees are located in the surrounding Arab states. For these reasons and perhaps many others, Team Arab really hates Team Hebrew. Team Persia hates Team Hebrew too, even though they have never openly engaged each other militarily or otherwise.

But let's call out some other characteristic of Team Hebrew. Obviously, they are Jewish, and as such are the only non-Muslim actors within this region vying for influence and/or control. Team Hebrew is also a strong, secular, well-established democracy as well as a fully developed country with extremely high standards of level. Again, all of those factors make it quite unique within the Middle East region. Team Hebrew is indeed a fully 'western' country in every sense of the word when it comes to development, economic and political systems, and even religious and cultural values.

Most importantly, Israel also has high levels of technology, especially military technology, and is an undeclared nuclear power. That is crucial. Team Hebrew is the only entity in the Middle East that has nuclear weapons. They are an undeclared nuclear power because the US and others insist that they do not openly declare this fact . . . otherwise everyone in the neighborhood will want a nuclear weapon too, thus launching a regional arms race. And nobody wants that right now. Or ever.

Speaking of the US, it should also be evident to you that Team Hebrew is a staunch ally of the US, the EU, and all western institutions in general (with the possible exception of the UN, since UN members often give Israel the smackdown in that forum.) The inverse holds true as well: the US has supported Israel openly and covertly for decades. Israel is regularly the top recipient of US foreign aid, even though they are a rich country in their own right, and have a powerful and well-trained military. The US has regularly shared/sold weapons, weapons technology, and military intelligence with Israel as well. And, yes, you can go ahead and make the assumption that this relationship pisses off all the other teams in this regional competition.

So why would I suggest that the Team Hebrew motives are easy to explain? Because they are fairly well defined and there aren't that many of them. Their primary objective? Maintain their territorial integrity. Keep the boundaries of their 60 year old state in tact at all costs. Second objective: have national security . . . that is, to be secure in their state by not having terrorist attacks or open declarations of war against them. Third objective: get all other neighboring states to recognize their right to exist, which of course helps out with Objectives one and two.

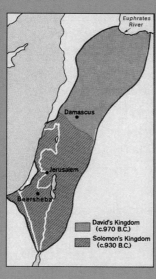

What the Hell Is the Deal with Israel?

Israel is the loaded topic of all loaded topics. There are so many emotions surrounding the formation and history of Israel, it is hard to be completely unbiased about the issue. If you lean too far in either direction, you can be quickly charged with anti-Semitism or, conversely, Zionism. But by the mercy of Elijah, here is the deal with Israel . . .

I won't get into biblical history too much, but will make mention of this: This area was the historic homeland of the Jews: 'The Promised Land' that Moses brought them to many millennium ago. Fast forward to the Roman Empire, who persecuted the Jews (one in particular you may have heard of: Jesus Christ) and eventually totally kicked them out of the area altogether in the second century AD. Since then, locals have been living there, hanging out for a couple thousand years.

The modern history of Israel begins around 1900, when Theodor Herzl (among others) began pressing for the creation of a national Jewish state—this movement became known as the Zionist movement. Jews began buying property in Palestine and forming small Jewish communities. In 1917, the British government issued the **Balfour Declaration,** which endorsed the establishment of a Jewish homeland in Palestine. Shortly after, Palestine became a *protectorate* of the British government (because of dismemberment of Ottoman Empire after WWI—see next chapter).

This caused a surge of Jewish immigration that continued until 1939, when the British government issued the **White Paper,** which limited (but did not stop) Jewish immigration to Palestine. This pissed off the Jewish community, who viewed the White Paper as a rejection of Zionism, and also pissed off the Arabs in Palestine, who wanted Jewish immigration to stop completely.

After World War II, when the horrors of the holocaust were revealed, there was a giant uprising of sympathy for Jews and for the Zionist movement in general. Simultaneously, Jewish armed forces in Palestine became more aggressively defensive of Jewish territory—attacking both British and Arab forces. The British decided that keeping Palestine as a protectorate was no longer in their interest, so they ceded control to the UN. The UN

That's it. That's all. Pretty easy to digest. Now I ain't saying its right or wrong, or good or bad, or that it will ever even happen. I'm just saying their objectives are pretty easy to identify and understand. All of Team Hebrew's foreign policies, international alliances, and strategic actions serve to accomplish one or more of those very simple objectives.

So Israel's occupation of the West Bank, of the Gaza Strip, and even areas within Syria referred to as the Golan Heights is maintained to achieve their national security goal. Israeli development of a strong military and nuclear weapons was done to ensure its existence by discouraging any more open attacks across its borders. Israel usually sides up with 'Team West' (particularly the US) when it serves their purposes to achieve those objectives. Usually, but not always. Because Israel sometimes goes against US foreign policy by negotiating with neighboring states (that the US hates) to achieve the 'recognition' goal. That is currently happening right now: Israel is meeting with Syria, much to the chagrin of the US, and for sure the issue of Syria recognizing Israel's right to exist is on the negotiating table. But we better get to the next, more complicated force affecting this region . . .

accelerated the development of a plan to partition Palestine into separate Jewish and Arab states. This formed the Jewish State of Israel, which was quickly recognized by the United States and eventually by most everyone else—but not any of the surrounding Arab countries. This established the 1947 UN partition borders (see map insert).

Violence erupted soon after the partition. Armies from Egypt, Syria, Jordan, Iraq, and Lebanon all clashed with Israeli forces. Jordan gained a foothold in the West Bank and Egypt gained a similar foothold in the Gaza Strip. This is important to note because these are still disputed areas today. A ceasefire was finally brokered in 1949—creating a new set of de-facto borders now known as the green line (see map insert).

Israel frequently spat with its Arab neighbors throughout the 1950s and 1960s. The culmination of this aggression was the 1967 Six-Day War, where Israel, using advanced weaponry from the US, went gangbusters and conquered the West Bank (including East Jerusalem), Gaza Strip, Sinai Peninsula, and Golan Heights (see map insert). Egypt and Syria were highly pissed about this, and attempted to regain their lost territory in the 1973 Yom Kippur War. This war was more of a stalemate—no territory changed hands. But, the Yom Kippur War was significant because the United States sided with Israel, pissing off EVERY Arab nation and inciting the 1973 oil embargo.

The next major shift in Israel's borders was peaceful. In 1979, President Jimmy Carter invited Egyptian leader Anwar Sadat and Israeli Prime Minister Menachem Begin to the United States and helped negotiate the Camp David Accords. This treaty returned the Sinai Peninsula to Egypt and granted more autonomy to Palestinians residing in occupied territory. Since 1979, most violence associated with Israel has been within its borders. The Palestinians living within Israeli territory have garnered significant international support for statehood. Recently, Israel has begun taking steps that seem to suggest that the formation of a sovereign Palestine is imminent. However, Israel is not prepared to cede the amount of territory that the Palestinians believe they deserve—and have even started construction of a wall encircling much of the disputed area in East Jerusalem.

TEAM ARAB

Now we are onto the real cultural anchor of the Middle East proper, and here's where it starts to get really messy. Team Arab refers to an ethnic group, just like Turks or Persians. However, this ethnic group happens to be the majority within the Middle East as an entire region, and many of the states/groups of this region are overwhelmingly Arab in descent. Maybe you've heard of Saudi **Arab**ia or the **Arab**ian Peninsula or perhaps even Aladdin and other tales of 'The **Arab**ian Nights'?

Before the advent of Islam, the Arabic ethnic group was centered in the Arabian peninsula, natch. Although the Arabs were originally primarily a nomadic people with an itinerant lifestyle centered around the use of the camel and an extensive network of desert oases,

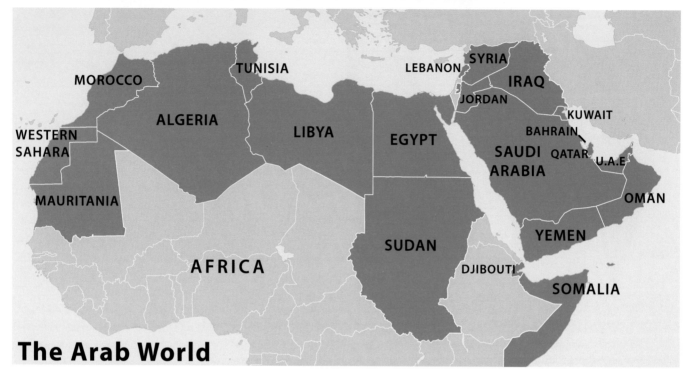

The Arab World

Arab world stretches far and wide, but their Arab League is shallow and useless.

there were a number of urban centers. These were mostly located in the western portion of the peninsula, al-Hijaz. Cities like Makka (Mecca) and Yathrib were important centers of commerce and trade and the former was also a crucial center for the pre-Islamic polytheistic religions were abounded. Muhammad himself was an important merchant in Makka and was well known in the region even before his religious undertakings began.

Within a century of Muhammad's death, the Arabs had expanded well into Sassanid Persia, pushed the Byzantine Eastern Empire out of the Levant, and were trading blows with Charles Martel in France. The expansion of Islam, except in the instances in which it came into contact with a resident imperial power, was overwhelmingly peaceful and local populations of Christians, Jews, and other random monotheistic religions willingly accepted their new rulers, as, especially in the case of the Byzantine Empire, Christian sects were persecuted terribly. Conversion was not enforced, but had concomitant economic benefits such as the relief from a poll-tax on non-Muslims, but this was not encouraged as it would rob the Arab polities of cold hard cash.

Politically, this "Arab Empire" was not terribly cohesive, especially with regard to the territories in Spain and northwest Africa. Eventually, after a couple of centuries, the core at Baghdad held only nominal sway over anything significantly placed away from it, but the religion itself had spread from France to the Oxus River. From there you can tie the story back into the 'end of the Golden Age of Islam' when Genghis Khan totally destroyed Bagdad thus effectively ending the Arab Empire reign. Then onto the rise of the Ottoman Empire which we have discussed above and will again in the next chapter: Team Arab essentially becomes just another component of the multi-ethnic empire that consolidates this region from about 1300 to 1923, when the last vestiges of the Ottomans are swept away and the modern map of the Middle East is drawn.

Of course, this new map of the Middle East is not a singular Arab entity . . . far from it. Of the new political boundaries drawn up after WWI, there are roughly 22 countries which are predominately Arab in ethnicity. How do I know that? Because in 1945 six of those countries formed an entity known as the **Arab League**, and membership has jumped to 22 in the intervening years. This League was formed to" . . . draw closer the relations between member States and co-ordinate collaboration between them, to safeguard their independence and sovereignty, and to consider in a general way the affairs and interests of the Arab countries."

Fellow monarchs discussing oil revenues.

In other words, the Arab states want to work together to achieve common Arab goals. In point of fact, at various points in the last sixty years, there have been several attempts to reunify their states under a pan-Arab banner. Let me go ahead and cut to the chase: it has never worked. The Arab League itself has to be considered a fairly dismal failure, as the member countries more often fight with each other than actually agree on any damn thing at all. They still get together once a year or so to discuss solutions to common issues like the Palestinian debacle, the Sudanese civil war, or the invasion of Iraq . . . but they never decide on anything nor do anything about it. I guess they at least have a nice all-you-can-eat hummus bar that keeps people coming back.

So that gets us up to now. Team Arab is still a potent force of influence in the region for various reasons.

1. Many Arab states are excessively rich off of oil production. With wealth comes power.

2. Arab culture is the incubator of Muslim culture (remember, Islam started in Saudi Arabia, where the two holiest cities of the religion are located.) That still counts for something on a planet where there are roughly a billion Muslims. Please note: Arabs are overwhelmingly of the Sunni division of Islam, in contrast to the Shia brand which is primarily found in Iran . . . more on that below.

3. Arab is the most populous ethnic group across the region, including such groups as the Saudis, the Egyptians, the Palestinians, the northern Sudanese, the Iraqis, the Lebanese, and the Algerians, just to name a few.

A few final points of analysis: Team Arab totally hates Team Hebrew, since the Palestinian debacle is now an Arab debacle. That hate has been softening for some Arab leaders though, as Egypt has officially recognized Israel and made peace with them, and Jordan might as well have, and Syria soon might. Ponder this: Egypt officially recognized Israel in 1979, and Egypt has been the #3 top recipient of US foreign aid every year since 1979. Hmmmm . . . coincidence?

The bigger issue that you might not now about is this: Team Arab also really hates Team Persia (Iran), and it is the competition between these two teams that has become the hottest current showdown. Team Arab is getting very wary of the growing power and influence of Iran within the region. And dig this: Team Arab is exceptionally worried about the possibility of Iran getting nuclear weapons . . . perhaps even more worried than Israel or the US! Team Arab will be working with the US and others to make sure that Team Persia does not get such weapons.

Speaking of which, the core of Team Arab lies in Saudi Arabia and Egypt . . . and as fate would have it, both countries are strong allies of the US (well, at least the leaders of the countries are.) You should know this fact well: the US generally supports Team Arab for various political (US hates Iran too) and economic reasons (they got tons of oil.) Got it all? Then let's get to that Iranian team now to see why they are so despised by the Arabs . . .

ANOTHER PLAID AVENGER INSIDE TIP: Virtually all Arabs are Muslims, but most Muslims in the world are not Arab. Does that make sense? Islam is a worldwide phenomenon now, and places like Indonesia actually have more followers of the faith than any single country in the Middle East. The reason this is confusing for outsiders is because Islam started in Arab lands, and the original and only true Koran is written in Arabic. So no matter where you go in the world, from Morocco to Malaysia, Muslims will be reading the Arabic Koran and praying in Arabic tongue . . . but that don't make them ethnically Arab. Of course, I'm so savvy that I can read Arabic numerals . . .

TEAM PERSIA

Onto the next, and final, of the major teams in our Middle East round-up. For this one we have to go back even further in time to tell their tale. Further back than the Ottoman Empire, further back than the Arab Empire, and, indeed, even further back than the advent of Islam itself. Team Persia's story goes back several thousand years, but we will just hit the high-lites here so that you can understand how very different and distinct this team is from all of its neighbors. Never heard of Persia? Well, in today's world we call it Iran . . . and while Iran is the core of this Team, there are other players on their side too. But let's start at the start.

Persia can track its origins back to 1500 BC when Aryan tribes (namely, the Medes and the Persians) settled the Iranian Plateau. Power goes back and forth between these groups until the Persians come out on top in 558 BC when Cyrus the Great beat out the competition and then went on to consolidate the peoples of the plateau and expand the empire outward into Lydia and Babylonia and eventually Egypt and beyond . . . making it the most powerful political entity of the time.

Later, Darius the Great tried and failed to incorporate the Greeks into the Persian fold . . . look up the epic Battle of Marathon as to how that went down. Also, go watch **The 300** to see an excellent, but not so terribly accurate, depiction of this Greek/Persian face-off period—Iran actually protested the release of the film as being racist and inflammatory.

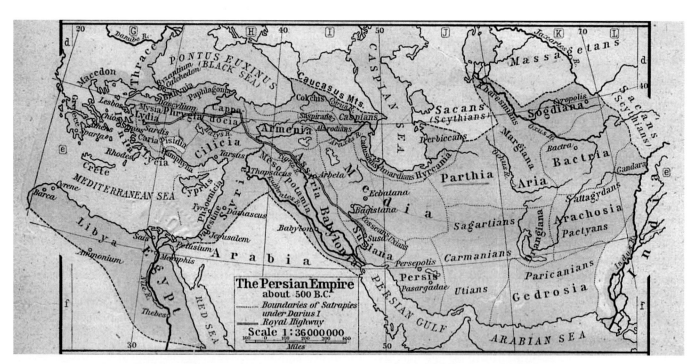

The 300 stopped them, and then Alexander whipped them.

Next name of note: Alexander the Great united the Greek city-states and led his famous campaign across Asia primarily to squash the power of the Persians for good; he was fairly successful in this endeavor, as Darius III was killed (and the empire with him) in 330 BC. While the entity lasted a bit longer off and on, it never regained its past power or glory. But Persians have a long, proud history that is still looked back upon with reverence and distinction. Thus, their ire at the negative depiction of their forefathers in **The 300**.

But let's now fast forward. The Arab/Muslim conquest of Persia in the 640's AD was to forever change their destiny. Not only did this convert the Persians to Islam, but it set the stage for the current Islamic sect differences that are still very much alive today. As referenced earlier in this text, after the death of Muhammad, the religion gets split into two main branches: Sunni and Shia.

Now, the liturgical and ritual differences between Sunnis and Shi'is, or Shi'ites are minimal and mostly unim-

Iran: the core of the Persian power, Shia power, and a whole lot more!

portant. The branching off of the Shi'a (literally, partisans) of Ali occurred when certain members of the early Islamic community disputed the line of succession following Muhammad's death. Most folks supported one of Muhammad's top men Abu Bakr, but others backed Ali, who was Muhammad's son-in-law. In this contest for power, Ali and then his son Husayn were killed and these early partisans were dispersed throughout the Islamic realms. The death of Husayn particularly became a focal point for the community, especially in modern times, with open manifestations of "passion plays" mourning him and his followers' deaths in the desert near present-day Karbala.

But what's all that ancient history got to do with modern day Iran? Just this: Iran became the haven for the supporters of Ali, and over time evolved into the core of Shia Islam. While Shia is the minority sect worldwide (world = 85% Sunni, 15% = Shia), it is the majority of followers in modern day Iran (Iran = 90% Shia, 10% Sunni) and that makes all the difference for our team competition.

Now let's make another jump forward. Persia was picked on and beat up on by Russia and Britain during the European powers' imperial battles for world control, however they always managed to maintain their independence and were never colonized. By 1906 they instituted a constitutional monarchy and by 1950 a dude named Reza Shah was on the throne and increasingly ruling with an autocratic iron fist. It should be noted that this dude came to power with the assistance of the US and the UK who had essentially deposed the prior leader (Dr. Mohammad Mossadegh) because he had nationalized the Iranian oil industry, much to the chagrin of western countries.

So foreign powers had to get involved in the Middle East to save their oil industries. . . . Hmmmm. . . . what is that old saying about history repeating itself? But this Shah guy is s little too over the top and pissed off too many Iranians, and the shit soon hits the fan. Or should I say Shiite hits the fan? Time for the Iranian Revolution! Check the box for details:

What's the Deal with . . . the Iranian Revolution?

Up until 1979, Shah Mohammad Reza Pahlavi was the constitutional monarch of Iran; he was happy exporting oil, quashing dissent, and resisting Soviet influence. The US and the Shah were the best of friends because he was basically a US puppet. He liked playing with big guns, and we liked supplying him with just such toys, just to make sure the Soviets wouldn't. But unfortunately for the United States, most people in Iran were very unhappy with the Shah. It seems that Iranians did not like living under a dictatorship.

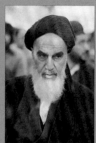

The Shah . . . and the Ayatollah.

Protests of the Shah's government began to occur, and the Shah ordered the military to shut them down. Hundreds of demonstrators, including students, were killed. This happened several times, and popular support against the Shah really took hold. So, a populist coalition of liberals, students, leftists, and Islamists escalated the protests to the point of revolution and ousted the Shah. We call this the 1979 Iranian Revolution or Islamic Revolution.

The primary political figure during the revolution was the Ayatollah Khomeini, a Muslim cleric who encouraged demonstrations against the US and Israel, whom he declared "enemies of Islam." In the following days, a group of young radical Muslim students took over the US Embassy and held 52 Americans hostage for 444 days.

The Ayatollah Khomeini was the most popular figure in Iran because of its strong Muslim background, but there was also a powerful secular movement. A power sharing system of government was attempted, but eventually Iran became a true Islamic Republic, with all of the power vested in the religious elite led by Ayatollah Khomeini. The United States became even more enraged, especially since it was unable to rescue the hostages, and cut all diplomatic ties with Iran.

To this day, there is no official US presence in Iran—no diplomats, no troops, no nothing. This is one of the reasons there is currently so much animosity between the United States and Iran. Many US leaders see Iran as a threat to Western stability in general, *especially* if they become a nuclear power. This is a critical issue in today's world, as Iran continues to be in the spotlight by developing nuclear technology—which they say will be used for peaceful purposes, but the West is convinced will be used to build a bomb. The rhetoric is running full steam on both sides right now.

Just know this: the US is all about shutting Iran down, either diplomatically or ultimately by force. The EU wants to shut them down, but only diplomatically. Russia is their ally, and wants to help them develop their nuke program for energy production, and China wants to do nothing about the Iranian situation because they are all about the sovereignty. So whatever goes down, don't look for it to be dealt with at the UN Security Council, which is already deadlocked before the process even begins.

And now we arrive at the present. The Iranian Revolution has been called the last great revolution of the 20th century, and for good reason. It is a grand experiment of Islamic theocracy with limited democratic elements, but it is in essence a blending of church and state into one big ruling system. It's really the first of its kind, and one of the reasons that other Middle Eastern countries are terrified of Iran is the fear that their revolution could spread . . . meaning that Iranian-style theocracy could sweep into Egypt or Jordan or Algeria and displace the systems/leaders that currently have the power. And no one wants to lose the power!

Now let's get to the meat and potatoes: Team Persia is a busy boy, and doing quite a bit to assert its power and influence across the Middle East . . . which severely pisses off Team Arab. These two teams HATE each other, and as I have alluded to earlier, are the biggest forces facing off within the region. This hate started in earnest when Saddam Hussein (with backing from other Arab states, the US, Russia, and Europe) invaded them, thus starting the decade long Iran-Iraq War which ended with about a million casualties. The hate between Arab and Persia exists to this day. Why so much hate? Dig this:

HATE number 1: As just mentioned, Team Persia has no problem exporting the ideals of its revolution to other places. Iran increasingly sees itself as the only true Islamic country of the region, the only real and true purveyor of the faith. It mocks the Arab countries for their morally corrupt leadership as well as for being stooges of US foreign policy. Iran is trying to assume a moral and ethical leadership role on issues like the Palestinian debacle, the existence of Israel, and any foreign intervention into Middle Eastern affairs.

Since Team Persia is the only fully Shia state, we have come to define Team Persia in this religious sense too . . . but they are not totally alone. I want you to be aware of a new entity that is named the **Shia Crescent**. It is based on a projection of Iranian influence and power to other Shia groups across the wider region . . . but please don't mistake this Persia/Arab animosity as a religious war of any sort. The Shia Crescent is simply a nice way to highlight areas that Team Persia has increasing influence in. Take a look at the map.

The map is showing you the percentages of Shia folks in selective states, and we should note a few

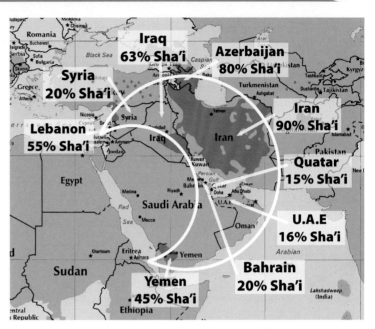

Shia Crescent: this ain't no Lucky Charm for the Arabs, or the US.

choice groups that make daily news and effect events. Iran is the core of this crescent, but its effective reach spans from the Persian Gulf countries all the way thru Iraq, which has a majority of Shia and is why Iran is helping fund and arm Shia militant groups in the current Iraq civil war. But the Shia vein also runs thru Syria: a country whose leadership belongs to a sub-sect of Shia, and therefore is malleable to Iranian Shia influences. To continue on the road, you get to southern Lebanon, where Shias also have a slight majority . . . and also where a radical Shia terrorist group named Hezbollah hangs out. Iran funnels money and guns thru Syria to Hezbollah to help them fight against Team Hebrew. You starting to get a sense of the Iranian deal here? Which brings us to . . .

"Israel? I do not recognize. Does not compute."

HATE number 2: Team Persia still openly utterly and completely hates Team Hebrew, and the current whack-ass, ultra-conservative President Ahmadinejad actually called for the destruction of Israel. Now, we've already pointed out that Team Arab hates Israel too, but some Arab leaders have recognized Israel, while still others have been softening their rhetoric about the Jewish state over the years. Meanwhile, Team Persia leaders have held the hardliner attitude of refusal to recognize, but also calling for its destruction. Hard core! That's why Iran supports Hezbollah, but it also supports Hamas down in the Gaza Strip . . . just to keep jabbing a sharp stick into the Israel flank at every available opportunity,

This also puts Iran in the position of appearing to be a true helper and defender of the Palestinians, reinforcing the idea that the Arabs are just a bunch of losers that can't look out after their own. And it makes them appear to be the only country in the region able and willing to stand up not only to Israel, but also to other outside forces . . . which brings us to the last . . .

HATE number 3: Team Persia is developing a nuclear industry. Now hold on! I didn't say nuclear weapon! But that is what all the other Teams think is going on. Iran has been pissing off its neighbors and world powers by its persistence in developing fuel to be able to develop a nuclear power industry, and this is the issue that is really causing the most consternation across the region. And outside the region as well. As of this writing, Iran has not broken any international law in its nuclear pursuit—it is not illegal to produce nuclear energy.

However, virtually all western nations (the US and the EU) have condemned the move harshly and are busy setting up international sanctions to stop the Iranians. For their part, Iran has claimed they have a god-given right for nuke energy, and nothing will stop them in their quest. Iran's open defiance sets them apart from all the other states in the region, and is seemingly a point of pride with Iranian leadership. Great. Like we needed another problem in this region.

And here's why it is a problem: Iran getting the tools to create a nuke bomb tips the balance of power in the region radically. No one else has the bomb (except of course Israel who won't admit it) and while most folks assume that Israel would be the country most frightened of a nuclear-armed Iran, in fact that's probably not quite true. Israel has the bomb too, making for an effective deterrent to ever be the target of an Iranian attack. Why would Iran nuke Israel, knowing that 100 nukes would be sent back in response? The folks who are really worried are Team Arab . . . 'cause they don't got no bomb! A nuke Iran would be stronger than any Arab country, and would contain the most powerful deterrent to prevent any attacks against their Persian motherland . . . including any attacks potentially from the US or others!

Sum up: Team Persia hates Team Arab. Team Persia hates Team Hebrew. Team Persia hates Team Foreigner. In return, all those teams hate Team Persia right back, and may be working with each other in order to stop any further rise of Persian power. You dig? So Arab states might work with the US and maybe even Israel to make sure the Persians get sidelined. Interesting shit. Or should I say interesting Shiite?

TEAM FOREIGNER

And now our job starts getting way easier. The major forces have now been outlined in perhaps too much detail, but we still have some other characters in this Middle Eastern drama that are powerful players affecting events. I don't have to spend as much time with these, because they are in the news on an hourly basis and if you don't know these cats yet, then you must be living under a rock. Team Foreigner consists of those states not actually from the region, but somehow find themselves here anyway.

With no reservation, the US in the primary outside entity that has dramatically altered events of the past decades. The US has supported kings, monarchs, dictators and dirtbags aplenty in its quest to influence events and resources in the Middle East that are of strategic interest . . . well, I guess all countries do that, but the US is the most powerful at this game. The Saudi royal family, the Shah of Iran, Saddam Hussein, and Hosni Mubarak all quickly spring to mind.

Foreigners love to party in the Middle East!

It also should be noted that Israel and Egypt are the number 1 and number 2 recipients of US foreign aid, and have been for decades . . . simultaneously, US companies have sold tens of billions of dollars worth of arms to Saudi Arabia. But the US is also a staunch ally and weapons supplier to Israel . . . damn! The weapons business must be good! Uncle Sam has now invaded Iraq not once but twice, and the US maintains a troop presence in multiple states of the region; a visible sign of its presence can be seen almost everywhere. The US led 'War on Terror' is actively engaged across the entire region (both overtly and covertly) to root out rebel/terrorist groups whose ideology conflicts with the US world view. And of course there are diplomatic interjections too: the US is typically the sponsor of most Israeli/Palestinian peace talks; the US is leading the trade embargo against Iran; the US is a builder of democracy in Iraq (well, at least they are trying.) The list could go on . . .

Special Envoy Blair . . . oh, Tony, you are always special in my book!

But of course they are not totally alone. The US does have its 'Coalition of the Willing' in Iraq which includes its typical lapdogs, the UK and Australia, along with 49 other countries. The UN is of course intimately involved in trying to help stem the tide of conflict in the region . . . albeit with not much results. And now there is something called the Quartet on the Middle East: a foursome of entities collectively working together to mediate the peace process in the Israeli-Palestinian conflict. The Quartet consists of the US, Russia, the EU, and the UN, and former UK Prime Minister Tony Blair is the group's current Special Envoy. Go get'em Tony!

Let's cut to the chase on this Team Foreigner. Team Persia hates 'em, especially the US. In return, Team Foreigner really hates Team Persia, especially the US. Did you know that the US and Iran don't like each other? Well, now you do. The US typically supports and sides up with Team Arab on a whole host of issues . . . but mostly on the hating Iran one. Unfortunately, the US position with Arab states gets extremely complicated because of course it is best friends with Team Hebrew. Let's rank the Teams in order of how much the US likes them:

1. Team Hebrew comes out on top

2. Team Turk is close behind (remember, they are a NATO member!)

3. Team Arab is supported by US on some issues, but not all

4. Team Persia comes dead last. And perhaps that's exactly how the US wants it right now. Dead. Last.

Starting to make sense? I doubt it. But let me add in one last complicating clause of this foreign influence. While many Arab state leaders support the US, and vice-versa, most people in those Arab states are increasingly pissed about US presence and their leaders support of US policies. This is making the water even hotter for a lot of these folks, as they become increasingly unpopular with their own people. One need only point out that Osama bin Laden's original mission was to drive the US out of the Saudi holy land . . . and not accomplishing that, he then turned to start attacking the Saudi government themselves for being corrupt stooges of the US. And the Saudis ain't alone, as there are other groups within the region expressing their displeasure in any number of violent ways . . . which brings us to. . . .

ADDITIONAL NON-STATE ACTORS

And now for the last. I won't go into great detail on these groups, but I did want you to be aware that there are other entities that are affecting the flow of events within the region . . . much smaller entities that are not states or governments. Therefore, these groups do not behave like states or governments, cannot be coerced the same way as states or governments, and cannot be effectively attacked or punished like states or governments can. That makes them very sticky entities indeed, and they are often thorns in the sides of the bigger Teams we have already talked about. But, they can also be used as tools by the big Teams to attack or influence one another as well . . . hmmmm . . . tricky, tricky, sticky, sticky.

I know that terrorists groups are probably the first things that come to mind, but there is actually a much bigger and more important one to tackle first: the Kurds. The Kurds are an ethnic group (check back to map on opening page again) that are located in the mountainous areas of Iran, Iraq, Turky and Syria. They are a nation of folks without a state . . . and they very much would like to have one. For over a century, the Kurds have dreamt of and petitioned big powers to have a Kurdistan country of their own. But they have been used, abused and betrayed by virtually every regional and world power in this quest. The Kurds are seemingly a damned bunch of people. And I mean damned in terms of doomed.

They have been sporadically beaten down by the governments of all the states that they occupy, mostly because no government wants to see a free Kurdistan. That would entail the loss of some of their own territory, and therefore no one is going for it. Team Turkey, Team Persia as well as components of Team Arab (mainly Syria and Iraq) actively work against any Kurd movement toward independence. You may remember that Saddam Hussein used biological weapons on these folks multiple times to keep them in their place. You may not have known that Turkey has also been fairly oppressive in keeping the Turkish Kurds down.

I bring up Team Turk in particular because they just invaded Iraq in February 2008, much to the ire of the US who is trying desperately to keep a lid on the Iraq mess. Why did the Turks go in? To root out a radical pro-independence Kurdish terrorist group named the PKK that has been responsible for multiple attacks within Turkey proper. Just so you can see how convoluted alliances can become in the Middle East, Team Turk is actually getting help from Team Persia in this effort, while the normally pro-Turk US is trying to stymie the effort. Geez! How confusing!

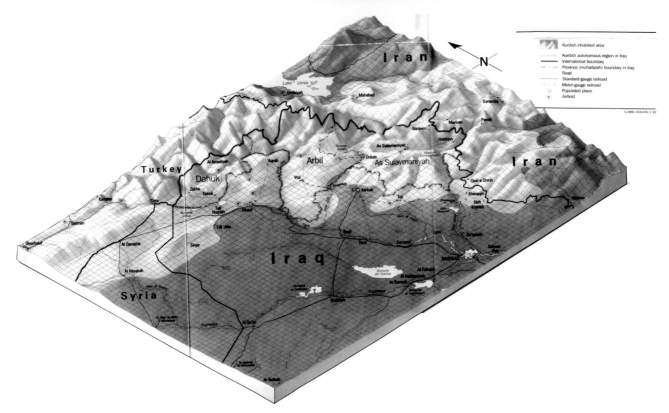

Kurdish folks hiding up in the hills . . .

Other even smaller groups of note are political parties/rebel groups/terrorists groups. Yeah, that's a mouthful. And I don't mean political party or rebel group . . . I mean political party AND rebel group. Entities like the Shia group Hezbollah in southern Lebanon, Hamas in the Gaza Strip, or various groups across the Middle East referred to as the Muslim Brotherhood all fit this description. What do I mean? Well, they are all political parties that actually put up candidates to run for office in all the countries they are located in . . . however, all of them also have militant wings of their party that actively go out and do violent shit. Violent shit like suicide bombings, rocket launches into populated areas, or open armed warfare against other entities or states.

Why would anybody vote for a political party that did shit like that? Mostly because in the areas where they are located, they are seen as actually fighting for the people as opposed to the ineffective and corrupt governments that are in charge. In both Gaza and southern Lebanon, the political party sides of Hamas and Hezbollah (respectively) build schools, run hospitals and soup kitchens, and generally protect the citizens, which seems like a pretty good thing. That seems like the types of things that the government is supposed to do, but is failing at. In such circumstances, the locals vote for those political parties . . . and why wouldn't they? An example: Hamas actually swept the Palestinian elections a couple of years ago because the alternative party, Fatah, was largely seen as corrupt, ineffective, and lackeys of western powers.

But wait a minute! We have a problem here! Because these same parties have those militant wings which do violent things . . . and as such are labeled as terrorist groups by Israel, the US, and the EU. And you know what happens to terrorists groups. They get embargoed, stone-walled, and cut down. So all the Western powers don't like these groups and try to shut them out of the political process, causing ever more conflict. Even though Hamas was democratically elected,

Part of the Non-State Actor Action Faction.

they were not recognized by the West, and all of the Gaza Strip was punished for their support of the group. It is a messy business indeed.

Some of these groups are simple to understand though. Al-Queda just is a terrorist group, with no aspirations for political participation. Hezbollah is kind a close to being in that category too, as they are mostly a tool of Iran just to cause trouble with Israel. And varying groups named Muslim Brotherhood can go either way: there is an Egyptian Brotherhood, a Jordanian Brotherhood, and a Syrian Brotherhood, et al. Many of the Brotherhoods have been banned from political participation in total, mostly because they are proponents of bringing Islam into the political process . . . meaning that they might want to eventually change the government structure to be more in line with the Iranian model, or with Islamic law, etc. And none of those Arab governments want that to happen, so they just label them as terrorists groups and ban them from politics, if not make their existence completely illegal altogether. Some of these groups have in turn resorted to the terrorist track . . . cause what the hell else are they gonna do after they have been banned from participating?

All these non-state players have the potential to cause varying degrees of trouble for the major powers, It all depends on who they decide to side up with to achieve their own objectives. And it appears that that can change on a daily basis.

CONCLUSION

So what you see from this Team breakdown is that we have had a series of empires which has controlled the Middle East at different times . . . first the Persians, then the Arab/Islamic, and finally the Ottoman Turk. While all of them are now Islamic, each of these three empires has resulted in a distinctly unique strong team—that are radically different from each other, with distinct ethnic character and political affiliations—that is vying for influence across the wider region.

Again, the three main Islamic historic entities still present in today's world are the Persians (now Iran), the Ottoman Turks (now Turkey), and the Arab/Islamic (now 20 indiviual Arab states with Saudi Arabia and Egypt as the core). These main three have been recently been joined by Team Hebrew (Israel), Team Foreigner (the US, EU, et al), and various other non-state actors like Team Kurd and smaller political party/terrorist groups. In the end, they are all fighting for their own agendas to either control territories within the region, control governments in the region, control resources in the region, or control the direction of the region as a whole.

Whew. That's it. What a freakin' mess. Let's get the hell out of this chapter now . . .

Black Sea

iARIA

Istanbul

İzmir

Ankara

T U R K E Y

Nicosia

GEORGIA
Tbilisi

CAUCASUS MTS

ARMENIA AZ
Yerevan

Aleppo

SYRIA

CHAPTER OUTLINE

Turkey

TURKEY IS A:

(a) Country

(b) State

(c) Nation

(d) Nation-state

(e) Region

(f) All of the above

F you! I mean, it's F to you. Turkey is like Japan and Russia in that it is a sovereign state in its own right with enough distinctions about it to set it apart from all of the places nearby, which makes it a Plaid Avenger world region. So what is the deal with Turkey? What's going on here? Why is it different enough to be apart from the Middle East—the region it has classically been associated with? Anybody from the Middle East and particularly from Turkey itself would say, "No way! We don't have anything in common with each other!" But here in the West, we just see Turkey and the Middle East as kind of a common whole. That is all changing, though. There is a lot about Turkey historically, presently, and in the future, that distinguishes it 100 percent from all other Middle Eastern countries. Does that mean it's more like Europe? Nope, it's quite distinct from Europe as well. A lot of people in Europe want to distance themselves from Turkey, but meanwhile, some want to embrace it. Turkey is in kind of a strange place in the world right now in that it has its own thing going on while at the same time it's acting as a bridge between two cultures and regions. And that's the Plaid Avenger keyword for Turkey: **the Bridge.**

As we discussed in the Middle Eastern region, there are lots of different ethnic groups in what is collectively referred to as the Middle East, and one of those is Turkic. Turkic is also a distinct linguistic group. Where are the Turkic people? Oddly enough, many people say, "Oh of course it's Turkey; they've always been in Turkey." Well, no, not necessarily. In modern day Turkey, they refer to themselves ethnically and linguistically as Turkic or Turks, however, this group is originally from Central Asia. They have not been in charge of what is now the present state of Turkey for very

Plaid Turkish Delight

1   oz Wild Turkey bourbon whiskey

1   oz sloe gin

1   oz apricot brandy

2   oz pineapple juice

3   oz 7-Up soda

Shake all ingredients (except soda) and strain into an ice-filled pina colada glass. Add 7-Up soda, garnish with fruit slices, add straws and serve. Like the wild turkey sez: Gobble, Gobble!

long in history, maybe only about 800 years. The folks who would become the Turks came from Central Asia, across what is now Iran, through Iraq, and into modern day Turkey about 1000 years ago. After a couple hundred years, they took over, their culture took hold, and they made it their own. Perhaps we get ahead of ourselves, but that's what makes them distinct . . . number one: a different ethnicity and linguistic group from all the surrounding countries. But the Plaid Avenger is calling it **the bridge.** Why and how is Turkey so different from every place around it?

Turkey is more western than virtually every other Middle Eastern country in terms of economic development. At the same time, they are not

Islamic people, but not Islamic state.

as Western as European countries. This is the first of many things that pitches Turkey out as kind of a "no-man's land," somewhere in the middle. They have a capitalist system that is fully integrated into world economic dynamics. Nobody would disagree with that. They are the strongest fully established, democratic Muslim country.

That's important enough to pause and restate: democratic, fully Muslim country. Perhaps the main reason why they are typically classified as Middle Eastern is their single commonality, which is Islam. Turkey's population is almost 100 percent Islamic. However, it is *not* an **Islamic state,** and that makes all the difference. Turkey has religious ties to its Middle Eastern brothers, but all other aspects of their society, like democracy and capitalism, make them very European. This duality reinforces the idea that Turkey is a bridge. Before we get to a more cultural background, let's talk Turkey physically.

PHYSICALLY . . .

It's pretty easy since Turkey is a single country. If we were to compare Turkey to the US, and overlay it with latitude consistent, we see that it stretches from the nation's capital here in the United States to Kansas City, Missouri. It's about the same latitude, and covers West Virginia, Virginia, parts of North Carolina, Tennessee, Kentucky, Indiana, Illinois, and parts of Missouri. It's a decently sized country. Given that its latitude is roughly the same as the states I just mentioned, Turkey has a pretty similar climate. It is humid continental with some humid subtropical in the southern parts. However, given that it borders the Mediterranean Sea, we know it must have some Mediterranean climate. Indeed, it does around its coastal fringes. Turkey has four distinguishable seasons, just like we get here in this part of our country.

The only other major physical factor to consider is that the terrain is quite different from here in the eastern United States. Turkey, as a whole, is a pretty mountainous country. It has an uplifted plateau in the middle, with some high mountains, particularly on its eastern borders, where you can find Mt. Ararat (16,000+ ft.) as you go into the Caucasus Mountains. Even over in the western part, the elevated plateau is on average over 6000 feet elevation.

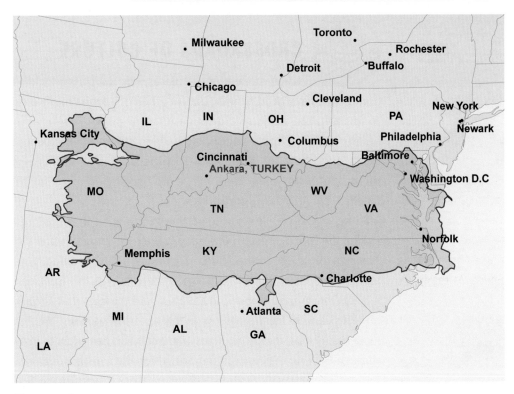

Size comparison

This is kind of an **escarpment,** as we talked about in South America and will again in sub-Saharan Africa. There are not a lot of coastal plains or flat areas in Turkey, so as soon as you get off of those nice, sunny Mediterranean shores, the terrain and the elevation make it quite a bit cooler, quite a bit faster. As you get to the far eastern side of Turkey, there can be fairly tough winters. It does have some Mediterranean and Black Sea frontage, which moderates things a bit, but it still is a fairly cooler place than eastern North America at similar latitudes.

Turkey is such a mountainous country because it is on the border of several different tectonic plates. It is at the confluence of the Eurasian, African, and Arabian plates, very much like we had several plates coming together in Japan. As with all geologically active mountain-building scenarios, it's an active earthquake region. Just in the last five or six years, Turkey has had some serious earthquakes, having tremendous impact in terms of human lives and property damage. That about wraps up the physical traits of Turkey, so let's get back to the cultural. Why is Turkey "the Bridge," or a crossroads of culture?

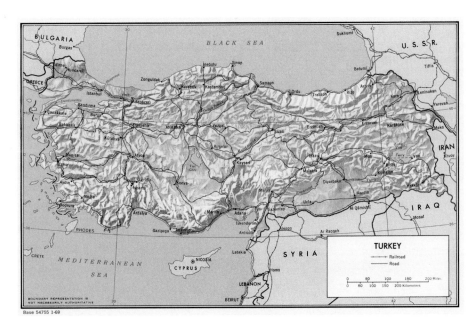

Assyria

Babylonians

Persians

Macedonians

CROSSROADS OF CULTURE

Turkey is one of those places, like the classic Middle East, where people have been hanging out for a hell of a long time. We can go way back to 1000 BCE to the Assyrians, a tough band of dudes. We've heard all the names before, and the Plaid Avenger isn't going to get into them too much. I want you to understand how the **Anatolian peninsula** has been a crossroads of culture throughout history. The Babylonians are hanging out here in control until around 1000 BCE, the Assyrians shortly after that.

So we've had people hanging out here for a good long time, people who became kind of the core of Western Civilization. The core cultural hearth for Western Civilization is here in the classic Middle East and Turkey. Eventually, the Persians come along. The Persian ethnic group, whose descendents live in modern day Iran, had a mighty empire around 500–600 BCE. These are the guys that Alexander the Great and all of his ilk were fighting against. In this historical situation, the Persians sweep from modern day Iran, their core, across the Anatolian peninsula to invade Europe proper through Greece. Turkey was the bridge for the Persians coming from the east to invade Europe in the west. As a result of that, Alexander the Great and his Greek buddies invade back. You may see reference to the Greeks calling this area **Asia Minor.** To combat the Persians, Turkey becomes the bridge of invasion for Alexander's forces out of Greece. They sweep over, kick the shit out of the Persians, and establish a European empire all the way into India, making use of Turkey as a crossroads for this. And we're not finished yet!

The Greeks are of course going to get beaten by the Romans, whose empire comes to include the Anatolian peninsula. To spare you the long blow-by-blow history of the Roman Empire, eventually, the Romans decide they need to establish a secondary capital in the East, as the Empire was expanding. The main capital stays in Rome of course, but the eastern, secondary capital is formed in Constantinople, where the Turkish city of Istanbul is today. After the disintegration of the Roman Empire, the eastern section of the empire becomes known as the **Byzantine Empire.** You've probably heard of the Anatolian peninsula referred to as "**Byzantium**" in ancient texts. This occurs between 300–500 CE.

Again, the Plaid is reinforcing that this is a crossroads. We've had the east coming from one direction, and the west coming back from the other. Turkey is always the central pivot point of these

The Greeks and Romans did their Turkish tours too . . .

movements. Not only was the Anatolian Peninsula the stage for the political division that results in the Byzantine Empire, it is the stage for a division of religion as well. We know it as the **Great Schism,** the split between the Catholic Church and the Eastern Orthodox Church in 1054. The Eastern Orthodox Church sets up camp, still in the Byzantine Empire, and spreads Eastern Orthodoxy into Russia, the Middle East, and Eastern Europe. We of course know the Catholic story, which is centered in Rome and spreads to most of the rest of Europe proper. But our story's still not finished!

Orthodox Byzantine boys in black getting their chant on.

We're taking it up to the time of Mohammad, peace be with him. Born in 570 CE, not in Turkey, but down in the Saudi-Arabian peninsula in the holy city of Mecca, where Allah used him as the vehicle for the creation of the Koran. This is where the religion that we now know as Islam started.

Where did it go? It diffused outward from the Arabian Peninsula to lots of places: Africa, Central Asia, South Asia, and also Turkey. A reversal takes place in the Byzantine Empire. Eastern Orthodox central is displaced on the Anatolian Peninsula because of the expansion of Islam from the east. In addition, the Turkic peoples from Central Asia have come into the area during this whole movement of Islam to settle into the Anatolian Peninsula, making this **the bridge** between Eastern and Western cultures and religions once again. This is a happening place, man, everything's been going on in Turkey! But it's not even Turkey yet!

ENTER, THE OTTOMANS

How'd it get to be Turkey? Well there's one more group we haven't talked about yet: **the Ottomans.** After the Turkic ethnic and linguistic group takes over what is now Turkey, they build a big empire: the Ottoman Empire. Starting in roughly 1300 CE, the little core that was only around Constantinople grows in all directions over the course of the next 400 years, to the point that they take over virtually the entire Mediterranean coast of Africa and much of the classic Middle East including the Arabian Peninsula and what is modern day Iraq. The Ottomans expand into the Tigris and Euphrates river valley, Mesopotamia, where the Babylonians once were.

So these Ottoman dudes take over the Black Sea area and even invade Europe proper; they're on a roll. This event perhaps impacts today's world the most: the introduction of Islam deep into European territory via the Ottoman Empire. This is primarily Eastern Europe, modern day Yugoslavia, Albania, Romania, Bulgaria, and Greece. The Ottomans, a predominately Islamic empire, controlled all of this territory. At the height

Romans

Byzantines

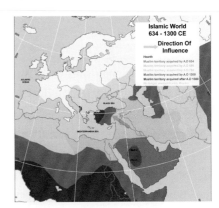
The growth of the Arab-Islamic Empire sets the stage for the Turks . . .

Ottomans

Turkey: Home base for Ottoman spread.

of their empire, they were knocking on the doors of Vienna. They even attempted to take Austria a few times. That's what we consider Western Europe now! They nearly conquered it several times, but never quite succeeded. Nevertheless, that gives you an idea of how far they penetrated into the continent, taking their culture, particularly their religious culture, with them.

This ties back to why we talked about southeastern Europe in particular being a trouble spot in today's world because of the infusion of so many different reli-

Side note: The Ottomans are the guys that brought coffee to Europe, via their face-off with the Austrians at Vienna. Ever heard of Viennese coffee? The brewing and consumption of coffee were passed across the battle lines during protracted wars over the centuries. We often think of the Austrians and Italians as coffee connoisseurs, but that shit all got introduced via our Turkish friends. And ever had Turkish coffee? Wow! It will knock your socks off man!

gions, ethnicities, languages, and groups of people. This is part of it, part of the same story. So Turkey is the bridge, the platform for the movement of people from Europe to the Middle East, but just as importantly, from the Middle East to Europe. Religion typically seems to be the sticking point for a lot of this; an issue that we see cropping up even in the modern era as Turkey tries to join the EU. More on that later.

FORMATION OF THE MODERN STATE

As you have guessed by now, the Ottomans didn't last forever. Though they were large and in charge and had an expanding empire from about 1300 to 1700 CE, from 1700 onwards, they go into a steady state of decline. Why happened? It has a lot to do with stuff we've already talked about, but to put it simply, these guys got behind the times. In the Middle

Sultans simply scoffed at backwoods Euro-trash.

Ages, they were superior to the Europeans in terms of technology, army, and firepower. They had the finest universities in all of Europe and the Middle East. All great centers of learning, the oldest colleges, as well as all scientific revolution and innovation during the Middle Ages, were happening in Ottoman-Turk territory. They eventually got a little insulated, headstrong, and arrogant, and saw the Europeans as a kind of backward race that they needn't mess around with that much.

On top of that, think about how they got so rich. What did they produce? Were they a big colonial empire producing and trading goods, building an economy? Nope. They largely obtained their wealth and sustained themselves by continually pillaging for **booty.** The Plaid Avenger is all about pillaging the booty. But in this context it means that through conquest of war, you take valuable stuff, like gold and other riches, from other places. That's okay for a while, but it eventually leads to a lack of economic infrastructure. A booty economy, unfortunately, can't stand on its own two feet in the long run. If the only way you get rich is just by taking stuff, when you get to the point that you can't take stuff anymore, you go broke.

Indeed, this is part of the reason for the collapse of the Ottoman Empire. They became **economically stagnant,** meaning they're not producing anything and they're not doing anything. This causes the Ottomans to get behind economically and technologically. While they're sitting around, stagnating, the Europeans are in full bloom: first the Renaissance, followed by colonialism and industrialization. The Ottomans on the other hand are starting to fall down just as the Europeans are starting to stand up, and those Euros stand up *big time.* This comes to a kind of ultimate conclusion right around 1900. This is an empire that's been around now for a good 600 years, and they've actually had an unbroken line of sultans. But that's about to change.

A **sultanate** is a monarchy, a royal imperial line of centralized power. That's the other thing that has been disintegrating through most of Europe at this time: monarchies themselves, and all centralized power structures. The Ottomans don't have a whole lot going for them at this point. Things are going downhill; there's internal dissent because the economy is not in good shape, and they're losing territories to the expanding Europeans. They have already lost Greece due to internal revolts and rebellions all across the Balkan Peninsula. By 1909, Abdul Hamid becomes the last of the unbroken line of Ottoman Sultans. The people had enough and said "We've got to change! This sucks!" Again, a very common theme we have talked about in other parts of the world, "We have to get rid of this guy! This system's not working, so let's get rid of HIM!" They depose the Sultan, but they're still on shaky ground.

In another part of this tale, which I haven't incorporated yet, the Russians and the Ottomans have had several wars. There has always been animosity between the Russians and the Ottomans. The Russians were always trying to expand out to get more shore frontage on the Black Sea, on the Mediterranean Sea, anywhere they could get so that they could build their naval superiority—and the Ottoman-Turkish territory was always a good target. The Russians were always trying to interject power into Ottoman territory. The Europeans, at the exact same time, were always trying to counter Russian influence in Ottoman territory. So this is another component of why Turkey becomes the bridge; it became a battleground for the competing powers of the Europeans and the Russians.

So after the Ottomans depose the sultan, they try to form something close to a democracy, or a republic as it were, and try to copy the European model. But they are very young, and very weak economically. So they're looking around saying, "Hey, who can we ally with? We're getting so weak that Russia could probably beat us. . . . Somebody be our buddy! Somebody sign a pact with us saying you'll come help us if Russia invades. Anybody! How about you guys in the UK, will you sign a pact? France? Spain? Italy? Germany? Come on, somebody help us out here!" At this point, the Ottomans are looked upon as kind of a redheaded stepchild of Europe. They're physically close to Europe. They dealt with European politics when they invaded Austria. It's not as if they're unknown; it's not as if they're a foreign territory that nobody knows about, but nobody wants to deal with them . . . because they kind of sucked.

German leader Wilhelm II helped out the Ottomans alright . . . helped them out of an empire!

The British and the French think, "Well, these guys are kind of losers. What are we supposed to do with these guys? We don't want to ally with them. We don't want to go to war with the Russians just for these guys. We don't want the Russians to win, but we don't want to engage them in open battle either, so we're just going to hedge our bets." Nobody wanted to deal with the Ottomans. However, Germany under Wilhelm I, knowing full well that it's about to start World War I says, "Hey, we'll help you poor bastards out! We'll be your buddy, because we don't like the Russians either. *We'll* be allies with you." So in 1914, they set up an alliance with Germany. Then Germany goes to war with everybody, and ultimately loses . . . Long story short: Oops! Bad alliance!

The Ottomans, having not chosen wisely, are basically dismantled at the end of World War I. In 1919, at the conclusion of World War I, something happens that the Plaid Avenger refers to as **The Peace to End All Peace.** It's actually a book title you should check out sometime; it's really sweet, even if a bit dry and a lot long. It explains a lot about why there's not peace in the Middle East right now and perhaps why there never ever never ever will be. What is the Plaid Avenger referring to? It's got to do with a bad job hacking up the turkey . . . and it wasn't even Thanksgiving Day.

CARVING UP THE TURKEY

The European powers that were victorious in World War I not only carved up Germany's Prussian Empire, but also carved up the Ottoman Empire. The way they carved it set up the political, ethnic, linguistic, and religious differences that still perpetuate conflict today. In other words, they take a map of Ottoman territory and say, "Okay, here's this section. You guys go to Greece. Let's call this chunk over here Romania. Oops, I spilled my coffee there. Let's just call that coffee stain Jordan. This over here, Iraq." Almost all the modern day boundaries in this entire area are drawn in part or whole during this redistribution or reallocation of land after World War I. What's left over is Turkey, and this is where we get the country of Turkey today. It always was the central core area of the Ottoman Empire, the piece where the actual ethnic Turks were located. Turkey has remained stable to this day partly because it was primarily Turk, made up of Turkic people. All the other boundaries sucked because in many cases the Europeans drew them arbitrarily, with no consideration of the cultures within the newly drawn borders. On top of that, a lot of the new states were given to European powers, which were to supervise

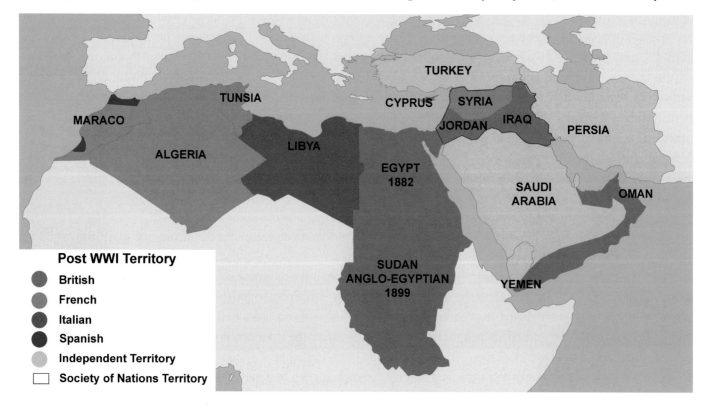

them as a "big brother." For example, the French became the "big brother" of Syria. The British became the 'big brother' to Egypt and the Sudan. These new "baby brother" states were called **mandates.**

See, all these European powers were still really into the colonialism thing, and the end of the war spelled more territory and more influence and more resources for them to control. I do need to point out one resource in particular that was just being discovered in parts of the Middle East during this period: oil. And even though oil was not as central to the world economy in 1919 as it is today, these Europeans knew it was worth a lot and therefore they wanted to control it. Ever wonder why one of the world's biggest oil companies, BP (British Petroleum), is from a country that has no oil? Check again at the mandate map above. Hmmmm . . . the UK had mandates on Jordan, Iraq . . . what a shock.

Anyway, the mandate system effectively meant that political control still rested with the European powers occupying these Middle Eastern lands even after the Ottomans went away. This is part of the problem with today's world, but we'll talk about that more when we get to the Middle East. That's "the peace to end all peace" in 1919. Essentially, these countries were carved up in such a way as to ensure perpetual conflict, which of course is precisely what has happened in the greater Middle East. But Turkey has actually held together quite nicely since the war . . . how?

AWESOME ATATURK

Another politically noteworthy event happens in 1919. This guy named Mustafa Kemal leads a resistance to the allies' plan to carve up Turkey. As the Ottoman Empire was carved up, a lot of folks wanted to carve Turkey up even more. They said, "If we don't completely eliminate them, they'll be a future threat, so let's chop 'em up!" But many Turks in the ever-dwindling territory decided to fight back against this total elimination plan, and one such man was a total bad ass known as Kemal.

Mustafa Kemal was an army officer and an ardent, fervent, nationalist. He was a big pro-Turkey guy who loved and believed in his country. He became very popular leading this resistance, and because of his movements with his brotherhood in the military, they stymied European efforts to carve them up further. He immediately sets himself up as kind of a national hero, and he eventually becomes a hell of a lot more. He continues with this struggle to regain full control of Turkey away from the allied European powers, and basically in 1923 succeeds at this task. That's a red-letter date to remember; 1923 is the foundation of the modern republic of Turkey by Mustafa Kemal.

After Mustafa declared the modern republic, he helps get what the Plaid Avenger refers to as the "Meiji Restoration of Turkey" rolling. What am I talking about? From 1924 to 1934, under the guidance of the main man Mustafa, Turkey completely transforms itself, not unlike Japan, from a primarily agriculture-based economy into what is now a more modernized and industrialized country. He pulls it completely into the modern framework of things, using the European model. He does a bunch, so I'll just fire it off for you. He revamps the entire government. The Ottoman Empire was a monarchy until that government was disbanded after World War I. Mustafa reinvents it, not even as a constitutional monarchy, but as a democratic republic. Period. He was elected in short order and set about revamping the country.

Under his influence, Turkey establishes a parliamentary system and laws modeled after those of Europe. The

What's the Deal with . . . Ataturk?
The power, the prestige, and the honor accorded to Mustafa Kemal Ataturk cannot be undervalued in Turkey of 1923, nor of Turkey in 2007. He is the man. He is the top man. He is the George Washington of Turkey, the father of the country, the baddest-ass badass, a military and political genius. He transformed an entire country from crap to THE SHIT in impressively short order. That's one of the reasons he was beloved. He was then, and he is today. He's the father of Turkey in the sense that he helped hold it together at its very formation, but even more so because he put it on the path of modernization.

Ataturk embraced the West even in style . . . snappy dresser!

Turks start building roads, and schools introducing Western-style education across the entire country, and modernizing their architecture. They redo energy production and transmission, telephone lines, communications. You name it, they did it. In ten short years, they really catch up. Now is Turkey a completely modernized, completely rich country like the rest of Europe? No, but it's pretty far down that path, and this is due to Mustafa and the movements that happened during his leadership.

Perhaps what sets Turkey apart from the rest of the Middle East the most is that Mustafa made it a staunchly **secular** state. Staunchly! Mustafa said, "*In this country, we're of Turkic ethnicity, we are of Islamic religion, but we will not be a religious state.*" I can't stress this enough. There is a separation of church and state at the outset. The government is the government, the church is the church, and the two will never mix. The United States may also have the separation of church and state, but it's more staunchly defended in Turkey than it is in the United States. That's a Plaid Avenger fact.

Mustafa went so far as to outlaw religious dress in public buildings, a law that still holds today. In fact, there was a court case in Turkey last year in which an Islamic woman wanted to wear her headscarf, and they say in Turkey, "Wear headscarves! Wear a full burqa if you want! You're just not walking into a government building with it on. Period." You cannot wear religious garb into the Grand National Assembly, the Turkish equivalent of Congress. YOU CAN NOT DO IT. If you even have a cross on a chain around your neck, that's got to come off too. That is the ultimate separation of church and state. We're going to see how that has propelled Turkey along its path and made it extremely different from the Middle Eastern countries in its neighborhood as this story progresses. That is a huge deal. The Plaid Avenger can't stress it enough.

Turkey is a proud NATO member!

TODAY'S TURKEY

But enough of ancient history, let's get caught up to the present. While Turkey was still doing its restoration—and getting along pretty good but not quite as far along as Western European nations—World War II breaks out. Turkey stays mostly neutral, but are actually chomping at the bit to fight. "Yeah, we want to get in! The Germans screwed us during World War I, so we want to come help you beat the shit out of them this time!" However, the Allies, including the United States at this time, thought it would be more problematic than helpful for Turkey to join the war. The US, UK, and France are all like, "Okay, thanks, but just hold on, we don't really need you right now. Just sit tight and don't side up with the Germans. We'll make sure nothing bad happens to you." Most of the war plays out like this, but in February 1945, when it was evident that the Germans had lost World War II, the Turks said, "We declare war on Germany too!" In a funny historical circumstance, they get to come to the victory party after the Germans are defeated. Since Turkey declared itself an ally, on the side of the good and righteous, it is a charter member of what becomes the UN after World War II.

They join the UN as a founding member in 1945. Something even more interesting is that in 1952, Turkey joins NATO, the *North Atlantic* Treaty Organization. Now we all know how much Atlantic territory Turkey has, but if you had to pick one single event that really makes Turkey different from all its neighbors, joining NATO is it. In one fell swoop, they embed themselves firmly in the Western camp. From this point forward, on the books, Turkey is a US ally. This becomes of particular consequence as we get into today's world, because there are NATO bases in Turkey.

Why is that important, Plaid Avenger? A lot of US operations into Iraq and Central Asia were made possible by bases in Turkey. When the United States fought the first Gulf War against Saddam Hussein, most of the planes carrying the bombs took off from Turkey. Joining NATO is the critical juncture, as I see it. Turkey says, "We're throwing in our lot, and we're throwing it in with the West. Yes we're Islamic like our Eastern neighbors, but politically, we're more like our Western neighbors."

MAJOR MILITARY

Being a NATO member requires that you have a strong and updated military in order to be a true member of the club, and Turkey does fulfill its duties in every respect. But that is not the only reason that the Turks have a strong military tradition, as well as having strong nationalistic pride of their professional soldiers. There's so much more, and it still plays in today's worlds . . .

See, during Ataturk's reign, he knew the only way to hold the state together and keep it from being dominated by the Europeans was to have an effective military deterrent. He therefore immediately modernized his military up the world standards. However, Ataturk had other motivations for a strong centralized force: to ensure the separation of church and state in his staunchly secular new republic. Maintaining the secular state is one of the primary roles of the Turkish military, and one that has seen the most action . . .

In 1960, 1971, and again in 1980, the Turkish military staged coups and took over the government. Now, from a Western perspective, we'd say, "Ooh, that's not very democratic. That doesn't look good." Most people would consider that a sign of an up-and-coming fascist military dictatorship. In Turkey's case, those

Don't mess!

people would be wrong. That is why Turkey is incredibly unique. The military has been strong since Mustafa "The Main Man" Ataturk, and it is seen as the staunch protector of secularism in Turkey. Every time there has been a military coup in Turkey, it has either been because the government has been excessively corrupt, or there's been an impending threat that religious folks are going to take over the government. In both cases, the military interjects and says, "Nope, our allegiance is to the state first." Therefore, you can't even really consider it a military dictatorship because there is no singular dictator in any of these circumstances.

The military says, "Our first role is to protect the state and the state's constitution, and that says we're going to be secular, and that's the way it is." In each of these coups, the military comes in, wipes the slate clean, and says, "Okay, do it over." I'm telling you this story because the military in Turkey is still seen by the Turkish people in a largely positive light. Turkey's pro-military stance is a sticking point for Turkey's membership into the EU. The EU feels that Turkey's military is too strong, a little too excessive for European taste . . . which brings us to the next current conundrum for our Turkish friends . . .

EU IRRITATIONS

A big issue today is the EU entry we just talked about, which started over 50 years ago, but in real earnest for over 20 years now. In 1987, Turkey started seriously talking about entering the EU. Again, they are a UN member; they're a NATO member; they're right next door to Europe; they're closing in on fully developed status. Twenty years ago, Turkey said, "Hey, that EU shit looks pretty cool. We'd like to be a part of that, looks good. We're your NATO buddy; we've helped fight

Turkey in the EU? Ah . . . promises, promises . . .

the Cold War with you. Let us in." This brings up a very important point. They were a US and European ally all during WWII and the Cold War, so Turkey very rightfully says, "Hey, we're your boy; we're your ally. We're here to help out! Haven't we been helping out for 50 damn years? Let us in the EU!" There has always been a little bit of foot dragging by the Western European countries to allow that to happen.

First, the EU told Turkey that their economy wasn't liberalized enough, so Turkey opened it up and diversified it too. Then the EU told them they weren't rich enough, so they diversified the economy. Then Turkey was accused of human rights abuses against the Kurds, so they passed laws against discrimination and calmed the Kurd situation down for a decade. Then the EU said that their military was too strong, and that was problematic for a true democracy, so the Turks divested the military of some of its constitutional power. Now the EU is saying talks are stalled until Turkey allows unfettered port access to the Turkic parts of Cyprus . . . nevermind that the Greek parts of Cyprus do not have to reciprocate this situation. Geez! Is this sounding like a round-around or what?

Plaid Avenger as Interpreter:

What the EU Says:
"Oh we're kind of worried that Turkey's not rich enough, not democratic enough, that they have issues persecuting their Kurdish minority, that they don't have enough human rights, that they have some human rights abuses."

What the EU Really Means:
"We're really worried about you guys being Muslims!" The Western European take on this, in the Plaid Avenger's opinion, is that they are worried about admitting an Islamic country. Yes, Turkey has a secular government, but it's nearly 100 percent Islamic, and all Westernized states are having problems with radical Muslims in the world right this second. They are all worried about people moving freely between an Islamic country and the rest of Europe. "If we let Turkey in the EU, then that means that anybody who gets into Turkey, who for instance is a radical extremist Muslim that wants to blow up European stuff, can come from Turkey and get anywhere they want to in the EU." Valid point.

What Turkey Says:
"We're working on all that; we've made great strides. We have settled a lot of disputes with the Kurds. We've given them autonomy and given them some rights. We're doing what we can, and yes, we are staunchly secular and we're going to remain that way. We're proud of our military and we're going to try and keep it strong, but we're willing to concede."

What Turkey Really Means:
"Hey you bunch of Christian whiteys, get off your damn high horse and let us into the Union. It's not the Christian Union, so quit jerking us around. We've been here helping you guys out as a staunch NATO member for 50 years. Just because we're not Christian, don't hold that against us. Please let us into the CU, I mean EU." It's largely seen by Turkey as a Christian-Muslim issue, so they know the real deal.

Nick is all for a Turkish Club Med . . .

What's the real deal with this EU inspired nonsense? I'm afraid it's outright cultural racism, for lack of a better phrase. A lot of Europeans are simply not comfortable having an Islamic member of their Christian country club. Remember back in the Western Europe chapter when I told you about the cultural friction developing in Europe? This is apparently part of the same story.

The Turkish population is actually starting to get fed up with the entire mess too. Public opinion used to be fairly high supporting their EU membership bid, but it has dropped steadily for several years now. Maybe 75% of the Turks were all for EU entry a decade ago, but it more like less than 25% today. I can't say that I blame them either. Turkey has sat on the sidelines and watched as state after state in what used to be the Iron Curtain territory get accepted into the EU, while the Turks continue to get put off. And insulted . . .

Most recently, Nicolas Sarkozy of France suggested that Turkey should become the foundation cornerstone of a 'Mediterranean Union,' comprised of states from North Africa, southern Europe, and the Middle East. In other words, Turkey should just start a different club, since they are not going to get into the EU club. I think you can probably figure out how that idea was received in Turkey.

KURDISH KONFLICT

To continue on with our current events in Turkey, I've just referred to one of the previous sticking points for EU entry: human rights, particularly for folks in eastern Turkey. What are we talking about here? The Kurds. The Kurds are not Turks; the Kurds are an ethnic group of people that we've referenced before in the Middle East chapter who have no state. They are a nation of people without, though they would like to have, a state. They are a nation of people who have been *promised* a state several different times in European and world history. But they never got it. It's an ethnic group of people located largely in the mountains of eastern Turkey, in Iran, in northern Iraq, and even in Syria. You may have heard of these guys because the US actually had a no-fly zone in northern Iraq to protect the Kurds from Saddam Hussein who actively mustard gassed them on several occasions.

Turkey's track record with the Kurds is somewhat sketchy, and here's where I'll have to piss off some of my Turkish friends. While they are kind of a modern state and

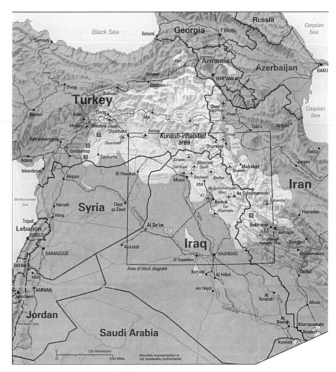

Kurdistan: a nation without a state.

there's a lot going on that's really good, the long track record with the Kurds is somewhat negative in that they have not been given equal rights. There's been an active campaign of discrimination (may sound a little strong but it's not too far off) over the last several decades. There have been so many human rights violations that a countermovement has arisen within **Kurdistan,** as the Kurdish areas are sometimes known. The **Kurdistan Workers' Party,** or PKK, is a radical group that has spearheaded this countermovement, unfortunately by using violence.

This is an extremist group that is actually considered a terrorist organization by Turkey, the US and the EU. They have had a campaign since the 1970s of blowing up Turkish stuff and Turkish people in order to fight for their rights, with an ultimate goal of gaining independent territory and national autonomy. This has been a main sticking point for Turkey as I've already referred to earlier, in that the European Union says, "You guys are picking on those Kurds too much . . . that's not good." At the same time, Turkey is saying, "Hey wait a minute! These guys are terrorists, just like you guys are dealing with terrorists!"

So this was a big sticking point for the Turks for decades, but it actually had begun to settle out in the last 6 or 7 years. The Turkish military captured Abdullah Öcalan in 1999, who was the head of the PKK and made plans for his execution . . . but in an obvious show that they were trying to be conciliatory to the EU, they said, "Okay, we won't kill him. We'll keep him alive in jail and even though he's a terrorist, we're not going to kill him." He's still in a Turkish jail today, probably wishing he were dead.

Since Öcalan's arrest, the conflict had died down, the number of terrorist attacks had diminished, and the Turkish parliament had passed lots of laws to try to equalize human rights and give these guys a little more power. Things in Turkey

Kurdish refugees

had been getting much better for the Kurds . . . but then that damn pesky American invasion of Iraq stirred the pot again. Apparently the PKK regrouped in northern Iraq and has carried out several attacks on Turkish soil in the last couple of years. And this has led to renewed trouble for everyone here in 2008.

Remember I told you that Turkey has a strong and proud military? Well, the Turks got pissed at these PKK attacks, and decided to act. Much to the displeasure of the United States, Turkey has conducted several bombing raids and now even has mobilized ground troops to go into Iraq and destroy the PKK forces. The US is not happy, mostly because the northern part of Iraq is the only damn peaceful part of the country right now, and no one wants to see more people with more guns getting into this mess. But those Turks are not sitting still for the fight, and future movements are probably inevitable. Keep an eye on that one my friends.

TURKS TRANSITIONED

Another big reason that Turkey deserves to be teased out as an independent region from its Middle Eastern neighbors or even its Eastern European neighbors is the situation of its people and its economy.

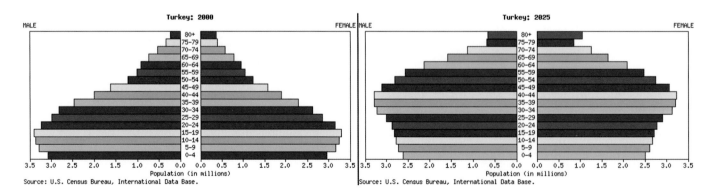

Let's look at the peeps. As you can see from the population pyramid here, Turkey, even just 30 years ago, was considered developing because of its explosive population. But wow, look how much has changed in the last 30 years. Their pyramid has basically rounded out, tapered off, and as you can project ahead by 2025, will become completely stable and even slightly shrinking. It would be exactly what we would consider a fully developed nation. Its population is pretty stabilized, and getting even better.

And the cash? Economically speaking, they're not the richest place in the world. They're not even rich by Eastern European standards. However, they're doing pretty well. They have a diversified economy—10 percent of an agricultural sector, and 30 or 40 percent of what we'd call an industrialized sector, which isn't too bad. It has an almost 60 percent service sector, and that's the type of thing we say, "Hey, that looks like the economy of a developed country." Indeed it does. It's yet another example that they are quite different from all the places around them, just for their modern situation if nothing else. They still are kind of on track to become part of the EU. As we've already suggested, the EU is running out of excuses to resist their admittance. The final assault of paperwork to become a full fledged member is supposed to be processed by 2015. This development and almost imminent EU membership puts Turkey in the catbird seat to expand economically. With no reservations, I say that from just about any measure you want to examine, Turkey will certainly be considered a fully developed country within the next decade or two.

Let's end this modern assessment with the strife over secularism. While you now understand that the secular nature of Turkey is what sets it apart from its Middle East neighbors, I should warn you that this status is being heavily debated in the society still. The country is almost exactly 50/50 split on the extreme nature of their secularism. The more western, urban populations favor the staunch separation of Islam from politics, but the rural populations are much more conservative in thought and perhaps want to change things a bit to incorporate religion into the state a bit more.

You know what? It's about exactly how the US is right now too . . . think about it. Red states with big rural populations vote Republican; blue states with big urban centers generally vote Democrat . . . an almost even 50/50 split in the last several

Turkish President Abdullah Gul: perhaps not so secular.

elections. Republicans would vote for school prayer, Democrats for getting rid of a nativity scene in a government building. That about exactly outlines the Turkish situation too, only with Islam instead of Christianity. Damn, am I good or what?

Prime Minister Recep Erdogan also accused of not being secular enough.

Back to Turkey: the current President and Prime Minister are from a political party that is more conservative, and more religious. Many folks from the other big political party are staunch secularists, and distrust the President greatly, fearing that he and his party are changing laws and possibly even amending the constitution to allow for more religious stuff in the government. Some opposition leaders have recently called for the President and Prime Minister to be fired and their entire political party to be banned on constitutional grounds that they are threatening the Republic's very existence. As absurd as that sounds, the case has been cleared to be heard by the Supreme Court. This is serious shit. Serious enough for the head generals to issue some veiled threats to government leaders to watch their asses . . . a house cleaning may be in order if the pendulum starts to swing too far away from the secular roots of the nation.

FINISH UP YOUR PLATE OF TURKEY . . .

If Turkey gets in the EU, which still seems likely at this point, their economy will grow. They will become even more incorporated as a member of Europe. They will perhaps become even more incorporated as a Western ally in this new war on terrorism in the Middle East. They will be distancing themselves from all of the radical elements that people in the West are frightened of in the Middle East, which will be to their great benefit. The Plaid Avenger is not making fun of anybody in the Middle East. I'm just saying what's going to happen to Turkey if they get into the EU.

If they *don't* get into the EU, things are going to swing the exact opposite way, and that's what's so fascinating about Turkey's position in the world today. They really are in the catbird seat, as the Plaid has mentioned several times now. If they go the EU route, they will become more Western, there's no doubt. If the EU turns their back on Turkey, Turkey is independent enough and economically strong enough, and it's certainly militarily strong and competent enough that it will say, "Fine. The hell with the CU (Christian Union). We'll C U later!" They will turn right around and become a leader within the Middle East. There's no doubt in the Plaid Avenger's mind.

That does not mean Turkey's government will become Islamic, but it will turn around and become a regional leader in the opposite direction. If it turns its back on Europe and embraces the Middle East, it would become, instantaneously, one of the wealthiest countries in the region. It would easily be one of the most diversified economic countries, and probably the one with the most ties to different parts of the world—and one that is not reliant on a single commodity for its wealth, like so many countries nearby are dependent on oil. That gives Turkey a lot more power. So **the bridge** of Turkey is actually strengthening. The Turks are gaining more power in today's world because they are becoming what the Plaid Avenger calls a **pivotal historic player.**

THE PLAYER

How are they a player? Turkey is a player because they've got two different directions they can. Just like we've talked about with Russia already—they can go China, they can go Europe. Turkey can go Europe, Turkey can go Middle East. They're already a strong NATO member, but they actually refused to help the US movement in Iraq. This actually came as a great surprise to the United States. The US said, "Hey, NATO member since 1952! Turkey, you're our boy! Sweet! We're going to launch our Iraq invasion from your soil!" And Turkey said, "No way in hell. It's not going to happen. We don't like Saddam either, but those are Islamic people about to get bombed. We don't support this war. You're not going to bomb people from our soil. It's not going to happen." What was the direct result of this? The challenge of, dare I say, *smacking down* the world's military and economic superpower's request? What were the repercussions? What happened? Jack shit nothing is what happened.

Turkey is *that* strong now; it is a pivotal historic player on the world stage, and we know that because nothing happened to them. The US even threatened to cut off international aid saying, "You're going to do what we want or we're not going to give you money anymore!" and Turkey said, "Fine. Don't." Colin Powell was really pissed off about that, and nothing happened. The threat of pulling aid was all smoke and mirrors; the US was powerless and it knew it. In fact, the exact same scenario played again when Turkey sent troops into

Erdogan: in a powerful position.

northern Iraq to get the PKK in 2008. The US begged them not to do it, but Turkey went ahead anyway, and the US was forced to support their old ally even though they weren't happy about it.

Turkey: the other, other, other white meat.

Add to that a strong sense of nationalistic pride, a strong and independent military, a strong and functioning democracy, and strong political leaders, and you have one hell of a world region. We'll have to watch them quite closely to see which other regions they end up becoming a major power in. It could be one, it could be several . . . because **the bridge** Turkey is strengthening, is a pivotal power player, is a region of its own with balls of its own.

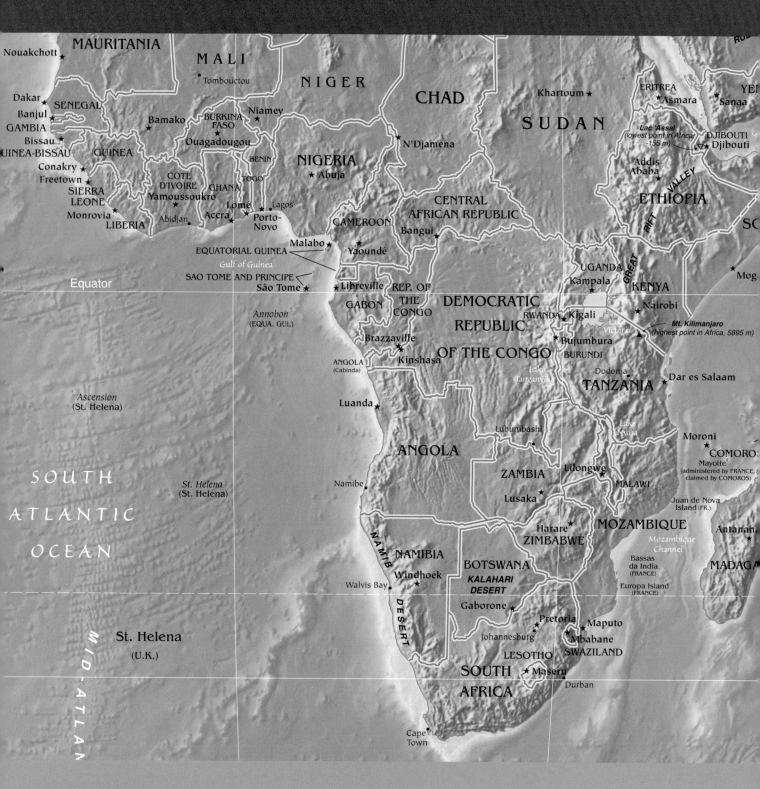

CHAPTER OUTLINE

Sub-Saharan Africa

20

SO let's move south from the Middle East into sub-Saharan Africa, what the Plaid Avenger could perhaps call the "Basket Case Region of the World." Does that sound too harsh? Am I too cruel? I don't think so. By really any measure, any standard to which we compare human life on this planet, the states of sub-Saharan Africa fall to the bottom of the list. What am I talking about? Things like life expectancy (some sub-Saharan African countries give you 29, 30, 31 years till you die), some of the lowest literacy rates in the world, some of the highest infant mortality rates in the world, and pretty much the lowest GDP figures you can find anywhere on the planet. Many people are living on less than a buck a day here. Really by all accounts, and not just those defined by the West, sub-Saharan Africa seems to fall in last place in the world race at this juncture in history. Why is that? Why is this the face of Africa? Let's find out.

Why this?

GIRAFFE HAIR

Africa is the second largest continent on the planet, dominated only by Asia the monster continent. This is a really big place that has a lot going on. Any place that has a lot of size comes with a lot of good stuff. Not only do you have really large tracts of land, those tracts of land have huge mineral resources of all different varieties. Crazy things like uranium, which is hardly used on the continent. Africa also has lots of diamonds, as you probably already know, copper, manganese, all kinds of mineral resources. There are some tremendous patches of oil, though not widespread. Overall, there are a whole lot of resources. But wait a minute! This isn't explaining why sub-Saharan Africa is poor. Hang on! We'll get to the poor part in a bit. So this part is a really huge place, so huge in fact that a lot of the regions we have talked about would fit easily inside the continent of Africa.

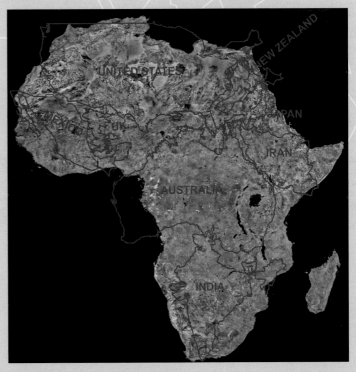

A big ass place.

What about some of the physical features of Africa? Some of us think, much as we did in South America, that this is a tropical place . . . and oh yeah, the Sahara Desert is in the middle of it. It's the largest hot desert on the planet and takes up most of the northern tier of Africa. And indeed, like South America, there is a huge tropical jungle in the middle part of Africa. It straddles the Equator, but not where many people think. Some think it's near the Sahara, but it's actually down below the bump of Africa and goes through the Democratic Republic of Congo as you can see on the map.

So there is tropical forest in this area near the Equator, which blends into tropical savannah both to the north and south. This savannah area comes to mind when most of us think about Africa, about the wild animals like cheetahs, elephants, and The Lion King and all that other crap people get happy about when they watch Disney movies. This is the commonly portrayed climate and vegetation of Africa: tall grass, and a few scattered animals and trees. And that's not all!

A pattern emerges as you move away from the tropical jungle areas near the equator. You jump into the savannah areas if you go north or south, and if you go north or south of that, you get into steppe. North or south of that gets you into desert. It's like there's a mirror at the equator. Things get more complicated on top of that! We have some full-on midlatitude climates like in the mideastern United States as well as Mediterranean climates near the south part of Africa and on the coasts. Because of some highland areas in Africa, there are also some places that are a bit cooler.

There are no major mountain chains in Africa to speak of. Africa is kind of an anomaly in the world in that it's pretty much the only continent in this world without a major mountain chain on it. It has *some* relief, but not a lot. Most mountain chains across the planet are the product of two tectonic plates getting together to bump and grind. In Africa, we have the opposite. There is no tectonic lovemaking going on here. The Arabian plate is moving away from the African plate, creating

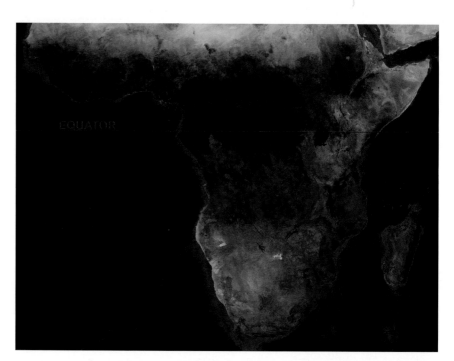

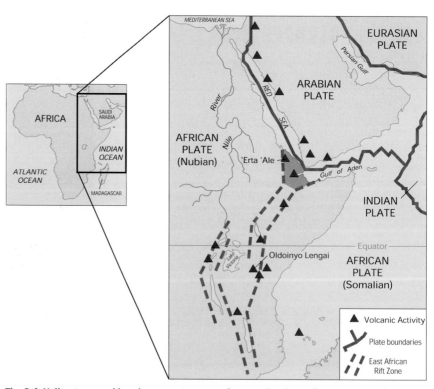

The Rift Valley is caused by plates moving away from each other. Africa is growing!

Africa's main physical feature, **The Great Rift Valley.** It is on Africa's eastern flank, splitting Ethiopia in half and going down into Kenya and Tanzania. The rift actually goes right through the middle of the Red Sea, expanding it. There are still some bad feelings bubbling up, in the form of lava. And when you have volcanic activity on the surface, it can make mountains. So there are one or two major mountains in Africa though there aren't any major mountain *chains*. Africa's getting back out on the scene with some new "assets" to attract another plate. Kilimanjaro is one of those assets, and it's pretty big at an elevation of around 19,000 feet. But there are no major mountain chains to speak of, no major dividing lines in Africa's interior.

However, like South America, Africa has escarpments, or big jumps of elevation right off the coast. This makes the interior continent of Africa as a whole hard to penetrate via water. It's actually worse than South America. The Congo River basin is the only serious channel through which to penetrate the continent and it's in the full-on tropical jungle zone, which makes it tougher to get into for various reasons. So as you can see, Africa is difficult to penetrate, much like South America, due to the escarpments all around the perimeter, and the serious vegetation and tropical rainforest in the river basins.

Again, let me stress the size of Africa. From north to south, it's about five thousand miles. From east to west, it's about five thousand miles. The sheer size of Africa even compounds movement across and within the continent. There are also other physical barriers like the Sahara Desert, which separates north from south quite nicely. For how long? Forever. The desert is one of the reasons why we split sub-Saharan Africa from the rest of Africa. It's such a big divider, the Plaid Avenger named the region after it. Countries in the Sahara Desert are already included in the Middle East for obvious reasons, like climate, Islamic influence, oil, and conflict.

Sub-Sahara, everything underneath the desert, is a totally different region. We don't have to look much further climate-wise because it's not predominantly desert. Religion-wise, there are some Islamic people sub-Sahara, but it's mostly a Christian area. When we look in the northern part of Africa, we see people of Arab descent. In the South, people are distinctly black African. We are drawing fuzzy lines between these two regions because the lines go right through the middle of some of the countries. This is significant when we think about current events in Africa. These fuzzy lines are bisecting Nigeria and Sudan, a couple of countries with big problems. The northern parts of these coun-

tries are predominantly Arab and/or Islamic while the southern parts are predominantly black and Christian. This has caused friction that will play out into the 21st century. The stories in progress here are far from over, as Sudan is in the middle of a civil war and Nigeria is not far off.

LAGGING BEHIND

Why is sub-Saharan Africa in such dire straits? Before the Plaid goes further, this is an awesome place to visit. Let me bookend this chapter by making sure you understand that I personally like the place. Africa is great. I think it has the most potential of any region today. It hasn't suffered the ravages of industrialization and modern warfare that the rest of the planet has. That may yet serve to benefit Africa . . . but not anytime soon. They are way far behind right now. But it's not over for them yet. History has a way of reversing itself through change, and Africa is a prime

Africa: 'The Dark Continent.' In more ways than one . . .

candidate for reversal. But let's face the facts. Right now, Africa is really hurting.

Why is it hurting so badly? Why is sub-Saharan Africa so poor? When I say poor, I mean the bottom of the barrel. We've looked at South America and its great wealth disparity in which there are few people that are rich and a ton of people that aren't. You can't even say that in Africa because even the rich people just ain't that rich. The wealth disparities are actually lower here because there are hardly any millionaires or billionaires hanging out in Africa. That level of wealth isn't concentrated within any class of people in Africa. How did it get to this point? Didn't I open this section by saying it's physically rich in land and resources and a lot of other things?

The operative term to think of here is "**marginalized.**" Marginalized is a term that I oft apply to sub-Sahara Africa. If you're like, "Hey what does marginalized mean?" I ask you, where is the margin of this page that you are looking at right now? Of course, the margin is on the edge, on the fringe. What do you do on the edge of a piece of paper or a page of a book? Not a damn thing. Nothing important, anyway. Maybe you scribble in the margin, write notes, doodle, or make love notes that say, "I heart the Plaid Avenger." You can do all this in the margin, but it doesn't equate to anything. To marginalize something, somebody, or a whole region, you just push it off to the edge and don't really trouble yourself too much with it, if at all.

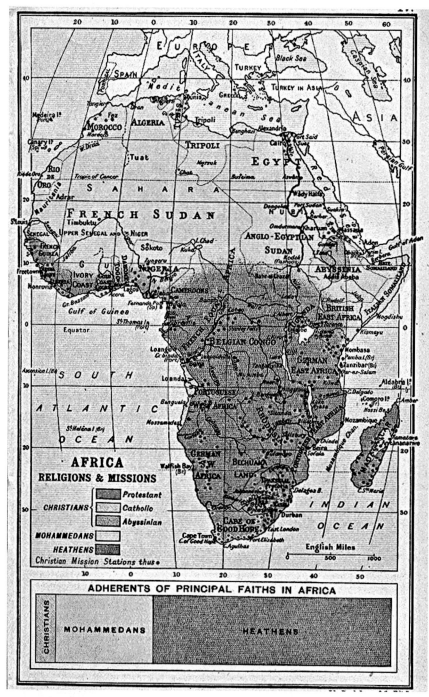

No wonder they haven't prospered! Godless Heathens! (circa 1914 map)
From *Literary & Historical Atlas of Africa and Australasia* by J. G. Bartholomew (1943)

Sub-Saharan Africa is maybe the only region on the planet (and you should never use extremes, but damn it, I'm using extremes) that has been consistently marginalized throughout history and into the modern day. It's true. Other folks in other places in other states in other regions just don't deal with sub-Saharan Africa. Yes, sometimes people give aid because they feel guilty about not making any economic ties, but there is no serious movement to really change things there. That's what I mean when I say marginalized. We deal with Africa only when we absolutely have to, which is rare.

How? How has it been marginalized? What are you talking about Plaid? All we have to do is step back into very recent human history. Let's go back 500 years. For a lot of regions we've had to go way back, but if we went back four or five thousand years in Africa, we'd see some pretty big kingdoms. That's a little known fact for most people, because history books largely ignore it. There were stand-alone groups of people that had civilizations. I'm not marginalizing Africa by ignoring this history; I just want you to understand what is going on in today's world, which has almost nothing to do with that part of African history.

The main thing people know or remember about Africa or read in Western textbooks is one significant economic activity, and one alone. Any clever guesses? That's right, **the slave trade!** We've already talked about it in South America and the Caribbean. The mass movement of Africans as slave labor from the continent to the New World from 1500 onwards has made an impact that most history books and textbooks completely ignore. It completely mystifies the Plaid Avenger that anyone can get through grade school or high school and not comprehend the damage the rest of the world has done to this region. Not to mention that it has now marginalized this region completely. We're the ones that did it!

What? Me Marginalized?

What do I mean? Think about this for a minute. We're going to play a game. Let's pretend space aliens are going to colonize Jupiter. First, they'll need some workers. They come to a certain part of the planet, let's say the United States. They're going to come and say, "Hey, we're recruiting some folks to help us colonize this moon and mine some gold." What kind of people would these slave traders take? Obviously, they would take strong people, healthy people, smart people. They would probably take anybody that had any real resource or utility about them, wouldn't they? Wouldn't you? Wouldn't you want the strongest, the best and the brightest as your workers?

So what would happen to the United States if within the next 300 years, this alien race took the brightest, strongest and the healthiest? I don't think you have to stretch your imagination a lot to realize that this would be a huge negative impact on any place. In Africa, this happened for a *very* long time. Think back to the numbers we looked

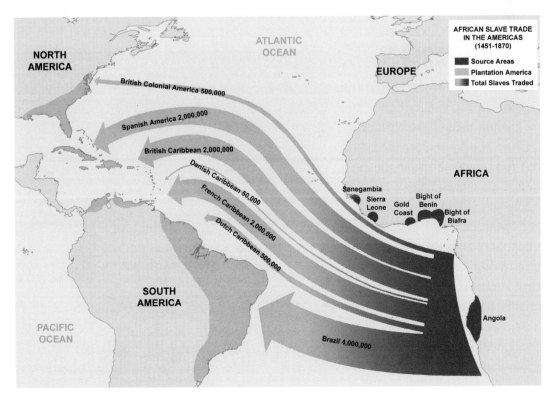

European bastards at work.

at in Latin America . . . you might have had 4–6 million (MILLION!) people taken from the coast of Africa to Brazil, maybe another 5–8 million more just to the Caribbean. We are talking about millions and millions of people.

Let's just think of the demographic impact on Africa after several hundreds of years of this type of depletion. What do they get in return? *Guns and liquor.* What a great swap! I wonder why Africa is poor now? I'm having some trouble here; can someone help me do the math?

At the exact same time this is happening, as we saw in the Middle East chapter, Africa is getting bypassed. We've talked about Chris Columbus, we've talked about Vasco Da Gama . . . what were these guys trying to do? They were trying to get to India. How did they do it? They bypass Africa completely. Keep in mind the term "marginalized." These European dudes were experts at marginalizing Africa—and I can't make fun of them, they're just trying to make some money. The whole point was to get the living hell around Africa as fast as possible. That was how they were going to make more money . . . by bypassing the Middle East and Africa altogether.

Africa was largely unexplored at this point. It didn't matter. The obvious goal of the rest of the world was to get around it. That's about as marginalized as you can get: "We don't know what's here and we don't even care; we just want to get around it!" So they bypass Africa, and it never gets fully integrated into European or Middle Eastern economies. And when they aren't being completely bypassed, people just show up to drop off firearms and liquor in exchange for people. Depletion of demographics cannot be understated.

Jupiter. Now recruiting workers!

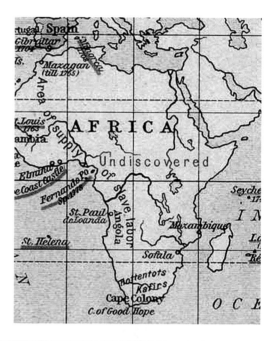

FINALLY "DISCOVERED"?

Africa is known as "**The Dark Continent.**" Some folks might think, "Oh, that's because people there have dark skin." Nice try, but no. The British coined that phrase because people were in the dark about Africa, knowledge-wise. Even up to a hundred years ago, people were like, "Uh, what's down there? I don't know . . . It's big. Oh, and there are people there because we took them during the slave trade . . . other than that we know jack shit about Africa." Again, we're talking about the 1800s. Not long ago. Back then, famous British explorers from National Geographic like David Livingston made much ado about "discovering" the continent and filling in the blanks on their wall maps of the world.

Dr. Livingstone, I Presume???
Who Is Dr. Livingstone and What's He Doing in Africa?
David Livingston was a Scottish Missionary who explored Africa in the mid-1800s. In fact, Livingston is credited with being one of the first Europeans to complete a transcontinental African journey. He also discovered Mosi-ao-Tunya Waterfall, which he renamed Victoria Falls after the Queen (the inconsistency of "discovering" and "renaming" didn't seem to bother anyone). Why did he do it? According to his statue, his motto was: "Christianity, Commerce, and Civilization" (presumably in order of importance). Ironically, this is also the motto of many members of the United States' government today.

This always cracks the Plaid Avenger up. Did people just not know that Africa was there? They did, how could they not? Africa is connected to the Middle East, the cradle of Western civilization. Traders from India and China bumped into the African coast long ago. Everybody in the Western and Eastern world knows that Africa is there; it's not invisible or anything. It's just largely marginalized. So when was Africa truly discovered? A couple hundred years ago the European powers that had colonized the rest of the planet already were finally like, "I wonder what's there on that enormous land mass just south of us. Hey, no one has actually claimed this shit yet have they? That's interesting, maybe we'll take it.

Maybe there's something there we can use now."

MASTERS TO BASTARDS

More specifically titled: Colonial Masters to Post-Colonial Bastards. This culminates into something that the Plaid definitely wants you to know, a red-letter date for Africa. Red for blood maybe . . . This date was 1884 when Africa was truly discovered, in that it was carved up for discovery, colonization, and imperialization by the European powers. 1884 is the year of **The Berlin Conference.** What's the Berlin Conference?

A PATCHWORK QUILT OF COLONIES

As the Plaid already suggested, the European powers had already colonized the New World, taken over South Asia, India, Australia, and made in-roads to China. They are pretty much in all the continents. This is the last place left, and being very civil nice white dudes from Europe, they said, "Chaps, let's all get around the table. We shouldn't fight about this. We all have plenty of problems around the world. So let's do this is in a very civil manner because we're civil guys. Let's put out a map of Africa and divide it up; we don't really need to fuss and fight about it." And indeed, that's what they do. As you might imagine from the title of it, it occurs in Berlin. It doesn't even happen on the continent that they were carving up.

Think real hard and try to tally up how many people from Africa were at this meeting . . . Think, think, think. Oh that's right: None! Not one single representative from Africa was present at this conference, the purpose of which was to carve up their continent, the second largest continent on the planet! This huge place was divided up very civilly. Some of it became French, some Italian, some British, etc. The Belgians got modern day Congo, a massively big place that would cover the eastern seaboard of the United States. Germans had some of the colonies down there as well. So did the Portuguese with Angola and Mozambique. A Patchwork quilt of European power got draped over the continent of Africa.

One question that always pops up in the Plaid Avenger's mind about this patchwork quilt is why? Why is it a patchwork? How come it isn't divided up into zones with the Brits on one side, the Frenchies on the other?

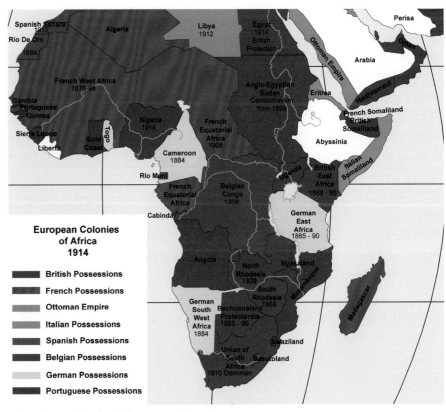

What a beautiful cake to divvy up to Europe!

Certain European powers had already made inroads into Africa, sure. But because the Germans sponsored the conference, the Plaid has always had a sneaking suspicion . . .

Here's the Plaid Avenger's Theory: The year 1884 is exactly 30 years before Germany decides to try and take over all of Europe. I can't help but think when I look at this map of Africa that what the Germans did is very intentional. In splitting Africa up into different chunks, you have multiple borders with the other European powers . . . borders that would have to be defended, borders that would require input of capital and men and guns. Indeed, if you look at the German territories themselves, you're like, "Oh, they butt up against all the other European powers, which by the way are controlled by the European powers that Germany attacked in World War I."

Here's a little known fact for you: in the outbreak of World War I, there was fighting in sub-Saharan Africa where the

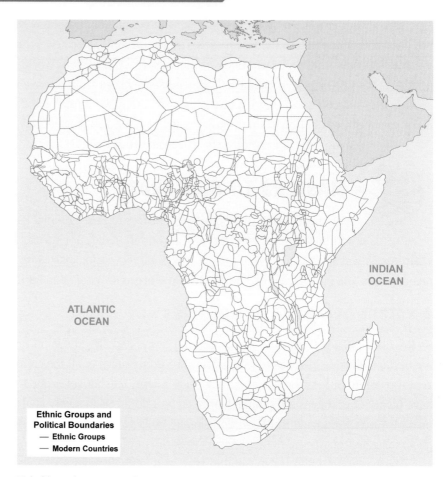

ATLANTIC OCEAN

INDIAN OCEAN

Ethnic Groups and Political Boundaries
— Ethnic Groups
— Modern Countries

Tribal boundaries ignored.

Germans made movements of troops to draw off resources from Europe. The Plaid Avenger theory is that this is a map that was drawn with conflict in mind. It was used to incite division within Africa as a political tool. It can't be proven, but it is certainly possible given what the wacky Germans were up to at this point in history. Remember, we are still discussing why Africa is so far behind, and this is one of the main reasons: internal conflict and dissent.

What was there before the European powers drew their big lines? There were as many as 10,000 ethnic groups and tribes, for lack of a better word, scattered throughout Africa with little to nothing in common with each other. They were all divided into what we see on the map. This creates a situation in which people were grouped into political bodies by an outside force with complete disregard for the political arrangements that they were already in. They might be grouped with folks that they may not like, neighbors with whom they might be engaging in active warfare. The lines drawn at the Berlin Conference were completely arbitrary.

This is a big source of dissent in today's Africa. Here we are 122 years later, and this is still problematic. Tribes that were one group in an ethnically defined territory are now in three different countries. You don't have to go too far back to see that a lot of the ethnic conflict, strife and genocide has been based in part on these folks being in political divisions that have nothing to do with where their ethnic groups are located. That's a really big huge deal. Here's the funny part: after the European powers decide to pull out of Africa, they maintain the old borders that were drawn arbitrarily in Berlin.

FREE AT LAST

So let's get into independence. What happens after independence? How did it even come about? As you can see from this map, most African countries are fairly new. They are the youngest countries in the world, meaning they gained their independence fairly late in the game in 20th-century history. As such, new leaders, new governments, and radically disparate ethnic groups within single states are having trouble.

We talked about the continent being split up into units by European powers. Now these "units" are all sovereign states. Most of them didn't have their "independence movements" in the conventional sense of the term. Mostly, we relate independence movements to violent insurrections that throw off the shackles of a domineering power by force. To be sure, there were protests and anti-colonial groups throughout Africa, but typically there were no great wars. In the 1960s, 1970s, and

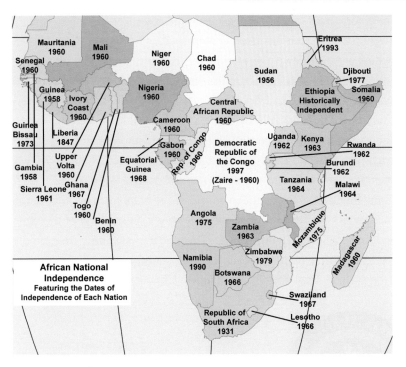

Young states with growing pains.

1980s, the European powers more often than not were like, "Oh, we can't have colonies. That's kind of ridiculous nowadays." So they just kind of grant independence to their African colonies. For instance, the Belgians sort of negotiated their way out of the Democratic Republic of Congo by saying, "Okay, you guys have fun! We're just going to walk out of here!"

So these young African countries are not very well established even in today's world just because they are young. They are also poor as shit from the start. Infrastructure was never that great, because of what the colonial powers did during their tenure: jack shit. When we think about colonial investment in places like India or Southeast Asia where France had Indochina or even in South America where the Spanish were, we typically think of the colonial powers setting up towns, with maybe some industries and businesses. The African colonial experience brings back the term "marginalized."

Pretty much all investment from the colonial powers in Africa, which wasn't much, was extraction-based. Yeah, they built *some* roads and railroads: but only to help get the products they wanted out of there. Yeah, they built *some* seaports, only to move the oil, the grains and the vegetables out. I'm pointing this out because this is tied into what's going on economically in Africa today. Even though they are all sovereign states, there was never a lot of investment in Africa's infrastructure. As a result, and a key point for you to know, countries in Africa typically trade with the outside world more than they do with each other. There are no major interstate systems through Africa. There are no established communications systems through Africa. This place is compartmentalized in all ways, shapes, and forms, and the investment that was put into infrastructure was minimal at best. There is not a lot of trade or communications between countries that are next-door neighbors. It is a major reason why Africa is poor today.

BASTARDS ON PARADE

Some states did have independence movements and rebel leaders who turn into independence leaders. People like, gosh I don't know, Robert Mugabe, who was a guy that took up arms to throw off the colonial yoke; he is now vilified as a bastard in today's world. People like Patrice Lumumba, who was a freedom fighter in what is now the Democratic Republic of

Congo. So what happened when these charismatic leaders took over there countries from the colonizers? Answer: simply put, only a shift in who's robbing the country. This brings up a term that has been coined specifically for the sub-Saharan African experience: **kleptocracy.** This unique term, which is now known the world over, is pretty much identified only with this region.

What does kleptocracy mean? Well "-ocracy" usually means "ruled by." So *demo*cracy means "rule by people." *Aristo*cracy means "rule by rich people." *Klepto*cracy, oh that's right, means "rule by thieves." Rule by thieves, a term coined just for sub-Saharan Africa. This refers to the fact that corruption has and continues to run rampant here. It has become an established way of life. It's probably the biggest African disease and the Plaid Avenger will go out on a limb and say it is the biggest reason why Africa is so far behind the times these days. Government corruption has destroyed Africa.

Once the good guys who fought for their country's independence 40 years ago got rid of the colonial yoke, they came down with the disease. It's not AIDS, it's not Ebola, it's POWER. It's the worst disease they've got. Even some of the most passionate and beloved independence leaders get the disease when they take power. Once power is gained, they simply cannot relinquish it. They cannot let it go. You can see leader after leader in country after country get into the system, become corrupt, and then find it impossible to escape the system. They don't want to leave. Many changed their country's constitution so they can rule indefinitely.

WHAT'S THE DEAL WITH . . . THESE AFRICAN DUDES RULING FOR SO DAMN LONG?
LONGEST RULING PRESIDENTS IN AFRICA

Name	Country	Years in Power	Total Years
François Tombalbaye	Chad	1960–1975	15
Milton Obote	Uganda	1962–1972, 1980–1985	15
Gamal Abdel Nasser	Egypt	1954–1970	16
Gaafar Nimeiry	Sudan	1969–1985	16
Mengistu Haile Mariam	Ethiopia	1974–1991	17
Juvenal Habyarimana	Rwanda	1973–1994	21
Mohamed Siad Barre	Somalia	1969–1991	22
Moussa Traore	Mali	1968–1991	23
Daniel arap Moi	Kenya	1978–2002	24
Ahmed Sekou Toure	Guinea	1958–1984	26
Albert Rene	Seychelles	1977–2004	27
Hastings Kamuzu Banda	Malawi	1963–1994	31
(Joseph) Mobutu Sese Seko	Zaire	1965–1997	32
Felix Houphouet-Boigny	Cote d'Ivoire	1960–1993	33
Gnassingbe Eyadema	Togo	1967–2005	38
Idriss Deby	Chad	1990–Current	18 (and counting)
Omar Hasan Ahmad al-Bashir	Sudan	1989–Current	19 (and counting)
Zine El Abidine Ben Ali	Tunisia	1987–Current	21 (and counting)
Robert Mugabe	Zimbabwe	1987–Current	22 (and counting)
Hosni Mubarak	Egypt	1981–Current	27 (and counting)
Teodoro Obiang Nguema Mbasogo	Equatorial Guinea	1979–Current	29 (and counting)
Jose Eduardo dos Santos	Angola	1979–Current	29 (and counting)
Moammar Gadhafi	Libya	1969–Current	39 (and counting)
Omar Bongo* (world record holder)	Gabon	1967–Current	41 (and counting)

As you can see from the chart, Africa is pretty much alone in the world when it comes to this. These are not monarchies, these aren't royal houses, these aren't even supposed to be military dictatorships. These are supposedly democracies where people have been in power for 20, 30, and almost 40 years. This is Africa's biggest problem: the addictive disease called political power. We can look on that chart and see leaders of particular note. Robert Mugabe in Zimbabwe, an ex-freedom fighter, a popular leader elected 26 years ago, he's still there. "Hi, Robert, how's it going?" "Hey Plaid Avenger,

Know Your Sub-Saharan African Bastards!

Idi Amin
Amin seized power in Uganda in a 1970 coup. Determined to purge the country of those who were disloyal, Amin set up the "State Research Bureau," which would be more accurately described as a death squad. The death squad targeted Christians, Asians, members of the Acholi and Lango tribes, academics, etc. Over the years, Amin became more erratic, at one point reportedly declaring himself the King of Scotland. Western media often portrayed Amin as a bumbling murderer. Amin finally lost power in 1979. Over 300,000 Ugandans were murdered or tortured during Amin's rule. It was also largely rumored that he was a cannibal, and that he found political enemies "delicious."

Mobutu Sese Seko
Mobutu was "president" of Zaire from 1965 to 1997. During this time, Mobuto executed political rivals, condensed power in the executive branch, and outlawed Christian names (he changed his name from Joseph). However, Mobutu's biggest characteristic of bastardness was his greed. He stole billions of dollars from the already poor Zaire economy. In 1985 it was estimated that he had $5 billion in Swiss bank accounts alone. Mobutu can be seen as a prime example of kleptocracy (rule by a thief). Mobutu was overthrown in 1997 (after supporting the Tutsi regime responsible for the Rwanda genocide) and Zaire was quickly renamed the Democratic Republic of Congo (DRC). The DRC is currently war-torn and screwed, both economically and politically.

Robert Mugabe
Mugabe has been in charge of Zimbabwe ever since it became Zimbabwe in 1980. During this time, he has quashed political dissent and been accused of gross human rights abuses. But he began to really get serious about destroying his own country about five years ago when he initiated a "kill all the whities" campaign in Zimbabwe in which the government confiscated white-owned land, and subsequently did little to nothing to protect the white minority when all hell broke out. In 2005, Mugabe's government initiated Campaign Murambatsvina—a program to destroy the shantytowns of Zimbabwe, leaving millions homeless. Here in 2008 he and his party outright lost the last election and are now beating and jailing all political opposition in the lead up to a 'run-off' in order to 're-decide' the prior election. Gosh. I wonder who will win? The Hitleresque mustache isn't helping his image abroad either.

Teodoro Obiang Nguema Mbasogo
Obiang became the defacto leader of Equatorial Guinea since he took power in a 1979 coup. Equatorial Guinea has since been described as one of the most corrupt, ethno-centric, antidemocratic, and repressive states on the planet. However, the good news is that Obiang has prostate cancer and may die soon. Not soon enough though: conservative estimates of the wealth he has stolen from his country are approaching the billion-mark. Since oil was discovered, his personal bank accounts have received hundreds of millions of dollars, and at the same time the standard of living and GDP of the rest of the population has plummeted. What an asshole.

I'm currently plunging my country into the toilet!" You can look at Equatorial Guinea. This guy, General Mbasogo, is closing in on full-on dictatorial powers since oil was found in the country. So corruption and kleptocracy are pervasive themes in these countries. They are both big reasons why this place is so far behind the times. I will throw in a few names just for personal reference whom I will later expand upon. Guys like Robert Mugabe. People like Joseph Mobutu who controlled the Democratic Republic of Congo for 30 years . . . oh, and a few others of note . . .

These guys siphoned off billions of dollars. Again we look at Africa and wonder, "Why are they so poor?" Well, a lot of these leaders robbed their countries blind. Some of these leaders are still doing it, which is why the Equatorial Guinea reference comes up. Joseph Mobutu, at the time of his death, had somewhere around 5 billion dollars stashed away in Swiss and Saudi Arabian banks, and lots of other places. He, as well as others, siphoned off wealth at phenomenal rates and didn't even have bank accounts in their own countries. They took that money somewhere else completely. It's really a sad scenario that has been repeating itself since the independence movements in sub-Saharan Africa.

ADDITIONAL AFRICAN AILMENTS

Now why else is there object poverty and conflict across this region? Well, corruption causes poverty which causes conflict. An additional complicating factor is that when countries are extremely poor, some unstable border wars and resource wars tend to crop up too. This has happened particularly in the Democratic Republic of Congo, as you will see in the International Hotspots Chapter, where there might be seven or eight different sovereign states involved in skirmishes in this one country. This is Africa's own World War now because there are so many resources that people want on the eastern side of the Congo that countries are just taking them. You might be like, "What? We live in the modern world. People can't just go into other countries and take stuff! A state can't do that!" Well it might not happen anywhere else in the world, but resource acquisition is definitely a compounding factor of conflict that still happens in sub-Saharan Africa. But that's not all: ethnic, religious, environmental global geopolitical factors and even health play a role in escalating misery in this place. Let's look at a few in more detail.

STRIFE OF ALL STRIPES

Let's talk about ethnic and religious strife. We already talked a little bit about ethnic strife between different tribal groups across Africa. This is still in play. You can easily cite countless episodes, similar to the Hutu-Tutsi genocide in Rwanda, which simply consisted of extremists from one ethnic group wiping out another ethnic group. On top of this, there is serious religious strife. I already pointed out earlier in this chapter, two countries of particular note that have problems with this: Nigeria and Sudan. These are prime examples of what I'm talking about when it comes to religious strife. Because Islam is so pervasive in the Middle East, it has crept into states in Northern Africa, leading to religious division in many states. The most classic example is Sudan. The northern part of Sudan is full of Islamic Arabs and the southern part of Sudan is largely non-Islamic Black Africans. The North Arab guys are in charge of the whole country, and implemented Shari'a law. This caused open rebellion in the

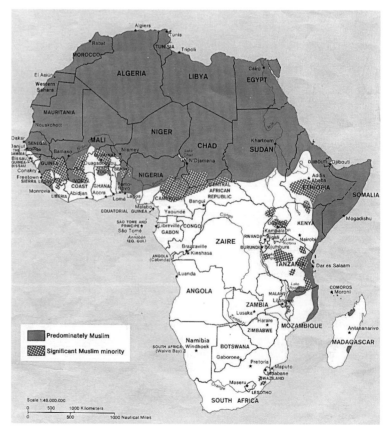

south and continues to incite harsh feelings and violent acts, to the tune of several millions of casualties over the last 30 years. In 2005 an agreement was made that the southern states of the Sudan will soon be able to get rid of those laws, but who knows how that will turn out. Historically, agreements haven't had a great track record whenever power is at stake.

We also see this in today's Nigeria, even though it's not in civil war. The northern part of Nigeria has certain substates that voted to go into Shari'a Law. That's all fine and dandy if you are Islamic but there are many other folks that aren't into that, and this has become a hot button issue in Nigeria. These Islamic folks in the northern part of Nigeria want to live by Islamic law but the government in the south says, "Wait a minute, we're the government. You can't have Islamic law overriding government law." So we have religious strife in Nigeria that cropped up big time when the 2002 Miss World Pageant was slated for Nigeria. There was a publicized case on the docket in which a woman in northern Nigeria was convicted of adultery. The Shari'a law dudes sentenced her to death by stoning, old school style. This became a firebrand issue with some of the Miss World contestants; you know how upright those ladies are, really caring about world events and all. But in this case, they actually cared and staged protests and such. They refused to go to Nigeria and indeed, they moved the whole pageant to London. So there are some real repercussions from this religious conflict in sub-Saharan Africa. It's something we should be paying attention to.

The main point that I'm stressing is that this is why there is conflict and division within sub-Saharan Africa. We'll throw in one more thing for those of you who saw *Lords of War* With Nick Cage. The issue of gunrunning fuels all conflict in Africa. Africa is one hell of an armed continent as far as individual weapons go. None of them have nuclear weapons or conventional missiles. Few of them even have conventional war weapons like tanks, but boy do they have guns on this continent! They've got all types of small arms from Russia, Israel, the US, France, you name it. Every gun producer has a big and avid market in sub-Saharan Africa. This place is armed to the damn teeth. This is such a travesty. In Africa, the poorer a country is, the more of their GDP they will dedicate to buying weaponry. This almost harkens back to the slave trade 500 years ago. What gets dropped off in Africa? Guns and liquor. No wonder there is instability in this region.

CLIMATE CHALLENGES

So let's get to a new topic. Why all the starvation in Africa? We've talked most about postindependence, why there is conflict on all scales, but why the starvation? Why do we see Sally Struthers' commercials telling us to give money for starving Africans? Why do we see mud covered children with flies crawling all over their faces. Why? What's the deal? Don't they have any damn food there? Can't they grow food? What are they, stupid? Are they lazy? What's going on? Why are these people starving death? There is no other part of this planet that has as much starvation in it, at least not as much as is portrayed on the news. Why is this place so hungry? There are lots of different reasons having to do with physical factors and economics.

Going, going, gone: Bye-bye arable land!

Number one is the **climate.** This is a tough climate. Savannah and steppe comprise a big component of this continent and these areas are affected radically by fluctuations in weather. Typically, when we see classic places like Somalia or Ethiopia, it's because they have had a seriously bad drought. One bad drought will single-handedly wipe out agricultural products within a single year. When they have back-to-back droughts, it becomes totally disastrous. That's why you have millions of people starving to death. Any dry climate is under increased pressure if it becomes even a little bit drier.

One thing that drought in Africa can lead to is **desertification.** This is mostly along the Sahara Desert. Desertification is even worse than drought because it is drought that becomes permanent. It is arid land that, for environmental reasons that we are still unsure of, turns into desert. It's a one-way street. Some parts of Africa, where people used to grow food and herd sheep and goats, have become desert. People have to move out. It's finished; you can't really do anything else afterwards. Humans can't live there; we need water and there's no water there. So we have to desert (as in leave or abandon) that desert (as in useless-ass sand). Also, look at this map for our Middle Eastern friends that we discussed last chapter, and think more about that issue of water I brought up—big trouble brewing.

On top of that, in areas of Africa with well-watered, tropical climates, you typically have a lot of **disease.** So another reason why this place is hurting, starving to death, with a high infant mortality rate, is that the climate is conducive to disease, not to mention the complete lack of health care. Thinking of tropical Africa brings to mind the nastiest diseases that hang out here, like Ebola and AIDS. These are diseases that mutated or developed in tropical Africa. Ones that you haven't even heard of, such as schistosomiasis, which features germs that can get into your skin and hang out in your bladder the rest of your short life until you are urinating blood. They've got eye worms, which are self-explanatory. They've got worms to penetrate every orifice you have. And here's the really good one, elephantitis: look up pics on the Internet if you really want to lose your lunch. Malaria is the number one killer in Africa and it

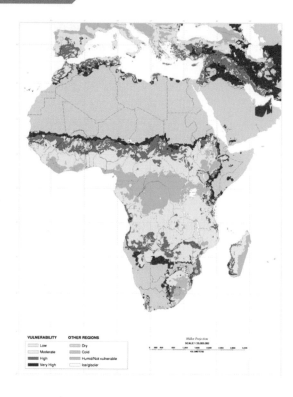

is a treatable and curable disease. That's where we get into the lack of health care. So why are they starving and why are they hurting? Reason number one is the combination of those two physical factors.

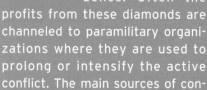
What's the Deal with . . . Conflict Diamonds?

Conflict diamonds are diamonds produced in active war zones. Often the  profits from these diamonds are channeled to paramilitary organizations where they are used to prolong or intensify the active conflict. The main sources of conflict diamonds include Sierra Leone, Liberia, the Democratic Republic of Congo (DRC), and Angola. Sierra Leone is particularly bad, because their diamonds are easy to mine and of high quality. Government and non-government forces have traditionally applied organized crime-like tactics to control diamond fields. In Sierra Leone, the children that dig for conflict diamonds are often executed for suspected theft or simply for underproduction. Another common punishment for suspected theft is the amputation of limbs. Go watch the movie *Blood Diamond* for a decent description of the situation. Spoiler: Leo Di Caprio dies in the end. Oh wait! That's not a spoiler, that's a bonus!

ECONOMICS: MO' MONEY? TRY NO MONEY: AFRICA NEEDS IT

We've already referenced reason number two for starvation. Africa is challenged by size and escarpments. This is not an economically diverse place or developed place because of its sheer size. Economies require movement and trade to grow. There's not a lot of infrastructure for this in Africa, and at this point, to build five thousand miles of road costs millions. Who the hell has that kind of money in Africa? It encapsulates 30 different countries. It is more than three times the land area of the US, including Alaska. It would take some serious cash to build enough roads to cross this continent. This is not an economically integrated place and it is not likely going to be in the future. They're hurting. We talked about the escarpments problem. It's hard to penetrate into the continent with ships. Economic activities, like agriculture, that benefit from movement in greater mass become very unprofitable and tough to do with no commercial shipping access. They have a strike against them in terms of the physical world and in terms of sheer size and escarpments.

Other economic challenges that play into Africa's lack of wealth go back to the colonial era. We've already talked about this. What did colonial masters invest in? The answer: nothing but extractive industries for raw commodities, which Africa is still known for in the world 122 years later. It started off with the slave trade, taking humans away from this country and hasn't evolved out much further. Now, it's just concentrated on taking ores and diamonds and oil out of this place instead of people. "Ok, we've got the stuff; let's just get it out of here the fastest way possible. Build a railroad station solely to get to the copper mine. What? We're not interested in an infrastructure for people! We just want the stuff out of there!"

Extractive economies are based on primary products. What are they worth? Jack-diddley-shit. Primary products aren't worth much. On top of that, many African countries are what we call **single-commodity economies** precisely because of this scenario. This problem exists in other parts of the world but nowhere in quantities as large as in sub-Saharan Africa. These are countries that upwards of 80, 90, sometimes 95 percent of the entire economy is based on a single primary commodity. For example, take Niger. Ninety-five percent of its GDP is from one thing, uranium. This is a substance that no one in Niger can use for anything. It's an export commodity that's pretty much what they make all their money on. Sao Tome and Principe: 90 percent cocoa. Zambia: 85 percent copper. Botswana: 80 percent diamonds. Now you might look at that and say, "Well that's good, at least they have something." Again, this is a primary commodity. Diamonds

Message to Plaid Avenger: African agent has acquired the conflict diamonds and is at rendezvous point . . . and she's a hottie . . .

are raw; they aren't worth that much. The worth comes from processing all these things, and here's a news flash: the processing typically occurs somewhere else. So they sell this stuff cheap. Speaking of diamonds . . .

Here's the complicating feature the Plaid Avenger wants you to understand about this single-commodity situation: what are diamonds worth if the world goes into recession? The answer: jack-shit. How good of a shape is Zambia going to be in if the price of copper plunges? They're in trouble. How about cocoa? Are you joking me? Your economy is based on freakin' chocolate? Wonka be damned! That is so variable and so subject to market fluctuation that it should be pretty easy for you to understand now that this is a place that is always on a knife's edge. It's not economically diversified, and on top of that, it's dependent on primary products.

COLD WAR EFFECTS IN AFRICA?

Here's another economic challenge making this place poor: the Cold War is over. During the Cold War, as we've pointed out multiple times in this manual to understanding the planet, the two sides, Team Soviet and Team Capitalist Democracy were vying for influence around the world. Those teams would make loans to or sell arms to countries to get them on their side. "Come on! Be on our team!" sub-Saharan Africa was no exception. So the teams, mostly led by the United States and of course Soviet Russia, made inroads and tried to make deals with the same corrupt leaders that I referenced earlier. "Hey, we'll lend you money if you say you won't join the other team." Some of these African leaders were really savvy and played both sides. I'm thinking of Joseph Mobutu Sese Seko from the DRC in particular, because he took money from everybody. And of course, he put it into his own bank accounts in Switzerland, which made the situation in the DRC even worse. He took guns from everybody too. What a bastard!

During the Cold War, money flowed in for just such purposes. Again, just like the United States sponsored the Marshall Plan in Europe, folks said, "We should make inroads to Africa because if we don't, then the Commies will. If the Commies help them out then they will be on Team Commie. We should help out. We should lend them money. We should try to do some projects for them." By and large, that's what happened during the Cold War, maybe not as much as other places in the world, but it happened in Africa. Investments were made. But guess what? The Cold War is over. There is no Team Commie vs. Team USA anymore. As a result, aid has simply dried up. There is no impetus, no reason, no economic drive for the United States to help out or do anything in Africa. And Russia, shit, they couldn't afford to do anything even if they wanted to. So this all kind of imploded overnight, and aid has completely diminished. But that's just the Cold War reason.

Aid is also diminishing for other reasons. One of the main reasons is corruption. See how things are tied together? Because of the corruption within the governments, not only due to corrupt leaders but also militaries, places like Somalia are in anarchy. Everyone is corrupt. There are aid organizations that want to bring food to starving kids and medicine to babies, but they simply cannot get anything to them because of internal corruption. There are distribution problems because of the road situation in Africa, but on top of that, you have corruption from the highest points of government all the way down to the local scale. If the US sends a billion dollars to fight AIDS in Zimbabwe, you can expect half of that to be swindled by higher-ups working in the bureaucracy. Okay, well that still leaves a lot of money, which you can expect to be swindled by the people on the ground that are supposed to be giving it out in the form of shots. Really everybody from the top down perpetuates the corruption.

What's the Deal with . . . Loaning Money to Chad?

As you know from Chapter 6, the World Bank is an organization that makes developmental loans to poorer countries. Also, you should remember that the World Bank often makes these loans contingent on "structural adjustments" in the recipient country. Long story short, the World Bank gave Chad a loan to build a pipeline. In return, Chad had to promise to put 10 percent of the profits into an account designed to fight long-term poverty. Everything was going well until the government of Chad decided that perhaps they, and not the World Bank, knew what was best for their country.

So, the government moved some of the oil profits from the long-term account (that the World Bank demanded) and invested them directly into schools and health care. Some of it may also have been invested in guns. Bad move. Why is this important? Because it deals with sovereignty. Chad thinks it is their sovereign right to use revenue how they best see fit. The World Bank, on the other hand, contends that it is their right as a loaner to enforce measures to insure that they get paid back. The Chad/World Bank loan was viewed as a new model for loans to Africa, where there have been many problems with government officials stealing revenue from the poor. Whether this model will be used in the future depends largely on the result of this dispute.

This has become a titanic problem in which people have gotten to the point of, "I'm just not going to donate, what's the point? It's not going to get to the people who need it." If you think this a Plaid Avenger personal comment, it's not. I say donate as much you can to Africa! Hell we've already freakin' screwed the continent for the last 500 years; we should have a moral obligation to go back and help. However, this corruption problem makes a lot of people suspicious, and we can see evidence of this in the last year. One suspicious party is the World Bank, which has said, "We are only going to lend money to your country if we come and give it out ourselves." There are places like the World Bank and the IMF that say, "Yeah, we're not going to lend you money until you change governments because you guys are too corrupt."

Transparency International, an organization that performs studies on corruption, places most African countries in its top 30 most corrupt places. Does this affect anything? We already know people don't want to send international aid because of the corruption, let's branch it out. How about international investment? Who the hell is going to build a factory for twice the actual cost because they have to pay everybody off? When Transparency International comes out and says, "Wow these ten countries are the ten worst and they're all in sub-Saharan Africa," most business people hear, "Oh, you'd be crazy to invest there. Can't afford that. You'll never make your money back." So all of these things are related to each other. It's hard to tease out single items, but the end of the Cold War is a big one, causing international investment aid to drop off simultaneously making this place even poorer. We'll end with one last huge-ass negative that is making the region poor . . .

AIDS

We're still talking about why this place is poor, why is it starving. The last issue we cannot possibly talk about enough is AIDS. I'm not a big fan of AIDS but we're going to have to spend a few paragraphs talking about it here, not for the same old same old reasons you've read about elsewhere. Yes, it's terrible, it's sad; people are dying of this disease. Everything you've heard is true. I want you to

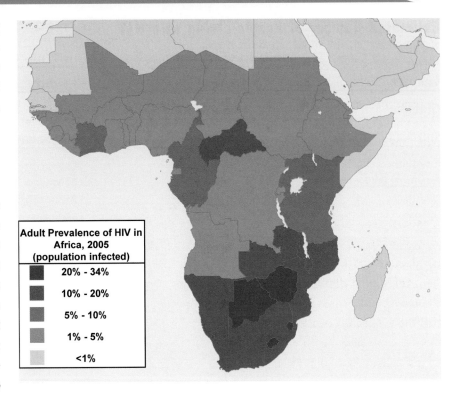

Adult Prevalence of HIV in Africa, 2005 (population infected)

20% - 34%

10% - 20%

5% - 10%

1% - 5%

<1%

think deeper though, because we're trying to project ahead about what's going to happen in sub-Saharan Africa. If we want to figure out what should and can be done about this region, we have to deal with this 800 pound gorilla called AIDS. It is massive and it is going to be so far-reaching into society that the mere idea that it's just a few people that are sick and dying is not even the tip of the tip of the iceberg. What are the true impacts of AIDS? We can look at the map on the next page and see that there are some places where a quarter of the population of the country is infected. Of course, that's liable to get worse in a lot of places. Even if it does get better, we're still talking about a fifth or a sixth of the population infected with AIDS.

What are the real impacts about which the world should be concerned? Why can't we all just put our head in the sand about Africa? Africa is in a state of crisis management, if not already, they certainly will be in the next 20 years. Why the crisis? AIDS is a terrible disease for a lot of reasons, one of which is that it doesn't kill you instantaneously. Wow. That sounds horrible, but I'm trying to get you to think deeper folks. If you get ebola, you're going to die now. If you get hit by a car, you're going to die now. AIDS is a disease that takes people out over a long period of time. They are sick for a long time, steadily deteriorating, ultimately becoming dependent.

Here's the big impact: You take a quarter of your population who typically used to be factory workers, farmers, mothers, fathers, teachers, firemen, soldiers, people who were actively creating wealth, and turn that quarter into dependents, sick, laying in a bed dying. That in itself should get you to think about how titanic this issue is in a lot of countries. Merely swapping a quarter of your population from providers to needers is enough to drop any country, including the United States. If this happened in the United States, it would be huge. A quarter? Hell, just ten percent! Taking them off the plus side of the chart and putting them on the negative side. This is making a massive impact in Africa.

Here's more food for thought: What age and socioeconomic groups typically come down with AIDS? If you guessed that it's people in the working class from puberty to about the age of 35, you're right. So people from about 15 to 35, people usually in the work force, are the ones getting sick. Africa is now being called the Orphan Continent because there are so many motherless and fatherless children who are in need. Of course, loss of this age group leaves a lot of old people who are too old to have sex since this epidemic broke out. So you have a society that is getting tilted demographically. You're losing the middle that you want and you are left with a lot of needy people, young and old. This is an epidemic that is causing titanic problems in many countries and it is only going to get worse.

Estimated Number of People Living with HIV

Country	Adults and Children 2005 Estimate	Country	Adults and Children 2005 Estimate
Global	38 600 000	Global	38 600 000
Sub-Saharan Africa	24 500 000	Sub-Saharan Africa	24 500 000
Mauritius	4100	Central African Republic	250 000
Equatorial Guinea	8900	Botswana	270 000
Mauritania	12 000	Burkina Faso	150 000
Djibouti	15 000	Burundi	150 000
Gambia	20 000	Chad	180 000
Guinea-Bissau	32 000	Lesotho	270 000
Somalia	44 000	Angola	320 000
Sierra Leone	48 000	Ghana	320 000
Madagascar	49 000	Cameroon	510 000
Eritrea	59 000	Côte d'Ivoire	750 000
Gabon	60 000	Ethiopia	850 000
Senegal	61 000	Malawi	940 000
Niger	79 000	Democratic Republic of Congo	1 000 000
Guinea	85 000	Uganda	1 000 000
Benin	87 000	Zambia	1 100 000
Togo	110 000	Kenya	1 300 000
Congo	120 000	United Republic of Tanzania	1 400 000
Mali	130 000	Zimbabwe	1 700 000
Rwanda	190 000	Mozambique	1 800 000
Swaziland	220 000	Nigeria	2 900 000
Namibia	230 000	South Africa	5 500 000

Source: 2006 Report on the global AIDS epidemic, UNAIDS/WHO, May 2006.

Why is this a potential time bomb? For all the things I just mentioned, we are only in the introductory stages of this. We have massive numbers of people infected. The true impacts, economically and demographically, have yet to manifest themselves. In other words, it is going to take another 50 years before this completely comes to a head. And that's providing they cured everybody from the get-go, starting right now. If no one got AIDS anymore in Africa starting today, there are still going to be countries that are closing in on collapse for lack of workers, lack of army, lack of firemen, lack of nurses, lack of doctors. This is a really big deal. There are huge numbers of orphans running through the streets, which usually equates to crime after a while. This is bad, bad news for many countries, especially places like Zimbabwe, Uganda, Botswana, which have the highest rates of AIDS in the world.

We can step back from this in the West and say, "Well, we won't go there. We just won't vacation there this year. I won't go see the African animals and everything will just be fine, sooner or later." No. We live in a globalized world, man. We live in a connected place. Once one state collapses it usually creates a vacuum, which pulls in other states into the anarchy as well. I think it's a safe hypothesis to go out on a limb and say that the collapse of one or two states in Africa could incite a war that pulls in multiple states vying for power and influence. This is how wars start, my friends. This is how it goes down. As far as I'm concerned, leaving Africa alone and letting it descend into anarchy is not an option that anybody in this world wants. Why would you, unless you are a total crooked bastard? So why is Africa in such dire straits? There you go. I just listed off a bunch of stuff. None of it is particularly nice, but it's the truth.

ALL IS NOT LOST . . .

I don't try to sugarcoat anything, but having gone through the plethora of problems, I think Africa has huge potential. I think Africa may be one of the best continents to be on in the next hundred years. Why is the Plaid Avenger saying this? There is a light at the end of the tunnel. Africa has a rich history; it's not as if they are completely lost and have never known anything else. No, some of the richest kingdoms ever known were in North Africa. There are also pockets of development in certain places today. Some countries are doing pretty well, so I don't want to categorize the whole region as collapsing; they aren't in that dire of straits yet. Here are some countries of note:

South Africa is doing pretty well. They have lots of internal problems, but economy and GDP-wise, they aren't doing too bad and they make some kick-ass wine. Nigeria is extremely oil rich. Yes, they have some religious and corruption problems but by and large, if you read studies about people in Nigeria, they really like their state. In fact, I read about a happiness index, conducted by the UN. They polled people around the world about their countries and their lives. Nigeria ranked number one in the happiness index. People were very happy to be in Nigeria; they loved it there. But perhaps not all . . . see the box. And Kenya, Tanzania, and others

are making bank off of Africa's biggest money maker outside natural resource extraction. What is it they've got? Tourism trade. People love to see those unspoiled landscapes and those giraffes, hippos and all that happy horseshit. The Plaid Avenger would rather put 'em on a hamburger bun and eat 'em, but some people like to go check them out. Have fun with that, until the hippo bites you in half . . . but that's another story.

On top of the pretty animals and landscapes, there is a finally a continent-wide movement for positive change: the AU. Now, don't let me exaggerate its current position; the African Union is not really a force to be reckoned with yet in any capacity. They formed a while back as the OAS (Organization of African Unity), and just recently changed its name to the AU primarily to be cool-sounding like the EU. It has aspiration to be a free-trade block like the EU and others, but it has largely been ineffective in this capacity since all of them together are shit-poor, thus increasing trade to other poor folks don't really help you

What's the Deal with . . . Oil Workers Getting Kidnapped in Nigeria? Recently, nine internationals were kidnapped while working on an oil platform in the Niger Delta. The kidnappers were members of a Nigerian rebel group (Movement for the Emancipation of the Niger Delta) that demands more oil wealth be returned to the communities from which it is taken. Nigeria is the biggest oil exporter in Africa, yet most of the country's 130 million residents live in poverty. Other attacks by the Nigerian rebels have reduced the oil output in the Niger Delta by 25 percent. The Delta is home to ethnic Ijaws, many of whom seek independence from Nigeria. This is all important because Delta oil is big business, and big business hates instability, so it appears like shit might start going down.

that much. Almost all African states trade more with countries outside of Africa than they do with their immediate neighbors.

While the trade stuff hasn't really worked out for the AU, here's what has: its armed forces. The AU now has a professional army that is composed of forces from every country on the continent. And it is fast evolving into a continent-wide emergency force that is increasingly being dispatched to Africa's hotspots. What's so great about that? Well, the outside world is extremely excited about this prospect for several reasons: 1) It is believed that Africans can better deal with African problems, 2) Africans know the area/cultures better and can more readily move around and more quickly react to changing field circumstance, and 3) If Africans take care of their own problems, then the outside world doesn't have to do it.

AU forces from Rwanda ready for action!

That last point is the crucial one. Remember, the world turned its collective back on the Rwandan genocide as it has also done in the past with Sudanese genocide, and countless civil wars, plagues and droughts which have caused unimaginable death counts. It really hasn't been in anyone's political interest to get involved in Sub-Saharan Africa, and one need look no further than the US's opinion about sending troops to Africa ever since *Black Hawk Down*. It just ain't happening. So lots of outside entities (including the UN, the US, and the EU) are all about giving shit-tons of money to help develop the AU force as a substitute for direct intervention. Probably not a bad idea.

Point is, that the AU now finally has a mission that they can all rally around, and that the outside world is eager to support with money and training. It ain't no NATO, and it ain't even no NAFTA or ASEAN either . . . but hell, it's better than nothing! And it could very well be the thing that once successful will lead to further political and economic integration of the member states. That would make it quite unique in the world, as being first a military grouping that eventually becomes something economic. We shall see.

THE LAST WORD . . .

So Africa has a few things going for it; it has some pockets of development and more importantly, it maintains its unspoiled character, which I think is a huge boon to Africa in the future. But if we look around the planet at places such as Russia, Eastern Europe, China, and India, we see places packed-ass full with people and have industrialized to the point of polluting their own environment, places where you can't drink the damn water anymore because it's so damn toxic. They're rich, but everything there looks like shit. Even in America, where we see big, wide-open spaces, there is some nasty evidence of the postindustrial era, cities collapsing and rusting down to nothing.

In Africa, unspoiled is the word to think of. Yes, perhaps people say about Africa, "Yeah, they're not industrialized and they're poor and that is why they suck." But I'm telling you to look at the long term, at the big picture here. In another 50 or 100 years, people may be coming in droves to Africa because it's the only nice place left on the damn planet where you can get to huge tracts of land and drive around for days and not run into anything. That's increasingly what I think people like to see. It's why the biggest sector of many of their economies is tourism. People want to see that stuff; it's cool.

You know, a hundred years ago, if you wanted communications, you built telephone poles or railroad systems or electric grids crossing your

entire country or continent. Well, we live in a different world now. Africa didn't develop and that's one of the reasons why it's not as far along. At the same time, they don't need telephone poles anymore. Africa is fully connected, without all the bullshit. Everybody just needs a cell phone. They can all be on the Internet without the landlines. So, yes they are behind and yes they are not as developed but they have basically leapfrogged. They have picked up all the best parts of the technology that's been created in the developed world, without all the baggage. They didn't have to industrialize and pollute their continent that much. They didn't build telephone poles and communications networks, and now they have that stuff anyways.

Finally, why is all not lost? As I suggested at the opening of this chapter, they are resource rich. They have shit-loads of stuff; stuff that people want. Maybe not so much oil although some countries like Nigeria have that too. Things like uranium, manganese, silicon, and copper. Africa has tons. They have tremendous amounts of resources. They also have animals and land if you want to consider those resources as well.

I like to think about sub-Saharan Africa as just in "downtime." That is, every region has been undeveloped, becomes developed, and reverts to undeveloped again. Countries go in cycles of development. Remember that the British were the kings of the world, and now they are the US's lapdog. China was the center of the world, then it sucked for two hundred years, and now it's climbing back on top again. Things change. Things have a tendency to turn around and indeed that may be what happens in Africa given the long scope of human existence. So they may be down, but not out. The Plaid Avenger will be partying there for sure, once they develop a few more types of alcohol.

The Afrikaner

¾ oz **Amarula Cream liqueur**

¾ oz **Amaretto almond liqueur**

¾ oz **dark creme de cacao**

¾ oz **Captain Morgan spiced rum**

Shake all ingredients in a cocktail shaker with ice. Strain into martini glass. Amarula Cream liqueur is a smooth cream liqueur made from a blend of fresh cream and the pulp of the exotic fruits found in the african marula tree (Sclerocarya Birrea). As dark and rich as the mother continent herself.

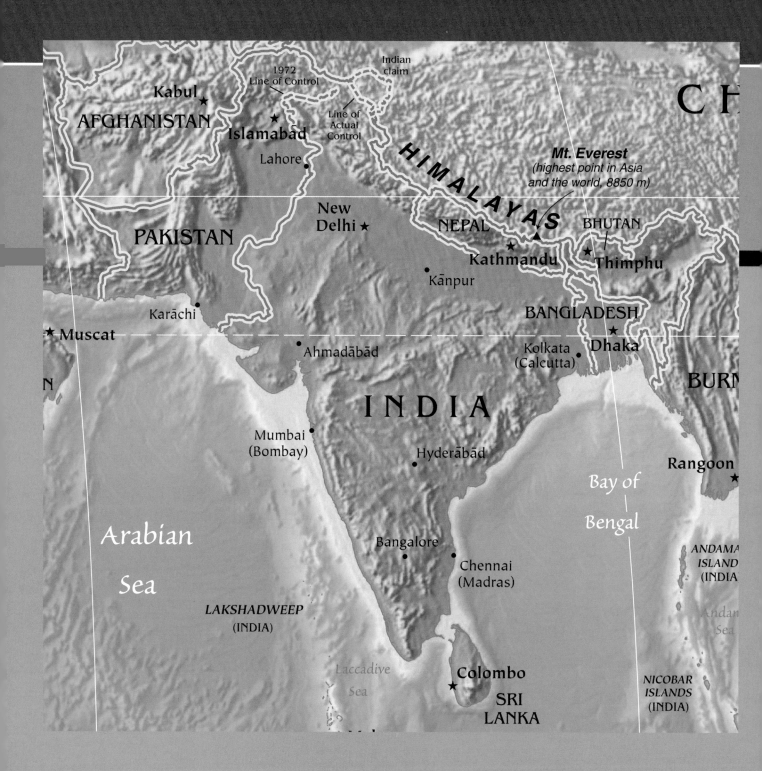

The map shows:

Kabul ★
AFGHANISTAN
Islamabad ★
Lahore •
1972 Line of Control
Indian claim
Line of Actual Control
HIMALAYAS
Mt. Everest
(highest point in Asia and the world, 8850 m)
PAKISTAN
New Delhi ★
NEPAL
BHUTAN
Kathmandu ★
Thimphu ★
Kānpur •
Karāchi •
★ Muscat
Ahmadābād •
BANGLADESH
Kolkata (Calcutta) •
Dhaka •
BURM
INDIA
Mumbai (Bombay) •
Hyderābād •
Arabian
Sea
Bangalore •
Chennai (Madras) •
Bay of Bengal
Rangoon ★
ANDAMA ISLAND (INDIA)
LAKSHADWEEP (INDIA)
Laccadive Sea
Andam Sea
Colombo ★
SRI LANKA
NICOBAR ISLANDS (INDIA)

CHAPTER OUTLINE

South Asia

SOUTH ASIA is often referred to as "the subcontinent" because geologically and plate tectonically, it is. A few million years ago, it was a separate land mass and has been slammed into the continent of Asia ever since. I point this out just so you can see physically what is going on here. We have the Himalayan Range, the highest range on the planet, because this little region is *still* actively being slammed into the rest of Asia. But South Asia is a subcontinent in more ways than just geological.

Indeed, if we looked around the rest of Asia proper, we would see that we can distinguish people we call Indians from India quite easily from the Chinese, or the Burmese, or the Vietnamese, and definitely the Japanese. These folks are different and it's obvious in the way people look, in the way they dress, the way they behave, and in the religions they have. How is South Asia separated from the rest of Asia?

Well first, what is South Asia? It is the big three: India, Pakistan, and Bangladesh, and the small three: Nepal, Bhutan, and Sri Lanka. We could also throw the small island nation of Maldives in there, but I won't say much about them. Thanks to the rising sea level due to global warming, the entire country will be underwater soon. Sorry guys!

India, Pakistan, and Bangladesh are the big three not only because they dwarf the other countries in this region in size, but also because they are in the top ten most populated countries on the planet. South Asia may not be a big place geographically, but it is certainly a very populated place: a dwelling place for loads of humans.

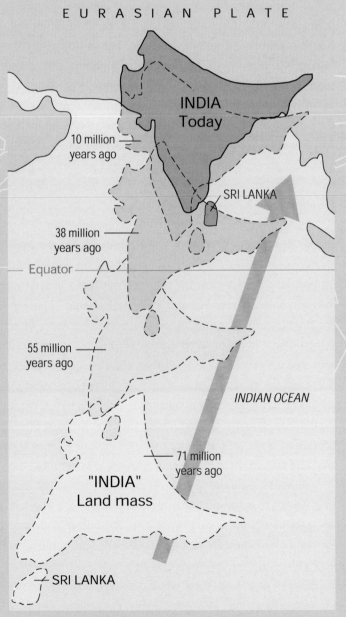

EURASIAN PLATE

INDIA Today

10 million years ago

SRI LANKA

38 million years ago

Equator

55 million years ago

INDIAN OCEAN

71 million years ago

"INDIA" Land mass

SRI LANKA

LET'S GET PHYSICAL

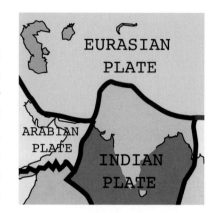

One of the reasons why we have this distinction of culture in South Asia is based somewhat on the physical world; South Asia as a subcontinent has been kind of isolated from the rest of Asia. Isolated how? If we refer back to our opening map we can see that it is isolated in a couple of ways mainly by terrain and climate, our old physical friends. It is isolated terrain-wise by the Himalayan Range, the mightiest, most powerful range on the planet. The highest mountain in this range is of course Mount Everest standing at 29,028 feet. All the other peaks that make up the range are in excess of 20,000 feet and in fact, the top ten highest peaks on the planet are all here.

The Himalayan Range is important because it serves as a barrier. It is difficult for folks from our part of the world to differentiate between folks from Vietnam and China for example, but to tell any of these folks from an Indian is pretty easy. The Himalayan Range is just too tall to transit. Do some people get through it? On pack mules, yes, but a very few; there has never been a lot of economic or human transaction across this barrier. Like the Andes, the Himalayan Range is one of the major barriers to human movement on the planet. The Himalayas are even bigger than the Andes and have kept things quite separate as cultures evolved in terms of religious systems, diets, languages, and ethnicities. It is all quite distinct from one side of the Himalayan Range to the other.

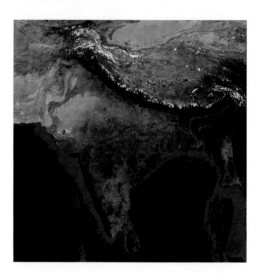

Even though we often only think about the Himalayas, if you follow the border of this region you get to the **Hindu Kush,** the **Pamir Knot,** and the **Karakoram Ranges.** All of these are really huge mountain systems that are on par with the Himalayans themselves. These latter ranges wrap around Pakistan and separate Pakistan from Afghanistan. If we go to the other side, the Himalayan Range kind of wraps down in between what is now India and Burma. The Himalayas are the biggie, but it is kind of a continuous system of hills that very nicely isolates this part of the world from the rest of Asia.

Climate starts to play a role as you progress westward out of this region, where you run into some pretty severe rainforest and jungle vegetation on the Burmese border. If you go in the opposite direction, you run into the Thar Desert and into more deserts as you go into Iran—so dry on one side and wet on the other. Sounds like a good martini . . .

Climate, vegetation, and terrain have really kept this place kind of isolated from the rest of Asia. Now having said that, I want to make a quick point that while South Asia has been *isolated* throughout history, it is not *isolationist.* This is an important point to consider. China, our friend to the north, has been an isolated country by design for many millennia. By that I mean they are distinctly different and want to keep foreign influence out and are only concerned about what is happening in their own country; they make a conscious effort not to be part of the wider world. India, Pakistan, and Bangladesh have been isolated physically, but not by choice. They have been open free traders with the rest of the planet for a good long time, mostly by sea via the Indian Ocean.

SLIPPERY WHEN WET

A final, distinct climate factor in South Asia is the **monsoon.** The monsoonal system was first identified and characterized in India proper. In winter, cool dry air moves from across the continent and flows outward over the ocean and keeps the climate kind of dry. During the spring and early summer, this system completely reverses. The winds change and start moving towards the land. They move from the warm wet waters of the Indian Ocean bringing warm wet air masses over the Indian subcontinent, and start to produce huge amounts of rainfall once the wet air masses slam into the mountains. The first terrain that they hit is the **Western Ghats.** The Western Ghats is just a small mountain range that floats down the western fringe of India. It doesn't take much; these mountains are maybe two to three thousand feet high, but it just enough to force up the air masses and drop tremendous amounts of

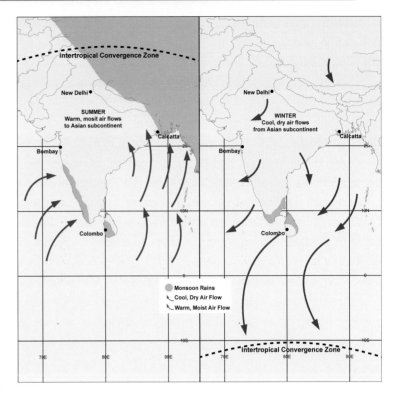

rainfall on the west coast of India creating a classic monsoonal system, dropping in excess of 80 to 90 inches of rain per year. As the rest of the air mass progresses inward it eventually bumps into the Himalayan Range; as that warm wet air is pushed upwards it has the same effect again resulting in heavy rain on the fringe of the Himalayas and in Bangladesh.

This system has really become a life cycle in South Asia. Grain harvests, movements of people, and whole economies are based on this, and when the monsoon rains are too early or too late it can spell disaster. There is really a pulse to the South Asian way of life that moves around this whole monsoon system. However, not all places in India get torrential rain during one time of the year and not the rest. It is really subtle, and it is different depending upon where you are in this part of the world.

Parts of the subcontinent get tremendous amounts of rain, while other places like New Delhi, the capital, are not so much different than Washington DC. They are in the midlatitudes and do have a kind of seasonal change, but it is a bit warmer and drier throughout the year. They don't get torrential rains but there is a strong rainy season. It gets dry in the winter, really dry into the spring, and then the rains come. The rains do tend to concentrate in late spring/early summer, not much different from parts of the United States. So just to give you an idea and make sure that the Plaid Avenger is not steering you wrong, we hear about monsoon Asia and monsoon India, and yes indeed it is a factor in the physical world there, but it's not uniformly distributed. There aren't tremendous amounts of rainfall in all places at once with dry seasons in between. It is quite a dynamic system, actually.

PEOPLE POWER

We've discussed the physical components of South Asia, but what about the people? Where are the people? In South Asia there are lots of people, hell-loads of people. India's population alone has now topped 1 billion. If we look at Pakistan, their population has now topped over 165 million and Bangladesh over 147 million. The point I am trying to make here is that all three of those countries are in the top ten of the most populated countries on the planet. Taken as a singular region, it is well over a billion and a half people. Someone do the math for me, what's a billion and a half of six billion? Isn't that closing in on a fourth maybe a fifth, or 20 percent of the world's population in this one region? This is of serious consequence when trying to figure out what is happening in the world.

Where are these people? Are they concentrated in coastal margins? Are they in big cities? Small villages? Are they in the mountains or the river valleys? The answer is yes! They are everywhere and live all over this place. In fact, to go out on a limb here, the Plaid Avenger spent quite a bit of time in India undercover for various missions, and there really is no place you can go in India proper that you can't find people at all hours of the day and night. This is a region that does not sleep. This is a busy place all the time with people everywhere. You can't run out into the woods and crap under a bush without ten people hanging out there doing the same thing. This place is bustling, it's happening, and it's happening nonstop. If we just look at a handful of countries like Bangladesh, India, and Pakistan, throw in China, Indonesia and Japan, we are looking at maybe 12 percent of the world's land area. On that 12 percent of the world's land area, 52 percent of its population lives.

Let's describe some of these people all packed in all over the damn place in a little more detail. Why are South Asians different from other Asians? When we think of India we typically think of Hindus. Is that a religion, a language, or an ethnic group? Let's sort some of these terms out.

Undercover agents at work.

HINDU OR HINDI?

Hindi is a language, and so we therefore think that's the main language of India. We are wrong already. Hindi is a language, one of maybe 15 or 20 major languages spoken in just this one region. Those are just the major languages; there are several hundred dialects and mixed languages through South Asia. This is very confusing for us from other parts of the world where we live in primarily single language societies. We assume there must be some linguistic commonality in this region. There is no majority language at the moment in India. In fact, if you want to cite a lingua franca of this region, that would be English. That's got something to do with India's English colonial period. English is spoken by a lot of folks, but perhaps only 15 to 20 percent of the population. Hindi is just another language of many spoken here, and indeed if you talk to folks from India, Bangladesh, or Pakistan, you will find that many of them speak several languages.

Major Religions
- Hindu
- Muslim
- Christian
- Tribal / Animist
- Buddhist
- Sikh

Arabian Sea

Bay of Bengal

INDIAN OCEAN

One of the first languages South Asians learn is their local dialect. Again, that can be one of several hundred dialects and mixed languages. The second one they learn is often something like Hindi, which can be used as a kind of lingua franca inside India. The third one is typically English for perhaps obvious reasons of economic advantage. So there are a variety of languages spoken and they exist in a kind of hierarchy of how they are learned. English usually wins out in today's world, Hindi is a far distant second, and a local dialect would be third.

So not all South Asians are Hindi, not even close. So, how about are they *Hindu?* They are not all speaking *Hindi*, but are they all *Hindu?* **Hindu** is a religious system, and we tend to think of Hinduism as a description of the religious lifestyle of people in India. When you are around Indian people, they now recognize the term Hinduism as describing their religion, but it does not really mean anything to them. It is not a self-defined term, like Christianity being based on the life and teachings of Christ. Hinduism is a kind of conglomeration of cultural beliefs that someone from the outside world said, "Well you guys speak Hindi . . . how about we call this Hindu?"

When we think of India proper, we think the majority of people follow Hinduism. However, the majority of people in Pakistan are Muslim. The majority of people in Bangladesh are Muslim. The majority of people in Sri Lanka are neither of the two. They are Buddhist instead. So we have a nice little mix of some Western religion and Eastern religion dancing around this place. Bhutan is primarily Buddhist with some Hindu, and Nepal is mostly Hindu with some Buddhist. So we have kind of a confusing mix of things going on here, but the two major power players of course are Hinduism and Islam.

VISHNU VS. MUHAMMAD VS. BUDDHA

How did this get to be? What is the deal with this religion stuff? Buddhism is primarily in Sri Lanka and Bhutan and in the Tibetan plateau just north of this region. The Buddha, Siddhartha, the main man in the Buddhist lifestyle, was actually a Hindu born in India. (In a similar vein, Jesus Christ was actually Jewish.) He eventually thought, "Hey, I dig Hinduism; I dig the lifestyle, except this whole life cycle and being reborn again and again, and always suffering and being reborn sucks!" So he invented his little reform movement to change things, think of things in a different way and be removed from the endless cycle of rebirth. Buddhism is a universalizing religion and as such, he wanted to spread it to other places and it spread itself right out of India. It had its heyday from about 300 BCE to 300 or 400 CE. It was in vogue. Everybody dug it for a while, but Hinduism eventually displaced it in India once again, and it largely disappeared. Now when we think of Buddhist areas, we have Sri Lanka and Bhutan here, but we also think of Tibet, China, even Mongolia and Japan as having a huge Buddhist influence. Buddhism moved on beyond India proper.

So where did the Muslims come from then? Well, it's the same deal if we think religiously. Muslims didn't come around until about 600 or 700 CE after the death of the prophet Mohammad. The empire, what I call the Arab-Islamic empire, expands out from the Middle East all the way over to the northern fringes of South Asia. For the next thousand years they will heavily influence South Asia. There has historically been some friction between the Muslims and Hindus, and it's still not over. Muslim-Hindu friction is far from a historical remnant. It is still a very real issue, typically where the majorities of each belief meet: on the Pakistan-India border. Again, Pakistan is predominately Islamic and India predominately Hindu. Tensions primarily arise in the western states of India and sometimes manifest themselves in violence.

CULTURAL HEARTHINESS

Like China, Mesopotamia, and the ancient civilizations in Middle America, the Indus River valley where we find India and Pakistan proper is an ancient cultural hearth. A civilization cropped up on its own, with its own big cities and architecture, mathematics, and unique cultural ideas. South Asian culture was perpetuated throughout the millennia in its isolated environment, allowing it to remain quite different from China, or even closer next door, Mesopotamia. These are very different places because of their spontaneous creation and uninhibited growth for extended periods of time. I am not going to bore you with a lot of details about ancient history in this part of the world because it is too rich, and like China, there is too damn much. So I just want you to know that throughout history in this part of the world we have multiple episodes of different empires and kingdoms, the formations of some of the biggies of philosophy. Some classics of world religion started out here. Hinduism started here and gave rise to the evolution of Buddhism. Islam was infused later to combine a unique cultural dynamic in this region.

HISTORICAL HAPPENINGS

Let's get back to the period that I was talking about earlier, the period of Muslim dominance. Yes we had Hinduism and Buddhism, but eventually the Muslims came to town around 1000 CE. This is a continuation of the expansion of the Arab-Islamic Empire, which began to spread after the death of the prophet in 632 CE. Islam makes its way into Afghanistan and with the help of the Mughal Conquest and a little bit later, ends up taking over virtually all of what is Pakistan and India in today's world. They create the Mughal Empire.

MUGHAL MANIA

The Mughal Empire dominated South Asia for about 800 years from 1000CE to about 1757CE. It was basically a hierarchy of Muslim rulers, a thin veneer of Islamic influence over the millions of Hindus that lived there. The ruling class was Islamic, but the majority of the population

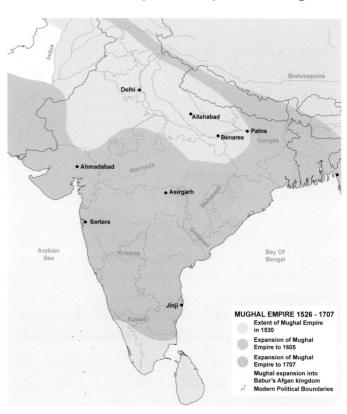

MUGHAL EMPIRE 1526 - 1707
- Extent of Mughal Empire in 1530
- Expansion of Mughal Empire to 1605
- Expansion of Mughal Empire to 1707
- Mughal expansion into Babur's Afgan kingdom
- Modern Political Boundaries

remained Hindu. I want to make sure you understand that because when we look at today's India, there are a huge number of Muslims in India today—around 150 million. That population of Muslims in Hindu-dominated India is actually larger than the population of Muslims in Saudi Arabia, Iraq, Iran, or just about any country. The Muslim minority in India is bigger than the Muslim majority in most other Islamic countries. So this is a significant demographic to consider, and it has its roots in this period of Muslim influence during the Mughal Empire.

The dominance after 1757 soon shifts. Small kingdoms and fiefdoms comprise this period of the Mughal Empire, like European feudalism or Japanese Shogunates, with princes and royal courts. There is kind of a main king, but there are sub-princes and sub-dukes under those guys that control smaller and smaller territories. The beginning of the end of this is around 1700, as foreign intervention starts to creep in. Surprise! Who would be responsible for this foreign intervention? Who would be sending out fleets of ships to go trade or establish in-roads in other parts of the world?

ENTER THE EUROPEANS

That's right, our old friends back in Western Europe, one up-and-coming colonial power in particular: the British. Actually, the Portuguese also came there and established a small trade province on the west coast of India, called **Goa.** These two European powers make inroads into South Asia for the main purpose of trading. You may have even heard of the British East India Trading Company, for instance. It was a company sponsored by the British government. They worked out a deal with the company saying, "Here is your charter, go out and establish trade with South Asia; we will insure the boats and we get a cut of your business."

Why would they want to do this? You should know very well by now. They want to get raw commodities—they want the good stuff. Stuff like spices, silks, and ceramics. This is not a new story; it's a continuation of the same old same old. The

Can you spot the European establishing trade links in this picture?

East India Trading Company, sponsored by the British, wants to get in here and get first pick on all the best stuff. They turn out to be very good at this.

These guys are not just partially successful; they are radically successful at establishing trade with South Asia because the Mughal Empire is winding down a little, doesn't have a very firm grip on things. Again there is only a small veneer of Mughals in control of that vast majority of Hindus in India, so their control weakens and it becomes fairly easy to get in and establish port cities and trading colonies. These cities start to grow into territories that the trading company controls. They essentially go into the next fiefdom or dukedom over and chat with the prince, "Hey, we're going to give you loads of money to trade some stuff with us. It's going to be good for you!" Lots of princes said, "Yeah, it looks good to me. I'll sign a trade deal, no problem!" So through diplomatic relations and strategic ties, the Brits make their way in and are way more successful than they ever dreamed. They end up controlling huge chunks of land after a while.

Eventually, disputes arise between princes who had some previous friction between their kingdoms. This trading company is so damn successful that, though it is set up exclusively for trade, it finds itself acting as a diplomatic entity between these feuding kingdoms. These disputes could potentially turn into violent conflict, and that would ruin trade completely. So the higher-ups at the trading post glance at their royal charter, and get Britain on the horn to let them know that things may be getting out of hand.

Great Britain looks at this mess and says, "Whoa, this is not your charter! What the hell is going on here? Sit tight, we're taking this shit over." A trading company is not fully equipped to handle colonization. That's why they're in the trading business. So the British crown sends in the warships and court jesters and everything in between and fully colonizes India. From then forward, we are talking about 1800 now, this whole territory of what is now India, Pakistan, and Bangladesh, is under the umbrella known as **British India.** It is an official British colony. There are some independent kingdoms left over that hold out and have diplomatic relations, places like Bhutan, the kingdom of Nepal, and Ceylon, which is now Sri Lanka. These guys hold out as independent territories and avoid the burden of colonialism. All the rest of it, the big three, are all one big land conglomeration called British India.

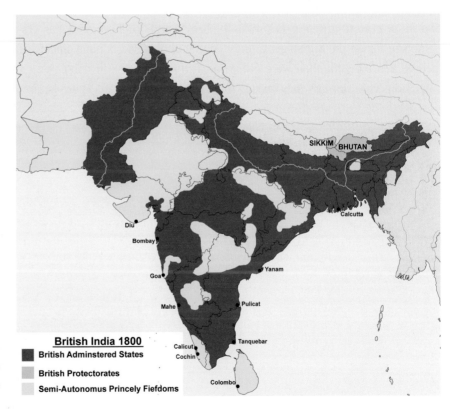

British India 1800

■ British Adminstered States

■ British Protectorates

■ Semi-Autonomus Princely Fiefdoms

India is the biggest country (I keep referring only to India because India is the power player—the Plaid calls it like it is); it has the biggest population, the biggest economy, and the biggest military. When we think of India and South Asia as a whole, it is not completely developed but it is certainly not in last place. It is much better off than other places like

Africa or even closer places in Central Asia or Southeast Asia. What is it that is different about South Asia that has kept it ahead of the pack when it comes to developing countries or developing regions? It has a lot to do with its colonial experience. Some things happened in British India that gave it its strategic advantage. Before I piss off my Indian friends, let me state for the record: Colonialism sucks! And the fact that the British were controlling your people probably sucked for a couple hundred years. However, there were some distinct advantages that have put India in the catbird seat today.

DROP THE WICKET, JAMES, IT'S TEATIME: ADVANTAGES OF BRITISH COLONIALISM

My Indian friends, you're not so bad off. **Number one,** it was a singular European entity that took you over. As such, there wasn't internal fracturing like in Africa or even to a lesser degree in South America or Southeast Asia. That's kind of a plus. At least you know exactly who to blame. **Number two,** the colonizer was Britain, which means you spoke the Queen's English. While at the time it may have been revolting to your great granddad, it has benefited you greatly in today's world. English is the lingua franca of business, travel, airlines, the international space station, and technology. Everybody speaks English when they deal with that stuff, and that has put you, Indians, on a strategic fast track. It is a great advantage to speak English and that's part of your colonial heritage.

There's a good chap, now fetch us a spot of tea!

What else did Britain do differently here than in other places that were colonized on the planet? **Number three:** Internal investment. That's a biggie. In Africa we pointed out that most investment was simply to extract the resources; just to get stuff out. We could even say that about the New World. When they get to the New World, or even to Africa or Australia, the British and other colonial masters don't really add too much in the way of infrastructure. When the British get to India in the 1800s, this is a huge place with a long history, with big cities, and millions of people, more people than were in Europe at that time. The British can't just wipe India clean and start again by building new industries, nor can they merely focus on extracting stuff. There is already stuff going on, preexisting economies and

---

What's the Deal with . . . the Great Mutiny?

Why two different names for the same thing? Well, it depends on who's telling the story. "Mutiny" has the connotation of something bad that needed to be suppressed. "War for Independence" has a more positive connotation of, "We are trying to be free." Try and figure out which group called it what. What was the Great Mutiny all about? It was obviously about independence, but amazingly enough it came to a head because of fat. Animal fat to be exact. Pig fat, cow fat, lard, all kinds of yummy animal fat put together in a big stew. Why would the British care about fat? They didn't. However the British, during their colonial days were pretty savvy about controlling the local populations, and one of the more savvy ways they did this was by employing locals in the army and the police force. Why would they do that, Plaid Avenger?

Here's why: When you are obviously from a different part of the world and your skin color is obviously different, and your religion is obviously different, and your language is obviously different, people are immediately on guard if you boss them around and tell them what to do. That sort of thing causes resentment issues to crop up. "This bastard thinks that he's better than me! I don't like being bossed around by an outsider. What the hell does he know?" The Brits were familiar with this human tendency. They knew that they could alleviate this problem by getting local people who look like the people there, talk like the people there, understand the problems and issues of the people there . . . and training *them* to beat down the locals! It's a brilliant system, it's easy to implement; the Brits did it all over the place, and it worked magically in India.

Back to the fat: Nobody was eating it; they were using it to grease the cartridges for their guns. Oh, that's not a big deal. How could that cause a mutiny? People in India at the time were of what two religions?

cultural systems. So the Brits focus in British India was updating the infrastructure, improving it, modernizing, and building railroads and communication systems across all of British India, some of which are still in use today.

So again, I cannot stress enough that colonialism sucks. I am sure South Asians would have preferred being on their own. But the British brought in a lot of perks, and if you look at colonial experiences around the world, British India's was really not too bad in comparison. In addition, the introduction of the Europeans in the America's decimated local populations; that didn't happen here either. The colonial story is radically different here in South Asia.

ADVANTAGES, SCHMADVANTAGES

Having talked about the advantages, it still sucks alright. The Indians are being ruled and controlled by a different people, a different culture. They are being ruled and controlled by whiteys from another place. These British dudes dress funny and talk even funnier, and they play these kind of strange games like cricket, and dance around playing croquet—pretty strange stuff. Who wants to be ruled by guys like that? Indeed, internal unrest develops fairly early on in this game. Many Indian folks weren't too keen on this from the get-go. They weren't so keen on the Mughals, and they were less keen on the British and wanted to get them the hell out of there. This comes to a head for the first time in 1857, when something called the **Great Mutiny** occurs. You might also see this referenced in India as the "First War for Independence."

MY MAIN MAN MAHATMA

Enter Mahatma. Everybody knows Gandhi. He's one of the coolest dudes in world history. Everybody loves Gandhi, kind of, so what's his deal? Gandhi was an Indian guy trained as a lawyer in Great Britain who spent some time in South Africa peddling his craft. He was a British citizen because all folks in the colonial system are citizens of the mother country. So when he was down in South Africa he became incensed because he realized that though he was a British citizen, he was still considered second-class by "true" British people (aka white British people). Gandhi had an awakening at this point and was like, "This sucks. I am not really a British person even though I went to school in Britain, I talk like a British person, I work with British people, but I am still not really British. The British don't think I'm British."

Most famous 'little brown man.'

That's right, Hinduism and Islam. What people would have problems handling cow fat and pig fat to grease the cartridges of their guns? That's right, Hindus and Muslims. Cows are sacred in Hinduism and pork is unclean to Islamic folks. In all of their wisdom, the British soldiers said, "Here's the grease for your guns, chaps. Cheerio!" The local soldiers said, "We hear it's made of pig and cow fat. We're not touching it." The British in all of their worldly wisdom said, "Do it or die." And the Great Mutiny began.

It was quelled fairly quickly and didn't become a very big uprising, but it is still remembered in popular culture. This was the first attempt to throw off the yoke of British Imperialism. The Great Mutiny, as coined by the British, and the War for Independence as coined by the locals, those being the Indian guys. Obviously the British are going to be ejected at some point, because they aren't there now. Ok, so how did British colonialism end if it didn't end with the Great Mutiny? Where did they go from there?

Oh! A circus! No wonder they mutinied.

He kind of got bothered by this and went back to the motherland where he realized the British were assholes. (Okay, excluding Monty Python.) He was Indian and wanted India to belong to and be run by Indians.

Gandhi started a peaceful movement to kick the British out. In other words, he started the movement saying, "You are going to leave. We're not going to shoot at you. We are not going to fight you, we are not going to beat you down with clubs and physically kick you out. We are going to make you leave without even raising a fist. With no violence."

Now how did he do this? Well, he did a variety of things. Of course he didn't do it by himself, but he was the driving force and most popular leader of this nonviolent movement. He not only ended colonialism in British India, he simultaneously and much, much, much, much more importantly ended **neocolonialism** at the same time. He realized the two things were inherently tied together.

What is neocolonialism? Neocolonialism is when a foreign entity controls your country, not politically, not physically, but economically. It owns a lot of the business and controls the flow of goods and services, and sets up things that are an advantage to their country and not yours. One of the reasons India is doing really well in the world today, while places in Africa aren't, is because neocolonialism is still happening in Africa and it was stopped in India.

When the British came into India it was during Britain's industrial era, and they needed raw commodities. They have all these weaving mills and industrial stuff and the industrial capacity to make things, but they need raw materials. Process the cheap raw materials into things that sell for more money. The best example of this neocolonial economic system in India is the wool the Indians had been spinning into their own cloth for 5,000 years. The British bought the wool from them for virtually nothing, processed it into nice crisp linens in their own British factories back home, which employed their own people. The folks in Britain can then make a good wage, and then Britain brings back the cloth to sell to the Indians for 100 times what they bought the wool for. This is really a fantastic deal; this is sweet. How can the Indians say no? They really can't because the British were in control of the country.

Gandhi was aware of this system when he started this nonviolent movement. He told everyone, "We need to kick these guys out of here. We could physically take up arms and kick these guys out, but the system is so skewed, we'd still be screwed. We need to fix it from the inside out. We need to end this neocolonialism crap along with the political colonialism. Hey! Why are you dudes buying this British cloth? What in the hell are you thinking about?" I am paraphrasing; Gandhi probably never said "hell" or "dudes." Back to Gandhi: "We are Indians; we have been making cloth since before there even was a Great Britain. Why are we buying cloth from these guys? Can someone explain this to me? It makes no sense whatsoever! Stop buying British cloth and start weaving your own again." Gandhi only wore homespun cloth he made himself for the entire second half of his life. His kind of skimpy toga was a symbolic gesture saying, "Hey look, this is all you need. You don't need any of that fancy stuff." In fact if you ever see pictures, a documentary, or even the movie Gandhi, you will see that he is often around a spinning wheel. The spinning wheel was a symbol for the peaceful independence movement. "Do it yourself; let's break from this economic cycle. Free yourself from this slavery and make your own cloth!"

Once people heard of this practical way to gain independence, the movement started to gain speed. Again we are talking about the late 1930s getting into the early 1940s, but it wasn't a nationwide deal yet. More people were talking about independence, but most folks were still talking about nothing. This little nonviolent movement was kind of a mosquito bite to the British, no big deal. As the movement progressed, the British started to pay attention. "We might want to start dealing with this Gandhi guy and figure out how to shut him down." So what did they do? They made the cloth cheaper. They make it so cheap that people can't afford not to buy it.

When Gandhi saw this he said, "Well ok, that got their attention! I have another idea. We are currently buying salt from the British. Hello, can I have everyone's attention? We have a ton of coastline where there is this substance called

The Mahatma

4 oz. Indian chai tea

1 oz Goldschlager cinnamon schnapps

2 oz Stoli vanilla vodka

In a pot, heat 1 cup water & 1 cup milk. Add 1/5 teaspoon chai masala. Add 2 teaspoons tea leaves. Stir occasionally & bring to a boil. Strain & add Goldschlager schnapps and Stoli vodka. Gandhi would not have imbibed, but the rest of us will. Ride the monsoon!

saltwater. It becomes salt when the water evaporates. Salt is free, why are we paying for it?" He got the word out and in 1930 organized a 'Salt March' to the sea, like a common strike, where everybody went to the coast and made salt. The movement actually grew in popularity and Indians set up salt producing shops on the coastline. Gandhi himself worked at them while he was at speaking engagements and rallying the people. This became a big deal and the British were starting to get pissed off because their profits were being cut in two by this salt boycott.

These things culminate in British discussions with Gandhi. "Hey Gandhi, lets work things out; we are your buddies." Gandhi refused: "It's time for you limeys to get the hell out." The British still did not think that it was too big of a deal. Gandhi tries a different tactic. By now he's gotten massively popular, and he encourages everybody in India, which at this time was probably half a billion people, to not go to work the next day. "Everybody skip work; we're having a general strike." The British, being very much in touch with the common people (can you smell the sarcasm?), actually had no idea this was happening. It was a smashing success. The whole country just stopped in one day.

This is when the British really see the writing on the wall and realize that the people actually do have the real power here. They can call a general strike, they can cease all economic activity, and they can shut down this country. They just did. They are willing to make it incredibly unprofitable for the British to be there. At the same time this is happening, World War II has broken out. If you know anything about World War II or read any of the chapters thus far in this book, you realize that it is kind of a big deal in Europe, and that keeps the British quite busy.

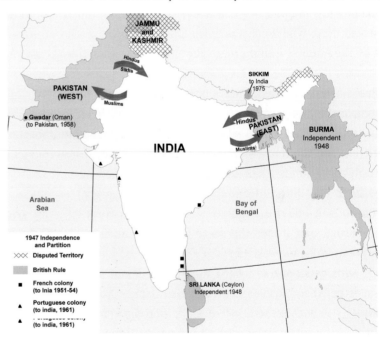

We know that Europe is essentially destroyed at the end of World War II. The British are spent physically, mentally, and economically, and all these protests are occurring in India at the same time and it just becomes too much. They dragged India along to support them in World War II, but the common perception on the street was "It's not our war. We are not getting involved. We are trying to kick you out of here. We are not coming to Europe to spill blood for you, ours or anyone else's." By 1945, the Brits pretty much had to throw in the towel; they just couldn't hold onto India anymore. They didn't have the resources to keep it under control, by force or otherwise. They had to rebuild at home. They started the concession talks for India to become independent, and in 1947, that is exactly what happened. In 1947 they drew it up on the conference table and handed over control to the locals.

PAK'IN OUR BAGS FOR THE PARTITION PARTY

But now the story gets complicated. A bunch of other people in the country wanted another kind of independence. "We want an India too, but not Gandhi's India. We aren't Hindus like Gandhi; we're Muslims." This brings us back full circle on the topic of religion. There is still a huge minority of Muslims in this country whose basic platform was, "The British suck, but here is the deal; we are a minority, and if the British walk out of here the Hindu majority will kick the living shit out of us. The only reason they haven't yet was because the British have been in control for a couple hundred years. If we don't get our own place, if we can't subdivide British India and get our own country, then we don't want the British to leave."

Ali Jinnah, Father of Pakistan

Here is where we have to introduce a new character in our play and that is a guy called Ali Jinnah. Gandhi is often credited with being the father of India, and Ali Jinnah is often credited with being the father of Pakistan. He was a Muslim in British India and was the one who was leading the fight for the formation of a distinct and separate sovereign state for Muslims. He was also British trained and schooled, a lawyer just like Gandhi, and a savvy politician. Gandhi was vehemently opposed to this, as were many others in India. However, when all was said and done that's how it had to go down. It got tense once Jinnah told Gandhi that he didn't want the British to leave. Gandhi didn't want that; he had been fighting for years to be free of the British, so he considered it the lesser of two evils. He and his party capitulated and said, "We want a unified state, but we'll settle for the split." (On a side note here there is actually a minority of people in India who actually hate Gandhi. They blame him for the country split.)

In 1947 Britain packed up shop, redrew the map, setup partitions, and sailed off. What we see here in this map is something similar to today's map. We've got Pakistan, India, and another place called Bangladesh, but on this map it is labeled as Pakistan East. The agreement set in place two separate homelands, areas for the Muslims in British India. Again as you see on the map, it is Pakistan East and Pakistan West, which are two different territories who at the same time were a singular sovereign state. It was Pakistan, but with an eastern and western side. India was for the Hindus, and Pakistan was for the Muslims. This is all fine and dandy on a map, but the reality is of course that Muslims and Hindus are living all over the damn place. This really got to a fever pitch that on this day of independence in 1947 when there was a mass migration of people. Tens of millions of people found themselves on the wrong side of the border and suddenly needed to move.

The Muslims in India were like, "Holy shit, we better get over to Pakistan East or West or we are going to get the hell beat out of us!" The Hindus in Pakistan East or West said, "We're on the wrong side; we need to get over to India proper." This is a very turbulent time, a bloody day in India's history. As you might expect, people were being uprooted from their homelands, places where their families may have been forever, and are now on the wrong side because of the new lines on the map. They rip up all their material possessions, all their family, and move. They are instantaneous refugees. The friction and the tension grew between these massive movements of people who were not necessarily enemies but certainly not friends, their differences accentuated by going in two different directions down the highway. This ends in violence: massive rioting. It is a nasty day in history, and it sets the stage for future tensions between India and Pakistan.

This gets back to what I was talking about with issues between Muslims and Hindus in today's world. This is still hot. In the last five years there have been three different massive rioting incidents. Unknown things spark the unrest and massive slaughters of Muslims, which then spark slaughters of Hindus, which are then avenged in mass slaughters of Muslims. This has gotten to be nasty business here in recent history. It has actually gone to full-fledged international warfare three different times since 1947.

The only date I want you to remember is the one in 1971 when it wasn't so much based on religious conflict as it was a political maneuver by Pakistan East. They weren't happy. They felt that Pakistan West was too far away to properly understand their needs. India helped fuel this internal dissent, which turned into

outright warfare between Pakistan West and India during which India helped convince Pakistan East to declare independence. And now it's Bangladesh. So, now we have three countries and now you understand why Pakistan West is almost 100 percent Muslim, why Bangladesh is almost 100 percent Muslim, and why India is somewhere in between with a vast Hindu majority. Occasionally, riots still occur today, mostly along that Pakistan/India border. I remember a few years ago when a trainload of about 40 Muslims got burned to death after some Hindus barred the entrances and exits and caught the damn thing on fire. This sparked about two months of retribution riots. This problem is a historical relic of the tension from long ago, still active in today's South Asia.

TIME FOR TODAY'S SOUTH ASIA

This is a mixed bag of states, an assortment of cookies. Are these places developed or are they developing? Who's got the money? Who's doing well? Who's not? When we look at South Asia, India is the premier powerhouse player with the most people and the biggest economy—one that is really exploding right now. Exploding like China? Not quite that hot, but it is developing fast. They are developing a middle class as well, so the developed/developing question is a tough call. Let's look at some issues to help us define their status.

THE LITTLE COUNTRIES

We have mostly talked about the three big boys in this region: India being the biggest giant and Pakistan and Bangladesh being the other two. What about the other countries, the three smaller guys, Bhutan, Nepal, and Sri Lanka?

Bhutan is easy. The whole country is like a Buddhist monastery. They have been hosting their refugee brothers from Tibet for quite some time. It is a home away from home for the Tibetan monks, including the Dalai Lama. Bhutan is a curious place in that it is trying to preserve its 11th century standards in the face of 21st century advancements. Until 1999, there was a nationwide ban on television and the Internet. Though the ban has been lifted, there are still active movements to prevent popular culture from the rest of the world intervening in their culture that is still an old school monarchy. Bhutan has held its own throughout the centuries. If you want to time travel, go there.

Nepal next door is perhaps even more fascinating because it would be similar to Bhutan a whopping 20 years ago, but now it is utter chaos. I want to end this little section talking about two poles of conflict on either side of this South Asian Region. The active conflict bookends: Nepal in the north and Sri Lanka in the south. Both countries are on the brink of civil war/collapse/insurgency where people are going to get killed en masse. Nepal in the last few years has had an increasingly bigger problem with a Maoist insurgency that wants to totally eject the ruling monarchy. Their primary mission is to change the government from a constitutional monarchy to perhaps communism, or maybe socialism. It's not very clear. What is clear in Nepal is that there is fighting, and over 11,000 people have died since 1996 when this insurgency got kicked off. There has been a rebel group scattered throughout the country that's been fairly effective in striking targets and generally causing chaos.

On top of that, in 2001, the heir to the throne went postal and shot the entire royal family over their choice of his bride. He then shot himself but lived for a little while longer. He was crowned king while he was comatose. That event fueled the fire for the Maoist rebels; they loved the idea of having a comatose king. They thought it was great and that they may be able to get control of the state by causing more chaos with no king to rule the country. When the comatose king died two days later, a lesser-known uncle became king and began pulling power away from more democratic institutions to himself, and he has been doing this under the guise of needing more power to fight the rebel insurgency.

In April 2006, in the government's effort to crack down on the Maoists, they pissed off the prodemocracy movement in the country. So what we have is this bizarre triangle of folks. Now the Maoists are teaming up with the prodemocracy people to overthrow the monarchy all together. And they pretty much accomplished this by 2008; the monarchy has been sidelined, elections are being held and the place is now starting to settle down quite a bit. It is still a very new democratic experiment for these folks, so future instability is entirely possible, and probable, as they figure out how to go forward.

Let's go to the other side of the South Asian region for the other still quite active conflict in **Sri Lanka.** We will talk more about Sri Lanka in

What's the Deal with . . . the Tamil Tigers?

In Sri Lanka, the rebel insurgents/terrorists have a killer mascot . . . literally. The dudes call themselves the Tamil Tigers. That's their political party. These guys are fairly vicious and by all standards they would be in the top tier of terrorist organizations for their practices. The Tigers have been blowing up people via human suicide bombs for quite some time now, a technique they mastered in the 1970s. In fact, they had women strapped with explosives, making attempts on the prime minister on several occasions. Several years ago they went into a political rally during the Sri Lankan presidential elections, walked into the winning candidate's victory speech and blew out the whole base floor of the hotel. They also have boats and have sunk several Sri Lankan Navy ships. This is some pretty serious shit and it has gone through phases where the rebels and the government have gotten together and tried to calm things down and things looked like there were going to go pretty well, but everything's disintegrating now.

Ethnic communities and religions

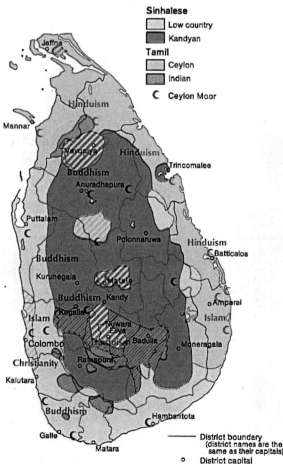

Sinhalese
- Low country
- Kandyan

Tamil
- Ceylon
- Indian

C Ceylon Moor

District boundary
(district names are the same as their capitals)

o District capital

the Plaid Avenger hotspots chapter, but let's introduce the situation here: Sri Lanka is a country that is bordering on civil war. Perhaps that's a bit strong, and my Sri Lankan friends may disagree, but they have been off and on for about 20 to 30 years now, all based on an ethnic division. In an ethnic enclave on the northern fringe of the island there are people called the Tamils. It's an ethnic group that actually came from India. The Sri Lankans proper, the people on the rest of the island, are the ones that run the government and have the real power. This has been a face off for several decades now in terms of the Tamils either wanting an independent homeland, a sovereign state, or more autonomy and more power.

So this is a summary of the two poles of South Asia outside the realm of the three giants. We have some conflict that is quite active, and may get much hotter. But back to the giants . . .

ENERGETIC INDIA

So are they developed or developing? India is currently the largest democracy on the planet. That looks like one in the plus column for developed. They are also currently in a transition from a socialist slant to full-fledged capitalism. They, like China, are kind of approaching something we may call "the wild west of capitalism." It is really a free market there now; things are really happening, and private enterprise is really exploding. On top of that, what you have is a lot of what used to be government-run

things becoming **privatized.** Privatized means the Indian government, during it's more socialist leanings, controlled things like the electric grid, train services, a lot of the main energy production industries, and in the last five or six years, they have started to sell this off to private investors. "We'll let private capitalists take that and we'll just tax it and perhaps make more money off of it." This big switch to capitalism is one of the reasons you have this infusion of capital from around the world. Again, we are talking particularly about India.

"Yes Plaid Avenger, my back office is always open for you . . ."

Why else is India bustling right now? They have several distinct advantages from British influence; one we already pointed out is that they speak English. India is well-equipped to embrace the world economically, and they are doing just that. Indeed when your computer breaks and you get on the phone to have someone help you fix it, who are you talking to? You are probably talking to someone from India. They are big into telecommunications now, into high technology, and the service sector. It is actually quite fascinating because they have whole divisions of technical support and telemarketers there that specifically train people to not just speak English, but to train them how to speak certain regional dialects of English. So if you go into a technical support center outside of New Delhi, the huge room with 500 to 600

people in it will be subdivided into what region of the United States they are receiving calls from. So there is a Midwestern section, perhaps a Californian section where they talk surfer dude language, or a northeastern section where they talk real fast with those Boston accents, or a southeastern quadrant where they talk with a long drawl, southern belle style.

We also talked about how the British invested heavily in their infrastructure, and that has benefited them in today's world too. Another thing that India is famous for is something called **back offices.** The hot word in today's world is **outsourcing.** What's that? It means there is cheaper labor there and more people to do it, so jobs move there because companies can save money. Unlike other places in the world, say China or other developing countries, these folks speak English, and most working age Indians are fairly well-educated. This is a huge advantage to India in terms of this outsourcing, but also something called back offices. Back offices actually have a bit of a longer history than outsourcing.

Back offices are companies that set up in India decades ago. When you go to the doctor, for example, he scribbles out your symptoms as you tell him you have herpes, and hemorrhoids, and ingrown hairs. The doctor is writing all this down and at the end of the day he hands it to his secretary to transcribe into a digital file. What has been happening in the US is that after the doctor closes down, the secretaries fax the notes to India to a back office where people who speak and read English transcribe the notes into a digital file, and then send them back. So what's

Indian lager of choice . . .

this back office got to do with it? Why was this whole system possible? Well, think about what I just said, as the doctor's office is closing in America, what is happening in India? That's right! They are waking up. It is a complimentary business arrangement, so doctors can get work done more efficiently.

But that's not all! India is fast becoming a center for IT technology development, not just basic manufacturing and low-level service sector stuff. Call centers combined with software development center . . . now that's a combo that everyone can rally around! India has an extremely large (and growing bigger everyday) pool of highly educated and skilled engineers, programmers, and entrepreneurs that are making it a desirable location for technology-oriented companies across the board. We are talking quaternary level stuff here brothers and sisters! Every country wants those jobs! And India is doing a great job becoming a real global center for emerging technologies . . . perhaps even better than China, and increasingly competitive with the US and EU.

Things are looking up for India; hell they were never looking down too much to begin with, but this is a place that is bustling right now. You've got a democracy, capitalism, international investment, and jobs here getting outsourced to our Indian friends. The result of all these things taken collectively is that you also have a burgeoning middle class in India as well . . . and that is a true marker of success in today's world. So obviously it must be a developed region. . . . right? Well, that's still a tricky call.

Remember the Plaid Avenger rule of thumb for development. Is it developed or developing? Say a country has all the appearances of a developed nation. They have the highest levels of technology. They have nuclear weapons. They have it all. But are they developed? The Plaid answer is probably not. We always have to consider is how the majority of people are doing there. How is the average Joe on the street living? While India has a lot of pluses going for it, it doesn't have that in terms of the average Sanjay on the street. The average man on the street is still living on about a buck a day. They've still got intense poverty across this region as a whole. Indeed while there is lots of good stuff happening and there's a growing middle class, there is still tremendous wealth disparity. Most people live in what we would call abject poverty. When you visit India don't be shocked; it is something that takes Westerners a while to become accustomed to— impoverished children, dirt roads, animals shitting everywhere. It is not something that people from the West can really get their heads around. You can even see this in big cities.

But let the Plaid throw in a disclaimer to finish this off: they do have a growing middle class, and that is one of the tip-offs that it is developing fast. A few people can get really, really rich and everyone else can remain dirt poor, so that's not a fully-developed region. But if that middle class continues to grow, then indeed things are going well, and that is what is happening in India today.

Here's another disclaimer to throw in: when you talk to folks from India in universities across the United States or even Europe, 20 years ago they would have come to the university to get trained and try and stay. They would come for engineering or science and look for a job in their host country because that is where the good jobs are. It's fascinating to the Plaid Avenger that now this trend is starting to reverse. Indian people are coming to America or Europe to get a degree and are then going right back home again because that's where the action is. While they could get a good job here, they can get a better one there. They are going to have to work a little harder; they may have to open up their own business, but this is where it's bustling and that's why you have the growing middle class. I am not just talking about computer technology and computer programming and all that other stuff. There are people going back and starting their own Gap stores and McDonalds. It is at that point where they are at the critical mass and people want to go back there and make a real fortune, not just a small fortune. India is on the development path, but it has a ways to go.

One last thing about India's position in the world today is a reiteration of the fact that the whole South Asian region is physically isolated, though not isolationist. India has been an independent player for the last 50 years; they are very careful about the countries they make allegiances with. India's independence from Britain actually coincides with the beginning of the Cold War. So what? I point this out because India never sided up during the Cold War. In fact, they are one of the few countries in the so-called Third World category that said, "No, we are not going to choose a side." Remember First World was the capitalist democracy, the Second World was the Commie Soviets, and the Third World referred to everybody who wasn't on team one or two. The term is a Cold War relic that had nothing to do with whether you were poor or rich, but whether or not you sided up.

The Indians are independently minded. I have been fascinated for a long time about why the US has not established stronger trading and strategic ties with India. Why would they? Well, India has a huge population and a huge potential market for businesses. And hell, the people even speak English! India is also a democracy just like the US. They have all kinds of traditions that are just like ours, so why have we not had a closer relationship with them? One of the answers is because of its independent status; they never got on our side during the Cold War or embraced our ideals; they never helped combat the "Evils of Communism." That's just a Plaid Avenger speculation, but it has some weight when we look to the other power player in the region and that is Pakistan.

PLAID AVENGER INSIDER TIP: Know this, world-watchers. The US-India relationship is changing fast, just here in 2008. The US is increasingly seeing India as not only a strategic business partner, but also as a partner in balancing the power of rising China. And don't forget terror! India is also seen as a partner in the 'War on Terrorism', as it is a great example of a multi-cultural, democratic state that other states should follow. Just this year the US has done a decades-worth of courting to the Indian government—not the least of which was a US-sponsored deal to help them out with their nuclear power industry, even though India has not signed the Non-Proliferation Treaty. We shall see how this proposed marriage works out . . .

PAKISTAN IS PACKIN' THE HEAT

Pakistan did side up in the Cold War, with . . . guess who! The US. And while India was independent, Pakistan needed a strong ally because they didn't have anywhere near the economy, money, or manpower of India. They sided up, and they ended out on top if you look at them today. There are a lot of countries around the world that would like to say that the US is their best friend, and Pakistan is in that position. They received tremendous amounts of foreign aid from the United States during the Cold War. They still receive vast amounts of aid from the US today, but for different reasons: the terror war thing. Unfortunately, this presents a major

The US on the job, helping beef up the Paki military.

problem for Pakistan: the US-led war is almost exclusively against Muslim extremists, and Pakistan is almost exclusively Muslim. The average dude on the street in Lahore is not a fan of the US. However . . .

Pakistan's administration has always been a staunch US ally, very pro-US, even though the people have not. Pakistan is currently fronting the war on terrorism for the United States in its fight to find Osama bin Laden and other Taliban rebels and extremists on its border with Afghanistan. This active role has earned it the number three spot for US foreign aid recipients.

Too bad all that great US foreign aid has been only directed at beefing up Pakistan's military capabilities to fight terrorism, because the country has quite a few other problems which are just as pressing . . . if not much worse. Its economy can be described as weak, at best. Its democratic institutions: weak, at best. Its political stability: tenuous, at best. Its potential for further extremism, more terrorism, and perhaps open revolution: HUGE!

There's no sense in getting into great political detail here, because the events are changing too rapidly and whatever I write will probably be out of date by the time this book gets into your hands, but we can say a few things that will stick.

President (formerly President/General) Pervez Musharraf is easily the most totally screwed world leader on the planet right now—and his season of hell has no happy ending in sight either. Mush used to be the head of all the armed forces, and as such took over the utterly corrupt Pakistani state by force in 1999 . . . and has led it ever since. He is a huge US ally and major player in the fight against global terrorism, but simultaneously is not much loved in the state he leads. Democratic forces at home and abroad (read: the US) convinced him to take off the uniform and just be President, so it at least looks like a functioning democracy. But things just continue to get worse . . .

Musharraf is trying to pacify the wants and desires of 170 million Paki citizens—that's the 6th biggest population in the world. It's also a devoutly Islamic society, including the whole spectrum of religious views from the mainstream to the seriously extreme. It's a society that has attempted to be a democracy since its inception back in 1947, with less than desirable results—the reason

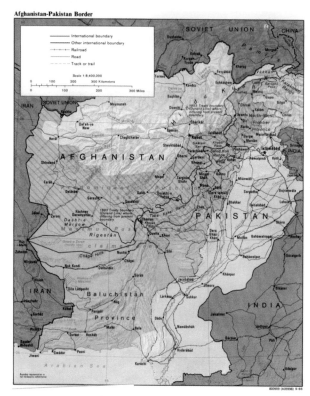

Afghanistan-Pakistan Border

The blue areas are not exactly fully controlled by either states' governments. If at all.

Mush as President and General: a screwed up position.

Mush took over the country in 1999 was because of massively widespread government corruption. And Pakistan is a nuclear power, with nuclear missiles that need to be controlled. And to fight terrorism, he has had to crack down on civil liberties in the country, which pisses off the locals. And to keep getting international aid, he has to suck up to the western powers, which pisses off the locals more. And, and, and . . . and this guy is screwed!

There have been several assassination attempts, and violent protests always seem to lurk just below the surface of this society. In just the last year, Mush basically fired the Supreme Court, sent in forces to slaughter a bunch of radicals that had laid siege to a mosque, lost further control over the western regions of the country to radicals and rebels, and had to hold the country together after a major political rival (who probably would have become the next Prime Minister) named Benazir Bhutto was assassinated. Damn! Talk about a full year!

Mush sans the uniform. Still screwed.

Virtually every political event that happens causes widespread protests by folks who are either pro-democracy, or pro-Islamist, or pro-independence, or anti-US, or just anti-Musharraf. Dude! Everything this guy does pisses everybody off here lately! Keep up with current events on this guy, but just know this for now: he probably ain't gonna be around too much longer. So many forces are working against him, and both the Pakistani people and the US government are growing impatient at him for lack of results...in either democratic reform and/or the war on terror. Honestly, I have no idea why the hell the guy even wants to keep the job...it is the shittiest position on the planet.

But all that internal turmoil and international pressure and the War on Terror is still not the whole story with Pakistan . . . we haven't even got to the Indian side of the country yet.

What's the Deal with . . . Kashmir? Nice Sweater! Now leave before I kill you!

The hottest example of continuing conflict between India and Pakistan is the instance of Kashmir. It's not a goat-wool sweater; it's a disputed territory. So what's the deal? You already know about the partition in 1947. When the Brits were there with Gandhi and the leaders of the future Pakistan, they were saying, "Ok where do you guys want to draw a line? Who wants to be Muslim and who wants to be Hindu? Who wants to be India and who wants to be Pakistan?" They kind of went region to region and asked regional leaders what side they wanted to be on. States said, "I am Hindu, I want to be in India," or "We are predominately Muslim and want to be in Pakistan." When it came to Kashmir (the proper name is Jammu and Kashmir), a little region nestled in the foothills of the Himalayan system, a mountainous, beautiful, rugged place where you could get killed if you visit, the people were mostly Muslim while the government was Hindu. The Hindu governors wanted to be in India, and the Islamic people wanted to be part of Pakistan, but the governors were the only ones that the Brits heard. It was immediately contested before the Brits even got on the damn boat to leave.

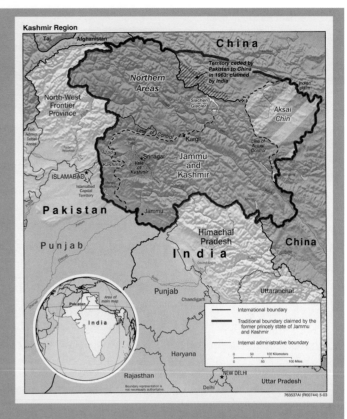

Kashmir Region

This is still the situation. It is still a very much disputed territory. The Indians say, "Hey, sorry! Kashmir is part of India." Pakistan says, "Come on, that's crap! It's a bunch of Muslims who didn't get a voice, and you guys screwed us!" As of right this second, closing in on the end of 2008, this is a fairly stable situation. Violence has flared up and there are extremist groups on both sides of this border who want to either make sure it stays in Indian hands, or see it reverted to Pakistan. There have been suicide bombings and assaults on Mosques and Hindu temples, most recently in late 2005. Things flare up from time to time and I guarantee we haven't seen the end of it yet, although that would be nice. Maybe if they all held hands and sang "Kumbaya" together in Jammu and Kashmir, everyone would chill out a little. A lot of folks in India, Pakistan, and the rest of the world would like to make sure that happens so that these two countries don't have a nuclear war.

India and Pakistan are two quite different tales altogether. We need to define the difference between India and Pakistan a little more because there is still potential for some serious conflict. We have the independent India (though it could be argued that they are not completely independent after buying arms from Russia at one point, making the US a little leery), and the US-funded and militarily-supplied Pakistan. About 30 years ago India entered the nuclear club after testing a bomb they called "Smiling Buddha." Pakistan immediately said, "Oh shit! We have been at war with that country a few times; we need nuclear bombs too!" The United States for the last 10 or 20 years discouraged them big time from doing this, but they went ahead and covertly ran a nuclear development program throughout the 1980s and 1990s, confirming their nuclear capacity by testing their first nuclear bomb in 1998. This development, two countries that essentially hate each other's guts both going nuclear, is cause for alarm for everybody outside this region. Things are stable right now, but people know that at any time some serious nuclear shit could go down. It's not probable, but still possible.

A typical freakin flood in beautiful Bangladesh.

BANGIN' BANGLADESH

I would be remiss in my regional duties if I did not at least mention the other giant of South Asia, even if it's not a major player in the neighborhood, nor the world. Sorry to my Bengali brothers out there, but we all know it's true. Bangladesh may not have a lot of regional or global power, but it still carries the titan status because of its huge population packed into a small little area: over 150 million folks (that ranks 6th in terms of most populated countries) squeezed into a state about the size of Iowa. Damn!

As you know from earlier in the chapter, Bangladesh started its life as the overwhelmingly Muslim 'East Pakistan'; but due to linguistic and racial discrimination along with lack of proper representation, the Bengalis declared and gained independence (with the help of India) in 1971. They have had a pretty rough road ever since . . .

Famines, natural disasters, droughts, floods, and widespread poverty have defined life in Bangladesh for its entire existence. Just about every year monsoonal rain systems totally trounce the area with floodwaters, which isn't hard to do since almost all of the land a flat alluvial plain that sits just slightly above sea level. Death and destruction seems to be a way of life. But that is only the beginning of the fun for this place! Bangladesh has been plagued by a weak-ass economy, political instability, and internal corruption, which has regularly resulted in coups and rapid administration turnover. As of right this second, the leaders of all three of Bangladesh's main political parties are behind bars and the government is being run by the military which took over by coup last year . . .

Hmmmm . . . I guess they still have a little in common with their Pakistani brothers after all . . .

MOMMY WOW! I'M A BIG KID NOW!

Now I'm not making fun of these countries here, but please do consider that they are all fairly young states, having achieved independence in 1947. They pretty much just celebrated their 60th anniversaries, but while these states may be youngsters in the modern world they have grown up fast and are global players already. In conclusion, when we think about South Asia, we do have to consider that India is the big power player. They are big into industry and technology. India is becoming a centerpiece for software creation and programming. In fact, there are now whole cities built up as IT centers, and a

India's got one now!

lot of computer programmers and computer programming companies from the United States are relocating there. Several years ago, California chip maker AMD said it was moving to India, causing a lot of senators to blow steam about taking away American jobs. AMD moved their *design center* to India. They didn't just outsource the low-paying jobs! They are moving the high-paying design work! That's a big deal! AMD sez: "There are more highly educated, skilled programmers in India than in the US. All the people coming to this country who are being trained in computer programming are Indians and they are going back to India. There are more computer programmers in India capable of this kind of work."

This is a major event. It is one thing to move cheap factory assembly jobs where people put TVs together for a nickel an hour. That kind of work is not going to be missed, but moving a computer chip design center is a big deal. AMD is not alone. A lot of global firms are hastening to India's back offices. India is bidding on the 2012 Olympics. Things like that mean they are joining the big boy club. They are happening and want in on the big action. Poor countries don't get the Olympics for a reason, and it is because they can't afford it. They just can't do it; Olympics facilities are expensive. When a country wants to do it, they can't be afraid of a price tag; it's about the prestige. In addition, India is now an associate member, along with China, of **ASEAN,** the **Association of Southeast Asian Nations.** South Asia is on the fast track to being in all the powerhouse trading blocs of the planet in the next hundred years.

In 2005, India started constructing its own aircraft carrier. They bought some others from Russia and Britain in recent years, but they are building a gigantic custom one. Now lots of folks who aren't military people, including the Plaid, are about love, not war. They say, "Who cares? What's the big deal?" An aircraft carrier is quite different from any other military hardware because it can be used as a projection of power anywhere on the planet. You are at the big boy table if you have an aircraft carrier. You don't just have armies of people in your country, you don't only have tanks in your country, you already have some planes with rockets that will go to other countries, but now you can put all that shit on a big platform that floats and take it anywhere on the planet you want. It is a true projection of power and only the big boy countries have that. India is hip and happening.

Pakistan is slightly different from India. It is a big country with lots of people and lots of problems, not the least of which is its relationship with the US which the folks in charge really like but the idea is very unpopular with the masses. This type of internal dissent is not something that goes away without a fight, so this is a big problem for Pakistan. On top of that, their economy is not in great shape. Pakistan is not growing nearly as fast as India. For those of you curious about military affairs, I should also tell you that India out-competes their Pakistan neighbors on all things military, and by an exponent. Indian army, aircraft counts, tanks, missiles, and even nukes are about 10 times that of what Pakistan possesses. So we are not talking about evenly matched entities if a war were to ever break out. Of course, nuclear weapons even the score fairly quickly, in that pretty much everyone in the entire region would die if it ever comes to that . . . but let's hope they don't! Things have been softening here lately . . .

There have been Pakistani and Indian peace talks over Kashmir in the last several years and there have not been any major outbreaks of religious violence for a while now. There was however a major event here that may have kept the lid on the tension and violence. This was an enormous earthquake in October of 2005. This thing killed 90,000 people and left another 3.3 million homeless. This titanic disaster was something that brought the two countries together even closer. India was first on the scene and offered tremendous assistance to Pakistan in and around the Kashmir area. Let's end this chapter on a nice note: Even though it was due to an earthquake, it has seemed to bring the countries together for a greater good and things are sitting pretty right now, and prettier for India, of course.

So relax, have some chai, and get ready to rock and roll into Central Asia . . .

CHAPTER OUTLINE

Central Asia

LET'S move to the center of the Eurasian continent. This is a place that has been mired in turmoil and been the centerpiece of world history for quite some time that suddenly found itself left behind. Central Asia is kind of a vacuum in the heart of Asia that, as opposed to going through, people go out of their way to avoid. But times are changing fast my friends, and Central Asia may have found a new home as the delicious meat center of a Russia-China sandwich . . . but I am getting ahead of the story as usual . . .

What is it about Central Asia that makes it a region? Is it a region? A lot of people may say that it's not a separate region, but it is to the Plaid Avenger and here is how I'm going to define it . . .

THE GAME PIECES

Central Asia consists of a core of countries that everyone might agree upon: the "-stan" countries that no one knows how to locate or pronounce. Kazakhstan is the big one, and then Uzbekistan, Turkmenistan, Afghanistan (I know you've heard of that one), Tajikistan, and Kyrgyzstan. Everybody would say "Yeah we think that's kind of Central Asia, or at least we know where you're talking about—all those places we can't pronounce."

Kazakh Hotties!

This may be the trickiest region to define because we have to take parts of another country in order to do it. We are going to take the western parts of China, including Xinjiang, one of the biggest, most significant westernmost provinces of said country. We must also take two other Chinese provinces, Tibet and Inner Mongolia, as well as the independent sovereign state of Mongolia. The Plaid Avenger calls all of these places **Central Asia.** It's a little tricky because you will say "Oh wait, you just took parts of China and China is its own country. It's a sovereign state." We're going to talk a lot about China in the next chapter, but what you'll find is that China has a very distinct east/west divide. Virtually all the people and businesses are in the east. All economic activity is on the eastern side closer to the coast. You can't consider the country divided down the middle; most inhabitants are as close to the coast as possible. Most of the transportation, communication, and government are there as well.

China proper, as it has been known throughout the centuries, is the eastern side of the country, but not the west. The west is quite different in terms of its population. It is sparsely populated and contains ethnic groups that are not historically Chinese. Consequently, religions there are very different from those in the east.

All the reasons eastern China has *little* to do with western China are the same reasons that western China has *a lot* to do with Central Asia. The dissimilar groups in parts of Mongolia and the "-stan" countries are thrown into this region called Central Asia. Why is it a region? What's homogeneous about the disparate group of countries, states, and Chinese substates? Let's get to work.

THE GAME BOARD

The most obvious similarities between all of the countries in this region lie in the physical attributes. Unlike other regions that contain a variety of climates and terrains, like South America or North America, Central Asia is relatively standard throughout. Like the Middle East, it is mostly desert and steppe, making it homogeneously dry across the board. There is really nothing else, no other climate

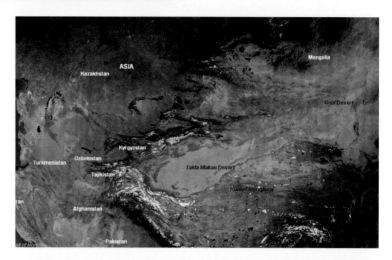

to speak of. You definitely won't find any big forests. There are patches of growth, but this region is mostly either grassland or desert, which has had a definite impact on how people have settled and survived for the last several thousand years in this region.

But before we get too deep into dryness, let's look at the terrain factor. This is one of the highest and toughest terrains on Earth. We already referenced the Himalayas when discussing the division of South Asia from the rest of Asia, and they play a big part here as well. It's not just the range itself—it's the whole Tibetan Plateau, which sits over 12,000 ft. above sea level. It has extremely high mountains. The **Hindu Kush Mountains** run through Afghanistan; the **Tien Shan** run through Kyrgyzstan and Tajikistan. These mountains seem wimpy in comparison to the Himalayas, but what they lack in physical harshness, they make up for in another kind of tactical danger. (Just ask the US military in Afghanistan.) This is not a fun part of the world. It is very difficult to get around, through, or across the plateau.

In addition to the Tien Shan, the Hindu Kush, and the Himalayas, we have the Altai Mountains in Mongolia. Although there are a few basins where things level out a bit, it boasts some of the toughest terrain on the planet.

The terrain and dryness go hand in hand. For the same reason that there are the monsoons in South Asia, Central Asia is nearly all dry. All the water that would float up north drops from the sky as the air is pushed higher by the Himalayas. This causes the monsoons, and makes for only dry air to make its way up the mountains and into Central Asia.

The dryness doesn't support much vegetation. A lot of Central Asia is what we would distinguish as "grasslands." We think "Oh, grasslands are good for things like wheat and barley." No, those are long grasses. Central Asia can't even sustain most of that stuff. There is only enough water in this ecosystem to support shorter grasses. Since the land can't support any type of large-scale food crops, it in turn cannot support huge populations. Much of the food that the locals eat nowadays has to be imported. This is a fairly stark environment.

Throughout the centuries one of the main perceptions we have had of Central Asians is that they are horse people. Why don't they raise cattle or something else? Well, the environment won't allow it. It can't be done because the vegetation isn't there for farmers to raise large amounts of cattle in one place, year after year. But short grasses can sustain animals that move around a lot, like horses, which is why the region's inhabitants are known for having them. More on that later . . .

LANDLOCKED

What is the most unique feature of this region? It's landlocked, which is another condition that makes it a homogeneous whole. In fact, some of these places are doubly landlocked. What is "landlocked" and why is it significant? What does this mean for the place as a whole? **Landlocked** means you have no tie to the

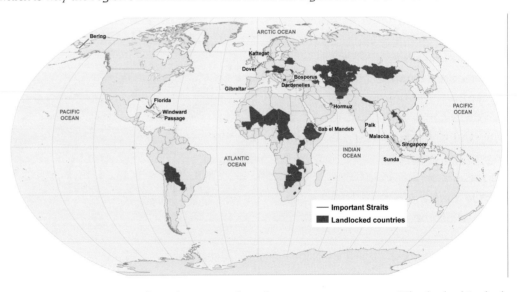

oceans, period. Not even a river system that goes to a place that can indirectly get you to an ocean. What's the big deal about that? In the good old days when people used to travel across the continent on trade routes, Central Asia's location in the middle of things was a bonus. Those days were good, but they are long gone, my friends.

In today's world, virtually all the world's traffic and economic activity happens via the oceans. If you don't have access to the oceans then you are not part of the world economy. Therefore, Central Asia is not part of the world economy today. It is what The Plaid Avenger calls a **marooned region.** It's not attached to what's going on around the rest of the planet.

Landlocked means you are economically stagnant and behind. As I mentioned before, some of these places are **doubly landlocked,** which means they are landlocked by other landlocked countries. That means that their economy is internal and they're not doing squat, with the possible exception of something like drilling for oil and making pipelines to places that aren't cut out of the world economy. A few of these places have that advantage. But places like

Kyrgyzstan are so far from anything that they cannot possibly foster any meaningful movement of goods or services across the Asian continent. It's just not going to happen. Being landlocked is a physical condition that has an enormous influence on what's going on internally and externally for Central Asia.

A Yurt: Central Asian party hut!

CULTURE CENTRAL

Let's look at some cultural traits that permeate Central Asia, the main one being religion. We look at Central Asia and typically think Islam, which is a good place to start. All of the "-stan" countries and the western provinces of China are Islamic. Islam spread there from the Middle East during the big growth of the Arab-Islamic Empire. These countries have been staunchly Islamic ever since. However, there are some exceptions in the region, such as the Tibetan Plateau and Mongolia. These are a couple of core areas for the "purest" kind of Buddhism in the world. When we talk about China, the Koreas, Japan, and

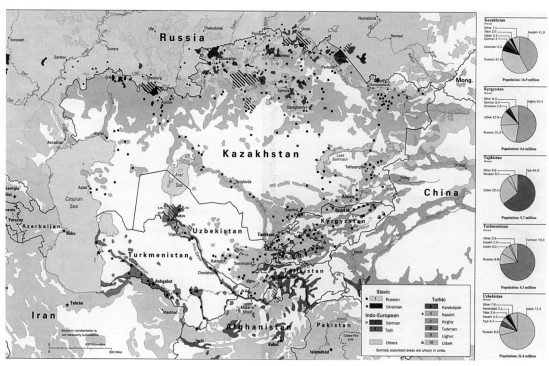

But who is in the white areas? Answer: Nobody.

South East Asia, Buddhism is there but it is usually incorporated into lots of local beliefs. In fact, in China it is called the **Confucian Complex,** which consists of Confucian religious and philosophical practices blended with Buddhism to form a unique belief system. But in the Tibetan Plateau and in Mongolia, pure Buddhism is the primary religion.

While this region is primarily Islamic like the Middle East, it is still different enough to be teased out of the Middle East. One of those differences is Western China. A lot of folks don't know this about Western China, but it is predominantly Muslim and it is comprised of an ethnic group that is not Chinese, but **Uyghur** (pronounced Weeger, kind of like Weezer). This Turkic ethnic group has been hanging out for several thousand years in what is now known as Western China, and they have embraced Islam.

They are quite different from everybody else in China—you don't hear a lot about them because they are kind of being repressed right now by the Chinese government. Lots of folks in the Uyghur community have been fighting for some sort of autonomous state or perhaps even a fully sovereign state. At this point China has deemed these guys Muslim terrorists. (Go figure.) This issue will come back into our story in just a little bit, but that's why we tease out part of China to put with Central Asia. These guys in this part of China have way more in common with Central Asia than with their own country.

PRANCING AROUND THE CONTINENT

We talked about the physical features of the region being dry and landlocked. What has this landlocked dry, arid, short grass steppe meant culturally to this region over the centuries? It has meant (again) that they are not a big agricultural region. They are mostly **nomadic;** that is, they pick up their Yurts (those big-ass white tents that you see) and move on a moment's notice to go to better grasslands for their horses. Some people native to this region are not sedentary and noncentralized, consisting mostly of small tribes of folks on the move. There have never been huge populations in this region. These guys have been forever focused on the horse not just as a main means of locomotion, but also as a way of life. I'm thinking specifically of the Mongols. Mongol domination at one point in history is one of the other unifying cultural factors of this entire region. The value of the horse in Central Asia can't be understated, especially for this group we call the Mongols.

Uzbeki Zorro!

The Mongols were the most kick-ass group of horse warriors that the world has ever seen. The Plaid Avenger would put money on these guys in today's world. Even now they would be a serious bunch of ass-kickers. What was so cool about them? What did they do that was so damned unique?

MONGOL MANIA

The Mongols are a small group of ragtag horsemen who rallied under **Genghis Khan** and started a campaign to conquer the whole damn planet right around 1200 ce. And Genghis is the one dude who got fairly close. Lots of folks have had that ideal such as, I don't know, Hitler and Mussolini? But this is a guy who actually came fairly close to conquering the whole damn world at the time.

Don't mess with the Mongols!

A couple of unique things about the Mongol Empire: It crossed the Eurasian continent for the first and perhaps only time in history, maybe even in today's world. They created a single empire that tied together the peoples of Europe and the peoples of the rest of Asia under a single umbrella. To my knowledge, this has not been done since. We could look at the modern world and say, "Oh yeah, people have interactions now," but not on this scale. This is a singular empire that placed white Europeans and Chinese people in the same state. What's so important about that? Perhaps nothing, except that this cultural interchange was all under a singular empire.

The Mongols set up this system where they were bad asses and under their rule it was said that a virgin with a pot of gold on her head could travel from one side of the empire to another unmolested and untouched. That may or may not be actually true, but it gets at the idea of Mongol citizens' safety. They had a good legal system that was strictly

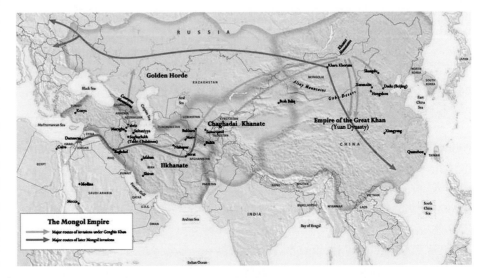

The Mongol Empire
Major routes of invasions under Genghis Khan
Major routes of later Mongol invasions

enforced. What that type of safety infrastructure creates is a lot of trade and cultural interchange. So you have this mass movement of goods, services, materials, and technologies across this Eurasian continent like never before, and perhaps not since. So the Mongol Empire was very unique in world history; it encompassed all of what is now China, parts of Southeast Asia, and parts of India as well as big chunks of the Middle East that stretched all the way into chunks of Europe. They sacked Baghdad in 1258, which marked the end of Middle Eastern expansion—remember that from a few chapters ago?

How did they unify all of these lands under one common empire? They were ruthless conquerors. Their environment propelled them into this rough way of life where they were simply bad-ass warrior dudes who could ride horses for days. These guys were totally brutal. One of Genghis Khan's sayings was "Submit or die." He didn't negotiate with anybody, period. No ifs, ands, or buts. Typical Mongol

Gengis Khan. Ok, not really because they didn't have cameras 800 years ago, but this guy is funny as hell as a replacement.

foreign policy would be going to a town and telling the inhabitants, "Here's the deal; you guys get down on your hands and knees and start begging for mercy right now. We'll circle around you, slowly making our way toward your homes, and decide if we'll kill you. But if anybody takes up arms against us we will kill every freakin' one of you down to the last man, woman and child. Blood will flow in the streets and we'll burn the town to the ground."

That was how they were successful in storming across the continent. But perhaps even more important to their success were their fighting tactics. They could cover HUGE amounts of territory in a day. They would ride horses continuously and would have stations set up so that whole cavalry units could get new horses and essentially ride nonstop for 72 to 96 hours. That is an amazing feat in today's world, much less a thousand years ago. The Mongols were so tough they trained their ponies so they didn't have to get out of the saddle to eat; they made cuts on the ponies' necks and drank their blood for nourishment. Drinking blood is not only a fun fact; it also accentuates this tough environment. What does their diet consist of? Mare's milk and blood. Protein rich! I think somebody should invent the Mongol diet because these guys are lean, mean fighting machines.

But if you go to Mongolia today, you'll see a lot of people doing these same things. Not in terms of raping and pillaging, but what they eat and what they do for a living has not changed much. They still herd goats, still drink funky milk, and generally are chillin' out on the central Asian plains.

So the Mongols ended up ruling much of the Eurasian continent, but their empire wasn't a superpower for very long. Their glorious reign was pretty short after Genghis Khan died. After that, they sort of stopped conquering, and eventually the Mongol Empire broke apart into separate "kingdoms" that affect world history in lots of different places: Kublai Khan rules China; Tamerlane was in Central Asia; descendants of the Mongols end up as the Mughal Empire in India, and even the Cossacks of Russia are lineage of the Mongols. But for a while, under the main man Genghis, the Mongols whipped ass and took names, making a pretty huge mark on history, especially military history.

PARKER BROTHERS INSPIRED . . .

There's one thing the Plaid wants you to know about in Central Asia because it is still kind of happening; it's called **The Great Game.** The Great Game, coined by some British guys as so many things on our planet have been, describes the major world power players' attitudes toward Central Asia in the last couple hundred years. That attitude has resulted in Central Asia becoming very much like the game of **Risk.** It's a platform or playing field for different countries to vie for influence. No one really wants it. No one wants to actually control it. They just want to make sure they have their fingers in there to ensure that other people don't control it. This is a scenario that arises during European imperialism, and even the build up to WWI and beyond.

THE CLASSIC ORIGINAL BOARD GAME . . .

Basically it's the Russians vs. the British vs. The Persians/Iranians vs. the French vs. the locals. All these colonial powers and others who are in the neighborhood, such as the Chinese and the Persians, all kind of jockey around Central Asia to make sure that no one else gets in. Everybody protects their own backyard. It's mostly the Russians who started up this game because they had been expanding their territory for hundreds of years, perhaps in a bid to expand their coastline. Among other things, they increased their influence by pushing into Central Asia. Many would say they wanted to push down into Iran to gain access to the Indian Ocean, which is one reason that the Persians don't want the Russians there.

As the Russians are coming down from the North, the British, who controlled British India at the time, are pushing up from the South, effectively buffering against Russian influence in the region. The Chinese don't want anyone in there so they are vying for influence to make sure that no one is encroaching on their territory. This becomes a big game where rulers are moving soldiers around on this very real chessboard. That's why it's funny in today's world to see the United States vying for influence in Afghanistan by pushing US ideals and working against Muslim influence—same story, different century.

Afghanistan is a good country to discuss for just a second. The Russians and the British found this out a long time ago; you just don't mess around in Afghanistan. Everybody, all these world powers, have tried very hard in the past and let me tell you what the historical scoreboard reads: Afghanistan: 1000, Outsiders: zero. No one from Europe or anywhere else has successfully occupied or influenced Afghanistan to do a damn thing, and it remains to be seen if the US/NATO is going to have much impact either. These groups of folks throughout Central Asia, particularly Afghanistan, have a fierce independent spirit. They understand that they are pawns in the game and they will have none of it. When the British went into Afghanistan to thwart the Russians, the Afghans kick the hell out of them. Then when the Russians come in 50 years later, they kick the shit out of them too. These dudes are tough; they have serious balls.

Not even a century later, the Soviet Union invaded Afghanistan in their bid to expand the communist sphere of influence even further. This time a new player joined the game: the US. The United States armed and trained a bunch of locals . . . let's call them the mujahedeen . . . to really stick it to the Ruskies in order to stymie the Soviet advance. And it worked great! That 1979 to 1989 Afghan campaign was to prove absolutely disastrous for the Soviets, and has been credited as part of the reason for their eventual collapse just two years later. Of course, those CIA trained mujahedeen then ended up becoming the Taliban and members of al-Queda which the US now finds itself fighting, but that is a different round of this unfolding drama. Isn't this region just a pack of fun? Kind of like playing nude lawn darts . . .

THE 21ST CENTURY EDITION!

Lots of the parties who were vying for influence in the last couple hundred years are some of the same players in today's world, with a few new entries—like the United States, the Taliban, al-Queda and a country that didn't even exist back then, now called Pakistan. And as in the past, no one really wants Central Asia but everybody is trying to expel other influences/powers. The Game is back on. For your own note, most of the powers originally got involved to curb the power and growth of pre-Soviet Russia. The British in particular didn't really want to get into the northern parts of India but felt compelled to in order to stop the Russian advance. The game to stop Russia is over, but there are three new reasons that the game is getting started back up:

1. THE VACUUM CREATED BY MOVING THE SOVIETS OUT

Russians under the Soviet umbrella actually do gain control of all of Central Asia proper except Afghanistan by the 1940s. All of those "-stan" countries became Soviet satellites. Afghanistan was never brought into the fray and that's why the Russians invaded them in 1979, much to their own chagrin for the next decade. Since the fall of the Soviet Empire in 1989, all of those former Soviet SSR's declared independence and became sovereign states again. So who is really in charge? For most of the -stan countries, this has resulted in authoritarian dictators/one-party states that are extremely open to outside influences, especially when there is money involved. How refreshing. Oops, I mean how exactly the same as always.

2. BECAUSE OF INCREASING FINDS OF PETROLEUM AND NATURAL GAS

These natural resources are items with which the world cannot live without as evidenced by the fact that people are still willing to pay 130 dollars a barrel as of June 2008. This oil and natural gas is not just in one Central Asian country, but in all of them. Every day it seems they increase their findings of potential natural reserves that these places have. Kazakhstan is kind of the leader of this. It's the biggest country with the largest amount in reserves.

Where is this stuff going? It's going everywhere. This game is back on because everybody wants that stuff. No one wants to control the places but they want the influence that the stuff brings. As described by the US's Energy Information Administration: *"Central Asia has large reserves of natural gas but its development as a major natural gas exporter is constrained because of a lack of pipeline infrastructure."* Now everyone wants a piece of the infrastructure-building action.

Who are they supplying? Kazakhstan's and Uzbekistan's stuff has mostly moved west into Russia and then on into Europe. Turkmenistan and Uzbekistan actually supply the Ukraine and other Eastern and Western European countries as well as Iran. Some of it floats south to or through Iran. Increasingly even Tajikistan, Turkmenistan, and Kazakhstan are building pipelines into China proper. Hmm, why would China want that stuff? Oh that's right! Their population is exploding and they can't ever possibly have enough oil and natural gas. These historically landlocked economies of Central Asia are in a prime position now. The one thing that they could move out of their countries to make money off of is being discovered in large amounts.

Source: Energy Information Administration

3. TERRORISM AND DRUGS

Why would anybody from the outside world be interested in vying for influence of drugs and terrorism? Ask the US government! That's the precise reason that the United States is there, quite frankly. The current US-led war in Afghanistan is

to try and stop the Taliban, al-Queda and any other radical extremists groups which may be there training, setting up shop, or otherwise trying to control the area. And I do want to be quick to point out that this is a US-*led* effort . . . the Afghan campaign is actually a NATO mission, of which the US is the biggest player. Why is that important? Because it shows that all other NATO members (namely all of 'Team West') are involved in the fight because they all believe that the anti-terrorism fight is a worthy cause that they will continue to pursue.

As suggested above, plus don't lose sight of the irony that the US and NATO are there currently fighting against forces that they helped train to fight the Soviets back in the 70's. Ah, the game continues. . . . Of course drugs are a bad thing too and Central Asia is historically one of the largest producers of opium, so lots of developed countries around the world in their **War on Drugs** have had their fingers in Central Asia long before the current conflict in Afghanistan. Unfortunately, in a war-wrecked country, drug production is one of the few (if not only) economic opportunities for these folks to embrace. It has been further complicated by the Taliban and al-Queda now using the drug trade money to help re-arm and re-equip themselves to do further battle against 'Team West.' Damn, could this mess get worse? Yep: while virtually all this product used to be shipped abroad to the rich, bored citizens of Europe and America, it has been increasingly used at home. Meaning: drug consumption and addiction has soared in Central Asia, Russia, and East Asia too.

So terrorism, drugs and petroleum products are the main reasons that Central Asia has become an area of much interest for folks around the globe who otherwise wouldn't give a flying rat's ass about this economically marooned region. There really isn't much else to this place to interest the outsiders. What's made this even more important in today's world is the **War on Terrorism.** It is the reason why the US is in Afghanistan, supposedly the reason they are in Iraq, and a reason why there are US military bases that had cropped up all throughout Central Asia—because of the fear that terrorism and extremism will be on the increase, particularly in this region. The United States is vying for influence here not to control the place, but to control the extreme elements within the place. The United States is worried about terrorists in this Central Asian society, but they're not the only ones.

The Russians are also worried because they have lost a lot of territory since the implosion of the USSR, so they are continuing activities in the region. Their long history of influence in the region, desire to maintain their status as a world power, and close ties between Russian/Central Asian economies give them more reason to stick around. They have their terrorist problems as well, mostly with Muslim extremists over in Chechnya but also here in Central Asia.

And then there's China. Here is a theme that's perfect for identifying western China as part of Central Asia and not as China proper. It is a little known fact that when the United States declared war on terrorism after 9/11 there were two countries

that IMMEDIATELY jumped on board and said, "Yeah we'll help! We agree that terrorism should be fought on all fronts!" Those two countries are probably not ones you would think of as the first in line: Russia and China. Russia says "Yes we've been fighting Muslim extremists for years. We call them Chechens and we are going to continue to beat the hell out of them in our war on terrorism." And in those footsteps, China said "Yes, we have Muslim extremist terrorists too. They are the Uyghurs out in the western states who have been blowing stuff up and making attempts at independence movements. So yes, US, we're going to fight the War on Terrorism too by continuing to beat the shit out of the Uyghur separatists in our country."

The terrorism thing is a rallying cry for a lot of countries to continue to be involved in Central Asia. This is a theme that is probably not going to go away any time soon. We've got Russia, China, and the United States in there vying for influence for oil, trying to control terrorism, and lots of other things. Who else may be involved in The New Great Game. For starters: the Pakistanis, who are huge US allies and are the ones fighting the truly active War on Terrorism on their own border. Pakistan's largest border is shared with Afghanistan and that border is a real hotspot for active conflict. People are shooting at each other there all the time. That is where everyone thinks Osama bin Laden is currently hiding. The US is moving money and guns around and sending soldiers to the area, but in Pakistan they are actually shooting people and making the kills.

Iran, which also fronts this region, is increasing its power on the planet by building nuclear facilities and playing up its role as a leader of Muslim Culture. It is also a major mover of natural gas and oil out of Central Asia to the rest of the world. They want to join the big boy club and are vying for influence as well. They have the advantage of being Islamic like all their Central Asian brothers. They are not puppets of the US, which is the way a lot of folks in this region view Pakistan. Because of this, Iran may end up being a major political player in this region in the very near future. Maybe not . . . maybe the US will invade them first, but I kind of doubt it right this second.

THE GAME CONTINUES TO EVOLVE . . . WITH NEW PLAYERS

To summarize, Central Asia is an isolated region both physically and economically, a culturally and economically marooned region as the Plaid Avenger calls it, which has been suddenly thrust back into prominence in the new version of The Great Game. Why? It's mostly for resources (oil and natural gas), but also for the fight against terrorism and the drug trade. We also see some of the old school elements of The Great Game here in terms of Russia not wanting to completely lose all of its influence in the region. The US military presence is actually seen as a direct threat to this historic Russian influence. Vlad "The Man" Putin is not too happy about it.

What's the Deal with Drug Production?

Hey man, want some heroin? If you want to get it cheap, why not go right to the source? In that case, you'd probably take a trip, no pun intended, to Afghanistan. Afghanistan is the largest producer of opium in the world, weighing in at almost 5,000 metric tons. That's 87 percent of the opium supply of the entire world. Quite impressive.

The funny thing is that under Taliban rule, opium production was much, much lower. Once the US intervened and knocked the Taliban out, with an almost audible "smack" heard round the world, opium production nearly doubled each year after 2001. 2008 was a world record breaker for most opium produced in the country . . . nice job guys! And here's a hint for you, most of that isn't going to the pharmaceutical companies that turn opium into legitimately consumed pain killers. This is hardcore stuff getting released into the streets, mostly to Europe and Southeast Asia, in larger and larger quantities. That's where the money is. It's untaxed, uncut, and a hell of a cash crop for this economically landlocked region, and production is only increasing despite US occupation.

What a pretty poppy garden these boys are tending . . . of opium poppies that is . . .

Luckily for him, his country is currently winning the fight. Some countries have requested the US troops to leave as soon as possible, and Uzbekistan recently just blatantly kicked them out. Many of the -stan countries are already reestablishing their old ties with Russia for security purposes, but they are also increasingly looking to Russia for leadership in the oil and natural gas industries. Vlad is happy again . . . The vehicle for this renewed Russian leadership is a supranationalist organization named the SCO, and you heard it here first, this group has huge potential to become a major global force in the coming decades. Best to know a bit more about it right now.

YOU GOTSTA' KNOW THE SCO!!!

Watch out! This coalition could be hot! The Shanghai Cooperation Organization (SCO) is an intergovernmental organization which was founded on June 14, 2001 by leaders of the People's Republic of China, Russia, Kazakhstan, Kyrgyzstan, Tajikistan and Uzbekistan.

Comrade Russia iz still vatching Central Asia . . .

Cooperation and organization on issues like natural resource extraction, counterterrorism, extremism, and separatism. Now holding joint military exercises, and thinking about a free trade pact. Though the declaration on the establishment of the Shanghai Cooperation Organization contained a statement that it "is not an alliance directed against other states and regions and it adheres to the principle of openness," most observers believe that one of the original purposes of the SCO was to serve as a counterbalance to the US and particularly to avoid conflicts that would allow the US to intervene in areas near both Russia and China.

How are they pulling this off? Well, in lots of curious ways that have tremendous potential for the future of these states, and the world. First, there have been very secretive discussions about these countries creating a common cartel

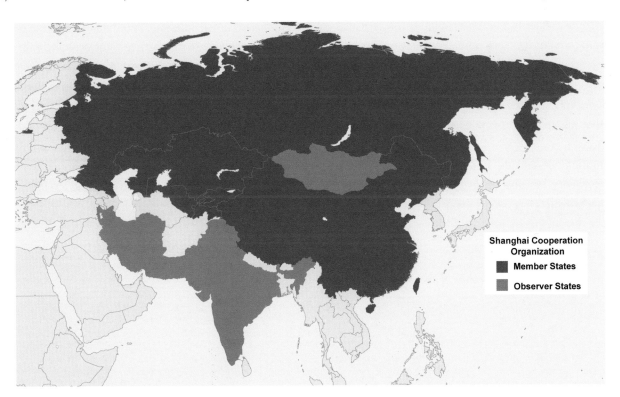

A hot ass trade block to watch.

based on their exports of natural gas . . . basically an Asian version of OPEC. Just as OPEC countries control the lion's share of exported oil, and therefore control the supply and price, the SCO countries combined control a significant amount of global reserves of natural gas. It is not a stretch of the imagination to see them pooling their resources together under a single umbrella of control . . . which would make them all even richer.

Second, the SCO states are strengthening their defense pacts with each other to ensure that no interference or invasion will be allowed from outsiders. In essence, they have formed an Asian version of NATO. The movement in this direction is why most US military bases have now been kicked out of SCO states, and also why the US request to become an observer state has been declined every single year. Its also why the SCO has starting doing the joint military exercises. By the way, don't start digging your backyard bunker in preparations for WWIII anytime soon: militarily these guys are still pretty clueless . . . okay, they outright suck. The main point is that they are just beginning to do these exercises, thus setting the trend for the future.

But let's get you even smarter: what current 'observer' state in the map above do you think is desperate to become a full member of the SCO? If you said 'Iran', then give yourself a cookie and a barrel of oil. Were Iran to join this 'Asian NATO' club, then the prospects of US/UN actions to prevent Iran from going nuclear would instantaneously become a world crisis. You dig what I'm saying here? It's a really big deal.

Organizing pipeline construction, conducting military exercises, and refusing to grant the US "observer status." Ouch!

This thing is on fire, and no one in our country has probably even heard of it. But I think you should . . .

THE GAME IS ON . . .

So terrorism is a problem which, despite US influence, is not going away; it's actually increasing. To be completely frank, Afghanistan is the only real hotspot and haven for most of the terrorism in the region right now, mostly related to the US/NATO war and the lack of any strong and stable government functionality. When you look at the rest of the -stan countries in this region, they are all strong-arm authoritarian types, being influenced mostly by strong-arm Putin in Russia and the fairly assertive commie crew over in China. As such, those states are extremely successful at repressing and/or eliminating terrorist elements . . . unfortunately they are also good at repressing any democratic and human rights elements too. I don't want to paint this region in an entirely negative light because they do have some positive things coming with some of the wealth accumulation due to their increasing natural gas and oil exports. One of the things I like people to remember is when we say, "Damn it, this sucks. Gas is going to be 5 dollars a gallon this summer. This is terrible. Oil is 130 dollars a barrel, this sucks!" Well, it may suck for you, but it actually means great things for Central Asia and any other oil/gas producing region. That means their revenues are expanding, and they've got a little more wealth, hopefully to spread around to their Average Joes.

Things may be looking up for the -stans. Economic integration in Central Asia has actually risen to an all time high for the last 500 years, because states are figuring out that they must work together in order to effectively build the infrastructure to get their petroleum products exported out to the rest of the world. With that type of cooperation comes increased trade

We ain't doing so bad . . . for a bunch of bad-asses!

and communications. That's why the Plaid Avenger really wants you to know all about that SCO . . . because it is becoming the most effective organizational superstructure to accelerate this process. I'm telling you, it's a big deal. Look for the SCO to not only become an OPEC-style cartel of natural gas in Asia, but also for it to become a NATO-style defense structure which many Asian nations might be keen to jump into. Trade and economic integration will follow.

Still, this is a place of fairly extreme economic disparity and massive challenges in terms of infrastructure creation, but at the same time, due to its Soviet influence, this is a region that is fairly literate. People are fairly well-educated and the illiteracy rates are some of the lowest in the world. If you look at how much money they make, it looks like they are impoverished like a lot of Sub-Saharan African countries. But in terms of standards of living, access to health care and literacy rates, they are not doing too badly. Russia and China as powerful bookends; an new Asian OPEC; an Asian NATO Things are not completely dire and could be looking up, although the authoritarian structure in the governments of most of these places may still keep the people down for a while to come. But that is a story for another time and another place.

Let's get to the next superpower on the planet . . .

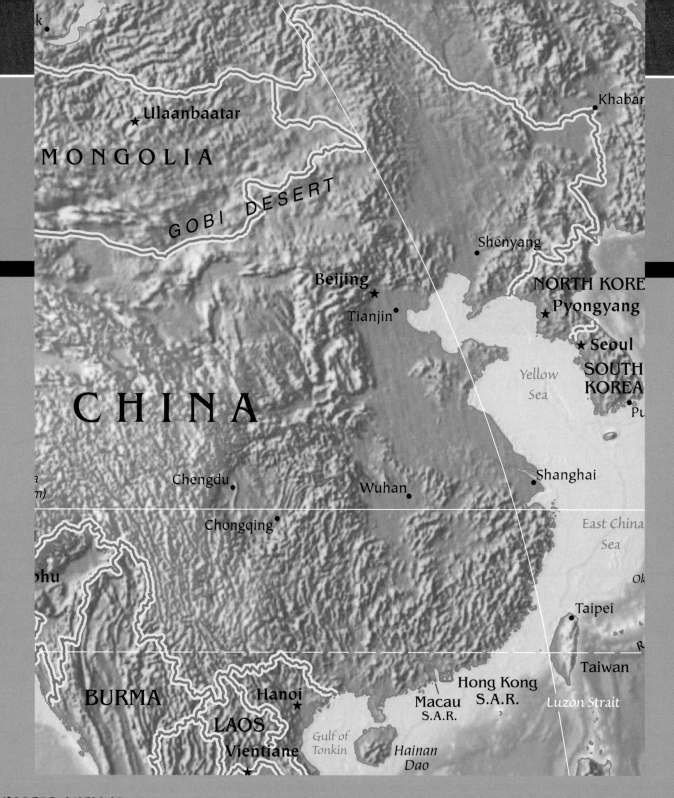

CHAPTER OUTLINE

East Asia

23

THE BEAST IN THE EAST

This one is easy. This region is the big bad boy on planet Earth right now, perhaps the next superpower. A lot of folks are scared that they're going to be *the* superpower and take over the Earth. I'm scared! They certainly are going to be *a* superpower. They are not going to be the sole superpower, but perhaps they are going to become the balance for US power on the planet. They are going to be the yin to the US's yang. My God that is good! Isn't that good? The main country we are talking about here is China, the main master-blaster for the 21st century. We are going to talk about why it is the powerhouse of this region, and the wider world. But also in this region we are going to take on North Korea and South Korea. And for those that aren't sure where it's suppose to go, Taiwan falls in this region as well.

Yin-Yang

1 1/2 oz Jagermeister herbal liqueur

1 1/2 oz Rumple Minze peppermint liqueur

Serve with alcohol chilled. Rocks glass or double-shot. Its up to you. Just use the force, and feel the balance as you imbibe. Your chi will be improved.

China and most of the planet consider Taiwan to be China's renegade province, but a lot of folks in Taiwan think they are independent. About 25 countries in the world recognize it as an independent sovereign state, and that number is dwindling fast, so no one really cares. Taiwan counts as part of China because I live in the real world, not Taiwan's pretend one. So that is our region.

Before we go any further, let's make sure we identify the specifics of our region from the map on this page. China is divided in half, and we have already taken out Western China and put it in Central Asia for lots of

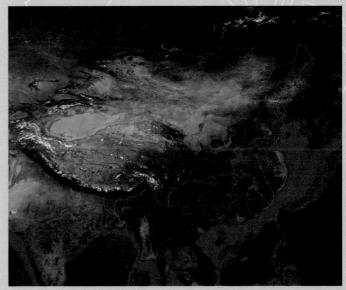

China and US: roughly same size, same latitudes.

reasons that you have already read about. The region we are going to call East Asia is made up of East China, the core of the Chinese Empire for centuries, Taiwan, South Korea, and North Korea.

PANDA FUR: THE PHYSICAL WORLD

As you see in the graphic on the previous page, China and the United States have some similarities. Which one is bigger? Which one is smaller? I don't know. It depends on what sources you look at. Some say China is the third largest country on earth and the US is number four. Some reverse that. Doesn't matter to me; it's pretty darn close either way. What you see in the chart on the next page is that latitude is held constant, so it's near the exact same size as the US, but the latitudinal range is a bit larger, i.e. it goes a little bit further pole-ward than the continuous United States and stretches further south of the tropics. Hainan Island there in the southern part of China would be about where Cuba is in our hemisphere. What does this equate to climate-wise? Well latitude being held constant, you know what climate is like on the east coast of the United States. That's about what the east coast of China is like as well. From north to south on the eastern seaboards of both countries, the climate regimes are identical.

But what's different? Here's the difference. The United States has an east coast like China, and a west coast unlike China. China has no west coast. Its western fringe is buried in the continent. Continentality has a different effect on the climate than coastal regions, as we already know. The Plaid wants you to know that when you travel from the coast to the western part of China, several things happen. The west gets cooler in the winter and oftentimes hotter in the summer. Elevation increases and terrain gets rougher and rockier as you move west (as you can see in opening map). You have the Tibetan Plateau in Western China as well as the Taklimakan Basin. These are areas that are way above sea level, particularly the Tibetan Plateau propping up the Himalayan Range, (the largest mountain range on the planet).

As you progress off the coast you will go upwards in elevation and the temperature disparity will increase. That means it will get hotter in the summer and cooler in the winter. **Continentality** means it will also get dryer, as there is less contact with large bodies of water. So temperatures get more extreme as you progress westward from the coast, getting drier and higher. This lovely clothing chart pretty much sums it all up:

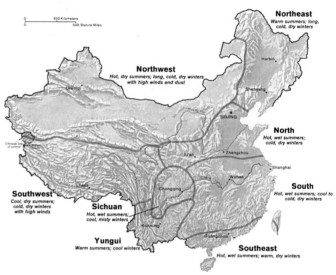

Clothing Recommendations for Travel in China

Winter
- North, Northeast, Northwest, and Southwest: heavy, warm clothing, coat, hat, gloves, boots
- South, Yungui, and Sichuan: mediumweight, warm clothing, light coat, rainwear in Sichuan
- Southeast: lightweight, warm clothing, sweater

Summer
- Northeast, Northwest, and Southwest: summer clothing, light coat or sweater in the evenings, rainwear in the Northeast for occasional rains
- North, South, Yungui, Sichuan, and Southeast: light, loose tropical clothing, sunglasses, rainwear

Spring/Autumn
- North, Northeast, Northwest, and Southwest: mediumweight clothing, light coat, hat
- South, Yungui, Sichuan, and Southeast: lightweight clothing, sweater, light coat, rainwear

PANDA PEEPS . . .

Ethnically, I want to consider why we subdivide China into separate regions. As we pointed out in the Central Asia chapter, we have a lot of different ethnic groups in China. In Mongolia, of course, there are Mongols. They also live in Inner Mongolia, a province of China. In the Tibetan Plateau there are Tibetan folks, and of great importance in the northwestern quadrant, we have some Cossacks and some Uyghurs (pronounced Weegers). This is the exact reason why we classify most of Western China as part of Central Asia. Those are the ethnic groups that are not Chinese.

As you can see, the vast majority of people in China are on the eastern side, particularly along the eastern seaboard. The vast majority of those same people are what we call **Han Chinese,** named for an ancient dynasty. The Han dynasty's rule spanned from 200 BCE to about 200 CE. They were a very popular dynasty, so popular that people started calling themselves by the dynastic name. They're still known today as Han Chinese. Which brings up the question, where are people in China?

We pointed out that most of the Chinese population is on the eastern side of the country. That is another reason for this east-west divide within China proper. The eastern side is where all the people are and where the ethnically Han Chinese people are. It is also where there's a more moderate climate with more moisture, which is essential for food growth. Where most of the food is grown is

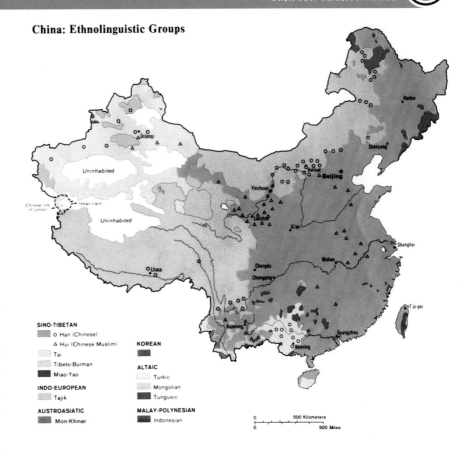

China: Ethnolinguistic Groups

SINO-TIBETAN
○ Han (Chinese)
△ Hui (Chinese Muslim)
Tai
Tibeto-Burman
Miao-Yao

INDO-EUROPEAN
Tajik

AUSTROASIATIC
Mon-Khmer

KOREAN

ALTAIC
Turkic
Mongolian
Tungusic

MALAY-POLYNESIAN
Indonesian

where most of the industry is, most of the cities are, and where most of everything is. This is not a coincidence. This eastern scenario is quite different from the situation for the western people who are not distinctly Han Chinese. In the western countryside, it is more sparsely populated, there is a much more rural base, and it is cooler, higher, and drier. So that's your East Asia round-out of climate, terrain, and ethnicity.

PANDA OF CHRISTMAS PAST

So why do we call it the powerhouse? Several things make China quite distinct in today's world—and I'm going to get to Korea, just be patient. China is by definition the world's oldest continuous state. Was it a state 4,000 years ago? I don't know, but it was something pretty damn close. We already talked about what a sovereign state is, but here I think the term that better applies is **nation-state,** a culturally distinct group of folks with a common culture that they all recognize and perpetuate in their defined area. That's what China has been for a long damn time. Have there been states as old, or older? Perhaps. Mesopotamia was right up there, but it's gone now. Ancient Egypt was there, but it's gone now. China has been there for about 5,000 damn years, and they're still here.

In order to understand China's history and current state we need know that they have been **isolationist** by design. This has been facilitated by the physical world. How so? Well let's look at China and some of the physical factors that we just talked about. It has been coined "the Far East" by European phrase, which just means it was on the other side of the planet from everything that Western societies were familiar with. Just by physical distance, it has been far away from a lot of history. It has the Pacific Ocean, the world's largest ocean, on one side of it putting some serious distance between it and anything else. If we progress around to the north of China, we get into big-ass deserts like the Globe. To the northwest lie big deserts like the Taklimakan Basin. These are some dry-ass places, and people tend to like water for some reason, so nobody's

China: Population Density

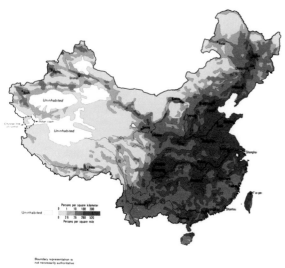

Agricultural Regions

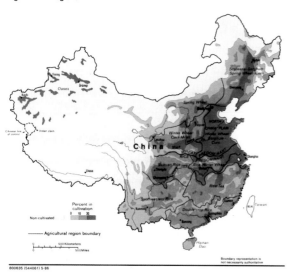

China: Industry

Can you detect an east/west pattern?

there. Keep going around to Central Asia where we get steppe and desert climates intermingled with some tough-ass terrain. Let's keep the tough terrain going in the southwest. We have the Himalayan Range, the largest on the planet, keeping things isolated. And to the south we have a thick rainforest and jungle environment in what are now Burma, Thailand, and Vietnam. The physical conditions of China alone kept things isolated. On top of that, they wanted to be isolated. Their physical environment provided everything they needed to thrive.

The last big theme I want you to think about when you go through this chapter is that China has historically been based on **authoritarian regimes,** centralized power in the hands of the few. Their 5,000-year history has been dominated by what we call an imperial period. That is an empire. All the big names you have heard of, like the Han dynasty, are **dynastic successions** of centralized power. Also consider that throughout most of history, China has been one of the most populous states, if not *the* most populous state, and it still is today.

CHINA IN WORLD HISTORY

Date	Status
1000 BCE	China is "the bomb"
500 BCE	China is "the bomb"
100 BCE	China is "the bomb"
YEAR 0	Jesus is born; China is "the bomb"
100 CE	China is "the bomb"
500 CE	China is "the bomb"
1000 CE	China is "the bomb"
1300 CE	Mongols invade; despite this, China is "the bomb"
1500 CE	Age of European Colonialsim kicks off; China is still "the bomb"
1600 CE	China is "the bomb;" Manchu Dynasty reaches largest extent ever
1800 CE	Shit starts to change . . . things turn to shit

What you see in the table above is the only real ancient history that I want you to understand about China. China, as both a distinct culture and a distinct state, has been the shit for most of human history. What do I mean by "most of human history"? Pretty much from about 2000 BCE right on up to about 1800, that's right, only 200 years ago. If you had been anywhere in the world and you said, "Hey, what country has the most going on, what country's got the most thriving economy, who's making the most money, who's got the highest level of technology, where is it happening, where should we go to invest?" The answer for all these things, throughout all of human history, would have been China. They have been a powerhouse of economic activity and population forever. Western history books are too wrapped up in their own shit to recognize this fully, but the Plaid will help you see. Learn this the first time and never forget it: Although we see modern China growing and we say, "Oh wow, look at them go! Isn't this great?" just keep it in perspective. They have been at the top for most of history. The United States has only been in existence as long as China has stumbled and fallen down, but now they are reasserting themselves. This is a theme I will get back to by chapter's end.

PANDA EXPANSION

As you can see throughout the historical expansion of China proper, the core of China has always been the eastern seaboard. While the empire has fluctuated and its borders have grown (sometimes retracted, but mostly grown), the core has always been maintained. I said earlier that the Chinese have been isolationists by design. Throughout most of history they know they're the shit; it's not as if they don't know the rest of the planet exists. They just ain't interested. People came to them for education; came to their cities because they are the most cosmopolitan and happening places. People came to trade with China because they wanted all of that cool shit China makes. China has historically been the center for tea production, ceramics, and porcelain—what do you call the stuff that your mom breaks out for fancy occasions like Thanksgiving? That's right! China! It's not called china because it's small and breakable, but because it's from China! The spice trade was also a huge market based out of China.

All of the stuff that the Europeans and the Middle-Easterners and lots of other folks around the planet wanted throughout history was produced in China. Trade was mostly one way: going out. As you know this is something that is true still today, but on top of that one-way trading, the cultural interaction was also mostly one way. Now yes, sometimes things come into China that are adopted and adapted into their culture. Sometimes even foreign invaders come into China and take over. But what China has been exceptionally good at throughout all of its history is maintaining its distinct sense of culture.

Even when invaded and taken over by other groups of people, like Mongols or the Manchus, China assimilated the foreigners very rapidly. It's kind of like an old out-of-hand saying that, "Anybody can go to China and do anything he wants, but they are going to be Chinese in the end." Everything gets **Chinafied** once it gets in there. This is because the Chinese have this isolationist design, very inward-looking and self-preserving. Take the Great Wall of China, for example. This is one of the major features of China that is a direct material manifestation of its isolationist design: a big-ass wall built to keep people out. The basic Chinese self image is, "We are China on this side. Keep the hell out. We don't need your stuff. We don't need your culture. We don't need anything from

you. We are the bomb. We are the center of the universe!" They really said that last part; there is a place you can go in Beijing called the center of the universe. That's pretty much the way they've seen themselves throughout history.

Does that mean that they never had interaction with anybody else on the planet, and that they were always alone? No, absolutely not. As I have already suggested, there has been trade throughout the centuries. The **Silk Road** provided exterior trade and contact with regions as far away as Europe. Why'd they call it the Silk Road? Well, like the fine china for which China was named, it wasn't self-applied; that's just what European traders called it. The

Hmmm . . . Chinese silk. I should investigate.

Silk Road was for people to get silks out of China to trade to the Middle East and Europe. The point is that China knows there is a world going on out there. They had contact with the other regions, but mostly kept to themselves. Not many records of Chinese exploration, economic entities expanding trade, or world conquests are to be found in their history.

They remained quite isolated and that was fine and dandy for the past 4,000 years, but when we get to the modern era, China meets its undoing. This is what we mostly want to spend our time on when we talk about more current history and where China is today. Isolationism, while very successful for virtually all of Chinese history, is going to unravel in the last 300 years, in a massively bad way. What are we talking about here? Up to the 1700s, global interaction and trade is there, but it is controlled by the state, and is mostly one way. China will sell you all the crap you want to buy, but they don't need any of your stuff. They say, "Keep all that. We don't need any of the goods you produce. Keep your culture too. We don't need that. We've got our own culture already."

Once the Europeans get to the age of worldwide exploration and colonization, China is one of the last places they get to. Trade was eventually established. Maybe you've heard of a couple of these distinctly European trade entities, like the Dutch-East India Trading Company and British-East India Trading Company. The British are the ones we already talked about back in South Asia; they ended up taking over all of what is now India, Pakistan, and Bangladesh. These are economic entities that are sponsored by Western European countries, but became a lot more. They got in and took over large sections of South Asia and Southeast Asia, and then they started working on the big bad boy that they haven't conquered yet: China. This is a slow process that's staved off consistently by the Manchus for as long as they can hold out.

About 1800 is a critical date to remember. This is the swing date. China is big and bad up until this point in history, then things start to go downhill. And the sliding board is steep, my friends. By the 1800s, trade companies have made inroads into China. At the same time, the Industrial Revolution changes the whole world in radical ways. We have machines making stuff in much greater volumes, which means for the first time, Europe can produce things like silk, maybe even pottery, for as cheap as China has always produced it. This shifts the balance of power away from China a little bit.

STONED PANDA

On top of that there is a big push for capitalism and free trade in the world, sponsored by the British. Adam Smith published the *Wealth of Nations* in 1776, an important red letter date for lots of different reasons, but this was the kick-off date for the whole concept of free trade. The basic premise of **free trade** is that all countries and all businesses ought to have a right to trade with anybody they want to. The British primarily sponsored free trade in the beginning because they have been trying to make inroads into China and get some trade action for years. China so far was very conservative in their dealings. The Chinese say, "Oh, you guys can buy all the stuff you want here, just leave us the money. You bring all your silver and you can have all of the pottery, silk, and spices that you want."

Lots of money had been flowing into China for a while and this was pissing off the Europeans who were like, "Hey, China has all the bank money. All of our money goes there, and then they don't buy any of our stuff." The British are looking around saying, "What can we do; how can we break into this market? They don't want any of our stuff like the textiles we are producing via the Industrial Revolution . . . what could we sell them? Damn, I can't think of anything . . . WAIT, I've got it: Opium! That's awesome, what a fantastic idea!" And that is exactly what the British end up doing. You'd think they were joking, but the new plan was to get everybody addicted to drugs and start selling it to them like gangbusters to reverse the flow of silver back to Europe. It worked perfectly. Once this influx of drugs was established, it was unstoppable. By the mid-1800s the British, the French, the Germans, Dutch, and Russians all had established trading ports, and the Manchu Dynasty started to weaken.

Opium War: the British win the right to sell crack.

Why did I bring up the whole story of opium? Because as the Chinese were weakening, they were like, "Whoa, what the hell is going on here? All of our people are addicted to crack. We can't have this. Yo, British dudes, back the hell up with that boat of crack. You can't sell that here. We refuse to let your ship dock up with all that opium." And the British said, "Oh, ok, then we declare war on you." Thus from 1839 to 1842 we have the aptly named **Opium Wars.** The British were fighting for the right to peddle crack to the Chinese. If you look back at British historical documents, they say the whole fight was over free trade. They gauged it all on something that makes them sound like sincere and honest brokers. Yeah bull; they were slinging crack. Millions of Chinese folks were addicted to it and it was disintegrating the social fabric of the nation. So the Brits fought a war and won the right to distribute opium to the Chinese population.

How did this happen? How did this mighty, mighty nation, that's been around so long, lose a war over crack to the British? Isolation is a dual-edged sword. Yes, through most of history it has kept China distinct, and for most of history they were ahead. But the other edge of the sword is that because they weren't paying attention to what was going on in Europe, they missed the Industrial Revolution. The Industrial Revolution, which goes hand in hand with military revolution, ended up giving the British a technological advantage. By the time the British show up with their gunboats and crack boats, they are militarily superior to the Chinese. This three-year war shouldn't have even lasted that long; it was a duck shoot. How do you say "quack" in Chinese?

ANGRY PANDA

This ends in 1842 and is a stunning defeat for the Chinese. Yes, empires have come and gone, and people have beaten each other up, and they've had some wars—but they have never had a foreign body of people from somewhere on the other side of the planet invade their soil, and whip their ass completely. They receive such a sound thumping in the Opium Wars that they are forced to basically cede all control of territory over to the Brits. The British forced China to open up all trade to all states in the world. In fact, they had this hilarious thing that was called, "no favored nation status." We think of that in today's world as the MOST favored nation status, but the British said, "You are going to have a **no favored nation status,** which means you have to trade with everybody, and any rights you give to one country you have to give to us all." They completely liberate the Chinese economy for every other country's taking overnight. This is a titanic blow to the Chinese culture, to the Chinese way of life, and to the Chinese economy. In this same peace treaty, concessions of the Opium War included the British picking up a fairly significant territory that you have probably heard of, Hong Kong. That was 1842, and the British controlled that right up until 1997.

In 1843, China ceded Macau to the Portuguese. Just to put this in historical context, the Chinese society starts to crumble at this time because of another thing the British and European colonial powers did; they made the Chinese pass a law that said you couldn't persecute missionaries from Europe. I'm not making fun of anybody's religion; be as damn Christian as you want to be, but think about what strain this is to a very independent culture that's managed to hold onto its own ways for a long time. The fabric of the Chinese society basically degenerates in a matter of a few decades.

ABANDONED PANDA

And on top of that, to put this all in historical context, what is happening in other regions nearby? Southeast Asia has already been subjugated by European powers. The colonial powers hold all of Southeast Asia except for Thailand. The British control

what is now South Asia. The British also have Australia at this point. Japan is a major issue to now consider from the Chinese angle. What's happening in Japan as this disintegration is occurring in Chinese society? Let's jump forward a little bit to say 1868. What happened then? It's in the middle of Japan's **Meiji Restoration.**

If you had to pick two events that most demonstrate the difference between the evolution of Japanese society and Chinese society, they would be the Opium Wars and the Meiji Restoration. The West is disgracing China during the Opium Wars and at the same time the Meiji restoration is occurring in Japan—as they embrace the West. We can stop right now. Take a breather from reading this book and think about this: Why is Japan the second richest country on the planet right now and why has China been playing catch-up?

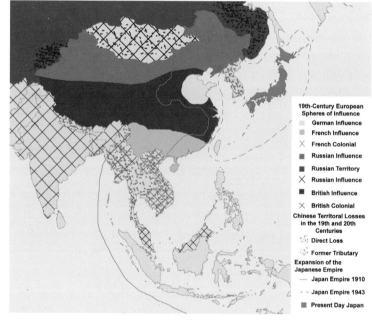

Why is Japan a fully developed nation and why is China still developing? Why has China been poor so long and been disgraced for the last 100 years while Japan has been kicking ass?

The answer to these questions has much to do with the Opium Wars and the Meiji Restoration. These two countries, once side by side, took two different paths at the same juncture in history about 150 years ago. Today's world reflects the two different outcomes of these countries' choices. To put the icing on the cake: In 1895, we have the **Sino-Japanese War** in which the Japanese thump the Chinese and take control of the Korean peninsula. Now, for the first time, we pull our Korean friends into the mix. Korea up to this point has been a little brother of China, a vassal state, which Japan has also been. Japan taking Korea is another titanic blow to Chinese civilization. A former vassal state, which has always been a subsidiary of China, has now crushed them in a war and taken control of territory. That was devastating to the Chinese.

Beleaguered Boxers held captive by cowboys

As you can see from the map on the previous page, in 1899 China is in dire straits because of its continued isolationist endeavors. What is China doing then? Are they playing catch-up with the rest of the world, like Japan? Are they embracing the West? Are they trying to adopt and adapt? Nope. In 1899 they have something called the **Boxer Rebellion:** a movement to purge out foreign influence. They say, "Hey everybody, wake up tomorrow and go kill all the whiteys!" This was in response mostly to interjection of Christian missionaries, but also to the shitty state apparatus that was under foreign domination, politically and economically. The Boxers were this kind of martial artsy, mystic group of dudes trying to reestablish

order in the Chinese society. Just to give you a sense of their cluelessness, the Boxers believed that if they prayed hard enough and were pure of heart that bullets would not be able to penetrate their bodies. Hmmm . . . I think you can already predict how this is going to turn out. They slaughtered some Westerners and besieged the Western diplomatic quarters in Beijing where they were basically holding people hostage.

How many country mascots can you identify in the thrashing of the Chinese dragon?

So how did the rest of the world respond? Check out the political cartoon above for the answer. They got a coalition of all the colonial powers together. The French, the Russians, the British, etc., all the great European powers were now working hand in hand like good brothers to go beat the hell out of the Boxer Movement and the Chinese Dragon altogether. And that's exactly what happened. To make matters worse, the US helps out—and worst of all, Japan is there too. Damn. Talk about salt in the wound!

Japan is growing in influence and is starting to take over the world after embracing Western ways, while China, at the turn of the century, is burying its head further in the sand and is trying to beat out the foreign influence. This is a big mistake, and the misery is not over yet, because they still have to get through the 20th century. So China, by 1900, is fully under control of colonial powers. The state is still intact, but only at the whim of European countries. Look again at that image above. The caption underneath reads "The real trouble will come with the wake . . ." how prophetic for a freakin cartoon made in 1900. But the dragon will have to sleep through a bit more trouble yet before its slumber is interrupted.

20TH CENTURY PUNISHES THE PANDA MORE

In 1912, the last Qing Emperor was removed from the throne, and the Republic of China was established. That marked the end of the Qing Dynasty and imperial lines altogether. This place is in chaos. Everything religious, cultural, economic, and

political is in shambles. People have just given up. This didn't happen overnight; it developed over decades. Chinese people have been saying, "What in the hell are we going to do about this?" In 1911 they finally say, "That's it; the whole imperial line is over. We are not doing that anymore. We need to at least try to catch-up with the West. Look, they have constitutional monarchies and republics over there. Let's do that! We can't do this empire thing anymore; ours sucks anyway." So they throw out the Qing emperor. You may have seen a movie called *The Last Emperor*, that's what it was about. What's the deal? Did they ever have a movie in Japan called *The Last Emperor*?

No, we already know that Japan still has an emperor, but this is when China departs. They give up on the whole imperial way and move toward something else, but it ain't going to be easy. In this state of chaos, nothing will happen overnight. They can't decide internally on what they should do, or who should be in power. The country breaks down into what is sometimes called a **warlord state.** Local military leaders take over, and there is no authoritative central government

The Last Emperor of China. No, not the dude, but that little kid.

to speak of. This plays out for the next 20 years, well into the 1930s.

This leaves people in China polling around looking for some answers. "What should we do? What type of system should we implement? The imperial system is gone and we're not going to do that again." Some say, "Let's embrace the US model, or the French model, or the UK model," and others say, "Hey, what about that Soviet model though? That looks pretty good too." This starts the face-off of ideologies within China. In 1928, the **Nationalists,** under a guy named **Chiang Kai-Shek,** are fighting for a repub-

Chiang Kai-Shek

lic. They defeat the folks fighting for a Communist state. The Nationalists also defeat or ally with or outright pay off all those warlord guys remaining in the northern states, uniting the country. But this is tenuous. Why is it tenuous? Because of another incursion I haven't mentioned yet.

Look back to the spheres of influence in China map. Look at what the Japanese are up to. This entire time Japan's empire has been expanding. I already pointed out they took over the Korean Peninsula back in 1895, but they didn't stop

How Now Chairman Mao? Who the Hell Is Mao?

Mao Zedong (Mao is his last name) becomes the leader of the Communist party in China in 1927 when he formed the People's Liberation Army. He and the Communist Party were largely seen as folk heroes and true Chinese nationalists during the Japanese occupation, as they conducted a guerrilla war against the Japanese aggressors throughout the entire conflict. It should be noted that the Nationalist Party led by Chiang Kai-Shek did little to nothing during the occupation, choosing instead to horde weapons and money given to them by the US—given for the sole purpose of fighting the Japanese.

After WWII and the brutal Chinese civil war against the Nationalist/Kuomintang party, the Communists took over mainland China in 1949 and declared the People's Republic of China. You can like him or you can hate him, but Mao is largely seen as "the George Washington of China" at this moment in history, because he declares that "the Chinese people have stood back up." Meaning: the two centuries of foreign occupation and humiliation are over.

Mao became the leader of China and was known as the "Four Greats": "Great Teacher, Great Leader, Great Supreme Commander, Great Helmsman." He became the supreme dictator of China and every Chinese person was required to have a book of Chairman Mao's quotations. He has been praised by many for unifying China and making it free of foreign domination for the first time since the Opium Wars.

However, Mao is sometimes credited as a lethal dictator. Because of some his projects—such as Anti-Rightist Campaign, the Great Leap Forward, and the Cultural Revolution—over 80 million Chinese people died. Part of the reason so many people died was that Chinese officials were so afraid of criticizing Mao that they told him that everything was going fine. Also for this reason, China did not start implementing capitalist reforms until after Mao died in 1976.

Fun Commie Fact: Mao started his own kind of communism, called Maoism, that stated that communist revolution needed to come from rural peasants. Marxist communism was designed for industrialized countries, like the ones in Europe.

there. The Japanese also staked out some claims of ownership of Chinese lands after they helped out quashing the Boxer Rebellion. They made further incursions into what is now Manchuria, and started to take control of some port cities. The Europeans were already doing it, so the Japanese wanted to play ball as well. Japan largely stayed out of the whole WWI conflict, the reason being that they were busy securing more empire for themselves over in East Asia. By the time all this chaos happens in China, when there is no real leadership and no one knows what the hell is going on, Japan has seriously invaded them.

This is the point—in between World War I and World War II—when the Japanese have secured real control over all the major facilities in China. This Japanese invasion is only perpetuating the chaotic state in China, and a civil war breaks out amongst the Communist and Nationalist forces again. During this civil war something called the **Long March** occurs where **Mao**

Zedong leads the Chinese Communists in a retreat through Northern China after they get the shit beaten out of them by the Nationalist forces. The fight should have been over after that initial ass-kicking, but somehow this guy named Mao pulled off a last-second, fourth-quarter win, which leads us to the question . . . who the hell is this Mao guy? See insert box on page 416.

In 1937, the Japanese army attacks China outright. This is the buildup to World War II. By the following year, Japan controls most of Eastern China. Remember that's where the most people are, the most businesses are, and where the most of everything is.

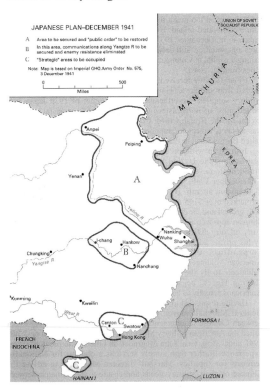

JAPANESE PLAN–DECEMBER 1941

A Area to be secured and "public order" to be restored
B In this area, communications along Yangtze R to be secured and enemy resistance eliminated
C "Strategic" areas to be occupied

Note: Map is based on Imperial GHQ Army Order No. 575, 3 December 1941

0   500
Miles

Japanese plans for the mainland. China was not happy.

Now, as this is happening we are going to go ahead and get into WWII. We have already talked about a lot of that stuff, so we don't have to reiterate it here, but I do want you to know this: WWII is disastrous for the Chinese. Recall from way back in the Russian chapter that the Russian losses were something like 10–20 million during World War II. But it's a lesser-known fact that the Japanese did one hell of a job slaughtering the Chinese at the same time. This mass slaughter has been barely acknowledged by Western historians and people like you. The losses in China may have been upwards of 20–30 million; hell it could have been 40 million. It's almost impossible to tell in hindsight because there are so many damn people there and their records weren't that good. Somewhere between 20 and 40 *million* Chinese were killed during the Japanese occupation in the buildup before and during World War II. And very, very few of those millions were actually combatants . . . in other words, they were unarmed civilians.

Many were innocent women and children who were slaughtered in nasty ways by the Japanese. I guess it was just another way they were trying to embrace the West. Japan tried the first kind of modern biological testing and biological warfare during World War II. Some of their experiments included dropping rats infected with bubonic plague from bombers over heavily populated cities to see how fast people would get the disease; they also poisoned water supplies in major cities to see how fast people would die. We also talked about the **Rape of Nanking** in which millions of people were slaughtered in the streets. The Japanese didn't want to set up internment camps. I am reiterating this again in this chapter because it's just that goddamn important.

When we think of the horrors of World War II, we usually think of the German atrocities against the Jews, and those were horrible, make no bones about it. But when China thinks of World War II, they think of the horrible atrocities which left a probably 8 or 10 times higher body count in their country at the hands of the Japanese. This makes for bad blood, my friends. It's still there today. Also remember that the Japanese have occupied the Korean Peninsula since 1895, an even longer time, under the exact same kind of brutal regime. The Koreans haven't forgotten either. All of Korea ended up being a work camp for the Japanese to get resources out of mines. All the

This really sucked for China.

What the Hell . . . Is the Story Behind Taiwan?

For most of its history, Taiwan was an island territory off the coast of China that was of no great significance. (Sorry my Taiwanese friends! You know its true!) However, Taiwan immediately became a Cold War hotspot when the Chinese Nationalists (Kuomintang), after losing the Chinese Civil War, retreated to Taiwan and set up a government called the Republic of China (ROC). Meanwhile, Mao and the Communists controlled mainland China and called themselves the People's Republic of China (PRC).

The leaders of both countries have long subscribed to the one-China policy (that there is only one China and Taiwan is part of China), each insisting on their own government's legitimacy. Of course, during the Cold War, capitalist countries recognized the ROC as the legitimate government of China and communist countries recognized the PRC as the legitimate government of China.

Today, the Taiwan situation is tricky. The Kuomintang lost control of Taiwan in elections in 2000, but the new president, Chen Shui-bian, still maintains that Taiwan is independent. However, most countries do not have relations with the ROC and the Taiwanese position has eroded over the past few decades as the PRC has gained international prominence. Because of its one-China policy, the PRC only participates in international organizations where the ROC is not recognized as a state. The United Nations, for example, expelled the ROC when the PRC was admitted. To make matters even more complicated, while most countries do not have official relations with the ROC (to not make the PRC mad), they do have informal relations with the Taiwan government. For example, the United States operates the American Institute in Taiwan, which is like an embassy. However, it is not officially called an embassy because America is not allowed to have diplomatic relations with Taiwan.

The Taiwan situation was really tricky for the last decade, because the Kuomintang lost control of Taiwan in elections in 2000 to President Chen Shui-bian, who was from a staunchly pro-independence party that regularly pissed of China by making moves to secure said independence. However, things have settled down considerably just this year as the KMT won the presidency back, and the new President Ma (that's right, just Ma...like your mother) has made great strides to mend ties with China proper.

Fun Fact: While the US officially adheres to the one-China policy, in reality it practices a two-China policy. Under the 1979 Taiwan Relations Act, the US sells Taiwan military weapons, and the language of the act warns the People's Republic that any coercive unification efforts would be "of grave concern to the United States."

FORMOSA
FROM THE LATEST AUTHORITIES
Revised by Rev. W. Campbell

resource extraction from the Korean Peninsula was shipped back to Japan. Now, why would Japan be building this empire, taking all these resources, enslaving the population of Korea, and taking over places in China? For the reasons we have already pointed out in the Japan chapter: They don't have any resources on their island, and to expand and get richer they've got to take stuff from other places. That's why they became an imperial regime.

The Japanese occupation is so horrifically bad that the Nationalists and Communists even team up at one point. They say, "Holy shit! This sucks so bad, there is no point in us fighting each other right now; we have to get these assholes out of here first!" They team up and kick out the Japanese. Of course it's the United States' involvement in the war against Japan in the Pacific that does most of the job, but the Chinese are doing some fighting on their soil as well, making life for the Japanese difficult. Finally, in 1945, it's lights out for Japan, literally and figuratively.

In 1946, after WWII is over, the civil war is back on again. The Nationalists and Communists that had teamed up said, "Hey alright, cool, the Japanese are gone. Yeah, the war is over, so let's hurry up and rebuild so we can get back to fighting each other to see who controls this place." Long story short, after this stretch of 150 years where China gets the shit pulverized out of it, the end result is that in 1949, the Communists win the civil war. Mao was a long-shot to win at several different points, but the Commies pull it out. The Communists win, and the People's Republic of China is established in 1949.

What happened to the Nationalist party that had a lot of supporters that fought that big-ass civil war? Did most of them get slaughtered? Nope; most of them withdrew to the island of Taiwan. Taiwan? I've heard of that place. . . .

So the Commies take charge, and start to pull the country up by the bootstraps. They have an agricultural revolution, and begin industrialization. The Communists start to make strides to rebuild their society, their country. But this isolationist vein, this antiforeign vein, so prevalent in Chinese history pops back up again in 1966–1969. This is what some call the **Cultural Revolution;** at least that's what it says in Mao's little red book.

The **Cultural Revolution** is very much like the Boxer Rebellion in that the sentiment was basically, "We don't like any of these foreigners. We don't like foreign influence, so let's purge it all out. Destroy all Western instruments, destroy Western literature, banish people that are from the West, persecute, imprison, or kill people who speak English or people who were Western educated." A real social upheaval and purge occurs within China. China regains a little sanity after World War II and the civil war, but it's not out of the woods yet. The last bad event for them, that I'm going to talk about, occurs in 1989. This is when hundreds of students are massacred during the prodemocracy protest in **Tiananmen Square.** This event puts us up into what I think most of you readers here will know about . . .

THE DRAGON AWAKENS: CHINA IN THE MODERN ERA

This is stuff you probably remember, or have at least heard referenced. This is the end result of the Chinese communist experiment: They had made some progress since the wars ended, but they've also had these internal purges and internal problems—and they are not really that rich yet. China is still kind of backwards and behind. To top it all off, they are persecuting democracy movements. How crappy is that? But this is where China begins to reevaluate some of its actions, because the world watched the Tiananmen Square massacre and said, "How horrific, how terrible! What's the deal with these guys? They are bastards!" Strangely enough, this is when everything starts to around for China.

ECONOMIC EXPLOSION

Things have gone on the upswing, but slowly. After Mao Zedong died in 1976, his subsequent successors in the Chinese government started to liberate the economy and adopt capitalist reform—something which Mao absolutely raged against his entire life. The first guy to take the country in this new direction was a cat named Deng Xiaoping. If we are going to credit Mao with bringing China out of its 'period of sorrow', then we really have to credit Deng with truly bringing China back to its restored position of wealth and power in today's world. It was Deng who pushed for capitalist economic reforms, put the country on the path of modernization, and pretty much gave up on the commie experiment thing that Mao had attempted.

As we already suggested many times in this book, Communism has never worked anywhere. It is a political and economic system that is just too complicated, and not one single manifestation of it anywhere has ever managed to work. It didn't work in Russia, didn't work in Vietnam (mostly because the US ruined its chances from

Deng and Carter in 1979. Well, at least one of them was a successful leader.

the get-go), hasn't really worked in Cuba, and didn't work in China.

But here is the big difference: in Soviet Russia, the USSR, in one fell swoop overnight they said, "Ok we are going to get rid of this. Anybody that wants to be out of the USSR, go ahead and vote yourself out." Then the Berlin Wall falls and the whole damn Russian economy falls with it. Make no mistake; the Chinese were watching those events extremely closely. This is one reason why the Chinese are liberalizing very carefully, very slowly, which they've been doing for the last 40 years. They have opened their markets . . . but slowly. They've allowed foreign capital investment . . . but slowly. They have privatized some industries . . . but slowly. Because when did Tiananmen Square happen? 1989.

Tiananmen Square: where all the action happens.

That's exactly when the whole kit-n-caboodle came crashing down for the Soviets. Mikhail Gorbachev, the leader of the Soviet Union, was actually visiting Deng in China during that incident. Chinese leaders rightly surmised that the reason the pro-democracy movement popped up at that time and that place was because people were supporting Gorbachev. Some college kids were like, "Yeah, Birthmark-head is opening up and liberalizing and making democracy in Russia. Let's all have a big protest here to support that!" The Chinese government said, "No! Look what's happening there; those guys suck! They're falling down and eating crap. We are not going to do that again."

Thus, the massacre. The Tiananmen massacre was terrible. The Plaid doesn't want any college kids killed, because hey, college kids are cool, but it was a very intentional move by the Chinese government. They said, "We can not allow this to happen because we can not allow our society to spiral out of control like the Soviet one did." If you think about it in hindsight, it was a calculated, conservative move. China is bustling in today's world while Russia is struggling to catch up. The Chinese have had infinite patience and since Deng Xiaoping took over as head of state after Mao died they started to liberalize and open up, but at their own pace, a pace that is massively accelerating right at that point in time.

TIANANMEN TURNAROUND: 21ST CENTURY SUCCESSES

The point of entry is the Tiananmen Massacre of 1989. It was bad and it got a bunch of bad press for China, but I'm putting it back in here as a turning point, because it doesn't happen again, and it won't ever happen again. "What's The Plaid talking about? You can't be talking smack like that shit!" I'm telling you, I know. The Chinese got too much bad press over that incident. They may very well have done it again, but they figured out, "Oh, we don't want bad press. We want people to invest here. We want to become part of the world economy. We want to have influence in the world. We want to have the Olympics here. We want to have the Miss Universe Pageant." You can't have any of that shit if you are killing your own citizens. So this is a great place to start in terms of the 21st-century turn-around for China, because it is the last time you are going to see a tremendous and bloody crackdown of that magnitude. The Chinese government has learned its lesson well—bad press equals bad investment strategy.

The government is still run by the Communist Party, but this is not a communist state as we suggested way back in the *Know Your Heads of State* chapter. True, communism is economics and politics put together, but there ain't a damn thing about this society that's economically communist. This is the wild west of free-market capitalism, my friends. Since the Communist Party is still part of the government, it's better to term the government a **one-party state.** True, communism is

"Plaid Avenger, I have the secret formula for Chinese economic growth . . . but I think I'm being followed . . ."

gone. Ain't nobody paying attention to that nonsense anymore. By the way, only about 2 percent of the entire Chinese population is a card-carrying commie. That's 2 percent of a billion and a half. What does that equate to? A decent sized number, but still jack. This is not a communist economy, and it is not necessarily a communist country; it is a one-party state.

Let's get to the entire decade right after the Tiananmen massacre, when China enjoys massive economic growth. There are huge influxes of foreign capital in the form of investments by multinational corporations. The Chinese are very particular about how this is happening and are controlling things very stringently. They've been saying "Oh OK Microsoft, Boeing, Exxon, sure you guys can come over here and start a company if you like, as long as you give us all the technology we want. In other words, we are going to get something out of this too; we're not just going to open our markets and let you come do what you want."

They certainly have gotten something out of their international relationships, but why would they want to be so anal about everything? Look where it's gotten them. In a single decade they've pretty much caught up. Granted, they are not on the technological level of the West yet, but they are catching up fast. So 1990 was the kickoff of massive economic growth, large amounts of foreign capital, foreign investment, and foreign business. Why would foreign business want to be in China? Oh I don't know. Would you like to be in a place to sell your product to a billion and a half people? Yeah, I thought so.

This 1990s economic growth is due not only to foreign investment, but also to private enterprise within China. Liberalization of government control led to growth in **entrepreneurs**—Chinese people starting Chinese businesses. And there are a billion and a half people there, man! They are emerging from a communist economic system where no matter how hard you work—or don't work—you are going to get paid the same. What incentive is that to work hard? There are no incentives. But put them in a capitalist environment. "Hey dudes if you work harder you get more money. You get more money, you get more shit, your life can be better." If you get a billion and a half people who desperately want more shit

and offer said stuff to them, man, watch out! This place is blowing up due mostly to entrepreneurial growth of private business within China. This economic explosion can also be linked to the growth of the Tigers, the thing we talked about way back in the World Econ chapter. Other countries in the vicinity have been gaining in all these categories too: international investment, international business, etc.

The reason companies had been going to Indonesia, Taiwan, or South Korea is that they had cheaper labor. China is the cheap labor pool of the planet. Businesses are flocking to it to take advantage of that. Every major business on the planet now has a presence in China. This has all happened in the last 15 years. This is an economy that is so damn hot that they typically have what we call double-digit growth. If they say the GDP growth is 11 percent or 12 percent or 13 percent that means the GDP next year will be 11 percent bigger than it is right now. Take what we have right now and multiply it by 11 percent and add it on next year. In countries like the United States and most of Western Europe, 3 percent or 4 percent growth is fantastic. In China, 10 percent,

12 percent, 14 percent growth is titanic, but they are consistently achieving it. The Chinese government's main problem right this second is not how to make their economy grow, they are trying to figure out how to put the brakes on it. "We're going too fast; shit is getting out of control. Let's cool it down, cool it down!" It is a situation of which every country in the world is envious. Who wouldn't like to be in a situation of growing too fast as opposed to slow growth, or no growth?

THE PANDA TAKES BACK ITS CUBS . . .

In 1997, China conducted training off the coast of Taiwan. This consisted of firing gunboats and some missiles over Taiwan's airspace. It was a very specific move at a very specific time to symbolize that China was ready to reassert itself. They didn't do it before. There was rhetoric and there was talk before, but now that the Chinese economy and military had caught up enough they said, "Ok, we're telling you what's going to go on. Taiwan is our territory. We are going to do something and see what happens." So it's a symbolic gesture, I think, and marks a turning point where China is ready to reassert itself militarily, if necessary.

In 1997, Hong Kong was returned to China. The British pack up all the shit that they claimed from the Opium Wars and sailed the hell out. The Chinese weren't really waving goodbye either. They just went to work pulling Hong Kong and its mighty capitalist economy back to the motherland. That same year, six months later, the Portuguese returned Macau to China. As eluded to earlier, Taiwan is now the final piece of the lost Chinese empire which is soon to be put back into its strategic place.

The new leader of Taiwan, President Ma, has made every indication thus far that he will be working to smooth out the relationship with mother China. In the first month he was in office, there have been high level meetings between Chinese President Hu Jintao and major Taiwanese leaders, they have agreed to resume commercial flights between the countries on weekends, and also agreed to triple the amount of tourist allowed to visit the island every day to 3000. This is the most open that communications and travel have been between these two entities since before 1949. That is big news, and please keep in mind that all of this has occurred just in the first month that Ma has been in office. I predict significant changes in his 4 year term in office. You know what? I'm just crazy enough to make a grander prediction: I believe we are seeing the beginning of the end of the historic dispute between China and Taiwan. Look for Taiwan to be firmly back in the Chinese fold within a decade.

World Trade Organization
Organisation Mondiale du Commerce
Organización Mundial del Comercio

But onto other issues. In the year 2000, the United States establishes **favored nation status** and trades with China. In 2001, China joined the World Trade Organization (WTO). This is a society on fire. We can add a few other things here such as: China is now an associate member of ASEAN, a member of the SCO, a member of APEC, and host of the 2008 Olympics. China is all over the damn place.

Here is a quote from the chief Chinese negotiator, Long Yongtu, regarding China's entry into the WTO: "the 15-year process is a blink of an eye in the 5,000-year history of China." I love that shit, man. That resonates with the Plaid. Awesome, awesome quote to get you to understand what is going on in this society. They're telling the world, "We are here for the long haul, friends. We are reasserting ourselves. We are going to reclaim our proper position in the world economy and the world politic. And 15 years, you think that's a long time? That ain't shit. We will sit here for 100 damn years, if that's what it takes. We are China. We have the patience of a rock. We will get it done." If it sounds like I'm getting too fired up about China, it's because this is *the* vibrant place right now. It's really happening.

To finish off our categorized date list of Chinese achievements in the 21st century, we have to include outer **space**. In 2005, China put a man in space. China now joins the most exclusive country club on the planet. It's a short list. Do you know it? It's the US, Russia, and now China. Not even Japan has done it, the mighty, mighty wonder to the east of China and the number two economy on the planet. How about Germany, the number three economy? Nope! They've never done it either. Nobody else has done it. Man in space. The Chinese are setting the stage. This is again like so many of these

Danger Will Robinson! China is here too!

other things I've mentioned: it is a symbol. China says, "We are in the big boy club now. We are the shit. We have got it going ON!" Think about it. There is no goddamn reason to put a man in space. It's all about prestige. They are reclaiming their world role. The 21st century is a whole different world for the Chinese.

And they aren't even satisfied with just putting a Chinaman in orbit for a few days. The Chinese have every intention on putting a man on the moon, and they have already announced tentative plans to build a permanent moon base! Holy green cheese! A freakin' moon base! Not even the US pulled that one off! Just to give you an idea of how serious this is, China was actually 6 months ahead of schedule when they succeeded in the manned orbit plan. Now they are slated to get to the moon by 2012, and appear to be on track. In what is assuredly a total random coincidence, the US upped NASA's budget times ten, and NASA then announced that they were now planning to build a moon base first. Space race is back on my friends!

I actually hope the Chinese base gets built first, that way once the US base is being worked on, the Americans will have someplace to order take-out from . . . but I digress as always . . .

BIG PLACE, BIG ECONOMY, BIG MILITARY . . . BIG PROBLEMS!

I know I have stressed this a million times, but let me stress it one million and one times, China is reassuming its place on the world stage. It is almost impossible for the United States to understand this scenario, because think about the timeline. The entire time the US has been rising in the world is the exact same time period China spent falling. Throughout all of US history, China sucked. But that's not looking at the big picture. They've been on top for 5,000 years. China is not saying, "Hey, we are growing and we're finally going to be a part of the world economy," they are saying, "We are taking back our place at the top." That is a much better way to phrase it, and a much better way for you to understand what's going on. In the same light, China is increasingly becoming a model to follow for other states all over Asia.

During the entire Cold War, we lived in a bipolar world. The US was one big power, and the USSR was the other. All the states in the world could choose one side or the other. Some chose neither, but that wasn't many. Nowadays, we are getting back to a bipolar world again. The US had a good run there for 10 or 15 years as the sole superpower in the world, but China is rising to meet it (not overtake it). Some countries in South America are now making strategic ties to China. In Africa, a lot of nations are making strategic ties to China. Certainly Southeast Asia is making strategic ties to China. It's just the way things are going down right now; China is the other option in a newly bipolar world.

How is China doing this? Their explosive economy is a big part of it—double digit growth now for a decade and a half. Part of that is entrepreneurship, which leads to a growing middle class. That's what you have to have if you are going to have an internal economic engine that keeps going. You've got to have that middle class that likes to buy a lot of stuff, and China is growing a big fat middle class right now. Here's some other cool shit that makes them appealing: China is on the permanent UN Security Council, which means since World War II they have had a world political voice. They are now in the WTO. They are a member of ASEAN and APEC and SCO. They are pretty much in all the big boy clubs. They are in the big boy space club too! On top of that they have what the Plaid Avenger has got to refer to as one suave-ass foreign policy.

SUAVE-ASS FOREIGN POLICY?

There are two parts to this. 1. For the last twenty years, China has been working to resolve all of its border disputes. Thirty years ago, China disputed all its borders with everybody. In today's world, that is going away. They are cementing ties with all their land neighbors, a pretty suave move, if I do say so myself. 2. They are setting up strategic ties with countries all over the planet, sometimes with no strings attached. It's a very odd

President Hu

Prime Minister Wen Jiabao

thing. In the US, this "no strings attached" business is looked upon with suspicion. China lends money to countries with no motive? We find this hard to believe. We always have a motive behind everything we do. We say, "Oh, we will lend you some money if we get something in return." But China just lent like half a million dollars to Palau, some Pacific nation no one has even heard of before. They build bridges and stuff in Africa. They have been throughout Latin American, Africa, Southeast Asia, and even India setting up economic ties, buying different resources and setting up free-trade options.

This is done primarily with an eye for **resource acquisition.** As China's economy continues to explode, they need more energy, like all big economies do. What types of energy? Coal, which they have a lot of, and oil, which they don't. You often see **President Hu Jintao** of China making his rounds. In Spring, 2006, he visited all of South America and actually came to the United States to visit George Bush. He went to Saudi Arabia, and then he went to tour all of the African nations. This guy gets around. His premier, **Wen Jiabao,** gets around even more. These guys are hustling around the planet right now.

DETRIMENTAL DIPLOMACY

One of the problems is this same suave-ass foreign policy. For those who are ultraconservative out there, and you think The Plaid is some liberal commie who is just supporting China no matter what, just hold on, you'll see. I said their policy was SUAVE. Suave doesn't mean morally or ethically good; I didn't even say it was good period. But it is very freakin' suave.

How is this suave-ass foreign policy detrimental for the Chinese? China does business for business's sake. They don't really worry about the details too much. Throughout this book we talk about the UN's permanent Security Council and China's role in it, and the issues of sovereignty. China is one of the strictest adherents to the ideas of **sovereignty.** They are all about it. They don't want to intervene anywhere. Actually, the Chinese have no troops in any country and they like it like that. They say, "Sovereignty is sovereignty. Whatever you do to your people, it's not our business." The reason they do that is they don't want anybody messing in their backyard anymore. They respect sovereignty because ultimately they want everyone to respect theirs. They don't want anyone messing around in their country because of what they are doing to the Uyghur people over in the western part of China. This means they will do business with states no matter what those countries may be doing to their own people.

I am thinking particularly of Sudan in today's world, and even Zimbabwe. Most of the world does not like, does not support, and does not want to trade with these two countries in Africa because they have fairly brutal records of persecuting people in their countries. The morally and ethically right thing to do is to refuse to support that state in any capacity. But China says, "We don't give a crap. We will trade with you. Hey, can we buy oil from you Sudan? Thanks buddy!" Perhaps their open policy is not such a great thing. This causes friction between China and other rich countries around the world. Developed countries say, "You can't do that," and then China says, "Hell yeah we can. We are a sovereign state." So the issue is a source of friction for a lot of the Western countries.

I should tell you that even this attitude has been changing fast in China just in the last year. China has been very keen to make a good if not great impression on the world with the Olympic Games they are hosting this year. But the world was not going to let them achieve this so easily. Growing attention to the Sudan situation in particular has cast such a negative light on China's dealings there that have been calls for an Olympic boycot . . . of at least the opening ceremonies if not the whole affair. This spooked China enough for them to allow the UN to move on the Sudanese situation without stopping it . . . remember, as a member of the UN Permanent Security Council, China has up to this point used its veto power to prevent anything from happening to its Sudanese buddies. That situation has now changes due to international pressure.

TUMULTUOUS TIBET

And speaking of frictional Chinese policies, there is the small matter of Tibet. Or should I say huge matter of Tibet. The area we refer to as Tibet has been various things at various times in the last thousand years: it was an independent kingdom, a vassal state, an autonomous region, a semi-autonomous region, a colonial holding, and a fully absorbed territory into a state we call China. For purposes of under-standing today's world, we need only concern ourselves with that last description . . . as part of Chinese territory.

During the heyday of the Manchu Empire in China, well over 300 years ago, Tibet increasingly came under the influence of the Chi-nese. But Chinese power was destroyed by internal factors and civil war combined with Western and Japanese imperialism in the 1800's. As China was falling apart, Tibet first became a pawn between West-ern powers (mostly Russian and British), and later began asserting its outright independence—and to keep the record straight for you, their 'independence' was proclaimed while China was self-destructing and the 'West' was preoccupied with World War 1. Basically, Tibet was largely just left to its own devices while all the other world powers were busy.

Long story short, once China got their act together (after WWII and their Civil War), they immediately starting re-establishing their presence in Tibet . . . and in fact had never renounced their claim of sovereignty on the area. The Dalai Lamas continued to partially rule in Tibet with, to some extent, autonomous power given by contemporary Chinese govern-ments, until the People's Republic of China invaded the region in 1949 and then took full control in 1959. The Dalai Lama then hauled ass to India and has since ceded temporal power to an elected government-in-exile. Which brings us up to date enough to understand today's world . . .

The current 14th Dalai Lama seeks greater autonomy for Tibet. Not outright independence, but greater self-rule auton-omy. The Chinese have interpreted this as a threat to their 'sovereignty'—and let's just call a spade a spade here . . . they

hate the guy! They hate that he is so popular. They hate that he is well respected, and even venerated, as a world figure. They probably even hate his sweet-ass flowing robes. And they really, really, really, really, really, really hate it when any world leaders meet with the Dalai Lama because the Chinese think that the more recognition the guy gets, the more the world will demand that China give back Tibet to him. Its a similar issue to their Taiwan situation—the Chinese want NO ONE to officially recognize the guy for fear that Tibet will someday claim independence.

What is the Dalai Lama really up to? Well, the dude now tours the world—and he is the first Dalai Lama to go abroad—spreading the Buddhist message and preserving Tibetan culture. He does officially lead the 'government in exile' from Dharamsala, India. He is a fantastic speaker, promotes world peace, wildlife conservation, and a host of other awesome shit that has won him great respect, acclaim, and even a Nobel Peace Prize. Let's face it: the dude is the Buddhist shizzle . . . how about we call him the Budd-izzel?

Fast forward to now: because everyone knows that all eyes are on China due to the upcoming Olympics, a bunch of Tibetan nationalists decided to catch the eyes of the international press by having some big protests and raising all sorts of hell . . . which predictably pissed off the Chinese government, and forced them to crackdown hard. Like the Sudan situation, the world has been putting pressure on China to deal better with the Lama and the whole Tibetan situation. Unlike the Sudan situation, China has told eveybody to go piss up a rope. They accuse the Dalai Lama of inciting the whole affair, and are more determined than ever to squash the Tibetans. And I must tell you bluntly, well over a billion Chinese citizens back their government on this one.

It's certainly an issue that is causing the Chinese some consternation, and it ain't over yet. We shall see how it plays out as the Olympics unfold . . . and beyond. Well, at least they've got Taiwan settled down for now, since the Tibet thing doesn't appear to be heading for a happy ending . . .

THE GOOD EARTH?

What are some other looming problems within China's society? There is tremendous growth, but although they are really rich and getting richer and the middle class is growing, there is still a tremendous **wealth disparity** in the country. With a billion and a half people, that's not surprising. There are folks getting left behind, and part of the reason is the conversion from the communist economic system to the wild-west free market capitalism. Every man for himself, baby!

In old Communist China the attitude was: "We have these old factories. Everybody works at them. Doesn't matter if they are productive or not. We take care of you. You got retirement, you got healthcare." Once they transferred to capitalist ways, "Whoops, now you don't have crap! Haha, sorry! This is capitalism dude. Go out and get it yourself." This is fairly degrading for a good proportion of the population that is not sharing this economic prosperity. There is a real distinct rural to urban split here. It is mostly the rural areas in western China that are getting left behind. The disparity has

Old China sez: "Me Chinese, me play joke . . ."

caused some anticapitalist sentiments and some poor areas to break out in revolt, to protest for more benefits.

There are also titanic environmental problems. Any society that is exploding this fast typically ignores the environment. So China is faced with gargantuan environmental pollution and degradation problems. Perhaps even more pressing are problems with lining up all their coal and energy resources. And let's not forget the health problems associated with pollution and lack of healthcare for lots of folks.

SARS? Avian flu? Don't blame me—I'm just a damn chicken!

Speaking of which: Where did SARS come from? Where did the avian bird flu come from? Where did the recent bubonic plague outbreak come from? Where did swine flu come from? Go down the list, and you'll see a lot of these things are coming from China. This is turning Chinese health from a *local* to a *global* issue. The Plaid is not trying to suggest I know why these things seem to start in China, because I don't. But the most virulent strains of a lot of the flu that circulate around the planet seem to come out of China. Chinese health is a global concern. Plus, the last several times they've had outbreaks of stuff, the government has tried to cover it up, and that's not what the world wants to see. The world wants to be prepared for a big epidemic if one is about to break out. This is not a perfect society precisely because of these sorts of problems, but it's still a society on the move.

Before we finish off this chapter, we don't want you to forget about China's little brother up here, Korea. It's actually kind of a happening place too, though for different reasons.

LITTLE BROTHER GROWS UP: THE KOREAS

Why am I suggesting this is China's little brother? Throughout the last 4,000–5,000 years, Korea has been kind of a vassal state to China. But Korea has a distinct ethnic group; in fact it is the most ethnically pure state on the planet. When you take a demographic survey and say, "Hey what ethnicity are you?" you don't have to go far because it is 100 percent Korean. It's the only place like that on the planet. Even the Japanese have 2 percent of something else. Korea is totally ethnically pure and very ethnically distinct, but it's still China's little brother because most of their adaptation throughout history such as their religious structure, political structure, and philosophical structure was borrowed from big brother China. That's why we see a lot of similarities in art and architecture and the way people think and act between China and Korea. It's not China; it is distinct, but it borrowed a whole heck of a lot from China. What's the deal with the Koreas today, and why are there two halves called North Korea and South Korea?

SO NICE THEY NAMED IT TWICE? WHY TWO KOREAS?

For most of its history, Korea was one unified country. However, it usually got pushed around by its more powerful neighbors. It was occupied by China in the first century BCE and by Japan in 1895, which basically turned Korea into a work camp for the Japanese. However, the final insult came in the waning days of World War II. After it became apparent that the Allies were going to defeat Japan, Russia moved troops into the northern part of Korea and the United States occupied the southern part of Korea. After the war was over, the US and the USSR stuck around to "help rebuild and reestab-

lish order" on the peninsula. Separate governments were formed in these occupation zones, established at the 38th parallel, which led to the initial territories called North and South Korea.

North Korea became a communist dictatorship supported by the Soviet Union and South Korea became a capitalist democracy supported by the United States. But no one really thought that this situation would last forever. It was never intended to be permanent. But now we had the first real Cold War "face-off" of ideologies put into place.

For a variety of reasons, the North Koreans thought they could easily take over South Korea, so the North Korean army invaded South Korea in 1950, starting the Korean War. To stop the spread of communism, America sent thousands of troops to protect South Korea under the leadership of General MacArthur. Even though millions of Koreans died, the result of the war was a tie, and neither Korea ended up conquering the whole peninsula. To this day, over 30,000 American troops are stationed in South Korea in case North Korea attacks again. This conflict became the first "hot spot" of the "cold" war.

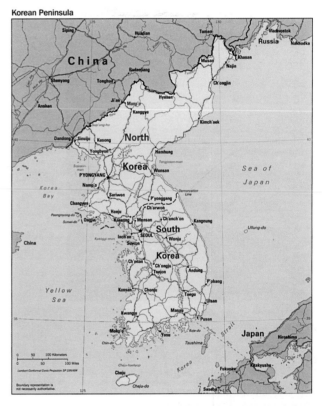
Korean Peninsula

"Let's go get those commies! I'm ready to invade the North!"

PLAID AVENGER INSIDE TIP: So how come it's not just one Korea? What does that have to do with Hawkeye Pierce? A really cheesy TV show named M*A*S*H* depicted the Korean War for the prime-time enjoyment of US viewers. The funny part? The Korean War lasted 3 years from 1950-53. The TV show lasted 12 years. That war was just so damn funny we had to watch it four times longer!

Since then, North Korea and South Korea have gone radically separate ways. South Korea is a capitalist democracy with the world's tenth largest economy while North Korea is still a communist dictatorship whose population is starving. However, there is a Korean reunification movement and the two Koreas are trying to reestablish relations with each other. A unified Korean team has even marched in the opening ceremonies of the past several Olympic Games. However, reunification will be difficult because the Koreas have been apart for so long and their economies and governments are very different. Also, many observers think that both China and the United States prefer that Korea be divided for geopolitical reasons.

Super-economy in the South; lights out in the North. Yep, that's Korea.

So the North-South Korea thing is a relic of the Cold War. It is one of the hot spots that flared up during the Cold War, where fighting actually occurred. What's going on in today's world with this battle of ideologies? Well, it is quite hilarious as you can see from this map of lights at night in the Koreas. South Korea: bright lights, big city. North Korea: lights out. This really underlines what's going on within these two "countries," and really shows who won the ideology battle of the Cold War. The Koreas sum it up so perfectly, so beautifully, that we have to point it out here. North Korea went down the communist path, the radical communist path. Now they are radically freakin' broke! They've got nothing. It is a society that is about to disintegrate under our good friend Kim Jong-Il.

I'm crazy!

I'm rich!

The opposite is South Korea, who embraced the democratic capitalist West and is now the number ten economy on the planet. We have three of the top ten economies right there in a nice little grouping of China, South Korea, and Japan. South Korea is a bustling and happening place. North Korea can't pay the light bill, but South Korea is going gangbusters.

Its funny that you don't know as much about South Korea, or hear about it that much in the news. But here is why: South Korea is a country wedged between the giants. Japan is the number two economy to its east and China the number four economy to its west. Oh, and to the north is the nutso nuclear-armed North Korea that catches lots of headlines too. In between those monsters South Korea looks

Korean hotties with drums.

What's the Deal with . . . the 6-Party Talks?

Those crazy Koreans do love to party! As long as its with six! The six-party talks is the name given to a series of meetings with six states—China, North Korea, South Korea, Russia, Japan, and the United States—to deal with North Korea's nuclear ambitions. These talks were a result of North Korea withdrawing from the Nuclear Non-Proliferation Treaty in 2003. The aim of these talks is to find a peaceful resolution to the security concerns raised by the North Korean nuclear weapons program. Five rounds of talks has resulted in jack-shit actually happening and little headway has been made disarming North Korea.

Why no movement towards a solution? Ummm . . . I think mainly because the leadership of North Korea is utterly and completely in freakin' la-la land. It should be noted that pretty much everyone agrees that North Korea is getting close to collapse, and bordering on completely hopeless. Their number one GDP earner is counterfeiting US currency. Does that count as sustainable development? What a joke!

Basically, the only thing this "country" has to its name is supposed nuclear weapons. That is the only bargaining chip they have to be taken seriously by the outside world. And patience from the outside world is growing thin . . . Of course, Japan and South Korea don't want them to melt down completely which could result in a nuclear weapon being launched. China and the US are fairly secure that no one in North Korea would be retarded enough to launch a missile in either of their directions, but everyone wants a peaceful solution to the mess. As of this writing, North Korea is preparing to do a missile "test" of their capabilities. We shall have to wait and see what response this brings . . .

Party?

like a little place, but it's not. It is big. China, South Korea, and Japan, to a lesser extent, are going to be the technological centers of the planet in the next 100 years.

These three countries have made that their mission, their goal. In fact, the South Koreans vowed in Spring of 2006 to put a robot in every home by 2020. No, this is not science fiction. It's not even fiction fiction. They actually said it! I believe they will do it too. They already have the fastest Internet connections on the planet, and have made Internet accessibility available to every single one of its citizens. They are not playing around man! South Korea is the most connected country on the planet per capita. All of the countries in this neighborhood have societies that are embracing technology with a vengeance. This is going to affect what's going on in the Web-world in the very near future. Soon you will see how these countries' technological expertise will impact the entire planet. Let it be known that these guys are hot and heavy with the technology sector, and they are transforming the playing field every single day.

And I shouldn't end this little discussion without giving at least a little positive press to our North Korean friends.

Actually, who gives a hell about those wackos, but you should know the reference to their "PARTY."

ENOUGH ALREADY ON EAST ASIA

I think you have got the picture now, and I'm probably going to repeat some things for the fifth time now, but let's do it again anyway. When we think about China, we think about one of the world's largest states, maybe the third largest state in the world. We also think of the world's largest military. Am I saying it's the best military in the world? No, the US has the best military in the world, but China has the largest free-standing army on the planet.

China also now has the number four economy on the planet. They just beat out France and the UK for the first time ever. They are in the top five, having jumped two whole slots in one year. The world economy power awards go to the US, Japan, Germany, and now China. But hey! China ain't alone in this region of big money: both Taiwan and South Korea are

New China sez: "Hahaha. I see China moon colony from here. We're so rich. This is fun."

bangin' out the bucks too, and all three of these entities are going apeshit with the newest and bestest technological sector development to boot. South Korea in particular has the highest level of high speed internet access in the world, and has also vowed to have a robot in every household by 2020. No, seriously . . . like I could make this shit up?

But back to the big boy: China is now also a member of all the world's most progressive and fastest growing trade blocs. Their middle class is growing just as fast as their prestige is growing. They are doing all the things the big boy countries do, like the Miss World Pageant, like the Olympics, like the space programs. This is a place that is really on fire. Yes it's got problems, but there are a whole hell of a lot of things going on in China that are right on target. China is back, and it is once again a world power to be reckoned with.

Along with the Taiwanese and South Korean titans, this region promises to be an epicenter of activity and excitement of all types in the coming century. If only somehow Kim il-Jong could be deported to Texas, then the whole region in its entirety could be totally kicking ass. Hmmmm . . . maybe I'll run that by W.

CHAPTER OUTLINE

Southeast Asia

CROSSROADS, CONFLICT, AND CUBS

Let's get it on! I am talking about the Thundercats, my friends, because this is where it's all going down: Southeast Asia, the **Archipelago Region,** a collection of peninsulas and islands on the southeastern quadrant of the Eurasian landmass. It's been a mover and shaker throughout the years, but it's one of those places we don't really know a whole lot about. A lot of big events have happened there in the last 100 years. Hell even in the last 50, the Archipelago Region is a place of crazy genocide, insane outbreaks of war, and massive movements of refugees into and out of the region. The last couple years have been interesting for the region: a lot of economic growth, a little political turmoil, and—oh yeah—two big-time natural disasters. So, what's going on in Southeast Asia?

PHYSICALLY ON FIRE

Southeast Asia is rugged and looks complicated, but it's actually quite simple to understand. The variation in terrain predominately runs north to south in this region. We have rugged mountains that run down as a continuation of the Himalayan Range, and turn due south through Burma and Thailand. There is another different chain that runs down the Vietnamese coast called the Chaine Annamitique. Damn the French and their language. The Northern parts of Vietnam, Laos, and Burma are mountainous along the Chinese border. Most of the Indonesian Archipelago has at least some mountainous terrain as a result of volcanic activity. It is yet another geologic hot spot in terms

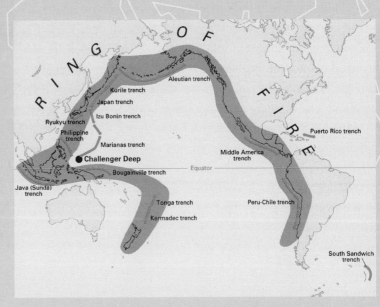

The Ring!: Areas of greatest volcanic and seismic activity.

of plate tectonic activity. The convergence of some pretty major plates makes this one of the most volcanically and seismically active regions on the planet. It is a definite centerpiece of **The Ring of Fire.**

You may have heard of Krakatoa, a volcanic island that freakin' exploded into oblivion in 1883. The blast was so titanic that the dust, ash, and smoke that entered the atmosphere created a haze that partially blocked out enough sun to cool world temperatures for about a decade. In addition to some volcanic activity, there is also seismic activity. This fosters the development of **tsunamis,** giant waves resulting from offshore earthquakes. I bring this up because unless you've been hiding under a rock, you've heard of the massive tsunami that occurred in the Indian Ocean on December 26, 2004, claiming more than 200,000 lives. Southeast Asia is geologically active and has some fairly tough terrain, but nothing like the Andes or the

Himalayas that keep people from moving around. Because of the seismic activity, Southeast Asia is a fairly dangerous place, particularly in Indonesia and most coastal areas, which just so happens to be where most Southeast Asians live. And, as if tsunamis and volcanoes weren't enough, Southeast Asia also occasionally gets hit by tropical cyclones (a.k.a. typhoons). On

May 2, 2008, Cyclone Nargis made landfall in Burma and killed *at least* 50,000 people. Why did I just emphasis *at least*? Because the a-holes in the Burmese governing junta spent 70% of their collective effort trying to hide the damage. What did they do with the other 10%? Answer: they tried to keep international aid workers out. More on this later . . .

The final factor for physical geography is climate. Almost every country falls below the Tropic of Cancer. Indonesia straddles the Equator. All of the countries in this region have what we would call tropical climates. We can visibly see all three subdivisions of tropical climates in Southeast Asia. There's a whole lot of **tropical rainforest.** Indonesia is primarily rainforest, the biggest

Tsunamis: Great for surfers, bad for Southeast Asia.

chunks of rainforest left on the planet aside from the Amazon. There's some **tropical savannah** in and around Thailand, Burma, and Cambodia. All along the coastal areas of Vietnam and Cambodia, you can get a taste of **tropical monsoon** climate as well.

If anyone remembers Forrest Gump during his little Vietnam adventure, he talked about the rain that started one day and kept going for six months. Forrest was right; it is a true monsoonal climate. Perhaps the second best example of true, big-time tropical monsoon outside of India would be here in Southeast Asia.

There's some fairly decent terrain north and south in the Burma to the Vietnam area. There is some tectonic activity with implications for disaster in Indonesia and around the coastal areas, and the region is home to a nice blending of the tropical climates. That's your physical roundup for Southeast Asia.

WHO'S THERE?

This is pretty easy. It's just a couple of handfuls of countries, so we'll go ahead and fire them off for you: Burma (there is a new name, Myanmar, established by the military junta there which I refuse to recognize, so we're going to go with Burma), Laos, Thailand, Vietnam, Cambodia, Singapore, Malaysia, Indonesia, the Philippines, and the Sultanate of Brunei. And, introducing to you now, the newest sovereign state on Earth, East Timor! Congratulations East Timor. Our plaid-thoughts are with you on this special day!

What is it that we want to know about this region? The subtitle of this chapter mentioned that this region was a crossroads. What is it about Southeast Asia that has made it a crossroads? Historically it has always been and still is considered a crossroads of all types of Asian culture. It has been the true melting pot of Asia. Influences from all over have made their way here and dropped off a lot of their cultural baggage, which has been picked up by the locals who were already there. This amalgamation of different things from different places in Southeast Asia makes it quite unique, but you can still pick out where a lot of these influences came from. What am I talking about?

BACK UP FOR BACKGROUND

What's the story on this part of the world anyway? All us Americans know is that we fought a war here that we lost, and that all our Nike shoes and clothing is increasingly made in this place. Well, let's back up the refugee boat for a minute and take a look at just a few historical/cultural artifacts that will help us understand the region better.

CHINESE INFLUENCE

Since forever, Southeast Asia has been a subsidiary vassal state of the Chinese. We've just finished talking about how the Chinese have been around for 5,000 years and for much of that time, border states have always been kind of "semi-china." But China has been the big dog, the one everybody looks up to or at least respects. Everybody on this part of the planet has known forever that the Chinese are the real power. This leads to pervasive Chinese historical influence, so much so that a lot of the folks currently in Southeast Asia (Thais and Vietnamese) were once in China proper. The Han Chinese influence kept pushing people further and further south until they were completely out of China's current borders. The Thais have reestablished themselves in what is now . . . that's right: Thailand!

Chinese influence is a dominant force throughout history and we will see at the end of this chapter that it still is today. Southeast Asia has been in the Chinese cultural sphere of influence for a very long time. Chinese philosophy, Chinese religion, the Chinese way of life, Chinese governmental standards and political philosophies have rubbed off in this region.

But it's not just the Chinese that have influenced the culture. Southeast Asia is an archipelago with small islands and big islands. In fact, Indonesia has 14,000 islands. These are coastal peoples, maritime peoples. What do maritime folks do? A lot of them end up trading . . .

SEE YOU AT THE CROSSROADS

Southeast Asia has been an epicenter of global trade for quite some time. I know this isn't something we often think about, but what was it that Columbus was trying to get to? He was trying to get to the East Indies, **The Spice Islands.** Why there? To get all the good stuff that all the European jackasses of the time would pay an arm and a leg for. "The Spice Islands" and "the East Indies" are just European synonyms for Southeast Asia, predominantly Indonesia, which was the destination to get all of the good shit. For a very long time, even before the Europeans came around, people from South Asia

(India) and people from China were trading stuff back and forth between each other, and a lot of times it was through maritime routes. As you might expect, all those maritime routes go through Southeast Asia. The people of the Southeast Asian islands became integral to this trade system very early on. There were Hindu traders from India who established trading posts in this area while they were trading with the Chinese, who also had a presence there. In time, there were Muslim traders too. The Europeans are going to come fairly late to this ballgame, but they show up and participate in the trade game.

Now why am I telling you all about this ancient trade? Why is it important for today's Southeast Asia? Well it's this crossroads idea, not just a physical crossroads of traders and goods, but a crossroads of all of the traders' cultures. When you go to Southeast Asia, you will see cultural influences that are obviously not local. Let's just pick religion. You can pretty much find all world religions in Southeast Asia. Even the Christians make their way to this part of the world via

European traders. In places like Burma, Thailand, Laos, Vietnam, and Cambodia, you will see old-school Buddhism in practice. In fact, some of the biggest Buddhist monuments and temples on the planet are located in this place. Buddhism came from India. What else came from India? Hinduism. You'll see a big Hindu component in all those countries also.

But wait a minute! We aren't finished yet. There are some other religions like Islam, for instance. Islam is predominant in Indonesia, Brunei (there being a "sultan" of Brunei might give you a tip off there), and Malaysia. Malaysia, Indonesia, and Brunei are predominantly and overwhelmingly Islamic, with Indonesia being the largest Islamic country on the planet. Then we go to a place like the Philippines. The Philippines, eastern parts of Indonesia and even East Timor the (region's newborn), are all predominantly Christian. The concept that there are both Muslims and Christians in Indonesia warrants pause for thought, because while most of the Eastern religions and Eastern philosophies get along with each other, typically those Western ones don't. So if you want to find religious violence in Southeast Asia, go straight to Indonesia where the Muslims and the Christians both cohabitate, though not very well.

You will see Hindu temples, Islamic mosques, Christian churches, and Buddhist temples all over this region. You can kind of say that about every part of the world; everybody is mixed up a little bit, but here you can see some very ancient places that really

Spices: the crack-cocaine of the 16th century

A little bit Hindu, a little bit Buddhist

Singapore for Dummies

Calm down, my Singaporean friends—I mean no disrespect. "Asia for Dummies" only implies that your average American could find his or her way around the island. And if you happen to be this average—or even slightly below average—American, this is the Asian country for you! Singapore is a global city—like London, Paris, or Tokyo. English is an official language—everyone speaks it. Singaporeans, in general, still like Americans (this is a disappearing quality in the World, enjoy it here while it lasts!). AND, they have couture shopping. And five star hotels. And great food. OH, and did I mention it's cheap (again, enjoy it while it lasts)—the exchange rate, even as of 2008, is still pretty damn good! You can even walk across the whole island in one day! It's a damn nation-city. How cool is that? They've got a semi-official national beverage called the Singapore Sling that is one part gin, one part cherry brandy, and one part pure delicious! And their national symbol? A MERLION! Half Mermaid, half lion. Who wouldn't want to crawl into the sack with that! Especially after a couple of Singapore Slings! Rawwwwnnnn!

So why is Singapore so Western? One answer is British colonization, but there is also a more complicated picture that goes back to the trading. Being a primary shipping and trading hub, Singapore acquired aspects of many cultures including Chinese, Malay, and Indian. Through the years, Singapore recognized the value in being international and has focused on projecting a positive global image. Singapore is still one of the world's leading trading ports—over 1 billion tons of cargo flows through every year. It is also home to some of the most elite universities in Asia.

One final word of caution to all my plaid traveling friends: DO NOT BRING DRUGS INTO SINGAPORE. All kidding aside, they will execute you for it.

reflect how long this melting-pot idea has been going on in Southeast Asia. As you might expect, I'm just using the example of religion, but language is also very diverse here as well. Ethnic groups are very diverse, as there's a huge presence of the Chinese, which we will get back to in just a little bit. This is a place that has been truly a crossroads for a long time and, I might point out, still is in the present.

!!CONFLICT!!

THE EASTERN
FRONTIER OF INDIA
AND NEIGHBOURING COUNTRIES
FRENCH AND ENGLISH EXPANSION
1805-1807
English Miles

The last historical section of the cultural crossroads has to do with European colonization. The development of Southeast Asia has been impacted heavily by outsiders. That may be something that the locals don't want to admit to, but it's a fact. All of those religions and a lot of the languages spoken here were imported from other places. A lot of the development in Southeast Asia, including the way the governments work, is also imported or at least heavily influenced by other places as well. The last big wave of influence comes from the European colonizers, who make their way through Siam, Indochina, and the Dutch East Indies.

Where do all these terms come from? These are terms that were invented by the European colonial masters who established trade and ultimately political control of this region. This group of masters included a little bit of everybody, kind of like in Africa where we have a whole bunch of countries represented. The British had possessions here, the French had a huge chunk of it, and the US even controlled the Philippines for a time after taking it from the Spanish. The Dutch controlled all of what is now Indonesia. The Portuguese had a colony named Timor, which is now East Timor, which is why it was separate from the rest of Dutch-controlled Indonesia. Even the Japanese had a hand in this part of the world, particularly during World War II.

So when did all this come about? Same old same old. When you get into the 1700s and 1800s, the Europeans start coming in and making themselves at home. It's not really a land grab, but it starts off just like it does in South Asia and in British India, where people set up ports of trade. As we've already suggested, Southeast Asia has been the center of trade for 1,000, maybe 2,000 years already, so the Europeans just want to get in the game. Quite frankly, they are shut out for a good long time because trade has already been established. But inevitably, the Brits and the Portuguese wear them down and start to make inroads. One thing leads to another over the course of a several hundred years and they end up controlling the territories outright.

I'll make a rundown here just to make it completely clear. The British controlled their British India. At the time British India consisted of Myanmar and Burma. The French controlled a part of this region as well, named French Indochina. The Brits also controlled Malaysia and Singapore (which is really just a tiny island adjacent to malaysia). The Spanish initially controlled the Philippines until 1898 when the US assumed control of the island nation. The Dutch controlled all of Indonesia and the Portuguese controlled what is now East Timor.

EVERYBODY has a hand in this region, though strangely enough, one country remains unoccupied. That is Siam, or modern day Thailand. This is a great piece of trivia, placed on government tests for employees trying to get into foreign service. The question is, "Which country was never colonized by a foreign nation?" The answer is Thailand. If you ask "Hey, what is the richest nation in Southeast Asia today? What's the most stable nation in Southeast Asia today?" you'll be directed to Thailand, more often than not. Coincidence? Probably not. But we're talking about this foreign influence and where it is going to go.

What's the Deal with . . . French Indochina?

French Indochina was a group of French colonial posses-sions in Southeast Asia including modern day Vietnam, Laos, and Cambodia. France acquired these colonies in the late 1800s and held them until World War II, at which point Japan kicked them the hell out and took Indochina for themselves. Japanese rule, however, lasted only until the United States dropped atomic bombs on two of Japan's most populated cities. With Japan's withdrawal, Indochina was theoretically free from colo-nialism. That is, for the three seconds before France attempted to colonize them again.

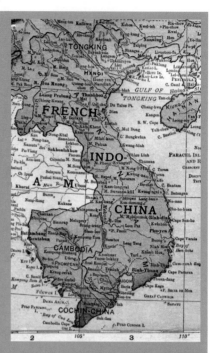

France found it impossible to regain control over Vietnam. This is par-tially because of a homegrown Vietnamese insurgent group of communist nationalists led by Ho Chi Minh. This group, the Viet Minh, had been fighting for independence even before WWII, then were fighting against the Japanese, and then quickly shifted their efforts to fight against the French once the Japanese were ejected. After years of devastating war, the Viet Minh had gained decisive control of northern Vietnam, declaring independence as the Democratic Republic of Vietnam in 1954. At the Battle of Dien Bien Phu, the French were forced to surrender. As part of the cease-fire peace agreement, Southern Vietnam (the State of Vietnam) was officially brokered by world powers (namely the US) until elections which were to be held the following year. It didn't go down that way, but that is a story for another box. . .

Poor Frenchies. Germany whipped their asses in Europe. The Japanese whipped their asses in Indochina. Then the Vietnamese whip their asses again in Vietnam. No more French Indochina after that last spanking.

MORE CONFLICT!

In 20th-century events, it gets very interesting in Southeast Asia, the location of some of the nastiest throw-downs in the last 50 years. Since the Europeans had their fun time with World War I, and then World War II because obvi-ously they didn't get enough the first go around, the world has largely been devoid of huge conflicts with massive death tolls . . . that is everywhere in the world except here in Southeast Asia. While we in the West are having our Cold War where Team USA faces off with Team USSR, we never engaged in active conflict. The guns remained cold, hence the name "Cold War." But there were several flare-ups, several hot spots, where people shot each other and where this ideological war reared its ugly head in active conflict. The Korean War we mentioned already. The other major flare-ups are here in Southeast Asia.

Before we can get to the tale of that aggression/transgression, we have to set up the scenario a little bit better, because some more violence occurs on the soil here during World War II. During the buildup of Japanese power, South-east Asia and Southern China became a battleground for World War II, mainly because of the Japanese occupation. Some fairly nasty Japanese war crimes took place in these regions as I've alluded to before.

How did this go down and why is this of particular significance? Southeast Asia has been a crossroads of trade and culture, and now becomes a crossroads of occupation. Unlike any part of the planet, this is a very unique trait of South-east Asia: it was taken over by the West and subsequently taken over by the East. This is the only place The Plaid has ever heard of that had European colonization that was then supplanted by Japanese occupation. Coming and going. Southeast Asia got it from both ends. That ain't no damn fun. That will probably leave a mark in the morning, and it certainly did at the end of the 20th century.

SMART GODZIRRA!

As you know, Japan built up its empire in the early part of the 20th century. Then in 1931, they start intruding into northeastern China and taking over the Chinese coast. They are still invading, fighting, and conquering into the 1940s. They start taking over the Philippines and before World War II breaks out officially, they have a presence in all Southeast Asian nations. How did they get away with this, and more importantly, how did they get away with this without firing too many bullets? Every country we have just discussed was controlled and occupied by the Japanese, but you don't really hear that much about fighting there.

The reason why it wasn't a big shoot-out for the Japanese to take over this place was because of, if you remember back to our lecture on Japan, the **Greater East Asia Co-Prosperity Sphere** established in 1938. To reiterate what that was about, the Japanese used a savvy piece of foreign policy, although they were holding guns

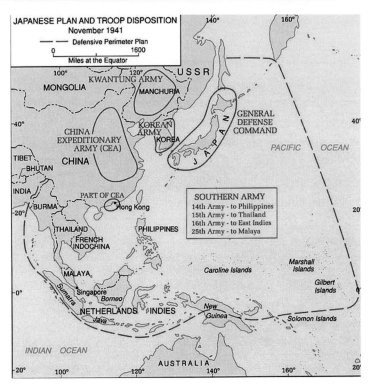

The busy Japanese.

at the time. They went to all these places like French Indochina, the Philippines, and Indonesia and said, "Hey, look dudes. Look at our skins. We're Asians. We are all yellow here, we're brothers. You've got a huge bunch of foreign white dogs on your soil that are controlling you. You're just their puppets. You're letting them treat you like punks! Come on, let's all get together as Asians and expel all the Yankee scum-dog pigs!" Many saw the Japanese as liberators at the time, so they were able to waltz through Southeast Asia without firing too many shots. Were the Japanese telling the truth? I think we all know the answer to this question: hell no! They were actually just planning to supplant the European colonizers, which is exactly what they did, in a fairly brutal manner. Work camps/death camps/prisoner of war camps were set up all over Southeast Asia.

BATAAN DEATH MARCH

The Plaid is giving you examples of some incredible atrocities perpetrated by the Japanese in Southeast Asia. We talked about them in China, about the death there, and we know about Japanese history against the United States in WWII, but a lot of people don't know about Southeast Asia. It's some fairly nasty business, as evidenced by the Bataan Death March, where more than 10,000 US and Filipino soldiers were marched about 100 miles from one camp to another across the Philippines. Many were not fed, and those who began to fall behind were executed or tortured.

Rounding up people and slaughtering them was a common occurrence all over Southeast Asia. A lot of this has not been forgotten by the Southeast Asian nations, but they are not as hardcore as the Chinese and the Koreans about it. The Chinese and the Koreans still really hate the Japanese. The Southeast Asians harbor some resentment but it is not as strong or as big of a deal to them. But it is a big of enough deal to talk about for a little bit.

Don't mess!

BURMESE RAILROAD

The Japanese essentially colonized Southeast Asia in the form of an imperial expansion, similar to how the Europeans did it long ago. These countries became colonies of the Japanese, but only for a short time. As I suggested when we were rounding up our talk about Japanese movements at the end of World War II, the Japanese were using Southeast Asia essentially as a launching pad for the next phase of their invasion, which was India. This brings us back to the *Bridge on the River Kwai.* In that movie the Japanese were building a railroad line across Burma to supply their invasion of India. We already know the outcome of World War II: the Japanese are going to lose, and in a strange turn of events, the colonial masters that were kicked out by Japan soon came back into control. Some countries declared independence at this time, but some of the old European colonizers come back to reclaim their territories. Of particular interest is the French reclaiming Indochina, which we already discussed as an event that leads up to the Vietnam War . . .

'NAM

Why is 'Nam the most infamous of all American wars? Why should it matter whether Iraq is or isn't like Vietnam? Why is everyone STILL talking about Vietnam? The answer is fairly simple—the Vietnam War was a complete freakin' debacle that everyone now realizes was utter bullshit. But it was bullshit that pulverized a small Asian nation while simultaneously ripping apart the social fabric of the US.

The Vietnam War was ultimately a civil war between North Vietnam (communist, led by Ho Chi Mihn) and South Vietnam (propped up by outsiders as democratic, pro-Western). After the Frenchies were ejected out of the territory in 1954, the UN-brokered peace agreement called for a general election across the entire country the following year. All intelligence reports indicated that Ho Chi Minh would win the election both in the north and in the south by overwhelming majorities. He was the main man in Vietnam. So what was the problem? Well, he was also a communist, and we all know how much the US hates commies. And by the way, who the hell is this Ho guy anyway?

Who the Hell Is Ho?

The Main Vietnamese Man! Another 'Father of the Country' dude. Take George Washington, add in Winston Churchill, Gandhi, Lenin, and Mao . . . and you will have Ho. When all is said and done, Ho is probably the most fierce nationalist the 20th century ever knew. He dedicated every second of his entire life to Vietnamese independence, and my friends, he is idolized still in Vietnam for his contributions. You'll see references to him as 'Uncle Ho'; he's just part of the family!

And what a resume! Left Indochina in his late teens to travel the world and ended up in France where he was one of the founders of the French Communist party, and began the propaganda campaign right there in Europe to expel the colonizing forces from his homeland. Invited to be schooled in Moscow after their little communist takeover, and was a tireless reader and writer for his vision of a free Vietnam. Was at one point imprisoned in China by Chiang Kai-Shek (remember him; leader of the Nationalist Party and hater of commies?) Organized the VietMinh forces to counter the Japanese invasion, and then later led those forces to oust the French.

Was the President of North Vietnam, and would have easily been elected President even in South Vietnam, were it not for outside interference. . . Since the US so despised commies, he was vilified in the US even before our major involvement in the war. Until very recently, the US was convinced that Ho was a puppet of communist China—despite the fact he had waged a border war against them too!

Mo' money? No, its Ho Money!

continues

Who the Hell Is Ho? *(continued)*

Extremely intelligent and savvy dude, but first and foremost a man of the people. Lived in a cave for a while during French occupation, and even after winning the war, Ho refused to live in the Presidential Palace; he worked in a traditional bamboo and grass thatch hut until he died in 1969—not living long enough to see his vision of a unified and free Vietnam materialize.

He also looked a hell of a lot like Colonel Sanders of KFC fame, but I digress . . .

The US could not allow the election to go forward, so we stalled, and then we helped our local picks cheat a little. A puppet government was put into place in the south, propped up by the US . . . actually a chain of puppet governments led by dictators. As a result, Ho in the north as well as locals in the south started agitating for reunification and expulsion of the foreign influences.

Violence flared up in 1957 and then things started to get violent. The United States, fearing that South Vietnam would be defeated and become communist, became more actively engaged in helping the puppet South Vietnamese government by sending more money, more arms, and more "military advisors" (aka US dudes with guns.) Perhaps the United States' main concern with Vietnam involved the **"domino theory"**—simply, if Vietnam went communist it would trigger a communist takeover throughout Asia. Once one country went commie, all surrounding countries would fall "like a chain of dominos." No, seriously, they believed this crap! By 1965, American troops were actively participating in the war by the thousands.

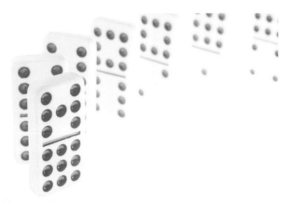

They failed to fall.

The main goal of the United States was initially to remove the communists from power in the North, but they also encounter a powerful communist guerrilla movement in the South—the **Vietcong.** So while the US was supposed to be "protecting" the South, they ended up "fighting" the South as well (sound familiar?). Vietcong guerrillas had no trouble blending in with the rural South Vietnam population, who were largely sympathetic to the Vietcong's nationalistic message.

Viet Cong soldier

The United States did many shitty things in an attempt to win the War. The US sprayed millions of gallons of Agent Orange (an herbicide that is now known to be toxic to humans) to destroy the Vietnamese jungles that helped protect the Vietcong. They also dropped massive amounts of napalm on villages they believed were harboring opposition forces.

In the end, the United States eventually got sick of dealing with Vietnam and left. North Vietnam took over South Vietnam, the whole country became communist, and the world did not end. The US military figured it out after we suffered over 200,000 casualties. As many as 4 million Vietnamese (Northern and Southern) were killed, with perhaps only 25 percent of those being active communist fighters. But perhaps the biggest tragedy is that the whole premise for the war was disproved. A communist Vietnam did not set off a row of dominoes, nor did it prove even the most remote threat to US domestic security.

Worst of all, we initially got into that mess to help out the French.

What's the Deal with . . . Pol Pot?

As one of the most egregious violators of human rights in recent memory, Pol Pot easily earned the Plaid-title of "Ass-munch of the Decade" for the 1970s. Pol Pot was the leader of Cambodia (or as he called it "Democratic Kampuchea") from 1975 to 1979.

The revolutionary movement that brought Pol Pot to power is largely considered the most murderous of the 20th century. Around 3 million Cambodians died from overwork, malnutrition, and state-sponsored executions. This equated to approximately 35 percent of the Cambodian population at the time.

Pol Pot's politics were a brutal offshoot of Maoist Communism. He attempted to tear down Cambodia's old political structure (which was in part established by French colonialism) to make way for an agrarian communist utopia. His tactics included suppressing religion and intellectualism. Citizens were executed if they failed to meet production quotas and also for more trivial matters like wearing glasses, being a monk, being intelligent, speaking a foreign language, being an ethnic minority, etc. Many of those executed were forced to dig their own graves and were then buried alive (many speculate this was done to conserve bullets). Although technically removed from power in 1979, Pol Pot continued to exert brutal influence on Cambodian politics (in one way or another) until his death in 1998.

See a depiction of this regime by watching the really historically accurate film *The Killing Fields*. Whew! Talk about a place that *should* have been invaded!

POL POT PIE

But Vietnam is not the only place for strange violence in Southeast Asia. Indonesia, in its movement into the modern era, has been run by dictators who were supported by the United States. Burma is currently run by an outright military junta. Lots of the other countries, however, are leaning toward democracies—places like Singapore, a very rich place, Indonesia, and the Philippines. Then you have some holdouts from the Communist era, such as Vietnam. Then we have two places closing in on full-fledged anarchy and chaos, Burma and Cambodia. Cambodia is the scene of one of the most horrific cases of post–World War II genocide under our good friend Pol Pot.

But enough of the death and destruction, let's get to why these places are hot in today's world . . . and I'm not talkin' tropical heat here, I'm talkin' cash money!

CUBS IN THE CATBIRD SEAT

Cubs? What? What the hell are you talking about? I'm talking about the cats. The tigers. Let's do Southeast Asia. What is happening in today's Southeast Asia?

This has a lot to do with things we have already referenced. There is Chinese influence, which is still big and may be growing as China's influence expands in the world. Lots of people migrate from China to Southeast Asia, set up businesses, and bring their families along. Is this good? It can be good. The Chinese often bring a lot of capital and set up businesses, but the negative is that that's the stuff the locals were probably going to do.

Indeed, there is some friction between ethnically Chinese people and all the other ethnicities within Southeast Asia. The Chinese are a major component of all the populations within Southeast Asia we talked about. Cause for concern? I don't know, but certainly cause for friction. Indeed, when the economies go south, say if Indonesia goes into a depression,

NUMBERS OF ETHNIC CHINESE IN EACH SOUTHEAST ASIAN

Country	Ethnic Chinese	% of Local Population
Thailand	9 million	14%
Indonesia	7.5 million	3.1%
Malaysia	7 million	25%
Singapore	2.8 million	76%
Vietnam	2.5 million	4%
Philippines	1.5 million	2%
Burma	1.5 million	3%
Cambodia	200,000	1.3%
Brunei	60,000	15%
Laos	50,000	1%

one of the first things all you Plaid news watchers will see are Chinese businesses being attacked. Chinese individuals become kind of a whipping post of anger that people rally around. "The damn Chinese, they're here taking our jobs!" The Chinese typically don't assimilate themselves into the culture of the countries they migrate to. Throughout Southeast Asia there are visible pockets of Chinese influence and businesses all over the place.

What else is going on in Southeast Asia today? Economically, it is a bustling and booming place, which is where **the Cubs** come in. You might have heard of something called the **Asian Tigers,** or **The Economic Tigers** referring to Hong Kong, Taiwan, South Korea, and Singapore, which have been exploding economically since the 1970s and 1980s. Growth rates have been astronomical in these places, making them very rich. The expansive growth rates are beginning to spread to places like Thailand, Vietnam, Malaysia to a certain extent, the Philippines, and Indonesia. That's why I'm calling them the **Cubs.** They are on their way to becoming tigers themselves, but they're just getting started.

Why are these places in Southeast Asia picking up economically right now? One of the reasons is **cheap labor.** Most businesses go to China for this reason, but if they don't go to China, they go to Indonesia, Thailand, or the Philippines. Because of this cheap labor, a lot of businesses and multinational corporations are relocating to Southeast Asia, if not outright starting whole new businesses there. I'll go out on a Plaid limb and say that all car manufacturers have a plant or two in one or more of the countries in Southeast Asia.

Why else are more businesses moving there? **Lax environmental laws.** Nike has been in Indonesia for a decade or two now. Apparently it makes more economic sense to ship leather from Brazil, cloth from China, rubber from Vietnam, and then manufacture it using cheap labor in the Nike plant in Indonesia before shipping it to the United States where you can still sell the shoes for $20 and still make a profit—but you go ahead and charge $150 anyway and make more profit. That's the way the economic world is working right this second, much to the advantage of multinational corporations, and the Southeast Asian nations, to some extent. Some of the losers in this process are places like Mexico. Some places in South America used to be cheap suppliers of labor, but they have gotten a little bit more expensive, so labor is moving over to Asia. Companies go wherever the labor cost is the lowest. How low can you go? Southeast Asia and China are winning the limbo right now.

The other factor in this is that Southeast Asia is a massive **supplier of raw materials** to the world. Where are the places that want raw materials more and more? We say, "Oh! Well it's the US and Western Europe, the advanced countries. We use all that stuff." Wrong! Think again. The world is changing. Japan is a huge importer of raw materials. When I say raw materials, I mean everything from oil to rubber to trees to tin to bauxite, everything. Southeast Asia has a lot of this stuff and even the stuff it doesn't have goes through their waterways and shipping channels.

Lots of stuff has gone to Japan, and as a result, the Tigers, like Taiwan, have become big processing centers. Wait a minute, who is the new big tiger? Who is the 800 pound tiger? Who is the 800 pound gorilla on top of the 800 pound tiger? That's China. China is now pulling in resources from all across the planet with an unquenchable thirst, and a lot of those things are coming from Southeast Asia, which is right next door. If they have something, China will use it. It's very similar to the situation between the US and Mexico. Mexico can't possibly produce enough shit to feed the United States'

Gorillas and Tigers: these guys are all kicking ass!

market. Southeast Asia is exactly like this right now and they don't have enough wood, enough rubber, enough aluminum, or enough vegetables. They can't possibly have enough. China will import it all. It is a phenomenal place for them to be, and it's one of the reasons why their economy is starting to climb out of the gutter and one of the other reasons why I'm saying this litter of cubs will soon be tigers. Claws up! RAWWWRRR!

This region is growing, but before I go any further, is this place bustling to the point that everybody is getting wheelbarrows full of gold and becoming fat-belly rich? No, of course not. One of the reasons why these countries are getting rich is because of cheap labor, typically meaning a lot of the wealth isn't filtering down to the lowest classes. There is endemic poverty here, lots and lots of poverty. There are some poor-ass people here, but economically speaking, looking at **GDP,** looking at foreign investment, they are starting to do pretty well. That doesn't mean they are out of the hole yet, they still have a hell of a long way to go. One of the things that may help them go that hell of a long way is . . .

ASEAN

I can't get enough of ASEAN because it is setting up—and this is a Plaid insider tip—to be one of the most successful trade blocs on the planet. It's hard to imagine how they aren't going to be at this point. One of the things that may take them to the level of development, and I'm talking about the region, is that ASEAN may become more than just a trade bloc. This is speculative of course, at best. What is **ASEAN?** ASEAN is a trade bloc, a free-trade zone that consists of all of the countries in Southeast Asia. Here's the

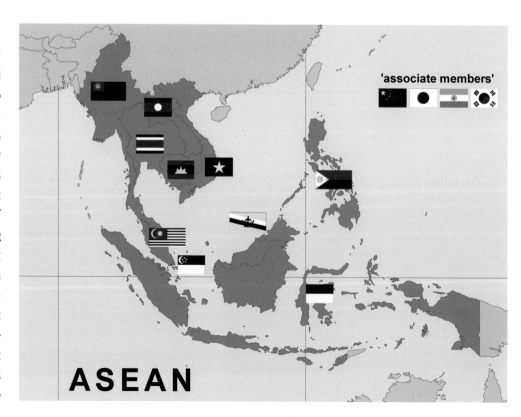

'associate members'

ASEAN

kicker. It's becoming so popular as a free-trade zone and is starting to incite so much economic activity that other countries want to get in the club. Yes, there are still some countries that want to get into the EU, but it's getting close to the end of its growth as a trade bloc. (Let's not even mention the FTAA because that idea is played out and probably won't happen.) All the other trade blocs are approaching their limits, but ASEAN is in position to keep expanding. How about China? Big plus. How about India? Another big plus. They are two associate members with a combined population of almost three billion people who want to be in this free-trade zone with Southeast Asia. How can this be a bad thing for them? Another associate member who wants to do more business is Japan, the number two economy on the planet. Any country in ASEAN is really sitting pretty. This is a trade bloc that is happening. I can't see how anything but good can come of it for the member countries.

BUMP IT TO THE NEXT LEVEL, BABY!

If you poke in and see what's going on within ASEAN, you'll find out pretty quickly that it's becoming much more than a trade bloc as well. They are starting to turn into something similar to the EU. It's only in the early stages of this, mind you, but it is becoming apparent already to me. Visit the ASEAN Website to see what I'm talking about. You'll see plans for hydroelectric power as part of a proposed ASEAN-wide power grid. Let me say that again: a joint electric grid for the entire region! That is crazy! Europe doesn't even have that, to my knowledge. If you are going so far as to do that then you got to think that if they are already talking about infrastructure in terms of roads and bridges and ports, they might simultaneously raise the standards of living for every country, which might mean an integrated healthcare system across the region. I don't know; it's hard to tell where they are going with this, but certainly they are already integrated in economic terms, and they don't have any qualms about free movement of people.

ASEAN Smoothie

- 1 oz. Amarula Cream liqueur
- 1 oz. DeKuger Strawberry liqueur
- 1 oz. Everclear alcohol
- 1 oz. Apricot brandy liqueur
- 1 oz. Nachtmusiek chocolate liqueur
- 1 small banana
- 1 scoop chocolate ice cream
-   several ice cubes

Blend all ingredients in a blender on high power until smooth. Pour into a very tall collins glass, garnish with chocolate shavings and a cherry, and serve. Toast to our Southeast Asian friends as their trade block explodes, as will the flavors of this smoothie in your mouth!

ASEAN is setting itself up to be something a whole lot more like the EU with maybe even less friction between the countries involved. This will, dare I say, be a stabilizing force within a region with a track record for serious conflicts. ASEAN has become a savior to these countries. It's hard to see any intraregional conflict cropping up here in the future, because once these countries become integrated in every way that they've proposed, conflict will be quickly resolved and made nearly impossible. Soon, nobody will be able to dredge up a reason to fight. Are there people who are unhappy there? I'm sure there are unhappy people all over the damn place, but there are no unhappy governments in this deal.

We talked about power grids and hydroelectric systems, possible healthcare systems and I'll go out on a limb and say that the regional stability that ASEAN provides may indeed be the impetus for a **common military**. No one has talked about that yet, but the Plaid Avenger is going to say it. I don't give a shit what other people may be saying. All I know is that it is a very likely possibility in the years to come. Here is a little quote for you: "Today, ASEAN is not only a well functioning indispensable reality in the region. It is a real force to be reckoned with far beyond the region. It is also a trusted partner of the United Nations in the field of development . . ." Who said it? Kofi Annan said it, former Secretary General of the United Nations, on February 16, 2000. A thumbs-up from Kofi can only mean good things. How awesome is Kofi!

I love Kofi. I love Aung San too. Hmmmmm . . . I feel a Plaid Avenger mission to free this babe is imminent. What? You don't know Aung San? Well, she is only the finest democracy-promoting babe in the Asian archipelago . . . fighting for freedom and liberty and justice for all in her home state of Burma. Speaking of which, there is only one cause of friction within the ASEAN countries, and that is Burma. Let's find out a little more about the situation there . . .

What's the Deal with . . . Aung San Suu Kyi?

Suu Kyi is a prominent prodemocracy advocate in Southeast Asia. In 1988, she founded the National League for Democracy in Burma after many prodemocracy demonstrators were killed and radically repressed. The military junta that was in power at the time had a pretty terrible track record as far as human rights were concerned. A general election was held there in 1990 as a result of the uprisings for democratization. Aung San Suu Kyi's non-violent democracy party won 90 percent of the vote. The junta immediately nullified the results and is still in power.

In 1990, her cumulative work and nonviolent tactics won her both the Rafto Prize and the Sakharov Prize for Freedom of Thought. A year later she was awarded the Nobel Peace Prize. So what's this hero of democracy doing today? Funny you should ask! She is currently sitting in a dark, damp prison cell in Burma. Why? Because Burma is ruled by a corrupt military dictatorship and her babble about human rights was pissing them off.

What is the international community doing to help this chick out? The other members of ASEAN (Myanmar joined in 1997) are sufficiently embarrassed and have pressed Myanmar to reform politically. The West has cut off almost all relations with Myanmar. The United States won't even officially call them Myanmar; they're still on the books as Burma. How will this help Suu Kyi? It probably won't. She's pretty much screwed, as are the rest of the people. Too bad they don't have a shitload of oil there, or we'd go and "free" them.

But I won't end by slamming the US the country is actually doing the most to help her and her country out. We have a 100 percent trade embargo against the country, and encourage everyone else in the world to follow. Unfortunately, our European friends and most of the world have not followed suit yet.

BURMESE BASTARDS

Burma is the redheaded stepchild right now that everyone else keeps in the closet because the world has put pressure on the Aung San Suu Kyi's situation. What? Who?

In 2007, political tensions once again flared and all international, humanitarian eyes were on Burma. The junta, in an unexceptional move, raised price on fuel and other basic necessities. But, this time it was the straw that broke the camel's back. Activists started to protest, the government broke them up, but then the monks started to protest. Thousands and thousands of monks donned saffron colored robes and marched through Rangoon (Yangon if you prefer the Manmarification) protesting against the junta. The world watched—thanks largely to cell phones and other digital cameras as no official reporters are allowed in the country—as the government debated whether to forcefully put down the giant protests. In a particularly moving moment, the monks marched to Aung San Suu Kyi's house (where she is under domestic arrest for bullshit) and she came out to receive them—in a sense, blessing the revolution and thanking the monks for their courage. Fortunately, although the junta did use some force, there were no massive slaughtering. Unfortunately, the protest failed to accomplish much other than to raise awareness. In fact, on May 29, 2008, the junta decided to add another year on Suu Kyi's prison sentence.

And, as mentioned earlier, Burma just got slammed by one of the most deadly cyclones ever. And, guess what, the first thing the junta did was deny anything was wrong! Seriously! The global community was poised to help and the Burmese government basically came out and said, "We don't need foreign aid. Everything's under control. Trust us. We're cool." Meanwhile their population is totally ravaged and in ABSOLUTE need of foreign aid. And get this, eight days after the cyclone, the government conducted a previously scheduled nationwide vote! Yep, don't mind the water, just proceed to the polls! This whole time, the entire world is flipping out just trying to send in aid. But goddamn sovereignty—the main rule is that you can only come in if asked. Long story short, the Burmese government didn't allow in foreign aid workers for two weeks after the disaster and even then it was only aid workers from ASEAN members nations. They waited another week before they allowed in aid workers from the rest of the world. Lots and lots of people died. Many may have been saved if Burma had a government that was interested in the well being of its citizens. OK, enough with the heartless bastards in the Burmese junta, back to ASEAN . . .

TERRIBLE TERROR POTENTIAL

We'll end on a negative note here, unfortunately. Terrorism is a real force to be reckoned with on the planet right now, as the US-led war on terrorism is quite active around the planet. This War on Terrorism is definitely not a Cold War. It's quite hot at the moment. One of the regions that people worry about but don't seem to hear about is Southeast Asia. Why would you have a War on Terrorism here? Maybe because Indonesia is the largest Muslim state in the world, and as such, is considered a hotbed of extremist activity. For those of you not in the know, several Western hotels and buildings have been blown up just in the last couple of years here . . . A bunch of Australian tourists got killed in a fairly nasty blast at a tourist hotel not long ago. There are also reports of extremist activity in the Philippines, Malaysia and lots of other places in Southeast Asia.

It has to do with physical geography too, because these very separate islands provide cover for lots of secret stuff to go on. There are a lot of terrorist cells in and within Southeast Asia, and because they can get on small islands and operate fairly independently without anybody checking them out; they are completely under the radar. I can tell you without reservation that Australia has been very worried about this for a while. They are probably the next country that will be outright attacked. They spend a lot of money and a lot of time trying to figure out where terrorists are and in case it's not clear by now, they're looking at Southeast Asia. They ain't looking in the Middle East, that's for sure. None of the terrorists there are a threat to Australia. However, there are some radical groups within Indonesia and in the southern Philippines. There is a rebel/terrorist group that has been kidnapping tourists for quite some time. Check out the news; you don't have to look too hard to find them. They are called **Abu Sayyaf.**

You can rest assured that Uncle Sam has been checking this out. The United States and everyone involved in the War on Terror has operatives checking out movements here. Another reason for worry is clashes between Christians and Muslims, which happened notably in the small island group called the **Maluku Islands** in Indonesia.

Southeast Asia has some negative things to deal with nowadays, terrorism being the big one. Australia, being a power player in the region, has taken on most of the workload for the antiterrorism movement and is supported by the United States and Europe. This offends some countries in Southeast Asia, namely Indonesia and even more so Malaysia. Those crazy bastards get really hot and bothered about foreign influence, even if it's on issues concerning terrorism.

ROUND-UP

So terrorism: bad. ASEAN: good. Southeast Asia: rockin'. Thundercats: Ho! This region has tremendous potential for economic growth as it becomes the newest 'workshop' of Asia producing shit tons of manufactured goods. Its placement between the make it well suited for both production and distribution of a variety of goods and services to Asia as a whole . . . having the giants of China and India on either side of you sure don't hurt either. The ASEAN grouping is set to explode into the 21st century, having put its century of conflict well in the rear view mirror.

Unfortunately, the region also has explosive potential of other kinds too. Volcanic, earthquake, tsunami, typhoon, and monsoonal activity are a very real part of life for Southeast Asians, and one that will never go away. In fact, it seems to be increasing here lately! This region continues to get pummeled with the most horrific natural disasters year after year. Coupled with Mother Nature's ire is the terrorist potential which seems to permeate many areas in this widely dispersed (and hard to effectively control) archipelago arena.

So the upcoming century will still be hot and active for Southeast Asia and ASEAN . . . let's hope its hot babes and hot economic growth versus hot lava and hot spots of conflict!!! And Aung San: I love you!

Level **Blue**

Status No active shooting. Arms build-up may be happening, but discreetly. However, political ideological differences on site make conflicts possible, and perhaps inevitable.

Level **Yellow**

Status Active violence by individuals or small groups is active, or getting very close to erupting. Arms build-up and other preparations are happening, and not discreetly. Political or ideological differences getting hot enough for active, organized forces to be on the move. Could go down any moment.

Level **Red**

Status GAME ON! Active violence by inviduals, small groups, and/or large organized forces like a state military are happening. Nothing is discreet, and open war may have been declared. People are shooting other people, and you can watch it all on CNN.

Plaid Avenger's Hotspots of Conflict

WHAT CAUSES HUMANS TO KILL EACH OTHER?

Since the end of the Second World War in 1945 there have been over 250 major wars in which over 23 million people have been killed, tens of millions made homeless, and countless millions injured and bereaved. In the history of warfare, the 20th century stands out as the bloodiest and most brutal—three times as many people have been killed in wars in the last 90 years than in the previous 500.

The nature of warfare has also changed. From the set-piece battles of the earlier centuries, the blood and mud of the trenches in the First World War, and the fast-moving mechanized battlefields of World War II, to the high-tech "surgical" computer-guided action in Iraq and Kuwait, war

One from the west: "And there went out another horse that was red: and power was given to him that sat thereon to take peace from the earth, and that they should kill one another: and there was given unto him a great sword."

—The Revelation of St. John the Divine: 6:4

And one from the east: "Now I am become Death, the destroyer of worlds."

—from The Bhagavad-Gita

as seen through our television screens appears to have become a well-ordered, almost bloodless, affair. Nothing could be further from the truth. During the 20th century the proportion of civilian casualties has risen steadily. In World War II two-thirds of those killed were civilians; by the beginning of the 1990s civilian deaths approached a horrifying 90 percent.

This is partly the result of technological developments, but there is another major reason. Many modern armed conflicts are not between states but within them: struggles between soldiers and civilians, or between competing civilian groups. Such conflicts are likely to be fought out in country villages and urban streets. In such wars, the "enemy" camp is everywhere, and the distinctions between combatant and noncombatant melt away into the fear, suspicion and confusion of civilian life under fire.

And people kill each other because of ethnic differences, religious differences, cultural differences, and any other thing that differentiates different groups of humans. Wars are also fought over resources, land, and political control of areas—particularly where states or empires have dissolved into multiple entities (British India, Yugoslavia). And now we have new wars with new dimensions the likes of which the world has not seen before: Battles of ideologies that span the entire planet.

Now perhaps you are thinking the Cold War was just such a conflict—and you would be right. But it was cold, as its name suggests. Here in the 21st century we have the "War on Terrorism," the "War on Western Imperialism," and the "War on Drugs," which are global ideological battles—but damned hot ones! People are actively shooting at each other in these wars, wherever they are sponsored all over the planet. That's the new part.

Conflict within states, conflict between states, and ideological conflicts in which the entire globe is the battlefield. We've got it all in our day and age. But we can't possibly cover all the active conflicts happening. The Plaid Avenger wants to pick out just a few situations that have global implications, as well as a few more than may be heating up in the coming year. The Plaid Avenger legend is worthy of a minute's review to clue you in to the conflict status, as of September 2006.

INDIA–PAKISTAN

HOT SPOT: KASHMIR

In 1947, after India gained independence from Great Britain, it was divided into two separate states because of large differences in their religious populations. India retained most of the subcontinent with its predominately Hindu population while Pakistan (and East Pakistan, now known as Bangladesh) formed as a home to South Asia's large Muslim population. From the beginning, friction has existed between these two giants of the subcontinent. Bloody clashes broke out the very day of independence, as millions of folks were on the move, shifting to the "proper" country that housed their religious inclinations.

Alright, so everyone's got their own bachelor pad, hanging out with their own crew. So not a care in the world, right? No cause we're forgetting about that tricky place that makes ridiculously comfortable fabric. The continued conflict between the two states is primarily over Kashmir, a small region about the size of Kansas, located in the northwestern part of the Indian subcontinent where the two countries meet. The Kashmir region was originally ruled by a monarch (or Maharaja) who gave India control of the region shortly after the nations split—the majority Muslim population of Kashmir did not agree with this move. Afterward, war erupted and continued until the UN arranged a cease-fire in 1949, by which time Pakistan gained one-third of the Kashmir territory. After India formally annexed the rest of Kashmir in 1956, the Muslim population was once more provoked to rioting, and fighting has continued ever since with a repeated pattern of attacks and cease-fires for the last 50 years.

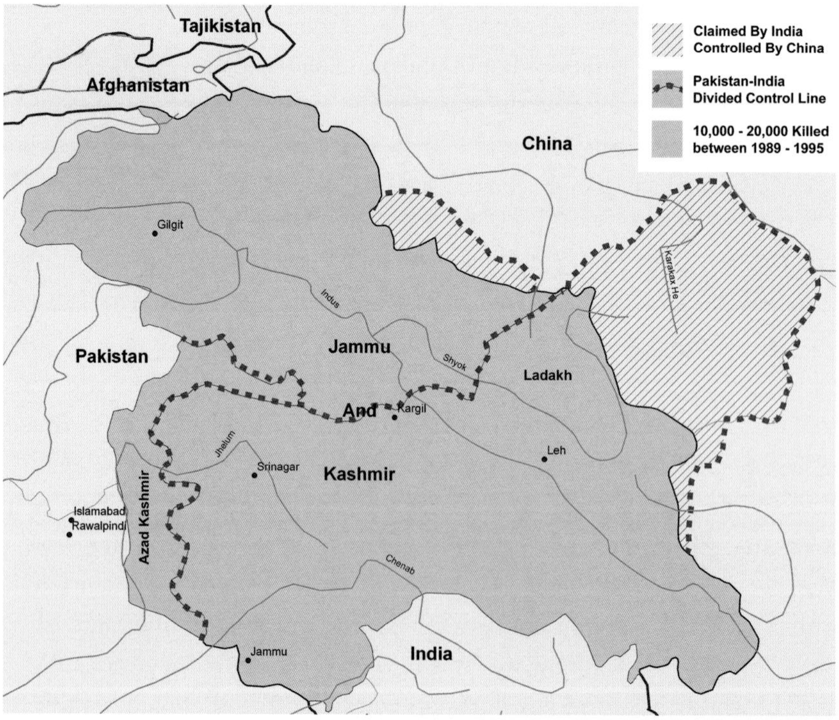
Tajikistan
Afghanistan
China
Claimed By India
Controlled By China
Pakistan-India
Divided Control Line
10,000 - 20,000 Killed
between 1989 - 1995
Gilgit
Indus
Karakax He
Pakistan
Jammu
And
Kashmir
Shyok
Ladakh
Kargil
Leh
Jhelum
Srinagar
Islamabad
Rawalpindi
Azad Kashmir
Chenab
Jammu
India

The situation intensified in the 1990s as both sides began testing nuclear weapons and gained global attention because neither state has signed the nuclear nonproliferation agreement. Although recent meetings have shown signs of a peaceful resolution, this conflict must be considered a political hot spot as India and Pakistan remain the only neighboring nuclear powers with hostilities towards one another. In a hopeful vein, a massive earthquake that rocked the area last year resulted in the two countries working together to provide disaster relief. Hopefully that sentiment will hold. But make no bones about it, the fuse could easily get lit again between these two and escalate rapidly.

DEMOCRATIC REPUBLIC OF CONGO (DRC)

HOT SPOT: EASTERN CONGO

The history of the Democratic Republic of the Congo has been a complicated one, full of instability, coups d'etat, violence, and name changes. When the "Republic of the Congo" gained independence from Belgium in 1960, a guy named Patrice Lumumba was elected president, but was overthrown in a coup d'etat in 1965 by Mobutu Sese Seko. Sese Seko, a dictator, was supported by the United States and Belgium, and controlled every aspect of life in the country. He even changed the name of the country to "Zaire" in 1971. After the Cold War was over, the United States did not think it was necessary to support Sese Seko anymore, so he was overthrown by Laurent Kabila in 1997, who renamed the country back to "Democratic Republic of The Congo-Kinshasa." The name of the capital city is added to the name of the country to distinguish it from the "Republic of the Congo-Brazzaville" which is a different country that is next door to "Democratic Republic of the Congo." Get it? Good. Someone explain this stuff back to me.

This new Kabila government immediately came under fire by rebel groups and has yet to establish any sort of stability. Kabila quickly lost control of parts of eastern Congo to Ugandan, Rwandan, and Burundian backed rebels while still receiving support from Angolan, Zimbabwean, and Namibian troops. The organization Human Rights Watch wrote that Congo is a human rights disaster area and "soldiers of the national army and combatants of armed groups continue to target civilians, killing, raping, and otherwise injuring them, carrying out arbitrary arrests and torture, and destroying or pillaging their property. Tens of thousands of persons have fled their homes, several thousand of them across international borders." In fact, the DRC conflict is

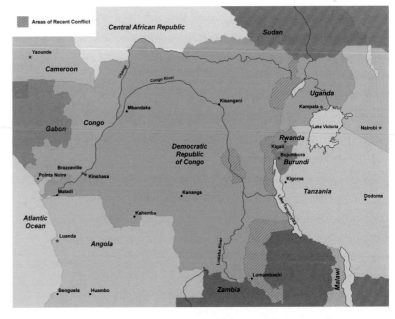

responsible for the establishment of a new category of war crime: institutionalized rape. Roaming groups of soldiers raping women with total disregard for laws or morals has left an entire generation of women physically and psychologically and another generation fatherless. In fact, the conflict in the Democratic Republic of the Congo has been called "Africa's World War" and 3.8 million people have died as a result of it. A peace treaty was signed in 2003, but the situation remains unstable and could devolve back into war at any time. In a couple years, you could be watching "Hotel Congo."

So why the fighting? Quite simply, money. This area is huge, massively huge, and filled with gold, diamonds, uranium and practically every commodity the developed world wants. Because there is no sense of nationhood and the leaders of the different factions are war criminals and thieves who are only looking to line their own pockets. The natural wealth of the Congo is taken out of the country, leaving a poor, uneducated population embroiled in turmoil. Things here are really bad and the near future holds few foreseeable good changes.

Some areas of the country are effectively controlled by the armies of other neighboring states. Or rebel groups from neighboring states. Or terrorist groups from neighboring states. Or local rebel groups. Or local warlords. Or . . . I think you are starting to get the point.

A huge-ass country with a weak central government; a valuable and tempting resource base; a hideout for rebel groups of all sorts; perhaps seven different states have forces in and out of the territory. What a damn mess. Could implode soon, and turn into an all-out territorial grab by all the involved parties: The DRC, Uganda, Rwanda, Burundi, Angola, etc.

SUDAN

HOT SPOT: DARFUR

Often times the conflict in Darfur, which is a province in western Sudan, is painted as a war between the Arab government and the black African commoners. But if you go to Darfur everybody looks black. What's the deal? Well, as Arabs began to dominate the government in the past century and gave jobs to members of Arab tribes, being Arab became a political advantage and some tribes adopted that label regardless of their ethnic affiliation. Nowadays, each tribe gives itself the label of "African" or "Arab" based on what language its members speak and whether they work the soil or herd livestock. The true division in Darfur is between ethnic groups, split between herders and farmers, who are fighting over the region's scarce resources.

Anyway, the Darfur conflict started in 2003 when two non-Arab groups, the Sudan Liberation Army and the Justice and Equality Movement, took up arms against the Sudanese government, alleging mistreatment by the Arab regime in Khartoum. In response, a government-backed paramilitary group called the Janjaweed began pillaging towns and villages inhabited by members of the African tribes from which the rebel armies recruit members. Janjaweed literally means "armed men on horseback" in Arabic and is not a Rastafarian pot-smoking army. The Janjaweed militia supported by the government in Khartoum are tasked with the job of removing all inhabitants who might make resource extraction difficult, or demand compensation. What resource extraction? Why oil of course! Southern Sudan is awash with oil, and the revenues it brings . . . which is perhaps the main reason that the government does not want any independence movements cropping up in these areas. So send in the Janjaweed!

Of course, the Sudanese government has denied helping the Janjaweed, especially because the Janjaweed have been accused of genocide and ethnic cleansing non-Arabs. Together with government troops, the armed Arab militia is responsible for the deaths of up to 50,000 African villagers and the displacement of another million from their homes in Darfur. It should be noted that both sides are accused of serious human rights violations, including mass killing, looting, and rapes of the civilian population. However, since the Janjaweed are better armed and funded, they are doing a better job of it.

So how come the world isn't stepping in to stop it? Well, mostly because China is a veto-wielding member of the UN Permanent Security Council, and simultaneously the biggest investor and consumer in the Sudanese oil industry. Starting to get the picture? Things may be changing here in 2008: the Chinese want to show the world how awesome they are as they host the Olympics, so they don't want to look like big assholes by holding up any UN movement on the situation while a possible genocide is occurring. The UN is now creating plans to launch a joint UN/AU force into the area to help stop the violence, and the Sudanese government is being pressured into going along with it. We'll see. It should be noted that there is separate civil war going on in the South of Sudan that has nothing to do with the Darfur conflict—similar roots and structure,

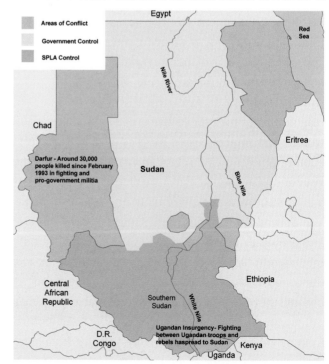

Areas of Conflict

Government Control

SPLA Control

Egypt

Red Sea

Nile River

Chad

Eritrea

Darfur - Around 30,000 people killed since February 1993 in fighting and pro-government militia

Sudan

Blue Nile

Central African Republic

White Nile

Ethiopia

Southern Sudan

Ugandan Insurgency- Fighting between Ugandan troops and rebels hasspread to Sudan

D.R. Congo

Kenya

Uganda

but technically a separate event. An event that's caused nasty ethnic purges off and on for several decades now. The two civil wars fought since independence in 1956 have left the country with fewer than ten years of peace in 50. Damn, Sudan's just a busy field of death: two conflicts for the price of one.

SRI LANKA

HOT SPOT: THE NORTH

Sri Lanka is a paradox; on one hand it has the highest per capita income in South Asia, with an ancient culture, and progressive economic and industrial sectors...on the other hand they have been courting a decades old civil war. The conflict in Sri Lanka has arisen because of differences between its two main ethnic and religious groups; the Sinhala-Buddhist majority and the Tamil-Hindu minority. For years, Sri Lanka was under British rule and the Sinhalese complained that the British were giving the Tamil preferential treatment. The Tamil claimed that there was no preferential treatment; they just got better jobs because they were better. When British rule ended, the Sinhalese majority decided to get back at the Tamil with the Sinhala Act of 1956, making Sinhalese the only language allowed in Sri Lanka, effectively blocking the Tamils from getting any good jobs.

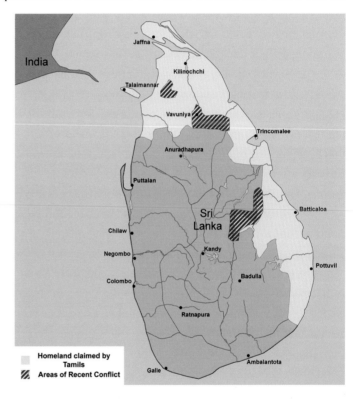

Homeland claimed by Tamils
Areas of Recent Conflict

To fight back the Tamil Hindu minority formed the Liberation Tigers of Tamil Eelam (LTTE), or Tamil Tigers for short, to gain independence. This terrorist organization has successfully assassinated several Sinhala prime ministers, used claymore mines in guerilla attacks, and continues to be responsible for attacks on the island. The Tamil Eelam pretty much invented and patented the practice of suicide bombing, and even has a group known as the "Sea Tigers" who have clashed with the Sri Lankan navy. To my knowledge, they are the only terrorist group that has their own Navy, air force, and military uniforms with a kick-ass tiger logo emblazoned across the chest.

Since 1983 the two sides have fought on and off in civil war. A 2005 cease-fire between the LTTE and the government held fairly well for a little while, but the situation was once more complicated because both sides accused each other of carrying out covert operations against the other. The government claimed that LTTE rebels were killing opponents and government soldiers, while the rebels accused the government of supporting paramilitary groups against the organization and assassinating Tamil journalists and civilians. The conflict there has claimed the lives of 50,000 and forced millions to flee to India on both sides. Today, access for journalists and human rights groups is strictly limited and the conflict seems nowhere close to settlement.

So why is it heating up again right now? The tsunami disaster of 2004 caused a breakdown of everything—including the peace process compounded with accusations that disaster relief/aid were withheld from Tamil populations by the government incited rioting and the civil war appears to be back on. With the national government unwilling to secede any territory or grant independence to a Tamil country, and the Tamils steadfast in their fight for independence, violent conflict appears inevitable for some time. It could get real hot, real fast on the tear-drop island.

THE BALKANS

Once known as the "powder keg of Europe" the Balkans once more may be expected to explode back into war at any time. The roots of the conflict are very deep, yet they can be directly linked to the independence of Slovenia and Croatia in 1991 from the state known as Yugoslavia. The area consists of three main ethnic groups and several loosely connected factions: the Serbs (Orthodox Christians), the Muslims, and the Croats (Roman Catholic) with links to Western Europe.

Once upon a time there existed the Socialist Federal Republic of Yugoslavia. Within that republic were six constituent states, Bosnia-Herzegovina, Croatia, Republic of Macedonia, Serbia-Montenegro, and Slovenia. The conflict begins when Croatia and Slovenia formerly announced their independence from Yugoslavia. This gave rise to surrounding states in the former republic in ousting their one-party communist states systems and electing officials with nationalist platforms. Here's the main problem though, all of those regions are pretty

much comprised of several different ethnic groups who believe they are misrepresented. A prime example of that is Kosovo, a region comprised of 88% Albanians with an ethnic minority of Serbs. The Kosovo-Albanians want to leave the Serbian Republic, while the Serbs within Kosovo are scared shitless of what will happen to them if they stay in Kosovo.

On February 17th 2008, Kosovo formally declared independence from Serbia. Serbia out-right rejects this notion and upholds that is illegal under U.N charter, while Albania, who strongly supported the KLA who fought guerillas wars against Serbia, was the first to support Kosovo.

Are you ready?-cause here's where it gets interesting. Technically speaking, Kosovo is a region within Serbia, which is an internationally recognized state by the U.N., which then gives Serbia the right to preserve its territorial integrity. The wrong words and the wrong moves could just push this region over the edge and start a war. No biggie right? Well, except for the fact that this is the same region that sparked WWI.

Dig this: The US and a dozen other EU countries (including the UK and France) have also recognized the Kosovo independence claim. Unfortunately for Kosovo, both Russia and China (which are both veto-wielding members of the UN Security Council) side with Serbia on this question of sovereignty. Hmmmm . . . I'm starting to see a larger world showdown over this tiny little province.

ISRAEL VS. PALESTINE

The Israel-Palestine conflict has very deep roots—stretching back thousands of years. In ancient times, the area that is now Israel was inhabited by Jews who had a degree of autonomy and self-governance. However, in 70 AD the Roman Empire, who controlled the land, burnt down the Jewish temple and kicked all of the Jews out of Israel. The next 1900 years were known as the Jewish diaspora, when Jews were scattered around the world and often persecuted for being Jewish. After a particularly atrocious bit of persecution in World War II (the Holocaust), European countries and the United States decided that it was time to allow the Jews to return to Israel and have their own homeland. The state of Israel was created in 1948 and Jews from all around the world migrated to Israel to be free.

The problem was that a new group of people were living in that area who were calling themselves the Palestinians. These Palestinians were mostly Arab and Muslim and by new, I mean that they had only been living there a few hundred years, not since biblical times. To make room for Israel, some of these Palestinians had to go. The facts are disputed as to exactly how and why it happened, but around 700,000 Palestinians left Israel in 1948 and settled in the countries bordering Israel, including Jordan, Egypt, Syria, and Lebanon. To make matters worse, all of the countries bordering Israel were Arab and Muslim, and their governments wanted to look tough on Israel to make their people happy. For this reason, The Arab countries demanded that Israel take the refugees back. Israel said no and these refugees quickly faced a Catch-22 situation: Israel would not let them come back to their former homes and the Arab countries they migrated to would not find them places to live either.

As you can imagine, the Palestinians turned violent quickly and began forming terrorist organizations to attack Israel. Again, to look tough on Israel, the surrounding Arab countries went to war with it twice. In 1948 and 1967 the Arab countries fought Israel and lost both times. After each of these wars Israel took more land, taking the West Bank from Jordan in 1967 and the Golan Heights from Syria in 1967. Israel still controls these areas and claims that it needs these lands because of the geographical and strategic locations of the sites for their national security.

The two most disputed territories are the West Bank and the Gaza Strip. These areas were not originally part of Israel in 1948, but were taken by Israel in the 1967 war. These areas are predominately Palestinian and the Palestinians in these areas want their own state. However each part wants different leaders. The Palestinian Authority (PA) has been the pseudo-government of this pseudo-state, and has been dominated by the political party Fatah since its inception. However, Fatah and the PA have become unpopular with the Palestinians because it is corrupt and not making any real progress on the big issues.

For this reason, the Islamic extremist organization Hamas continued to gain popularity in parliament, and a major rift occurred in the summer of 2007: the democratically elected Hamas completely 'took over' the government of Gaza Strip, and kicked out their Fatah opponents. So now this pseudo-state of Palestine is even divided amongst itself: The Fatah dominated PA controls only the West Bank, while the Hamas party controls the Gaza Strip. Let's make it even messier: Hamas has a history of supporting terrorism in Israel, and many western governments (the US, the EU, Israel) consider Hamas a terrorist organization, and as such will not deal with them.

The situation only looks like it will worsen since Israel closed off the Gaza Strip to all flow of good and traffic except that which is essential to stem the daily barrage of cheaply made rockets that fly from Gaza into Israel. This is a move intended to punish the more militant Hamas, while Israel, the US and the EU are holding up the PA as the true leaders of the Palestinian people in a desperate bid to try and normalize relations. But even that is not working out so well . . . the Gaza embargo which is starving citizens to death has become a debacle for all parties involved, and is stymieing the peace process further. Expect this one to get even messier. Hell, you don't have to expect it: just watch it unfold.

WAR ON TERROR: GLOBAL MANIFESTATIONS

US IN AFGHANISTAN

U.S. involvement in Afghanistan is still fresh in our memories—oh right, cause we're still there. The story however is a long one. In 1996, the Taliban, a fanatic Islamic extremist group, took control of Afghanistan, which had before then been a mishmash of warlords fighting for power. On October 7, 2001 NATO (led primarily by the US) began its military campaign against Afghanistan known as *"Operation Enduring Freedom."* The invasion was in direct response to the 9/11 terrorist attacks and under the belief that Afghanistan was harboring the same terrorist that planned the attacks. With the help of a rebel group called the Northern Alliance (which gains much of its funding through opium sales), America and its allies established a new, secular government in Afghanistan. This invasion sparked off what is now known as the Global War on Terror.

The main problem in Afghanistan has been the unsuccessful implementation of its established government. Afghani's are arguing that the ruling government is comprised of ethnic Tajiks, while the majority of Afghanistan is Pashtun. The Pashtun's are freaking out cause they think the Tajiks are too westernized with their skintight jeans and pink Armani t-shirts, creating a secular government. The Pashtun's would prefer a Pashtun-dominated Islamic based government, which is strongly supported by its neighbor in the north Pakistan. A reoccurring problem the U.S. is seeing is the failure of its exported form of democracy in the Middle East *(See: U.S. in Iraq)*.

A recent surge in Taliban activity has many speculating that the U.S. and its NATO allies are failing in reconstructing Afghanistan. A clear example of that was on April 27th 2008 when Afghan President Hamad Karzai survived a failed assassination attempt. Failed yes, but a victory for the insurgents, as they were at least capable of getting close to Karzai. This is putting immense pressure on Karzai's administration to successfully establish and proclaim an effective government.

A particular problem posing itself against the Afghan government is the sharp increase in production of opium, which can be processed into heroin. Can't be that big of a problem right? Afghanistan is a war torn country, when the hell are you ever going to have time to grow opium.

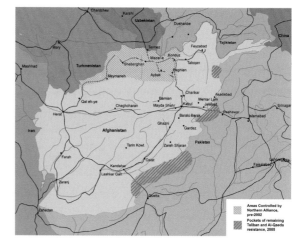

Areas Controlled by Northern Alliance, pre-2002

Pockets of remaining Taliban and Al-Qaeda resistance, 2005

Well apparently there's something in the air because Afghanistan produces 92% of the worlds opium and 80% of the world's heroin. But lets get down and dirty with the problem itself. The Taliban and al-Queda have used the opium trade to re-equip, re-supply, and re-organize themselves, and as of this writing in 2008, have turned the tide of the battle back in their favor.

Yes, you are reading this correctly: the Taliban is currently gaining ground and beating the NATO coalition. Damn! The US has been outright begging other countries to contribute more to the cause, and the Brits, Aussies, and even the Frenchies have recently pledged to increase troop levels. If the French are sending in more troops, and the Americans want them to, then you know the situation must be dire!

We call Afghanistan a "country" because it occupies a space on the map of the world, but it isn't really one. For years, Afghanistan has been a battlefield for rival warlords and ethnic groups. Every time somebody has tried to set up a strong central government (Soviet Union in the 1980s), war has broken out. People in Afghanistan are used to war and are good at defending their homeland. America better take some lessons in history before it tries to impose a government that those folks don't want.

US IN IRAQ

Ever since Saddam Hussein invaded Kuwait in 1991, he has been one of America's worst enemies. In the first Gulf War, American forces drove Hussein out of Kuwait and destroyed much of Iraq's army. When asked why he didn't pursue Hussein to Baghdad to finish the job and remove him from power, former President George H.W. Bush told a group of Gulf War veterans, "Whose life would be on my hands as the commander-in-chief because I, unilaterally, went beyond the international law, went beyond the stated mission, and said we're going to show our macho? We're going into Baghdad. We're going to be an occupying power—America in an Arab land—with no allies at our side. It would have been disastrous. We're American soldiers; we don't do business that way."

After George W. Bush (the other president's son) was elected President in 2000, he decided that American soldiers **did** do business that way. So America unilaterally attacked Iraq, went into Baghdad, and occupied the country—America in an Arab land. But a funny thing happened on the way to Baghdad. Hussein's forces did not even show up. The war was a cakewalk; it was almost too easy. People wondered where Hussein's famous "Republican Guard" had disappeared to.

Then the sinking truth set in. Hussein had intentionally told his army to stand down. They knew they never would win a traditional ground war with US forces, so they dispersed and began an insurgency, fighting a guerrilla war with bombings and sneak attacks. Hussein was eventually captured, but since America declared "Mission Accomplished" more than 2000 American soldiers have died in Iraq, with new attacks happening daily. Insurgents have even kidnapped foreigners and beheaded them on television.

Public support in America could potentially decrease because nobody wants to subject their children to guerilla warfare. Furthermore, one of America's justifications for invading Iraq was that Saddam had WMD (weapons of mass destruction), but when American forces found none in Iraq many people felt bamboozled and lied to.

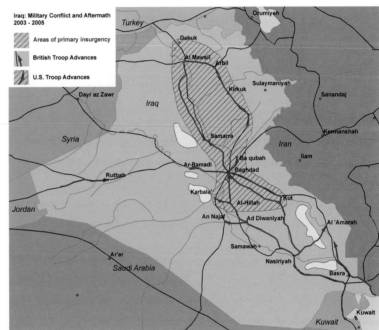

This place is a mess. America wants to establish a democracy in Iraq, but that will be difficult because Iraq consists of three rival ethnic groups that do not get along: The Kurds in the north, the Sunnis in the middle, and the Shi'ites in the south. Good luck getting those guys to agree on a government. Good luck indeed.

US VS. IRAN

Iran and the United States have been enemies since the 1979 Iranian Revolution, when Islamic extremists overthrew the US-backed Shah and took control of the government. When the fanatics took over, one of the first things they did was raid the American embassy in Tehran and take 52 Americans hostage for 444 days. The images of the hostages on TV made Americans furious at Iran. Iran has also funded terrorist groups world-wide, including Hezbollah, which was responsible for bombing a Marine barracks in Lebanon in 1983 and killing 241 American marines.

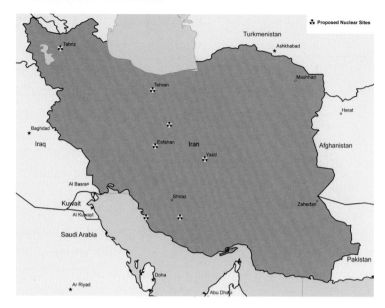

Iran has the dubious distinction of being listed by the State Department as the top state sponsor of terror worldwide, making it a natural target in the war on terror. To make things worse, Iranian officials are not only hostile to American values like liberal democracy and freedom of expression, they are also hostile to America's main ally in the Middle East, Israel. The President of Iran, Mahmoud Ahmadinejad has even said that Israel should be wiped off the map and other clerics are famous for their anti-Semitic rhetoric about Israel. No wonder George W. Bush called Iran part of the "axis of evil" in 2002.

Despite years of talking shit, the United States may finally have an excuse to attack Iran. In 2006, Iran admitted that it was enriching uranium to build nuclear power plants. Iranian officials claim that they are just doing this for nuclear power, but some American officials are concerned that this is just the first step in developing a nuclear bomb.

Obviously, American policymakers are scared to death of Islamic extremists, known for supporting terror and threatening Israel, having nuclear weapons. There has already been talk of a US invasion of Iran. This is being resisted big-time by China and Russia, both of which are doing big deals with Iran for energy importing and exporting. So this situation has got some beyond-the-Middle-East, whole-world repercussions as well.

Iran's air force and navy are shaky at best, and the United States could take it in a couple hours with some surgical bombing. A ground war is another story. Unlike Arab Muslims, who usually consider themselves more Muslim than nationalistic, Iranian people are very nationalistic and would resist an attack violently. I cannot conceive of anybody in the US government being dumb enough to attempt a ground war in Iran—but we should never underestimate the capacity for ignorance, I suppose.

I believe the worst case scenario that we might see would involve surgical bombing of the nuclear production facilities—which will serve to infuriate the Iranians, and piss of the Russians and Chinese as well. The Iranian government has also said that it will step up terrorist attacks (especially in U.S. occupied Iraq) if force is used against them. As of 2008, the US has been on a fairly successful diplomatic campaign to isolate and punish the Iranian regime until they give up on the nuclear development stuff. The EU and many other US allies have pushed for a major trade embargo against the country. And the US and Great Britain actually froze all Iranian asset and bank accounts within their repective countries. Of course, the Iranian response is to claim that they have a god-given right to nuclear power . . . although I'm not sure I've ever read any religious texts in which the Almighty specifically outlines his/her beliefs on fusion. Or is it fission? Oh well. The rhetoric is heating up, and this one could get ugly, quickly. And everyone is going to be involved one way or another.

NORTH KOREA VS. ?????? THE US? SOUTH KOREA? JAPAN? EVERYBODY?

North Korea is America's worst enemy in the Far East. They are communist; they possess about 5,000 tons of biological and chemical weapons; they administer death camps where 200,000 political and religious criminals are worked to death; and they are also run by a crazy dictator (Kim Jong II), who is not averse to funding his burgeoning **nuclear**

program using money laundering, heroin smuggling, and counterfeit currency. George W. Bush has said, "I loathe Kim Jong Il. I've got a visceral reaction to this guy, because he is starving his people. And I have seen intelligence of these prison camps—they're huge—that he uses to break up families and to torture people. It appalls me." Bush even included North Korea in his "axis of evil" speech in 2002.

The whole conflict started in 1950 when communist North Korea invaded South Korea and America sent troops to defend South Korea in the Korean War. Ever since then, North and South Korea have endured an uneasy peace and the United States has stationed more than 30,000 American troops in South Korea in case North Korea tries to invade again. However, the thing that scares American policy-makers most about North Korea is the fact that they are building nuclear weapons.

To resolve the nuclear issue, there has been some diplomacy, but the Korea issue is complicated. At first, North Korea wanted the US to sign a peace treaty that would formally end the Korean War (which never hap-

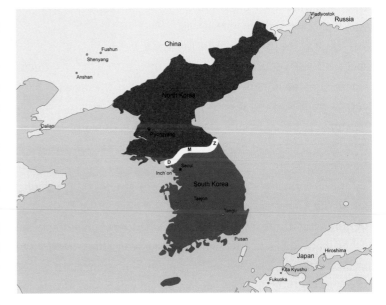

pened), but now they just want security. Unfortunately, Kim Jong Il and his advisors have decided that the best way to gain security is to threaten their neighbors with nuclear attacks and threaten that they are not averse to preemptive war. The US wanted to resolve this whole issue in the form of six-party talks involving themselves, North Korea, South Korea, Japan, China and Russia, and in November of 2005, the last round of these talks was held and an agreement was reached to provide North Korea with financial aid if they stop their nuclear program. But Kim won't finalize the deal unless the US drops its demands regarding his country's trade activities. The US responded to this by saying that the trade and nuclear issues are separate and they refuse to merge the two.

North Korea is not much of a threat militarily and would probably get their asses kicked by South Korea in a war. Or really a war with anybody. In fact, much of their population is starving. But with atomic weapons, and the crazy rhetoric that Kim Jong Il is famous for, many people are scared of North Korea. But, as former secretary of state Madeline Albright said of him, "I don't think he's delusional . . . we had very peculiar information about Kim Jong Il—that he was a recluse . . . he's not someone who only is interested in watching bad movies." Nukes, nuts, and nothing to lose: not a good combination.

RUSSIA VS. CHECHNYA

In the Northern Caucus Mountains lies a little place called Chechnya. Every hiccup in Russian history has been quickly followed up with screams of independence from Chechnya. The Russian Revolutions of 1905 and 1917: INDEPENDENE! World War II: INDEPDENCE! The Soviet hockey team losing to the Americans in the 1980 Olympics: INDEPENDENCE! Chechnya has been a part of Russia for a long time but the Chechens have never really been happy about it. When the Soviet Union collapsed in 1991, Chechnya declared independence and formed its own government. Unfortunately, this government was run by criminals and Chechnya quickly devolved into a state of chaos and wide-spread corruption. Russian President Boris Yeltsin saw this situation and believed that since Chechyna was so chaotic, Russian troops could easily take it back. So in 1994, 40,000

Russian troops entered Chechnya. They got their asses kicked because they had no idea what they were getting themselves into and they eventually signed a peace treaty with Chechens rebels in 1996. This was the First Chechen War.

The treaty however proved useless, as Chechnya rebels, dissatisfied with their appeasing government, took matters into their own hands and began a series of terrorist acts against Russian targets. Russian troops were once again mobilized and sent in to Chechnya in 1999 beginning the Second Chechen War. Although a majority of the fightinig occurred between 1992 and 2002, the war is still technically going on today. Here's where shit starts to get sticky.

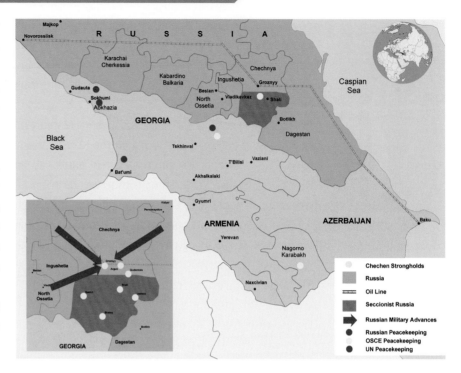

Chechnya is predominatly Sunni Muslim and some of those crazy rebel guys starting to become affiliated with Islamic extremists, you might have heard of one; does al-Qeada ring a bell? As of 2006, no country recognizes the independece of the Chechen state.

There actually was a lot more world attention on the plight of the Chechens, and world sympathy for their cause, before the 9/11 attacks on the US and the start of the Global War on Terrorism. Due to their tactics—suicide bombs, blowing up public trains and buildings, civilian targeting—their "soldiers" have been more and more classified as terrorists rather than rebel freedom fighters. Their reputation took a particularly nasty turn when some of these rebels took over a primary school, blew the building up and shot a bunch of kids. Bad move fellas. You start killing kids, and no one is going to side up with your cause, no matter how damn good it is. Want to know more? Look up the Beslan School Siege. Bad business. And it is due partly to this bad blood that this affair will likely get hot again soon.

ANTITERRORIST GOVERNMENTS ON THE PLANET

After the September 11, 2001 terrorist attacks, the United States announced a "War on Terrorism" and China, Russia, and a number of other countries eagerly signed on. Many were curious as to why China and Russia would so eagerly support the United States in a war on terror, especially since these countries are usually competitors on the world stage and rarely agree on foreign policy objectives. It turns out that China and Russia were excited about the war on terrorism because it gave them an opportunity to suppress separatist movements in their own countries. Any group can be called terrorist, especially if they engage in violent acts against the government, so Russia and China went ahead and engaged in military action against Chechens and Uyghurs, respectively, as part of the global war on terror.

Now the US is seen with all its military might and current active operations as the biggest player in the global fight against terrorism. The Plaid Avenger is not so convinced. What states are really out in the trenches every single day, day in and day out, foiling potential terrorist plots and apprehending terrorist suspects. My Big Three spring to mind.

WAR ON TERROR: HARDEST WORKING ANTITERRORIST STATES ON THE PLANET

Pakistan, Saudi Arabia, and Egypt have several things in common. They are all extremely important players in the Middle East region and all contain mostly Islamic populations who have a visceral dislike of American policies. They are also similar in that they are ruled by pro-Western, pro-American leaders who are hated by much of the population because of their perceived mismanagement, corruption, and subservience to America. For this reason, the leaders in charge of these places are often forced to curtail freedoms and suppress Islamic extremist movements. When America was attacked on 9/11 the leaders in these countries were very excited to sign up for the war on terrorism because it gave them the opportunity to crush dissidents in their own countries in the name of a good cause.

PAKISTAN

Prior to September 11, the Pakistani army was overextended in its region and knew that its support of the Taliban and al-Qaeda, by implication, was unsustainable. Since Pakistani forces were nearly bankrupt, the United States began providing President Musharraf with the resources and support necessary to take on these forces in exchange for Pakistan's support in the war on terrorism.

Pakistan began cooperating with the US by sharing intelligence, and capturing al-Qaeda terrorists to be handed to the US. They are said to be the most committed nation in the GCTF, Global Counterterrorism Force. Pakistan has provided several key logistical air force and naval base sites, provided over 70,000 troops to the Afghan border, and has launched several successful operations to take out foreign terrorists. They are, however, being repaid for their contribution to the war with billions of dollars in grants and assistance money along with unspecified numbers of fighter jets and military training.

Some conflicts have arisen recently, including the deaths of innocent Pakistani civilians from US bombings in northern Pakistan on multiple occasions in early 2006. They occurred as a result of bad intelligence

Mush on board.

identifying the area as the possible hideout of a senior al-Qaeda member. Despite his people's growing hostility toward the US in response to the attacks, Musharraf could only defend his collaboration with the US, asking that the people cease support of guerilla resistance toward American occupation of Afghanistan. Although it does seem Musharraf is being pushed around by the United States for its own economic and strategic interests in the region, he knows their assistance is critical to combating religious extremism and succeeding in the war on terrorism.

Know this for now: Musharraf has plummeted in popularity, and Pakistan is on the brink of total instability. Don't look for Mush to be in power for too much longer, and the whole US/Pakistani relationship will change when the next leader comes to power. Which will be soon.

SAUDI ARABIA

Saudi Arabia is one of the most Islamic countries in the entire world. It was the birthplace of Islam and every year millions of Muslims come to Mecca for the required pilgrimage. Not only are most Saudi Arabians devout Muslims, Islam is the only legal religion in Saudi Arabia. And not only is Islam the state religion in Saudi Arabia, a particular extremely conservative type of Islam called Wahhabism is the dominant form found in the country. The ruling monarchy of Saudi Arabia tries to make their citizens as happy as it can, but it also wants to remain chummy with the United States, who is a big consumer of Saudi oil and a supplier of their weapons.

This duality has caused some tension in Saudi society. The monarchy is reluctant to allow democracy in Saudi Arabia because they are afraid they will lose power. This lack of democracy has angered many Saudis, especially the emerging large middle class of professionals, who are calling for political and social liberalization. In recent years, the populace has become increasingly frustrated over growing unemployment rates, corrupt leaders, and a lack of political rights. This tightrope walking was made worse with the war on terror. It turned out that 15 of the 19 hijackers in the September 11 attacks were Saudi Arabians, so the Saudi government had to step up antiterrorist activity to play along in the war on terror.

The inevitable forces of Westernization may eventually force the monarchy to give its people some rights. That may or may not

Abdullah on board.

be a good thing for the United States. One thing is for sure: the Saudi government is walking the beat every day to prevent terrorist attacks—attacks targeting THEM, not the US or anybody else. Several plots have been foiled in the last years, including one attempt to blow up a major oil refinery outside Riyadh.

Plaid Avenger Fun Fact: Saudi Arabia spent $34 billion on weapons and updating their military just in 2007. That equates to 8.5% of their GDP for the year. It also made them the 6th highest spender on military expenditures in the world. Hmmm . . . I wonder why?

EGYPT

Egypt has been a very tense society for years. Some of the first Islamic extremist organizations, like the Islamic Brotherhood, were formed in Egypt. The famous Sayyid Qutb, who is considered the intellectual daddy of Islamic extremism, was Egyptian. Gamel Abdel Nasser, who was one of the first Arab leaders to begin giving the finger to the United States and the West, came to power in Egypt in 1952. Egypt was widely seen as a bastion for Arab nationalism and anti-Western rhetoric. For the most part, regular Egyptian people have supported these anti-Western leaders.

However, for most of its recent history, Egypt has been ruled by pro-Western and pro-American leaders. When the president of Egypt, Anwar al-Sadat, signed a peace treaty with Israel in 1978, which was extremely unpopular in Arab and Muslim world, Islamic fanatics assassinated him. When Hosni Mubarak came to power after Sadat's assassination in 1981, he had the dirty job of suppressing all of the Islamic fanatics, Arab nationalists, and all of the other "troublemakers" in Egypt. For this reason, Egypt has very little freedom of speech, large amounts of corruption, and a terrible economy. Egypt has elections, but nobody is allowed to run against Mubarak, so he wins every time. Mubarak is a friend of the United States, but many Egyptians do not like him, so there is a chance we will see some conflict in this country.

. . . and Hosni on board.

All three of these leaders typically make The Plaid Avenger's Top Ten Leaders Most Likely to be Assassinated List, aka The World Leader Death Watch. Now you know why. Hell, Musharraf had to dodge bullets on three different occasions already. The other two aren't in public enough to even be shot at . . . and for good reason! Hang in there, Mush!

CHAPTER OUTLINE

1. Political Teams
2. Military Teams
3. Economic Teams
4. The Final Final

Team Play: Evolving Power Centers of the 21st Century

26

OKAY my friends its long past due to wrap up this blundering batch of buffoonery I call a book. And what better way to round up a world region text than to back up from the entire planet and assess exactly how these world regions are interacting with each other . . . either working with each other, against each other, or forming up teams to cancel each other out. It's such a delicious stew of international intrigue that is much like high school except these states have nuclear weapons and control the planet. Other than that, it's the same old same old human nature. But I digress . . .

Let's once again look at the major players that are affecting the course of events on our planet strategically, politically and economically. Then we'll call it a day.

LET'S MEET THE POLITICAL POWER PLAYERS!!!

No sense trying to pretend otherwise: the US is still the undisputed heavyweight when it comes to a single entity with the absolute most political power. To put it simply, what the US wants, the US gets. An example: There was never any credible threat that any other country was going to attack the US because of its recent invasion of Iraq. Most countries, institutions, and people on the planet may have been staunchly opposed to the US move, but the fact is that no one was actually going to do anything about it. That is raw political power, and the US is the only state that has been able to wield that sword solo for a couple of decades.

But, the world is changing fast my friends. The US still has the power, but other states and groups are rising fast to match their diplomatic skills with Uncle Sam. With no reservations, I tell you that we are moving from a uni-polar world (only one power, namely the US) to a multi-polar world (with many major powers.) This is the setting of transformation that we find ourselves in here at the onset of the 21st century. Politically speaking, let's take a look at the major forces that shape decision-making across the globe, and who teams up with who in order to get their agendas pushed. I will identify the major players, their motivations, their agendas, who they like and who they hate, and see how that is translating into current events that are going down around the globe.

SAMMY SOLO

America has long been a team of one. Its physical isolation far from the rest of the world has forever insulated it from the global events in which it participates . . . or declines to participate in. Its entire history could be viewed as a wavering cycle of either isolation (in which it does not get involved in global events) or full-on engagement (in which it is full-on the predominate player.) Take a wild stab which side of the spectrum it is on right now.

When Uncle Sammy decides to go for the global gusto he has seemingly unlimited energy, money, military, and ambition to get the job done . . . regardless of world opinion. Now, for the last hundred years, the US usually has a global coalition of participants that back it up. Let's call them Team West for right now. In WWI, WWII, the Korean War, the Cold War, the first Iraq War and countless others, the US served as a team leader that rallied the world to victory. Or at least something close to it. Point is, that mostly the US didn't have to stand alone because the UK or the EU or NATO or the UN or Team West was there to get its back.

However, since the end of the Cold War—circa 1990—Sammy has increasingly worked on his own to achieve his agenda. Why? During the last 50 years, it was the US and the USSR in a bi-polar world of competition, giving the world at least two options to choose from. But now it has been a couple of decades that the US has stood completely alone at the top of the heap . . . alone at the top of this uni-polar world. In this time, the US quickly grew accustomed to the role of sole political power, and therefore has increasingly acted alone whenever it really wanted something that the rest of the players would not support.

And I'm not just picking on the Bush administration either: the Clinton administration acted unilaterally on several different occasions as well, either to stop perceived terrorism in Africa or perceived genocide in the Balkans. The dynamic duo of Cheney and Rumsfield just took the US even exponentially further down this unilateral path (willing to act alone), with the most extreme example being the aforementioned current Iraq War. Beyond even a willingness to act alone, the US for over a decade has actually preferred to, so it does not have to waste time with negotiation and organization and cooperation that is required by international diplomacy.

The times are a changing though. No matter who becomes the next American President, the US is already leaning back to diplomacy and coalition-building as the most effective tool for international action. We can see this unfolding currently as the US is working exceptionally hard to rally world support on the growing threat of an Iranian nuclear industry . . . and it is having much success. The entire EU backs them on it, and even Russia and China are starting to come around to the US view point after lots of wrangling and back-room debates. The NATO-led Afghan mission has also been recast as needing more international support as opposed to being primarily a US military force.

So Uncle Sammy had a solo run in the sun for a while, but it appears that in this newly forming multi-polar world his future role may be as primary leader of Team West. Okay, who the hell are they?

TEAM WEST

Throughout this text I have thrown around the concept of a core world culture that is primarily steeped in western traditions and values. It's finally time to identify just exactly who is on this 'Team West.' Obviously, the core of the team is Western Europe, the place where 'Western Civilization' was born and evolved . . . thus the team name. *'Western civilization'* encompasses the big ideas on which our lives are based. I'm talking about the big things here: things like philosophies, legal systems, economic systems, medical practices, writing systems, and particularly religions like Christianity and all its sub-sects.

However, the true adhesive of this team is based on common ideologies. All the members of Team West also share particular values such as liberal democratic governance, emphasis on individual human liberties/rights, and the free market/capitalist system. These are more important to consider than the other stuff, since there are some non-

European actors on this team . . . and while they are not Christian or European or even white, they are staunch believers in the team's principle values. That's why they are on the team. Okay, so who?

Joining Western Europe we have Eastern Europe . . . and let's just go ahead and refer to the team elements of both regions as the EU. The EU countries may have been the historic core of Team West, but the all-start quarterback of the squad is now the US. But there are even more players on the team! Canada and Australia always show up to the game, as does Japan . . . yes, that's right, Japan is definitely part of Team West even though it is in the east, and Asian to boot! It shares all the West values, and has staunchly supported the US and the team ever since the end of WWII. One other surprise entry: Turkey. As a staunch secular democracy, capitalist country, and NATO member, Turkey also primarily sides up with Team West, even though it is Muslim. Primarily, but not always. We could even count Israel on Team West too, although for various reasons it does not usually openly participate in most of the Team's competitions.

How does it work in today's world? Well, when the Team comes up with a desired policy or goal (how about we pick 'the War on Terror'), the US usually leads the charge, and will often be supported on the UN Permanent Security Council by having the UK and France back them up. The EU as a whole typically is on board too. Then when it is time for the real action to go down, Canada, Australia and Turkey will jump in to join with the EU and US troops . . . and Japan will voice its support for the endeavor, and perhaps even supply money or materials to aid the effort (remember, Japan does not have offensive military capacity.) Then the team hits the field and tries to score the goal. Got it? Good.

Team West is a potent force today, mostly because it consists of most of the planet's richest countries, some of the most powerful and technologically advanced militaries, as well as having 3 out of the 5 nuclear powers. Can you feel the power yet? No? Well, also consider this then: all NATO countries are on Team West, which essentially means that NATO itself is a tool of Team West's arsenal. And NATO kicks ass.

An example as referenced above, the team's quarterback, Uncle Sam, is currently leading the charge against Iran to embargo the state and possibly have eventual military strikes against them. The EU is already on board, as is Canada, Japan, Australia, and even perhaps Israel, which has been conducting military exercises as part of the propaganda campaign designed to scare the shit out of the Iranians. See how it all works my friends? Then let's get on to some other entities which are not part of this team . . .

THE BEAR

We already had a whole chapter on Russia, so I can keep it brief here. It was largely assumed that Russia would inevitably join Team West after the collapse of the Soviet Union in the early 1990's. It does share most of the common cultural characteristics of Western Civilization, but somehow it has always remained just on the fringe of that grouping . . . just always slightly different, with a distinct 'not European' component. After the demise of the USSR, Russia was a second

rate power, with even less prestige, that was really at the mercy of international business and banking and stronger world powers like the US, the EU, and NATO. Russia pretty much just had to go with the flow, even when events were inherently against its own national interests . . . like the growth of NATO for example. But of course all that has reversed in the last eight years under the judo-chopping long arm of Vladimir Putin. He, along with shit-tons of revenues from the Russian oil industry, has brought the Bear politically back to a position of strength. He plays hardball in international affairs now, and has reinvigorated a Russian national pride that has long laid dormant. In short: the Bear is back . . . Grrrr!

So now that the Bear is strong again, it has been re-thinking the whole joining Team West business . . . and it appears it is declining the invitation. Russia prefers to be an independent player in order to be a global power again, as well as to achieve its own unique foreign policy goals. And it is in a prime position to do this.

Since the Russians supply one-third of European energy demand, this gives them all sorts of economic and political leverage over their Eurasian neighbors. Piss off Russia, and you might not have heating oil next winter. But the Europeans aren't the only ones who need oil. Look eastward and you see Japan and China both vying for petro resources too, so Russia is really sitting pretty right now. The Russians are forging economic and strategic political ties to their east as well, mostly with China. They are at a historical east/west pivot point and they are straddling the fence about which relationships to make or break. I think they're being extremely savvy and are going to avoid taking sides in anything.

We can see this rift between the Bear and Team West in a variety of ways in today's world. The US and many Europeans express concern or outright criticize Russia for becoming too authoritarian under Putin, thus detracting from their democracy and human liberties . . . which is of course one of the foundations of Team West. The US and EU also accuse Russia of using oil as a political weapon to get its way . . . a not entirely false charge, but is that illegal?

In return, Russia usually counters most US movements at the UN Permanent Security Council, where it of course holds veto power. One need look no further than the current Iranian issue, where the Russians have been quick to dismiss Team West's fears of Iran's nuclear ambitions, and has promised to veto any severe embargoes or military action against Iran, and even is helping the Iranians build their nuclear power industry. Russia is increasingly working together with China economically, diplomatically, and militarily too, which is perhaps unsettling to the other world teams . . .

Yep. The Bear is a center of political power not to be taken lightly . . . but is there really ever a situation that a bear would be taken lightly? And while I would never brawl with a bear, I would be even less likely to disagree with a dragon . . .

ENTER: THE DRAGON

Just as with the Bear, the Dragon has been resurrected as of late and is on the fast track to becoming a major world political power. As you undoubtedly deduced from the chapter on China, the state had a rough go of things for most of the 20th century, from internal destruction to civil wars to colonialization to wartime atrocities to counter-productive communist policies. But since the capitalist reforms of the 1970's China has really turned things around and become an economic powerhouse of the globe . . . remember, it jumped two whole slots just last year to become the 4th largest economy on the planet.

With that economic clout has come global political power. The Dragon has been very focused on rebuilding itself for the last few decades and therefore was not that interested in exerting itself in the global political structure, except of course when it was in its own interest to do so (think of any issue dealing with the status of Taiwan.) China also is the staunchest supporter of sovereignty in the world, so its attitude towards global issues/conflicts outside of its own territory has typically been 'live and let live,' although 'live and let die' may be a more appropriate descriptor. China does not like to get involved in the affairs of other states no matter how horrific the situation, and in return wants no one poking their noses into Chinese business. You dig?

Now this would all be just an asinine academic excursion but for one thing: China is one of the veto-wielding members of the UN Permanent Security Council. So when international action is called for by Team West to punish Iraq or Burma, the Chinese position is usually to play the spoiler and veto any actions by the UN, or at least dumb-down the UN action to the point that it is ineffective or useless. Need an example?

Take Sudan, Zimbabwe, and Burma. Most of the world does not like, does not support, and does not want to trade with these countries because they have fairly brutal records of persecuting their own people. The morally and ethically right thing to do is to refuse to support that state in any capacity. But China says, "We don't give a shit. We will trade with you. Hey, can we buy oil from you Sudan? Thanks buddy!" Perhaps their open policy is not such a great thing. This causes friction between China and other rich countries around the world. Developed countries say, "You can't do that," and then China says, "Hell yeah we can. We are a sovereign state." So the issue is a source of friction for a lot of the Team West countries.

I should tell you that even this attitude has been changing fast in China just in the last year. China has been very keen to make a good if not great impression on the world with the Olympic Games it is hosting this year. But the world is not going to let it achieve this so easily. Growing attention to the Sudan situation in particular has cast such a negative light on China's dealings there that have been calls for an Olympic boycott . . . of at least the opening ceremonies if not the whole affair. This spooked China enough for it to allow the UN to move on the Sudanese situation without stopping it . . . remember, as a member of the UN Permanent Security Council, China has up to this point used its veto power to prevent anything from happening to its Sudanese buddies. That situation has now changed due to international pressure.

So with the number four economy on the planet and increasing international pressure to pony up and accept some global responsibilities, China's star is on the rise politically too. China's steadfast respect for the power of sovereignty still trumps all, and thus the Dragon will be very hesitant to throw its weight around in the international arena. China still does not commit very many troops to UN functions, and will hesitate from any unilateral action on its own part, and also mostly stall multilateral actions even when sponsored by the UN. While the Dragon does in theory support the US-led 'War on Terror', it will continue to stymie any major efforts by Team West to transform other countries, either by invasion or persuasion. With its UN veto-wielding power, it more often than not will be siding with Russia to counter major moves by Team West while strengthening its hand at home and in its immediate neighborhood. And that is done with an eye towards countering another global power in the Dragon's 'hood' . . .

TEAM HINDU

I would be remiss to not include the other significant growing power center on our planet, and that would be our Indian friends. Like China, Team Hindu is a burgeoning economy here in the 21st century and that economic power will increasingly be translated into political power . . . that's right, India will soon be another major axis of planetary political power. But I don't want to exaggerate the circumstances! India is on the rise for sure, but currently is nowhere near the economic, political, or military power of a Russia or China . . . yet. Stress on the 'yet.'

India is soon to be a major power player because it has a whole lot of unique attributes which will soon force it to be a player. Let's quickly list them: India will soon be the most populous state on the planet (China is now, but not for too much longer). India has a vibrant and growing economy, and it is simultaneously diversifying nicely. It is a nuclear power, and, yes, it has nuclear weapons. India has a significant military, certainly the strongest in the region. As part of that, India has an aircraft carrier. That means it has a means of projecting power abroad. The only other countries in the neighborhood that fit that description are China and Russia . . . who are both power players already.

However, unlike their Chinese and Russian counterparts, Team Hindu actually shares a lot of attributes/ideals/goals with Team West. India is a strong, established democracy (the biggest in the world actually) and a supporter of free market principles and global trade. India, like Team West, has human rights/individual liberties as a foundation stone of its society. India is an avid supporter of the 'War on Terror' and as such does quite a bit at home to thwart extremism of all sorts. Hell, they even speak English for Pete's sake . . . how much more western could they get?

Well, I'm pushing it a bit far now . . . they are not western, and do maintain their own distinct culture as well as their own distinct take on foreign policy and global affairs. But look for them to become a stronger and stronger voice in the near future. President Bush has met with Prime Minister Singh multiple times during his presidency in an effort to warm relations between the two titans. The US was actually working very hard to get a deal signed with India in order to help them out with their nuclear power industry.

Hmmm . . . why do I keep bringing up the nuclear issue? Oh that's right! The US and Team West want to legitimize the Indian nuclear position (they never signed the nuclear non-proliferation treaty), so as to further isolate and 'delegitimize' the future Iranian one. See how this shit works?

So Team Hindu may still be a minor world player right this second, but that status ain't gonna last for too much longer. They are one of the five potential additions to the UN Permanent Security Council, and given their 'western' tendencies, I would look for their membership to be supported by Team West. I would also speculate that Team Hindu will likely be increasingly siding with Team West on global issues of the future . . . albeit with a more reserved tendency to use force. Gandhi taught them way too well . . .

POLITICAL TEAM SUMMARY

Uncle Sammy has been the sole political superpower on the world stage, but that brief era is coming to a close. The rise of China, India, and the rebirth of a strong Russia preclude the US from acting unilaterally in the future. The likely US response is to rebuild its base of allies and become a stronger leader of Team West. And Team West will be strong.

China, and increasingly Russia, has a tendency towards authoritarianism and an emphasis on the trump card of sovereignty and therefore does not completely share in the value systems of Team West. As such, these two power players are a likely alliance that will balance/counteract the Team West influence on global affairs. Team Hindu does actually have much more in common with Team West, and will likely be an ally of the West in future global issues.

This section has merely been a summary of the **MAJOR** power players on the planet. Of course there are other states and entities that will affect global events and influence the direction of the planet in a myriad of ways. Brazil, South Africa, Islam, and ASEAN all spring to mind. We simply focused on the most powerful, most organized, and most influential teams that are/will be the major shapers of global political policy for the near future. These are the teams that will decide how to conduct the global 'War on Terror' and the global 'War on Drugs.' These are the teams that will decide all major UN actions, including the possible expansion of the UN Security Council. These are the teams that will shape all major global policies on global warming, fighting global crime, and conducting global war.

Yep. They are the majors of political power. But what about other types of power?

MILITARY MACHINATIONS

Now you might think that political power immediately equals military power . . . and you might be right. Might does sometimes make right. And there are many individual powerful states on the planet right now. However, the alliances of military power that have occurred between states has been accelerating greatly in the last decade . . . and these military power centers have themselves become an important component of understanding how the planet works. So let's just brief over the major military entities on the planet and how they interact with one another.

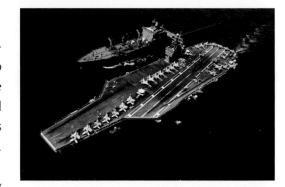

THE BIG BOYS WITH THE BIG TOYS

The US is the undisputed heavyweight of military power, military technology, and military spending. Look back at the table in Chapter 6 to check out military expenditures for 2008 and you can quickly calculate that the US alone accounts for half of the total world spending on all things military. Damn! That's some power! However, China actually has the largest standing army, and is spending fast to catch up with the US. And even they are not alone.

Let's just call a spade a spade here. The most powerful state military entities in terms of global reach are the US, the UK, France, Russia, China, and India. Why those? Those are all the states with mostly modern militaries, the money to make them stronger and keep them up-to-date, the ability to project that power outside of their own countries, and they all have nuclear weaponry to boot. Places like Israel and Pakistan may have many of those qualities, but not all. Certainly Israel, Pakistan, Turkey and Brazil are powerful regional entities, but I would not necessarily call them powerful global ones. That make sense?

All the big boys, except India, are also on the UN Permanent Security Council, which means they all have a big voice in how that organization is run too. For this section, just know this: the big boys are all countries that have, or could, act unilaterally from a military standpoint. But that's not really the way things go down too much anymore . . .

ARMED ALLIANCES

Mostly, use of military force in global conflicts occurs as a coordinated effort between states as part of a bigger institution/entity. Most of these groups have already been discussed throughout this text, but let's hit them up one last time and make some predictions for the future use of military power across the globe, but also how these entities will be working with, or against, each other in shaping global events.

THE UN

Most member states contribute troops, supplies, or money to the UN for its active military missions. Since any active mission must clear the UN Security Council, the big boys described above get to decide where those missions will be allowed to happen. Have you figured out where virtually all UN missions have occurred? If you said 'Africa' then give yourself a gold star! Why there? Because it's the only place that all the major powers can agree on to have a UN presence in. China would never allow a UN military mission to Burma (their ally), Russia would never allow a UN mission to Kazakhstan (their ally) and the US would never allow a UN mission to Canada . . . okay, maybe that one would fly, but you get the picture.

UN Secretary General Ban Ki-Moon

The only places that UN troops end up in are typically poor, developing countries in which no major power has a vested interest, and therefore no one on the Security Council will veto. The DRC Congo, Liberia, Haiti, Lebanon, Ivory Coast,

Chad, Ethiopia, East Timor and Kosovo are all excellent examples of current UN deployments that lack vested interest of major power players. However, Kosovo should throw up a red flag to you, as I have explained earlier in this text how it has become a hot-button issue between world powers.

But dig this: that mission was agreed upon by Russia back in the late '90s when it was in a significantly weakened state . . . it would never let something like that go down now! Same thing goes in reverse though: the UN mission to poor, undeveloped Sudan has been held up by China for years, because it formed a vested interest in the place when Chinese companies started developing Sudan's oil fields. Only increased international pressure has forced the Chinese to allow a mission to happen . . . but in a much more limited capacity; that is, a smaller force with more constraints on what it can do.

And that brings us to the last point about military maneuvers of the UN: they are largely weak and ineffectual. The big powers can never all agree on any single issue, and therefore any mission which gets passed is typically watered down to the point of nothingness . . . if there is any action taken at all. Remember the Rwandan genocide? What a freakin' debacle! The major powers couldn't even form a plan of action on that huge mess, even though no one had a vested interest in the place. The entanglements of getting military missions passed through the UN system is the major reason that the US typically bypasses the UN altogether and goes straight for . . .

NATO

Easily the most powerful and effective military arrangement on planet earth right now. And the preferred choice of the US, since the US is the primary player and most influential member in the club. In other words, the US has a much easier time getting actions sanctioned by NATO than by the UN. You know all about Article 5 and how the group works, so let's cut to the chase.

NATO is essentially the military arm of Team West. Yes, the whole Team, not just the US. Think about it. Kind of makes sense, doesn't it? All members of NATO are part of Team West, and even Japan and Australia (non-NATO members) often help out NATO missions with supply and support services. This is what makes Team West so potent: a combination of common ideologies with an organized and powerful military structure. They can get the job done, and more often than not can agree about what the job is.

This is significant in today's world because NATO has done a major mission shift to now incorporate the 'War on Terror.' As you know, after 9/11 the US invoked NATO Article 5 in order to get the club to help out with the Afghanistan mission, which of course they did. The current war in that state is a NATO war, not a US one. That sets the stage for many more NATO engagements in this global war on terrorism in the future. Granted, NATO will not dive head first into every US anti-terror effort: it is important to note that NATO did not support the current US war in Iraq. However, they may

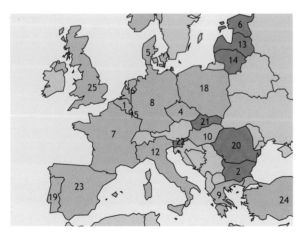

eventually come to the US's assistance in this situation too. So NATO has become stronger over the years and has increased its mission to a global reach, which is fitting since they are the most effective global military in the world. Look for India to start helping with any future NATO endeavors too.

So what's not to love about NATO? Well, if you don't necessarily agree with all the foundations of Team West, then you might be a bit leery of NATO's power. Russia is the obvious antagonist of NATO, and this has been in the news big time in the last year. Vladimir Putin openly threatened to re-target missiles at the Ukraine if they attempted to join NATO, and also to more generally re-target the nuclear arsenal at Europe as a whole if NATO proceeded with its missile-defense systems being built in Eastern Europe. Russia is invited to most high-level NATO meetings in an effort to placate the Bear, but it appears that Russia has other things in mind. It is not looking to ever join NATO because perhaps it has an alternative . . .

SCO

Of course! From Chapter 22! Russia + China + all of Central Asia. That's the SCO: the anti-NATO! Okay, okay okay, that is a bit too strong of a descriptor, but the Plaid Avenger wants you to be smart about the world, not politically correct. The hell with that! Let's get to the goods.

Though the declaration on the establishment of the Shanghai Cooperation Organization contained a statement that it "is not an alliance directed against other states and regions and it adheres to the principle of openness," most observers believe that one of the original purposes of the SCO was to serve as a counterbalance to the US and NATO, and in particular to avoid conflicts that would allow the US to intervene in areas near both Russia and China. How are they pulling that off?

SCO states are strengthening their defense pacts with each other to ensure that no interference or invasion will be allowed from outsiders. In essence, they have formed an Asian version of NATO. The movement in this direction is why most US military bases have now been kicked out of SCO states, and also why the US request to become an observer state has been declined every single year. It's also why the SCO has started doing the joint military exercises.

However, it is a very young organization, so I wouldn't call them a military powerhouse on par with NATO just yet. But dudes! Dudettes! The alliance does consist of two nuclear powers, Russia does have the second largest nuclear arsenal on the planet, and China does have the largest standing army! While I do not predict this entity doing anything aggressive anytime soon, I also do not think it's a stretch of the imagination that the US and/or NATO would be extremely hesitant to ever attack any of the SCO members . . . even the dinky ones . . . for fear that the defense alliance might strike back. I mean, that is the whole point of a defense alliance after all.

So the US/NATO strikes a terrorist cell in Uzbekistan, which then forces the SCO to counter-attack. Hmmm . . . That sounds like a WWIII scenario to me! Don't get too worked up yet though; these guys are still organizationally pretty weak, and their mettle is untested. Would Russia and China really counter a US attack? Only time will tell. Actually, let's hope we never have to find out.

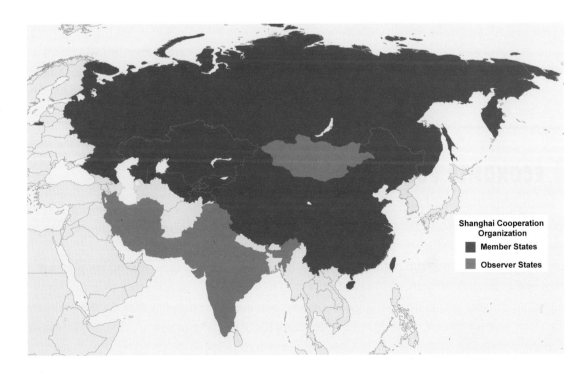

Shanghai Cooperation Organization

■ **Member States**

■ **Observer States**

The more important issues have to do with those observer states of the SCO, particularly Iran. As suggested in Chapter 22, Iran would just love to be a full-fledged SCO member so that it could have an insurance policy against western aggression. Iran thinks that the SCO membership will somehow shield it from any UN or NATO or US attack. But it ain't a full member yet, and Russia and China are not likely to grant it that status, because no one involved wants to get into a global power battle over the antics of asinine Ahmadinejad. Again, let's hope that is the case.

The SCO is a fascinating study on the future of Eurasia, and the world. Be sure to keep up with them as the entity continues to evolve. We already have two major power players in the club, as well as the entire region of Central Asia. India is also an observer member: a position which again sets it up as a future power player on the globe. Iran really wants to be part of the club, which effectively moves SCO power and influence into the Middle East as well. These guys are just all over the place!

OUT OF AMMO

Summary: the UN is weak, NATO is strong, and the SCO is evolving. All three will be the primary military alliances which shape future conflicts around the globe, both the small ones and the big ones. The UN is likely to expand the Permanent Security Council, which will make them even weaker from a military standpoint; more voices at the table means less things that can be agreed upon by all. NATO is nearing the end of its expansion period, having pulled in most of Eastern Europe, and stands more powerful than ever given its new global objectives. The SCO is young and ineffectual so far . . . but that means it has the most growing to do, and possibly the greatest future potential of them all.

Of course each individual state has its own military might, and the big boys will continue to dominate the game in the global competitions. Smaller powers like Israel, Brazil, Pakistan, Saudi Arabia, and Iran will continue to build up their military might and will affect regional politics in their prospective neighborhoods, but won't have global reach. I suppose I should also throw in smaller and smaller military entities like rebel and terrorist groups, which of course can shape regional or even global policy in general by their actions. I know they are the ones that seem to be the big deal every single day when you read the headlines of your newspaper, but the reality is that they are militarily just a pin-prick to the big boys and to world affairs. Many pin-pricks can add up though.

I did want to give a final shout-out to my AU military brothers as an up-and-coming force for regional power as well. The African Union as a whole may be largely ineffective in terms of economics or politics, but the AU military is starting to gain some steam. It is increasingly being used for peace-keeping efforts all around Africa (it is a critical part of the UN mission in Sudan), and is getting a lot of support from the big power players to keep on getting bigger and better. Indeed, perhaps it will be a strong and professional pan-African army that will help the region as a whole put itself back together, fight corruption, and build a stability that will allow for economic investment and growth. Wouldn't that be grand? And speaking of economics . . .

ECONOMIC POWER PLAYERS

Another facet of global competition is the quest for more dollars . . . more dollars for your country, more dollars for your country's businesses, more dollars for your country's citizens. Mo' money, mo' money, mo' money! Do we have Team play at the global scale for economics too? Why sure we do!

To be sure, economies are made up of businesses, which are made up of people, and all people have different personal incentives and goals and ambitions and opportunities to make money. I'm not going to get down to the abstract, philosophical reasons for why people do what they do, or even why countries do what they do. When the rubber hits the road, it's really every man for himself, or in this case every state for itself, since states are first and foremost beholden to their citizens to make sure that their economy is as strong and rich as possible. Some states are obviously way better at

this than others, sometimes at the expense of other states. But that is the way the proverbial cookie crumbles.

However, even though every state looks out after itself first, some states have figured out that they get richer when working with other states. And the economic 'centers' of the planet do shift according to who is doing the best, producing the best, or growing the fastest. We can look at what entities and 'Teams' are major forces for economic activity in the world, how they compete with each other, and what the future might bring in terms of cooperation or collision. Sounds like fun, huh? Then let's expound about some economies . . .

BIG BOYS WITH BIG TOYS: PART DEUX

Why not stick with the pattern? We can identify the individual states with the biggest economies for starters. The US is by far and away the biggest economy in the world, larger than the next three economies combined. And you know the next three: Japan, then Germany, then China. The rest of the top ten gets rounded out with other rich European countries, but watch out! A simmering South Korea is making its way up the ranks and soon will break into the top ten as well. So why should we care about these economies with big numbers?

Well, because money is power! And rich societies are typically stable and happy societies . . . typically. And who doesn't want to be in a rich society? Levels of richness effects all sorts of things like political power, military might, standards of living, but also global patterns like commodity chains, trade routes, distribution of economic activities, and even immigration/emigration patterns. Yeah, I know, big shock: people migrate from poor states to rich ones. Go figure.

Where these super-economies are located also has a lot to do with how economic alliances go down, how competitive these states are with each other, and how powerful they can become. Don't believe me? Then let's revisit the EU . . .

EUROPEAN UNION

The EU has a dozen of the top world economies within its ranks, but individually none of them can compete effectively with the US economically. But hold the phone! Take all of the EU states together as a single entity, and you are suddenly looking at the richest organization on the planet! Even richer than the US in terms of GDP and GDP per capita. The EU as a singular entity has increased trade among its member states, increased trade abroad, and become much more effective at attracting international investment. That's what everybody wants to do! Which is why these supranational organizations based on trade have become so popular lately . . . and rich.

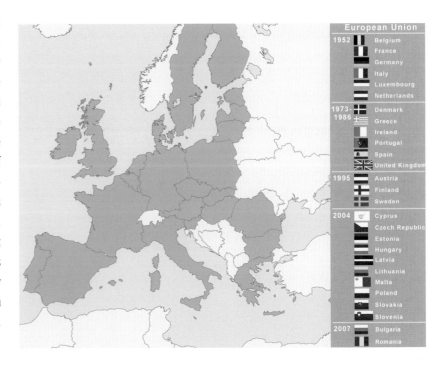

European Union		
1952		Belgium
		France
		Germany
		Italy
		Luxembourg
		Netherlands
1973–1986		Denmark
		Greece
		Ireland
		Portugal
		Spain
		United Kingdom
1995		Austria
		Finland
		Sweden
2004		Cyprus
		Czech Republic
		Estonia
		Hungary
		Latvia
		Lithuania
		Malta
		Poland
		Slovakia
		Slovenia
2007		Bulgaria
		Romania

Before we get to those other, a few more points on the EU. Like NATO, the EU seems to be at the end of its expansion streak. It has pretty much absorbed all of Eastern Europe, and the only likely future members are the states that were formerly Yugoslavia (no real economic gain for the EU here), the Ukraine (big potential gain here) and finally Turkey (big gain with some big risks here.) The former Yugoslavian states are economically weak and have little to offer even when strong. The Ukraine is an agricultural and manufacturing powerhouse with a huge land area and population that would radically affect the EU. Turkey is almost exactly like Ukraine for all the reasons just listed, but promises to be divisive within Europe as a whole because of its Islamic culture . . . look back to chapters on Western Europe and Turkey for more details.

So some possible gains, but really the EU is at a breaking point already where lots of folks think they can simply not get any bigger and maintain any sort of effective control and economic cohesion. But they do have a lot to work with already. Creating this union has been the only thing not only keeping Europe afloat, but making it a global powerhouse to compete with the US, and of course a rising China. The EU will continue to bust ass to fine tune its EU program—because it knows it has to in order to continue to compete with the economic prowess of Asia as a whole.

And I'm not just talking about China here folks . . . all of Asia is on fire with economic growth, from Korea to Indonesia to India. The center of the economic game is shifting. For hundreds of years, the Europeans were the center of the global economy, eventually forfeiting their top slot to the powerhouse Americans who have held onto it for about a century. But nothing ever stays the same forever, and the 21st promises to be the Asian century for being the economic center of the universe.

This transition is already well underway, and the Europeans do not want to get left totally behind as the Asians start kicking economic ass and taking names. In the 1990's when the USSR folded up shop and the EU expansion began in earnest, there was even talk of eventually incorporating Russia into the EU . . . what a continental powerhouse that would be! Russia is such an important part of the EU economy that it is already invited to major summits and consultations on EU policy, even though it is not a member . . . and right this second it doesn't appear that it will ever be, by choice. Because the Bear is straddling the fence, already looking to the other side of the continent for alternative companionship, which brings us to . . .

SCO

What? Back to the SCO! Remember them? I've already told you that this group may eventually be an anti-NATO, but they also started the organization to be a regional trade block. With the Eurasian titans of Russia and China as the bookends, this is increasingly looking like the team to beat.

As you already know, the SCO is building infrastructure like roads and pipelines across the member states, mostly to facilitate natural resource extraction. Remember I told you about the possibility of them becoming a natural gas cartel akin to OPEC? Well, that may very well be the building block that turns into increased trade among the nations, but more importantly will facilitate trade to other parts of the world. Central Asia has done well to throw in its chips with the SCO . . . otherwise they would be marooned in the middle of the continent fending for themselves. That trade block shit really works for some states! Instead of being on their own, those states are now a central hub of export supplying petroleum products to the eastern and western sides of the Eurasian continent. Damn! Silk Road back in action!

More important than salvaging Central Asia is the blossoming relationship between Russia and China. You know from the political power players section above that both Team Bear and Team Dragon typically find themselves as the opposing end of a lot of Team West initiatives, so they have a common alliance of sorts already. Both states are avid supporters of sovereignty, and don't want anyone messing in their backyards. So the evolution of a friendship between the two . . . and then the creation of the SCO . . . is a predictable development. Again, Team West and the EU were hopeful that Russia was going to join their squads eventually, but it doesn't look like that is going to happen, perhaps ever.

Russia is strong again, but it's no powerhouse economy on its own. Hanging out with the big boy China certainly is beneficial to the Ruskies, especially since the Chinese demand for natural resources and energy supplies is insatiable! So now the Russians find themselves in the enviable position of supplying energy to the powerhouse EU and the powerhouse China and Japan to boot. Economy is thriving. Life is good. And it is probably will be getting a lot better . . . Because as that world economic focus shifts to Asia, Russia stands to continue to benefit even more. The Bear will be increasingly dining on Mu Goo Gai Pan and sake shots as it rolls over to economically embrace the Dragon . . .

THE DRAGON AS ASIAN LEADER

I've been stressing that Asia as a whole is on fire with economic activity, and with no doubts you know that China is the main engine for all this explosive exponential economic energy. Team Dragon has been cranking out double digits in terms of increases in GDP growth year after year for over a decade. That is crazy talk growth! Their manufacturing, industrial and service sectors have been blowing up as they crank out everything from toothpaste to Nike shoes to rocket parts for NASA space ships. They have become the workshop of the world.

But this you know already, so why am I bothering to repeat? Because with no reservations I tell you that China will become the world's largest economy in the next 50 years. It will displace the US from the top slot . . . although you have learned enough from this book already to know that this shift does not equate to China being truly richer or better off than the US. But they will have the biggest economy, and more importantly, will continue to be a focus for international investment, as well as increasingly a center for evolution of new technologies.

And here is the real deal about being a world economic power player and the focus of world economic energies: more things happen in your neighborhood. Huh? You know what I'm sayin'! With this increase in energy comes an increase in interest, an increase in investment, an increase in education, and an increase in technologies. The best-est and smartest peoples are attracted to where the flame is burning the brightest. The newest innovations in all sorts of technologies almost invariably occur in hot, happening societies where the action is . . . and that center of action is increasingly Asia!

Team Dragon is being looked upon as not only a very desirable trading partner among other Asian states, but as a model of success to be duplicated. Most Southeast Asian economies are now tied into China, as are the Koreas, and even the Central Asian countries via the SCO as described above. China is truly regaining its historical legacy as the center of the Asian universe.

And Asian countries are not alone. Japan (okay, they are Asian too, but very western!) is turning more to trade/invest/compete with China, as is Russia, as is Australia, and yes, even as is the US. Japan and Australia in particular have publicly pronounced that they know they must work together more economically with China if they are to continue to thrive; both countries' foreign policy initiatives have shifted immensely to suck up to China more, even though both are still part of Team West. Hey man, money talks!

Caption: Tigers back with the Dragon!

I call it Team Dragon because I want you to know that it really has become more of a team affair. Yes, China is the center of the action—but remember, there are other economic powerhouses in this 'hood.' Taiwan, South Korea, Singapore, and Hong Kong were once titled the 'Asian Tigers' because they too underwent decades of phenomenal industrialization and economic growth. Those tigers have now come home to roost under mother Dragon . . . this place is a veritable smorgasbord of animated animals! And they are getting rich! Throw Japan into the lot here, and you have a whole cluster of top world economies here . . . with one big difference:

Most top twenty economies are in Europe, and Europe is about played out. The rest of the top twenty world economies are Asian, and they are just getting warmed up! Damn! Look for Asian states to totally dominate the world economic measures of wealth in the coming decades. For sure, China will soon be number two, Japan will be number three, and South Korea will be number ten. And they are all next door neighbors! Are you starting to get a fever for the flava' of East Asia?

So major growth, major competition, and major shifts in economic focus and economic policy around the world as Asia rises. Don't get all sad on me though . . . your region is still good too! The US and Europe will still be rich, don't worry about that! And there are just a few other entities I want mention before escaping this escapade.

SOME OTHER ECONOMIC ENTITIES OF NOTE

I've mentioned ASEAN back in the chapter on Southeast Asia, and a supranationalist organization with more potential for economic growth than I can imagine right now. Smack dab in the middle of the powerhouse China and Japan to the north and growing power India to its west (all of which are associate members), the ASEAN core might well become the epicenter of an Asian EU. Wow. That would be insane. It's still a ways off, but the point is that this group is in a position of it being almost impossible for them to NOT grow economically right now. Southeast Asia is starting to absorb a lot of manufacturing jobs not just from abroad, but directly from China too. It's good to be close to the top dogs. Speaking of ASIAN top dogs . . .

As with the rise in political clout, Team Hindu stands to become an economic powerhouse in its own right, although it is going to take a bit longer than their other Asian brothers. It's that damn big population that makes things problematic for them to advance as fast! But advance they will nonetheless, but for different reasons than others. Namely, India is fast becoming a high-end technological center for growth in Asia and the world.

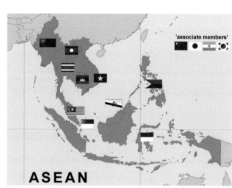

ASEAN

China and other Asian nations have focused first on becoming agricultural and manufacturing giants, then incorporating more and more service sector and quaternary activities as they get richer.

India is on rather the reverse course: it focuses heavily on increasing its service sector, and especially on new technology stuff. Computer programming, information technology, and engineering applications are fields that India is specializing in immediately. While international business may be attracted to China or Indonesia for their low wages, international business is attracted to India for their lower wages AND highly educated and skilled service sectors. Why pay a European programmer when you can pay an Indian programmer half as much? Look for Team Hindu's star to rise fast in our technologically-focused world.

Finally, I will reference the Latin Lefties. Team Lefty if you like. You can love him, you can hate him, or you can depose him in an illegal coup, but Hugo Chavez does kind of 'represent' this Latin America shift to the left that has taken on a bit of a revolutionary flavor. While the leftward swing is a political thing, it also heavily incorporates an eco-

2008 Political Positions

MEXICO
CUBA
BELIZE
HONDURAS
GUATEMALA
EL SALVADOR
NICARAGUA
COSTA RICA
PANAMA
VENEZUELA
COLOMBIA
ECUADOR
ECUADOR
PERU
BRAZIL
BOLIVIA
PARAGUAY
CHILE
URUGUAY
ARGENTINA

Far left
Left leaning
Center right

Just look at all that leaning!!!!

nomic component . . . which is why I include it here in this section. I won't go so far as to suggest that Team Latin Left is an economic power of global significance, but it is one of global interest since it represents a significant shift in thinking, and strategic economic alliances.

What am I talking about? Team Lefties have a common denominator: a desire for greater social services/wealth redistribution via the state structure. They ain't communist, but they are pretty far to the left side of the Socialist spectrum we discussed in Chapter 4. The so called 'Bolivarian Revolution' has resulted in a couple of things I want you to note: a movement away from outside free trade unions, namely the FTAA, which is currently dead in the water. And that is related to the second big thing: a Team Lefty shift away from the US as its sole economic influence . . . and shifting towards China (of course) but also the Middle East and Sub-Saharan Africa.

Interesting turn of events. Need proof? In May 2008 China joined the board of the Inter-American Development Bank, which is a major source of funds for Latin American countries to finance projects for the social and economic development for the region. Damn. First Asian member of that group. Uncle Sammy ain't happy about losing influence in his backyard. But Team Dragon doesn't mind spreading its love around.

FINALLY THE FINAL FINAL FINAL SUMMARY

So now we have identified the major forces that shape the future of our planet by battling it out every day politically, militarily, and economically. Or sometimes cooperating with each other too. Either on their own or within international organizations, the most powerful sovereign states plan, buy, sell, trade, agree, disagree, fight, make peace, plot, unify, embargo, or bitchslap each other in various ways to achieve their objectives. It ain't a pretty process, but it's the only one we got until smarter folks like you make it better.

Does it appear that I have forgotten large parts of the globe? Oh no my friends, I have not forgotten anyone! This chapter was about major movers and shakers, and that list is not all inclusive. Sub-Saharan Africa is at the whim of the international system until they straighten their shit out. The Middle East as a region is doomed for eternal conflict and a variety of debilitating internal problems until they set their shit straight too. Most of the sub-regions of Latin America are doing okay, but do not impact world events in a major way. Eastern Europe has effectively become part of Western Europe. Regions like Turkey, Japan and Australia play more of a role within the ranks of Team West than they do on their own.

But history is not done my friends! Unpredictable events can shake things up quickly in today's world and change the course of states, or regions, or the whole damn planet. Even with my super-human powers of insight and alcohol absorption, I could not have predicted the attacks of 9/11, the massive Asian tsunami of 2004, or the horrible outcome of another Indiana Jones movie release. Events like these have huge repercussions for the region in which they take place, but are also felt throughout the world in the form of global policies and actions that are implemented due to the event itself.

That's why it is important to keep up with your planet. You have taken a very large step in the right direction by reading this book. And congratulations on that feat of endurance and patience. But the game is far from over. Stay involved and educated about what the hell is going on in the world so that when the time comes you can make the biggest impact for positive change . . . no matter what it is you decide to do in life.

Lots of people ask me how I keep up with the events and actions of the planet. Well, I do a lot of on-the-spot super hero action within these regions on a daily basis. But when I'm at home in the underground lair, here are a few of the websites I keep up with, so that I can keep up with the world:

- http://news.bbc.co.uk/ for daily lightweight international news
- http://www.iht.com/ for more in-depth daily international news

- http://www.worldpress.org/ for deep in-depth weekly assessments of major news events. On this site you will also find hotlinks to every single digital newspaper on the planet from every single country that has them.

You can tune in to CNN anytime to check out the daily arcane domestic political party finger pointing nonsense, and up-to-the-minute status of Britney Spears' baby mama drama. Mainstream American news sources are not really worth much else.

Always read at least two different news sources about every story you are learning about; make sure one news source is from inside the country where the news happens, and one that is outside the country where the news happens. It's the only way to get a balanced view of what's actually happening on the planet.

To be unaware and ill-informed about the world around you is to be a passive player in the game of life. Keep your head in the game. Stay informed. Read. Pay attention. Write a letter. Protest. Help someone in need. Start a revolution. Hell, just make the world a better damn place. Peace.

And party on!

Image Credits

CHAPTER 4

Page 50: All images © 2007 JupiterImages Corporation; **Page 51: left:** photo by unknown (ca. 1920), from Library of Congress; **center:** White House photo of Paul Morse; **right:** stipple engraving by MacKenzie (ca. 1805), from Library of Congress; **Page 52: top:** photo by unknown (ca. 1920), from Library of Congress; **bottom:** stipple engraving by MacKenzie (ca. 1805), from Library of Congress; **Page 54: left:** photo by unknown (ca. 1920), from Library of Congress; **left center:** photo by Warren K. Leffler, from Library of Congress; **center:** White House photo by David Bohrer; **right center:** photo by PHI (AW/NAC) Martin Maddock, U.S. Navy, from Defense Visual Information Center; **Page 55: left:** Government of Argentina; **left center:** photo from Official Russian Presidential Press and Information Office; **center:** Dept. of Defense photo by Tech. Sgt. Jerry Morrison, U.S. Air Force, from Defense Visual Information Center; **right center:** Dept. of Defense photo; **right:** stipple engraving by MacKenzie (ca. 1805), from Library of Congress; **Page 56: top:** photo by Jack Delano (ca. 1940), from Library of Congress; **bottom left:** Dept. of Defense photo by SSGT David Nolan; **bottom center:** U.S. Air Force photo by Airman Ryan Ivacic; **bottom right:** U.S. Air Force photo by Staff Sgt. Vincent Mouzon; **Page 57:** © 2007 JupiterImages Corporation; **Page 59: left:** © 2007 JupiterImages Corporation; **right:** © 2007 JupiterImages Corporation; **Page 60: top left:** © 2007 JupiterImages Corporation; **top right:** © 2007 JupiterImages Corporation; **bottom left:** © 2007 JupiterImages Corporation; **bottom right:** © 2007 JupiterImages Corporation; **Page 61: top right:** © 2007 JupiterImages Corporation; **middle left:** © 2007 JupiterImages Corporation; **middle right:** © 2007 JupiterImages Corporation; **bottom left:** © 2007 JupiterImages Corporation; **Page 63:** National Archives & Records Administration photo; **Page 65:** map courtesy of Katie Pritchard; **Page 66:** map courtesy of Katie Pritchard

CHAPTER 5

Page 68: Dept. of Defense photos; **Page 70:** © 2007 JupiterImages Corporation; **Page 72: top:** © 2007 JupiterImages Corporation; **bottom:** all photos © 2007 JupiterImages Corporation; **Page 73:** © 2007 JupiterImages Corporation; **Page 75: fig. 5.1:** courtesy of Katie Pritchard; **Page 76 & 77, fig. 2.2:** NASA/Goddard Space Flight Center Scientific Visualization Studio; **Page 78, fig. 5.3:** map courtesy of Katie Pritchard

CHAPTER 6

Page 81: © 2007 JupiterImages Corporation; **Page 82:** flags: *The World Factbook;* **Page 83: top:** map courtesy of Katie Pritchard; **bottom:** map courtesy of Katie Pritchard; **Page 84:** map courtesy of Katie Pritchard; **Page 85:** map courtesy of Katie Pritchard; **Page 86: top:** map courtesy of Katie Pritchard; **Page 87: top:** OECD logo used by permission; **middle:** © 2007 JupiterImages Corporation; **bottom:** © NATO; **Page 88:** © Royalty-free/CORBIS; **Page 89: top:** NATO logo used by permission of NATO; **middle:** © NATO; **Page 90: top:** © NATO; **bottom:** *The World Factbook;* **Page 91: top:** Frank and Frances Carpenter Collection, from Library of Congress; **bottom:** Copy-

right © African Union, 2003. All rights reserved. Used by permission; **Page 92: top:** U.S. Air Force photo by Tech. Sgt. Jeremy T. Lock; **middle:** flags: *The World Factbook;* **Page 93: top:** flags: *The World Factbook;* **middle:** WTO logo used with permission

Part 2 opener: map courtesy of Katie Pritchard

CHAPTER 7

Page 98: map source: *The World Factbook;* **Page 100:** NASA/Goddard Space Flight Center Scientific Visualization Center; **Page 101:** map source: *The Cambridge Modern History Atlas 1912,* courtesy of the University of Texas Libraries, Perry-Castaneda Library Map Collection; **Page 102:** U.S. Marine Corps photo by Lance Cpl. Kelly R. Chase; **Page 103: top:** map courtesy of Katie Pritchard; **bottom:** all images © 2007 JupiterImages Corporation; **Page 104: top:** photo by M.B. Marcell (ca. 1911), from Library of Congress; **bottom:** U.S. Air Force photo by SSGT Jacob N. Bailey; **Page 105: top:** Dept. of Defense photo by U.S. Navy; **bottom:** U.S. Navy photo by Mass Communication Specialist 3rd Class Kathleen Gorby; **Page 106:** U.S. Navy photo by Mass Communication Specialist 3rd Class Geoffrey Lewis; **Page 107:** Library of Congress; **Page 108:** art by John C. McRae (ca. 1620), from Library of Congress; **Page 109:** U.S. Navy photo by Chief Warrant Officer 4 Seth Rossman; **Page 110: middle:** photo by *The New York Times* (ca. 1954), from Library of Congress; **bottom:** map courtesy of Katie Pritchard; **Page 112:** U.S. Dept of Agriculture, from Library of Congress; **Page 113:** © 2007 JupiterImages Corporation; **Page 114:** map courtesy of Katie Pritchard; **Page 115: middle:** U.S. Air Force photo by SSGT William Greer; **bottom:** U.S. Air Force photo by A1C Tanya M. Harms; **Page 116: top:** created by Acme Litho. Co., New York (ca. 1910), from Library of Congress; **bottom:** created by Leslie-Judge Co., New York (1917), from Library of Congress; **Page 117:** created by United Cigar Stores Company (1918), from Library of Congress; **Page 118: top:** U.S. Government Printing Office (1943), from Library of Congress; **bottom:** created by National Printing & Engraving Co., Chicago (ca. 1880), from Library of Congress; **Page 119: top:** created by American Lithographic Co., New York, from Library of Congress; **middle:** Illinois Co., Chicago (1917), from Library of Congress; **bottom:** American Lithographic Co., New York (1918), from Library of Congress

CHAPTER 8

Page 120: map source: *The World Factbook;* **Page 122: left:** originally published by Thomas B Noonan, from Library of Congress; **left center:** Library of Congress; **right center:** Library of Congress; **right:** Engraving by W. Holl after painting by Franz Hals, from Library of Congress; **Page 125: top:** *Blue Marble: Next Generation* image produced by Reto Stockli, NASA Earth Observatory (NASA Goddard Space Flight Center); **Page 127: left:** National Archives & Records Administration; **right:** National Archives & Records Administration; **Page 128: top:** Farm Security Administration, Office of War Information Collection 12002-27, from Library of Congress; **bottom:** maps courtesy of Katie Pritchard; **Page 129:** maps courtesy of Katie Pritchard; **Page 131:** created by James Montgomery Flagg (1918), from Library of Congress; **Page 133:**

Library of Congress; **Page 134:** map by Katie Pritchard; **Page 135: top:** Library of Congress; **bottom:** International Monetary Fund; **Page 136: top:** Government of Argentina; **bottom:** Bundesregierung/Laurence Chaperon

CHAPTER 9

Page 138: map source: *The World Factbook*; **Page 141: top:** © 2008 JupiterImages Corporation; **bottom:** map source: *The World Factbook*; **Page 142:** map source: The World Factbook; **Page 143: top:** map source: The World Factbook; **bottom:** map source: *The World Factbook*; **Page 145: top:** phioto © 1941 by J. Russell & Sons, from Library of Congress; **bottom:** map source: *The World Factbook*; **Page 146: top:** map source: *The World Factbook*; **bottom:** map source: *The World Factbook*; **Page 147:** source: *Nuclear Weapons and NATO: Analytical Survey of Literature* by U.S. Dept. of the Army, courtesy of University of Texas Libraries Perry-Castaneda Map Collection; **Page 148: top:** map source: *The World Factbook*; **bottom:** map source: *The World Factbook*; **Page 149:** map courtesy of Katie Pritchard; **Page 150: bottom left:** map by U.S. Central Intelligence Agency, courtesy of University of Texas Libraries, Perry-Castaneda Map Collection; **bottom right:** map by Katie Pritchard; **Page 121: left:** Dept. of Defense photo by Tech. Sgt. Cedric H. Rudisill, US. Air Force; **left center:** © NATO; **right center:** © NATO; **right:** photo from Official Russian Presidential Press and Information Office; **Page 152: left:** official portrait of the president of the Ukraine; **right:** © Herbert P. Oczeret/epa/Corbis; **Page 153: top:** © 2008 JupiterImages Corporation; **bottom:** © 2008 JupiterImages Corporation; **Page 154: top:** © 2008 JupiterImages Corporation; **bottom:** from *Former Yugoslavia: A Map Folio* (1992) by CIA, courtesy of University of Texas Libraries; **Page 155: left:** White House Photo Office Collection (1971), from Library of Congress; **center:** © Lucas Jackson/Reuters/Corbis; **right:** © Herbert P. Oczeret/epa/Corbis; **Page 156:** CIA map, courtesy of University of Texas Libraries; **Page 157:** map by Katie Pritchard

CHAPTER 10

Page 158: created by Strobridge Lithography Co. (1895), from Library of Congress; **Page 159: top:** © 2007 JupiterImages Corporation; **bottom:** *Blue Marble: Next Generation* image produced by Reto Stockli, NASA Earth Observatory (NASA Goddard Space Flight Center); **Page 160: top:** created by Strobridge Lithography Co. (ca. 1898), from Library of Congress; **bottom:** created by Strobridge Lithography Co. (ca. 1896), from Library of Congress; **Page 161:** map source: *The World Factbook*; **Page 162: top:** created by W. Holland (1803), from Library of Congress; **bottom:** map source: *The World Factbook*; **Page 163: top:** scanned from Helmolt, J.F. ed. *History of the World* (New York, Dodd, Mead & Co., 1902); **top middle:** from *Harpers Monthly 1883, vol. 67* (page 99), Library of Congress; **bottom middle:** engraving by A. Muller (1879), Library of Congress; **bottom:** scanned from Helmolt, J.F. ed. *History of the World* (New York, Dodd, Mead & Co., 1902); **Page 164:** from the George Grantham Bain Collection, Library of Congress; **Page 165: top:** lithography by M.A. Striel'tsova (ca. 1918), from Library of Congress; **bottom left:** *New York Times*, 1919, Library of Congress; **left center:**

Tsar Nicholas II (1915) by Boris Kustodiyev; **right center:** Library of Congress; **right:** photo ca. 1909, **Page 166: left:** Library of Congress; **right:** photo from *Liberty's Victorious Conflict: A Photographic History of the World War* by The Magazine Circulation Co., Chicago, 1918; **Page 167:** map source: *The World Factbook*; **Page 168:** from New York World-Telegram & the Sun Newspaper Photograph Collection, Library of Congress; **Page 169:** U.S. Signal Corps photo, from Library of Congress; **Page 170: top:** photo by U.S. Office of War Information Overseas Picture Division, Library of Congress; **bottom:** map source: *The World Factbook*; **Page 171:** photo by U.S. Office of War Information Overseas Picture Division, Library of Congress; **Page 173:** © 2007 JupiterImages Corporation; **Page 174:** official White House portrait; **Page 175: top left:** Library of Congress; **top center:** U.S. Signal Corps photo, from Library of Congress; **top right:** photo from Franklin D. Roosevelt Library, Library of Congress; **bottom left:** White House Photo Collection, Library of Congress; **bottom left center:** © Bettmann/Corbis; **bottom right center:** © Bettmann/Corbis; **bottom right:** White House Photo Collection, Library of Congress; **Page 176:** White House Photo Collection, Library of Congress; **Page 177:** photo by Earle D. Akin Co, 1909, from Library of Congress; **Page 180:** map courtesy of Katie Pritchard; **bottom:** photo from Official Russian Press and Information Office; **Page 181: top:** © NATO; **bottom:** © NATO; **Page 182:** map from U.S. Dept. of Energy; **Page 183: top:** © NATO; **bottom:** cover of *The Great Train Robbery* by Scott Marble, 1896, from Library of Congress

CHAPTER 11

Page 185: top: map source: *The World Factbook*; **bottom:** Blue Marble: next Generation image produced by Reto Stockli, NASA Earth Observatory (NASA Goddard Space Flight Center); **Page 186: top:** Dept. of Defense photo by Mass Communication Specialist Seaman Bryan Reckard, U.S. Navy; **middle:** Dept. of Defense photo by Tech. Sgt. Rob Marshall; **bottom left:** created by Hiroshige Ando (1859), from Library of Congress; **bottom right:** © 2007 JupiterImages Corporation; **Page 187: top:** Tsuta-ya Kichizo (1858), from Library of Congress; **bottom:** U.S. Navy photo by Photographer's Mate 2nd Class Nathanael T. Miller; **Page 188: top:** Library of Congress; **bottom:** Library of Congress; **Page 189: left:** Dept. of Defense photo by PHI (AW) M. Clayton Farrington, U.S. Navy; **right:** photo by Mathew B. Brady, from Library of Congress; **Page 190: left:** Heinoya (1870), from Library of Congress; **right:** Dept. of Defense photo; **Page 191:** art by Rivinger (1860), from Library of Congress; **Page 192:** map source: *The World Factbook*; **Page 193:** photo by U.S. War Department Signal Cops, from Library of Congress; **Page 194:** Office for Emergency Management, Office of War Information; **Page 195: top:** image created by James Montgomery Flagg for Office of War Information Domestic Operations Branch, from National Archives & Records Administration; **bottom:** from the George Frantham Bain Collection, Library of Congress; **Page 196: top left:** photo by Office of War Information Overseas Operations Branch (August 9, 1945), from National Archives & Records Administration; **top right:** Dept. of Defense photo, Dept. of the Navy, U.S. Marine Corps; **bottom right:** photo by U.S. Army, from Library of Congress; **Page 197: top left:** photo from NASA; **top left center:** photo ca. 1918, from Library of Congress; **top right center:** International Monetary Fund; **top right:** Dept of Defense photo; **bottom:** all photos © 2007 JupiterImages Corporation; **Page 199: top left:** © 2008 JupiterImages Corporation; **middle right:** Dept of Defense photo; **bottom left:** Dept. of Defense photo; **Page 200: top:** Dept. of Defense photo; **bottom:** Dept. of Defense photo; **Page 201: left:** Dept. of Defense photo by Helen C. Stikkel; **right:** Dept. of Defense photo; **Page 202:** all photos © 2008 JupiterImages Corporation; **Page 203:** Library of Congress

CHAPTER 12

Page 204: map source: *The World Factbook*; **Page 205: left:** *Blue Marble: Next Generation* image produced by Reto Stockli, NASA Earth Observatory (NASA Goddard Space Flight Center); **right:** NASA/ Goddard Space Flight Center Scientific Visualization Studio; **Page 206:** all images: © 2007 JupiterImages Corporation; **Page 208:** all images: © 2007 JupiterImages Corporation; **Page 209:** ca. 1915, Library of Congress; **Page 210: top:** Dept. of Defense photo by Tech. Sgt. Jerry Morrison, U.S. Air Force; **bottom:** © 2007 JupiterImages Corporation; **Page 211:** © 2007 JupiterImages Corporation; **Page 212: top:** Dept. of Defense photo by R.D. Ward; bottom; © 2007 JupiterImages Corporation; **Page 213: left:** stereograph (1919), from Library of Congress; **right:** poster by Farmer's (1915), from Library of Congress; **Page 214:** lithography by Cincinnati Lithography Co., from Library of Congress; **Page 215:** all images: © 2007 JupiterImages Corporation

CHAPTER 13

Page 216: map source: *The World Factbook*; **Page 217: top:** photo ca. 1867, gift of Oliver Wendell Homes, from Library of Congress; **bottom:** photo by William Henry Jackson (ca. 1885), from Library of Congress; **Page 218:** map by CIA, courtesy of University of Texas Libraries; **Page 219:** all maps: from CIA, courtesy of University of Texas Libraries; **Page 220: top:** map courtesy of Katie Pritchard; **bottom:** Library of Congress; **Page 221: top:** map source: *The World Factbook*; **bottom:** photo from the Frank & Frances Carpenter Collection, Library of Congress; **Page 222: top:** © 2008 JupiterImages Corporation; **Page 223: left:** Library of Congress; **right:** courtesy of Brazilian Embassy; **Page 224: top:** scanned from Helmolt, J.F. ed. *History of the World* (New York, Dodd, Mead & Co., 1902); **bottom left:** Library of Congress; **bottom left center:** photo from Sistema Internet de Presidencia de la Republica de Mexico, from Primer Informe de Gobierno (State of the Union Address); **bottom center:** courtesy of Brazilian Embassy; **bottom right center:** photo by Warren K. Leffler, from Library of Congress; **bottom right:** Government of Argentina; **Page 225: top:** photo ca. 1900, from Library of Congress; **bottom:** from *Judge, February 15, 1896*, Library of Congress; **Page 226: top:** photo ca. 1900, from Library of Congress; **bottom:** photo by Elias Goldensky (1933), from Library of Congress; **Page 227:** photo by Warren K. Leffler, from Library of Congress; **Page 228:** both photos by U.S. Drug Enforcement Administration; **Page 230:** map courtesy of Katie Pritchard; **Page 231:** Government of Argentina; **Page 232:** maps courtesy of Katie Pritchard; **Page 233:** © 2007 JupiterImages Corporation

CHAPTER 14

Page 234: map source: *The World Factbook*; **Page 236: top:** from *Historical Atlas* (1911) by William Shepherd (pp. 186–187), courtesy of University of Texas Libraries; **bottom:** map source: *The World Factbook*; **Page 237:** from *Historical Atlas* (1911) by William Shepherd (p. 106), courtesy of University of Texas Libraries; **Page 238:** all maps: *The World Factbook*; **Page 239:** all maps: *The World Factbook*; **top right:** © 2007 JupiterImages Corporation; **Page 240:** all images © 2007 JupiterImages Corporation; **Page 241:** © 2007 JupiterImages Corporation; **Page 242: top:** © 2007 JupiterImages Corporation; **bottom:** all maps: *The World Factbook*; **Page 244:** map source: *The World Factbook*; **Page 245: top:** from George Grantham Bain Collection, Library of Congress; **bottom:** from George Grantham Bain Collection; **Page 247: map source:** U.S. Drug Enforcement Administration; **bottom:** Government of Argentina

CHAPTER 15

Page 248: map source: *The World Factbook*; **Page 249: top:** from *This Dynamic Earth: The Story of Plate Tectonics* (online edition) by W. Jacquelyne Kious and Robert I. Tilling, prepared by U.S. Geological Survey; **bottom:** © 2007 JupiterImages Corporation; **Page 250: top:** © 2007 JupiterImages Corporation; **bottom:** from *Historical Atlas* (1911) by William Shepherd (p. 213), courtesy of University of Texas Libraries; **Page 251:** map courtesy of Katie Pritchard; **Page 252: top: left, left center, center right center:** all images © 2007 JupiterImages Corporation; **top right:** photo by U.S. Drug Enforcement Administration; **bottom:** photo by Capt. Charles Davis, U.S. Marine Corps, from National Archives & Records Administration; **Page 253: top:** *UnifruitCo Magazine*, October 1948, from Library of Congress; **bottom:** ca. 1920, from Library of Congress; **Page 254:** U.S. Air Force photo by Tech. Sgt. Sonny Cohrs; **Page 255:** official U.S. Marine Corps photo; **Page 256:** Dept. of Defense photo; **Page 257:** map courtesy of Katie Pritchard; **Page 258:** © Christian Poveda/Corbis; **Page 259:** © 2007 JupiterImages Corporation

CHAPTER 16

Page 260: map source: *The World Factbook*; **Page 261:** from *This Dynamic Earth: The Story of Plate Tectonics* (online edition) by W. Jacquelyne Kious and Robert I. Tilling, prepared by U.S. Geological Survey; **Page 262:** all images © 2007 JupiterImages Corporation; **Page 264: top:** © 2007 JupiterImages Corporation; **bottom:** photo by Jack Delano, from Farm Securities Administration Collection, Library of Congress; **Page 266: top:** photo by C.B. Waite, from Frank and Frances Carpenter Collection, Library of Congress; **bottom:** created ca. 1915, from Library of Congress; **Page 267: top:** map source: *The World Factbook*; **bottom:** created ca. 1830, from Library of Congress; **Page 268:** map source: *The World Factbook*; **Page 269: top:** © 2007 JupiterImages Corporation; **bottom:** map source: *The World Factbook*; **Page 270:** © 2007 JupiterImages Corporation; **Page 271:** photo by Warren K. Leffler, from Library of Congress; **Page 272: top:** Dept. of

Defense photo; **bottom:** © 2007 JupiterImages Corporation; **Page 273:** top: Dept. of Defense photo by SGT Michael Bogdanowicz; **Page 274: top:** photo by U.S. Drug Enforcement Agency; **middle and bottom:** © 2007 JupiterImages Corporation; **Page 275: top:** © David Brooks/ Corbis; **bottom:** photo by U.S. Drug Enforcement Administration

CHAPTER 17

Page 276: map source: *The World Factbook*; **Page 277: top:** *Blue Marble: Next Generation* image by Reto Stockli, NASA Earth Observatory (NASA Goddard Space Flight Center); **bottom:** © 2007 JupiterImages Corporation; **Page 278: top:** scanned from Helmolt, J.F. ed. *History of the World* (New York, Dodd, Mead & Co., 1902); **bottom:** *Blue Marble: Next Generation* image by Reto Stockli, NASA Earth Observatory (NASA Goddard Space Flight Center); **Page 279: top left & right:** *Blue Marble: Next Generation* image by Reto Stockli, NASA Earth Observatory (NASA Goddard Space Flight Center); **middle left & right:** © 2007 JupiterImages Corporation; **bottom:** NASA/Goddard Space Flight Center Scientific Visualization Studio; **Page 280:** map source: *The World Factbook*; **Page 281: left:** photogravure by G. Garrie, 1903, from Library of Congress; **right:** etching by Max Rosenthal, 1902, from Library of Congress; **Page 282: top:** Government of Argentina; **middle:** U.S. Air Force photo by SSGT Karen L. Sanders; **bottom:** map courtesy of Katie Pritchard; **Page 283:** map source: Office of National Drug Control Policy; **Page 284: bottom left:** U.S. News & World Report Magazine Photograph Collection, from Library of Congress; **bottom center:** Government of Argentina; **bottom right:** Government of Argentina; **Page 285:** map courtesy of Katie Pritchard; **Page 287: top:** © 2007 JupiterImages Corporation; **bottom:** scanned from Helmolt, J.F. ed. *History of the World* (New York, Dodd, Mead & Co., 1902); **Page 288:** map courtesy of Katie Pritchard; **bottom:** Dept. of Defense photo by Tech. Sgt. Cherie A. Thurlby, U.S. Air Force; **Page 289: left:** photo by PHI (AW.NAC) Martin Maddock, U.S. Navy, from Defense Visual Information Center; **right:** Dept. of Defense photo by Helene C. Stikkel; **bottom:** www.g8russia.ru/

CHAPTER 18

Page 290: map source: *The World Factbook*; **Page 291: top:** photo by PHAN Christopher B. Stoltz, U.S. Navy, from Defense Visual Information Center; **bottom:** U.S. Marine Corps photo by Sgt. David J. Murphy; **Page 292: top:** *Blue Marble: Next Generation* image by Reto Stockli, NASA Earth Observatory (NASA Goddard Space Flight Center); **bottom:** map source: CIA map courtesy of University of Texas Libraries; **Page 294: left & right:** © 2007 JupiterImages Corporation; **Page 295:** map courtesy of Katie Pritchard; **Page 296:** map scanned from *Atlas of the Middle East* (CIA, 1993), courtesy of University of Texas Libraries; **Page 297:** map source: CIA map courtesy of University of Texas Libraries; **Page 298:** map from *Iraq: A Map Folio* (CIA, 1992), courtesy of University of Texas Libraries; **Page 299: top right:** © Daniella Zalcman; **top left center:** Dept. of Defense photo by Tech. Sgt. Jerry Morrison, U.S. Air Force; **top right center:** Dept. of Defense photo by Sgt. Curt Cashour, U.S. Army; **top right:** © European Community, 2008;

middle left: Dept. of Defense photo by R.D. Ward; **middle left center:** Dept. of Defense photo; **middle right center:** © European Community, 2008; **middle right:** Dept. of Defense photo by Helene C. Stikkel; **bottom left:** Dept. of Defense photo; **bottom left center:** www.g8russia.ru/; **bottom right center:** Saudi Information Office; **Page 300: top:** from George Grantham Bain Collection, Library of Congress; **bottom:** map scanned from *Atlas of the Middle East* (CIA, 1993), courtesy of University of Texas Libraries; **Page 301:** map scanned from *Atlas of the Middle East* (CIA, 1993), courtesy of University of Texas Libraries; **Page 302:** photo from National Archives & Records Administration; **Page 304: top:** from Library of Congress; **bottom left:** Girsch & Roehsler (1892), from Library of Congress; **bottom right:** photogravure by G. Barrie after P. Baretto (1902), from Library of Congress; **Page 305: top & bottom:** © 2007 JupiterImages Corporation; **Page 306: top:** map from *Historical Atlas* (1923) by William Shepherd, courtesy of University of Texas Libraries; **middle:** created by Jacques Louis David, from Library of Congress; **bottom:** © JupiterImages Corporation; **Page 308: left:** © 2007 JupiterImages Corporation; **right:** from George Grantham Bain Collection, Library of Congress; **Page 310: left:** White House photo; **right center:** Dept. of Defense photo; **right:** Dept. of Defense photo by R.D. Ward; **Page 311: left:** Dept. of Defense photo by Staff Sgt. Shane A. Cuomo, U.S. Air Force; **middle:** Dept. of Defense photo by Spc. Katherine M. Roth, U.S. Army; **right:** Dept. of Defense photo by Lance Cpl. Samantha L. Jones, U.S. Marine Corps

CHAPTER 18 ADDENDUM

Page 312: map scanned from *Atlas of the Middle East* (CIA, 1993), courtesy of University of Texas Libraries; **Page 313:** Dept. of Defense photo by TSGT Jim Varhegyi; **Page 314:** map scanned from *Atlas of the Middle East* (CIA, 1993), courtesy of University of Texas Libraries; **Page 315:** photo from the George Grantham Bain Collection, Library of Congress; **Page 316:** maps from *The World Factbook*; **Page 317:** maps from *The World Factbook*; **bottom:** photo from Frank & Frances Carpenter Collection, Library of Congress; **Page 318:** map courtesy of Katie Pritchard; **Page 319:** White House photo; **Page 320: top:** photo from George Grantham Bain Collection, Library of Congress; **bottom:** map from *Historical Atlas* (1911) by William Shepherd, courtesy of University of Texas Libraries; **Page 321:** CIA map, courtesy of University of Texas Libraries; **Page 322: left:** © Bettmann/Corbis; **right:** © Bettmann/Corbis; **Page 323: top:** CIA map adapted by Katie Pritchard, courtesy of University of Texas Libraries; **bottom:** © Daniella Zalcman; **Page 324: top:** ca. 1917, from Library of Congress; **bottom:** Dept. of Defense photo; **Page 326:** CIA map, courtesy of University of Texas Libraries; **Page 327:** Dept. of Defense photo

CHAPTER 19

Page 328: map source: *The World Factbook*; **Page 330: top:** © 2007 JupiterImages Corporation; bottom: © JupiterImages Corporation; **Page 331: top:** map courtesy of Katie Pritchard; **bottom:** CIA map, courtesy of University of Texas Libraries; **Page 332: left:** maps from *The World Factbook*; **right:** by Elihu Vedder, 1896, Library of Congress;

Page 333: left: stereo by Underwood & Underwood, 1907, Library of Congress; **right:** maps from *The World Factbook*; **Page 334:** map from *The Cambridge Modern History Atlas*, 1912, courtesy of University of Texas Libraries; **bottom:** © 2007 JupiterImages Corporation; **Page 335: top:** from George Grantham Bain Collection, Library of Congress; **bottom:** from George Grantham Bain Collection, Library of Congress; **Page 336:** map source: *The World Factbook*; **Page 337:** from George Grantham Bain Collection, Library of Congress; **Page 338: top:** © JupiterImages Corporation; **bottom:** Dept. of Defense photo by R.D. Ward; **Page 339:** Dept. of Defense photo by Tech Sgt. Jim Varhegyi; **Page 340:** map courtesy of Katie Pritchard; **Page 341: top:** Government of Argentina; **bottom:** CIA map, courtesy of University of Texas Libraries; **Page 342: top:** Dept. of Defense photo by PH2 (AC) Mark Kettenhofen, U.S. Navy; **Page 343: top:** © NATO; **bottom:** © NATO; **Page 344:** Dept. of Defense photo by SSgt. Jeremy T. Lock, U.S. Air Force; **Page 345: top:** © NATO; **bottom:** © 2007 JupiterImages Corporation

CHAPTER 20

Page 346: map source: *The World Factbook*; **Page 347: top:** CDC photo by Dr. Lyle Conrad; **bottom:** *Blue Marble: Next Generation* image produced by Reto Stockli, NASA Earth Observatory (NASA Goddard Space Flight Center); **Page 348: top:** *Blue Marble: Next Generation* image produced by Reto Stockli, NASA Goddard Space Flight Center); **bottom:** from *This Dynamic Earth: The Story of Plate Tectonics* (online edition) by W. Jacquelyne Kious and Robert I. Tilling, prepared by U.S. Geological Survey; **Page 349:** NASA/Goddard Space Flight Center Scientific Visualization Studio; **Page 350:** map from *Literary and Historical Atlas of Africa and Australasia* by J.G. Bartholomew (1913), courtesy of University of Texas Libraries; **Page 351:** map source: *The World Factbook*; **Page 352: top:** NASA/JPL/University of Arizona; **middle:** map from *The Struggle for Colonial Dominion*, courtesy of University of Texas Libraries; **bottom:** photo by Sophus Williams (1884), Library of Congress; **Page 353:** map source: *The World Factbook*; **Page 354:** map source: *The World Factbook*; **Page 355:** map courtesy of Katie Pritchard; **Page 357: top:** caricature by Edmund S. Valtman, from Library of Congress; **top middle:** Dept. of Defense photo by Frank Hall; **bottom middle:** Dept. of Defense photo; **bottom:** © European Community, 2008; **Page 358:** CIA map, courtesy of University of Texas Libraries; **Page 359:** © JupiterImages Corporation; **Page 360: top:** USDA map; **bottom:** photo ca. 1911, from Library of Congress; **Page 361:** © JupiterImages Corporation; **Page 362:** © JupiterImages Corporation; **Page 363:** map courtesy of Katie Pritchard; **Page 365: bottom:** © JupiterImages Corporation; **Page 366: top:** Dept. of Defense photo by Airman 1st Class Marc I. Lane, U.S. Air Force

CHAPTER 21

Page 368: map source: *The World Factbook*; **Page 369:** map from U.S. Geological Survey; **Page 370: top:** from *This Dynamic Earth: The Story of Plate Tectonics* (online edition) by W. Jacquelyne Kious and Robert I. Tilling, prepared by U.S. Geological Survey; **middle:** © JupiterImages Corporation; **bottom:** *Blue Marble: Next Generation*

image produced by Reto Stockli, NASA Earth Observatory (NASA Goddard Space Flight Center); **Page 371:** map courtesy of Katie Pritchard; **Page 372: bottom:** map source: *The World Factbook*; **Page 374:** map courtesy of Katie Pritchard; **Page 375: top:** photo by Underwood & Underwood (1903), from Library of Congress; **bottom:** map courtesy of Katie Pritchard; **Page 376:** U.S. Army Air Forces photo (ca. 1942), from Library of Congress; **Page 377: top:** created by Maurice Merlin for Works Project Administration, from Library of Congress; **bottom:** created by Courier Lithography Co. (1899), from Library of Congress; **Page 379: top:** map courtesy of Katie Pritchard; **bottom:** © Bettmann/Corbis; **Page 380:** map source: *The World Factbook*; **Page 381:** Dept. of Defense photo; **Page 382: left:** CIA map, courtesy of University of Texas Libraries; **right:** © 2007 JupiterImages Corporation; **Page 383: top:** © 2007 JupiterImages Corporation: **bottom:** © United Breweries, Ltd. Used with permission; **Page 385:** Dept. of Defense photo; **Page 386: top:** CIA map, courtesy of University of Texas Libraries; **middle:** Dept. of Defense photo by Cherie A. Thurlby; **bottom:** Dept. of Defense photo by Helene C. Stikkel; **Page 387:** CIA map, courtesy of University of Texas Libraries; **Page 388: top:** Dept. of Defense photo by Staff Sgt Val Gempis; **bottom:** Dept. of Defense photo

CHAPTER 22

Page 390: map source: *The World Factbook*; **Page 391:** Dept. of Defense photo by SSgt. Jeremy T. Lock, U.S. Air Force; **Page 392: top:** *Blue Marble: Next Generation* image produced by Reto Stockli, NASA Earth Observatory (NASA Goddard Space Flight Center); **middle:** Dept. of Defense photo by SSgt. Cherie A. Thurlby, U.S. Air Force; **bottom:** Dept. of Defense photo by Sgt. Michael A. Abney, U.S. Army; **Page 393: top:** Dept. of Defense photo by SSgt. Joseph P. Collins, Jr., U.S. Army; **bottom:** map courtesy of Katie Pritchard; **Page 394: top:** photo ca. 1915 from Sergei Mikhailovich Prokdi-Gorskii Collection, Library of Congress: **bottom:** CIA map, courtesy of University of Texas Library; **Page 395: top:** Dept. of Defense photo by SSgt. Jeremy T. Lock, U.S. Air Force; **middle:** photo ca. 1915 from Sergei Mikhailovich Prokdi-Gorskii Collection, Library of Congress: **bottom:** map source: *The World Factbook*; **Page 396:** photo from Sergei Mikhailovich Prokdi-Gorskii Collection, Library of Congress: **Page 397:** Dept. of Defense photo by Spc. Jerry T. Combes, U.S. Army; **Page 398:** map source: U.S. Energy Information Administration; **Page 399: top:** photo from Enduring Freedom CD Collection by Joint Combat Camera composed by Army, Navy, Marine, and Air Force photographers, from Defense Visual Information Center; **bottom:** Dept. of Defense photo by Cpl. Justin L. Schaeffer, U.S. Marine Corps; **Page 400:** Dept. of Defense photo by SSgt. Jeremy T. Lock, U.S. Air Force; **Page 401: top:** Dept. of Defense photo by SSgt. Jeremy T. Lock, U.S. Air Force; **bottom:** map courtesy of Katie Pritchard; **Page 403:** Dept. of Defense photo by SSgt. Jeffrey Allen, U.S. Air Force

CHAPTER 23

Page 404: map source: *The World Factbook*; **Page 405:** *Blue Marble: Next Generation* image produced by Reto Stockli, NASA Earth Observatory (NASA Goddard Space Flight Center); **Page 406:** CIA map, courtesy of University of Texas Library; **Page 407: top:** CIA map, courtesy of University of Texas Libraries; **bottom:** © 2007 JupiterImages Corporation; **Page 408:** CIA maps, courtesy of University of Texas Libraries; **Page 409:** maps courtesy of Katie Pritchard; **Page 410:** © 2007 JupiterImages Corporation; **Page 411:** wood engraving in *The Illustrated London News* (1858 March 6, p. 233), from Library of Congress; **Page 412: top:** © 2007 JupiterImages Corporation; **middle:** map source: *The World Factbook*; **bottom:** stereograph by Underwood & Underwood (1901), from Library of Congress; **Page 413:** top: lithography by Joseph Keppler (1900), from Library of Congress; **bottom:** from George Grantham Bain Collection (1902), Library of Congress; **Page 414: left:** photo ca. 1945, from Library of Congress; **right:** © 2007 JupiterImages Corporation; **Page 415: left:** map by Mark D. Sherry from *The China Defensive Campaign* brochure, courtesy of University of Texas Libraries; **right:** stereograph by Underwood & Underwood (1901), from Library of Congress; **Page 416:** map from *The Scottish Geographical Magazine* (Volume XII: 1896), courtesy of University of Texas Libraries; **Page 417:** photo from U.S. News & World Report Magazine Photograph Collection (1979), Library of Congress; **Page 419: top:** © 2007 JupiterImages Corporation; **bottom:** © 2008 JupiterImages Corporation; **Page 420:** WTO logo used with permission; **Page 421:** © 2007 JupiterImages Corporation; **Page 422: left:** www.g8russia.ru/; **right:** © European Community, 2008; **Page 423: top:** map source: *The World Factbook*; **bottom:** photo from House Committee on Foreign Affairs; **Page 424: top:** © 2007 JupiterImages Corporation; **Page 425: top:** CIA map, courtesy of University of Texas Libraries; **bottom left:** photo by U.S. Information Agency Press and Publications Service Visual Services Branch, from National Archives & Records Administration; **bottom right:** photo by U.S. Information Agency Press and Publications Service Visual Services Branch, from National Archives & Records Administration; **Page 426: top left:** NASA/Goddard Space Flight Center Scientific Visualization Studio; **middle left:** © Toshiyuki Aizawa/Reuters/Corbis; **middle right:** U.S. State Dept. photo; **bottom:** Dept. of Defense photo by John Byerly; **Page 427:** National Archives & Records Administration; **Page 428:** © 2007 JupiterImages Corporation; **Page 429:** all images © 2007 JupiterImages Corporation

CHAPTER 24

Page 430: map source: *The World Factbook*; **Page 431:** U.S. Geological Survey map; **Page 432: bottom:** © 2008 JupiterImages Corporation; **Page 433:** © 2007 JupiterImages Corporation; **Page 434: top:** © 2007

JupiterImages Corporation; **bottom:** © 2008 JupiterImages Corporation; **Page 435:** map from *Cambridge Modern History Atlas*, edited by Sir Adolphus Ward et al. (London; Cambridge University Press, 1912), courtesy of University of Texas Libraries; **Page 436:** map from *Historical Atlas* (1923) by William Shepherd (pp. 186–187), courtesy of University of Texas Libraries; **Page 437: top:** map by Jennifer L. Bailey from *Philippines Campaign* brochure, courtesy of University of Texas Libraries; **bottom:** poster by Office for Emergency Management War Production Board, from National Archives & Records Administration; **Page 439: top:** © 2007 JupiterImages Corporation; **bottom:** Dept. of Defense photo by SSgt. Herman Kokojan, U.S. Air Force; **Page 440: top:** © Bettmann/Corbis: **Page 442: top left & right:** © 2007 JupiterImages Corporation; **bottom:** map courtesy of Katie Pritchard

CHAPTER 25

Page 447: © 2007 JupiterImages Corporation; **Page 448:** map courtesy of Katie Pritchard; **Page 449:** map courtesy of Katie Pritchard; **Page 450:** map courtesy of Katie Pritchard; **Page 451:** map courtesy of Katie Pritchard; **Page 452:** map courtesy of Katie Pritchard; **Page 453:** map courtesy of Katie Pritchard; **Page 454:** map courtesy of Katie Pritchard; **Page 455:** map courtesy of Katie Pritchard; **Page 456:** map courtesy of Katie Pritchard; **Page 457:** map courtesy of Katie Pritchard; **Page 458:** map courtesy of Katie Pritchard; **Page 459:** White House photo; **Page 460: top:** White House photo; **bottom:** Dept. of Defense photo by A1C William M. Firaneck

CHAPTER 26

Page 462: bottom left: from Library of Congress; **all others** © 2008 JupiterImages Corporation; **Page 464: top:** lithograph by Illinois Co., Chicago (1917), from Library of Congress; **bottom:** ca. 1917, from Library of Congress; **Page 465:** © 2008 JupiterImages Corporation; **Page 466:** © 2008 JupiterImages Corporation; **Page 467:** © 2008 JupiterImages Corporation; **Page 469: top:** Dept. of Defense photo; **middle:** © 2008 JupiterImages Corporation; **bottom:** © NATO; **Page 470: top:** NATO logo used by permission of NATO; **bottom:** map source: *The World Factbook*; **Page 471:** map courtesy of Katie Pritchard; **Page 473: top:** © 2007 JupiterImages Corporation; **bottom:** map courtesy of Katie Pritchard; **Page 475: top:** © 2008 JupiterImages Corporation; **bottom:** © 2007 JupiterImages Corporation; **Page 476:** maps courtesy of Katie Pritchard